For
Clio and Cordelia
Julia and Natalie

PETER N. STEARNS
CARNEGIE MELLON UNIVERSITY

HERRICK CHAPMAN
CARNEGIE MELLON UNIVERSITY

European Society
in Upheaval

Social History Since 1750

THIRD EDITION

MACMILLAN PUBLISHING COMPANY
NEW YORK
Maxwell Macmillan Canada
TORONTO

Editor: Bruce Nichols
Production Supervisor: Betsy Keefer
Production Manager: Jennifer Mallon
Text Designer: Robert Freese
Cover Designer: Blake Logan
Cover Art: T. Hesketh, "Warrington High Street." Warrington Museum and Art
Gallery. The Bridgeman Art Library/Art Resource.
Photo Researcher: Chris Migdol

This book was set in 10/12 Baskerville by V & M Graphics, and was printed and
bound by Book Press.
The cover was printed by Book Press.

Copyright © 1992 by Macmillan Publishing Company,
a division of Macmillan, Inc.

Printed in the United States of America

Earlier edition, entitled *European Society in Upheaval:*
Social History Since 1800, copyright © 1967 by Peter N. Stearns;
copyright © 1975 by Peter N. Stearns.

Macmillan Publishing Company
866 Third Avenue, New York, New York 10022

Macmillan Publishing Company is
part of the Maxwell Communication
Group of Companies.

Maxwell Macmillan Canada, Inc.
1200 Eglinton Avenue East
Suite 200
Don Mills, Ontario M3C 3N1

Library of Congress Cataloging-in-Publication Data
Stearns, Peter N.
    European society in upheaval: social history since 1750.—3rd
  ed. / Peter N. Stearns, Herrick Chapman.
      p.   cm.
    Includes index.
    ISBN 0–02–416201–9
    1. Europe—Social conditions—18th century.   I. Chapman, Herrick.
  II. Title.
  HN373.S68   1992
  306'.094—dc20   91-18753
                                                     CIP

Printing: 1 2 3 4 5 6 7   Year: 2 3 4 5 6 7 8

Acknowledgments

We would like to thank our editors at Macmillan for their support in this project, as well as Richard McCance at Carnegie Mellon University for his help in preparing the manuscript. We are indebted to our students, both graduate and undergraduate, who with their questions and research have enhanced our understanding of social history. And we wish to thank our colleagues at the Pittsburgh Center for Social History and in the history department of Carnegie Mellon University. We feel privileged to be a part of the exciting community of inquiry they have created.

Contents

ACKNOWLEDGMENTS   *v*

CHAPTER 1

Introduction   *1*

Managing the Complexity of Change: Social
    Structure, Chronology, Geography   6

CHAPTER 2

Preindustrial Society in Europe   *14*

Agricultural Society   16

    Agricultural Methods   17
    Land Tenure   21

The Rural Classes: The Aristocracy   25

    Structure of the Aristocracy   28
    Aristocratic Power   30
    Aristocracy as Ruling Class   32
    East and West   34

The Peasantry   35

    Peasant Tradition   37
    Stability and Tension   45

The Cities   46

    The Bourgeoisie   49
    The Artisanry   53
    The Urban Poor   58
    Popular Culture   59

A Status Society: For or Against   61

Changes in Europe's Agricultural Society   63

CHAPTER 3

The Forces of Change: The Late Eighteenth Century as Turning Point   67

Sources of Change   70

Population Growth   72

   Causes of Population Growth   74
   Effects of Population Growth: Commercialization   77
   The Propertyless   81
   A Sexual Revolution   83

A Balance Sheet   85

Two Revolutions   87

   The Industrial Revolution   88
   Causes of Industrialization   90
   The Spread of Industrialization   92
   The Nature of Transition   93

CHAPTER 4

Early Industrial Society   97

The Spread of the Industrial Revolution   98

   Immediate Effects of Industrialization   100

The Agricultural Classes   105

   Market Agriculture   105
   Methods and Products   106

The Aristocracy   109

   Economic Base   109
   Social Status   111

The Peasantry   115

   Economic Pressure   116
   Peasant Rebellion   119
   Toward New Equilibrium   124

Urban Society   128

   Growth of Cities   128
   City Population   130
   Material Conditions   131
   City Government   132

The Rise of the Middle Classes   135

   The Conundrum of the Middle Class   137
   The Traditionalist Sector   138
   The Middle Class   139
   The Professions   142
   Middle-Class Politics   145

Middle-Class Economics 149
The Middle Class and Lower Classes 150
Middle-Class Culture 154
Middle-Class Families and Women 160
The Middle Class and Social Change 165

The Urban Lower Classes   166
The Artisans   167

Stability of Habits 168
Forces of Change 169
The Reactionary Impulse 172
The Self-Help Impulse 173
Political Interest 175
Mutual Aid 176
Protest 178

The Working Class   180

Material Conditions: Progress or Decline? 182
Work 186

Servanthood   189
Family Life   191

Leisure and Values 194
Discontent and Protest 195

Early Industrialization and Protest   199
Gender   204
Conclusion   208

CHAPTER 5
Mature Industrial Society   *210*

Technology   212
Big Business   215

Big Business: Some General Social Effects 218

Economic Redefinitions   220

Weaknesses in the Economic Structure 224
The Major Economic Forces 230

Political Change   231

The Rise of Democracy 231
Mass Education 234
Welfare Reforms 237
The New Relationships of State and Society 242

The Upper Class   242
The Peasantry   248

Cooperation and Peasant Politics 250
World War I 254

Urban Society   256

The Middle Classes   256

   Middle-Class Disgruntlement 258
   Shopkeepers: The Borderline Middle Class   261
   Signs of Discontent   262
   The Middle Class and Its Values 265
   The Lower Middle Class 267
   Economic Values and Social Status   269
   The Leisure Ethic   271
   The Middle-Class Family   275
   Middle-Class Women 277

The Working Classes   279

   A New Security   282
   A New Kind of Work   284
   Life Off the Job   287
   Discontent   290
   Strikes   291
   Trade Unions   293
   Socialism   297
   World War and Depression   300

Mature Industrial Society and Eastern Europe   304

   Mature Industrial Society: An Interim Assessment   308

Mass Culture and the Leisure Ethic   310

   Decline of Traditional Values   311
   New Beliefs   313

World War I and the Collapse of Industrial
   Society   317

   Economic Effects   321
   Social Chaos   324

CHAPTER 6

The Consumer Society   *331*

   Toward a New Social Structure   336

   The Expanding Role of the State   341

      The Welfare State   342
      The Crisis of the Welfare State   347
      Nationalization and Economic Planning   348

   Economic Development   351

      Postwar Growth   351
      A New Age of Troubled Economies   358

   Social Change   360

      A Vanishing Peasantry   361
      The Middle Class   363

The Working Class 366
The New "Underclass" 369
Changing Patterns of Protest 370
Eastern Europe 372

Gender Relations and the Family   374

New Roles for Women 375
Innovations in the Family 377
The New Feminism 380

New Forms of Protest   382

Student Protest and a New Radicalism 382
*Environmentalism, the Peace Movement, and
  the "Greens" 387*
Ethnic Nationalism and Regionalism 391
*Immigrant Rights, Racism, and the New Ethnic
  Minorities 396*

Revolution in Eastern Europe   401
Conclusion   408

CHAPTER 7
Conclusion: Patterns and Complexities   413

Bibliography   418

Index   443

CHAPTER **1**

Introduction

The basic fact of European history since 1750 has been an unprecedented social upheaval. Every age is a time of change, and Europe had not been static in the previous centuries. But in the last two hundred and fifty years a new kind of society has formed, as different from its predecessor as agricultural society was from the hunting culture with which humans first began to fight for survival. Beginning in the eighteenth century, demographic, economic, and political forces arose that were truly revolutionary in their intensity. The population of the European continent began to expand rapidly and, in addition, grew exceptionally mobile. Europe became urbanized; for the first time in human history the majority of people lived in cities, and the countryside was partially urbanized as well, as a city economy and culture spread outward. The economy of Europe was transformed. Production expanded greatly, and new methods of marketing and transport arose. Finally, governments gradually adopted new methods and policies, often spurred by pressures from below as new groups gained political consciousness. The result was an increasingly active government that sought change in many areas—agricultural methods, the organization of cities, industry and technology, and more conventional matters such as police and military structure. Population growth, the industrialization of the economy, and the growth of the state—here were the most obvious motors for change.

The result was a transformation that touched every aspect of life; and in many ways the less familiar changes were more important. People became sexier. They had intercourse more often, both in and out of marriage. Their bodies changed. Modern European man is taller, is heavier, and has bigger feet than his premodern counterpart. The modern woman is taller as well, but her physical image and physical reality stressed greater slenderness. The age of puberty declined, ultimately by as much as eight years; in 1700 most lower-class girls began to menstruate only at age eighteen to twenty. These basic biological changes seem an integral part of industrial development and are occurring today in other parts of the world, such as Japan, where a similar social upheaval has been underway for some time. The list of fundamental transformations is lengthy, and this book covers many of them in detail. Preindustrial society had a different notion of work from modern society. It had little specific sense of leisure aside from sporadic festivals; the notion of vacations and daily, off-the-job recreation was born in the nineteenth century.

Some of the developments that have been part of building and maintaining an industrial society in Europe have been widespread, common in general terms to virtually the entire population. By 1900 most Europeans were attending school. Literacy became almost universal. Cities gradually drew in the majority of the population and increasingly set the tone for much of the economic and cultural life of the remaining rural sector. Birth rates dropped and infant death rates declined dramatically, creating a new kind of demographic structure by the twentieth century. Consumer interests expanded as personal and group expressions. The list of general trends is considerable. Furthermore, in many cases it describes patterns that begin to be discernable late in the eighteenth century and persist, sometimes expanding in intensity, into the latter part of the twentieth century. A heightened pace of work and growing specialization, for example, can be identified as part of early industrialization and continues to describe many of the work trends of Europe's advanced industrial society of the 1990s.

Some historians, emphasizing overlapping trends of this sort, describe developments in European society over the past two hundred and fifty years as a process of modernization. Obviously, it is true that Europe was more traditional in 1750 than it is today. Rather than speak of a single, coordinated process, however, this study emphasizes several more specific forces for change. European society responded at key points to major demographic shifts, first a massive expansion of population and then the declining birth rate. It was transformed through the process of industrialization, which introduced radical new technologies and organizational forms. It was shaped by the expansion of the state, as governments reached into more intimate contact with the populace and redefined their own functions. Finally, society was progressively transformed by the rise of science and the emphasis on rational knowledge, which altered formal intellectual life but also redefined popular beliefs and dominant political movements.

The idea of four major processes of change — demographic, industrial, political, and cultural — strikes a balance between complexity and coherence in dealing with the transformation of European society. The processes affected each other: industrialization built on the new labor force created by population growth and on aspects of the scientific outlook, while encouraging the development of new government roles. Relationships were not, however, tidy. For example, key groups attempted to use the state to resist industrialization or to compensate for its effects on their accustomed status. Some effects of industrialization, including the production of more devastating weapons of war, ran counter to some of the optimistic assumptions of science about the human capacity to understand and control.

Basic processes of change have certainly not joined to produce a symmetrical chronology. Certain factors were more important in some time periods than in others. Demographic change thus marked the latter eighteenth century, while technological shifts seized center stage by the early nineteenth century. The growth of the state, facilitated by revolutionary purgings around 1800, nevertheless played a more obvious social role in the late nineteenth and twentieth centuries. This mixed chronology, which must be captured by a careful periodization that moves through a preparatory transition to early industrialization to more mature forms and new technical and political issues, restates the central idea that the key forces of change, while not entirely random, did not form part of any serendipitous master plan.

The basic processes of change were conditioned by two other major factors. One was geography. Europe was not a single entity in 1750 but a complex cluster of countries and regions. People did not initiate or respond to the forces of change uniformly across the continent but in ways that varied significantly from one part of Europe to another. The state, for example, played a greater role in promoting change in Germany and eastern Europe than in Britain because of differences in political traditions, the social composition of these societies, and the timing of industrialization (since late starters in industrial development such as Germany relied on government initiative to help catch up with early starters such as Britain, where the state played a smaller role). Although the state expanded everywhere in Europe as a force shaping society (and it did so in similar ways throughout the continent), the particular pace, extent, and fashion in which this happened varied from country to country. Much the same thing can be said about other basic processes of change.

The second conditioning factor involved social divisions. The processes of change not only acted on society, but they also stemmed from it. Yet society, even in a single region, was not a homogeneous unit. It consisted of various social groups and also of divisions between men and women. The processes of change often redefined both social structure and gender relations. Social classes formed that were rather different from traditional groupings, and then the structure shifted further over time. The same held true for gender. At some points interaction with new technological or political forces created greater gender gaps, at others gender differences diminished. The basic point is clear: Change needs to be traced through the interaction with various groups, not as a uniform social force and not as a framework simply imposed on the population without the kinds of variation and modification that human agency entails.

A basic theme does survive the complexities of geography, time period, and social grouping: European society did change in fundamental ways from the later eighteenth century onward, as an industrial structure was forged and then variously refined. Fundamental change does not mean uniformity or even the complete obliteration of traditional behaviors. It does mean that, across Europe and for every population segment, virtually every aspect of life had to be rethought to some extent at least once between 1750 and the present, and in most cases several times.

Changes of this magnitude inevitably produce strong reactions. One reaction, characteristically, is apprehension. Europeans at many points have looked to a real or imagined past in preference to the society they saw taking shape around them. For example, polls in France as late as the 1950s revealed that the majority of the population believed that people lived longer in the past than in modern society, apparently assuming that the stresses of industrial life, in contrast to the peaceful existence of the countryside, reduced longevity. The facts were quite different. While longevity has not steadily increased over the past two hundred and fifty years, it has extended at several junctures, only rarely worsening for any population group. But the point is most Europeans, even today, are ambivalent about change, seeking it in some respects but fearing its consequences in others. Certain groups, throughout the process of change, have been positively antimodern, specifically attacking the values and institutions of change, and although they rarely win out they play a consistently important historical role.

Europe's fundamental changes have involved continuing tension between efforts to protest and efforts to adapt. The history of protest itself is divided between attacks against change and agitation for gains within its framework. In either case resistance is dramatic and has readily drawn the attention of historians. It is easy to assume that great change caused great unrest and that even when people were not taking to the streets they were just waiting for a chance to rise up. The theme of adaptation is also important. People learned to live with change, sometimes surprisingly quickly, although often with a certain amount of tension. One of the basic questions in the history of modern European society is why adaptation was so widespread, for there are areas of the world in which it is still not clear that modernization can take hold at all.

Fundamental changes in European society have inevitably caused hardship, which no amount of adaptation could have arrested. The insane form one example, by no means insignificant. It is impossible at this point to compare rates of insanity from premodern to modern society. They have not necessarily gone up. But insanity in modern society is identifiable; it is feared, and from the late eighteenth century its worst victims were increasingly institutionalized. In preindustrial society the insane were normally treated within family and village, for the boundary line between normal and abnormal behavior was less clear. Modern people, more rational, perhaps in some ways more fearful, try to isolate the deviant. The suicide rate has probably gone up, although we need real caution here, for the rate varies greatly from one modern country to the next, generally along the same lines that one finds in preindustrial rates. In Europe the countries with the darkest winters, notably in Scandinavia, along with Austria had the highest suicide incidence in the seventeenth century and they still have today. But it is possible to argue that the stress of basic change pushes more people to the brink of despair, or over it, than was true before 1750. Assessing the balance sheet of social change is an important exercise for which modern Europe provides vital evidence. Several gains are striking, but the darker side must not be neglected.

This book deals with Europe's modern evolution from the standpoint of social history. Social historians are concerned with changes in the values and behavior patterns of a whole society or large groups within it. They deal with many of the same phenomena that interest intellectual, political, economic, or diplomatic historians, but they do so from the perspective of how basic changes in the past shaped and were shaped by social groups. The social historian examines changes in formal ideas, such as the Enlightenment, for example, as these ideas affect the thinking of artisans, lawyers, peasant women, or midwives, rather than just a handful of leading thinkers. Social historians may study a law, not for the purpose of understanding the details of its writing and passage or even necessarily to see how it was debated in parliament, but to trace its impact on various groups of people. And there are major areas of behavior of interest to the social historian that have little bearing on conventional political or intellectual history but that are important for understanding people—family ties, for example, or the development of new recreation patterns.

Social history thus has a rather different focus from other branches of history. It is an approach more than a special set of topics, for the social historian attempts to cover every aspect of society, politics as well as toilet training, in terms of what it reveals about widely held values and behaviors. Relatedly, social historians do not treat lower-status social groups, such as peasants or workers, either as irrelevant to the basic stuff of the past or as social ingredients entirely defined by the master chefs in the leadership categories of business and politics. All major social groups have an active history that embraces more than formal political machinations or the spread of great ideas. Social history and the assessment of fundamental processes of change through its lens involve tracing strains and adaptations in family life, sports, crime, as well as the more familiar historical arenas. Social historical research, much of it focused on modern Europe, has added immensely over the past two decades to our understanding of how societies work, though some important research areas are as yet barely sketched. This book seeks to convey some of the resulting new knowledge as well as the challenge that remains, as accumulating new findings permit a grasp of the dynamics of social change in some of its most dramatic manifestations.

The development of industrialization and the expansion of the state since 1750 in Europe have embraced all of the interconnected institutions and behaviors of the whole society. As a social history this book captures the main lines of these transformations with the only historical perspective that reveals their scope.

Managing the Complexity of Change: Social Structure, Chronology, Geography

Europe in 1750 was divided into a number of social groupings. Subsequent changes altered the nature of the groupings, but society remained far from homogeneous. Not only economic position but also family structure and religious life divided the major social classes of every country.

The term *social class* is used very broadly as a descriptive category. It denotes people who have a similar style of life and social status. Sometimes they also share vigorous common consciousness. In 1900 only a minority of workers belonged to class-conscious organizations such as unions or socialist parties. Some members of the broader working class disagreed vehemently about political goals, for although there is usually a general relationship between class and political outlook, politics is not the best way to define a class. But workers shared a roughly common employment situation, similar recreational patterns and attitudes toward work, and a comparable family life. And in all these respects they differed from other classes at the time. Finally, although they did not necessarily share a positive sense of class unity, they knew they were different from nonworkers. They would regard both peasants and businesspeople as outsiders, whether they felt a sense of class conflict against them or not.

European social classes were defined by several fundamental factors whose combination tended to change over time. The continually renewed process of class formation is a key feature of modern social history. In traditional society, status was a central criterion. Many groups were marked off by law, so that they had different rights, different taxes to pay, even distinctive styles of dress. With early industrialization legal status was largely erased, but a sense of status continued to define many groups who would try to distinguish themselves by intermarriage and special patterns of consumption. The perpetuation of the old notion of status most obviously differentiated aristocrats from big businesspeople in Europe, well into the recent period, for aristocrats tried to set themselves off even when they no longer had legal privileges or unusually high incomes. But similar distinctions marked artisans off from factory workers and, to an extent, professional people, like lawyers, off from businesspeople.

Type of work often supplemented descriptions of status. The key traditional distinction was between people who worked with their hands and those who did not, and this remains important today. In particular it came to mark off the lower middle class from the working class, even when levels of earnings were not much different.

Increasingly, in industrial society, money was the great determinant of social class. It also played a role in preindustrial society, within the status groups. Rich peasants, for example, must be discussed somewhat separately from ordinary peasants, and the latter from landless laborers, even though all were usually in the same legal category. By the nineteenth century earnings and property ownership spoke more loudly, and groups with the same earnings could rarely stay apart too long. Hence aristocrats and big businesspeople, artisans and the better-paid factory workers increasingly coalesced into single classes because of shared economic position.

By the twentieth century stratification became more complex. Not only law but also property ownership had disappeared as the major criteria of social divisions. They still had influence, directly and through tradition. Ongoing industrialization did not neatly replace one kind of social definition with another. But increasingly job position was the key, not only dividing manual from nonmanual workers but also differentiating the latter in terms of position in a bureaucratic hierarchy. Earnings would usually reflect the main distinctions, but sometimes less sharply than before.

All of these distinctions must be explored more fully as we discuss the major stages of modern European social history. For now the main point is that we are looking for ways to define groups that shared values and styles of life, for this is the only way to grasp social reality. There were, of course, trends that cut across class lines. Religious beliefs or, later, nationalism were shared by many groups. Family patterns, though rarely the same at any one time, could be copied, so that it is possible to talk of some trends in family structure quite apart from class. But at any given point, even in the present day, social classes

differed in important respects even when they were moving in the
same direction. Any effort to label a period's culture in monolithic
terms usually means that only one or two social classes are being considered, at best. A good example is Victorian England, which has been
praised or blamed for its harmony, rigid morality, and optimism. The
definition almost completely ignores the lower classes, while over-
simplifying the middle and upper classes as well. One of the key
achievements of social history has involved bringing social diversity to
the fore, by exploring the complex ideas and behaviors of even upper-
class groups more fully and above all by giving lower classes serious
attention as historical actors even when their voices were not raised in
active protest.

How many social classes should be considered? In English history a
longstanding tradition once prevailed, for the nineteenth and twentieth
century, of dividing into threes: upper, middle, and lower. This trinita-
rian impulse is lazy and inaccurate, taking only the grossest kind of
economic divisions into consideration. We will require a more elaborate
framework, given the various criteria that set groups off from each
other. Moreover, within even more limited social classes there was often
a division, admittedly fuzzy, between elements that could basically accept change and those that were frightened by it. The lower middle
class, for example, has often been seen (particularly in Germany) as a
backward-looking unit, terrified by big business and impersonal organization. In fact, the group was divided, even though it shared a similar
life-style in other respects. Here and in other cases social classes constantly tended to pull apart, between those who tried to adapt to
change and those who tended to react against it. Finally, factors of age
and sex must be introduced. Age has yet to receive due attention, but
we are beginning to know something about the history of age-defined
groups like adolescents (a creation of modern society) and the elderly.
Sex considerations are more obvious, and special attention needs to be
given to women within each major social class, particularly, but not
exclusively, at those points when reaction to basic change widened the
gap between male and female roles and identities.

Periodization, fortunately, is somewhat simpler than social structure
in capturing basic stages of change. Because it is less concerned with
single events and great people, social history does not need a detailed
chronology. What happened in a decade is more important than what
happened in a year, though big events can have impact. This book
utilizes a fourfold periodization for the development of modern European society, after an initial section on the preindustrial setting. It de-
rives from a combination of the major changes in demography, state
functions, and dominant cultural trends along with the stages of industrialization and related alterations in the structure of class and gender
identities.

It is increasingly recognized that essential aspects of the industrialization process were taking shape in western Europe from about 1750 onward in the form of population increase and the spread of new forms of manufacturing. From this base, starting about 1820 (a bit earlier in England), flowed industrialization itself. This second phase of industrialization saw only a minority of the population touched by the factories directly, but it witnessed the most rapid urbanization. Together the first two stages of industrialization, 1750–1820 and 1820–1870, constitute the periods in which change was most bewildering and the institutions of society were most severely challenged.

From about 1870 onward industrial society matured. Family life stabilized to a degree and a new demographic structure took shape. New tensions arose as key social groups defined their interests more clearly, and continued innovation in technology and social organization produced its own strain. In fact, the last two decades of this third phase of industrial development saw much of European society in disarray. Staggered by World War I, the social structure that had been tossed up by mature industrialization was no longer adequate. Many people viewed the 1920s as signalling a new, and horrible, kind of society. In fact, the basic trends were not novel but cruelly distorted by the impact of the first total war.

Gradually, by around 1950, a fourth phase of change emerged. Some have labeled it *postindustrial* or *postmodern*, claiming that the very basis of industrial society has been overturned. It is more accurate to view it as a new stage within a basic process of ongoing industrial development, bringing striking new successes in Europe but also a new array of problems.

Geography is the final ingredient in the framework within which modern Europe's basic change can be approached. Europe, a relatively small continent, is bewilderingly diverse in terms of geography, climate, ethnicity, and historical tradition. Many social historians find it difficult to deal with more than a single region or city; this level of detail has a longstanding tradition in French social history, for example, where even a single village can be the focus of a massive monograph. At one level of historical reality the small region has to be isolated. Peasants in the poor, mountainous areas of the Auvergne differed greatly from wheat growers in Normandy. Peasants in vineyard regions are almost always more independent-minded than those who raise grain. Workers in Birmingham, where shops were fairly small and skill levels high, behaved quite differently from textile workers in Manchester; they even voted differently. Distinctions of this sort could be multiplied, but we lack the space to make them. And there are general processes that can be identified across the small regional lines, even if they would need refinement when applied to any given area.

We also take relatively little account of national distinctions. In many

TABLE 1–1. European Zones of Social Development

	Early Industrialization	
	West	*West Central*
	Britain, Scandinavia, France[a]	West Germany, Northern Italy, Low Countries, Northern Spain, Czechoslovakia[a]
Preindustrial patterns: Aristocracy	Early open to economic and political change; parliamentary tradition	Strong; big role in bureaucracy; efficient; some links to middle class
Peasantry	Independent land tenure; low traditional birth rate; much market production; relatively wealthy	Independent land tenure; less wealthy
Urban	Relatively large commercial cities; strong middle class; weakened artisan guilds	Smaller commercial middle class, larger professional element; strong artisan guilds
Patterns of change	Early industrialization; early decline of birth rate; early decline of religion; high level of desire for mobility, rising income; restrained political extremes	More state role in industrialization; more resistance to change; more persistence of religion; rise of political extremes (socialism, nationalism); lower levels of protest based on personal acquisitiveness

[a] Indicates middling position, close to next group over.

respects, for social history, these have far less reality than the internal re-gional divisions. The basic process of change and the nature of the key social classes cut across national lines, despite undeniable differences in political structure. Nations could particularly identify different versions of the expanding state but they are not the essential analytic units.

Above the national level certain large regional variations must be

Later, Induced Industrialization		Incomplete Industrialization	
East Central	East	South	Balkans
Austria, East Germany, Baltic States	Russia, Poland, Rumania, Hungary[a]	Southern Spain, Southern Italy, Ireland[a]	
Strong manorial aristocracy	Strong; economically inefficient; linked to state	Urbanized; absentee; inefficient	No large native aristocracy
High birth rate; mainly large estates; some large independent peasants; high traditional poverty	High birth rates; tightly tied to large estates; few large or independent peasants; poverty	Sharecropping; declining economy; poverty	Partially herding economy; few tools
Middle class dependent on state; small business element; small cities; strong guilds	Essentially no manufacturing cities or independent urban classes	Strong guilds; large professional middle class	No specialized artisanry; small merchant class
Later but successful industrialization; lack of rural protest; strong urban resistance to industrialization; open to fascism	Heavy state role in industrialization; lack of independent middle class, high rural unrest; open to communism and/or authoritarianism	Not open to nineteenth-century industrialization; high levels of rural unrest and/or religious fervor; long-standing population growth and/or emigration	Not open to nineteenth-century industrialization; gradual growth of nonindustrial cities, more artisanal specialization

consistently noted (see Table 1–1). The big division is between eastern and western Europe. Germany from the Elbe River eastward, most of the Hapsburg monarchy, and Russia constitute the bulk of the eastern zone. With due allowance for special Mediterranean traditions, the southern half of Italy and the southern half of Spain had a similar social framework, with the big qualification that levels of urbanization were far higher. The eastern–southern zone was characterized by large landed estates and, even at the end of the eighteenth century, a tight manorial system. Both peasantry and aristocracy were profoundly different from their western counterparts as a result. The preindustrial middle class was distinctive as well. Indeed it barely existed in eastern Europe, given the small size of cities, whereas in southern Europe it was highly traditionalist and tied to the aristocracy. Although important parts of this zone had a solid manufacturing tradition, as was true of Russia and parts of the Balkans, the area was not easily open to fundamental changes. When industrialization came it had to be copied from the West. It caused more tension as a result, and in some cases (as in the south) was less successful. Certainly the chronology was different. This area of Europe entered the first phases of industrial development only around 1870, so that patterns around 1900 in many ways mirrored those of the West a century before. Industrial maturity was reached only in the mid-twentieth century. Again we can talk of some common processes, but we will have to call attention consistently to differences in stage of development and in the precise form involved.

For all the complexities of time, place, and social diversity that make generalization difficult in European social history, the effort to draw broader conclusions about basic processes of change in the recent history of Europe has considerable importance for understanding the modern world. Since 1750 the emergence of new demographic structures, industrialization, the redefinition of knowledge, and state expansion not only transformed European society but also affected social relations across large stretches of the globe. At the same time, the process of change in Europe has proven to be unique. It was in western Europe that each of these four basic processes of change first began, and even today their counterparts have emerged in only a few other parts of the world and under different conditions. Only in North America and on the Pacific rim of Asia have people created industrialized societies to a degree comparable to what Europeans achieved. And even so, the European experience contrasts in important ways with these other cases. In Europe fundamental social change took place within the context of a long-established society with well-defined institutions and well-entrenched peasantries and aristocracies. North America offered a different setting that lacked such deeply rooted social customs and agrarian classes. If Japan shared with Europe a roughly similar history of aristocratic dominance, it nonetheless differed sharply in its cultural and political traditions. It is important to comprehend the particularity of social change in Europe both to see European history from a global perspective and to understand what is unique and generalizable from the European past. Finally, Europe remains, at the end of the twentieth century, an important, dynamic society. Despite the relative decline of Europe as a political and economic force during the twentieth century and the horrors that Europeans created and suffered during the world wars, these societies have displayed a remarkable capacity for recovery and renovation. Parts of Europe clearly count for a great deal in the modern world as the century draws to a close. And the peoples of Europe remain the makers and subjects of change.

CHAPTER 2

Preindustrial Society in Europe

At least on the surface European society was not changing very rapidly in the decades around 1700. Population growth was slight in most areas, though it hit relatively high levels in Russia. Social mobility seems to have been modest, as most people stayed in the station of life into which they were born. The size of cities increased somewhat and urban influence on the economy may have increased. In Holland there were significant improvements in agricultural productivity; in France a few new manufacturing procedures were developed. But these developments had scant significance for most European people.

Discussion of premodern society as of about 1700 can convey a false sense of stability. In England, for example, population growth, economic expansion, and concomitant social tensions had been considerable into the mid-seventeenth century. Here and in other parts of Europe major unrest around 1648 suggested substantial social change. Cities had expanded, and with them two crucial new social groups, the artisans and the bourgeoisie. Improvements in agriculture allowed general if moderate population increase off and on from the tenth century until about 1650 when there was a brief pause. In western Europe peasants had freed themselves from the tightest manorial restrictions and had altered their family structure. The British rural population, in particular, focused on free farming with considerable movement between villages.

Several fundamental developments marked European society from the sixteenth century onward. As European merchants gained increasing dominance in world trade, overall prosperity increased in Britain and the western part of the continent. More and more people became involved in some commercial exchange, selling at least a portion of their product to the market. Growing commercialization, in turn, produced signs of a new social structure, in which a majority of rural and urban property owners faced a growing minority of propertyless laborers available for work on a wage. This new proletariat produced growing concern about crime and poverty, reducing traditional patterns of community responsibility. Popular beliefs changed, partly because of the religious upheaval caused by the advent of Protestantism and Catholic response. Many people began to place new value on the family, in contrast to a traditional focus on the community. Acceptance of beliefs in magic, and particularly in witchcraft, declined, especially after the early seventeenth century. By the eighteenth century witchcraft trials had ceased, and in places like northern Germany references to magic as a treatment for disease had vanished. European society, in sum, was in the process of extensive redefinition in commercial and social structure and in habits of thought. While most of these shifts dated back to the sixteenth century, many persisted into the eighteenth century, meaning both that European society around 1700 was hardly traditional in some timeless sense and that it was not standing still.

All of this formed a crucial basis for later change; it was no accident that western Europe was the seat of the initial replacement of agricultural society. Industrialization, in other words, resulted from fundamental shifts earlier; it did not spring full blown from a stagnant setting. But the common image of preindustrial society as relatively stable is not wrong, if the modern period is taken as the measurement, for change before 1750 occurred within an essentially rural, communal structure. In some areas of Europe the basic structure of a preindustrial society lasted well into the nineteenth century. So although we focus on the early eighteenth century for a definition of this society in western Europe, many themes will carry through to 1850 or beyond for the east and south; the chronological range will thus be considerable.

A first sketch of European society around 1700, before the advent of the changes that directly ushered in the Industrial Revolution must, clearly, balance two images. The first is a society much different from the one that had emerged just a century later, under the spur of early industrialization and other forces — a society more rural, with more emphasis on community customs, with a more clearly dominant aristocracy. The leap from preindustrial to even tentatively industrial was massive. The second image, though, involves a society that, while agricultural, was quite different from most other agricultural civilizations, quite different from Europe itself just two centuries before. It is legitimate to focus first on the more stable features, turning then to the changes that were altering the social landscape, but in fact the two aspects were simultaneous.

It is essential to have some notion of the nature of preindustrial Europe and its complexity in order to grasp the causes, impact, and

basic meaning of the Industrial Revolution and great social changes it
entailed. Causes will be addressed more directly in the following section, but the main question is obvious: Were industrial patterns somehow forced on a reluctant populace by factors beyond their control,
disturbing a cherished routine? Or did they flow from the complexities
of European society even though many traditional institutions were
hostile to change? Determination of the nature of European preindustrial society says much about potential reactions to change regardless of
cause. If we see preindustrial communities as well integrated, giving
their inhabitants an automatic sense of identity, then the impact of
urban and industrial growth must have been severe. But if preindustrial
communities are seen as impoverished and authoritarian, perhaps
many people welcomed the chance to try something new.

Certainly an evaluation of preindustrial society continues to enter our
judgments of our own day. Ironically, it is not only conservatives who
display nostalgia for past values lost; many radicals also assume that
things were better before industrial capitalism reared its ugly head.
Contemporary impersonality is contrasted with the tight personal relationships of the preindustrial world. The modern family is seen as
loose to the point of anarchy, compared to the embracing family structure of times gone by. Old people, now shunted aside by a utilitarian
society, are held to have had an integral place in peasant life. And so
it goes. It is generally agreed that preindustrial society was very different from its successor, and in some aspects of life this is all that can be
safely concluded; for it is as anachronistic to measure traditional society
by modern values as to judge the direction of modern life by, say,
degrees of religious fervor. We can note also some areas of continuity,
for many groups tried to preserve traditional values even in quite new
settings. But it is difficult to avoid some value judgments about the
quality of life in preindustrial society, for the contrast tells us so much
about what we have become.

Agricultural Society

The basis of European society in 1700 was agricultural. Everywhere
the leading social class — the aristocracy — depended ultimately on agriculture for its economic support. And everywhere the most numerous
class was made up of the peasants and associated rural artisans who
lived in small towns, in villages, and sometimes on isolated farms. In
1800, 95 percent of the Russian population and 80 percent of the
French population was rural. Even in 1850 France was still 75 percent
rural, Germany 65 percent, and Austria 82 percent. And as late as
1900 Russia was 88 percent rural, Greece 85 percent, and France still

over 50 percent.[1] Throughout the nineteenth century, then, though in declining proportions, agriculture and activities directly related to agriculture remained the source of support for the majority of people throughout most of Europe. Focus on the industrialization and urbanization of Europe leads naturally to a tendency to neglect the continued importance of rural life. The agricultural basis of society must be understood particularly when considering society before the Industrial Revolution, prior to any massive inducement to leave the countryside for the city.

Agricultural Methods

In 1700 agriculture was almost everywhere designed primarily to feed the owners and workers of the land on which production took place. Certainly there were outside markets for agricultural production. Cities depended on the possibility of buying food. Even areas in eastern Europe, notably Poland and the Ukraine, exported grain to the more urban West. Obviously, producers near cities had frequent market contacts. Regions with specialties such as wine growing had some local exchanges at least and often sold more widely. Areas on navigable rivers were naturally more exposed to market opportunities than other regions. Finally, some exchanges were necessary even for agricultural communities themselves. Salt and metals had to be brought in. Wealthy peasants in parts of Austria and Germany bought meat imported from Hungary.

Nevertheless, even in comparatively wealthy and urbanized countries most peasants were concerned primarily with production for their own needs. This is why their agriculture is often described as a subsistence economy even though they produced enough extra to support the upper classes and to feed the cities. Even many large estates produced for only a local market, and almost all estates filled most of the consumption needs of the local labor force. In general, only the spread of an urban economy after 1750 created a sufficiently massive market to induce peasants and landowners to concentrate on production for distant sales rather than for local consumption. In eastern, and to a lesser extent southern, Europe the rise of cities in the West after 1800 did create a potential market for export even before industrialization occurred locally, and agricultural systems were accordingly altered early in the century. But almost everywhere in 1700 agriculture was still intended above all for local consumption.

This fact explains a number of the key features of preindustrial agriculture. Agriculture was not, in 1700 and even after, designed

---

[1] The term *rural* is not totally accurate here because in most countries it includes all residents of agglomerations with less than three thousand inhabitants. Although the bulk of this category was indeed rural, a minority were small-town artisans and bourgeois dependent on rural society only indirectly.

primarily to maximize production. In a predominantly nonmarket situation maximization simply made no sense. The local market was finite, traditionally at least. The number of people to feed in a village or on an estate could not expand rapidly. Undue attention to production would be a waste of time because there would be no way to dispose of a major increase. Efforts had to concentrate primarily on assuring existing standards for the existing population. Agriculture was designed, particularly for the peasants but also to a degree for the aristocracy, to maintain traditional (and often rather low) levels of consumption and to support the structure of rural society more generally. Notions of expansion and progress came hard to the rural producer.

The character of preindustrial agriculture showed most clearly in the methods employed, which were largely traditional and severely limited the productive capacity of agriculture. There were no major improvements in agricultural methods in Europe between about 1200 and the 1680s despite huge changes in other economic fields. Even after major improvements in method were developed, beginning in Holland in the 1680s and in England in the eighteenth century, they were extremely slow to spread, for producers could see no need for them. Farm machinery was nonexistent. Only a few simple tools aided the various processes of planting and harvesting. Sometimes the wooden plow was pushed by hand; even when it was drawn by oxen, women and children followed behind, manually distributing the seed. Harvesting was done by hand with a sickle for cutting. The scythe was known but not widely used despite the fact it would have saved on labor; it cut the grain too low, and peasants wanted to leave stalks for their animals to graze on. Peasants thrashed their grain by flailing it or walking on it.

With such simple methods, the amount of land that any one family could cultivate was obviously very small, and production was low. In a good year the methods did allow production somewhat beyond the needs of the producers themselves. It was on this margin that aristocrats lived, governments taxed, and preindustrial cities survived. But the margin was small indeed, and it was curtailed by the traditional practice of leaving much of the land fallow each year. This was the only way known to replenish the fertility of the soil. In most areas one-third of the cultivated land was left fallow annually; in some parts of southern Europe half the land was set aside. In the eighteenth century alternative methods of restoring nitrogen to the soil by planting clover or turnips were initially developed, but such methods were used by only a few large estates in England and northern France. Similarly, new systems of drainage that allowed the utilization of fields previously too wet for cultivation and improved the yield in existing plots were confined initially to Holland and the British Isles.

Finally, most villages possessed, usually as commons land, substantial tracts regarded as unsuitable for cultivation; at most they were devoted to occasional forestry and scrubby pasture land. Large sections of most countries, particularly on the Continent, had never been opened to agriculture at all. Only developments in the nineteenth century would show that cultivation of many of these areas was possible. In the meantime, agriculture before industrialization was characterized not only by simplicity of tools and methods, but also by a real limitation of the amount of land that was used at any one time.

Preindustrial agriculture was also dominated by the need to produce almost all the foods needed locally. Most villages were isolated from major markets. Only rutted wagon tracks connected them even to other villages in the neighborhood. Outside merchandise was a rarity and was usually either brought by itinerant peddlers or available on regular but infrequent market days in the area. Actually, shops were unknown in most villages. Most goods needed for day-to-day consumption had to be locally produced. Even individual families typically attempted substantial self-sufficiency in what they themselves produced.

Primary attention had to be given to a starchy staple, traditionally one of the cheaper grains, such as rye or oats, which was used for bread. Only in a few wealthy regions, such as parts of northwestern France, was wheat widely cultivated. In addition to the staples, however, a variety of other products were necessary. At least a few animals were kept for fiber, hides, and milk as well as for meat. Many regions raised grapes for wine; in other areas grains were used for beer and liquors. And of course each area sought its fuel in woods nearby. Most families made their own clothes and built or maintained their own housing. Some important activities required a degree of specialization. Shepherds, millers, and sometimes a variety of artisans, such as blacksmiths, took charge of work no one family could do for itself, but they too engaged in more general farming of their own. Such specialization remained almost entirely local. Only for a very few products or services did a village or estate have to look beyond its borders.

This was another important deterrent to maximization of agricultural production. Regions failed to concentrate fully on the products for which their soil and climate were best suited. Some regions had to attempt production, such as wine growing or meat raising, for which they were ill adapted. Small estates and villages with highly diversified agriculture were inefficient and uneconomical in all their products, resulting in poor quality and high costs even in the villages themselves. And the tendency to self-sufficiency severely limited the consumption standards of most localities. It had only been in the seventeenth century that most French peasants were able to consume wine because of pervasive poverty and the difficulty of importing specialized goods. Areas ill suited to production of a major staple were doomed to poverty regardless of their potential for more specialized production.

The starkest tragedy of rural life was the famine, to which preindustrial agriculture was peculiarly vulnerable. When crops failed even in a single locality, widespread starvation could result, because of the difficulty of bringing in food from other areas. Those who did not die went hungry. Many had to go into debt to tide themselves over, and because rural loans were risky, the interest rates were high, up to 60 percent a year. Hatred of the money lender was thus widespread, and because Jews served as lenders in much of eastern and central Europe, peasant anti-Semitism was widespread. But there was no doing without some help in a crisis, for rural charities or relief programs were almost nonexistent. It has been estimated that a famine of some degree of severity occurred once every four years in the rural world, because of bad weather or other conditions. Its impact was exacerbated by the necessity of saving one seed of every four produced for planting next year's crop, for this was low-yield agriculture. Rural society was thus poor and open to frequent crises. Poverty varied with the region, growing greater as one moves eastward across the map of Europe, but no large group of peasants was immune from potential tragedy. Poor diets, along with various epidemic diseases, kept the average lifespan of the rural population low; almost half the children born would die before they reached the age of two.

Even in a rich agricultural country like France many peasants lived badly, quite apart from famine years. Their housing was mean and small, with earthen floors, inadequate light and air (the French government taxed cottages by the number of windows they had, which forced even wealthy peasants to do without ventilation in their eagerness to foil the state), and crude construction from clay or logs. Animals frequently shared the small space. Poor chimneys filled the house with smoke in winter, and diseases such as tuberculosis were widespread. Clothing was crude, of rough wool or linen, and lacked variety. Many peasants went barefoot or at most had a pair of wooden shoes. Many ate only starches, drank only water, for meat and wine were too expensive except on the most important feast days. Most peasants had an inadequate diet; some did not even consume enough calories to sustain an active life. In Ireland it was estimated that a quarter of the population starved to some extent every year; here and in other countries much of the peasantry virtually hibernated in winter because their energy was so low. These were the worst conditions, but even richer farmers and members of the local aristocracy lived in circumstances that modern people would judge poverty-stricken.

The conditions of preindustrial agriculture also encouraged a distinctive attitude toward work, on the part of peasant producers and also many landlords. Intense work was not seen as a virtue. Peasants worked hard, in terms of long hours of often heavy physical labor; this was true of women and children as well as men. But there was also a great deal of what a modern economist would call underemployment, for many people clung to existence without enough land to keep them busy all the time. More generally, people mixed what we might see as leisure activities with their work. Agricultural laborers gossiped or sang in the fields together. On cold winter nights peasants in various parts of France gathered to sing and tell stories in a barn, but repaired tools or did sewing all the while. Finally there were days apart from work altogether. In the Orthodox countries of the east as many as eighty to a hundred days were taken off each year for religious festivals. Catholic areas were only a bit less relaxed, and Protestant peasants, with fewer religious festivals, developed or revived secular holidays such as May Day. Festivals emphasized community solidarity; they allowed feasting and games and elaborate role reversals that ridiculed local landlords and provided release from normal reality. The memory of the festival could linger for a people not wedded to frequent gratification. This was a distinctive kind of life with an undeniable charm, for sociability relieved what were usually rather boring jobs. But there was a vicious circle involved as well. Agricultural producers could not work too hard because their diets were typically deficient, particularly in protein. They could afford little meat. Because they did not work intensely they were inhibited from increasing their production. This was a deeply rooted work system that made a great deal of sense, particularly because there was no known way to avoid a natural calamity that could wipe away years of hard labor.

Land Tenure

Nothing better illustrates the character of preindustrial agriculture than the way land was divided and owned. Correspondingly, a change in land tenure patterns was one of the prerequisites for any major alteration of agricultural methods. Hence Great Britain, the one area of Europe in which a rapid rise in agricultural productivity was taking place during the eighteenth century, was also the scene of tremendous changes in landholding. On the Continent substantial changes were also taking place, but usually they confirmed and extended earlier methods. Systems of rural tenure and labor still conformed to the character of preindustrial agriculture.

There were, of course, a variety of systems of tenure. In certain areas, such as parts of central France, land was worked on the basis of individual farms and might even be enclosed by fences; the plots were relatively small and the methods and the tenure itself highly traditional. In general, however, two primary systems of tenure existed in Europe. Both systems could be found in most regions. Both had some support in tradition; even in the most recent patterns, such as Russia, several centuries of development had led to the estates existing in the eighteenth century. The two systems were vastly different, however, and so were the resulting positions of peasantry and aristocracy. Furthermore, each system was dominant in different parts of Europe, and in the second half of the eighteenth century each tended to increase at the expense of the other in its areas of dominance.

Roughly speaking, northwestern Europe was an area of small holdings in which peasants directly controlled at least half of the cultivatable land. Most peasant plots were still part of a large estate, and some manorial dues and services were owed to the lord; these taxes could take a big chunk of peasant earnings (30 percent in France, for example). However, peasants could usually buy, sell, and leave the land without difficulty. There were important large holdings as well that depended on peasant labor, but these did not involve the majority of the rural population. From the Elbe River in the east to the Atlantic in the west, from Tuscany and northern Spain to Scandinavia, most rural residents based their life on small plots of land operated as part of a village structure.

In eastern Germany and beyond and in southern Italy and southern Spain large estates dominated. The major exceptions to this were the areas of modern Serbia and Bulgaria, where most peasants were free from noble control of any sort. But around 1800, in eastern Prussia, for example, about 62 percent of the land was held directly in large units. The rest of the arable land was operated in a village system, over which landlords usually had manorial rights. Even on the large estates, villages often administered the land; this was generally the case in Russia. But ultimate control rested with the landlord, and in many cases he regulated the estate directly. Certainly the social and economic character of these regions was determined by the preponderance of large estates.

The older of the two systems was that of village small holding. Many villages and their basic tenure patterns dated from early medieval times. The system was highly traditional and in many ways was a typical expression of peasant agriculture and social structure. It therefore had some importance even outside its stronghold in western Europe. In England, where a rather new organization of agricultural labor was taking shape in the eighteenth century, village tenure had flourished earlier and still hung on in some cases. In eastern Europe, where the system was overlaid by the dominant large estates, small holding had existed earlier and persisted in a minority of cases. In Russia, when the emancipation of the peasants cut down the large estates in 1861, village small holding was resumed under government encouragement. And in France, western Germany, northern Italy, and elsewhere in the northwest the system was clearly dominant by 1700. Furthermore in France and neighboring territories the revolution of 1789 removed the last restrictions on peasant ownership of most of the land. In western Germany, to be sure, many peasants remained under some manorial obligations well into the nineteenth century, but they were imposed over a small-holding system.

The typical holding in the regions of peasant tenure was tiny indeed. The average small holding was only nine acres in France. In Russia, where the climate was far less favorable, the average peasant holding after emancipation was about twenty acres. Holdings of this size were usually manageable by a single peasant family, with some extra help at harvest time. And they were sufficient to support a family, except in regions of low fertility or in years of bad harvests. However, peasant tenures were by no means uniform. Only in a few mountain villages was there anything like equality, and here equal holdings may have resulted from the fact that there was little wealth there to tempt the greedy. In France at the end of the seventeenth century only about a tenth of the peasantry owned the "average" small holding. A smaller number had much larger plots. A village of a hundred families would include one or two big farmers who owned the plows and oxen and employed labor on their land. A larger number had only a plot or two and had to do something else to eke out an existence, most commonly hiring out to the farmers or the aristocracy as laborers. There were few people who were absolutely landless, though their numbers were growing.

In 1700 the most important small-holding regions, such as northern France and western Germany, were characterized not only by small average plots but also by division of holdings into separate strips and by a substantial portion of land held in common. Each village was surrounded by several basic fields, usually three in the areas where one-third of the land (that is, one of the basic fields) was left fallow each year. The individual family possessed one or more small strips of land in each of the fields. When peasants left land to each of their sons, the strips were repeatedly divided, leading to the patchwork of several plots still characteristic of many parts of France today. Furthermore, another part of the land around the village was owned by no individual but by the village as a whole. In 1800 one-sixteenth of all the land in France was thus devoted to village commons. Both the commons and the division of land into individual plots clearly expressed the purposes of village agriculture.

Village agriculture provided some minimal protection for all members of the community. The commons were used for cooperative grazing and, where forested, provided wood for the whole village. The village itself determined the use and organization of the common land. The commons also served to protect the poorer members of the village. Often peasants with only a garden plot scraped out a living by gathering wood, tending flocks, and even cultivating part of the commons. Division of individual plots into strips protected owners by giving them holdings in different places. If disaster overtook one section, no one family would bear the entire burden. If one section was more fertile than the others, all landowners would share in its fertility. In a few areas this general concern for sharing was extended to periodic redistribution of the land according to need. In Russia after the emancipation a minority of villages redistributed land as often as every ten years according to family size; there was no real private ownership at all. This was, of course, an exceptional development; most village tenure, as we have seen, involved substantial inequality. But universally there remained the desire to offer some collective control and protection.

Finally, division into strips required cooperation. The plots were too small to farm individually, and they could not be fenced in. The village collectively decided times of planting and harvesting. Few peasants could afford their own oxen, so when plowing was to be done it was a joint venture. The plow itself was hard to turn, which was one reason land was laid out in long strips, and the turning, too, required village help. The village, and village tradition, determined what land would be left fallow. Animals in collective flocks were allowed to graze in all the fields after harvest.

The need for joint effort was another reason that village agriculture was not easily adapted to change. Its collective framework allowed little room for individual initiative. The small size of most plots offered scant margin for risk or capital for unusual investment. But there was some collective security for all members of the system. In preindustrial agriculture this had to be the primary goal of small producers.

The other major system of tenure presented many contrasts to the village structure. Most obviously, land holdings in eastern and southern Europe were typically quite large. Junker estates in east Prussia, for example, averaged three hundred acres, and some ranged as high as two thousand. Again, great variety and inequality prevailed, but the scale was quite different. The estates were capable of significant output, which was above all designed to benefit the owner. The estates usually produced most of what their laborers required for consumption. But production did not end there; estate agriculture made sense only if a significant surplus was available for the profit of the owner. Estates therefore tended to expand in importance in the areas they dominated as market possibilities increased. In the early nineteenth century German and Russian landlords eagerly took advantage of the markets created by a rising population and by the urbanization of western Europe and extended the estate system. They purchased many small peasant holdings and forced other peasants, still legally serfs, to include their land in the lord's domain. Well into the nineteenth century the estate system showed a dynamism that was less evident in the small-holding system.

The methods used on the estates were not greatly different from those used in village agriculture. To be sure, more complex equipment could be employed on these large holdings, and some was introduced by the early nineteenth century. There was experimentation with new specialized crops, such as sugar beets in eastern Germany. Some Junkers even built their own refineries and distilleries to capitalize on their substantial production. But on the whole it was not new equipment or products that gave vitality to the estates of eastern and southern Europe; rather, it was a system of servile labor.

Serfdom was virtually unrelieved in the areas of large estates until 1848 at the earliest. Efforts at reform, as in Prussia during the Napoleonic period, came to little. In fact, many estate owners sought to increase the severity of the impositions on their peasants to provide additional income. Except in Prussia after 1807, landlords continued to control the movements of their labor force so that peasants could not leave the estate without permission. Heavy quotas of work service were required, sometimes as much as two days a week, often backed by floggings and other punishments. The resulting cheap labor was the basis of landlord profits. Aspects of the system were to continue in most areas, except Russia, even after serfdom was abolished. Although increasingly pressed, the large-estate system usually endured unless abolished by political means.

This meant that, with rare exceptions, large-estate agriculture was only a bit less conservative than peasant agriculture. It was so easy to exploit workers that little thought was given to more fundamental economic improvements, even when market opportunities increased. Absentee landlords in southern Italy and southern Spain simply took over half their peasants' produce, under the sharecropping system. Although often poor themselves, maintaining at best a shabby gentility, they could not be bothered with the kind of investment and planning that would have created a new production system. Elsewhere a minority of landlords during the eighteenth century began to talk of agricultural improvements, for the idea of change was in the air. But talk was cheap, and the improvement societies formed in Russia had little impact on practice. Even where the middle classes purchased landed estates, as occurred widely in France and southern Italy during the eighteenth century, they typically imitated the aristocracy, at most trying to increase peasant dues without investing in new equipment. For they saw land less as a way to make more money than as a sign of social prestige, and the aristocratic work ethic that they were imitating did not call for much attention to economic detail.

So both of the main systems of land tenure were geared mainly to preservation of the status quo. It would take quite a jolt to prod either the average peasant owner or the average landlord into making major changes.

The Rural Classes: The Aristocracy

The fortunes of the aristocracy were based on agriculture, even when the most prominent members of the class spent their lives in the cities. This was Europe's ruling class. Its wealthiest members overshadowed even the richest businesspeople. It dominated the political and religious establishments. But its roots were on the land, and ultimately, despite persistent and clever use of its other sources of power, the aristocracy declined as the land lost its economic vitality.

In preindustrial society the aristocracy was a legal status group more than an economic class, for as we will see there were really two economic categories within the aristocracy. Legal privileges were extensive. In most countries regional parliaments met to discuss taxation and other measures. Composed of three or four legal estates, each with an equal vote, they gave aristocrats substantial political voice; for the class itself constituted the second estate outright, and it heavily influenced the first estate, composed mainly of upper clergy drawn from aristocratic families or appointed under aristocratic influence. In some areas only aristocrats could own land; this was true in East Prussia until 1808. Generally, even in western Europe the class had special hunting rights that allowed them to ride roughshod over the peasants' fields in search of game. They had special courts for themselves, and normally ran the local courts that had jurisdiction over crimes committed by peasants. They had privileges of dress; only aristocrats could legally carry swords. At an extreme, this led to the anomaly of impoverished nobles, forced to till their own small estates, proudly wearing their weapons as they pushed the plows.

Legal privilege was linked to a distinctive value system that placed the aristocracy on top of a rigidly hierarchical society. The fact that many other groups, including peasants and businesspeople, accepted this hierarchy is another way of saying that the aristocracy was the ruling class, for not only its leaders but also its values predominated. The aristocracy was rooted in a sense of separate and superior status, passed on by birth and recognized in law. This feeling was particularly intense among those aristocrats of ancient vintage, descended from the fighting nobles of the Middle Ages. But actually most aristocrats were of more recent creation. Many people were ennobled in the seventeenth and eighteenth centuries for service to the state. In some areas, particularly Russia, this practice continued through the nineteenth century; Lenin's father, for example, was ennobled for state service. Usually these new aristocrats were able to gain some land, though in Russia many were quite poor and dependent on their salaries as state bureaucrats. In France, Prussia, and even Russia the service aristocracy increased its landed holdings in the eighteenth century. But the main point is that, no matter how new, aristocratic families quickly picked up the belief in inherited birthright. One of the great strengths of the class, well into modern times, was its ability to persuade new entrants and even nonmembers of the importance of gentle birth.

The aristocracy viewed the whole of society in terms of inherited status; where a man was born, there he was to remain. The class took pains to enforce its sense of inherited distinctions in society. It rarely intermarried with other groups, particularly in eastern Europe. Occasionally financial need might compel an alliance with a business family, but this was frowned on; merchants were seen as tainted by their daily preoccupation with earning money. From the peasants, on whom the class depended for its primary income, great respect was exacted. In the Baltic regions they addressed their lord as "Father." And aristocrats as landlords attempted to take a patriarchal approach to their tenants and serfs. Rarely did they deign to collect dues directly; this was left to middlemen, in England as in southern Italy. And peasant anger was more likely to be directed against these agents than against the owners. For, in addition to the deference that many in the lower classes felt for their social superiors, the aristocracy carefully granted favors to the rural poor. It could give servant jobs to daughters. As local magistrates it could settle peasant disputes. And it gave out periodic favors and tips. Landlords even attended rural festivals where their role was mocked by peasants mimicking noble airs, for the landlords shared this culture to an extent and used their tolerant patronage to cement the reality of power. Well into the eighteenth century the aristocracy was able to enforce its view of a society based on inherited status.

Ancestry alone did not, of course, complete the definition of the aristocrat. It was assumed that birth transmitted certain unique virtues. The qualities regarded as aristocratic varied with the region and type of aristocracy, but there were certain common features. The aristocrat was expected to maintain a particular sense of honor. In Prussia aristocratic honor was given legal recognition and an aristocrat's word was accepted in court without affidavit. In most places sense of honor was expressed in dueling. Aristocratic honor abhorred commercialism and usually commerce itself, although individual aristocrats invested boldly, ran coal and iron mines, and carefully supervised estates.

The aristocrat cultivated physical bravery; everywhere military service and leadership were typical expressions of the aristocratic code. The aristocracy also clung to a belief in noblesse oblige, in a superior aristocratic ability to care for the lower orders of society. This led them to expect, and through the eighteenth century usually to obtain, the leading places in government. It could also lead them, even in areas of great aristocratic exploitation of labor, to claim and even to implement feelings for the poor. In Russia, for example, the nineteenth century saw many aristocrats make efforts to improve the health and education of their peasants while exacting servile dues.

Finally, the aristocracy felt itself to be the bearer of a distinct and superior code of manners and culture. It was a leisured class, devoted to activities inaccessible to the crowd. It strove to maintain a peculiar style of life. This effort took the forms of dandyism for the British court aristocracy, of widespread gambling (which provided excitement and showed scorn for money), of the adoption of French language and culture by many Russian nobles, of distinctive homes and clothing in many areas, and of the perpetuation of exclusive hunting rights almost everywhere. In the concepts of distinctive honor, manners, bravery, and public service, the aristocracy saw the fulfillment of its superior status.

Structure of the Aristocracy

The special position of the aristocracy rested on several factors. The class was a small one. In Hungary 25 percent of the Magyar population claimed aristocratic status; a large segment of ethnic Poles were aristocrats. But these were exceptional cases. Generally, reliance on inherited status and the relatively expensive style of life severely limited entry. In 1789 there were only 400,000 French aristocrats, a substantial number but less than 2 percent of the population. About the same percentage applied in Russia, and in most of Germany less than 1 percent of the population was aristocratic.

Despite its small size the aristocratic class was divided into distinct subgroups. There were some impoverished nobles, like the *hobereaux* in France who proudly maintained their titles while serving as gamekeepers or beggars. In Poland and Hungary this type was particularly important, often owning a tiny plot of land; the Polish *golota*, or barefoot nobility, comprised the largest segment of the class.

More generally important were nobles' younger sons. In most parts of Europe the aristocracy carefully maintained a system of primogeniture, whereby the eldest son inherited the main title and estates. This was vital if a family was not to dissipate its wealth, but it left the massive problem of what to do with surplus male children. Some of them could acquire lesser noble titles and enter the government, military, or clergy. Britain was unique in allowing younger sons to go into business without losing their claim to aristocratic status, for the British aristocracy was unusually tolerant of commerce. Elsewhere the problem of placing younger sons was acute, for the aristocracy had a high birth rate.

Gender distinctions were sharply drawn in the aristocracy. Marriages were vital to ally different families, and they were carefully arranged with scant choices to either party. Women went to their husbands' families upon marriage, the common practice in patriarchal societies. Key family decisions were the province of husbands and fathers. Some aristocratic men engaged in double-standard sexuality, insisting that their wives be faithful while conducting their own excursions. Women's tasks concentrated on marriage, birthing a suitable number of heirs (and the birthrate in the class was higher than that of other groups), and serving as ornaments to social occasions. Behind the scenes, aristocratic women had informal power in their influence over husbands or sons and their role in operating a complex household with numerous servants. Some women gained an education. The official difference in power between men and women not only colored aristocratic family life but also set something of a tone for the larger society, such as in family law.

In terms of overall social structure, the two main groups of aristocrats were the *gentry* and the *magnates*. The gentry were small landlords with local rather than national political influence. They named judges and parish church officials. In eastern and southern Europe they made local laws and provided rudimentary police services. In England they served as local judges, the justices of the peace. They received dues and work services from the peasantry on their estates. In western Europe, where servile obligations were relatively low, they used tenants, share-croppers, or paid labor to work their estates. In any case, revenues were usually sufficient for a distinctive style of life.

The gentry lived simply but well. Their manor houses were plain but solid. They hunted, held lavish feasts and dances, and often gambled. They married among their own kind, although sometimes a match with a merchant's daughter was sought for economic reasons. This was not a cultured group, although some in government service obtained extensive education. But there was no question of the firm position of the gentry. Even the magnates were scorned as urbanized and vain.

At the top of the aristocracy was a handful of magnates of great wealth and sophistication. In Hungary, around 1800, out of a total of 75,000 aristocratic families, there were at most two hundred magnate families. This was an elite group. It had few contacts with lower levels of nobility. Intermarriage between magnates and lesser aristocrats was unlikely. Both groups had more contacts with the local middle-class elements of roughly comparable wealth than they had with each other. Despite shared legal status and many common values, the differences within the aristocracy could seem overwhelming.

The magnates were distinguished, basically, by the massive economic power behind them. They were the possessors of the most extensive estates in both eastern and western Europe and, correspondingly, of the most imposing family backgrounds and titles. They left the detailed administration of their estates to paid overseers and spent most of their time in the cities. English aristocrats had a six-month "season" in London, when they sponsored the leading balls and concerts. The Hungarian magnates long preferred to live in Vienna. The income from their estates freed the magnates to devote much time to leading positions in the state, the army, and the church. They traveled extensively; the Continental tour was an accepted part of the education of leading young aristocrats in Russia and England alike. Great attention was given to polished manners and dress—interest in careful codes of polite behavior was growing around 1700 as Europe's aristocracy became more "civilized." Far from these aristocrats were the violence, vulgarity, and simplicity of the lesser nobles. The aristocrat's education was exten-

The eighteenth-century aristocracy and its opulent style of life. Growing
prosperity, increasing refinement of manners, and a desire to distinguish itself
from potential social rivals marked aristocratic life. This cartoon, by the British
artist Hogarth, dates from the 1740s. *(Hogarth, "Taste in High Life," engraving.
Bettmann Archive.)*

sive; Baltic aristocrats, for example, had tutors for their primary
schooling and then went on to private secondary schools and often to
a university. In general, education was designed to provide grace and
polish. Training in the classics and attention to sports were designed to
produce general ability and distinction. Well rounded and cosmopolitan, the upper aristocrats could recognize their peers in any country,
which was one reason their group long resisted nationalistic loyalties.
And in almost every country the group remained in control of the
major institutions of society well into the nineteenth century.

Aristocratic Power

In combination, gentry and magnates constituted the leading political
class of preindustrial Europe. They ran many cities as well as rural
areas, serving as judges, representatives in the regional parliaments,

and chief executives. They dominated the top positions in the larger political units. Rarely could a nonaristocrat rise to high office level in the military. Dukes and princes ran the armies of the eighteenth century; their leadership ultimately prevailed over the upstart forces of the French Revolution and Napoleon. Beneath the magnates a host of younger gentry, particularly those excluded from the main inheritance, served in the next echelon. Here were important sources of jobs and income and also the fulfillment of the aristocratic code of honor and bravery. No one else could serve as well.

Aristocrats also claimed a particular responsibility for the church. Here the obligation to care for the lower orders of society could be expressed. Here younger sons, trained already in at least the rudiments of the classics, could find a suitable income and social position. It was relatively easy for aristocratic churchmen to arrange for their peers to fill the leading posts in the established churches. Furthermore, religion was an important part of aristocratic life. Some aristocrats, especially in the West, dabbled with irreligion in the eighteenth century, but this was a short-lived trend. Thus, in the latter eighteenth century, the upper echelons of the Catholic, Lutheran, and Anglican churches were dominated by the aristocracy. In 1789 all French bishops were aristocrats. And everywhere the aristocratic dominance of the established churches was a major factor in promoting social and political conservatism within the churches. For as the aristocracy served the church, so it expected service in return.

The most important institution in which the aristocracy took a leading and traditional role was, of course, the state. There was some ambiguity here. There were traditions of state service for both old landed families and more recent bureaucratic nobles, but there was also hostility to the growing central power of most monarchies, which cut into local privileges.

The basic political tradition of the aristocracy was one of a weak central government supplemented by the local political power of the aristocrats themselves. Since 1600 particularly, the central state had developed greatly, from France to Russia, and had deprived nobles of full power over law courts, taxation, and the like. It was always tempting to defy the central state and seek a return to localism. Through the *parlements* many French nobles fought the state during the eighteenth century; their resistance, expressed in the Assembly of Notables of 1787, set the stage for the French Revolution. Even later the localist tradition was maintained by people like Alexis de Tocqueville.

However, it was in eastern Europe that the localist impulse remained strongest. Most regions still had diets, the regional parliaments, controlled by the aristocracy, with substantial powers over taxation and regional administration. In Russia, by the 1760s, the government had greatly increased local aristocratic power, particularly legal power, over serfs. But this only whetted the appetites of many gentry to cut down the central autocracy still further. In Poland and Hungary the size of the nobility and the fact that central government was foreign led to even more active resistance well into the nineteenth century.

But by 1700 the aristocracy rarely indulged its penchant for anti-monarchism, for it needed government jobs. Frederick the Great, while strengthening the Prussian state, confirmed the Junkers' local power and continued to rely on bureaucrats drawn from the class. Some posts were outright sinecures, paying good money for no real service. In other cases, where nobles served as diplomats or finance ministers, important work was done, but almost always the aristocratic cachet was essential. Only with the French Revolution was there a real effort to drive aristocrats from the government, and ironically, this only confirmed the links between monarchs and nobles elsewhere; for when both were attacked, what was more logical than to combine in defense? Thus well into the nineteenth century, even in western Europe, including France after 1815, the aristocrats filled the main administrative posts. And where national parliaments existed they won control as well. In Britain the House of Peers was by definition aristocratic; more important, until about 1850, over half the members of the House of Commons came from the same class, which was adept at wielding influence and even buying votes in a system where suffrage was extremely limited.

Aristocracy as Ruling Class

Individual aristocrats brought great talent to their leadership functions. Some were economic innovators, playing a role, during the eighteenth century, in introducing new agricultural methods and even opening up new coal mines and factories. It was a British earl who first put rails in a mine, to haul coal. Many statesmen served well. The cosmopolitanism of the class was particularly important. It played a major role in keeping wars within some bounds of reason. Leading magnates might seek to aggrandize their state, but not at the cost of totally disrupting the European diplomatic system. The 1815 Treaty of Vienna, which balanced the interests of the states so neatly (while ignoring newer forces, such as nationalism), was a classic aristocratic peace.

But as a ruling class the aristocracy was losing any special claim to dominance, well before the French Revolution. Its military prowess was no longer distinctive. During the eighteenth century the newest, most potent branch of the military was the artillery corps; but leadership here required technical training, and few aristocrats, except very minor ones like Napoleon Bonaparte from Corsica, were willing to take the trouble. So artillery was badly used, until the French Revolution brought new blood into the system. Despite individual exceptions, particularly in Britain, the aristocracy had difficulty adapting to new social goals. In particular, it could not spearhead economic change because this would conflict with its sense of honor. All ruling classes are parasites in the sense that they depend on winning disproportionate rewards from the hard work of the bulk of the population. The aristocracy not only sucked up huge wealth but also depended on maintaining values that no longer had a vital role to play. The class was on the defensive by the eighteenth century. Its death pains were prolonged, and in some cases distorted a whole society, for the power of the class was great.

The ambiguous position of the class—great power combined with declining functions in a society that was increasingly commercial—was revealed by the aristocratic resurgence of the eighteenth century, which in one form or another touched most of Europe. There were several causes of the resurgence. Population growth hit the aristocracy hard; there were more younger sons to provide for than ever before, and posts in schools, the church, and the military did not expand accordingly. Prices rose, and to maintain an expensive style of life nobles had to increase their resources. There was a growing sense of middle-class competition for economic and social status. This was particularly true in the West, but even in Russia the rise of a small entrepreneurial class in the eighteenth century spurred the aristocracy to protests and some competitive activity, leading the state to reduce the merchant group. Finally, the weakness of the central state in France and the growing sympathy of governments in Prussia and Russia led aristocrats to believe that they could regain some political powers that had been taken away by powerful monarchs during the late seventeenth century.

Here, then, was both need and opportunity. And the aristocracy did make gains. But with few exceptions—these mainly in England, where the class helped revolutionize the agricultural system toward increasing production for the market—the aristocratic resurgence was defensive and backward-looking. In politics and religion this meant a growing effort to exclude all outsiders, even the rare talented newcomer, from positions; never had such an outright monopoly been attempted. In economics the resurgence consisted primarily of an effort to tighten the manorial screws. Traditional burdens on peasants were increased in an effort to counterbalance the price rises. Hence French nobles tried to raise manorial dues, and in Russia the *obruk*, or work-service obligation, was increased after 1760. Finally, in the social sphere the aristocracy tried to mark itself off from commoners with growing rigor. In France accessions to noble rank from below, previously a normal means of recognizing business success, were virtually eliminated after 1750. Even British nobles tried to draw away from the middle class, forming their own exclusive clubs and cultural groups. By the end of the century musical activities in London, for example, were largely an aristocratic preserve, whereas they had previously been open to the middle class as well.

The aristocracy thus displayed great activity but little power to inno-

vate. Unfortunately, there was a huge gap between the decline of essential aristocratic functions and the surrender of the class to new
forces. Everywhere a battle had to be fought, with the aristocracy showing great resilience. In eastern Europe the power of the class retarded
the process of fundamental social change well into the twentieth century.

East and West

The bitter battle of the aristocracy to retain its class supremacy involved
the whole of Europe until the mid-nineteenth century, but it is vital to
remember how varied the odds were from eastern to western Europe.
Manorial controls were at their apogee in the east, whereas western
aristocrats depended on remnants of their dues plus outright money
rents. Except in England and Ireland, western aristocrats controlled a
smaller percentage of the land than was the case in the east and south.
Hence they had to be more flexible in their defensive action. They
were inevitably more open to new economic methods, on the land but
also in industrial investments. In England, where the class was most
active commercially, they played a major role in economic change. Ultimately, aristocrats in western Europe would also have to come to terms
with a strong middle class, interacting with their representatives in parliaments and government bureaucracies.

In the east and south a manorial economy and legal privileges remained the basis for the class. Even when legal adjustments were
required, aristocrats sought to maintain a traditional stranglehold on
their labor force. In 1807 a reform law allowed peasants in East Prussia
to leave the land and soon thereafter they were permitted to redeem
their land from manorial dues. But the Junkers held sway even so.
They managed to have the new local administrative districts coincide
with the boundaries of their own estates, so they lost no local political
power; now, instead of holding courts as manor lords, they were judges
paid by the state. They expanded their landholdings by buying out the
poorer peasants. Indeed peasants could escape their dues only by turning over at least a third of their land to the lord, so either way the
Junker won. In fact, few peasants could afford freedom at this price
and serfdom remained well intact until after 1848. In other parts of
eastern and southern Europe changes in the manorial structure were
insignificant before the mid-nineteenth century, except where obligations were actually increased. Four years before the French Revolution
destroyed the legal privileges of the aristocracy in much of western
Europe, Russian nobles gained the power to buy and sell serfs and to
inflict any punishment on them short of the death penalty.

So the gap between the two regions was obvious. Aristocratic adaptation in the West, though often subtle and successful, contrasted with

intransigence in the East. At the top of society, the differences between
the two main zones of Europe were actually increasing in the decade
prior to industrialization.

The Peasantry

Interpretation of the peasantry is the most important item in any survey of preindustrial society, simply because they were so predominant
in numbers. Although not all rural residents relied mainly on farming,
agricultural peasants constituted at least 60 percent of any preindustrial
population. We have seen that they were poor and that they worked
hard, though not intensely toward maximum output. Did they have
values and structures that compensated for poverty? Many historians
have argued that they did and that industrial society, by overturning
peasant values and communities, involved some tragic losses. The argument has merit, and many peasants, fearful of city life, would probably
have agreed. But we must be careful to distinguish fact from fancy. We
have already seen that although peasant economic tradition carried
over some sense of offering protection to all members of the community,
it did not prevent intense suffering and inequality. Peasants did have
institutions of great importance and these worked well for many of
them. But their success was varied. The reality of peasant life can only
be captured with an appreciation for this variety.

For one thing the peasantry had an internal class structure. The big
farmer, the middling landowner, and the near landless laborer were
the three main units, and they could cordially detest each other. Their
careers were not static. Even under Russian manoralism there was a
range of inequality in income and land ownership of 150 percent
among peasants in 1858, with the poor paying a disproportionate
amount of manorial dues and taxes. But to be a rich peasant was apparently chancy; on one estate only one-fifteenth of the rich peasantry
retained their status between 1813 and 1856. In France peasant mobility seemed less extensive, and a rich farmer's family could probably
hold out fairly well. But mobility as well as intravillage tension pointed
up the profound divisions within even the agricultural group. There
were also, in the average village, a handful of nonagricultural people.
The ordinary village had a teacher or scribe (to help illiterate peasants
take care of legal business) and/or a priest or pastor; it also had an
innkeeper or some other businessperson. Thus 1 to 2 percent of the
rural population was middle class. A larger number were artisans, and
some villages specialized heavily in some branch of manufacturing such
as shoes or clothing. Indeed more manufacturing was done in the
countryside than in the cities in Europe's preindustrial economy; this

meant that at least 5 percent of the rural population were artisans, and other peasants did part-time manufacturing work. Even in the typical agricultural village the blacksmith and the miller played an important role. They were more likely to be literate than the ordinary peasant; they had more urban contacts, for they had to deal with city people to buy supplies and tools. The village, with usually no more than 250 to 450 residents, thus had a complex occupational structure. Rural people did not constitute a single class; even peasants did not, in economic terms.

Two other divisions among the peasantry must be mentioned. There was a vast difference in status between married and unmarried adults. In western Europe's preindustrial rural society, 30 to 50 percent of all adults never got married. These were younger sons who could not inherit land, poor daughters, and the unattractive or handicapped who could not find a mate. Their status was very low. Unmarried women, save those in Catholic countries who escaped to a convent, probably worked as servants either for one of the richer farmers or for their own brother (and their sister-in-law). Unmarried men were often agricultural laborers, but they had somewhat greater opportunites to go to the cities, at least part of the year, to earn a bit of money as unskilled construction or transportation workers. Unless they left the village permanently they remained, like the unmarried women, part of a family economy, contributing their income to the family fund; but they too were an inferior part. In dealing with the importance of the peasant family it is vital to remember that almost half the adult population did not have full rights in it.

Rural society also had a distinctive age structure. Children began to work at age six or so. They were a vital source of labor, and this is why rural tradition so commonly stressed the importance of having a great many of them. But children did not necessarily grow up or reach effective adulthood until their mid-twenties. Only when they could inherit land and marry were they really adults. Of course they matured late sexually, reaching puberty only in their late teens. But village society was not designed for the young in terms of independence and power. Age tensions would add to class differences, and the confrontation between a man in his mid-twenties, wanting to see himself established in village society, and his father could be bitter indeed, for the older man had to die or retire before the young could achieve independence. The adult male peasant had twenty to twenty-five good years to enjoy his status, for middle age was the prime of life. It was not that he would die young necessarily. The shockingly high death rates of rural life were among infants. If a man or woman reached twenty, the chances of living until sixty were pretty good, only about 20 percent less good than they are today in modern France or the United States. So there were elderly people in the village. Christianity urged great respect for the elderly, but in times of crisis villagers often turned against their elders, as in the witch crazes that particularly singled out elderly women. Grandparents could help babysit while their adult children worked in the fields. And usually men or women fifty years old would still have younger children of their own to help out, for child births continued into the mid-thirties for women and peasant fathers usually had their last child at about age forty. This was undoubtedly one of the chores that set aside the unmarried young adults in the village. The fact remains that older peasants were an economic liability. Although almost as likely to be alive, they were far less likely to be healthy than their counterparts today. There was the simple matter of teeth falling out, for there was no easy replacement, which in turn meant immense difficulties in digestion and for anyone who cooked for the elderly. There were, undoubtedly, vigorous patriarchs who continued to help out in the fields and ruled their families with a stern hand. There were also old peasants who had to plead with their children, or more commonly write out careful contracts to make sure they would still have a garden plot to support them even though they were no longer capable of running the family.

Key village traditions thus operated against a backdrop not only of poverty but also of class division and generational tension. They worked as well as they did because they were economically essential. We cannot be as sure that they provided emotional satisfactions.

Peasant Tradition

The foundation of peasant society was family and village, both of ancient date. Their traditional basis was vital, for peasants thought in terms of both institutions almost automatically, with little sense of alternative frameworks. Peasants had no sequential historical sense, for they learned from stories (and storytelling was one important function older people did have), not from books, and peasant legend, passed orally from one generation to the next, could jumble memories chronologically. They liked to believe that their lives maintained ancestral patterns. Hence peasants might claim the family was supposed to cherish its elderly even when they cordially disliked their own fathers. They might see the village as an egalitarian institution, owing equal support to all its members, even when the village had long since failed to live up to these standards (if indeed the standards had ever been more than myth).

The basis of the family, however, was economic, not myth. A peasant went courting in eighteenth-century Bavaria. He chose a woman whom he undoubtedly knew from childhood. (In a typically small village there were no more than ten to twenty people in their early twenties, which did force some suitors to go to another village.) But he also, if he

wanted to woo successfully, picked someone of roughly his own economic level. Hence children of rich farmers married children of rich
farmers. Sometimes there was no preliminary courtship at all, for an
intermediary "marriage broker" did the job. Often village youth got to
know each other in groups, for they could not be sure which individuals
would be allowed, by parental negotiators, to pair up. But finally the
couple met and the suitor was given about half an hour to propose.
Then the parents came in to see if they had taken to each other. If so,
the final negotiations began. The woman's parents had to make sure
the son was going to inherit an appropriate amount of property and
the man's parents had to be guaranteed a proper dowry (and woe to
the peasants who had too many daughters, for they could lose their
wealth simply trying to marry them off). As it began in economics, so
the family continued. In agricultural work there was a certain division
of labor, the man working the fields (with his sons, when they passed
infancy), the woman and daughters managing the house, caring for the
animals, and raising a vegetable garden (they also went to the fields at
planting and harvesting time). A rural French mason noted what he
expected of his wife:

> We know there are countries where women marry with the oft-realized
> hope of having to work only in the house; in France, there is nothing of
> the sort. Precisely the contrary happens. My wife, like all other women of
> the country, was raised to work in the fields from morning until night
> and she worked no less after our marriage.[2]

Where necessity required, a husband might go off to earn some money,
as in doing seasonal construction work, or his children might serve in
a richer farmer's house. Any cash was turned over to the head of the
household. Teen-aged children were in fact often sent out to work as
servants and laborers for other families. This helped a village economy
correct excessive imbalances in wealth; a poor man with many children
could survive only by sending some of his progeny to a richer neighbor
who had few. This may have had the added advantage of getting rid
of older children at a time when they were beginning to resent their
parents' authority. They would be kept under strict discipline as employees in another house.

With its economic base the family was a tightly knit unit, normally
broken only by death. It was normally an extended family, in the sense
that uncles, aunts, and grandparents normally interacted with a given
parent–child unit. Contrary to some impressions the extended family
rarely lived under the same roof. As we have seen it was not necessarily
ruled by an elder patriarch. In parts of the Balkans and Russia, the

---

[2] Charles Noiret, *Mémoires d'un Ouvrier Rouennais* (Rouen, 1836), pp. 4–5.

extended family nevertheless served as an economic entity, pooling all earnings under the direction of the family's head; in Serbia this unit was known as the *zadruga*. Even in western Europe members of the family stood ready to help each other out. Above all, if only from its role in providing a rudimentary division of labor, the family gave peasants their primary sense of identity. They worked and lived not for themselves but for the family. This was a concept instilled very early. Infants were a burden to peasant society, for they were an economic drain until old enough to work. Busy mothers had little time to spare. They fed their infants when they wanted to, not when the infant demanded. Typically they wrapped the baby in swaddling clothes, so that the baby could not move around, often hanging from a peg on the wall while they worked outside. Lack of attention was not a matter of economics alone. Half of all infants would die; it was risky to invest emotion in them until it was more certain they would survive (though of course this was something of a vicious circle, for more attention might have saved more of them). And they had to be taught deference. In the seventeenth century the dominant image held that the infant was a little animal, whose will had to be broken. Peasant methods of child rearing assured that most children would learn to respect their parents' orders and would identify with the group, not the individual.

The family's economic and emotional role was rather general across peasant Europe, despite great diversity in particular customs. In western Europe, however, peasant society since the end of the Middle Ages had developed an additional trait that complicated family life: late marriage. In eastern and southern Europe peasants married around age twenty (that is, quite soon after puberty) and had many children, most of whom died. In peasant society everywhere, unwanted children might be killed by exposure or abandonment. But western European peasants, freer from manorial controls, were more concerned about protecting their property and so wanted fewer children; they continued to practice abandonment until the nineteenth century, but they needed other regulation as well. Although some methods of birth control were known to peasants—notably, using animal bladders as condoms—the most general practice was a delay in marriage until the woman was near her mid-twenties and the man was somewhat older. And village society strictly prevented sexual intercourse before marriage, for illegitimate children would rock the local economy, too. The western European peasant family was thus, typically, a property unit as well as an economic one and accustomed to rather severe sexual restraint to preserve its functions. Peasant families tried to have six to eight children, well below the biological maximum. Late marriage helped limit births appropriately so that the peasant family would have enough children to help with the work and support old age, but not too many to provide for (after infant deaths took their toll).

The emphasis of this distinctive European-style family on the nuclear household involved more than late marriage age and the fact that a minority could not marry at all. Peasant families in principle were patriarchal. The woman moved to the man's house, as in the aristocracy, and the man officially "ruled" the home. Peasant sayings often reflected assumptions of male dominance: "It is easier to replace a wife than a cow."[3] Yet the peasant family's small size meant that husband and wife had to work together closely, often developing affection and sharing decisions in the process. Certainly, the peasant wife's vital work role gave her a family position far closer to equality than that of her aristocratic counterpart, and a strong-willed peasant woman could wield substantial family authority.

Above the family stood the village, a collection of several extended families who were themselves often closely related. Varying in population, but nowhere composed of more than a few hundred people, villages served a large number of functions. They were, of course, residential groupings. Only in a few regions did peasants live on isolated farms. Normally their houses clustered in a village and their fields spread around it. The village was an economic unit producing most of the goods the peasants required. The village itself directly organized much economic activity. Many villages, as in Britain before 1750, appointed shepherds and cowherds, decided what crops to plant, and governed the use of the commons. Villages also often settled land disputes among their members. After 1861 the Russian central government even used villages as units of government responsible for approving sales of land. Although this is an extreme case, clearly the village served in many ways as an important governing unit. Finally, villagers monitored the behavior of peasants. The close supervision explains, for example, why there was relatively little sexual intercourse before marriage.

Further, villages usually had a definite governing structure. In some cases villagers actually met to make major decisions; in Britain before 1750 a three-quarters majority was required to determine what crops should be planted. Russian villages in the late nineteenth century had assemblies composed of all heads of families, which in turn elected elders as officers. Elsewhere leadership was sometimes less formal, composed of the wealthier farmers, for generally the village was capable of exercising definite direction over its members while claiming some basis of consensus.

The communal tone of village life extended to recreation. Festivals, religious celebrations, and even weddings involved the whole village. Typically, although specific customs varied, village participation in weddings extended to a celebration around the house of a newlywed couple in some form of charivari. Village leaders usually gave the job

---

[3] J. A. Millot, *La Gérocomie* (Paris, 1807), p. 98.

of organizing more formal festivals to the younger people, which may have alleviated their discontent at lack of independence and of sexual outlets; the young were allowed a certain amount of prankishness on these occasions. But older people had their role to play as well, telling stories in the evening. In village festivals, operated carefully according to longstanding traditions (in southern Italy some villages celebrated the defeat of Muslim invaders, which had occurred nearly a millennium before, as if it had happened the previous year), we see much of the communal charm of rural life, for here was one area where class and age distinctions blurred. We see the corollary as well: One had to go to these festivals, for the village insisted on communal loyalty. If, in France, the head of a family failed to contribute straw for a ceremonial bonfire on the local saint's day, he was subject to severe public ridicule and popular tradition held that, soon after, he would break a leg or see one of his children die. Accustomed to communal loyalty the peasant would not perceive these requirements as a burden, however, for village life provided no real sense of individual privacy.

Few peasants had much experience beyond the village. In the poorer

The festival. This painting depicts a community wedding festival in Belgium by the Flemish painter Pieter Brueghel. The painting is from the seventeenth century. (*Pieter Brueghel the Younger, "Village Wedding." Ghent Museum/Art Resource.*)

regions a number of males had to wander off to seek work each year. In Spain up to 10 percent of the peasantry spent part of their time annually serving as carters, hauling goods to the cities by mule or donkey. The isolation of rural villages should not be exaggerated, and it bore far more heavily on women than on men. Furthermore, there were peddlers and even local fairs that provided entertainment and news as well as goods, but both were infrequent. Characteristically peasants distrusted towns and wandering traders as much as they enjoyed them. Both represented forces outside the village and so could not be fully understood. Similarly, agents of the central government reached the peasants only infrequently in the form of tax collectors, recruiters, and rural police. They were known and often disliked, but they were not a regular part of peasant horizons. Even the church affected the peasant primarily by reinforcing localism. The church was a village church, the priest usually a peasant from the region who possessed little education.

In this situation, then, peasants' first loyalty was inevitably given to their immediate area. Even dialects and costumes were fairly local, although both extended well beyond a single village. Peasants had little interest in national politics. Their political focus was on the village and local aristocracy; in larger terms they were apolitical. Furthermore local peasant politics was personal. Issues revolved around personalities in the village and, when votes were taken, they were by public declaration. The peasant did not deal with principles or abstract issues. Hence, well into the nineteenth century, peasants had no demonstrable interest in matters such as civil liberties or governmental structure. There was, generally, a traditional loyalty to the king as protector of the people. Even when peasants rose in protest, as in France in 1789 and in Russia as late as 1905, they would commonly express their affection for the king and blame the king's advisers for any wrongs. Such risings were over economic grievances rather than political ones, and when land reforms were granted, as in France by 1793, the peasants lost interest in further revolution. Political revolts by urban elements were commonly ignored by the peasants, as in the French Revolution of 1830 or the Neapolitan rising of 1820. In these and other cases the issues involved were irrelevant to the peasantry. Similarly, peasants had little active concern for other areas and peoples. There might be some traditional hostility to invaders; Balkan peasants, for example, often disciplined their children by threatening to call in a Turk. From Alsace east the Jew was known and disliked as an outsider and a moneylender. But aside from a few highly traditional general views, peasants found their standards and goals within their immediate surroundings.

Peasant localism strengthened, and was strengthened by, the pervasive traditionalism. The decisions made by village or family about economic or social matters were based primarily on local custom. The peasants' reliance on custom was quite natural. It expressed their isolation from other groups and regions and their need to rely on oral sources of knowledge. Peasants were predominantly illiterate, though a growing minority could read. In 1800 only 11 percent of the peasants of one Irish county could read at all; in France during the Restoration, less than 30 percent could read. Again this was an oral culture and people learned by listening, which meant that peasant knowledge was primarily a matter of traditional beliefs and practices orally transmitted. Aspects of the tradition were ancient indeed. Certain pagan rites and superstitions persisted everywhere. Old medical lore was carried on. Invasions, plagues, and revolts from previous centuries might be remembered as yesterday because they were carried on as part of a living tradition.

Ceremonies of marriage and burial involved an elaborate ritual, varying of course among regions but always grounded in tradition. In parts of Ireland in 1830 a bride was supposed to flee with the best groom on a horse; the groom would ride after and seize his "prize." Elaborate precautions were taken against the presence of witches, who might produce a childless marriage by their spells. Ceremonies existed to cure barrenness and disease. Pregnant women sometimes took mud from long ditches called "Priests' Beds" to avoid a painful labor. Various omens were taken to indicate good or bad luck in ventures such as marriage. Many ritualistic precautions were developed to protect newborn infants against bad fortune and evil spirits; often they intermingled Christian and pagan practices. No general statement can cover the huge variety of peasant rituals; but these rituals entered deeply into the life of the class.

Peasant traditionalism was not mindless. Peasants dealt with health issues, for example, by means of active choices, deciding by their own evaluation of the illness and the practitioners available whether to use a folk remedy, a local wise woman, an astrologer, or a doctor. This medical eclecticism gave peasants a real sense of control over certain medical problems as well as a chance to talk over a number of troubling issues with someone regarded as an authority. (Only the young did not participate in this medical eclecticism; parents, though they might grieve over a child's death, did not have enough belief in outside remedies to take sick children to medical practitioners.)

Another vital ingredient of traditional peasant culture was an ambiguous view of social hierarchy. Unless impelled by unusual distress, such as a severe famine, peasants accepted social inequalities both within the village and outside. They saw local nobles as natural leaders in the world outside the village, a world that was not of great interest in any event. Many serfs believed that it would be positively inappropriate for their masters to do manual labor. Often they followed their lords into battles that had little to do with their own interests; and when given the vote, during the nineteenth or twentieth century, peasants typically responded by electing their landlord or priest. Daily signs of deference abounded. British laborers tugged at their forelocks as a sign of respect when their landlords rode by.

This deference had several sources. Peasants were too busy with their daily work, often too poor and hungry, to think about protest. They were carefully schooled as children to respect authority; it was easy to carry over loyalty to family to loyalty to landlord or king. Sensible landlords, for their part, played by the rules of the hierarchical game. They were courteous, if patronizing; they left the dirty work of tax collecting to subordinates; they provided services of charity and mediation.

Peasants could also harbor anger at injustice. The egalitarian strain of rural tradition could be carried against rich farmers in one's own village, but more often it was turned against the landlord class or the tax collectors of the state. In many times of stress individual peasants behaved with deference during the day, and then went out to burn their landlord's haystack at night. More rarely there were general risings, in times of bad harvest. Peasants had a vital sense of natural justice. They could claim that their landlords had no rights over them, that they alone owned the land. This was the *jacquerie* tradition that went back to the late Middle Ages. Peasants could attack the property, manorial records, and even the persons of landlords. This was the tradition that sprang up in Russia during the great Pugachev rebellion of 1773–1775 and in France in the rural revolution during the summer of 1789. More common were local grain or tax riots, in which peasants would try, through violence, to insist that the government owed them protection in times of crisis. Often, as in France during the late seventeenth century, the state organized grain convoys to feed the cities during famine years. Peasants, attacking these convoys, were seizing grain and also expressing a sense that the state should protect them.

The peasants most commonly able to express the belief in natural justice were those with middle-sized plots of land. The farmers were too rich to bother with protest, the near landless too poor to feel fully part of the rural community—and a community sense was vital to preindustrial protest. Women often led bread riots, for they were seen as responsible for the family nutrition. Often other village residents played a key role in organizing unrest. Rural artisans, particularly, were potential leaders of the more sweeping efforts. Their literacy and urban contacts set them off from the ordinary villagers but could be vital in converting vague grievances into positive actions. For protest came hard to the ordinary peasant. It could play a significant historic role; when roused, peasant anger was hard to quell. Both deference and the protest tradition fed the peasants' political legacy to the decades in which industrial society took shape.

Stability and Tension

Peasant social structures and traditions were designed above all to provide stability. From marriage customs though village economic decisions peasants sought to perpetuate the world into which they had been born. Individual peasants changed. Not only was there social mobility, there was also a certain amount of geographic movement. Records of English villages show a surprising number of people born in other communities. Again, this was not a changeless society, but it had no culture to accommodate change. Given the frequency of disasters, like famine, it was more important to try to protect what one had than to think about improvement. Protest itself, when it occurred, was based on past standards: We want the rights we had in the past, or the grain we had last year.

Poverty, economic uncertainty, and social conformity were softened by a pervasive local religion. We cannot assume that all peasants were sincerely religious. The poor, particularly those who had to travel to seek work, may have paid little attention to the church. There were signs during the eighteenth century that peasants who lived near cities, where the culture was more secular, were irreligious, and this sentiment may not have been new. Generally, however, religious and peasant life were closely intertwined. An impoverished French village, run by an absentee landlord, beset by frequent migration and family tensions, was held together only by religion, which gave inhabitants a sense of a higher, if mysterious, purpose to life. Religious ritual was an integral part of village festivals and personal celebrations such as weddings and funerals. On occasion peasants displayed an intense religious emotion; this was a common response to famine or plague. More normally religious rituals provided emotional, even aesthetic, satisfaction. For married women, churchgoing was one of the only activities that took them out of the home.

The village had other devices to defuse tensions. Drink was one. Peasants could not afford to drink a great deal (even in France, wine drinking became common only after 1600), but on feast days and special times of tension liquor provided some release. Agricultural laborers were given drink after the harvest was in. Russian peasants in the nineteenth century, involved in the intense bickering over property lines that bedeviled peasant society, often settled cases in the village court by giving both parties an abundant dose of vodka. Nicknames often helped. Balkan communities well into the twentieth century expressed both humor and dislike by derisive name-calling. Festivals provided an occasion for socially controlled violence as well as drinking. Rough games pitted men from one village against men from another, or married men against unmarried. Many were little more than brawls.

But not all tensions could be controlled. Some villagers, lacking property or hating their parents or in trouble with the village council for displaying too much independence, had to leave. They might head for a city or sign up for long stints in the military (service contracts ran up to twenty-five years). But some roamed the countryside, and bands of beggars, even outlaws, could strike fear into the hearts of the village. There was violence within the village. Peasant property was normally respected, for village safeguards here combined with the need, in a subsistence economy, to avoid senseless destruction. But rates of personal violence could be high; up to 74 percent of all village crimes were acts of violence. Lacking local police, many peasants took revenge into their own hands. Family feuds, as in southern Italy, constituted an extreme of this practice and could lead to frequent bloodshed. Unwanted infants were often killed, usually by exposure, when peasant methods of birth control were inadequate. There was insanity in the village as well, if only because inbreeding could cause congenital madness. The "village idiot" was not a myth, and he or she often had company.

Village conformity thus exacted some toll. Certain kinds of peasants, particularly at certain stages of life, might be open to an alternative. But the attractiveness of village structures made it difficult to think in terms of novelty. Most peasants had a sense of identity so rigidly enforced that it inhibited choice. The massive changes of the nineteenth and twentieth centuries, necessarily challenging key rural values, would find many peasants ill prepared for change. They would drive some to acts of despair.

The Cities

While urban society was more recent in origin than rural, it too had a long history in Europe. The cities themselves were old. Their systems of government as well as many of their physical facilities had been established centuries before. The two principal urban classes—the *bourgeoisie* and the *artisans*—had both originated in the Middle Ages. Both classes had been renewed and added to since that time, but many of their institutions and values were extremely traditional. However, the cities were not closed to innovation. Social structures could not be totally rigid; the very physical proximity of a large number of people of varying positions caused a certain tension. The cities themselves were expanding even in the seventeenth century, though at a relatively slow rate, and their wealth was increasing. Finally, the leading urban class was usually mobile in the preindustrial period. The bourgeoisie in western Europe was based on wealth, primarily nonlanded wealth. Though by no means totally venturesome, the class as a whole did tend to try to expand its wealth to improve its social position. Despite important traditional features, then, the cities were sources of considerable dynamism around 1700. Indeed, from the cities emerged many of the innovations that created a radically new social and economic climate during the eighteenth century.

The urban map of Europe at the end of the eighteenth century was rather complex. Cities scarcely existed in eastern and southeastern Europe. There were a few centers, sometimes rather new, such as St. Petersburg. Some commercial activity took place in these cities, but the level was low. The few major cities of eastern Europe existed primarily as political and administrative centers. Cities that lacked these functions were of little importance; Athens, for example, had dwindled to a population of only a few thousand under Turkish rule. Correspondingly, the urban classes of eastern Europe were both tiny and weak. Commercial middle classes and artisans scarcely existed; much of the scanty trade that did go on was in the hands of foreigners. There was a bureaucratic middle class in Russia, but it was tiny and lacked independence. In terms of social structure cities were unimportant in these areas. Along with the large estates and rigorous serfdom of the countryside, the effective absence of cities was one of the defining characteristics of eastern European society.

In western Europe important cities did exist. Urban population in Scandinavia and Spain, at the extremities, was less than 10 percent of the whole, but significant commercial and artisan classes were present. In France, the Low Countries, and Britain, about 20 percent of the population lived in cities. It was in those areas that cities had been expanding in size and wealth. Even in western Europe, however, most individual cities were small. There were a few giant centers; Paris had a population of 700,000 at the end of the eighteenth century, one-sixth of the urban population in the country as a whole. The rest was scattered in smaller cities. Only Lyons had more than 100,000 inhabitants. A few other centers approached this figure, but far more had populations of only 5,000 to 10,000. The largest cotton-manufacturing city in France, Rouen, had fewer than 80,000 residents in 1815; vital regional commercial and administrative centers such as Toulouse had fewer than 50,000. In France and elsewhere the average city was modest in size, and such cities were widely scattered over the country as a whole.

The physical organization of the city reflected its size. Cities were compact. Traditions of crowding together for defense and ease of building remained. Many cities still tried to live within defensive walls, even as they expanded. Streets were small and narrow. Houses were also narrow, usually attached in rows. Crowding pushed members of different social classes into close proximity. Many houses were divided into apartments, with wealthy burghers occupying the lower floors and poorer artisans the upper floors. A large city, such as London, did have residential areas more clearly separated by wealth and profession, but even there important residential mixing occurred. Systematic segregation by class would arrive only with industrialization.

City governments generally undertook only limited functions before the Industrial Revolution. In England regulation of hygiene and trade scarcely existed. Police forces were rudimentary, fire prevention and transportation left entirely to private hands. On the Continent, central governments took a greater role in city life, and this was to increase in the eighteenth century. They undertook some housing regulation and fire prevention. More streets were paved, more sewers covered. Police forces spread to small towns.

Even on the Continent the dangers and difficulties of urban life were numerous. Crime and violence were common. Disease was widespread and epidemics frequent. In fact, almost every city before 1800 experienced more deaths than births in a given year; population was maintained or increased only by immigration from the outside.

The economics of most cities were as simple as their physical facilities. Local trade and artisan manufacturing were the economic bases of the typical urban center. Small shops sold foods, clothing, tools, and various luxury items to residents of the city and surrounding region. Products were commonly manufactured and sold in the same shop. Even so, few people were employed in a given shop because the operation was on a very small scale. Only a few enterprises reached out for more than local markets. Major cities like Paris produced some luxury goods for sale all over the world. Some other centers had a specialized production destined for wide distribution. Lyons exported much of its silk production; on a more modest basis, Thiers sent cutlery all over France. Even in these cities the units of production involved only a few workers. But above these units, large merchants exercised important control, bringing in raw materials and arranging for the sale of the products.

Many cities were centers of a rural textile-manufacturing system as well. Large merchants again brought in raw materials, but in these cases sent them out to peasant homes all over the surrounding region. Foremen served as middlemen, allocating raw materials and collecting cloth. Only a few finishing operations took place in the city; but the city was the economic center of the industry, and to the city flowed the profits. Only in a minority of cities did merchants engage in extensive putting-out production; only the most dynamic centers manufactured more than could be sold close to home. Most entrepreneurs and workers alike were involved in small operations in which neither complex tools nor complex business organizations were needed. For every far-flung export concern there were hundreds of tiny shops relying on the manual skills of one or two workers and the simplest of business and accounting procedures. Again it must be remembered that the typical urban resident lived not in a major production center but in a city with less than 10,000 inhabitants, content to serve a local economy.

The Bourgeoisie

At the top of the urban social structure were the bigger merchants and some related professional people, particularly lawyers. They did not necessarily run the city. Many units were controlled, like agricultural estates, by nobles or churchmen. The society and culture, though not the government, of bigger centers like London were dominated by aristocrats. The wealthier businesspeople might share in this culture, but at some distance. Concerts were advertised as being open to nobles, gentry, and "others," and seating was often segregated. In smaller centers the business community usually had a greater role, and merchant guilds ran the government of places like Mulhouse, Frankfurt, and Elbeuf. But at best wealthy urbanites had only local power and prestige.

In many cities the leading businesspeople constituted the *bourgeoisie*, a term that initially referred to a city resident. This had in fact become a legal status group, not unlike the aristocracy. It had special voting rights and tax privileges. Often it was quite small, reflecting the fact that old merchant families were prone to set themselves up rather like an aristocracy and fought the admission of outsiders. The term *bourgeoisie* has come to mean much more, of course, denoting a capitalist middle class. In preindustrial cities, though individual capitalists flourished, the bourgeoisie as a whole cannot be described in this way. We can see the seeds of a middle class, but not the class itself. Even the term *bourgeoisie* is too narrow, for not all business and professional people had the legal status of this group. It is nevertheless useful to employ the term for the premodern group as a means of distinguishing it from its industrial successor.

The bourgeoisie in this broader sense was an economic grouping in part. It was richer than the artisans and lower classes of the cities and less wealthy than the aristocratic magnates. But a successful businessperson might rival the earnings of the gentry, which is where the law came in: at the top, the bourgeois was bourgeois because they lacked noble title and noble rights. The class was a large one in the cities, representing up to 20 percent of the urban population, or about 3 or 4 percent of the total population of western Europe. Its members ran the larger businesses and manufacturing establishments. It sent some people into the government bureaucracy, at the middle if not the top levels. It was literate, and a few of its members went to secondary school and even the university; some lawyers and doctors, for example, were university trained.

However, although its outlines can be roughly defined, in many ways this was not a class at all. Its professional segment lacked many of the modern attributes of professions, although it loomed large as a percentage of the bourgeois, contributing over half the class in Prussia and other areas of central Europe. There were in fact only three premodern professions: law, medicine, and the clergy. In Catholic countries the clergy had its own legal privileges, and as we have seen its upper ranks were dominated by the aristocracy, its lower by bright peasants who had some special calling and/or the sponsorship of a local notable. In Protestant countries the clergy had more ties with the bourgeoisie. Service as an Anglican minister, for example, was a highly respected career for the son of an English merchant. But to obtain the necessary university training and placement it was common to seek aristocratic sponsorship; many ministers initially served as tutors for noble families. Hence, though they received training that can be called professional, clerics formed something of their own group even when not a legal estate, closer to the aristocracy than to the bourgeoisie. The leading lawyers also served the aristocracy; for the most, complicated transactions involved the landed estates. And although some were highly trained, others entered through an apprenticeship system that won them scant prestige. More doctors were trained entirely through apprenticeships and had a rather low status. Neither doctors nor lawyers had any means of assuring the quality of their colleagues (there were no examinations, no licensing) save through individual sponsorship, and no ways of limiting their numbers. Nor did they have much sense of professional cohesion, though some doctors assailed other kinds of medical practitioners.

Some preindustrial professionals were quite talented. But those who did well generally profited mainly from aristocratic patronage or from service to the state. Particularly in central and eastern Europe, bourgeois elements filled important bureaucratic posts because they had training and expertise that many aristocrats were unwilling to acquire. But as bureaucrats they were directed by aristocratic ministers and were sometimes themselves ennobled.

For their part the larger merchants were unable to provide a distinctive definition to the bourgeoisie. In big cities like Paris they typically aspired to become nobles themselves, for until the mid-eighteenth century if one amassed enough money one could hope to buy a title. In the meantime the wealthy merchants tried to imitate an aristocratic lifestyle, rather than develop a separate sense of values. This was why so many bought land where it was legal for them to do so. If they acquired an estate they liked nothing better than to rule as lord of the manor. Some won local government functions, as was the case with notaries in France and Italy who had great local prestige. Well into the nineteenth century a number of businesspeople essentially agreed with the aristocracy that commerce was degrading, and sought a more respectable way of life. The same impulse could even impede their money-making efforts in the city. In Paris, for example, aristocrats were more daring in their investments than bourgeois businesspeople, who typically put their money into real estate at a very low (2.5 percent) return. The concern for investment security and respectability must have kept many businesspeople from reaching their real goal— amassing enough to buy a title.

All of this means that the preindustrial bourgeoisie was not capitalistic in the modern sense or resentful of aristocratic dominance. But most businesspeople, particularly in the typical smaller centers, had no chance to aspire to the aristocracy. There was a bourgeois culture, although not a modern one. In the first place, the bourgeoisie had a clear sense of distinction from the lower classes. Here businesspeople probably shared aristocratic values, but because they lived in the city, where the poor were more menacing and not a part of a clear hierarchy, their views could take a fearful turn. The poor were inferior and there was no remedy for their condition. As the Bible helpfully commented, "the poor will always be with us." At most they deserved charity when times were particularly bad, and the bourgeoisie had a traditional, paternalistic attitude that would lead them to donate clothing to the poor, give occasional tips to their servants, and grant alms to the many beggars of the city. For their part the poor were supposed to be respectful and grateful. But the bourgeoisie was conscious of another urban group as well, the criminal class, for there were sections of the cities like London and Paris that were too dangerous to enter. Criminals were permanently degenerate; here, too, there was no remedy to propose. But the perception of two groups within the lower orders was confusing. Charity was fine, for example, but it should be carefully monitored lest it go to the undeserving, barbaric element. By the same token the bourgeoisie lived close to some elements of the poor and even shared in their culture. London merchants, for example, gambled and went to cock fights along with journeymen. This ambiguous class outlook, combining shared urban culture, charity, and fear, would long influence middle-class perceptions.

In business the bourgeoisie valued security and organized to protect themselves against risk. Many merchants were grouped in guilds that limited competition. In Frankfurt merchant guilds ran the city council, which alone had the power to grant citizenship in the city; and only citizens were allowed to conduct business. What was sought was a safe income and a legacy for the children. Women often helped with accounts or tended shop. Children were brought into the business early. Sons often did clerical work, planning to rise to ownership when their fathers died or retired; there was no real clerical class as a result. The bourgeoisie was comfortable, immensely impressed with the importance of owning property, but not, for the most part, eager to amass great wealth. It valued a certain simplicity in manners, differing thus from

The patriarchal family. Entitled "The Family Repast," this painting shows a bourgeois household being served a meal. The painting suggests a good deal about the status of children in relationship to parents and of girls and women in relation to boys and men (with a bit of age hierarchy among the children added for good measure.) This painting was done by the Le Nain Brothers in the mid-seventeenth century. *("The Family Repast," copy after Le Nain Brothers, France. Courtesy of The Cleveland Museum of Art, Gift of Mrs. Salmon P. Halle in memory of Salmon Portland Halle.)*

the imitators of the aristocracy. Clothing was somber, quite different from the flamboyance of the aristocracy, though more elaborate than the dress of the lower classes; French burghers wore knickered breeches, whereas the lower classes had only trousers, a distinction that would be given political meaning by the French Revolution, which designated the urban mobs *sans-culottes* — "without breeches." Bourgeois food was abundant but simply prepared.

This middling bourgeoisie had something of its own ethic. It stressed the importance of family life and sober behavior. It wanted disciplined respect from children and modesty from women (who were supposed to be subservient to their husbands while also playing a vital business role). Family and economy were intertwined in this group too, and marriages were carefully arranged to provide economic security for the new family; dowries and inheritance thus loomed large. The bourgeoisie valued hard work and condemned idleness. It frowned on spendthrift behavior and praised savings. But it also disliked excessive ambition. This was a group quite satisfied with its position in the middle of society; in Germany it was in fact called the *Mittelstand*, or middle order. Those who tried to rise too far were taking too great a chance; modest achievement was preferable. Regular religious practice was part of bourgeois respectability, and the class gave important financial support to urban churches and religious charities.

In sum, the bourgeoisie had certain values that could carry over into a modern middle class. The "early to bed, early to rise" ethic could form the basis for a dynamic capitalism or a challenge to the idleness of the aristocracy. But the attachment to modest property had a role for the future as well; it would keep many bourgeois from ever accepting some of the newer features of an industrial society.

The Artisanry

Right beneath the bourgeoisie was the artisan class. Indeed there was some overlap, and a successful artisan master (a wealthy goldsmith, for example) bore much resemblance to the bourgeois. But the classes were largely separate. Artisan guilds rarely had much voice in urban government, although economically they served many of the same functions.

The artisanry was the largest urban class, usually about 40 percent of the city population. Wealthier than the urban poor it lived close to the subsistence level in most cases; it was highly vulnerable to economic crises, for when harvests failed food prices rose and demand for manufactured goods fell off as well, hitting the artisan hard. So it was not so much a distinctive average income that defined the artisan class as the possession of a definite, traditional economic skill. Artisans made lace and embroidered fabric. They wove and finished cloth, particularly expensive cloth like silk, with luxurious patterns. They worked as tailors, printers, bakers, and butchers. They were the leading construction workers in the city, carpenters, painters, roofers, and masons. They made furniture; they made tools and other metal objects. In other words, they comprised the basic labor force of the urban economy, manufacturing most of the products required locally as well as some important items for more distant markets. Their methods of work were largely traditional. They worked with simple tools, lacking elaborate mechanical contrivances. They worked at home or in small shops, usually with no more than five other craftspeople. There was little division of labor in the artisan's work. A few young workers, particularly apprentices, often served relatively menial functions. They carried raw materials and finished products, swept the shop, and assisted in some of the more difficult procedures of the artisan. Aside from this, artisans typically carried their operations through by themselves, from preparing the materials for production to taking care of the tools. The complexity of the operation and the simplicity of the equipment meant that real skill was required. Artisans invariably underwent an important period of training, usually in a formal apprenticeship program. Even relatively simple jobs, such as lace making, required at least a year of apprenticeship, and more complex trades involved up to seven years of training.

Artisans built their lives around their work, spending long hours on the job. Their family life and work intertwined. Women helped with some manufacturing processes, but more commonly kept accounts and sold goods. In some cases their functions required them to be more literate than their husbands. The family lived in the shop. Artisan masters normally housed and fed journeymen as well as apprentices, extending the familial atmosphere. Not uncommonly the journeyman married the master's daughter, a good way to assure the boss's favor. Artisanal organizations favored the sons and brothers of existing craftspeople anyway, which enhanced the association of family and work. As with peasants there was little life outside the job, save for occasional festivals. Again, artisans did not work intensely, except for short periods; these bursts would be followed by slower work that allowed talking and singing with fellow workers. Many artisans, particularly those who worked in heat, causing them to perspire heavily (bakers and blacksmiths, for example), drank regularly on the job. The artisan valued his opportunity to mix what we would call recreation with labor.

Urban artisans resembled village craftspeople in many respects. Their skill and training, their relatively common literacy, and their work patterns could draw them together, and many a rural blacksmith or mason could move into urban crafts without much difficulty. But urban artisans had an organizational experience that was much different from rural patterns. They were less individualistic in a way, and certainly more accustomed to grouping in the interests of economic protection and sociability. The key artisan organization was the guild, which served many of the same functions as the village did for the peasant in attempting to provide security but also closely regulating social life.

Most guilds had the legal power to deny workers the right to practice a trade unless they were admitted as members. Through this device guilds typically tried to limit the number of workers in a given trade in a city; the guild existed not to maximize production but to protect the standard of living and the economic opportunity of its members. By limiting the number of workers it tried to assure employment for all. It also tried to restrict production so that artisans would receive suitable pay and prices for their work and products. Guilds therefore maintained strict controls over the methods used in work and generally prevented any major innovation in technique. This not only stabilized earnings but also upheld the value of traditional skills. Opportunities for the ambitious and clever might be limited as a result, but such opportunities were irrelevant to the guild's primary goal of protecting the welfare of all its members.

Moreover, important mobility was provided within the structure of many guilds. Artisans were divided into three major categories: apprentices, journeymen, and masters. Artisan tradition, and to some extent continuing practice, held that all artisans should have the opportunity to pass through all three stages during their production lives. The period of apprenticeship was, of course, vital to the artisan's position. Beginning usually in the early teens, the apprenticeship provided training for the job. A fee commonly had to be paid for the privilege of entering apprenticeship, and a stiff contract bound apprentices to their tasks. However, tradition and guild supervision attempted to ensure fair treatment of the apprentice. The master was required to feed and house apprentices and train them to the level necessary for full participation in craft production.

After apprenticeship artisans typically became journeymen, working for wages, often supplemented by food and housing provided by the master. Young journeymen typically spent a year or more wandering from city to city aided by the guild at each step, to gain skills and experience. These wander years also helped prevent labor gluts in particular cities. Following some years as journeymen, in which hopefully some savings could be accumulated, artisans might be able to buy or inherit a shop and equipment, becoming masters in their own right and often employing other journeymen. This did not mean that the masters became separated from their work, for masters worked beside their employees in most cases. Under guild rules and protection, artisans were provided with a social and economic ladder they could climb as they gained skill and capital.

Guilds offered, then, some economic security and defense of skills. They helped limit the gap between master and journeyman. In addition, they provided some political experience, as guild appointments were made by vote of all the masters. In some cases artisan guilds had some voice in city governments. Certainly the general recognition of guilds by city and even national governments gave the artisan significant contact with politics more generally.

Guilds were social groups as well, sponsoring a variety of functions and supervising a number of rituals. Many guild statutes set forth detailed funeral regulations, stating who should attend, who should bear the body, how many candles were to be lit, and so forth. Although artisans had more chance for independence than peasants, particularly when they traveled, guild membership restricted not only economic initiatives but also personal privacy.

Guilds expressed and provided many of the values maintained by artisans well into the industrial period. However, the picture should not be overdrawn. In the first place, not all urban artisans were involved in guilds. Further, certain populous trades were never organized in guilds; this was particularly true of work in which women were primarily involved. Women had a few guilds of their own in lesser trades, like lace making; in the Middle Ages, they had joined men in some more important guilds. By 1700, however, women had been forced out of the top crafts and attendant organizations. Their work supplemented that of a husband or father, in one artisanal version of the family economy, or women worked alone, usually in a low-paying craft and without guild protection. Artisans in the main had developed a fiercely male definition of prestigious work by the eighteenth century, which they would carry forward later on. Even in the masculine crafts certain cities never developed a full range of guilds. On the whole, however, the major artisan professions still had a guild tradition and important guild structures.

More important was the fact that the guild tradition periodically broke down even in the key professions. Usually two related conditions were involved. First, newcomers to the city, in periods of urban growth, could overwhelm guild limitations and create competition for jobs and wages among journeymen. In England by the eighteenth century most guilds had totally lost the power to restrict the number of workers in a craft or even to control techniques of work. When journeymen were overabundant it was tempting for masters to convert the guilds to their own ends alone. This had often happened in French and Italian cities and was to occur more massively with industrialization. Guild ideals held that masters should be roughly equal, and to this end guild regulations often limited the number of journeymen that any one master could employ, as well as holding open the promise of mobility. But when journeymen were cheap, individual masters often sought to advance their fortunes, at the same time using guild organization to block all but their own sons from rising to mastership. A class wedge could thus be driven within the artisanry. Even here, however, guild traditions were not irrelevant, for the typical response of journeymen was to form their own associations to bargain with the masters and achieve some of the goals guilds were supposed to provide. In seeking to protect wages and limit the number of apprentices, journeymen's associations were a midway point between guilds and craft trade unions. But in 1700 guilds themselves had rarely broken down entirely; they were particularly strong in central Europe. Artisan shops remained small and most craftspeople had personal contacts with the masters that prevented a complete class rift.

Journeymen and masters alike had a definite sense of status. They expected to be treated with respect, even by their social betters. Just as the bourgeois marked themselves off from artisans by distinctive clothing, so artisans wore emblems of their trade to distinguish themselves from the poor. Family organization resembled that of the propertied classes, peasant and bourgeois alike. Artisans married late, for it was improper to found a family without a suitable economic position, preferably a mastership. Marriages typically involved the same kind of economic calculation we have seen among other groups. Brides were supposed to have a dowry, grooms a skill and good prospects for the future. From this base stemmed the association of family and work, which was typically passed on to the next generation when the son was sent into his father's trade. It was in fact the father's responsibility to provide the funds to pay for his son's apprenticeship as well as to set up dowries for his daughters. Here was another reason for late marriage, which would limit the number of children born to the family.

Finally artisans had political expectations that were somewhat more precise than those of peasants. Artisans were not accustomed to asking for direct voice in government, although occasionally they did attempt this on the urban level. They did expect the state to help them out during economic slumps. In the typical preindustrial economic crisis, the artisan needed cheaper bread, for prices rose precisely as income went down. The response was often a bread riot, in which bakers were attacked for price gouging. But the artisanal protest tradition could spill beyond this. Sometimes rich businesspeople were attacked, for artisans had an egalitarian resentment of wealth that could burst out when times were bad. And indirectly artisan rioting called for state action: The government was supposed to bring in enough grain to drive prices back down again. Where possible the state did exactly this, for artisanal rioting was feared. As with the peasantry the basic artisanal protest tradition was backward-looking. It asked for restoration of conditions that had prevailed before, not for new gains. This is why it could occur only in economic crises, for there was no expectation of progress to motivate agitation in good times. But the protest tradition was important nevertheless, and artisans would carry it vigorously into the modern period.

It is tempting to idealize the artisan's life, in comparison with later conditions of manufacturing work. Skilled, respected, able to rise to independence, this might be an enviable lot. Certainly the values involved were important, and many artisans would long try to preserve them as the foundation for their social life as well as their definition of economic justice. But the system did not work well for everyone. Journeymen had personal contact with their masters but they were by the same token intensely dependent on them, directed about from day to day and supervised not only at work but also at meals and guild festivals. As was the case with the peasantry, a large number of journeymen could never marry because they did not acquire sufficient independent means. Many artisans, even masters, were desperately poor, though of course there was great variation from one individual to the next. Many ate little but starchy foods, and the quality of food was often spoiled. Housing was characteristically crowded, especially because the home was also shop and journeymen's dormitory. Health suffered. Many painters and printers died early from lead poisoning. Weavers were particularly subject to chest diseases because they pushed their looms with their chests. Indeed many artisans were deformed by their trade, and were more identifiable by their bent walk or gnarled hands than by the costumes they wore on festival days. Crowded housing, poor diets, and the miserable sanitary conditions of most cities caused a high infant mortality rate. Most urban artisans could expect more than half their children to die before age two; they were even worse off in this respect than the peasants. When a craft was destroyed by industrialization—and many were not, as we will see—important losses occurred that many craftspeople would try to protest. The chance to escape traditional constraints could attract some artisans as well.

The Urban Poor

Artisans were definitely not the worst off in a premodern city. Approximately 20 percent of the urban population were domestic servants, mainly though not exclusively males. In Elbeuf, for example, approximately 250 members of the bourgeoisie employed 194 servants in 1785, and of course aristocratic households in larger cities would add to this number. Servants had some economic security, for they were normally assured of board and room. Though their money wages were low, some were able to save. They could also imitate some of their masters' habits; many learned to read. Given hand-me-downs by their employers or dressed in livery, servants might be proud of their dress. A few successful servants might indeed rise in society, using their savings to buy an inn or some other business. But the typically modest bourgeois household was not the basis for material comfort. Housing was miserably crowded, and only poor food was provided. Servants as a whole were a highly dependent group. They could not risk protest; they had at least to pretend subservience. They had virtually no free time from their job, for they were expected to help set up the household in the morning and put things to right at night.

But at least the servants had some compensations for a hard existence. A vast number of floating urban poor had nothing. In the larger cities, the final 20 percent of the population was composed of unskilled, transient labor, and even smaller centers had a substantial group. These were people who did the cruder kinds of dock work—those who hauled carts and wagons, carried bricks or stones on construction sites, or dug ditches. Their functions were vital to the city, but their rewards were minimal, for they offered only their muscles, with no special skills or training.

The unskilled were paid low wages and also subject to irregular, degrading employment. Normally they were hired on a day-to-day basis, flocking to a city square (for example, the Place de Grève in Paris, from which the French word for *strike* ultimately came), where they would compete for attention from a hiring boss. Some had to offer bribes to get any work and all had to be carefully docile to any employer. Many drifted from one city to the next, or back and forth from the countryside. Unskilled construction workers traditionally came into Paris from several poor rural areas every summer, hoping to earn enough to tide their families through a hard winter. Southern Italian laborers wandered even farther in search of urban work.

The poverty of the unskilled could almost surpass description: ragged clothing combined with the meanest housing, often in cellars or attics or in hovels outside the city walls, plus meager food. Unless they had a rural base the unskilled could rarely afford a family, and many did not earn enough to form a marriage even in the countryside. Many had to beg. Some had to turn to crime. This was a desperate existence.

Yet the urban poor could not protest. They lacked the resources to take time off from their quest for work. Their diets afforded them no energy for an unusual effort. And they lacked community structures, which were essential to protest in premodern society. They moved about too frequently even to know many of their neighbors. They had no standing or traditions in the city and no organizational experience. This deprived them of leadership of their own. More than this, the urban poor were rarely able to join a riot started by others. Rioting required a sense of purpose in society; struggle for survival was not enough. So except for individual acts of defiance such as theft, the urban poor could not protest their plight. The group remained isolated and disorganized in the city, vital to the city's economic life, vaguely feared by the propertied classes, but otherwise ignored.

Popular Culture

Preindustrial cities had their own rituals and entertainments, beyond those organized by individual classes, that even the very poor could share to some extent. Urban popular culture expressed many of the hardships and uncertainties of material existence; it might also provide some distraction from them.

The culture was violent. As in the countryside, urban groups not infrequently engaged in brutal brawls. Rival journeymen's organizations, with no apparent differences save separate names and symbols, often came to blows. Apart from direct fighting, popular entertainment frequently had a violent element. Animal fights were prized, as in bear baiting or cock fighting, with bets placed on the winners. Public executions could gather thousands of people, as the state intended, so that the example would be clear. Whether they sympathized with the criminal or simply enjoyed the macabre show, the public rarely stayed away. There were popular songs, often with a romantic theme, and other casual entertainments as well, but the theme of violence was noteworthy.

Death played an important role as well. Cemeteries, located around churches and dotted through towns, were a constant reminder. Few people, urban or rural, were unused to death; virtually every family saw several children die. Hence the rituals associated with death were essential. The ultimate degradation was burial in a common ditch, and a family had failed when one of its members had to end in this way. A proper funeral soothed the tragedy of death; it could even add a bit of interest to the routine of living, for death was too common to be the subject of prolonged lament. The urban poor also shunned hospitals if they could because these were seen as places where one died among strangers, a judgment that had considerable basis in reality. Like peasants, urban inhabitants were eclectic in their choice of medical treatments. Suffering higher death rates, they were particularly vulnerable to plagues and epidemics, which periodically added a note of stark terror to urban life, causing the wealthy to flee altogether. Reactions of this sort were mixed with a certain amount of fatalism about God's will.

This was in an important sense a conservative culture, designed to palliate tragedy but not to seek improvement. Where change was suggested it was often feared; vaccination against smallpox, for example, introduced during the eighteenth century, met widespread resistance in the cities. Fear of the unknown was enhanced by the suspicion of outsiders, for the urban poor had little experience of help beyond casual charity from the upper classes or established institutions of society. In the cities even the church was often resented as the creature of the rich, and the poorest elements of the city proved readier to riot against the priests than against any other target. For the charity given by the rich and the church was known to be patronizing, and even when it had to be accepted the necessity was disliked. Worthless in the eyes of the larger society, the poor would have liked to close themselves off from it to defend their self-respect.

The changes associated with industrialization inevitably shocked the common people of the cities, and some, because of their traditionalism, were slower to take advantage of new opportunities than any other element of society. New urban leaders directly attacked the most common recreational outlets of the city's poor. But other values had to be preserved, at least until the physical quality of life in the cities underwent enough improvement to warrant a culture based on some hope. Elements of the preindustrial popular culture survive among the very poor even in cities today.

A Status Society: For or Against

The complexity of preindustrial society is obvious. Even the poverty, which has to be emphasized, was not absolute except for a minority in both city and countryside. Economic uncertainty was more widespread, rooted in the impossibility of controlling the conditions of agricultural production—hence the protective quality of most economic organizations, from peasant family to merchant guild. For all but the aristocracy and the bourgeoisie, life was full of hard physical toil. For men this was qualified by a work culture that intermingled elements of sociability and a slow or mixed pace. This was true of women in field and shop as well. But married women owed not only their productive labor but also frequent childbearing. To produce three or four children living to adulthood the peasant or artisan woman had to have seven or eight births, which were normally spaced two years apart. Thus the average married woman spent fourteen to sixteen years of her life carrying, bearing, or recovering from having babies. Apart from the physical strain, which resulted in frequent death in childbirth, there was the emotional anguish of infant death, which no amount of fatalism or ritual could entirely overcome.

To some extent the economic limitations of preindustrial existence restricted the affectionate quality of life. Economic arrangements came first in the family, and romantic love, though sung in popular ballads and hailed in aristocratic culture, was an accidental result. Infants were seen in terms of labor potential, and not given much attention until this potential could be realized; this was particularly true in southern and eastern Europe. Quarrels over property could poison family relations at a later stage; here western Europe, with its more property-conscious peasantry and bourgeoisie, faced greater tensions. Even death could not be given too much attention. When a married woman died she was typically replaced, for where there was property it was not hard for a widower to pick up another mate. Widows faced greater problems: preindustrial society discouraged women from remarrying lest inheritance be complicated, and conditions for older women may indeed have deteriorated around 1700. Given late marriage age and a slightly shorter adult life span, the average marriage may have lasted only fourteen years—considerably less than in the modern day, for mortality is more inexorable than divorce. We cannot know how much affection a husband lavished on his wife or parents on their children; undoubtedly there were great individual variations, as there are today. But we cannot assume that the family existed primarily as an affectionate unit.

Preindustrial society did provide other compensations for physical hardship. Religion gave hope for the afterlife. Preindustrial people had a concept of a "good death," in which an older person could expire over a several-week period (typically from a respiratory disease) at home and surrounded by family, making peace with any members with whom there had been dispute. While good deaths were not the only kind that occurred, the notion brought solace to the dying person and the family alike when it did apply.

More generally, the multitude of small organizations, beginning with family and ranging through village and guild, protected from loneliness and gave an automatic sense of identity, though it is important to remember that a large minority of individuals were not fully embraced by these organizations. Protection entailed intensive personal supervision of life. How one could work, whom one could marry, when one could have sexual intercourse, what one could do on holidays, all were precisely regulated, except for the minority of people who led a precarious existence roaming from one place to another. But except for the wanderers there is little sense that supervision was resented, for no alternative model of existence was available.

Furthermore, regulation was alleviated by some opportunities for spontaneity. Festivals sponsored a certain amount of roughhousing and vandalism, plus the activities that mocked reality including men cross-dressing as women. Europe's common people maintained a certain earthiness, delighting in farts and belches. Sexual activity, supervised to prevent unwanted births, was often and openly discussed. Other bodily functions could be indulged. Some rituals, indeed, mingled such actions in a culture where sexuality was not particularly privileged. In Wales, for example, courtship involved, among other things, a man's urinating on the woman's dress as a mark of possession.

Ownership, community, and ritual gave the majority of the population some stake in the existing order. Deference from below and paternalism from above cushioned the basic framework of a hierarchical society. Protest was extremely important but it occurred usually within the social framework, not against its foundations. Rarely did a preindustrial group toss up egalitarian arguments, though this had occurred among small radical sects in the Reformation and the English Civil War. More important, the bulk of the populace had some property or expectations of property. It might be highly qualified, particularly given the overlay of manorialism in eastern and southern Europe. But most peasants had at least a partial sense of land ownership; most journeymen owned their tools and could aspire to mastership; the bourgeoisie was propertied by definition. Younger people were kept in line by the expectation of inheritance. More than legal status, which defined the outlines of social groupings, property ownership, despite its various objects and gradations, served as the key to societal organization, and this principle would be brought forward in the first stages of industrialization even as legal privilege was attacked.

Women, to be sure, did not own much, though widows in many areas gained property rights. Their inequality with men was manifest, given the patriarchal family structure and unequal division of the most prestigious work. Their vital economic role in the family economy, however, gave many women an important voice in the conditions that most directly affected them, and their roles in bread riots showed how this role could extend to larger economic demands. Save in some aristocratic circles, there was no clear movement for a redefinition in women's status.

Few groups, indeed, professed active interest in changing the social boundary lines around 1700. The people who endured the most intense physical suffering were too remote from the prevailing organizations to have a voice. Individual discontent could be alleviated by mobility— moving to another village or to the town, moving up in society by purchasing an aristocratic title. Because some movement was possible at various levels, most commonly from one age group to the next as skills or property was acquired, the basic social order seemed acceptable and there was no need for an ethic of mobility. The aspiring bourgeois wanted to imitate the aristocracy, not displace it. The itchy journeyman hoped to become a master, not destroy mastership. There was change in life, or expectation of change, without an ethic of individual striving. Protest traditions were vital, but they more commonly attacked crises associated with the established order rather than the order itself. Only jacqueries periodically reached further.

The stability of preindustrial life was about to be challenged. And there were a number of groups who might be ready to take advantage of a new social structure, even if they were not overtly discontent in the preindustrial system. Women, youth, the poor, aggressive personality types at any social level, all might find reason to try something new. Others would resist. Cherished institutions, the property stake, and the very means of childrearing that stressed loyalty to authority and custom, all promised stern opposition to change. Literally none of the major preindustrial social groupings believed in change as a matter of principle. Even the bourgeoisie, as a class, sought to defend, not challenge. The small organizational units that defined institutional life were all predicated on maintenance of custom, not innovation, and their close supervision of their constituents made deviation difficult.

Changes in Europe's Agricultural Society

The basic structures of preindustrial society in western Europe remained intact in 1700—the dominance of aristocracy and predominance of peasantry, the family economy and the tight community bonds for work and leisure, even a strong tendency to invoke tradition as justification for action. Within this structure, however, important shifts had been occurring, particularly from about 1500 onward.

Europe's growing dominance on the seas, and in worldwide trade, obviously increased the size and wealth of merchant groups. It lent new importance to manufacturing, for Europe could now import cheap goods from overseas in return for sales of manufactured products. Gradual improvements in technology brought metalwork, then textiles to the highest levels in the world. Some cities and regions developed important specializations in manufacturing for the market. Merchant capitalists recruited growing numbers of rural workers to produce manufactured goods like nails or cloth, often combining this work with some agriculture. The number of wage laborers grew, particularly during the sixteenth century when a 3 percent overall population increase created greater landlessness. At the same time, commercial development brought greater prosperity to peasant farmers and artisans who did own property. Also in the sixteenth century, observers in England commented on the growing number of well-built chimneys and glass windows in rural housing, along with more abundant bedding. Not only here but in Holland, France, and Germany as well craftspeople began to decorate walls and cabinets, designed for otherwise ordinary folk, with graceful popular designs.

Religious disruption, and particularly the rise of Protestantism, plus new scientific ideas changed the ways many people thought. By the seventeenth century Protestant leaders were urging a more broad-ranging definition of the purposes of family life. Still units of production, families were also supposed to provide moral instruction for children under a father's guidance, and active friendship, including sexual enjoyment, for husbands and wives. Growing commercial development also prompted greater attention to family, particularly as men began to regard each other somewhat more competitively and sought more interaction around the secure familial hearth. Greater prosperity enabled many families to begin to provide more elaborate table settings and to purchase imported products such as sugar, coffee, and tea, which helped to focus greater attention on the family meal as a ritual occasion designed for enjoyment and active conversation. Revealingly, cookbooks, which had until about 1650 concentrated on instruction for preparing festival meals for a guild or village, now began to focus on family fare. With these encouragements redefinition of the family began to occur in Catholic countries like France as well as in Protestant areas.

New knowledge of nature and attitudes toward it also left a mark. The idea of controlling environmental problems through organized planning, rather than prayer and ritual, gained ground. Thus it was during the seventeenth century that fire companies were established along with commercial insurance to reduce risk. Lost-and-found bureaus were set up in cities so a person might go there to find a lost object rather than turning to a traditional "cunning man" who would seek lost items through magical divination. It was in this new popular culture that active belief in witchcraft began to decline, with trials ending in most previously active centers by the late seventeenth century if only because magistrates, a relatively educated sector, withdrew their support from the whole concept.

Changes in beliefs were prompted by a rapid spread of literacy among a growing minority of western Europe's population headed by urban groups. Protestantism promoted literacy as did the printing press. During the sixteenth century literacy tripled in many areas, and the process continued steadily thereafter.

Adding to the basic forces of commercial and cultural change was the growing efficiency of many governments by the late seventeenth century. Leading monarchies—the absolutism in France was the classic example—developed larger and better trained bureaucracies. This shift did not totally alter the rather loose relationship between state and society, though it typically produced pressure for higher taxes. Governments did begin to regulate economic activity more directly; by the eighteenth century they could even encourage basic changes in agriculture. They also developed better controls over movements of people and animals across borders, which could affect traditional plague contagion and so population size. Stronger governments also drew more popular attention toward expectations that the state should intervene against dire hardship, particularly in cases of famine or high food prices. Popular protest began to take on a more political tone. This was especially true in Britain, where the seventeenth-century civil wars revealed widespread popular claims to rights of expression, but it also surfaced in France, where by the 1680s grain riots routinely invoked government assistance.

Changes of this sort, occurring a century or more before the merest glimmer of the Industrial Revolution, altered European society profoundly, reaching from marriage to economic life. The changes were both dynamic and unsettling. They were also, however, extremely uneven. They did not affect eastern and northern Europe. In Russia, change was also occurring around 1700. It involved some increase in metallurgical manufacturing, but under state sponsorship with reliance on serf labor; commercial development was curtailed. The aristocracy was encouraged to develop more Western cultural interests, which drove a further wedge between them and the peasantry who disliked their Frenchified airs. The rigors of serfdom tightened. There were significant developments, but not the same sort that were occurring in western Europe.

Even in western Europe change was spotty. Some villages shifted to considerable production for the market with the alterations of outlook and social structure this implied, but others, sometimes little distance away, remained locked in an essentially self-sufficient economy.

Change meant different things for women than for men. Particularly in Protestant regions, the importance of family for women increased, if only because a separate religious life, in celibate convents, was now abolished. Within the family women began to take on more responsibility for mealtimes and other family rituals, but perhaps a bit less productive work. Men were disproportionately involved with some of the new forces, such as commercial activity and contacts with cities or growing literacy.

In addition, change was conditioned by new social divisions. The growth of the landless element, while it helped fuel more market production based on wage labor, also heightened anxieties about the irresponsibility of the poor on the part of many property owners. The idea of traditional community responsibility for charity, while still visible, diminished steadily. New institutions, notably the prison, first introduced in Holland around 1600, were devised to isolate and punish the most irresponsible poor as fear of crime mounted periodically. New social divisions emerged in the cultural sphere as well. Beliefs changed more rapidly among wealthier, educated groups than among the lower classes, though there were some common trends. Europe's elite became more suspicious of popular culture, terming it crude and superstitious. Landlords grew uncomfortable with their attendance at rough popular festivals, and they increasingly resented the festival customs of mocking the ruling classes. They still showed up, in 1700, but now as an obligation undertaken reluctantly. And they pressed for more orderly behavior.

The deep-running changes in Europe's agricultural society helped prepare for further upheaval to come as the first signs of industrialization, late in the eighteenth century, would spring from many of these currents. At the same time, the change trends, carving new divisions in Europe by region, class, and to some extent gender, guaranteed that any later shifts would have an uneven impact on European society, as both levels of effective power and basic outlooks increasingly diverged.

CHAPTER 3

The Forces of Change: The Late Eighteenth Century as Turning Point

Europe in 1700 was an unusual kind of agricultural society marked by extensive trade. Western Europe by 1800 was well on the way to abandoning its primary focus on agriculture, creating a much more revolutionary kind of social base. This chapter pinpoints the transitions that took shape in crucial decades of the eighteenth century. These transitions were built on the shifts that had been accumulating before 1700, but they went much further.

A number of related developments reshaped the economy and, to some extent, the character of society in western Europe from about 1750 to 1820. Economic relationships became still more widely commercialized, based on selling labor and goods for money and maximizing profits where possible. Commercialization also meant more impersonal economic dealings, with strangers in unfamiliar market settings. Although cities did not yet grow with unusual rapidity, urban influences spread along with the market economy. Entertainers from the cities fanned out into the countryside. By the end of the eighteenth century, for example, professional jugglers and other urban-based sideshows were a regular part of village festivals in France. Urban influence also showed in new patterns of sexual behavior and, in certain areas, a decline of religious practice. A new sense of time gained usage, as work, at least in urban manufacturing, was measured by the clock. Timing by sunset and sunrise was giving way to hour-by-hour punctuality; the growing sale of clocks and watches showed that more and more people were adopting this time sense, even if against their will. This preliminary phase of industrialization increased the division between propertied and propertyless people, which came as a particular shock in the countryside. This period also saw the birth of a more modern political sense, as elements of the bourgeoisie and the urban artisanry learned to demand rights of political participation.

Most fundamentally, new personality types were clearly emerging at a number of social levels. Diaries revealed a new concern with appearing cheerful, against traditional beliefs that a certain amount of melancholy was normal. Some peasants as well as merchants learned to think in terms of rationality and innovation, casting aside a traditional outlook. A new sense of individualism was even more widespread. People began to express and indulge their egos as individuals, reducing their identification with customary groups. In many villages, as one example, a few aggressive, indeed greedy, peasants began buying up more land, even trying to acquire some of the common lands. Their goal was more production for the market and more profit. Their efforts split village life, earning bitter resentment from other peasants.

These vast changes began in a setting that seemed in many ways rather placid. Western Europe between 1650 and 1730 appeared in a number of respects to have settled down. Population growth eased, hysterical persecutions of witches ended, religious conflict died down after the fires of the Protestant Reformation. Changes in the eighteenth century did extend previous shifts, including the growth of trade, Europe's dominance in the world economy, and new patterns of personal beliefs. At the same time, the sharp new upheavals that took shape after 1750 had some limitations. Even when the industrial and political revolutions of the late eighteenth century are added to earlier trends, we must recognize that European society in 1820 was still highly traditional in many ways. Even revolutionary upheaval did not quickly destroy older values and institutions. This was one of the ways change could be accepted. Young people were constantly more open to it than old, and this generational process helped cushion the impact of change. When young people in the villages adopted new styles of dress or began to drink coffee and tea, the old might grumble, but so long as they could maintain their consumption habits, they did not feel too threatened. But young people, too, mixed tradition and innovation, preserving many preindustrial structures, notably the family, in a new setting. Change and continuity may constitute a trite theme but it is a constant one in the modern upheavals of Europe.

The new round of change, often called *protoindustrialization* to distinguish it from the technology-driven Industrial Revolution that lay mainly in the future, was confined to western Europe: Britain, France, Scandinavia, Germany, the Low Countries. Its major features were also present in North America. This Atlantic region was already accustomed to market dealings, with a bourgeoisie that, if not highly dynamic, was at least attuned to trade and finance. Peasants already engaged in some trade. The commercialization process simply altered the balance of their economy; from marginal, sales to the market became increasingly central. Comparable commercialization was impossible in eastern Europe. In the Balkans peasants had almost no market experience. They viewed nature with superstitious awe. Tools, to them, were objects of worship as much as implements of production, and elaborate ceremonies were built around the ax or the stove. Only a few objects, in terms of tools and furnishings, were owned by the peasant household, probably less than a fifth as many as in the peasant cottage in western Europe. A new attitude toward things and toward nature was essential before further change could occur, and this came about only gradually in the nineteenth century. The Balkan region was an extreme case. Commercialization in the Russian countryside was suggested in the eighteenth century, as manufacturing spread and some peasants began to serve as commercial agents, hinting at a rural middle class. But the aristocracy, fearing this kind of innovation, assumed control of rural manufacturing by the end of the century, so neither the position nor the values of the peasantry could change greatly. Earlier changes in western Europe—the growth of cities, the reduction of aristocratic economic power, the partial independence of both peasants and artisans—created the only setting in which protoindustrialization could initially occur. The aristocracy could not block the process. Peasant tradition, though real, did not prevent new efforts to subjugate nature or introduce new forms of work. In both city and countryside, tools, though respected, could be changed.

The key manifestations of protoindustrialization involved extensions of market production, particularly in manufacturing, even in advance of radical new technology. Rural people churned out textile and metal products under the orders of city-based merchants, who supplied raw materials and sold the product, offering a wage as reward. From protoindustrial manufacturing came a wider use of money. People at various levels gained interest in consumer goods, particularly clothing; revealingly, increasing thefts of clothing mirrored the new passion for adornment. Traditional community structures yielded to more individualistic motives and to the growing gap between owners and wage earners. From this setting, in turn, full-scale industrialization would take shape, though only in Britain did this process advance significantly before 1820. The more general tide of eighteenth-century change, affecting social structure, work habits, even personal motivations, was more widespread.

But what caused a new round of change from the mid-eighteenth century onward? It is possible to see change imposed on the bulk of the populace, against their will: a group of greedy capitalists forced the common people into new ways. This leaves the question of where the new greed came from, but presumably this could be tracked down. The approach has some merit, as we will see, but it is too simple. Change came from decisions made by a whole variety of groups in the population. The decisions had unexpected consequences and their impact was severe in many ways. But they were not simply forced down the popular throat. And their results were correspondingly ambiguous. If the common people were merely forced to change, we would expect massive problems of adaptation. If, as we will contend, some innovation resulted from voluntary and widespread popular action, some adaptation was prepared in advance. The preparatory phases of industrialization have often been seen as a massive attack on a happy, traditional society, even an overturning of the natural human way of doing things. This view, particularly common in England, is nonsense. Preindustrial society was not so uniformly happy. Its ways were not "natural," for after all, only hunting and berry picking were natural to original humans. The transformation of preindustrial society did involve great strain, but it brought some rapid benefits as well. Otherwise, people would not have been so stupid as to participate in the process.

Sources of Change

Before the protoindustrialization process began at any general level, there was a massive revolution in the realm of formal ideas. The scientific revolution of the seventeenth century produced a belief in progress, reason, and the possibility of grasping the simple laws of nature. In the eighteenth century this mentality was carried forward in the Enlightenment, and philosophers held that human affairs could be ordered as rationally as they believed physical nature already was. The Enlightenment asked for political reform and material progress. Its image of the human being was very much like the model of the modern person as developed by social scientists in the twentieth century: secular, scientific, progressive, and so on.

The connections with other new developments were not always clear-cut, however. New science, for example, did not directly produce new inventions. Only in the nineteenth century was the linkage made. Eighteenth-century industrial techniques were worked out by artisan tinkerers, who had no contact with scientific thought. James Watt, the inventor of the steam engine in the 1770s, came closest to such contact, for he made precision instruments for scientists at the University of Glasgow. But his steam engine did not embody existing scientific ideas; at most he imbibed a belief that progress was possible and that step-by-step thinking produced new knowledge. Early industrial capitalists seized on Enlightenment ideas. Matthew Boulton, who first produced the new steam engines, joined a scientific society and talked about industry as the basis of world progress. But these interests occurred after his success as an entrepreneur; it is hard to argue that they caused it. The Enlightenment had a more direct role in the first signs of modern political consciousness. Belief in political reform spread to many sectors of the bourgeoisie in France during the second half of the eighteenth century via Enlightenment tracts. Lawyers and other professional people were particularly receptive. By the 1790s a more radical reform interest, also Enlightenment-derived, reached artisans, whose leaders began talking in terms of social contracts and popular sovereignty.

There is no question that a host of changes in popular beliefs developed or solidified during the early eighteenth century. The practice of swaddling children began to die out, which meant that parents had to find new ways to supervise infants and perhaps take new interest in their individual development. Naming of children, relatedly, became more individualized, with less use of parents' names or the names of older siblings who had died. The functions of home were further redefined, as family meals continued to gain importance under the supervision of the wife and mother. A more novel development involved the family's emotional base. Love became more acceptable as a motive for marriage itself, again at various social levels. It was no longer unheard of for a young woman to persuade her parents that an arranged match should be called off, however advantageous to the family in economic terms, because she did not love her suitor. Formalized gardens and new attitudes toward animals, reflecting a pragmatic approach willing to use animals dispassionately but also a new aversion to random cruelty, exposed new beliefs in a more benign and controllable environment.

Ideas about nature, self, and family, in other words, continued to change rapidly as a result of Europe's previous commercial growth and cultural changes such as religious reformation and the new science. While connections between the new mentalities and the further developments introduced in the 1750s were not always explicit, they fed into a willingness to consider further innovations. Fascination with the new manufactured clothing, for example, had some relationship to more romantic courtship patterns and a more explicit sense of oneself as an individual, and the clothing interest in turn fed the extension of textile manufacturing and the willingness of workers to seek wage-paying work.

The state, particularly on the Continent, also played a direct role in eighteenth-century change, though without intending to contribute to any fundamental transformation of society. From the late seventeenth century most European governments had been extending the scope of their operations. They tried to increase their contact with distant sections of their country, curtailing the regional power of aristocrats. Bureaucracies were expanded, and bourgeois elements were brought into some of them. Most important, the government began to deal with activities that had previously been left to the control of local and private groups. Many states codified laws on a national basis, establishing clear and presumably rational standards to replace local traditional rules. Governments felt active concern for the economic health of the nation. At the end of the seventeenth century, governments from France to Russia tried to introduce new industries and techniques. Several governments, such as the Prussian, encouraged better agricultural methods; they sponsored drainage projects and supported new products such as the potato. To promote commerce, several states provided clearer standards in currency and in weights and measures; Britain even established a semiofficial national bank. Efforts were made to cut down local tolls and other barriers to a national market. Roads and canals were extended. There were even direct attempts to encourage population growth.

In none of this, however, was there any intention of altering basic class structure. There was some talk of governmental responsibility for the well-being of all subjects. Some rulers increasingly saw their interests as separate from those of the aristocracy and other traditional bodies, such as the national churches; hence nonaristocratic bureaucracies and religious tolerance grew. But above all, Continental governments wished to develop their economic and military power. This required reforms in military techniques and recruitment. It required an improved economy, particularly in the manufacturing sector. It required greater governmental efficiency in many respects. But this was not a revolutionary purpose. Governments avoided challenging major privileges, especially those of the aristocracy, because such challenges might weaken the cohesion of the state. In eastern Europe, as we have seen, nobles were able to increase their power. Governmental action did spur some economic and administrative change, but for a full-blown economic transformation, some new impulse was necessary. Even in the economy, governments often prevented innovation by formulating elaborate rules on production methods that supported the craft and merchant guilds. So we must look elsewhere for the basic motor of change.

Population Growth

The massive expansion of Europe's population was the most important disruptive force of the eighteenth century. Elements of every social class were forced to innovate in order to survive. There were, to be sure, areas of substantial population growth that did not adapt; indeed the eighteenth century saw a population explosion outside of Europe as well. Within Europe demographic upheaval in Spain and Italy did not produce new social structures. Again only western Europe had the essential preconditions to alleviate population explosion through new economic structures, and even here the shock of demographic revolution was chilling.

In virtually every area of Europe the population increased by 50 percent to 100 percent in the eighteenth century, with the greatest growth coming after 1750. The Hapsburg Empire grew from 20 million to 27 million people; Spain rose from 5 to 10 million, and Prussia from 3 to 6 million. France increased from 20 to 29 million, Britain from 9 to 16 million. Growth continued throughout the nineteenth century. Some areas such as Italy and the Balkans even increased their rate of growth after 1870. In Europe as a whole, population rose from 188 million in 1800 to 401 million in 1900. This was an upheaval of truly impressive proportions. Its significance may be measured by comparing the rate of expansion with the 3 percent increase in Europe's population during the entire century between 1650 and 1750. Clearly, a demographic revolution occurred after 1750.

The expansion of population was European in scope. Certain regions, even whole countries, experienced an unusually rapid rise. Britain and Germany approximately tripled their populations during the nineteenth century after an even faster rate of increase in the late eighteenth century. France barely doubled its population between 1700 and 1900. Obviously, differences in degree must be noted. Distinctions in date are equally important. The demographic boom in western and central Europe was most intense between 1750 and 1850; French population began to rise as early as 1680. The factors promoting this boom touched eastern and southern Europe in a more limited way, and it was the period after 1850 that saw the most significant increase, with the spread of western techniques of midwifery and vaccination playing a leading role. By 1900 virtually every area of Europe had contributed to the tremendous surge of population, but each major region was at a different stage of demographic change.

The unprecedented increase in population was the most important feature of demographic change, but it was not the only one. In the century and a half after 1780, Europe sent 40 million people to the two Americas, Asiatic Russia, and other areas. Emigration was one of the clearest expressions of the turmoil that increasing population brought to European society. In the first generations of demographic rise economic opportunities failed to keep pace with the population. Emigration was most intense when population grew most rapidly and tended to decline once industrialization developed sufficiently to absorb most of the increase. Britain and Ireland supplied most of the emigrants at first, reflecting the intensity of population pressure in the two islands. The agricultural crisis of the 1840s convinced many German peasants that the land could no longer support them, and a wave of German emigration ensued. Eastern and southern Europe provided most emigrants at the end of the century. By 1914, 17 million people had emigrated from Britain and Ireland, 4 million from Austria-Hungary, 2.5 million from Russia, and 10 million from Italy. Only a few countries, such as France, largely escaped the movement.

Though only a minority of Europeans actually emigrated, the movement affected a far larger number. The wave of emigration greatly increased Europe's influence in the world. It brought new economic opportunities and new knowledge to many Europeans. Equally important, it disrupted many families, many villages, and exposed countless people to contact with new ideas about the possibility of mobility and change. Information and myth about the possibility of emigrating and the nature of life in new lands had significant effects on many villages and towns. They represented one aspect of the change in outlook that population growth brought to European society.

The populations of Europe not only grew in the nineteenth century, but also changed in physical character. Health improved. In 1800 the life expectancy of a Frenchman at birth was twenty-eight years; by 1900 it was almost fifty. Physical size increased. In western Europe the average man was about five feet tall in 1800. A century later average male height had increased by six inches, and weight was accordingly greater. Women grew less, but their health improved, particularly with dramatic reductions in maternal mortality late in the nineteenth century. For both genders, physical deformity became less common as diet improved and many forms of manual labor were lightened by the introduction of machines.

The demographic revolution thus serves as a backdrop for social change well into the late nineteenth century. But its consequences were most dramatic during its initial decades. And it is here that we must seek the basic causes of the process.

Causes of Population Growth

The population explosion resulted from a break in the traditional, if approximate, balance between births and deaths in European society. In England between 1700 and 1750, approximately 32.8 people were born annually for each 1,000 inhabitants, and 31.5 people died. Similarly, in Lombardy in the late eighteenth century, 39 people were born and 37 people died for each 1,000 inhabitants. Clearly, major alteration had to occur either in birth or mortality rate before the expansion of population could begin. In fact, both rates changed: families began to have more children and a lower percentage of the population died each year. Lower infant death rates meant more people living to produce children of their own, though falling adult death rates also increased the number of older Europeans. Much is still unknown about the precise developments in population rates in the eighteenth and nineteenth centuries, but certain general features seem clear. During the period 1750–1800, for example, the population of England grew at a rate of over 1 percent a year. Approximately 80 percent of this can be accounted for by a decline in mortality; by 1800 only 27.1 per 1,000 people died per year. But there was also a startling rise in the number of children born annually.

Several basic factors contributed to a decline in mortality rates in the eighteenth century. In central Europe and in France deaths in wars declined. Epidemic diseases became less common. Plagues still occurred; in the 1830s cholera killed a large number of people in western Europe. But the historic pattern of periodic decimation by epidemics, like the fatal wave of influenza in western Europe in the 1720s, was really broken. Better methods of hygiene, particularly in the cities, accounted for some of this decline. English cities kept streets cleaner in the late eighteenth century and paid more attention to sewage disposal. In parts of England vaccination reduced the incidence of smallpox, a major traditional killer. There was also an improvement of border controls against entry of diseased persons and animals. The growing efficiency of the Hapsburg government was particularly important in blocking the traditional route of plagues from the Middle East into Europe. But we should not exaggerate the importance of human agencies in this process. Certainly no major medical advance was involved. The decline of epidemic disease occurred outside Europe as well, for the eighteenth century saw a break in the traditional plague cycle, as had occurred before in human history. The germs would regroup and attack again in the nineteenth century, but by this time Europeans had learned new ways of dealing with disease, particularly through improved sanitation.

More important than reduction in disease was reduction of famine in the eighteenth century. Better diets improved health, which helped increase sexual activity (hence the birthrate rise), and still more important, reduced mortality. A number of factors improved the food supply. New agricultural methods were developed, particularly in England and the Low Countries, from about 1690 onward. Better methods of drainage opened up new lands. Increasingly, cultivation of nitrogen-fixing plants replaced traditional systems of fallow on some of the large estates. By growing plants like turnips every few years, all cultivable land could be kept in use, which brought as much as a 33 percent increase in agricultural production. New equipment, such as seed drills, also improved yields. In eastern Europe the governments of Prussia, Russia, and the Hapsburg lands fostered colonization of wilderness regions. The Russians expanded cultivation in the rich lands to the south and west, and new areas of Hungary were opened up to agriculture.

But the new lands did not account for most of the increased food supply. Nor, certainly, did new agricultural methods, for although these were known and discussed they were not widely adopted until the nineteenth century. The most important new development was a simple one: the introduction of the potato and, in southern Europe, maize from the New World. The potato's advantages over traditional grains were legion. It could be grown in three or four months, instead of ten, and in poor soil. Its yield was more than two times that of grain per acre, and so it was particularly ideal for small holdings; an acre in potatoes would support a family of five or six people, plus one animal, for the better part of a year. It could be cultivated by hand. It had high caloric and nutritional value. The qualities of maize were somewhat similar, though it was not widely grown in northern Europe. Italian peasants grew maize on their garden plots while they raised wheat for their landlords, subsisting on a corn meal polenta, which is still widely used in southern Italy even though it may cause pellagra. Maize also supported population growth in Spain, southern France, Hungary, and possibly the Balkans during the eighteenth century.

For the area in which population growth triggered industrialization, however, the potato was the chief agent. Population growth indeed varied somewhat with the rate of adoption of the tuber; France, for example, was slow, whereas the impoverished peasantry of Scotland and Ireland expanded massively as they converted to the new crop. England, in the middle position, nevertheless had at least a third of its population subsisting on the potato by 1844. Ironically, peasants had long resisted the potato, which had been brought from the New World, as an oddity, well before the eighteenth century. Traditional fear of novelty was at the root of their resistance. The Bible did not mention the crop, therefore it could not be good. It was held to cause typhoid fever. Russian peasants, in a slight variant, believed it produced cholera, which is one reason the potato did not catch on there until after 1850. But eighteenth-century governments and enterprising landlords promoted the crop, for increased population was a source of military and economic strength. And peasants gradually converted on their own because the potato initially answered two traditional needs. It helped assure against periodic famines, and grain failures in the eighteenth century played a major role in spreading reliance on the new crop; and it protected the peasant with only a garden plot, particularly in areas where landlord dominance or repeated division of plots through inheritance left a family with insufficient land to survive. A sensible decision, to adopt the potato, and one that had immense consequences.

The initial causes of population growth in western Europe lasted little more than half a century. By the early nineteenth century the rate of growth was slowing. But expansion would long continue, even increasing in terms of absolute numbers. Basically this momentum resulted simply from earlier growth. More people reaching childbearing age in 1800 guaranteed still more children reaching childbearing age by 1820 even if the birthrate slowed up a bit. By the nineteenth century the undeniable spread of agricultural improvements supported the new population. Ireland suffered demographic disaster in 1846–1848 when the potato crop failed, and never regained its peak levels of total population as death and emigration turned the country backward. But the rest of Europe, despite periodic famines, could now produce even more traditional crops than before. By this point industrialization itself also provided new jobs and wealth. Finally, by the later nineteenth century genuine medical improvements, particularly in the care of children, entered the scene. By 1900 death at infancy had been reduced to about 10 percent in western Europe. The discoveries of Pasteur and others from 1860 onward heralded additional improvements in medicine and hygiene. So populations still grew. But in fact most families in western Europe, by the second half of the nineteenth century at least, were trying to reduce their birthrates. Although demography still had a dynamic impact, the real revolution, resulting from a few simple decisions and an odd combination of circumstances, had already taken place.

Effects of Population Growth: Commercialization

The population increase of the late eighteenth century shook established behavior. Jean Koechlin was a rather ordinary master weaver in Mulhouse in precisely this period; not particularly dynamic, not an obvious industrial pioneer. But he had twelve children, all of whom survived to maturity. He needed jobs for his sons, dowries for his daughters. So he began to spread his textile operations to the countryside, ultimately directing a large putting-out operation. Koechlin's sons, in turn, more genuinely possessed of a risk-taking entrepreneurial spirit, set up large cotton factories and were industrial magnates by the mid-nineteenth century. Here is an unusual success story, but something like it occurred many times, which is why population growth is so vital to the understanding of economic change. New numbers provided a new labor force and new markets, quite obviously; they also provided new motivations.

It is impossible to say why some families, undoubtedly a minority, responded to population growth through innovation. Previous social position had something to do with the pattern. Large farmers probably had an advantage over other peasants as they converted to more market production in order to support their brood. Relatively few people rose literally from rags to riches under population's spur. Established merchants often clung to traditional business practices; only a minority of the bourgeoisie expanded trade and manufacturing. By the same token traditional centers of production often declined in relative importance. Their leaders, satisfied with preindustrial standards, simply did not take the trouble to innovate. Cities outside the traditional merchant and guild orbit, some of them, like Mulhouse, with no special physical advantages, could rise quite quickly. Here was the beginning of the remaking of Europe's urban map. Most artisans tried to cling to old ways. A few did not, and it was from French and particularly British artisans that most of the early industrial inventions came. A few cases of dramatic mobility occurred over time. A landless English peasant in the early eighteenth century sets up as a domestic weaver, possibly making a fairly good wage. His son becomes a foreman in the system, distributing raw materials to the workers and picking up the finished product. His son, in turn, sets up as a small manufacturer, for by now the family has a modest capital. And either he or his son, for by now we are near 1800, starts a factory. Population growth increased the fluidity of western European society.

Ultimately the economic innovators would coalesce into a modern middle class, but this was yet to come. For the eighteenth century, what must be emphasized is a division in virtually every traditional class, between those who sought change and those who resented the new pressures placed on them.

The aristocracy was sorely pressed by population growth. Although the class had traditionally generated much larger families than the poorer masses, it was not accustomed to seeing so many sons and daughters survive. Established positions did not increase apace. The army officer corps, for example, did not grow as rapidly as the aristocratic population. Here was a major source of the aristocratic resurgence during the eighteenth century. By trying to monopolize both church and state the class helped convert aspiring bourgeois into a middle class, with a consciousness of its own rights and values. By responding defensively, the aristocracy provoked a new class struggle. The French Revolution and related political battles elsewhere became middle-class movements for this reason. But individual aristocrats innovated more positively. They could be found introducing new mining techniques or new agricultural methods.

In England the aristocracy found new wealth through the enclosure movement, which was at its height in the sixty years after 1760. The movement involved the withdrawal of massive tracts of land from village tenure. Landlords, predominantly aristocratic, not only withdrew their own lands from peasant farming but also bought up much of the land of poorer peasants. Government acts, burdening many peasants with obligations to fence in their own land, literally forced many small owners to sell. By the early nineteenth century over 67 percent of British farmland was included in large estates. And the British landlords, unlike their Continental brethren, were not content with merely expanding their holdings; they fenced in their land, thus separating it from any remnants of village agriculture. They installed tenant overseers, often drawn from the more ambitious ranks of the local farming population, and paid them well to organize the estates on a basis of rational exploitation. Fallow fields were replaced by fields planted in nitrogen-rich turnips or clover. Drainage was installed. Cattle raising was extended and the stock much improved. Agriculture was geared to produce effectively for the market and to earn the highest cash return possible. Workers were ill paid, to be sure, but the system did not depend on serf-type labor; in fact, with improved methods, the productivity of labor was greatly increased.

The peasantry produced agricultural innovators as well. It was a desire to get ahead that produced the rationalizing tenant managers of estates in Britain or Normandy. Other peasants wanted to take advantage of the market on their own, for the class was obviously pressed by population growth and had to find new ways to support its children. Rising prices for marketable grain (up to 100 percent in some areas during the eighteenth century) provided their own lure for the ambitious. The large farmers in France began in many areas to attack village agriculture. They tried to buy out small holders to provide a better base for market production. They sometimes moved part of their operations onto common lands. This was the beginning of a very long process of change in village agriculture, for there was no revolution in peasant mentality. Even by 1789, however, the traditional middling peasant was demonstrably upset at the incursions of the big farmers. And a large class of propertyless peasants had been produced. Some families sold out, particularly of course in England, through the pressure of enclosures. Others simply had no land to distribute to a growing family. Here was a sharpening division, really unprecedented in terms of village traditions, between owners and nonowners.

Something of the same division widened among urban artisans, though with equal gradualness. Faced with population pressure artisan masters were tempted to try to expand their operations a bit, breaking with the guild system. In France and England artisan shops became larger, masters more like small businesspeople and less like fellow craftspeople. In some of these shops the new sense of time was promoted, for punctuality would increase production. Tasks might be divided a bit more than before, for specialization of labor raised productivity as well. A few shops were indeed on their way to becoming small factories, even without new equipment, and their owners to entering a new middle class.

The bourgeoisie produced its own set of innovators, always with the constant need to compete for new resources for a growing population. Professional people suffered from population pressure. Plum jobs in bureaucracy and church were not growing fast enough, and the aristocratic resurgence offended this group particularly. From lawyers, minor provincial bureaucrats, and even some nonnoble priests would come the articulation of the political aims of the middle class, as Enlightenment principles were translated into demands for new political power. A reform of the state, with bureaucracy open to talent instead of aristocratic privilege, was one of the most obvious ways for alert professionals to meet the demographic crisis. The impulse was to spread well beyond the borders of France, though it was in the French Revolution that this particular response had its greatest historic impact. But this was not the only professional recourse. At the end of the eighteenth century professionals in several areas began to form associations and talk about improvements in training. In Prussia, improvements in the training of Lutheran ministers contributed to a growth of professional consciousness generally; the new ministers, proud of the training, would commonly use their position to send their sons into better-paying professions such as the law or university teaching. Professionals generally pressed for expansion of secondary schools and universities; by 1800, partly because of the obvious need for better-trained bureaucrats, partly because of the impulse of the French Revolution, this expansion occurred. Finally, even before 1789, new professions were being suggested. Innovations in artillery as well as new economic development created the need for trained engineers, and on the Continent several training centers were established. This was a very early stage in the development of the professions, but it started trends that would accelerate later.

Innovative business elements of the bourgeoisie busily established or expanded banks and trading operations. In France and England colonial trade increased dramatically. But the most important eighteenth-century response to new pressures and opportunities was the dramatic expansion of the system of domestic manufacturing in the countryside—the core of the protoindustrial process. Urban merchants invested in raw materials, particularly in textiles, but also in production of metal tools, nails, and cutlery. They sent these materials to rural producers, who spun thread or wove cloth or forged knives in their own homes. Some of the producers marketed their own product, but increasingly, as the eighteenth century wore on, they served as paid labor and simply returned the finished items to the merchant, who arranged for sale. There were opportunities for great profit in this system, since the rural producers bore much of the risk. They invested in the spinning wheel or loom. It was easy to lay them off when there was a slump, for the skills involved were not great and were easy to replace. New centers of domestic manufacturing, like Mulhouse or Zurich or Elbeuf, along with port cities involved in the colonial trade, supported a booming business community—the embryo of a modern, capitalist middle class.

The Propertyless

Population growth increased social divisions in western Europe, which in turn created new antagonisms and greater diversity in social practices, including sexual behavior. Although not everyone in the propertyless class was impoverished, many people were. Population pressure vastly expanded the propertyless class and produced terrible hardship. The structure of a Bavarian village in 1817 reveals a common pattern. Of the family units only five were large farmers who employed labor on their own; forty-three had about 25 acres, enough to live on easily; forty-eight averaged 12.3 acres, which was not enough to support children over twelve, who would therefore have to find something else to do with their labor at a very tender age; seventy-four were even worse off, with 8.2 acres; seventeen had mere shacks; and some day laborers owned nothing at all. The landless or near landless lived in great material misery, and nutritional standards declined in some cases, for ironically the potato kept some people alive who before would have perished with so little land. Rising numbers of people who had to seek paying jobs often drove down the wages of agricultural workers. The big cities were filled with growing numbers of unskilled workers, too. Begging and crime increased everywhere. London, particularly, was never more thief-ridden than around 1800, when bands of impoverished children were organized to pick pockets.

Key groups of propertyless people suffered acutely. Many women, unable to marry a peasant or an artisan with property and so participate in a family economy of the traditional sort, had to seek other recourse. Many flocked to the cities. London, which had a surplus of men in the seventeenth century, saw a surplus of women by 1750. Unmarried women, in turn, particularly grew likely to seek menial jobs as domestic servants (increasingly a female occupation), to have illegitimate children, or to join the ranks of full-time prostitutes. The elderly were another growing category of the poor, some forced out by younger children who took control of scarce property when their parents turned decrepit. Alms facilities everywhere were strained by the increase in the numbers of impoverished people.

The growth of propertyless paupers led inevitably to rising rates of crime and begging, heightening fears among propertied people about the basic social order. Perceptions of society as well as economic realities became more divided.

Some of the propertyless found compensations. They lived under great compulsion, and some must have resented not only material hardship but also the lack of traditional status quite keenly. But elements of this group could adapt in their own fashion. Bavarian farmers found their laborers increasingly uppity, immoral, and money-grubbing. They criticized them for wearing flashy, city-style clothes. There were several important aspects to this judgment. In the first place, the growing nervousness of the owners showed obviously, for they distrusted people without property. This became a durable element of class tensions in countryside and city alike. Second, the propertyless, although never rich, were not always impoverished. The agriculture of the late eighteenth century was labor intensive. New equipment, when used at all, required more work than before; this was true, for example, of the seed drill. In addition, the most modern estates employed more labor than traditional agricultural units involving the same amount of land could have done. The enclosed estates of England thus displaced small landowners and really destroyed what was left of the English peasantry, but they did not displace labor. Women as well as men found paying jobs planting, harvesting, and tending stock. This is why, sometimes at least, agricultural laborers were able to buy new clothing. The propertyless were opening up a new style of life, which is what most obviously offended the propertied.

This theme was still more obvious among the rural domestic manufacturing workers, who usually earned better money wages than agricultural labor. This was a vast group, embracing hundreds of thousands of workers, women and men alike, around each major center. Some worked only part-time, but certain families and even whole villages virtually abandoned agriculture, except for garden plots, in favor of this newly expanded system. It took some venturesomeness to set up as a manufacturing worker, which is one way to approach a changing outlook amid the rural lower class. Many had little alternative, of course, for domestic manufacturing was an essential resource for an expanding rural population, now that there was not enough land to go around. But once involved in the system the typical domestic manufacturing worker changed his or her habits rather dramatically. These workers began to buy city-processed food products such as coffee, tea, and sugar. They adopted a more urban, and more revealing, style of dress, with more brightly colored clothing. The concern for dress was important because it provided a new kind of status, a new interest in life, and would be taken further by the industrial working class. Domestic manufacturers reflected urban influences on their lives in other ways. They might resent their lowly propertyless position, but some began to learn how to use the market system to maintain a good wage. Scattered strikes and riots occurred among both rural and urban producers during the eighteenth century in an effort to bargain with employers; here was at least the suggestion of a new pattern of protest. Indeed many of the propertyless were changing their conception of society more rapidly than their employers, which is why the owners found them disrespectful.

Finally, key groups of domestic manufacturing workers married at an earlier age because with no property to defend, the traditional waiting period no longer made sense. Able to earn money even in their late teens they were less subservient to their parents' authority. They began to seek more sexual pleasure.

A Sexual Revolution

There were several signs of a major change in sexual behavior that began in the late eighteenth century and continued into the nineteenth. Marriage rates increased in a number of areas. With new sources of income people who previously had to remain single were able to form families, which increased their status and gave them emotional support. The age of puberty began to fall. Boys' choirs were harder to maintain because voices were changing earlier. The age of menstruation also began to drop. Earlier puberty reflected better average nutrition. It also stemmed from the wider contacts, the greater sexual stimuli, possible in an expanding society. The traditional village horizons, in which there were just a handful of possible sexual partners in a given age group, were broadening as population grew, and there was more economic interaction with cities. Illegitimacy rates increased. From about 2 percent of all births in traditional society, illegitimacy rose throughout the protoindustrialization areas on both sides of the Atlantic, from about 1780 onward, reaching a peak by 1870 of as much as 11 percent in some cases.

Increased sexual activity occurred within marriage, too. This contributed to the rising birthrate. It also caused a major change in the customary cycle of births and conceptions. Traditional peasant society produced a peak of conceptions in May and June, which meant that far more babies were born in February and March than at any other time of the year. Why this pattern prevailed is hard to determine. Traditional spring fever, the advent of better weather, the greater privacy possible when children could be playing outdoors, all may have contributed. Probably the most important factor was the desirability of minimal interference with a mother's labor service. Giving birth in midwinter, when there was no agricultural work to be done, made good sense in a subsistence economy. It was not a good choice so far as infants were concerned, for the early spring and summer constituted the period when food was in shortest supply and parental attention was most distracted by jobs in the fields. So March-born babies were smaller and less intelligent than the average. With the spread of urban influence, for the conception cycle had never been so seasonal in the cities, and manufacturing work that could be done even in the winter, sexual intercourse could occur more regularly through the year. The traditional conception and birth cycle began to smooth out, though there are still traces of it even in the twentieth century. Here, too, was a sign that many Europeans were becoming sexier. In this case, by producing births at more favorable times of the year, the change may also have improved the size and intelligence of the population.

Peasant society had been sexually restrained. It had successfully prevented sexual intercourse outside of marriage. It had severely limited sex within marriage because of the need to regulate the timing of children. At the same time, sex was often openly and raucously discussed in a society that did not particularly privilege sexual acts over other bodily functions.

Now the setting changed, most obviously concerning the frequency of sexual activity but to some extent its meaning as well. As part of political reform, laws against fornication were repealed. More important, parental controls over sexual behavior were reduced. Something of a new youth culture was springing up, particularly among the propertyless, who, with nothing to inherit, had every reason to seek new satisfactions in romantic love. Women as well as men might find pleasure in these changes. A young Bavarian woman suggested her new sense of freedom when asked why she kept having illegitimate children: "It's okay to have babies, the king has okayed it."[1]

The clearest signs of change in sexual behavior occurred among the propertyless. This was the group, certainly, that produced the new rates of illegitimate births. But the decline in the age of puberty and the suggestions of more sexual activity within marriage may have affected the respectable property owners as well. New sexual pleasure denoted a greater sense of individualism, a desire for personal satisfactions, that could be the first step in the formation of a new kind of outlook.

The importance of sexual expression, particularly among young, propertyless people, was not simply physical. Many young men, deprived of access to traditional kinds of status, used sex to assert power over women and to provide a new means of assurance of manhood. Women, sometimes coerced, might agree to sex in hopes of marriage, now that their traditional channels to security were disrupted—for example, with the decline of the peasant dowry. Whatever the motives, sex began to loom larger as a recreational outlet, at least until full adulthood.

The sexual revolution had a number of obvious drawbacks. Older people, particularly among the propertied classes, began to lament the immorality of the young and the poor (another modern theme that would prove quite durable). More directly, greater sexual activity produced more children to take care of, and in many cases poor people began to have the most children, the reverse of traditional patterns. This in turn contributed to the tensions of an expanding population. It seriously conditioned the later life of women. The young woman who

---

[1] J. Michael Phayer, "Lower-Class Morality: The Case of Bavaria," *Journal of Social History*, 8 (1975): 83.

delighted in her new sexual freedom at age twenty became a mother worn out by the necessity of caring for six children, of perhaps eight who had been born to her, at age thirty. The late eighteenth century saw a number of efforts to counter the effects of the new birthrate and the greater survival chances of infants. There was an increase in child abandonment and exposure of children. In a number of countries baby farms were patronized by various social classes; ostensibly designed to nurse infants, the "farm" saw most of their charges die from ill care, which is presumably what their overburdened parents wanted. Only in the second half of the nineteenth century did the baby farms disappear. Some abortion occurred. In 1839 over 10 percent of all women arrested in Paris (156 individuals) were charged with infanticide, and about 1 percent more with abortion. Yet still the average size of the family increased.

A Balance Sheet

The spread of protoindustrialization had ambiguous results. Rising crime suggested immense personal hardships and dislocation. Violence often increased faster than crimes against property, suggesting that many poor people used traditional crime methods more frequently in response to change; it was hard to innovate even in expressing anger. And it was not only the poorest who were bewildered. Within each segment of society that produced an adaptable element there was a majority that found change unacceptable. The small peasant landowner who wanted nothing more than to perpetuate his family plot now found himself burdened with more children than he could provide for, pressed by his farmer neighbor who wanted to alter village agriculture in order to produce for the market or by a business-minded miller who increased his charges for processing grain. The urban influences that could liberate some peasants infuriated others, who found unwanted city people, strangers, trying to do business with them. In some cases two rural regions side by side had quite different reactions to new commercial pressures. In western France, a wine-growing area accustomed to selling to the cities adapted to domestic manufacturing and other urban contacts quite well. Right next to it was a region, the Vendée, of large estates run by absentee landlords. Here, new trade, involving contact with urban outsiders, was profoundly resented, and the peasants of the Vendée were to rise up against the French Revolution essentially as a protest against a host of innovations in the name of more traditional bastions such as the Catholic church. But within a given village, different personality types, even different age groups, produced similar distinctions. And, of course, many individuals had ambivalent reactions, appreciating, say, the new urban entertainers who embellished their

festivals but disliking other trappings of change, and above all, the re-
lentless pressure of rising population against a limited land supply. To
protect themselves, peasants resorted more frequently to collective action in what became a rising tide of rural riots. There were several
hundred small riots in Russia in the 1790s. A new current of agitation
took shape in southern Italy after 1810. French peasants rose more
massively in 1789. Their direct object was to end the remnants of manorial obligations, but they were also concerned about the activities of
the big farmers and the urban businesspeople. In this case they won
and lost; manorialism was abolished but this only increased the pace of
economic change. Further rural agitation was inevitable.

Artisans could also be ambivalent about economic change, but here
protest took even clearer shape. In Britain, Holland, and of course in
the larger French cities during the Revolution, artisans began to re-
quest political rights in order to defend their traditional values. Guilds
were abolished in France in 1791, a middle-class revolutionary achievement. Journeymen did not object to this, for the guilds had been taken
over by the masters anyway, but they did want new associations to defend their rights. This being denied, by another 1791 law that forbade
all economic associations, French journeymen launched an intense, if
sporadic, effort to win control of the state in order to defend traditional goals of protected wages and prices and a traditional economic
system. British craftsmen, particularly in London, who sought the vote
had similar goals in mind. For the most articulate artisans, political
agitation for a voice in the state followed from a desire to attack economic change. Here, too, the battle was just beginning.

Within all the lower-class groups—artisans, peasants, and landless
laborers—some elements sought to profit by new commercial forms,
some to protest them, and some doubtless did a bit of each, depending
on the economic conditions of any particular year. Some people, the
rising urban capitalists but also the rural spinners who bought fancier
clothing, began to think in terms of new pleasures. And amid all the
disruption important continuities with the past remained. The domestic
manufacturing system preserved the family economy. It gave new opportunities to women, who normally contributed their earnings to the
family fund; women did all the domestic spinning and some ancillary
weaving operations as well, almost always within the family context.
Many young people did not receive traditional parental support; they
avoided some controls as well. But more of them formed their own
families than ever before, for the economic functions were not lost.
Villages and guilds were not working as well as they had in traditional
society, but they had long performed imperfectly and they remained
viable throughout most of Europe. The Bavarians who had illegitimate
children still went to church, believing themselves good Christians, and
attended village festivals. They upset their priests—for the church was

quick to attack new behavior, leading the charge against immorality —
but they did not believe they had changed.

In other words the sense of upheaval was not yet overwhelming.
Even protest was based on an idea that past values could be restored.
Immense dislocation and hardship were important realities. But some
people found traditional problems alleviated by the new economic
trends. Domestic manufacturing cut underemployment in some rural
areas. Rising marriage rates and reduced sexual restraints answered
longstanding tensions in the rural culture of western Europe. Many
people, whether aggrieved or not, could believe that traditional values
were still functioning or were within reach of recapture. Without these
ambiguities, change could not have proceeded, and in some areas of
Europe, despite population pressure, it was stillborn.

Two Revolutions

From this volatile mixture two further challenges erupted at the end of
the eighteenth century. From France political revolution extended
many of the new governmental functions that had been initiated earlier; it also gave reality to the demands for political participation that
had been simmering among urban bourgeois and artisans. In England
the first Industrial Revolution had even more sweeping implications.

An aristocratic attempt to wrest more power from the monarchy,
part of the class's resurgence in France, triggered political revolution in
1789. The revolutionary process would extend for over a decade. Artisans and peasants acted on grievances new and old. The artisans focused on material insecurity and sought government protection against
economic change; the peasants attacked their landlords. But the revolution's direction was assumed by elements of the middle class. In terms
of personal aspirations many of the leaders were rather conservative
bourgeois. They used the revolution to take over landed estates and
high posts in the bureaucracy, creating a ruling elite whose interests
were not totally different from the aristocracy. But the political measures this group introduced truly revolutionized the legal structure of
society. By the autumn of 1789 the legal and economic basis of the
aristocracy had been attacked. Manorial rights and privileges were destroyed; where peasants held land directly, they now owed neither dues
nor work service. The principle of equality under the law undermined
the legal basis of the aristocratic order, and government service was
theoretically open to anyone with the necessary ability. The church was
stripped of lands and privileges; religious tolerance was extended.
Guilds were abolished and all combinations of workers forbidden. It
was now legal for anyone to set up economic operations and to use any

methods desired. In sum, the Revolution altered the structure and personnel of government and drew new groups into political consciousness. It removed the legal basis of the old regime by replacing hereditary and group privilege with equality under the law. At the same time, the Revolution placed ordinary people in more direct contact with the state, owing not only taxes but often military service as mass conscription was introduced. The Revolution promoted a capitalistic market economy not only in manufacturing but also to a degree in the countryside. In all these ways the Revolution provided the political basis for the social development of the nineteenth century.

The Revolution was not confined to France. Its principles had wide appeal to various groups, and the appeal was to increase in the next generation. In 1793–1794 merchants and artisans agitated in Holland for a revolutionary change, and there was stirring elsewhere in western Europe. In the east, where there was no significant urban element, the Revolution had repercussions among other groups. Some peasants in Bohemia, Hungary, and even Russia learned vaguely of the Revolution. Some aristocrats in Russia and Poland, chafing under autocracy, were attracted by ideas of the rights of people. Quite generally and for very diverse groups the Revolution promoted an idea of change and showed the path that change should take. Invocation of revolutionary principles was basic to most political agitation in the next century. Furthermore, French armies directly carried the gains of the Revolution to many areas adjacent to France. Guilds and feudal privileges were abolished in the Low Countries, western Germany, and northern Italy. Equality under the law was proclaimed, law codes rationalized, the church weakened.

Beyond these areas, monarchist statesmen were impressed by the revolutionary ferment and tried to prevent comparable disorder at home by timely reforms. Even after this the memory of revolution lingered, leading conservative statesmen to sprinkle their repressive measures with some reforms. More important, the military and political efficiency of the Revolution appealed to rulers in their own terms. Efforts to rationalize bureaucracy were undertaken in Prussia and Russia; new interest arose in improvements in commerce and agriculture. Not all these changes were effective; some were revoked after the Revolution. But a door had been opened to change in every corner of the Continent.

The Industrial Revolution

At about the same time, during the last decades of the eighteenth century, the Industrial Revolution was taking shape in Britain. It built on the same forces that had fueled protoindustrialization—growing demand for goods, businesspeople eager for profits, landless workers who had to accept jobs even in new settings.

The basis of Britain's Industrial Revolution was the application of mechanical power to manufacturing. At first this power often came from water wheels, but the invention of the steam engine about 1770 allowed far more massive mechanical power to be developed. By providing powerful pumps the steam engine allowed deeper mine shafts to be sunk, greatly increasing the amount of coal available for mining. In metallurgy steam engines were soon applied to power the bellows for blast furnaces and to operate automatic hammers and rollers for metals. Productivity in metallurgy was also greatly expanded by the substitution of coal and coke for charcoal in smelting and refining. The new fuels were cheaper than charcoal and could fire larger furnaces and ovens. Through a combination of these technical improvements the output of iron could be vastly increased. Furthermore, the spreading use of steam helped create a growing need for coal and iron to build and power the new machines. Rapid growth of production in both industries, based on important new techniques, was a fundamental feature of every industrial revolution.

Steam engines were applied to many other industries as well. Grain mills and sugar refineries used a large number, though more traditional methods survived for a long time. Far more important, and more extensive, was the mechanization of textiles. Unlike mining and metallurgy, textile production was well developed before the Industrial Revolution; need for cloth was basic to life, and protoindustrialization had drawn hundreds of thousands of people into its manufacture. Far more workers and entrepreneurs were involved in the industry and a far more valuable total product was created than in the heavy industries. Therefore, although technical changes in mining and metallurgy were vital and the output in these industries increased far more rapidly than in textiles, the mechanization of the textile industry was the change that affected the most people and the greatest product in the early Industrial Revolution.

The initial inventions of the Industrial Revolution were developed largely within the textile industry. Well before a practicable steam engine was produced, British inventors had devised major changes in both spinning and weaving. At first these improvements were designed to increase productivity in domestic industry with no change in the source of power. The flying shuttle, invented in 1733, raised the productivity of manual weaving about 50 percent by having the shuttle, which carries threads across the loom, return automatically instead of requiring another weaver to push it. The spinning jenny, developed a few decades later, wound fibers around a spindle automatically, permitting a single spinner for the first time to operate several spindles. In other words, inventions in textiles decreased the need for direct manual operation in certain key stages of production. They were therefore adaptable to mechanical power. First in spinning, then in weaving, water and gradually steam power were introduced to provide the motive force for production. By the 1780s the basic processes existed in England for a technical revolution in the textile industry, although the development of power looms was not yet complete. Along with new methods in mining and metallurgy, they ushered in the first stage of the Industrial Revolution in Europe.

The early Industrial Revolution involved not only technical change but also a new organization of industry, which followed from the new machines but had advantages of its own. Basically, the process consisted of concentrating the forces of production in larger, more compact units.

First, the workers themselves were concentrated in a factory. Utilization of water or steam power required that workers be gathered around the wheel or engine. Instead of being scattered in small shops or their own homes manufacturing workers were assembled under direct central control. Greater supervision was possible under this system. Division of labor could be substantially increased, raising productivity by having each worker specialize in one small part of the productive process. The factory system, in other words, had advantages even aside from the utilization of mechanical power. Early factories were generally rather small, often using only about twenty workers; but they steadily grew as the size of engines and machines increased, and as better methods of supervision were developed.

The factory system concentrated capital as well as workers into units of unprecedented size. The new machines were expensive. Factory buildings themselves cost money. Never before had manufacturing required the assembly of capital on such a large scale. In domestic production workers themselves had usually bought the equipment and the housing; the manufacturer needed only operating capital to buy raw materials and pay initial wages. With new machines and plants far greater investment was necessary. In metallurgy and mining, where machines were particularly expensive, most new firms were launched only through the participation of a number of wealthy people in some form of expanded partnership. In the textile industry an individual family could often set up a small unit with its own funds, supplemented by some borrowing and perhaps a temporary partnership. Subsequent expansion was usually financed by the profits of the firm itself, and the textile industry has retained traces of family ownership to the present day.

Causes of Industrialization

A number of general factors entered into the Industrial Revolution in every area. Certain factors were necessary to stimulate the movement; others were needed for the stimulus to be successfully answered. Britain, obviously, possessed the needed combination at the earliest date. Involved were features of government, population, class structure, past wealth, and physical geography. The combination was complex; only such complexity could account for the fundamental economic change.

The key factor in causing the Industrial Revolution in any area was the creation of a new level of need for manufactured goods, for everywhere industrialization was a response to other changes. Even the major inventions resulted from a preestablished need for new techniques. Hence the expansion of domestic production usually preceded the adoption of mechanical methods and encouraged the development of new productive devices.

New need, or market, for manufactured goods arose from a number of sources. Population growth was essential. In every major case population growth antedated industrialization by several decades, providing a major new market stimulus. Countries where population growth was relatively small, such as France, saw their industrial possibilities correspondingly limited. Changes in taste added to popular demand for clothing. Rising export opportunities also added to available markets. In western Europe and particularly Britain the expanding colonial trade of the eighteenth century was an important stimulus to manufacturing.

Improving transportation, finally, encouraged the growth of national and international markets. Britain, with a large fleet and an exceptionally extensive network of navigable rivers, had far better transportation facilities than the Continental countries in the eighteenth century. Improvements in roads and canals in western Europe in the same period provided general, though more limited, transportation possibilities. Outside western Europe the Industrial Revolution could not occur until after a railroad network was established. In France and particularly in England transportation and market possibilities were sufficient to allow initial industrialization before the railroad.

With new markets as stimulus, a region's response depended on several factors. Basic raw materials were needed. Britain had an exceptionally favorable supply of cotton from colonial sources, but it was access to coal and iron that was crucial to industrialization. Britain had substantial deposits of each and they were close together or linked by rivers and sea.

Available labor was provided by population growth and the new food supplies. Already increasing numbers of workers had been freed or forced from agriculture, when they turned to domestic manufacturing. Now some of them were lured or compelled into factories. The lure was, initially, higher wages than other work provided. The compulsion, broadly speaking, was the havoc factories created in the domestic manufacturing system. Vastly more efficient than rural work (a laborer in a spinning factory was up to one hundred times as productive as a cottage spinner, because of the power-driven machinery), early factories quickly displaced rural production in spinning, which hit working women particularly hard. The same process in weaving was more gradual, but again displacement occurred. Amid continuing population growth, this forced many workers into the factories. Labor force formation was not always easy even so, for few workers were yet willing to move long distances. A domestic manufacturing group might be displaced but cling to the countryside amid growing poverty. Britain again had advantages here. The enclosure movement, although it did not reduce available agricultural jobs, did limit the flexibility of the countryside to absorb increasing numbers of poor people. In areas of small holding, like post-revolutionary France, outmoded domestic workers could hang on, thanks to garden plots and the potato. Britain, in essence, was able to urbanize its poverty with unusual speed. Immigration from Ireland also fed the early factory labor force.

The Industrial Revolution required capital. Britain and western Europe possessed substantial holdings of commercial capital resulting from internal and colonial trade. Britain also benefited from an extensive banking system.

And one final, less tangible ingredient was necessary. An area could industrialize only if it possessed individuals willing to take the risks of engaging their work and funds in unfamiliar and risky ventures. Competition was rugged in early industry, and failures were frequent. Only relatively hardy souls were willing to engage in this process.

The new entrepreneurs in one sense constituted the culmination of the changes in business mentality that had been occurring during the eighteenth century, prodded by population growth, amid a minority of the bourgeoisie in western Europe. The pioneers of industry came almost entirely from the ranks of innovative artisans, domestic manufacturers, and wealthy farmers. Only a few aristocrats or lower-class elements entered the picture. Even established merchants generally held back, preferring safer investments and customary routes to prestige. Formation of an early factory required more spunk, however, than operation of an expanding farm or domestic production system, because the techniques were far more novel and the capital investment greater. Special factors might contribute to this new version of the entrepreneurial spirit. In England Dissenting Protestants, blocked from access to government posts and social prestige, tried to compensate by building industrial empires. Calvinists in Alsace similarly took a disproportionate role in French industrialization. But Catholics, in Belgium and northern France, could manifest a similar spirit, talking of glorifying God by hard work and good profits.

The Spread of Industrialization

The Industrial Revolution was barely under way by 1820. Even in Britain it involved only a minority of businesspeople and manufacturing workers, and most of the population was still in agriculture. On the Continent only a few, essentially experimental, factories had been set up. In most of Europe the legal changes introduced by the French Revolution had to be assimilated before industrialization was possible. Even with expanding population, a factory labor force could not be formed until manorialism was destroyed, for otherwise workers were not free to leave the land. Guild restrictions had to be abolished for new techniques to be widely introduced. Some areas were too poor in capital to industrialize, even when the legal reforms had been enacted. Others lacked the needed resources or transportation. Italy, for example, was extremely poor in coal. Germany and Russia had abundant supplies of iron and coal but lacked natural means of transportation to combine them; this was why the railroad was an essential precondition for rapid industrialization there after 1840.

But many of the causes of industrialization were widespread in Europe. Population pressure, in particular, provided an almost irresistible stimulus in terms of new markets and the need to innovate. Furthermore the dramatic example of Britain's industrial success served as a cause by itself after 1800. Businesspeople and governments found it hard to avoid imitation. British profits and successes in wars against revolutionary France prompted various Continental leaders to investigate the obvious model for industrialization. Britain itself, and then other early industrializing areas, provided ingredients initially lacking. Even by 1820 Britain had new capital to invest, entrepreneurs eager to set up factories abroad, skilled workers ready to earn good wages elsewhere. Impelled by the basic forces of change as they had emerged by the eighteenth century, but also by the spur of Britain's lead, the Industrial Revolution fanned out on the European continent after 1820, spreading steadily farther east and south.

The Nature of Transition

Sweeping changes were part of Europe's social history before the eighteenth century. Indeed, one reason for the quick and decisive reactions to the spur of population growth involved the previous shifts in economic and political structures and habits of thought. Nevertheless, the decades between about 1750 and 1820 stand out for the explosive quality of change, as western Europe began to set the framework for the world's first industrial society. Demographic upheaval added to other motives in triggering new levels of commercial manufacturing and new divisions between property owners and landless proletarians. With the French Revolution, the state expanded its functions in the wider society, adding another important dimension to the lives of ordinary people as they encountered new appeals for taxes and military service — new inducements to add patriotic loyalty to their sense of what their relationship to the state involved.

Many of the forces for change applied broadly in Europe, but differences in timing and in prior traditions kept regional diversities strong. While novel political ideas spread widely, for example, only the French lower classes had a new revolutionary tradition to appeal to directly in future protests. Artisans throughout western Europe faced growing commercial demands, which threatened to undermine traditional apprenticeship and mutual fellowship in favor of speedier work patterns designed to increase output even at a cost to artistry. English artisans, however, who had long lacked an active guild tradition, found it easier to form new groupings of journeymen to defend mutual interests than did their counterparts in Germany, where masters maintained a tighter guild organization and where journeymen and apprentices lacked strong social bonds. France emerged from the decades of transition with a strong and in some ways rather conservative property-owning peasantry, while Britain's enclosure movement displaced smaller farmers in favor of large commercial estates. Even aside from the big divisions between western and eastern European society, then, regional disparities often seemed to override common trends.

Social divisions complicated the picture as well. Middle-class families reacted to change by developing new kinds of training for their children, stressing more formal education and purchasing newly-available educational toys and books even for the very young. Childhood in the lower classes was also changing, but more in the direction of new work experiences and some new freedom from parental controls. A few new interests, such as the first attractions of consumer pleasure, cut across class lines, but specific standards and meanings varied significantly.

The complexity of trends amid often growing regional and social disparities should not, however, obscure the fact that western European society was profoundly shaken during the key transition decades, capped as they were by outright political and industrial revolution.

A key sign of the depth of change, though also of the division it provoked, involved a host of essentially traditionalist reactions, which became more visible by 1820 when many people called for a restoration of various older social ideals. Conservatism surfaced directly at the political level, in reaction to the French Revolution and the defeat of Napoleon's armies in 1815. Most European aristocrats and religious leaders hoped for an end to political protest and a reassertion of the virtues of church and king. Particularly fervent centers of upper-class conservatism, like Prussia, even reversed earlier reforms to tighten landlord control over an ongoing manorial economy.

Other groups moved to defend older values in other ways that might ironically involve new political demands. Many artisans and peasants groped for a definition of a traditional moral economy that they could use against new technologies and more commercial work relationships. The focus rested on appropriate definition of a job. Many

The impact of the factory on the urban setting and the environment. This painting of an unusually large establishment features Borsig's machine hall in Berlin in 1847. (*Carl Eduard Biermann, "Werk Borsig an der Chausseestrasse," 1847. Berlin Museum.*)

workers, both rural and urban, saw work justified in terms of some personal control and creativity, as against direction by others in the name of profits. They looked for a link between work and wider family and social contacts, as against impersonality, and for a pace that permitted both competence and a chance of conviviality. The application of the idea of moral economy to the kind of work situations gaining ground under protoindustrialization and then in the early factories produced a host of specific attacks against new equipment, greedy bosses, impersonal or abusive foremen. In some cases artisans called for a return to guild traditions and often they reached for some new kind of work utopia. The overarching fact was that almost every group in western Europe, by 1820, had to come to some conclusions about the directions of their work life as they risked cutting adrift from traditional standards. A few rejoiced in change wholeheartedly, far more sought to alter or reverse what they saw happening, and still others simply worried. Not long after 1820 a successful French businessman voiced a conundrum that would have appealed to many Europeans: "If progress were not inevitable, it might be better to do without it altogether."[2]

---

[2] René Sédillot, *La Maison de Weudel de Mil Sept Cent Quatre à Nos Jours* (Paris, 1958), p. 23.

CHAPTER 4

Early Industrial Society

The spread of industrialization and the impact of the legal and political changes of the French Revolution set the framework for the next stage of social change—when the effects of new technologies gained increasing priority. This was the period when cities began to grow rapidly, so that what had previously involved a partial urbanization of outlook now involved literal movement to urban centers. This enhanced the pressure for agricultural change, and new methods spread widely to meet the opportunity provided by a growing urban market and the disruptions caused by population growth and legal reform.

Yet the result was not a fully industrialized society. Class structure hovered uncertainly between preindustrial and industrial forms. This chapter covers a roughly fifty- to seventy-year period of growing industrialization that began in western Europe early in the nineteenth century. Having started in Britain in the late eighteenth century, industrialization spread to the Continent, where social and economic change proceeded in different ways and at different paces in various countries and regions.

Between 1820 and about 1870, the Industrial Revolution dominated social relationships in western Europe, though it was only in Britain, even by the end of the period, that a near majority of the population had come to reside in urban areas and work in the manufacturing economy. Despite the diversity in patterns of economic change on the Continent, however, it was during this half-century that the nature of industrial life began to emerge. Some of the new industrial experiences proved very durable, their traces abundantly visible still today. Other innovations, though vigorous and vital to the early industrial period itself, were transitory, a part of the special climate of anxious experimentation as unprecedented trends of work and residence took hold. A similar kind of early industrial society took shape in parts of eastern and southern Europe a bit later, allowing some cautious juxtaposition of developments there around 1900, with west European patterns a half-century before.

The Spread of the Industrial Revolution

Within any country the development of industrial production was extremely uneven after 1820. Established industries changed at very different rates, for many workers and entrepreneurs resisted innovation. Cotton spinning was quickly transformed whenever industrialization began, for cotton was an easy fiber to handle on machines, and cotton production, being relatively new, had few entrenched interests to resist change. Within a decade after industrialization reached a given area, all cotton spinning was done by mechanical means. This had already occurred in Britain by 1800; it would occur in France and Belgium by 1830 and Germany by 1840. Wool spinning followed, but linen lagged because of difficulty with the fiber, and a sense of routine in the industry prevented rapid mechanization. Weaving always took longer to change, although it too followed the pattern of cotton first, then wool, then linen, then silk. Power looms were less productive than mechanical spindles, so manual workers could compete for a longer time. It took fifty years or more for hand weavers to admit defeat in an industrial country.

The new methods of mining and metallurgy spread rapidly, but traditional firms, employing only a few workers and using simple tools, persisted for several decades. In France, where technical change began around 1820, half the iron produced still came from charcoal ovens in 1848. Many industries were not initially affected by new methods at all. Food processing, the building trades, tailoring, and the like were nowhere significantly altered until after 1850. These were the industries most solidly organized in a preindustrial craft structure.

Furthermore, in any country there were diverse regional patterns. Areas near coal supplies—northern England, northern France, the Ruhr—changed quickly, but other regions long continued to use traditional procedures. They suffered competitively, of course, so that industrialization everywhere heightened the regional concentration of industry. But stagnant backwaters, such as southern England, still contained large numbers of people.

Particularly during the first decades of industrialization this meant that several manufacturing economies coexisted in a single country. Crafts and even domestic production could expand, though never as rapidly as the factory sector. A more rapid death for the traditional forms might have been a kindness, but lack of knowledge, shortage of capital, and positive resistance to change combined to give industrialization an uneven pace.

In terms of the national roster Britain was of course the leader. The initial inventions had been widely introduced by 1780, and by 1850 the major manufacturing industries had been transformed. The pioneering period was over, for Britain possessed enough trained workers, managers, and investment capital to insure the continuation of industrial advance. Belgium and France effectively began their industrialization about 1820. France was held back by relatively slow population growth and a shortage of coal, but its major industries were transformed by 1870. The French growth in manufacturing production was slightly slower, per capita, than that of Britain or Germany; a more dramatic spurt began in the 1890s. But the transformation even before then was comparable to early industrialization elsewhere. It included also particular emphasis on efforts to increase commercial production in the artisanal sector—often to the dismay of the craftspeople involved. Germany began to industrialize in the 1840s and reached substantial industrial maturity about 1900. Sweden entered the Industrial Revolution about 1850; Italy, Austria, and northern Spain about 1870; and Russia clearly in the 1890s. All were to reach industrial maturity in the twentieth century, with the Italian process taking the longest time. By 1900, then, most of Europe was caught up in some phase of the Industrial Revolution, with only the Balkans relatively untouched. Obviously the chronology of the first industrial stage varied with the region. The dates 1820–1870 fit Britain and western Europe. Central Europe underwent much the same process about twenty years later, the east and south almost fifty years after that.

Furthermore the nature of industrialization differed from one major region of Europe to the next. The later the industrialization, the more important the heavy industrial sector. All industrialization from the German onward were preceded by railroad development; in Russia's case railroads began to be widely built a full two decades before industrialization. Railroads provided an obvious market for coal and iron, and this fact, if no other, assured the predominance of these industries in most of the later cases. In France, Britain, and Belgium lighter industries, particularly textiles, played a greater role. These industries were inherently less concentrated than mines or metallurgical firms, for their equipment was less complex. Early industrializers thus had a less bureaucratic industrial structure, more opportunity for relatively small businesses.

The later the industrialization the greater the role of government. In Germany, and even more in Russia, the lack of a large preindustrial bourgeoisie and of massive commercial capital required the government to play some of the role private entrepreneurs did elsewhere, and these were areas of a strong state tradition anyway. Governments in the later industrializations promoted change not only to catch up with other societies economically but also because of the military strength that the factory industry and railroad networks could provide. Foreign capitalists also took a greater hand in late industrialization; almost half of Russia's industrial capital came from abroad before 1914. Industrialization had to be induced, for commercial development had not gone far enough for it to occur spontaneously. This not only meant the absence of vigorous native entrepreneurial spirit; it also meant that potential workers were less attuned to a market economy. On the whole, induced industrialization caused greater shock than was the case in western Europe, where its roots went deeper in terms of preindustrial social change. It might be rapid and successful, as in both Russia and Germany, but it offended more traditional sensibilities. It was also true that later industrializers imported relatively sophisticated equipment from the west, so that technological change was less gradual. Here, too, was a source of disturbance. Economic development in a country like Germany could outstrip more general social change, a disparity with serious implications.

Differences in timing and emphasis are important in grasping the industrialization process, not only during the nineteenth century but into the present day. At the same time, some general features were shared. Key causes of industrialization were similar even though after the British case the factor of imitation was always added. Some common effects flowed from industrialization in every case as well, ranging from creation of a new kind of working class to widespread shock and dislocation among many other groups. Even in Britain, the majority of the population undoubtedly viewed many aspects of industrialization with disfavor still in the 1820s; even here, it took time for attitudes and other social institutions to catch up with economic change.

Immediate Effects of Industrialization

The first three generations of the Industrial Revolution witnessed continuing economic innovation. New machines, once introduced, were quickly improved, becoming larger and more productive. The number of spindles on spinning machines steadily rose during the early nineteenth century. Weavers were given one, then two mechanical looms to operate. The average size of the factory steadily increased, in part because of this growing sophistication of equipment. It was early discovered that large engines were more efficient than small. More important, the large firm had other advantages over a small enterprise. It had greater control over its supplies and might in fact produce its own raw materials. There was an increasing tendency for cloth producers to add a spinning plant or for metallurgists to acquire a mine. Large size permitted greater control of markets. A big firm could afford a better marketing organization, sometimes dictating terms to its buyers; in France the seven big producers of rails were fixing prices by mutual agreement as early as the 1840s. So the process of industrial concentration, with its implications for economic power and the development of managerial bureaucracies, began quite early, even though the average firm remained small.

The introduction of machines and factories had a number of more obvious economic consequences. Where new techniques often increased the productivity of an individual worker ten or fifteen times, or where many new workers were added to the manufacturing force, as in coal and iron, production rose greatly from the first. In 1800 Britain produced twenty-six pounds of iron per person; in 1880 it produced 260. The nation's gross production rose twenty-seven times between 1800 and 1860. Germany's per capita output of iron rose from 41 pounds in the 1860s to 170 in 1890. Coal production rose even more strikingly. Even France increased its output from 1 million to 13 million tons between 1840 and 1870. Prussia's coal production rose from 1.5 million tons in 1825 to 20.5 million in 1865. Output in certain other industries rose comparably. The machine-building industry grew from almost nothing to a position of major importance in the early stages of industrialization. Sugar refining in France increased 900 percent during the July Monarchy alone. Even textiles, which had been widely manufactured by older methods, expanded greatly. During the July Monarchy, French production of cotton and wool cloth doubled. In every branch of industry touched by the new methods a sharp rise in production was one of the major results of the Industrial Revolution.

The rise in production was accompanied by a change in the balance among industries. Industry as a whole, of course, became the major producer of wealth in society by the third or fourth decade of the Industrial Revolution; agricultural production also expanded in value, but it could not keep pace. Within manufacturing certain traditional products declined because they failed to adapt; some had been heavily staffed by women workers, which contributed to basic shifts in the economic relationships between the genders. The linen industry, hit by the competition of cheaper machine-made cotton cloth, faded in importance. Lace making and a few other artisan activities lagged for similar reasons. The importance of the textile industry as a whole steadily declined in the face of rising heavy industry, but textiles remained dominant until after 1850. A steel industry arose almost from nothing. The chemical industry, at first confined to the production of dyes, expanded and later in the century developed into an industrial leader.

Increasing production drove prices down fairly steadily. On the whole, rising productivity allowed industrialists to meet the need to lower their prices without diminishing their own profits. In individual cases, however, falling prices put real pressure on companies, and there were many business failures. Particularly before 1850, when business activity was not accompanied by a sufficient increase in the supply of money, the downward trend of prices was severe indeed. Between 1830 and 1848 prices of cotton goods in France fell 66 percent, of woollen goods 31 percent. After 1850 prices of manufactured goods still declined, but at a much slower rate because of the increased availability of precious metals. Nevertheless, the general tendency was clear, and price drops in turn opened new markets for a variety of goods previously too expensive for ordinary use. Significant changes in consumption patterns resulted. One observer in France hailed 1830 as a revolutionary year not because of the political upheaval, but because at about that time ordinary urban workers found they could afford stylish cotton clothing. In France and elsewhere in the west around the same period forks became a common utensil in the average home. Increasing availability of goods, through falling prices, was a necessary result of the Industrial Revolution.

Cheapness alone, however, did not insure sales. New marketing techniques were also necessary. National and even international trade rose greatly, further displacing earlier local patterns. The international trade of every industrial country expanded rapidly. In 1820, two million tons of goods entered British ports; by 1870 British ports handled fifteen million tons. Every industrial country quickly became involved in literally a worldwide network of imports and exports. Major companies set up factories in leading cities all over the world. Within an individual country the effects of expanded production on market structure were even more revolutionary. New facilities for mass marketing everywhere followed industrialization. Firms sent out trading agents, and contacts were set up in centers all over the country. In rural areas small shops gradually replaced itinerant peddlers; there was too much to sell to rely on occasional opportunities. Similarly, local fairs declined in favor of permanent wholesale and retail outlets. In larger cities the department store developed, a clear symptom of the need to find new ways to sell masses of goods. Beginning in Paris in the 1830s, the store specializing in diverse arrays of products spread all over urban Europe during the nineteenth century.

New transportation facilities, essential for the expanding markets, everywhere accompanied industrialization. At first the main emphasis was on increasing numbers of ships, improving paved roads, and building canals. Then in the early nineteenth century in Britain the omnipresent power of steam was applied to transportation as well as to manufacturing itself. The steam locomotive, invented in the 1820s, was first economically applied in a line between Liverpool and Manchester in 1830. In the 1830s local lines were built in Britain, Belgium, Austria, and between Paris and Versailles. During the next decade Britain and various German states began to build a more general system. France planned such a system, completing it in the 1850s and 1860s. By the

1870s the major countries of western Europe had a substantial network of trunk lines. Local lines had been established in Austria and Italy, and plans existed even in more distant regions. Along with the telegraph, which spread during the 1830s, the railroad provided more rapid communication of news as well as transportation of goods and people. It cut into local isolation and allowed more effective contact between central governments and outlying regions. Most important of all, it represented a major development in industry's quest for more widespread and substantial markets.

Improvements in shipping increased trade and communication among nations and continents during the nineteenth century. Before 1850 both iron and steam had been applied to shipping. This improved the speed of shipping and increased the capacity of each vessel. After 1870 ships were sufficiently large and rapid to allow intercontinental competition even in agricultural goods.

But the economic focus of this first industrial period lay in production, not in marketing or distribution. Leading economists stressed the virtue of increasing production; an extreme liberal, J. B. Say, even asserted that sales would take care of themselves. Industrialists themselves devoted most of their attention to problems of investment and technology. The Industrial Revolution was first and foremost a change in the technique and organization of manufacturing goods. It was stimulated by new market opportunities. But, once started, the process could outstrip the growth of the markets.

It was natural that the disposal of products caused the greatest economic difficulties of the early Industrial Revolution. European society was still poor. The resources of the masses were barely if at all above subsistence level. Their numbers were increasing, and their ability to consume rose gradually as prices fell. However, no change in consumption power occurred in the nineteenth century to correspond to the real revolution in ability to produce. Many of the economic difficulties of the century, and even beyond, were based on this disparity.

The disparity between what society could produce and what it could consume gave rise to fierce competition for the available markets. An atmosphere of conflict permeated the early Industrial Revolution. Even successful entrepreneurs felt hemmed in by the forces of competition. As transportation improved, the sense of competition from distant areas grew. Particularly on the Continent, where British rivalry was keenly felt, a desire for tariff protection resulted. Everywhere competition encouraged pressure on working conditions because of the need to reduce prices and seek sales that would keep pace with production.

The most agonizing symptom of disparity between production and consumption was the frequency of economic crises in the nineteenth century. In the first half of the century such crises generally occurred as a result of bad harvests, which decreased the income of peasants and raised food prices generally, leaving everyone less able to buy manufactured goods. Crises of this sort were not new, but their effects were felt keenly when a larger percentage of the population had moved into the cities. Production declined, prices of industrial products fell, and employment, profits, and wages dropped.

Most people managed to survive, though death rates rose in working-class sectors in the worst depression years. Difficulties in sales induced many entrepreneurs to undertake major technical improvements in the hope of cutting costs; such improvements set the stage for the next expansion of production and of consumption. During a crisis itself, however, there was real misery. And crisis years were frequent. Major slumps occurred in the late 1820s, in 1837, in 1846–1847, in 1857, and other declines occurred in certain localities and industries even more frequently. Crisis seemed to be a part of industrial life. It created a sense of insecurity among manufacturers and workers alike.

On the whole, however, industrialization steadily created new wealth through its expansion of production. This new wealth was by no means uniformly spread, but it came to benefit most elements of the population. Within a few generations it reduced the numbers living on the borderline of subsistence from a majority to a minority in the industrial areas. At the same time the Industrial Revolution changed the residence of the average person in Europe. It changed the type of work people did; it changed their pace of work. Along with population expansion and a new legal structure, it freed or forced the population of Europe from traditional ways of action. None of this was accomplished without difficulty and hardship; none of it occurred overnight. The novelty of industrial development dominated virtually every aspect of society during the nineteenth century.

Ironically, during the early industrial period most people remained outside the factory system, even outside the burgeoning cities. Only after 1850 in England and after 1870 in Belgium and Germany did factory production predominate. What industrialization did for most people was to heighten the commercialization process already spreading in the eighteenth century. New wealth, new markets, a new transportation system brought change to every sector of society. They deepened the sense of disturbance that had been growing in the previous period. In this period, preindustrial social classes and institutions remained supreme, but they now faced growing population pressure, a heightened pace of change, and more and more evidence that the social order of which they were a part was doomed. Artisans worried that they would slip into the factory labor force, old-fashioned merchants that would be eclipsed by the new big-business types. Even apparent advantages of industrialization, such as rising wealth, might be resented. Important adaptation occurred in this first period, but it was hard to perceive amid the loud, anguished clamor for a return to older patterns.

The Agricultural Classes

Market Agriculture

During the nineteenth century the system of market agriculture almost entirely displaced the traditional system of local subsistence production, already challenged in previous periods. Peasants and landlords alike depended increasingly on sales to distant markets. Production expanded to take advantage of new opportunities for sales. The growing trend toward market agriculture was spurred by population expansion and particularly by the rise of cities as part of industrialization, both of which extended the potential market. The changes in transportation also furthered the process. Railroads and rapid and capacious shipping allowed more substantial shipments of food to population centers. New manufactured goods were brought to rural areas, attracting many landlords and peasants to the sort of production that would allow them to buy outside goods. Changes in law also encouraged market agriculture, as the old rural regime yielded to revolution or reform — in western Europe after 1789, in central Europe after 1848, in Russia in 1861. Abolition of manorial dues meant that landlords increasingly depended on commercial profits from their land rather than on traditional revenues. Peasants were released from the protection of their former lord. No longer were the charity and other services of the lord readily available. Again, the only major recourse was to produce increasingly for the market. In many countries peasants were also subject to new taxes by governments once they were considered free agents; their needs for cash rose. German and Russian peasants also required some cash, for a certain period, to pay the redemption fees demanded for the abolition of manorial obligations. Both opportunity and necessity existed for the development of market agriculture.

Substantial profits could be made on the market. Demand for agricultural goods rose steadily and prices remained favorable until the 1870s; producers in a country like England, where methods were relatively advanced, knew a golden period of earnings. However, market agriculture involved certain pressures and even risks that were new to most peasants and landlords. Production for the market meant subjection to the whims of demand. Areas increasingly specialized in cash crops rather than general production, which improved productivity but also heightened vulnerability to market forces. The railroad brought the products of one region into competition with those of another. Despite rising consumption, this competition increased steadily during the nineteenth century, to the detriment of less efficient producers.

Ironically, sometimes tragically, the economic traditionalism of the agricultural classes was peculiarly ill suited to such radical novelty. Changes did occur; European agriculture vastly increased its production and efficiency. By 1830 England, for example, produced two to three times as much grain as it had in the eighteenth century. Huge cities could therefore grow, and famine became a thing of the past after 1850 in all but a few eastern regions of the Continent. Such immense development put real pressure on the customs and structures of agricultural existence and even on the economic well-being of many producers. Much of the life of the agricultural classes during the nineteenth century was determined by the clash between new economic forces and a highly traditional way of life.

The increasing pace of economic change, added to population pressure, heightened the division of all the agricultural classes between adapters and nonadapters. At all levels many people sold out. In the most tragic case, small peasants were tempted or bullied, as soon as they acquired legal freedom, to sell their plots, for the abrupt abolition of manorialism plus new needs for cash to pay taxes left many confused. In Prussia 100,000 small holdings disappeared between 1815 and 1848. The same collapse occurred in southern Europe after 1850. Here was the source of new class relationships, confirming the trend toward separation of owners and nonowners and the growth of a rural proletariat earning low wages in the employ of farmers or estate owners. Peasants were not the only ones to suffer from change, however. Many aristocratic landlords could not adapt to new methods and were forced to sell out to others in their class or to upstart merchants from the cities. Isolation and failure played a vital role in weakening the aristocracy and in embittering important segments of the class.

Finally, the countryside was increasingly conditioned by the exodus to the cities. This reduced further population pressure, which was a blessing. It removed some people who could not make out in the new economic setting, and their problems of adaptation now became part of urban development. Temporarily it gave the village new contacts, as many emigrants returned to tell of their experiences in the cities, even in foreign lands. In key periods of rural unrest these contacts played a vital role in articulating discontent. In the longer run, however, too many departures were permanent, driving out of the villages a dynamic, younger element. This weakened the ability of rural society to respond to innovation, for gradually some villages became a haven for older people whose hostility to change only increased with age.

Methods and Products

Market agriculture required major changes in agricultural methods, equipment, and products to meet the need for greater efficiency. Existing land had to be used more fully. Better drainage methods spread, allowing use of marshy land. The planting of nitrogen-fixing clover or turnips increasingly permitted the suppression of fallow land on the Continent, as it had in Britain in the previous century. Common lands were gradually divided and cultivated at great cost to peasant traditions and to the livelihood of many poor peasants. In addition, animal and chemical fertilizers were developed early in the nineteenth century, and their use slowly spread, increasing the yield of the land.

Changes in agricultural equipment also heightened productivity and decreased labor costs. Such a simple improvement as the use of the scythe instead of the sickle raised the productivity of harvest workers by up to 50 percent. More massive equipment became available also, but it spread slowly. Heavier, larger plows were manufactured. Threshing and reaping machines were invented. In agriculture, as in industry, it became increasingly possible to substitute machines for human power and labor.

Further, market agriculture's cash-crop specialization meant that general production of many foods became inefficient. Europe became increasingly divided into grain-growing, wine-growing, and stock-raising areas. Such areas were dependent on the market for the purchase of foods that they did not raise. Although this specialization greatly improved productivity, it had certain dangers. Failure of one crop could wipe out one's whole livelihood; for example, great misery resulted from the destruction of French vines by the phylloxera disease in the 1860s. Constant attention was necessary to keep a specialty crop up to rising standards of quality. Particularly in stock breeding, improvements in the product occurred fairly steadily in the nineteenth century. Changes in consumption patterns could threaten the profitability of a specialty crop. Sheep-growing areas were hit by the rise of cotton fiber and the declining popularity of mutton. Growing wealth in western Europe caused a general movement away from the cheaper grains, such as rye, and toward wheat by the mid-nineteenth century. Again, substantial adjustment had to be made by producers.

More productive methods, better equipment, and new crops created great possibilities for agricultural development during the century. They were encouraged by government information programs and by many agricultural societies, which tried to introduce and expand a variety of new techniques. Nevertheless, in many cases development was very slow. By 1870 only one-third of even the large farms in northern France had threshing machines, and only after 1890 did such equipment become common. Not until about 1880 did use of mineral fertilizer expand significantly in France. In all these cases it had required decades of spreading information plus a new rise in competition to produce major change in equipment. Similarly, many of the necessary changes in crop specialization occurred only slowly if at all.

Ignorance and traditionalism accounted for much of the lag between

Traditional methods in the fields. These gleaners picked up grain in the village fields after the harvest using arduous labor to avoid waste. *(Jean-François Millet, "The Gleaners," 1857, oil on canvas. Louvre, Paris. Alinari/Art Resource.)*

what was possible and what was done. The illiteracy of many peasants and the aristocratic hostility to commercial activity favored the status quo in most areas. Furthermore, major improvements in equipment or the quality of the crop required capital. Peasants and small landlords alike had little monetary capital; what they owned was the land itself. Credit facilities were not extensive in rural areas. In the early part of the nineteenth century loans still could only be obtained at rates of interest up to 60 percent. Later, government and cooperative funds were established to ease the situation, but credit remained tight. Finally, many peasants' plots were too small to apply machines successfully. Even simple improvements, such as the suppression of fallow, proved impossible for many farmers. They did spread, causing the great increase in production, but they ruined many peasants and aristocrats in the process.

Despite the transformation of agriculture, the agrarian classes were unable to maintain their traditional importance in society as a whole. Their production sank steadily as a percentage of total national output, and agriculture employed a declining share of the total labor force.

Most of the population increase in western and central Europe after 1820 went into the cities. The agricultural classes grew only slightly in the century as a whole, and in a few areas, such as France and Britain, they began to decline in absolute numbers after 1870 as improved methods and increased competition curtailed the need for labor. In the extreme case, only 10 percent of the population of Britain depended on agricultural work by 1900. It was easy for those who remained in the countryside to feel that modern life was passing them by.

The Aristocracy

Economic Base

The decline in the relative importance of agriculture hurt aristocrats severely, particularly in western Europe. Control of much of the land no longer assured them economic supremacy. Their average earnings were rapidly challenged by the owners of industry. In 1800 the British aristocracy controlled almost 20 percent of the annual production of the nation; by 1850 it commanded less than 10 percent. It became increasingly difficult to maintain a style of life distinguished by luxury. Some aristocrats attached themselves to the rising fortunes of industry despite the general prejudice against commercial activity. Few of them actually managed enterprises, but a number invested and served on boards of directors. However, aristocrats never rivaled the middle class for control of industry, and by mid-century in western Europe their wealth could be matched by the top businesspeople.

This meant also that the class had to abandon its pretense of serving as principal patrons for the arts. They had to admit middle-class rivalry in sponsoring musical events. Authors now made money by writing for the middle-class public, not a noble patron. Throughout western Europe the first half of the nineteenth century saw something of a battle between the two classes for cultural leadership, with the aristocrats typically defending classical styles and the middle class forming groups to support the newer Romantic trends. But war could be only temporary, for the aristocracy, no longer the dominant economic class, could not prevail.

Concomitantly, the changes within agriculture challenged aristocrats directly. The demands of market agriculture for commercial ability and technical innovation touched even eastern Europe during the early nineteenth century. There were definite attempts to adapt to market opportunities. Junkers and Hungarian nobles increased their landed holdings at the expense of the peasants. Production for export did rise. Some eastern landlords introduced crop rotation and even machinery quite early. By the 1840s Baltic aristocrats began converting to stock raising in the interests of improving their markets. And generally the use of wage laborers spread. However, only a few individuals modernized their agriculture substantially. There was relatively little general change in method; in Hungary, many nobles depended primarily on extending servile work obligations for their commercial product. Nowhere was there so fundamental a conversion to market agriculture as was occurring in Britain.

Yet a conversion was increasingly necessary, even aside from market pressures. In western Europe by 1800, in central Europe by 1850, and in Russia after 1861 manorial dues were abolished. Aristocrats who had depended on dues lost much of their traditional income by this change. Even when landlords retained domain, adaptation was essential, for revenues now depended on sales to the market.

Many landlords retained considerable power over peasant labor. Russian nobles received redemption payments in return for the abolition of manorial dues in 1861. Elsewhere some peasants continued to pay rents. In southern Italy and southern Spain many peasants were so poor in land and capital that they became sharecroppers for the lords. Here and in Prussia many landlords successfully pressed peasants to sell out after outright manorialism ended; in southern Spain three-quarters of the peasantry was landless by 1890, earning about nine cents a day as agricultural laborers. In none of the large domain areas except Russia did the abolition of manorialism break up the big estates, and even in Russia the lords kept much of the best land. The Romanian abolition of serfdom in 1864 actually destroyed peasant small holding and divided almost all the land into large estates for the first time. There and elsewhere freed but landless peasants were available for cheap labor.

However, the traditional sources of income were irrevocably lost. Peasant labor had to be paid in cash, even if wages were low. In the south sharecropping meant little if the sharecropper's product was not profitable. In other words, the abolition of manorialism inevitably forced the landed aristocracy to participate in market agriculture. Even where the class exploited peasants shamelessly it could decline.

Most landed aristocrats were unable to respond to the new conditions of agriculture. They failed to introduce new equipment and new crops. Many went heavily into debt to compensate for the inadequacy of their income from the land. Many became impoverished or eked out only a meager living on the basis of sharecropping or tenant returns. Many lost their land. Even in the early nineteenth century, when market conditions were excellent, many aristocrats had to sell out to more dynamic landlords from the middle class or from their own class. They lacked the capital and technical knowledge to keep going. In Prussia a third of the Junker estates were sold out between 1815 and 1848 alone. By 1885 about 87 percent of the east Prussian estates had changed hands. In 1855 only 55 percent of the land was in aristocratic hands, and by

1889 the figure had declined to 32 percent. Except to a limited extent in Russia, estates were seldom broken up; the peasantry did not gain in the large estate regions. But increasingly many estates were administered by the middle class or a few rich aristocrats on a commercial basis. Only in scattered regions, such as England, where aristocrats converted to radically new methods, or the Baltic provinces of Russia, where new methods were combined with semimanorial control over peasant labor, did aristocrats avoid major competition from new landlords.

Social Status

Aristocrats faced a crisis of legal and social status. Their sense of superior status had depended on high incomes and consumption power, both of which were now under attack; it had also depended on real legal privilege. The abolition of manorialism and the establishment of equality under the law, following on the principles of the French Revolution, destroyed such diverse privileges as exclusive hunting rights, the right to try certain crimes in manorial courts, and the right to have one's word accepted in other courts without challenge. Some privileges remained. Suffrage systems based on ownership of property, particularly landed property, gave aristocrats disproportionate voting power in many countries. France retained such a system until 1848, Prussia until 1918. On the whole, however, the legal status of aristocrats was little different from that of other citizens by 1815 in western Europe and by mid-century elsewhere. This fact, along with growing economic pressure, made it increasingly difficult for aristocrats to maintain their traditional feeling of hereditary superiority.

Two general lines of action could preserve some sense of special status. The social exclusivism of the class could be asserted against the rise of the middle class, and special political powers could be maintained or even augmented, which could provide income as well as status.

Everywhere in the early and mid-nineteenth century aristocrats tried to protect their distinctiveness in new ways. They made more formal use of their titles than before, when an appropriate social order could be taken for granted. They formed exclusive social clubs, in which they could conduct distinctive activities such as gambling. Intermarriage with the middle class may have declined, as in Germany; it was certainly disapproved. Rigid social barriers were maintained against contact with nonaristocrats in hunting groups and at dances. Until 1918 Prussian nobles used a rope to separate themselves from the middle class at any dance. After 1815 Parisian nobles began to build a purely aristocratic suburb, the Saint Germain quarter. Aristocratic schools often sought to exclude the nonaristocrats and continued to stress subjects such as classics that were suitable for refinement and leisure rather than for economic utility. German universities maintained an aristocratic code of honor in their dueling societies. Wealthy urban nobles perpetuated and even increased when possible their association with cultural activities. In a variety of ways, then, large and small aristocrats continued to seek a distinctive pattern of life and society.

In addition to its stress on style of life, the aristocracy tried to maintain its special political importance. The class continued to believe in its peculiar fitness to rule. Political activities allowed aristocrats to exercise their traditional concern for the well-being of society. They brought jobs that were dignified and provided income. Political power could be used to defend traditional aristocratic values such as religion and military prowess. Hence in countries like Germany poor aristocrats crowded into universities and the bureaucracy after 1815, competing with middle-class professionals and often worsening standards of training. Political jobs also allowed defense of the agricultural interests. Junkers could push for free trade to help their exports and subsidies to large estates; French nobles sought and obtained agricultural tariff protection.

Further, through politics some of the more objectionable features of the middle class could be attacked. In the early nineteenth century many aristocratic politicians in Britain and France encouraged the passage of legislation limiting the rights of employers over workers by defining conditions of child labor and hours of work. In Britain the Earl of Shaftesbury promoted the Ten-Hour Law of 1847; in Germany aristocratic parties supported restoration of guilds after 1848 and later backed the first social insurance laws in the 1880s. Only a minority of aristocrats took an interest in these efforts, and a fear of the unruliness of the masses increased in the class as time passed. However, aristocratic paternalism and hostility to the middle class, expressed through the use of political power, provided one of the foundations for more vigorous state regulation of industry in the nineteenth century. Here, as in many other ways, the aristocracy tried to use its political voice to support traditional position and values.

The aristocracy retained a number of types of political power in the nineteenth century. It continued to dominate the military and generally tried to limit the opportunities for nonaristocrats to enter the ranks of officers. Control of some of the leading positions in the state churches gave aristocrats another important form of institutional power. Aristocrats generally defended the established church with great vigor during the nineteenth century as one means of protecting tradition and stability in society. During the French Restoration (1815–1830) aristocratic politicians passed a law decreeing the death penalty for sacrilege in the Catholic church, and the British House of Lords long resisted measures passed by the Commons to allow Jews to become members of Parliament or to permit nonconformists to enter the universities. It was in government, however, that the main aristocratic power lay; even church and army were increasingly defended by political means. Nobles retained considerable local authority. In Russia and Prussia the local administrators established after the abolition of manorialism were usually aristocrats. In Spain landlords continued into the twentieth century to nominate local officials. Their nominees controlled much of the local police and were therefore able to intimidate the peasantry; they could also defend the aristocrats' interest against the central government. In France and Britain many regional administrators were aristocrats until 1850 or beyond, and many more were subject to aristocratic influence. Despite changes of regime in France, for example, the regional prefects changed little in social type between 1815 and 1850; they were not exclusively aristocratic, but the aristocracy played a considerable role.

The aristocrats had legislative power in government also. Their local popularity and prestige encouraged their election even in countries where universal suffrage was established. In 1905 one-twelfth of the British House of Commons was aristocratic; this was a notable decline from the figure of one-sixth in 1860, before the establishment of universal male suffrage, but it was a significant figure nevertheless. In France aristocrats played major roles in parliaments in such crisis years as 1848 and 1871 because of their local prestige among new peasant voters. Furthermore, many legislative bodies preserved an even greater role for aristocrats until 1914. The British House of Lords retained a full legislative veto until 1911. Suffrage limitations in Italy and systems of class voting in Prussia and Austria, by which every class (as defined by property) got the same number of votes regardless of its size, returned large numbers of nobles to legislatures in these countries until the late nineteenth century and even after.

It was in central administration, however, that the real political power of aristocrats lay. Even after democratic parliamentary regimes were established in Britain and France, administrators tended to be appointed by co-option rather than by determination of the populace or legislature, which reserved many of the principal roles for aristocrats. In eastern Europe, where the power of parliaments and democratic bodies was small, aristocrats played a fuller role in administration. There the principal ministers as well as the leading diplomats and civil servants were aristocrats. In France the aristocracy saw its hold on the ministries weakened after 1830 and largely destroyed with the establishment of the Third Republic in 1875. In England nobles shared the ministries with commoners throughout the century. Even in France and England, however, many of the chief administrative bodies beneath ministerial rank, such as the diplomatic corps, remained largely in the hands of the aristocracy.

Aristocratic dependence on administrative positions made the class an increasingly conservative force. There were three notable exceptions to this. In Poland and Hungary resentment against foreign rule and the deteriorating economic position of the gentry caused a rise of rebellious nationalism after 1815. There the lesser aristocrats had little political power to defend, so it was understandable that Polish risings in

1830 and 1863 would be led by nobles. The liberal, nationalist Hungarian revolution of 1848 was primarily a rebellion of the gentry. Only after 1867, when the Hungarian aristocracy won great national and local political power, did the switch to conservatism come. In Russia some members of the gentry, particularly educated bureaucrats and military personnel, had grievances against the autocracy; a few of them led the abortive December rising of 1825. By the 1830s liberal gentry were forming the first elements of the discontented intelligentsia, but this radicalism was not characteristic of aristocrats generally, even in Russia. And by the 1860s in Russia even the minority was being weaned away from opposition to the tsar. The factors in this process were familiar ones. Economic difficulties increased with the abolition of serfdom; the gentry depended on state help. Local political power grew; the gentry filled most of the positions on the *zemstvos*, the new regional assemblies.

Generally, aristocrats provided the principal support for formal conservative groups during most of the nineteenth century. In France

Continuities in the life and work of the peasantry. This French painting from 1853-1854 shows young women sifting corn, using traditional methods and by all indications indulging a rather traditional pace of work. *(Gustave Courbet, "Winnowers," 1853-1854. Musée de Nantes, France.)*

many nobles defended the Bourbon, or legitimist, tradition of monarchy into the 1870s and later despite three intervening regimes. In Prussia the aristocrats also gathered increasingly around the king. Politically as well as religiously, the class defended traditional institutions and through them their own customary leadership.

By 1870 the position of the aristocracy had been altered substantially. Land remained a source of power but an increasingly shaky one. Social distinction remained also, but it had to be defended with new and formal devices. Titles were generally recognized, usually supported by the government. Only in Norway had aristocracy been fully abolished. Interestingly, legal protection for aristocratic titles ended in France in the 1870s, with the result that many middle-class people added the aristocratic "de" to their name. This diluted the aristocracy but also reflected its ongoing social cachet. In politics the nobility retained great power and used it consciously to defend the whole range of aristocratic interests.

The important legal and economic decline of the class was a vital aspect of social change in Europe throughout the nineteenth century. By 1870 most aristocrats in western Europe had to abandon efforts to defend their class as a separate entity, and to join forces, however grudgingly, with other conservative elements. At the same time, before 1870 and even afterward to some degree, the resiliency of the aristocracy was also an inescapable fact. Even in the economic sphere all was not lost. Certainly in politics and administration the nobility remained the dominant element except in some parts of western Europe. The class felt increasingly beleaguered. Its actions were often belligerently defensive. Because it was dying but not dead, the class remained a surprisingly important social force.

The Peasantry

Changes in the situation of the peasantry during the nineteenth century in some ways mirrored those within the aristocracy. Both classes were traditional and tradition-minded. Both were faced with major economic and legal change. Both defended many of their customs against change and with some success. Aristocrats and peasants both remained more religious and more politically conservative than did urban classes during the same period. Both were opposed to certain values of the triumphant middle classes and to the rise of the urban masses. Unlike the aristocracy, however, the peasants were not a traditionally privileged class. Less conscious of social status, many were able to adapt more fully, if gradually, to the needs of market agriculture. Poor, even destitute, they were capable on occasion of turning violently against existing society, against the aristocracy itself, in a way most aristocrats could not because of their continuing stake in the existing order. Peasant life altered fully as much as did that of the aristocracy, but the alterations inevitably took vastly different forms.

It is vital to remember that, even by 1870, the majority of Europe's population, aside from Britain, was still peasant. The class diminished steadily in importance but remained massive. The war between tradition and change in the rural world, though often silent, was a basic factor in overall European society despite industrialization's command of center stage during the mid-century decades.

Certain aspects of peasant traditionalism persisted. Local festivals continued to constitute one of the major forms of peasant recreation. Even in England peasant songs and folklore were continued into the 1840s. Many French peasants retained age-old superstitions in dealing with childbirth or illness. Distrust of distant regions, including the city, was still common. A great attachment to the land remained. Many peasants gave up or left their land reluctantly, usually under the pressure of considerable misery. If they could, they commonly tried to counter economic novelty by confirming their hold on the land and even acquiring more.

Traditions of village and family unity loosened during the century, but still remained a vital focus for peasant life. Many villages maintained some supervision over local agriculture and law. Village courts in Russia continued even at the end of the nineteenth century to rule on land and inheritance disputes on the basis of quite local customs. Peasant families maintained tighter traditional links than did families in other classes, and peasants typically had more children per family than other classes did. Religious practice remained important for most peasants, although there were de-Christianized rural areas in several western countries. In southern and eastern Europe peasants might respond to new pressures by a wave of religious fervor. Old Believers in Russia, though not new, continued to insist on a return to a purer church, and in Italy small sects, notably the Lazzaretti, gained peasant converts with the hope of an imminent millennium that would restore equality and dignity to the land. Even in western Europe material acquisition remained a less important goal for the peasantry than for the urban classes. An interest in material gains developed, but most peasants seemed content with a lower standard of living than that prevailing in the cities. Traditional recreation, the land, the family, and the church provided satisfactions that supplemented the material standard of living.

Economic Pressure

Major alterations in peasant existence were brought about by massive pressures that the peasant could neither resist nor fully understand. Population growth was the most general and fundamental problem.

Decline of domestic manufacturing increased the economic pressure. New legal and market systems encouraged the growth of a landless element. And market agriculture brought great difficulties even to peasants who owned substantial land.

Throughout Europe the land available per person continued to contract, with the worst problems spreading to the east and south. The number of peasants in European Russia doubled by the end of the nineteenth century with no notable expansion of the land under cultivation. Real land hunger developed in such circumstances, violating village and family traditions of a stable relationship to the land. Common lands were no longer capable of supporting the growing number of landless people. The opening up of new lands, through drainage and suppression of fallow, did provide new jobs for both men and women, but in every country there was a decade or more when demand did not keep pace with population given the simultaneous decline in domestic manufacturing. By 1780 many British rural laborers were dependent on charity for survival. In 1830 the introduction of harvesting machinery provoked a major riot from laborers in parts of England, trying to defend the jobs and wages they had. This was an unusual expression of collective consciousness, which followed from the high level of agricultural commercialization in Britain. But a less articulate crisis mentality prevailed elsewhere. The 1840s and 1850s were the crucial decades in Bavaria, as crimes against both persons and property rose even in prosperous years. Here and elsewhere in western and central Europe the agricultural laborers were not capable of formal protest. In the 1848 revolution, for example, landless peasants in Bohemia, lacking leadership, talked of their own sinfulness and the need for a purer religion; reflecting changes in the village structure they also asked for a hereditary right to cultivate some common lands. But they did not raise basic demands. In these same areas emigration to cities and abroad, along with the related rise of successful industrialization, soon reduced the worst pressures. An important landless element remained but they were not to be heard from for some time. Even in Prussia, where there were two million landless by 1849, only vague grumblings could be discerned. Continued deference to landlords or village notables, fear of going to the city and satisfaction at clinging to rural existence, the enervating impact of poverty, all must help explain the relative quiescence of this group after a decade or two of disorganized crime and unrest.

In eastern and southern Europe the landless loomed larger numerically, for far more people were dispossessed after manorialism was abolished. Rural crime rose rather persistently in Ireland before 1848, and later in southern Europe. In central and southern Italy this fed into more organized brigandage against government agents and the wealthy landlords or their minions. In Italy, where 3.275 million peasants had less than 2.5 acres of land by 1894, the landlords' officials could enter some estates only under armed guard. Even in Russia, where peasants received most of the land after emancipation, the pressure remained intense. Population growth was not matched by migration outlets and the law still tied many peasants to their village. Aristocratic landlords, though controlling only a minority of the arable land, had the best soils. Furthermore, some of them were bought out by a commercially minded middle class, and by 1900 one-seventh of the large holdings were in non noble hands. Finally, throughout eastern and southern Europe these changes, occurring late in the nineteenth century, took place in a framework of declining agricultural prices. Small wonder that their impact was more severe and durable than previously in the West. Apart from formal protest, increased drinking, growing hostility to the church as a tool of the upper classes, as well as crime marked the dilemma of the rural poor.

The peasantry that did have land, though impeded by traditionalism and lack of capital, might adapt more positively. Many did produce for the market; many did enjoy the more diversified goods available as the commercial economy spread. Peasants did not become like city folk; they maintained contact with distinctive traditions. But they were not all averse to a gradual adaptation to new ways. Their key activity was the attempt to purchase new land to take advantage of market opportunities, for this made sense in terms of traditional status as well. Hence in western Europe they nibbled at the holdings of their poorer brethren and at the common lands. Even in the large estate areas of Prussia a minority of peasant farmers did well, which helped reduce tension. And in Russia the emancipation of 1861 provided the average peasant with over twenty acres, albeit not always fertile ones. The continuing restrictions were galling. Russian peasants could not leave their village without village permission. In some villages land was to be redistributed every ten years; these repartitional villages allowed no permanent ownership. The obligation to pay redemption to the state, at rates sometimes higher than the rental value of the land, was terribly burdensome to all. But here, too, adaptation occurred, and a minority of peasants was able to buy new land during the last three decades of the nineteenth century. Only in southern Europe was the division among the peasantry almost nonexistent because of the pervasive large estates; there was a difference between a sharecropper and an outright laborer, but it was not great. Elsewhere a minority, varying in size according to the previous land tenure systems, could make do.

Peasants in Ireland undertook their own version of the adaptation process. Pressed by growing numbers and diverse discontent during the first decades of the nineteenth century, they were devastated by a brutal potato blight in 1846–1847. Many died; hundreds of thousands emigrated. Those that remained converted to a pattern of very late marriage, thus limiting births, as Irish population never recovered its former numbers. The majority of landowners also became more ardent in their attachment to a vigorous Catholicism.

This was a distinctive pattern, the result of Ireland's economic woes and its near-colonial status under British rule. Gradual adjustment to market pressures, including growing division between successful peasant-farmers and the landless laborers they employed, was the more common trend, bolstered by the gradual spread of education in the countryside and by new kinds of contacts with the growing cities. By the 1860s peasants in a few bellwether areas, like Holland, were beginning to form organizations that could fund a fuller conversion to market agriculture, as they set up dairy operations that could serve a wide export zone.

Peasant Rebellion

In the early stages of the transition to a more commercial environment a middling group of peasants, with some village allies, played a crucial role. While the long-term trend pushed peasants to convert to market conditions or to enter an agricultural proletariat (or, of course, to leave the land altogether), we must recognize an intermediate phase in which middling peasants were being squeezed but still tried to make do. Their neighbors might want to buy them out but land was their life. Taxes and other money obligations were rising rapidly. Real conversion to the market was impossible because of lack of sufficient land and capital. A future of landlessness seemed ominously close, the final degradation. Add to this middling group domestic manufacturing workers, not yet displaced, who also saw the handwriting on the wall as they were increasingly hardpressed by their employers, suffering declining wages and growing periods of unemployment. Add, finally, village artisans, like blacksmiths, who faced competition from factory products and who could play a particularly good leadership role. This was the formula for massive peasant rebellion in most parts of Europe during the early Industrial Revolution. The richer peasants did not join in, though they might sympathize; English farmers, for example, supported their laborers' demands for better treatment in 1830, claiming that they had adopted new machines only because competition forced them to. Except in England and, later, southern Europe, the landless laborers were generally too disorganized to be effective rebels. But middling peasants and their manufacturing allies were strong enough to make a last attempt to restore a better rural society. They won some victories, particularly when they attacked the manorial system; here they had major historical impact. But they lost the war because they could not stop the advance of industrialization and, when they gained the downfall of manorialism, they actually opened the way to further change.

A rising tide of riots focused on the apparent causes of misery. Merchants were often attacked during periods of high prices as a result of the increasing dependence of peasants on outside purchases. Here traditional protest focus was simply heightened by the new commercial trends. In 1795 British peasant women rioted in a number of market towns. In the years of poor harvests in France, such as 1828 and 1847, peasants often attacked shops and grain convoys. Grain dealers were attacked in Italy in 1898, again a symbol of resentment against the condition of market agriculture.

In periods of agitation peasants often refused to pay taxes or redemption payments, as in Russia in the late nineteenth century. Rioters sometimes attacked tax offices; more than resentment was involved in such attacks, for peasants often burned records in the hope of eliminating the hated assessments. Domestic workers frequently attacked factories and machines. This Luddism, though not confined to peasant manufacturers, was often an important concomitant of more general peasant discontent.

The most bitter and extensive riots, sometimes a part of major revolution, were directed against the landlords. This was often the focus of crime. Poaching and thefts were the responses of many English peasants to the hardships of the late eighteenth century. In Russia 144 landlords and 29 stewards were killed between 1835 and 1854. Generally much rural crime expressed the idea that the land belonged to the peasant and that the lords' property could be legitimately attacked in these new times of hardship. When it was most purposeful, peasant agitation tried to destroy manorial obligations and to acquire more land. Such agitation was usually precipitated by a year or two of bad harvests and resulting misery, but it sought more than temporary material relief. In response to population pressure the peasants sought more land and outright control of the land they already had.

Peasant risings against landlords employed many methods. Refusal to pay rents was a common preliminary to an actual rising. Angry and violent attacks on the house and more rarely, the person of the landlord were part of many riots. Rioters usually stole from the lord's property. Peasants on large estates often went on strike. Two features of the major risings were most indicative of the basic purpose. The records of the landlord were pillaged and burned to destroy manorial and sharecropping obligations where these still applied; or government offices collecting redemption payments were similarly treated. Peasants wanted to remove the burdens placed on them by the lords and felt that no compensation for this removal was justified. Furthermore, peasants often took over part of the lord's land and cultivated it. Here was a naked expression of the land hunger of the peasantry during its time of crisis.

Peasant risings were often apolitical, though they typically expressed a rural version of the moral economy ideals. They might coincide with political revolution, as in France in 1789, Germany and Austria in 1848, and Russia in 1905, but many peasants had little concern for political goals. Most commonly, they expressed their loyalty to their traditional monarchy, blaming bad advisers for any mistakes the government had made. If they obtained their demands concerning manorial payments, they were content; hence after 1793 the French peasantry largely lost interest in the revolution. When Italian and Austrian peasants won abolition of manorialism in 1848–1849, they tended to ally with conservative monarchies against further urban agitation.

Many, perhaps most nineteenth-century peasant risings lacked any formal doctrine. Russian peasants actually resisted the efforts of university students to spread agrarian socialism during the later nineteenth century. There were, however, important cases in which an ideological element was present.

Peasants in some French regions had acquired active political allegiances by the time of the revolution of 1848. The peasant majority, manorialism having ended long before, seemed politically quiescent, supporting conservative candidates when given the vote. In some regions, however, peasants vigorously defended republican values by their votes and by rioting when the republic was set aside in 1851; some even supported socialist doctrines. Several of the politically active rural regions featured substantial landless elements, open to the idea of using politics to protest their lot; some, in southern France, also maintained a tradition of resistance to dictates from Paris.

Southern Italy offered a second case of peasant politics, as some new political experience accumulated by the later nineteenth century and as pressures on the land built intolerably. Sicilian peasants accepted the leadership of urban socialists during the Fasci revolt of the 1890s, and they expressed demands for equality of bread and work and even the realization of a new fraternal order in the countryside. Peasants saw in Socialist concepts a way to express their old ideals of sharing and equality. Finally, in Andalusia in the same period peasants found a doctrine, brought in by foreign and urban agitators, that expressed many of their own hopes. Andalusian peasants were massively converted to at least some of the slogans of anarchism. They tried to free themselves from the encroachments of the central state by eliminating government in favor of purely village rule. They wished to divide all the land equally. By these means misery would be destroyed and a perfect social order established. Both southern Spain and Sicily were areas in which peasant poverty and lack of land were particularly acute; there was really no way for even a minority of peasants to adapt to change. Both were areas of traditional resentment of the state; southern Italians in particular resented controls and high taxation from the new northern-dominated government of united Italy. Both were areas of religious fervor that could carry over into the new ideologies. Even in these cases, although doctrine was brought in by outside agitators, the basic purposes of the peasants continued to be expressed. More commonly, doctrine was neither needed nor available, as even in protest peasants sought their own goals in their own way.

Whether politicized or not, the organization of peasant risings was vague and informal during the early industrial decades. They usually spread from one locality to another by imitation rather than by advance planning. Leadership even among Spanish anarchists was local because the movement was hostile to organization. There were no special funds to support peasant agitation and it was difficult to sustain the agitation for more than a few months. Rebellions might recur, as they did in Spain about once every ten years after 1870, but they usually burned themselves out fairly quickly. In its organization as well as its main purposes, peasant agitation drew from the traditional importance of the land and local structures, which is why landed peasants and artisans played the key role. Peasant rioters in Russia in 1905 came clearly from the middling landed group; anarchist leaders in the Spanish villages were most often craftspeople.

Regional patterns and dates of protest varied greatly. British peasants rioted frequently up to about 1850. They used some distinctive methods, notably burning of buildings. They might attack merchants, as in 1795, or new taxes and tolls, as in the 1843 Rebecca riots in western Wales. As we have seen, the 1830 riots in Kent and elsewhere were directed against threshing equipment in the name of just wages. Some rural domestic workers attacked the source of their competition, the new machines and factories. In this Luddite agitation, beginning in 1811 and cropping up occasionally later, small groups of weavers and others destroyed many machines in northern England by well-coordinated night attacks. The Luddites developed a doctrine based on the presumed virtues of manual methods and an egalitarian work setting.

In France the major rising occurred of course in 1789. Although manorial dues were abolished in the autumn of 1789, agitation continued until redemption payments were eliminated in 1793. Even after this there were brief local riots in famine years until the middle of the nineteenth century. Domestic workers, pressed by increasing factory competition, occasionally struck and rioted locally. In many of the poorer regions, such as the mountainous Auvergne, peasants rioted during the ferment of 1848 with intense unrest persisting through 1851. But most peasant regions were now immune to major agitation and some actively opposed the urban risings of 1848.

German peasants rioted occasionally in the early nineteenth century; banditry also increased. In 1848 peasants in many sections of Germany and Austria followed the lead of revolution in the cities and attacked their manorial lords. After two years of bad harvests peasants in several areas, especially in the southwestern part of Germany, pillaged and burned many castles and record repositories. In eastern Germany there was less revolutionary activity, but peasants were restless and some urged a redistribution of property.

Southern and eastern Europe witnessed some major peasant riots in the early part of the nineteenth century, but there agitation increased after 1870. Because of the deteriorating conditions in agriculture generally as well as the unusual poverty and pressure on the land in these areas of big estates, the period of agitation was often more extended than it had been in western Europe. In Andalusia anarchism spread after 1870. There were a number of major strikes by workers on the latifundias; anarchists even seized land and tried to set up an idealized village government and economy. The Sicilian revolt of the Fasci in 1893 followed three years of declining wheat production and wine prices and a concomitant rise in unemployment. Peasants tried to seize the land, claiming it was theirs by a tradition of possession akin to the possession of common land. Rioting broke out again in 1898 in Sicily and central Italy against grain dealers and bakers; many town halls containing tax records were attacked.

Riots were frequent in the Balkans in this same period. Romanian peasants rose several times in their hunger for land; a major outburst in 1907 resulted in thousands of deaths. Bosnian peasants rebelled against their Muslim landlords in 1875; they were spurred by a crop failure and by their resentment at having to surrender up to half their crop to the lords. There was one distinctive element in some of the Balkan agitation. Nationalist doctrines attracted increasing numbers of peasants as a means of expressing the common grievances. Nationalist agitators found considerable support among the peasantry on Bosnia, Serbia, and Macedonia. Peasant nationalism was directed particularly against the Muslims because they were landlords and unbelievers, but it could be turned against other outsiders such as the Austrians. The assassin of Franz Ferdinand in 1914 showed how peasant hardship could take a nationalist form: "I have seen our people going steadily downhill. I am a peasant's son and know what is happening in the villages. . . . All this had its influence on me and also the fact of knowing that he [the archduke] was a German, an enemy of the Slavs."[1]

Russian peasants engaged in some riots in every year of the century; between 1826 and 1849 there were about sixty local outbreaks a year. After 1856 petitions to the government or to landowners for freedom from servile obligations increased, spurred by the discontent of soldiers returning to the villages from the Crimean wars. News that the government was going to emancipate the peasantry and then dissatisfaction

[1] Joachim Remak, *Sarajevo: The Story of a Political Murder* (London, 1959), p. 77.

with redemption payments and lack of land caused a rise in the numbers of riots. In the first months of 1861 alone there were 1,340 outbreaks. This number was unusual, but in succeeding decades a great deal of agitation occurred, particularly in years of bad harvests and famine, such as the 1870s. In Russia as elsewhere, a combination of population pressure and dissatisfaction with legal changes created a high pitch of discontent. The culmination came in 1905, when peasants rose in many areas, spurred by bad harvests and the failures of the war with Japan. They pillaged landlords' forests and estates, refused to pay rents, and burned records in the familiar pattern. Peasants in the repartitional communes, who lacked firm individual ownership of land, were most active in the rising, which extended over a two-year period. After 1906 the pace of rioting declined quite notably until war and revolution brought renewed agitation to the countryside in 1917.

At some point in the nineteenth century, peasants in most areas tried to protest their changing situation, drawing on a tradition of recurrent unrest and on their vivid belief that the land belonged to them and that a vaguely egalitarian framework should define the local community. They tried to defend and increase their traditional attachment to the land by attacking outside ownership and obligations. Their level of discontent was high, just as the pressures on them were considerable. The period of protest, whenever it occurred, marked a major turning point in the lives of the peasants.

Toward New Equilibrium

The period of protest in almost all cases reached an end during the nineteenth century. Only in a few areas, notably in southern Europe, did conditions remain so stagnant that the protest period extended well into the twentieth century. In France and Britain risings were over by 1851. German and Austrian peasants were largely quiescent after 1848, and Russian peasants were relatively calm between 1906 and the 1917 revolution. Peasants who still had land were largely able to adapt the new conditions of agriculture. The landless had to knuckle under or leave.

A number of factors combined to relieve the pressures on the peasants. The full abolition of manorial dues and redemption payments was crucial in satisfying much of the peasantry in France after 1793; in parts of western Germany, northern Italy, and the Low Countries soon thereafter; in Austria and Germany by the 1850s; and in Russia after 1905. This abolition often resulted directly from peasant risings. It helped placate peasants particularly where individual holdings predominated, as in western Europe after 1848 and in Russia after 1905. But even in east Prussia a minority of peasants had satisfactory hold-

A handloom weaver in the nineteenth century. The contrast with the factory setting and the poverty are obvious, but many traditional workers tried to hold on. *(Louis Paul Henri Serusier, "The Breton Weaver," oil on canvas, 1888. Musée du Haubergier, France.)*

ings. Peasants who owned land now owned it free and clear, although in Germany some rental fees were still paid.

At the same time the rise of new factories provided an outlet for most of the excess rural population. Certain areas, such as Brittany, remained poor and overcrowded because they were too far from industrial centers; it was still difficult to travel very far. On the whole, however, industrial growth absorbed those who could not find a place on the land, sometimes with the help of emigration. In Germany, for example, the expansion of cities accounted for almost the entire increase of the total population after 1840. This alleviated discontent even in the eastern areas of large estates. In addition, domestic production was viable now only as a supplement, for older workers and women; and though this continued to involve many thousands of people, the full-time workers had given up. Here, even more than with middling peasants, the ongoing process of industrialization finally shunted aside leading protest groups, after a bitter period of transformation.

Alleviation of population pressure and the traditional obligations to landlords created a new environment for peasant agriculture in much of Europe. The landed peasants not only continued their quest for more land, gradually dividing common lands into private ownership and partially consolidating scattered strips, but they also increased their specialization for the market, some going into truck or dairy farming. Their effort was aided, after 1850, by the development of better agricultural credit through government and cooperative banks. Consolidation of the land was also encouraged by the state, and though peasant traditionalism retarded the process, some units were big enough to allow individual economic decisions about land use and to permit grazing of animals or use of machines in cultivation. All this naturally heightened the divisions between owners and nonowners, but even the landless might benefit as the cessation of population pressure stabilized their wages.

Nowhere was the readiness for adaptation of a large minority of peasants more dramatically apparent than in Russia after the 1905 revolution. Between emancipation and the revolution peasants had been held to a rather tight village agricultural system; villages made economic decisions and protected common lands and the division of holdings into strips. After 1906 the government, under the leadership of the reformist statesman Stolypin, tried to alleviate peasant discontent by releasing peasants from the hold of the village. Peasants could, on petition, abolish common land and repartitional communes and could consolidate strips. Taking advantage of these possibilities, most peasants withdrew their land from repartitional communes; almost half applied for some consolidation of strips. In a very short time the new economic interests of the peasant leaders became clear.

The final ingredient of the first stage of peasant adaptation to industrial society was the cessation of periodic famines. Their own improved production plus better transportation through railroads eliminated famines even when there was a poor harvest locally. In western Europe, 1846–1847 represented the last case of real starvation in the countryside. In normal years also the extension of the market system gave many peasants increasing access to urban goods, ranging from coffee and sugar to more stylish clothing.

For all these reasons the great age of peasant protest ceased toward the end of the early industrial period. It revived in Russia during World War I; its bases remained active in southern Europe and the Balkans, in part because these areas had not industrialized significantly yet. The countryside was not forever to be quiet. Peasants could gain new political interests.

But on the whole, by the middle of the nineteenth century in western Europe, peasants managed to forge a unique blend of the old and the new, and there were hints of the same combination in Russia after 1906. Their villages retained recreational functions. Their family structure had been jolted when they realized they could not provide land or jobs for all their children. In Russia after 1906, for example, children were free to leave home without parental consent after the age of twenty-one; previously they had been pledged to their father's authority and turned over their earnings to the family fund. But an individualistic strain, even outright migration to the cities, did not destroy the peasant family. Some peasants, as in France and Ireland, rather quickly reduced their birthrate to maintain the relationship between children and land. In industrial society, as the 1851 Republican uprising in parts of rural France suggested, more durable political protest would surface in France and elsewhere later on. In other areas large peasant families long prevailed and the belief in the economic importance of big broods remained. Large numbers of male peasants in southern Germany, for example, sought to get a woman pregnant before marriage, saying they wanted to make sure of their deal. This was not age-old tradition. But greater economic opportunity, including the chance to leave the countryside, let peasants indulge their customary desire for children and child labor more fully than before.

And peasants still protected themselves somewhat from the outside world. Government directives, aside from taxation and military recruitment at least, could be avoided; hence what the state wanted for agriculture, in terms of new methods and more commercialized tenure arrangements, differed considerably from what it got. There were increasing urban contacts, through market agriculture and the return of now urban relatives, but these did not totally break through the combined envy and distrust that peasants felt for the city. With their attachment to the land and village life, peasants stood apart from the conditions and values of all major urban classes.

None of this should suggest perfection or permanence. The successful peasants were in many ways lulled by their own image, which conservative politicians carefully enhanced, of the superior virtues of rural life. They preferred land over standard of living. And their moderate conservative adaptation escaped the rural laborers who worked for landlords or rich farmers. What is clear is that, despite some hints of new political interests in a few areas, a time of quiet descended in the final decades of the early industrial period. Whenever the old spurs to protest — manorialism, famines — were gone, peasants made do with an adapted tradition. Some of the least protected or more aggrieved elements simply left. Governments learned how to conciliate some peasants and repress others. This equation would ultimately change, as new problems emerged and new voices were raised. For the time being, however, a recognizable peasant society had been preserved.

Urban Society

Growth of Cities

Urbanization was a natural result of population growth and industrialization. Expanding population, and factory competition with domestic manufacturing plus rising agricultural productivity, released hundreds of thousands of people who were not needed and could not be supported in the countryside. Improved food production, along with better transportation, made it easier to supply urban populations.

The most rapid rates of urban growth occurred in the new factory centers, for mechanized industry required a large pool of labor. Many of these cities were essentially new, for factory location was increasingly determined by access to coal, and many of the coal-rich areas had been only sparsely urbanized before. And the peak rate of urban expansion corresponded to the rise of the factories, usually two or three decades after the Industrial Revolution began — 1820–1840 in England, 1850–1870 in France, 1870–1890 in Austria, and so on.

Other types of cities grew in the nineteenth century, without necessarily developing an elaborate factory system. Cities with port facilities were encouraged by the Industrial Revolution because the expansion of trading and exports increased the need for commercial outlets. Even in agricultural areas market opportunities spurred the growth of some big centers, such as Budapest. Trade, banking, and government encouraged the growth of traditional political centers such as London, Paris, and Amsterdam, and newer ones such as Berlin, more than industry itself. So urbanization and factory industry should not be too closely linked, and some cities grew faster than their purely economic functions warranted. In this there was real tragedy, for traditional migration patterns brought many peasants to the capitals, flooding them with unskilled workers, at a time when the most dynamic cities were trying to recruit labor. This was an obvious source of the unusual crime and unrest in the political centers as well.

One of the reasons for the growth of big cities, whether new or old, was the stagnation of many regional towns, which resulted in a major change in Europe's urban map. Improved transportation and marketing reduced the need for purely local trading and manufacturing cities. Even artisanal production tended to move from local towns to a small number of cities, such as Paris. The railroad itself operated most efficiently between large centers. Even when lines were built it was uneconomical for trains to stop and start too often and the initial systems of trunk lines long left many cities without service, usually doomed to decay. Similarly, the need for a pool of labor and massive capital and commercial facilities dictated the expansion of cities best located with regard to resources and transportation. Urbanization involved, then, the concentrated growth of some new industrial cities and of major centers generally. Many older towns, such as Norwich in Britain and Vézelay in France, actually declined as part of the urban movement. Even when a regional center merely stagnated, urbanization could again cause tragedy, as established groups could no longer rely on their local position to feel important.

Overall, however, the main fact of urbanization was the sheer rate of growth involved. Favored cities expanded rapidly. In Britain, many northern manufacturing cities, such as Leeds, Birmingham, and Sheffield, grew by 40 percent between 1821 and 1831. Between 1801 and 1851 Birmingham grew from 73,000 to 250,000, and Liverpool expanded from 77,000 to 400,000. Manchester rose from 25,000 to 367,232 between 1772 and 1851. London also continued to grow but at a slower rate. French industry and population expanded less rapidly. Between 1830 and 1851 four-fifths of France's population rise went into the cities; between 1851 and 1871, eleven-twelfths did so. Some industrial centers grew with great rapidity but never to the size of the British giants. Saint-Étienne rose from 16,000 to 56,000 between 1820 and 1850 and Roubaix from 8,000 to 34,000 during that time. The great growth of Paris overshadowed the provincial centers during most of the century, making French urban development far less balanced than was the case in other countries.

In Germany urbanization had clearly begun by the 1860s, for it was that decade that city growth first absorbed the whole German population gain. Berlin and the industrial centers in Saxony and the Ruhr grew most rapidly. In 1870 there were eight cities in Germany with populations of more than 100,000; in 1900 there were forty-one, and five were over the half million mark. Scandinavia and the Low Countries entered their period of urban growth around mid-century also, and eastern Europe soon followed. Austria's city population rose from 18 percent to 32 percent of the total between 1850 and 1890. During the last three decades of the century Warsaw grew by half a million, and the industrial city of Lodz rose from 31,000 to 310,000. Russian cities grew rapidly, with Moscow rising by 400,000.

In 1800 Europe had 21 cities with a population over 100,000; in 1895 it had 120, and their inhabitants represented 10 percent of the

European population as a whole. Several areas, in fact, were over half urban. Britain passed this point in 1850, and by 1900 over four-fifths of its people lived in cities. Germany was over half urban by 1900, France by 1930; and the trend spread widely.

City growth slowed down in most countries after the first decades of industrialization, though there was still substantial increase. By that time the nature of the cities and their place in society had been radically altered. New urban areas had risen, more massive agglomerations than had ever before been known. For a great chunk of Europe's population the most distinguishing feature of the early industrial period was the move to the city and adjustment to its life.

City Population

The initial decades of urban expansion depended largely on immigration from the countryside. The cities themselves had only scant margins of births over deaths in this period; they were not capable of significant natural increase. In some of the fastest-growing centers two-thirds of the residents had been there less than fifteen years. Many rural residents were attracted to the cities by the opportunities and excitement of urban life, but more were forced to come. Population pressure, loss of land, and more productive agriculture made many peasants unnecessary in the countryside, and factory competition displaced domestic manufacturers. After a period of declining wages and lengthening periods of unemployment, huge numbers of rural people sought refuge in the cities. Often they went first as transients, hoping to return to their village after a period of factory work. Gradually, their contacts with the countryside declined and they became fully urban.

Some of the cities' new residents had traveled long distances from their homes in towns and villages. Large cities such as Berlin and Paris drew from all over the country. Barcelona attracted thousands of southern Spanish peasants. A substantial number of foreigners came into many cities. Irish peasants sought work in the new British centers, and Belgians and Germans helped build up towns like Roubaix and Mulhouse; Poles later came into the Ruhr.

But one of the themes of rapid urbanization was an effort to cushion shock. Some long-distance migrants were simply unusually venturesome. Others expected to return home after earning a bit of money, planning to support the family economy or even buy land. Particularly before the railroad most migration was short-hop. That is, a displaced young peasant son moved twenty or thirty miles nearer a city, where the economy was more commercialized and jobs more plentiful. His children, in turn, moved into the city. Correspondingly many cities (the capitals are the leading exceptions) drew primarily on their own regions even as they expanded rapidly. Finally, some long-distance migration followed traditional patterns. Young servant women coming to Paris, for example, originated disproportionately in poor agricultural areas that had traditionally sent servants to Paris; only their numbers had greatly increased. None of this should minimize the jolt of urbanization. Cities provided a distinctive way of life. But not all people moved blindly into a strange environment. They took it one step at a time, often hoping to pull out as soon as possible. This is one reason they could survive the shock.

Cities were strange, bustling, hurried. They had been different from the countryside before, and the new urbanization sharpened some of the differences. The city population was young. The bulk of the immigrants from the countryside were between twenty and forty years old, the age at which one had the vigor and courage to tear up ties with the village or town. The youth of the urban population in turn contributed to the dynamism of the cities. The immigrants were at the most economically productive age, and this helped build the prosperity of the new cities. The energy of the young newcomers might also contribute to rising urban agitation.

In the cities illegitimacy and crimes against property had long been higher than in the countryside. Urbanization extended these trends to a larger population. The percentage of women was higher in the city because of a higher male death rate and the fact that the ratio of males to females at birth was lower than in rural communities. In vigor, in composition, and in many basic habits the people of the new cities were different from the people of the villages. There were many vital distinctions in class and behavior within the city, but urban life imparted some common features to city residents as a whole. Above all, cities were messier and more exciting places for all concerned.

Material Conditions

The most obvious general influence in the rising cities was the material setting. The great influx of immigrants put real strain on urban physical facilities, which had often been poorly developed even before. A positive deterioration of conditions occurred in many cities during the first period of urban growth. British cities, which had been paying growing attention to street paving and to covering sewers in the late eighteenth century, could not build rapidly enough to keep pace with their rising population. An increase in urban mortality rates was the inevitable result. Rapidly growing French cities such as Mulhouse had similar problems, but centers that expanded more slowly, such as Lille, managed to improve their facilities throughout the period. Later in the century similar material pressures occurred in the cities of southern and eastern Europe.

New numbers created a great need for housing. Old buildings were divided and redivided; the poorest families had only one room or even had to share a room with another family. New buildings were hastily thrown up, providing cramped, flimsy accommodation. Rents soared, doubling or even tripling in a decade or two. Intense crowding, inadequate conditions, high prices—these were the inevitable consequences of the influx to the cities.

The expansion of cities created needs for transportation as well. New streets had to be built. Many older streets were still unpaved, and the new ones were often little more than rutted paths. Vehicular transport was in private hands and expanded only slowly; the carriages and horse-drawn omnibusses were too expensive for most of the new residents. The crowding of the cities was partly due to the need to be within walking distance of the place of work, and even so some new workers had to walk many miles each day.

New population meant increasing need for wells and for sewage disposal; these too were provided only slowly and inadequately. Many sewers remained open, and many rivers were increasingly polluted by the disposal of wastes. This was in fact the peak period of urban water pollution, unmatched even in the twentieth century. The poorer areas of most cities were unbelievably filthy and smelly. They were naturally subject to disease and even epidemics, such as the cholera epidemic that raged through western Europe in 1832.

Danger from fire and from criminals was also high. Cities had few police facilities. In 1848 Berlin had two hundred police officers for a population of 400,000, and this was one of the best-policed cities of Europe. With unlighted streets, huge numbers of new and poor inhabitants, and few regular police patrols, it was small wonder that crime rates rose rapidly. The pressure of population on already limited facilities created a vast array of urban material problems in the cities.

City Government

Cities moved from increasing material distress to greater control during the early industrial decades. Gradually, private groups and particularly urban governments themselves developed new concepts of what a city should be like. They tried not only to catch up with the needs created by a rising population but also to go beyond what older cities had offered. New systems of fire prevention and of mass transport were developed; new ideas of police action and government inspection arose. By the mid-nineteenth century in western Europe, and soon after elsewhere, new institutions were transforming urban life.

In many cases the development of novel urban activities was promoted by changes in city government. New elements in the middle class, such as factory owners, sought urban political power. In Britain this change was slow. Manchester was governed as a noble manor until

1844, when the administration was opened to election by middle-class property owners. Even before then, however, industrialist groups had supplemented the manorial officials with activities of their own, especially in matters of police and hygiene. Cities elsewhere in western Europe were more abruptly freed from the control of aristocratic or church officials. The French Revolution established election procedures for mayors, with the franchise usually limited to property owners. Most cities in France and the Low Countries were governed by middle-class administration. The mayors of most factory centers were usually industrialists, but older elements of the merchant class controlled other cities. In eastern and southern Europe urban administration was opened to new personnel later in the nineteenth century; Moscow won a middle-class government after the 1905 revolution.

National governments, too, played an increasingly active role in the cities; in central Europe this continued the earlier trend. By 1850 the British government began to suggest and then require the establishment of local boards of health and education. The French government, more active in local affairs, played a major role in such projects as slum clearance.

Municipal governments took a hand in the matter of housing. By the 1830s French cities established some inspection of houses and even closed some of the worst slums. During the Second Empire the national government sponsored housing projects in Marseilles and elsewhere. In Paris the prefect Haussmann tore down huge slum areas to build a network of boulevards. The object was to eliminate the twisted, crowded streets that were so easy to barricade in revolution and to replace them with avenues down which troops could march and fire. The result was a major change in the housing and transportation of Paris, and also a considerable reduction in the possibility of riot. In Britain cities were empowered to inspect houses in 1851 and to clear slums in 1865; by the 1890s minimum standards of space and sanitary facilities were established in all houses. Elsewhere in Europe, in many German cities for example, stronger traditions of government action promoted regulations even earlier.

Cities also began to build parks. Paris removed many old cemeteries, health hazards in themselves, and replaced them with parks. At the end of the century Vienna tore down its peripheral walls and substituted a ring of boulevards and parks.

Problems of transportation were attacked by private companies and city administrations. Increasing controls were placed on bus companies. Streets were broadened and paved. Most important, commuter trains and later subways offered rapid transport at a low price. By the later part of the century rapid transportation and municipal housing regulations had greatly reduced urban congestion; the boundaries of cities spread and suburbs proliferated beyond them.

Urban governments also attempted to deal with crime and public hygiene. Gas lighting was installed on many city streets by the 1830s. Police functions were greatly expanded. New forces, such as London's bobbies, set up in 1829, provided far more numerous personnel. Cities also established fire departments, long supplemented by private brigades such as those provided by many insurance companies. Cities built new covered sewers quite rapidly and worked to improve the water supply. They began to clean the streets. Municipal officials checked water supplies, market conditions, and slaughterhouses. Schools, factories, and hospitals were also subjected to city inspection. Many cities required vaccinations of all residents.

The result of these various efforts in housing and hygiene was a major improvement in urban health. By the 1830s French cities had a large annual surplus of births over deaths. German cities such as Frankfurt achieved a similar surplus in the 1840s. Everywhere urban mortality rates fell much more rapidly than rural after the first shock of urban growth passed, and in a few countries, such as Austria by the end of the century, they had actually dipped below the levels of the countryside.

So the cities were not helpless even as they received their great onslaught of new people. Some government patterns were suggested that were later taken over by national states in their own response to industrialization, for cities forecast a host of welfare and regulatory measures. But for urban residents, old as well as new, the early industrial period was dominated by confusion and material horror as traditional facilities were overwhelmed by new numbers of people. Adaptation might occur, even among some of the poorer elements, but it was hacked out in an exceedingly harsh environment. The material problems of the city affected all classes. The rich began to separate themselves from the poor far more rigorously than before. The modern city was socially segregated, and middle-class elements quickly led a movement toward distinct residential suburbs. Some people feared crime, though their imagination often exceeded reality. Still more tried to flee dirt and pollution; it was no accident that most of the wealthy quarters shifted to the west of the center city, for prevailing winds came from the west and conveniently blew most industrial filth on the older sections in the center and the east. This kind of reaction left each urban class somewhat isolated in its efforts to come to grips with city life. The poorer classes obviously, but also the new middle class had to deal with an environment that was unexpected and to a significant degree out of control. Finally, the speed of urbanization not only created new social classes but overwhelmed older groups with new numbers; there was no chance for any large element to maintain the contact with tradition still possible for rural landowners.

The responses to material problems, though they did alleviate the worst distress, raised important issues in their own right. Expansion of government control could limit freedom of action. New police forces could make a small dent on crime, but under middle-class control, they spent about half of their time trying to limit popular recreations such as gambling and drinking—and they were cordially detested by many workers. Sanitary reform brought doctors into a new role as experts, extending their influence over middle-class health practices but also their power to regulate lower-class behavior. The city environment continued to pose important problems for the varied, often hostile groups involved.

The Rise of the Middle Classes

The rise of the middle classes is a familiar theme, expressing the most important change in social values and power alignments in the early industrial period. The middle class was not the most rapidly growing segment of society, but it outstripped all the purely traditional elements. The growth of business and of governmental activities increased the need for professional people, and relevant educational opportunities expanded sometimes faster still. Between 1809 and 1842 attendance at French *lycées*, which had been set up primarily to train bureaucrats, doubled. Russian university enrollments rose from 1,700 in 1825 to 4,600 in 1848. Some of the students involved were aristocrats, but there was a growing middle-class element. In Britain the professional ranks grew by 185 percent between 1803 and 1867. A distinct lower middle class arose as retail shopkeeping expanded everywhere. This was a vital economic function, now that there were more goods to distribute, and shops replaced fairs, peddlers, and some craftspeople as the purveyors of goods. From almost nothing, this group grew to about half of the mid-century middle class in cities such as Paris. The upper middle class profited from new economic opportunities, too. In Paris the wealthiest segments of the middle class rose from 2.4 percent of the population in 1820 to 3.6 percent in 1847, and the city's population itself had risen during the same years. Middle-level businesspeople, new factory owners and wholesalers, proliferated as well. This was no tiny elite. Although it did not quite keep pace with urban growth, it rapidly increased as a percentage of the overall population. In Britain, for example, the middle class grew by 223 percent, compared to the 206 percent rate for the population generally.

New numbers meant new wealth, and although the lower income levels of the class grew more rapidly than the top segment, there could be no doubt that the class commanded a rising share of the national income. The very rich in the class also increased their wealth per capita; an upper-middle-class family in Paris was richer in 1848 than its counterpart thirty years before. Many industrialists and bankers gained great fortunes. Even more modest manufacturers could steadily increase their living standards. The Alsatian Thierry-Mieg began with a small textile operation and within twenty years was earning three hundred times as much as the average textile worker he employed; at which time he proudly noted, "My fortune is made."[2]

New numbers and new wealth were capped by a reshuffling of positions. Most middle-class people came from propertied backgrounds—sometimes rural; there were few rags-to-riches stories. However, there was social mobility *within* the middle class, both up and down the social scale. Between 1820 and 1848 most of the richest middle-class families in Paris were replaced by new families drawn from lower in the class. The same process occurred in Vienna. Industrialists in smaller cities gradually shunted aside traditional merchants, who were unwilling to innovate. The majority came from among well-to-do farmers, former artisan masters, or supervisors in the putting-out system; they had not been born to their station. Toward the end of the early industrial decades opportunities decreased somewhat. The new upper middle class closed its ranks, and manufacturing families often monopolized even the new techniques. But for several decades talent and luck could really pay off in measurable mobility.

The rise of the middle class was thus very tangible. And the class could be measured off from other groups. There was a bit of fuzziness at the bottom. Perhaps 15 percent of all shopkeepers were close to the artisan level, intermarrying with this class and sharing its living standards. By the same token some master artisans claimed middle-class status, if they owned their own shops and directed a few employees. Factory supervisors and business clerks were another ambiguous group, and many supervisors had working-class origins. But on the whole distinctions were clear. The early industrial middle class owned property. The average big-city shopkeeper possessed at least twenty times as much capital as the average artisan. Most married within their own group; in Paris approximately 80 percent of the daughters of shopkeepers married shopkeepers during the period 1820–1848. At the top, only a few wealthy businesspeople could rival the aristocratic magnates until late in the early industrial period, and of course they were untitled as well, and frowned upon by aristocrats who were trying to defend their own position. The middle class was a growing group, definable in fairly clear economic terms, advancing in many ways—it should be easy to go on to talk about the class's clear triumph and the new values it stood for. In fact, there were at least two middle classes,

---

[2] Georges Mieg, *Une Lignée Mulhousienne: Jean-Ulric Thierry-Mieg et ses descendants* (Mulhouse, 1914), p. 39.

an old and a new, and traditional motives could intrude on apparently new economic functions. In the formative period for industrial society, middle-class elements warred with each other, and while newer ideas gradually triumphed they compromised with other values.

The Conundrum of the Middle Class

The middle class did not grow uniformly with industrialization. Where the state took a prominent role in industry, as in Russia, the business segments remained small and dependent; professional elements were long more important. The new middle class varied in size and strength as a function of the previous size of the nonaristocratic property-owning groups.

Luddite acts, though undertaken by only a small number of crafts-people, met with tacit approval from many middle-class elements. Shopkeepers sometimes cheered the machine breakers on, and magistrates were often inclined to be lenient. Most middle-class elements, even England, did not like the raw new factories and would have voted against industrialization.

In 1848 the Bavarian government sponsored an essay contest on the state of society. Contributors were mainly middle class: teachers, pastors, master artisans, even some local businesspeople. Almost uniformly they damned the changes they saw around them. The lower classes were immoral, witness their fancy clothes. The rich were getting too rich. "Destruction of these machines . . . would be the most beautiful way to get the disastrous things off the face of the earth."[3]

This was a sentiment that many manufacturers themselves might echo, or almost. In 1840 a young French industrialist, Motte-Bossut, impressed with what he had learned in England, set up one of the first big spinning factories in Roubaix. His parents, owners of a putting-out system with modest wealth, invested in his plant (he was their son, after all) but refused ever to set foot in it; such a gigantic operation was immoral. Another manufacturer in the same city urged that mechanization be limited and that England's horrible example be avoided, for above all the middling property owner should be protected from voracious capitalism. But other French industrialists wanted nothing better than to beat the English at their own game; to Motte-Bossut, England was "the center of the universe."

The middle class constantly criticized itself, or so it seems on the surface. Middle-class publicists, including many women, berated the average middle-class homemaker for idleness, living beyond her means, and frivolity. They were wrong, as we shall see; but the homemakers

[3] Edward Shorter, "Middle-Class Anxiety in the German Revolution of 1848." *Journal of Social History*, 2 (1969): 193.

read the criticisms, for they hungered for guidance. Happily they did not follow the moralistic advice, but they may have been troubled by it.

"Middle-class" political regimes were rarely clear-cut. "The" middle class was not liberal. Many were hostile to liberalism, and most distrusted pure liberal theory. The middle class was not yet eager to seize political power directly. When the whole class got the vote, as occurred for all intents and purposes in England in 1832, they elected about the same types of people as before, including many aristocrats. More commonly suffrage reforms divided the middle class, with only the top property owners gaining the vote. In the July Monarchy in France only about 250,000 males could vote, with landowners predominating. In Italy only 2 percent of the population could vote from unification to the 1870s. To go from "middle-class" to a defined political interest is usually misleading. The rise of the middle class was a vital feature of early industrial society but it entailed a rise in complexity as well.

The Traditionalist Sector

Tensions in the middle class arose inevitably from the mixed origins and roles of the urban groups who owned property but were not aristocratic. The old bourgeoisie, in the first place, did not simply roll over and die. Small-town big shots—the local judge, the miller—carried on even as their towns declined in relative importance. Even in large older cities (Rheims is an example) big merchants, although adamantly refusing to adopt factory equipment, long dominated the town's social life and kept the new industrialists at a distance; some industrialists, because of the stigma of novelty, long preferred to call themselves merchants. Even small manufacturers might see no point in innovating beyond a certain level because their goals were not really new.

In the second place, the cities were filled with former rural property owners—the middling peasant who had sold out, the former village teacher or grain merchant. For the countryside had concealed a large number of business and professional people, along with landed peasants. Some of these, on reaching the city, hoped to attain new heights; some joined the innovators. Far more hoped to preserve old values in new ways, now that the rural economy was so confused.

A case in point is the shopkeeping group. As noted, their economic functions were new. Many brought their capital in from the countryside; in Paris 60 percent of the shopkeepers were of rural origin. This much they would venture, but no more. They saw their business strictly in family terms. Women and children worked the same long hours as men, preserving even the traditional pace of work by building their whole lives around the sporadic activity of the shop. There was no desire to expand, and, overall, the shopkeeping group improved its economic position not at all during the nineteenth century. The group asked nothing more than to remain in the middle of the social scale.

The ministry was another channel for traditionalists. Many small-town bourgeois and artisans became Catholic priests or Lutheran pastors. This was mobility; it was certainly a respectable alternative to remaining in a stagnant job. Hence the peasantry was increasingly displaced in this profession by more urban elements, who often scorned the countryside and hoped for positions in the city. This was a particular source of tension in the German Lutheran church, for peasants did not like the new type of pastor. But the ministry remained a conservative force; its members were eager to preserve the old social order, not to adapt to the new.

Ministers and their families were key proponents of traditional values in early nineteenth-century Britain—which involved them directly in criticisms not only of lower-class behavior but also of other middle-class interests such as material greed. Novels and advice literature from these sources promoted a nostalgia for real or imagined rural values, and could make a middle-class readership seriously question the quality of industrial life.

In the long run the most traditionalist segments of the middle class would be economically differentiated from other sectors, becoming notably poorer and less mobile though still defined by their property ownership. In the early decades of industrialization some of the innovating elements of the middle class were, however, little better off. Values, more than economics, marked the split.

Finally, middle-class traditionalists provided some of the moralizing tone that has often been attributed to the middle class as a whole. Churchmen particularly led the charge against profit seeking and more luxurious styles of life. Religious writers attacked the real or imagined frivolities of middle-class women. Many traditionalists early on tried to restrict their birthrate, for they wanted to be able to pass on their property intact, not divide it among too many children. This promoted an ethic of sexual restraint, as well as a relatively late marriage age, for abstinence was one of the only sure ways this group knew to limit births. This group, though profoundly uneasy about change, lacked direct outlets for frequent protest; it was too respectable, too conscious of defending its property, to take to the streets save in a few major revolutions in 1848. Even in petitions traditionalists rarely attacked the middle class directly, since in the early industrial period they could make do; they were losing ground but were not displaced. Their full agony would come later, when society was more fully out of hand according to traditional norms.

The Middle Class

Many elements of the middle class accepted change. They had their anxieties. Big businesspeople could talk of the evils of cities and the unbearable tensions of risking a new investment. Homemakers might read the religious magazines even as they tried to work out a new style of life. The uncertainties surrounding innovation created some links between the rising middle class and the traditionalists, particularly in the first generation of industrialization. Later, businesspeople shook off some of the fears and spoke more consistently of expansion. In another shift away from tradition, the principal women's magazines in Britain deliberately avoided a religious tone after 1850.

Fear nevertheless played a significant role in middle-class life. The class was surrounded by signs of failure—the growing and visible number of people who lacked property and, with this, security and respectability. The decline of property ownership associated with early industrialization could terrify the group that defined itself in terms of ownership, for a downward plunge seemed only too possible. Fear prompted middle-class people to attempt new kinds of self-control, as well as supporting innovation in business and professional life. Fear helped account for the revulsion middle-class people might feel with regard to groups that lacked the requisite qualities for success—workers, people of "inferior" races, in some respects even women. At the same time, however, middle-class people did not usually acknowledge their fears, particularly by the late nineteenth century. Their preferred public stance emphasized confidence and control.

For the middle class thought in terms of science and material progress. It was sure a better world was being built through industrialization. Members of the middle class hoped themselves to rise in society. They were eager to acquire a new standard of living. They were conscious of the need to save money, since this was the source of investment funds and dowries for daughters, but they were quickly open to new pleasures as consumers. They wanted better furnishings for their homes. They wanted new recreational outlets, like the fancy bars that sprang up in Paris around 1850 or the music gardens in London that drew a fashionable crowd of young clerks and professional people for drinking and dancing. At the top, the upper middle class indeed began to separate itself from the rest of the group by a really luxurious standard of living. Successful businesspeople bought large mansions and had at least three servants. They increasingly took over patronage of concert groups. This kind of wealth came only to 5 or 10 percent of the class, though the numbers were sufficient to make a real change in the cultural tone of society. The bulk of the middle class had to be content with more modest improvements, but the desire for new pleasure was there even so. Ultimately this would be the source of a new leisure ethic. In this first industrial period the middle class spent long hours at work, twelve or more a day, and its work ethic overshadowed all else. But there was room for experimentation with a new style of life. Although set apart most obviously by property ownership, the bulk of the middle class pulled in three or four times the annual income of the working class—£200 in England, for example, compared to £60 for a skilled worker.

This margin, though not as great as might be imagined and inadequate for elaborate recreational expenses, served as a source of innovation in the household.

Finally, the middle class was open to the idea of mobility for others. Its myth was not the traditionalist lament that the poor were uppity and immoral when they were seen wearing fancier clothes, but rather the fiction of the self-made person. Few people actually did rise into the middle class in this period from below. As we have seen, recruitment was almost entirely from the ranks of existing property owners. Only 10 percent of entrepreneurs in Berlin had other than solid middle-class backgrounds. But a handful of examples were genuine: Cail, ultimately owner of a machine works in Paris, who started as an apprentice metal worker, or Joseph Brotherton, a successful manufacturer who was the only member of the House of Commons of working-class origin. And the idea that people could and should rise by their merits was central to the middle-class ethic, in contrast to the traditionalist impulse to want everyone to remain in their place.

Increasingly the innovative elements won out, in public discourse and to some extent in private conviction. Their newer values converted part of the middling class and even part of the aristocracy. They had a number of important weapons even though, at the start of the Industrial Revolution, they formed a decided minority among urban property owners generally. Success bred imitation. The traditionalists might rail against large fortunes but the fact was the new fortunes were there, tempting toward mobility. Hence although most shopkeepers remained stagnant, they sent perhaps 30 percent of their sons into the higher ranks of the middle class, and many sons of Lutheran ministers used the scholarships to which they were entitled to enter better-paying positions like law or teaching that commanded greater prestige in industrial society. Generational changes thus muted some of the conflict that existed between the various groups in the middle class.

Moreover, there was overlap between the values of traditionalists and innovators, for both appealed to a fund of bourgeois wisdom. They could agree on the importance not only of property but of hard work, savings, and respectable moral behavior. They agreed that the family was the proper basis for society and the goal of economic effort. They agreed that sons should be given a good start in life, through some education and a solid inheritance, and that daughters deserved a dowry to launch a proper marriage. They agreed in marrying relatively late, the men often in their late twenties, so that the family would start out on a proper footing. Important differences existed, for the traditionalists thought in terms of passing on the same station in life whereas the newer middle class strove upward. But there were similarities in what children were taught, which gave some basis for sons and daughters in a traditionalist family to decide to move beyond their parents' station.

Furthermore the middle class issued its own propaganda. Although religious literature was widely read in the first industrial decades, so were works such as those of Samuel Smiles in England, which preached a slightly different ethic of success. Hard work, respectability to be sure, but crowned by steady advance up the social ladder. This was a classic self-help approach produced in every industrializing country. Workers who saved their money and restrained their animal appetites could go from rags to riches. The literature was widely read by shopkeepers and artisans; Samuel Smiles, for example, won his main audience in these groups. Here was another way that the idea of social mobility and technological advance spread widely. Furthermore, similar values crept into the educational system under middle-class sponsorship. In the eighteenth century Prussian schoolbooks stressed the importance of social hierarchy and respect. By the 1840s they had switched emphasis to discussions of hard work, material progress, and self-disciplined control of impulse; they criticized selfishness and irreligion too, but clearly the balance had changed.

By the mid-nineteenth century the most advanced industrial areas were ready for industrial festivals. Beginning with London's Crystal Palace Exhibition of 1851 millions of people could be drawn to displays of the most modern machinery and the new arrays of material goods these machines spewed forth. By no means was the whole society converted to an ethic of material progress; even the traditionalists still held out to some extent. But given the combination of example and propaganda, it was hard to resist the middle class entirely.

The Professions

A crucial element in the development of the modern middle class was the conversion of the professions to a new outlook, in which claims to education and science displaced traditional status. There are real ambiguities here. Many people entered professions to achieve respectability in older social terms. Aristocrats, as we have seen, might take this path, and professionals retained more contacts with the aristocracy than most segments of the middle class. Even some businesspeople admitted the greater prestige of the professions by sending a son to the university so that he could become a lawyer or government bureaucrat. This pattern was developing as early as the 1840s in France and Germany. By the same token respectable professions like law were often overcrowded while new ones, such as engineering, had many unfilled jobs. The prestige of the professions rested on job security, at least when a government post was in the offing, and on the older place of the professions in the bourgeoisie. Professionals did not make as much money as successful businesspeople, so their high status had to have these partially anachronistic roots.

For their part professionals were constantly tempted to distrust the world of business. This was the only highly educated group in the middle class during the early industrial period, for most businesspeople sent their children to work after at most a few years of secondary school. It was not hard to see the business world as filled by money-grubbing, ignorant people. In turn, businesspeople often distrusted professionals as theorists, for they had a pragmatic streak that called any elaborate intellectual life into question. Professionals saw their role in local government threatened, as businesspeople used their greater funds to capture the mayor's office and the city council. Factory owners partially displaced professional people as leaders of local social groups. Professionals in a city artistic or philanthropic society had to pay increasing deference to the power and wealth of businesspeople. In Mulhouse the young chemistry teacher Achille Penot began a career of public service by attacking the industrialists who dominated the city. He investigated the conditions of the poor and found them horrible; and he said so. The local industrial society, which was proud of its devotion to spreading knowledge of new scientific and technical developments, responded with horror: they had been attacked by one of their own. So Penot tactfully withdrew his first book, was readmitted to the society, and thereafter made more modest suggestions for reform, such as better treatment of child labor, while writing panegyrics to the local industrialists.

So there was tension between professionals and businesspeople and they had somewhat separate worlds. The professionals' concern for their prestige showed vividly in their tendency to live beyond their means. At best they saved a bit of money for their children's education (and this was another group that early reduced its family size, so that it could afford the proper education); as much as 25 percent of capital could go to this purpose. But the professionals also wanted a fancy house and servants. Even Karl Marx, eking out a living as a journalist, had two servants. The professionals' impulse to spend for show, which endures to the present day, derived from their reaction to the world businesspeople were creating, in which money was the key to social position. Lacking elaborate property, for their capital was in their training, they tried to put a good face on it even at the risk of constant money worries.

But the main point is that they came to accept and even propagate the middle-class set of values, at least in this first industrial period. Penot did swallow his pride and work within the businessperson's framework, where he could in fact tactfully push for change. Professionals might lament their inability to match businesspeople's earnings, but they tried for a similar style of life.

Above all, professionals began their own kind of occupational modernization in this period. Three key elements were involved: formation of professional associations to defend standards, insistence on regular formal training capped by an examination, and, usually a bit later, a state licensing procedure. In 1832 the British Medical Society was formed, against an older, looser group of London physicians; its impulse immediately was to push for better training and a clear association of medicine with scientific advance. In 1858 the Medical Act provided state licenses and examinations. In addition, universities in London and Edinburgh began to provide more careful medical training, in contrast to the older tradition of a gentlemanly liberal education followed by a bit of apprenticeship. Somewhat more slowly, lawyers followed this same pattern. And other groups joined in. Surgeons, formerly associated with barbers, advanced their status and income by professionalizing. They formed their own societies, improved their training, developed new specializations such as gynecology. Pharmacists professionalized; in 1815 British apothecaries won a law that established examinations and licensing. As the century wore on, architects, engineers, and upper-level teachers joined the professional ranks, while accountants moved toward the same goal (achieving it only in the twentieth century). A few groups, admittedly, tried but failed. Primary school teachers talked about better training and licensing but were never able to enforce these on the majority.

The modernization of the professions, both old and new, had a distinctive flavor. Licensing and examinations were designed among other things to restrict entry; here was a guildlike approach that actually restricted mobility into the professions, for the requisite training was expensive. But the process meshed with an industrial society in other respects by increasing the training levels and associating the professions with scientific advance. Here, obviously, was the way professionals maintained themselves in an industrial age.

There were several more specific reasons that professionals chose to innovate during the early industrial period. In their schools, particularly on the Continent, they encountered consistent barriers to the free flow of ideas. Conservative governments restricted reading matter and fired liberal teachers. Suppressions of freedom of the press obviously mattered to an educated group. The frequent student riots of the early nineteenth century in western Europe and later in Russia and Italy set the stage for more persistent reform agitation. In their jobs the professionals encountered other barriers. Young lawyers in Germany who sought to enter the bureaucracy were forced to spend years in junior positions, or even on waiting lists, while their clothing and morals were carefully supervised. Relatedly, there was a constant tendency toward overproduction of professionals. It was easier to get through the universities than to find jobs afterward; this was one reason for the intense competition for bureaucratic posts in Germany. All this tempted middle-class professionals to think in terms of capturing the state and turning it to new purposes. If the aristocracy was reduced, if the state took over manorial functions, there would be new jobs for lawyers and judges. If the state encouraged economic growth then well-trained bureaucrats would be in the driver's seat, for with their knowledge they would easily outperform the aristocratic dilettante.

The modernization of professionals, which allied them, even if somewhat uneasily, with businesspeople, had immense consequences. It was the professionals, with their interest in formal ideas, who served as the main propaganda agents for the middle class. (Samuel Smiles, for example, was a doctor.) It was they who helped revise the schoolbooks. And above all it was they who, if only for their own interests, served as the political arm of the middle class in the final period of class struggle against the aristocracy.

The majority of the members of radical political societies such as the *Carbonari* were from the professional element, and middle-class revolutions were led by professional people. Journalists directed the French revolution of 1830. Professors led the delegation to urge reforms on the king of Prussia in 1848, and lawyers took the major role in the activities of the Frankfurt assembly. As parliamentary regimes spread, professional people again took a leading part as middle-class representatives. In all these activities the professional group worked for interests that the business elements also supported; but it continued to be the most politically conscious segment of the middle class..

In eastern and to an extent southern Europe professional people served as an embryonic middle class by themselves by the beginning of industrialization, in the absence of a large, independent business group. By the mid-nineteenth century nonaristocrats were entering the professions in Russia in substantial numbers. Many were sons of Orthodox priests, another instance of the transfer from older to newer forms of professional mobility. By the end of the century there were over a half-million doctors, lawyers, and related professionals, many employed by local government agencies. In the typical pattern they too began to form professional associations and also raise political demands, playing a major role in the 1905 revolution.

Middle-Class Politics

Generalization about middle-class politics is difficult. Many businesspeople had no particular political interest. They did not necessarily clamor for political rights. And they certainly did not insist on direct monopoly of political power. When they acquired the vote, as in Britain in 1832, they were content to let aristocrats continue to hold key ministries. But they did insist that government, no matter who ran it, fulfill certain key goals, and in this way they contributed to the continued alteration of the state. Very generally, most politically articulate members of the middle class were liberal. They wanted freedom of the press and of religion. They certainly wanted the state to get out of some traditional activities, such as support of guild restrictions and manorialism. Middle-class reformers worked further for the abolition of the slave trade and for state-sponsored education.

But the middle class also valued order. Riots ruined shops and factories, strikes and crime impeded the conduct of business. So the class supported restrictions on workers' rights to associate and the provision of new city police forces. It saw education as a means not only of training workers in new skills, which would make them better workers and possibly capable of rising in society, but also as an acculturation device that would make them docile. So the schools should teach religious and moral values, discouraging drink and disorder. Prison reform, similarly was meant to be humanitarian; the middle class could grow appalled at the brutality of traditional punishments and pushed for reductions in torture and the use of the death penalty. But prisons should also teach criminals proper values and should keep them hard at work, for work was a panacea. Middle-class liberalism was thus a double-edged sword. It advocated new freedoms and was based on a genuine belief that people could be good. But it wanted the state to educate and rehabilitate, and in this way sought new political controls over the lives of the lower classes. Even lower-class entertainments had to be supervised. New middle-class city governments quickly abolished bear baiting and cock fighting as brutal and sometimes moved against gambling as well.

The middle class wanted an efficient state that would not waste money. There was a profound suspicion of government, a holdover from the age when aristocratic elements had used the state to restrict economic growth. Even after obvious anomalies such as guilds had been destroyed many middle-class politicians had to fight the aristocratic effort to win special support for agriculture. British businesspeople, particularly, were driven to a high level of political interest by their opposition to the Corn Law of 1815, which set high tariffs on grain and therefore, by making food more expensive, increased their wage costs. Their political agitation helped lead to the suffrage reform of 1832, and twelve years later the Corn Laws were abolished. There was a general impulse to believe that, if the state would leave people alone and keep its activities to a minimum, the public interest would be best served.

But the middle class also saw new, more positive roles for the government. This view was stronger in Germany, where the government was traditionally active and relatively efficient, than in France or England, but the impulse was fairly widespread. Reformers who wanted to moralize and control the lower classes usually turned to government support. It was the state that could outlaw gambling. It was the state that could undo some of the worst effects of industrialization, by regulating child labor, for example. Most elements of the middle class, including many industrialists, came to accept the notion of some minimal state regulation in the general interest, and child labor laws were passed throughout western Europe during the 1830s and 1840s. Though not fully enforced, they did limit the age of entry to work and the hours children could be employed. Still more obviously the state could promote the economic interests of the middle class by providing tariff protection for industry, transportation facilities, and the like. Urban administrations were urged to build streets, drainage systems, parks, libraries, and schools. The growing vigor of city governments was due primarily to middle-class demands and interests.

The middle class came to recognize that the kind of state it wanted could only come from middle-class participation. Typically, politically active elements of the class pushed for municipal reforms that would give them control of city governments; and they advocated national suffrage systems based on property qualifications that would associate the vote with success in business. Correspondingly, they urged a parliamentary system that would give their representatives a voice. Parliaments were installed in all middle-class revolutions, from France in 1789 to Russia in 1905 and 1917, and the power of parliament was jealously protected and promoted by all major middle-class parties, such as the Prussian Progressives in the 1860s. Only with a constitutional, parliamentary regime did the middle class feel that its political interests could be realized.

Middle-class political interest was increasingly attached to the concept of the nation as well as to the ideal of parliamentary rule. This was the class to which nationalist doctrines particularly appealed. The middle class saw the nation as a vital economic unit. It needed a national market for its goods and national protection of its economic interests. Nationalism also gave the class a focus distinct from attachment to traditional dynasties and aristocratic political principles. After the revolution of 1830 the new king, Louis Philippe, ruled not by hereditary right but as king of the French. In Britain, France, and Belgium, where national existence was established by the 1830s and where the middle class participated in government, nationalism was expressed in pride in existing national institutions and the belief that one's own nation was morally superior to others. Elsewhere, as in Germany and Italy, the middle-class interest in nationalism obviously worked for political change. Middle-class political groups sought national unity along with constitutional, parliamentary regimes. In parts of eastern Europe a small middle class was often instrumental in introducing nationalism. Greek and Serbian merchants were exposed to nationalism in trade with the West during the French revolutionary period. Bulgarian merchants, a new group after 1850, inspired much nationalist activity.

Middle-class intellectuals spread nationalist ideas in many areas. Here again a passion had been aroused in the middle class that was to have profound political consequences.

During the first half of the nineteenth century, and later in parts of eastern Europe, the middle class was dissatisfied with existing regimes, although few members of the class agitated actively. Where there was sufficient liberty of the press, middle-class newspapers attacked governmental conservatism and aristocratic rule. In Restoration France and before 1832 in England, meetings were held and groups formed to agitate for reform of the suffrage, greater protection of liberty, and real limitation of the role of the aristocracy in government. In Spain, Italy, and Germany middle-class activity could not be so open, but there were some publications and discussion groups that condemned the established order. A minority of the middle class, drawn particularly from young professionals and students, went beyond discussion and actually joined groups for agitation. Masonic groups in Spain, the *Carbonari* in Italy, and the *Burschenschaften* in Germany drew significant numbers into vigorous political discussion and sometimes protest.

In certain circumstances the middle class countenanced direct action, even revolution, in pursuit of its political goals. It is incorrect to say that the class itself revolted. Businesspeople were seldom on the streets in revolutions, although they might shut their shops and encourage their employees to riot. The interest in personal security was too great for participation in actual violence; and after revolution broke out, the class was quick to form and join national guard units to preserve order. There was, nevertheless, a series of middle-class revolutions in the first half of the century in most western and central European countries. Middle-class intellectuals prepared the doctrines for these revolutions, doctrines that were accepted quite widely in the class. Middle-class groups typically provoked the revolutions and controlled the revolutionary governments, which sought liberal parliamentary and nationalist goals.

Most of the revolutions failed to establish a government wholly conforming to the middle-class ideals, but even where revolutions were directly defeated, as they were in Germany and Italy in 1848, the succeeding years brought some of the reforms the middle class desired. Parliaments were established, although their powers were limited. Middle-class economic interests were promoted, and national unities were achieved. The middle class did not rule in its own right; it shared power with the aristocracy and compromised its principles with those of the old regime. Nevertheless, a major political role was now assured.

After 1848, in fact, the era of middle-class revolutionary activity was over in western and central Europe. The class had made sufficient economic and political gains that it could be relatively content and the revolutions themselves had heightened its interest in order. Particularly in 1848, the agitation by the urban lower classes, culminating in such bloody riots as the June Days in Paris, attached the middle class to existing governments even when such governments were not fully satisfactory. The class did not lose an interest in parliamentary rule and other reforms, but efforts for change worked within the legal structure. In most countries the class had won some freedom of the press, through which opinions could be expressed. It had won a parliament, albeit often a weak one, in which further changes could be proposed. It had gained new bureaucratic jobs. After the 1848 revolution thousands of new judgeships were created in Prussia, and the Austrian bureaucracy expanded mightily to fill the void left by the abolition of manorialism. The middle class had dislodged the aristocracy from total control. It would now defend its interests in a calm and orderly way.

Middle-Class Economics

What the middle class did economically was more important than what it thought about the economy, but a general outlook was significant as well. Traditionalists in the middling class most typically wanted an economic structure based on small, family-owned units. They valued a wide distribution of property. This could lead them to a laissez-faire view, in which the virtues of free competition were praised. Certainly liberal economists in the early industrial period urged the good effects of individual effort, which through competition would produce more and more goods at lower and lower prices. But the traditionalists feared freedom too, and might turn to the government for assistance.

The leaders of the middle class rarely thought in strictly laissez-faire terms. They used the theories on occasion, particularly to defend against government interference or criticism of industry from the outside. Liberal theories were popularized in many middle-class journals, which spread the ideas and slogans. But the middle class was interested in promoting security as well as individualism and it differed from the traditionalists in being open to new forms of organization. It steadily modified the family firm approach by developing larger, more bureaucratized business units. And, even in this early industrial period, it went beyond the individual firm.

Cooperation was one means of reducing competitive pressure. Industrialists' associations developed early to share technical information or even to allocate markets and supplies. The middle class also sought government encouragement for the economy. Except in Britain almost all entrepreneurs insisted on tariff protection. They might feel that internal competition was valuable, but they certainly had no desire to face foreign goods. Most businesspeople also sought government encouragement of exports, provision of better transport systems, and the like. A smaller number of manufacturers sought government controls on quality and on conditions of work in the interest of modifying excessive competition. There were even proposals, fairly common during the July Monarchy, for example, for a system of government licensing aimed at restricting overproduction and crises. The middle class remained fundamentally optimistic about the course of the economy, for usually its purposes were being realized; but it was not wedded to a concept of complete individualism. Its openness to new forms of organizational control would become progressively more important.

The Middle Class and Lower Classes

The middle class did not innovate as fully in its view of the lower classes as it did in politics or economics. There was a great deal of ignorance of working-class life, particularly as businesspeople and professionals moved to separate areas of the city in order to avoid the worst urban problems. Many never penetrated the poorest quarters of the city. They saw some workers and beggars, but knew nothing of their life, so it was easy to accept general stereotypes. Their own servants were often dirty and ill mannered, in their view, which might enhance the barriers to understanding. There were many gaps between the middle class and the urban lower classes. Speech was different. Many artisans and workers had distinctive accents or dialects; some were even foreign. The middle class usually prided itself, after the first generation at least, on pure pronunciation. The class stressed cleanliness and respectable clothing. Workers, in contrast, were often dirty, ragged, even diseased, and to middle-class eyes they were unpleasant to look at. The middle class urged hard work, whereas many workers valued leisure and took time off when they could. The middle class valued saving; the lower classes had little to save and often preferred to spend any margin for enjoyment. The drinking and sexual immorality of many workers were widely criticized. The lower classes seemed often disorderly because of their penchant for rioting and the roughhousing in which many workers engaged.

All this led the middle class to a firm belief that workers were inferior. It brought some to a fear that the poor were becoming increasingly degenerate and brutal. The middle class was prone to exaggerate crime waves and, at an extreme, to see the urban poor as virtual animals who had to be controlled.

This was not the most common view, however. Exaggerated optimism was at least as widespread. The middle class was uncomfortable with poverty; this was one of its innovations in outlook, even though it produced few quick results. The class was thus open to arguments that poverty was not really there. Publicists often exaggerated improvements in clothing or diet. Great stress was laid on political reforms that freed the workers from the restrictions of guild and manorial lord. Technical developments such as gas lighting were assumed to be of benefit to all. Many observers claimed that workers could always earn enough in good times to cover their needs in bad. Others noted the beneficence of the factory system in giving work to women and children, who would otherwise be left without resources and without proper discipline. Mine owners might claim that their employees gloried in the possibility of working in a soothing pit, sheltered from the glare of sun and the beating of rain. The tendency to see a silver lining in every lower-class cloud relieved the consciences of the middle class and dulled any willingness to take positive action for reform.

However, optimism was not the only reaction of the middle class to the problems of the poor. The class could not be blinded to some of the horrible features of working-class life. Employers, after all, did see their own workers in the plant at least. Crime, riots, and begging indicated that all was not well. Government investigations of the conditions of child labor, carried on in Britain and France in the 1830s and 1840s, were covered by the press, and private reports by doctors like James Kay in Britain and René Villermé in France received considerable publicity. Local middle-class groups also sponsored surveys of labor conditions. Only the most fatuous members of the middle class persisted in asserting that all was well.

Confronted with the evidences of lower-class poverty, the middle class sought a scapegoat. Some said the fault was with the cities; others blamed foreign countries or distant regions for unfair competition that forced conditions down. Some still maintained that poverty was inevitable: did the Bible not say so? Many employers were honestly if occasionally saddened by their workers' lot but felt powerless to do anything about it. Many blamed the conditions of the poor on the poor themselves. There was a deep-seated belief that poverty must somehow be the result of moral inadequacy. Anyone with merit could advance in middle-class society. If workers would save, they would be protected from misery and could even rise; middle-class pamphlets pointed out how easy saving was. If workers would stop drinking, they would have both more money and more energy. Some manufacturers in France claimed that workers spent a quarter of their income on drink and that if they gave up drink they might be rich. If the poor had a decent family life, they would work harder, train their children better, and avoid the exhaustion of sexual debauchery.

The view that the poor were immoral justified a great deal of neglect of social problems. Why help those who would not help themselves? In 1834 the British parliament passed a new Poor Law designed to make poor houses as unattractive as possible. As the poor were to blame for poverty, they should not be encouraged to take charity. Middle-class city governments quickly outlawed begging, a major departure from traditional urban life. The same belief in the immorality of the poor

Middle-class contacts with the working class. Middle-class people served both as demanding employers and uplifting moralizers for workers—sometimes in the same person. This engraving features factory children being called to Sunday school by a "serious" factory owner. *(The Bettmann Archive.)*

justified such political measures as restricting the vote to the well-to-do. Society was fundamentally a hierarchy with the meritorious rising to the top. The same view of the immoral poor conditioned many of the reform efforts that were made. This approach, harsh and unfeeling as it was, came closest to being innovative. For it had some optimistic roots: If workers could reform morally, they might become civilized; that is, just like the middle class. British manufacturers, who began their conduct of factories with a traditional belief that workers were inferior but deserved help from charity, moved increasingly to a view that workers could or should take care of themselves, like any human being. This excused neglect: Workers were responsible for industrial accidents, even when no safety devices were provided. But it left workers considerable personal freedom. Some, by showing ambition, could win the respect, even friendship of the employer. Finally, on a more general level, the moralistic approach could lead to reform efforts. It obviously supported the effort to spread education. As one English observer noted, "Virtue is the child of knowledge, vice of ignorance: therefore education, periodical literature, railroad traveling, ventilators, and the art of life, when fully carried out, serve to make a population moral and happy."[4] Industrialists actively promoted technical training, if only out of self-interest, and although there were a few that felt education was dangerous, in giving workers new ideas, the expansion of schools, by private associations and by the state when in middle-class hands, was extremely rapid. Reformers also worked for limitations on child labor, for it was hard to argue that workers could improve themselves when they were committed to hard labor at six or eight years of age. Efforts to encourage saving were in the same vein. So was the periodic belief that workers could be political allies. The middle class, responsible for much harshness toward the poor, was also responsible for many efforts at amelioration. The real reformer was rare. Most middle-class people spent little money or effort on moralization programs. But the ameliorative streak did produce some results and it did leave the middle class open to later change.

Neither harshness nor reform efforts characterized the most typical approach toward the poor. The middle class did not, in this period, fully abandon more traditional attitudes. Although uncomfortable with poverty, it did not believe that much could be done about it. Although disliking charity, not only because it cost money but also because it provided no basic remedy, the middle class saw no other solution, and continued to rely heavily on it. Hand-me-downs and tips to the servant, a bit of money for the worker who was sick, an annual contribution to a charity fund—these were all that could be done. The poor were not seen as unusually degraded, but rather as naturally inferior people. Of course they drank too much, of course they were sexually immoral, but these were really the simple pleasures necessary for a life of hardship. Workers were often compared to children, who could be allowed a bit of frivolity but who should also be controlled by their natural superiors. As long as they were grateful and did not trouble the social order, they deserved charity when they fell on hard times.

In the bigger factories this approach, combined with the need to tie skilled workers to the firm, produced a paternalistic program that was often quite ambitious, particularly on the Continent. Companies built houses for their workers, set up aid programs for illnesses, constructed clinics, and so on. The result could be of real benefit to workers, but it could severely limit their freedom as well. For workers who offended their employers could be evicted from their homes; if fired, they would have no right to claim the money they had contributed to the company

[4] Archibald Prentice, editorial in the *Manchester Times*, April 2, 1851.

insurance funds. All of this followed from the interests of the firm in having a stable, docile labor force, but also from the broader view of workers as inferior and incapable of helping themselves.

During the first industrial period the failure to rethink its basic social outlook, even if modified by hints of a new approach, did not have serious repercussions for the middle class. Servants stole a bit or made fun of their masters behind their backs; workers sometimes robbed materials from the factory. Both groups changed jobs often, to maintain a sense of freedom. But general attacks on the middle class were rare, and individual efforts like crime or disrespect simply heightened the belief that the lower orders were irresponsible. The recurrent unrest of the period was not usually directed at the middle class specifically. Riots and strikes did target middle-class firms, and major revolutions like in 1848 produced a surge of lower-class unrest, which challenged basic principles of the industrial order and terrified some middle-class observers. Still, an acute fear of class conflict remained episodic in the early industrial period, and the middle class could hope that neglect, charity, better education, or paternal guidance — or some combination of these approaches — would keep unrest at bay and allow continued economic progress as the class was wont to define it. Only in the next stage of industrialization would the class's social outlook be thoroughly tested.

Middle-Class Culture

The middle class had sufficient funds and education to develop cultural interests, and middle-class values accordingly had great influence on the general development of the arts in the nineteenth century. At the beginning of the Industrial Revolution the cultural interests of the middle class were relatively simple. The tastes and habits of many members of the class reflected those of their parents in lower levels of the middle class or in rural society. Few businesspeople had substantial resources for cultural activity, and fewer still had time. In London, for example, even substantial businesspeople could not afford to attend concerts regularly until after 1840. On the Continent, particularly in the larger cities, there was a tradition of theater-going even for the lower middle class. But in industrial cities, and in Britain generally, simple amusements were the rule.

Artistic interests centered around the home and were largely confined to furnishings and decorations, items useful in daily life that provided some status among friends. The middle class sought comfort, neatness, and some sentimentality in its decorations. Typical of this taste was the Biedermeier style, which dominated German bourgeois furnishings and paintings during the mid-nineteenth century. The Biedermeier style stressed simple, manageable furnishings that would not take up too much space, decorated without great imagination or luxury. Wallpaper was crowded with picturesque designs; it was cheaper than it had been in the eighteenth century and became common in middle-class homes for the first time. Paintings in middle-class homes were generally either portraits or sentimental country scenes. Again, the interest was in a setting that would be at once comfortable and respectable. The class had neither the time nor the background for ostentatious designs.

The reading interests of the middle class also centered in the home. Men kept up with political and economic news in their newspapers and journals. Both newspapers and magazines increasingly stressed accounts of technical and scientific developments. Many middle-class views on progress were reflected in and furthered by this reading. Beyond this there was a general interest in stories suitable for family reading. Families often read aloud in the home. Newspapers and magazines provided serialized stories for such reading; authors such as Charles Dickens derived most of their income from these stories, sentimental narratives that were particularly valuable to women, whose formal education was slight. Such a magazine was *Die Gartenlaube* in Germany, which jumped from 5,000 subscribers in 1853 to 225,000 in 1867, as the middle class rose to greater prominence. *Die Gartenlaube* offered articles on science and education, the paths to progress; it editorialized against traditional superstition and for humanitarian causes. Its stories stressed the moral value of family and property. It condemned the aristocracy and often in stories portrayed the idleness and immorality of nobles as a shocking, but somewhat exciting, contrast to bourgeois virtue. Novels for the lower middle class in Germany went even farther in sensationalism, as well as sentimentality, although they too were always careful to let morality triumph.

Apart from home decoration and reading, the principal cultural interest of the middle class in the early nineteenth century was religion. In cosmopolitan centers such as Paris, where educational levels were unusually high, the middle class inclined to skepticism in matters of religion. Generally, however, the class maintained a firm tradition of church attendance and religious interest. Some industrialists came from intensely religious backgrounds. The Nonconformists in England entered industry in large numbers and long preserved their religious fervor. Protestant leaders of industry in Alsace and Switzerland tried to combine work and prayer. Some began each workday in the factory with collective prayer and Bible reading; many attributed their economic success to the will of God. Catholic manufacturers in northern France displayed similar religious intensity. Later, fervent Old Believers played a major role in early Russian industrialization, again combining religious zeal and economic activity. Church attendance was important to the middle classes during the early industrial period; for women particularly, religious practices provided an important outlet. Children were trained in the principles of religion and often were sent to church schools.

Middle-class socializing, Paris, around 1860. A social gathering with a familial air, from an early photograph. What does the scene suggest about gender relations? *(The Bettmann Archive/BBC Hulton Picture Library.)*

The middle class had little interest in theology and ceremony. Doctrines of sin and the afterlife were accepted but were not the focal points of middle-class religion. In fact, the middle-class values of material success and the ability of the individual to improve tended increasingly to contradict the traditional stress on otherworldly goals and original sin. Beyond this the middle class was generally opposed to the political powers of established churches. In countries where there was a tradition of a dominant state church, as there was in France and the Scandinavian states, the middle class proved particularly hostile to religion generally. In Britain and Germany the multiplicity of religions reduced the political issues surrounding the churches, although even there important conflict arose. The middle class resented religious intolerance and its enforcement by a state. It resented the power of aristocrats in the established churches. Neither traditional theology nor church politics attracted the middle class to religion.

Religion did fulfill three vital functions for the middle class. It provided a social focus; for most women church attendance was one of the only regular contacts outside the home. Religion was regarded as useful for the masses; it promoted morality and the acceptance of hardship on earth in the expectation of reward in heaven. Most important, religion served as a source and sanction for morality for middle-class families themselves. The class sought sermons and religious reading that would explain the beauty and utility of moral behavior. This did not add up to intense religious interest necessarily, though it gave churches a new source of funds, and while many people found vital spiritual satisfaction in religious beliefs, middle-class religious interest declined.

Outside of home and church, the cultural activities of the middle class were few during the first decades of industrialization. Many women did a bit of painting or took music lessons. Music was not widely pursued except as part of church services or family entertainment; by 1800 most homes in the English upper middle class had pianos. Theater attendance was generally uncommon; in England many businesspeople felt that it was a waste of time, and some regarded it as immoral. Not until 1850 did the British middle class begin to show an interest in drama. When it did, it applied to the theater the tastes it had developed in reading. It wanted sentimental and instructive plays, and it insisted on more comfortable theater seats.

These early limitations in middle-class culture were not permanent. They did, however, contain certain important principles. The class demanded that literature and art be moral. Erotic references were unacceptable, and governments during the period often tried to ban works such as *Madame Bovary*, which seemed too daring. Literature was to portray the value of hard work and thrift and show how these qualities allowed people to rise in society. It was to avoid subjects such as crime and was not to dwell on life among the poor, for such topics could not offer proper lessons for family reading.

Cultural products were also to be useful. They should provide information. The class did not care for flights of fancy; it preferred moderately realistic portrayals. Purely aesthetic experiences were not sought; art should decorate and represent, or it was a waste. Sentiment was entertaining and informing, but great emotions were dangerous. Scientists were particularly esteemed among intellectuals because their functions were so obviously useful; in fact, the middle class tended to confuse science with technology and praise both as motors of progress.

Other intellectuals and artists were regarded with some suspicion, for they seemed preoccupied with abstract theories and were not motivated by a proper respect for wealth. Middle-class reading often contained portrayals of the wildlife and subversive quality of some artists. The legend of the Bohemian artist was being born and would increase middle-class doubts about the morals and motives of writers and painters. Indeed, the rise of the middle class as the dominant shaper of cultural tastes contributed to a rebellion among some artists by the middle of the nineteenth century. Many painters and poets, often themselves of middle-class origins, sought ways to shock the middle class by rejecting convention and experimenting with the radical life-styles, sometimes including the use of drugs. The Bohemian antagonism with middle-class culture cut both ways.

The middle-class cultural canons of utility and respectability shaped its active educational interests in the early industrial period. Initially most members of the class had only primary schooling, plus some technical training. By the second or third generation of the Industrial Revolution, however, the cultural interests of the middle class broadened notably. Middle-class families still touted education as providing useful training as well as moral values, but some now saw it as a channel to wider social and professional prestige. By mid-century in Britain and France and a bit later in Germany, the intense efforts of the middle class to found businesses had paid off in secure and rising incomes. The class had more leisure, for many businesses now had large staffs, which reduced the time required at work. The class developed the inclination to enjoy itself, although the stress on hard work and saving did not disappear.

The religious interests of the class tended to decline as material success became greater and as other opportunities for recreation arose. The class did not abandon the churches. It still regarded them as morally and socially useful, but its religious zeal abated. By the second generation it was noted that factory owners in Zurich had become somewhat apathetic in religious practice; the same trend appeared later in Russia among middle-class Old Believers. By 1850 religious interest had declined notably in Britain, even among middle-class women, without turning to explicit hostility. In the second half of the nineteenth century some churches tried to accommodate the new interests of the middle class. Modernist movements in Protestantism and the rise of Reform Judaism were attempts to harmonize religion and science and de-emphasize unappealing doctrines such as original sin and the possibility of damnation. These trends reflected the middle class's continued attachment to aspects of religion as well as their characteristic lack of traditional piety.

After the first generation or two of industrialization, the wealthier elements of the middle class began to patronize music, art, and literature extensively. New levels of education played a great role in this process. Sons of successful business families were given more education and were sent to more traditional schools. In the early nineteenth century the middle class derided the classical stress of traditional secondary schools. Middle-class magazines urged the importance of science, modern languages, history, and other useful subjects, and the class sent its sons to schools that provided such subjects. About mid-century, however, the focus changed. Business families in France began to abandon the cheaper colleges in favor of the more prestigious and more classical *lycées*. The great British public schools were investigated in the 1860s and did introduce some modern subjects; but although they changed only slightly, the upper middle class supported the schools eagerly once its sons could enter them. The educational interests of the upper business group, the leading professional families, and the aristocracy increasingly merged. The bulk of the middle class could not follow this pattern; its education remained more limited and utilitarian. In fact, it was cut off from the upper-middle-class families by the new educational gap.

To demonstrate their social prestige middle-class families sought clear, almost official canons of taste. They shunned cultural innovations that might prove socially unacceptable in favor of firm, respectable standards. As vacations and travel became fashionable, travel guides were printed, and travel agencies formed to arrange safe and respectable itineraries for the increasing numbers of eager but inexperienced middle-class tourists. In the 1840s Thomas Cook opened in London the first major travel agency. Spas such as Brighton and Folkestone were patronized in imitation of aristocratic resorts. They might be dull, but they became symbols of status.

The middle-class delight in identifying socially acceptable institutions led to growing support for opera companies and symphony orchestras, institutions that enjoyed aristocratic patronage as well, as the funds and interests of the class expanded toward mid-century. Permanent symphony orchestras were established in many cities for the first time. Concert prices were reduced, which allowed many middle-class families to attend, and the new numbers and wealth of middle-class patrons increased the professionalization of concert music. German symphony performances even in Beethoven's time had usually involved a temporary collection of semiprofessional musicians, and the quality of playing was often very poor. The expansion of middle-class culture promoted a real improvement in musical performances.

The new patrons of art preferred works that met the conservative standards set by established academies, such as the British Royal Academy. Aside from portraiture, middle-class purchases of art were concentrated on the old masters, whose paintings had clear prestige and would be trophies as well as decorations. The new interest in the old masters was so intense that the forgery of masterpieces became a substantial business.

Middle-class libraries, similarly, were heavy with the older, safer works. The upper middle class in Paris in the 1840s bought more eighteenth- and seventeenth-century classics than contemporary works.

Magazines and books like J. C. Louden's *Encyclopedia* in Britain gave guidance for taste in furniture. The interiors of wealthy homes were elaborate and often showy. They scorned unity of design for an interest in accumulating decorative objects. Heavy furniture and fringed curtains were combined with Chinese figurines. An impression of wealth and profusion, with a continued interest in comfort, dominated many middle-class homes.

In many ways the architectural standards of the nineteenth century best exemplified the taste of the rising middle class. Expensive, ornate mansions became badges of middle-class wealth. Standards were again sought in the past. Imitations of classical and even byzantine style rivaled re-creations of the Gothic. These imitations, however, were usually modified to reflect a new interest in massive form and luxuriant detail. The French architect Viollet-le-Duc restored many Gothic buildings in France and England, often adding battlements and ornamentation unknown to the Middle Ages but appropriate to the new age of luxury. If the nineteenth century cannot be viewed as a triumph of creativity in popular arts, it can be seen as a vast development of a self-conscious interest in culture. The middle class, massive in numbers, rose from simple, traditional taste to an eager search for cultural prestige.

Finally, growing interest in dancing, choral concerts, and cafés gave new impetus to what might be called a professional recreational industry. Though not rich enough to contribute to formal architectural styles, sometimes too poor to furnish more than a single room with any luxury, the bulk of the middle class had a bit of money to spend on entertainment and it was beginning to move this interest outside of home. Here was the beginning of what would constitute important new definitions of what leisure is for.

Middle-Class Families and Women

It was within the context of the family that the middle class made its final contribution to social change in the early industrial period. Indeed its action here was more significant than its impact on formal culture, for this was an area of vital importance to the class as a whole.

The tight official structure of the middle-class family is well known. Children were expected to be respectful and discipline was strict. Careful economic arrangements were made for them. On the Continent legal marriage contracts stipulated levels of dowry, and many weddings were carefully arranged with an eye to economic advantage. Many a textile fortune was made when a spinning plant married a weaving mill, in the persons of their respective male and female heirs. In England, dowries and contracts were less general but economic interest was seldom absent. Many businesspeople everywhere liked to marry their daughters to professional men; this gave the professional some needed capital and the businessperson a sense of prestige. In western Germany, about half of the women married to government bureaucrats in the early nineteenth century were from business families. Concern for the future of sons was obvious, in the effort to provide secure foundations for the family firm followed by inheritance, and/or in the interest in a solid education. The desire to assure the family's future gave much of the sense of purpose to the hard work and economic innovativeness that characterized the class.

For married women, relationships often seemed formal as well, but a middle-class woman had to hope for marriage (and the vast majority did marry) because there were few respectable jobs open for women in the period. Yet women were typically considered inferior to their husbands in law. In England a married woman had no independent legal standing and could neither testify in court nor divorce her husband. Any earnings or property belonged to the husband. Much public culture, including that promulgated in many novels, suggested that women should cultivate their beauty, wear stylish clothes, learn social graces such as the piano, and in general serve as ornaments in the home. There undoubtedly was a sense in which businessmen, edgy after a long day spent in a rather novel and competitive economic effort, liked to return home to an attractive, submissive wife. Hamburg businessmen, for example, sought to marry women who would embellish the home with embroidery and rely on the male; one wife, taken to London on a trip, dutifully burst into tears whenever she lost sight of her husband.

Women were also supposed to be guardians of morality. Here too might be an important refuge from the cutthroat business world. Certainly the morality publicists urged on the middle class was often severe. Particular attention was given to sexual restraint. There was a widespread belief that undue sexual activity was damaging to a person's health, that sex involved expenditure of vital energy that could not be replaced. Certainly most doctors claimed this to be true. Women were held responsible for restraining their husbands, for their own sexual drives were believed much slighter. They were also expected to train their children to be sexually pure, for not only premarital intercourse but above all masturbation were dangerous as well as disreputable. Elderly adults were also supposed to refrain from sexual activity. Much of this sexual ethic was quite traditional, from classic authors onward, simply receiving greater publicity in the nineteenth century with an expanding readership. There is no question, however, that middle-class concern about youth sexuality increased, a sign of fears about lower-class behavior and about the cost of having more children than the family could provide for.

It is not hard to embellish this picture of a middle-class family caught in a network of inhibitions, ruled by the husband-father in authoritarian fashion. Unquestionably legal structure and the opinions of prudish doctors and publicists played a role in the actual family life. However, the real developments in the middle-class family went in more complex directions and would begin to change both culture and law. Many innovations were spearheaded by women.

Toward children, middle-class families became increasingly attentive and affectionate. Concern began with infancy. Mothers were no longer willing to let the infant cry, as had been previous practice; a crying child needed loving attention. The practice of leaving infants in the care of others declined. Parisian mothers, long in the habit of sending babies out to the countryside to be wetnursed, began by the mid-nineteenth century to keep the wetnurse in the home, where she could be supervised, or to nurse themselves. British mothers almost entirely abandoned wetnursing and either nursed themselves or adopted bottle feeding. New attitudes toward the infant led into a revision of disciplinary ideas. Physical punishment was increasingly replaced by discussion. Children were indeed to be respectful, but they received more love (and took more of their mother's time) than before.

Older children were something of a problem. The middle class did marry rather late, for economic reasons. Females, and particularly males, married several years after puberty. Males might find some sexual outlets through prostitutes or even abuse of the family's female servant; such practices were frowned on and certainly not universal, but many a French schoolboy spent part of his holidays in a local brothel. Middle-class girls and women, needless to say, were supposed to remain chaste until marriage. So the middle class did have to promote a rigorous sexual ethic for one stage of life, modified by a double standard for some young men; the particular concern over masturbation, whose evil effects were held to range from sterility through brain damage, reflected this tension.

Between husbands and wives there was a growing division of labor. Except in the small shops, women stopped participating in their husband's business after the first generation of industrialization. But this did not deprive them of functions, for the household was increasingly complex and women made the major decisions about family consumption patterns. The middle class, by definition, embraced growing numbers of people who had a disposable income, well above subsistence, for the first time. Wives administered much of this. Their desire for respectability meant a great deal of hard work, for the typical middle-class family could afford at best a single servant (indeed, despite the rapid growth of the servant class there were fewer servants than middle-class families even in the mid-nineteenth century). And not only child care but also notions of cleanliness were changing, perhaps in response to the filth of the cities. Women put more effort into cleaning clothes, dusting furniture, scrubbing floors. They also sponsored gradual improvements in the household. By the mid-nineteenth century middle-class homes were acquiring indoor plumbing and a separate bathroom; flush toilets would soon follow. Other new equipment was added, notably the sewing machine. Middle-class women were thus open to new technology, and their efforts spurred an important segment of the economy. Indeed it was to women, as the main agents of consumption, that advertising was principally directed. Finally, successful operation of the household required planning. Women learned to keep accounts and budget books. They bought major items on time, for a sewing machine was too expensive otherwise. In all this they asked for a great deal of advice from women's manuals and magazines.

For, although confined to home and family, middle-class women were developing a new outlook. They were becoming consumer-oriented. They were learning to think in terms of rational organization and careful calculation, just as their businessmen husbands were increasingly doing on the job. They were beginning, again hesitantly, to strive for material progress and technical improvements. Largely confined to a domestic sphere, middle-class women could develop important new ideas.

New attitudes were also developing in the field of health. Women were becoming less fatalistic about pain and disease that had previously seemed inevitable. Increasingly they switched from midwives to obstetricians for childbirth. They consulted health manuals. They bought quack medicines because they were advertised as being scientific. They made some mistakes in all this. Sometimes indeed they caused their children's death by overfeeding, the first reaction to prosperity, or by dosing them with harsh drugs. But their interest was in improving the health of their children, and gradually they had some success. Fewer developments benefited their own health. Women did welcome the reduction of pain in childbirth that came with the use of chloroform, although ironically many doctors opposed this.

But the most important development in the middle-class family came with the reduction of the birthrate. By the 1820s in France, if not before, and at least by mid-century in England and Germany the number of children born to the average middle-class family began to drop steadily. There were obvious economic reasons for this. Given the need to provide education and dowries, too many children were an obvious burden. The new concern for the individual child was possible only when there were fewer children to command attention. And women wanted more time for their other functions and, quite possibly, less exposure to the pains and risks of childbearing. Probably wives and husbands in most cases jointly decided to limit their families to three or four children, but occasionally women may have decided on their own. For from about 1820 onward devices were introduced that allowed artificial birth control. Sponges and diaphragms were widely used by women, and their quality steadily improved. With the vulcanization of rubber in the 1840s condoms, which had long been known, also became more reliable and cheaper. Some middle-class women may have suffered a certain role confusion as their families became smaller, for motherhood had long been their proudest function. More commonly, concern for the quality of the child replaced concern for quantity. All of this represented an important step in the redefinition of family life, and it would later spread more widely in society.

The new orientation of the family did cause strain. It was hard to keep pace with a consumer economy with a limited budget. Rents rose rapidly, which hit the middle class hard just as it was trying to improve living standards in other respects. Many had to flee to the suburbs, which were cheaper but involved commuting expenses; by the 1860s suburban populations were growing more rapidly than urban from London to Vienna. The desire for better family health outstripped the quality of medical practice, and many women suffered from health problems. A few, overburdened by their functions, turned to drink or, more commonly, the use of opiates, for opium-based drugs were widely sold. More commonly, women were able to adapt, particularly when birth control began to relieve their lot.

But what of marriage partners? They did not see each other as often as in a traditional bourgeois family, for the man's work increasingly took him away. But division of family labor was modified by a certain mutuality in decision making. At the same time marriage, though still based in part on economics, became somewhat freer; a couple made its choice with less parental guidance and with more chance for mutual affection. Within marriage sexual pleasure probably increased. The most rigorously prudish advice was often ignored. Birth-control devices, though they spread only gradually, certainly reduced one customary inhibition on the woman's part, and were advertised as doing so. For actual middle-class culture was by no means entirely strait-laced, and the married couple was urged to enjoy sex. Even a prosaic English doctor suggested: "During connection both husband and wife should endeavor to be in a happy state of mind. The wife especially should have happy thoughts when having connection."[5] A more radical writer,

[5] Henry A. Allbott, *The Wife's Handbook* (London, 1886), p. 57.

widely read in the English middle class around 1820, was more explicit: "The hypocrisy, the cruelty that would stifle or disguise a passion, whether in the male or in the female, is wicked, and should be exposed, reprobated, and detested. Young Women! Assume an equality, plead your passion when you feel it, plead it to those to whom it applies."[6]

We are far from knowing the state of sex life in the early industrial middle class. Obviously there were criticisms of the class's life-style, from both religious and medical observers, and this may have caused some confusion. The need to avoid sex before marriage (at least for women) could hamper response once marriage occurred. But it is safe to assume that a new, more affectionate, and actually sexier relationship was developing in some middle-class households. And this new relationship began to be reflected in changes in law. The legal rights of married women were improved in several measures in Britain from 1857 onward, culminating in the Married Women's Property Act of 1870, which gave a married woman the right to own her own property.

The Middle Class and Social Change

Thus the middle class was caught up in a host of changes, of which economic innovation was only the most obvious. It sponsored an important new stage of political agitation. It took over the principal patronage of cultural activities, though with directions that were as yet less clear. There were gaps in the pattern of change, particularly in the outlook toward the lower classes. And the middle class, though now preeminent in defining social values, had not wrested full power from the aristocracy. Finally, the rift between innovators and traditionalists complicated the pace of change, and again not only in economics. The revolutions of 1848 revealed, particularly in Germany, that the traditionalist sentiment could be used to support a conservative regime, against the political goals of the rest of the middle class. But increasingly the framework of society was being set by the middle class, and its pioneering efforts, whether good or bad, were being extended to the most widely publicized standards for the definitions of family functions and the position of women.

It was the middle class, finally, that increasingly shaped the conditions of the lower classes, as employers of most urban labor and as self-appointed guardians of a new kind of work ethic that stressed assiduousness, efficiency, and tolerance of new techniques.

---

[6] Richard Carlile, *Every Woman's Book or What Is Love?* (London, 1826), p. 8.

The Urban Lower Classes

The early Industrial Revolution compelled two quite different reactions from those who now found themselves in the urban labor force. The most obvious was the need to adapt to, or protest, novel conditions and a new level of exploitation. Factory workers new to both city and power machinery were the most rapidly growing social group. Right behind them were servants, almost entirely female. In both cases population had outstripped economic opportunities in the countryside, so like it or not something radically new had to be undertaken. But a large group of workers, still growing if more slowly, were not new to their jobs, and many of them were not new to urban life. Artisans remained a distinct force in urban society. They faced change too, but from a more established position. There is no possibility of discussing a single working class at this point. It is not even entirely clear which of the two main situations — total novelty or the need to defend established ways against threat — was more troubling.

Finally, there remained the urban unskilled, whose ranks were swollen by immigration into traditional centers such as Paris. Their lot, bad before, was now shared by more people. Some were young, both male and female, and cut off from parental direction as they moved to the city. Some were unable to get factory work, for cities like Paris had few factories as yet. Others worked as servants but were raped by an employer and then fired for having an illegitimate child, and so tumbled into the urban dregs. With new numbers, the slum sections of all the older cities became increasingly foul. That crime went up among this group is hardly surprising. Urbanization seems to have brought a fairly steady rise in thefts, fraud, and suicides, though little or no increase in murders (the murder rate dropped in cities like Paris) and a decline in arson (the traditional rural crime). However, lesser interpersonal violence (assault and battery) rose, and especially rapidly during the fastest period of urban growth. Here was a sign of tension that went well beyond the very poor, though it must be remembered that cities were not the only center of personal violence; many rural areas experienced higher rates. In some cases (this has been argued for England) crime of all sorts went down again once the peak urban growth had passed, for more of the "criminal element" could find regular jobs. More commonly the increase in crime rates simply slowed. But we know little else about the condition of the urban poor in this period, and it obviously should not be assumed that most of them turned to crime. Their existence and extreme poverty could affect the attitudes of the middle class, as we have seen. They could affect the consciousness of other lower-class elements as well, for one might protest out of a fear of falling into this group or remain self-satisfied because it had been avoided.

The Artisans

Artisans remained the largest urban group for several decades. Widely distributed in cities generally, they were particularly prominent in major centers such as London and Vienna. As late as 1850 there were as many artisans as factory workers in Great Britain. In the 1860s artisans represented 60 percent of the Prussian manufacturing force. In France artisans maintained a greater importance than in other European countries. At mid-century there were only 1.306 million French workers in firms with over ten employees, and many of these were, of course, domestic manufacturers. The remainder of the industrial population, including 1.548 million employers and self-employed, worked in firms averaging two employees. Twenty years later, at the time of the Commune, the bulk of the Parisian workers were artisans. Of approximately 500,000 workers in a population of 1.8 million, 100,000 were construction workers; 110,000 worked in jewelry, furniture, and other luxury industries; 34,000 were printers; 41,000 worked in food processing; 115,000 worked in clothing and textiles, mainly in small tailoring and dressmaking shops. This was an unusual concentration; Paris served really as a center for craft production, exporting artisans' wares all over the world. But even factory centers in 1870 depended on artisan labor for most food-processing, clothing, and construction work.

Until about 1850 in Britain and until at least 1870 elsewhere the number of artisans increased in proportion to overall population growth; for as population expanded and wealth increased with both agricultural and industrial improvements, the need for artisans rose. Industrialization itself fostered the development of some new small-shop crafts, notably in machine building. Flourishing cities required more carpenters and masons, more butchers and bakers, more tailors and shoemakers. With a very few exceptions early mechanical processes were not applicable to the kind of work done by urban artisans; in some cases they have not been widely applied to this day. A few urban branches of textile manufacturing, such as finishing of wool cloth, were quickly affected. The printing industry underwent increased mechanization, although in this case artisan skills were not entirely displaced. Some female artisans, such as lace makers, were affected by the rise of competitive factory products. For the most part, however, it was rural home workers, not urban artisans, who were displaced by the new industrial processes. The decline of a few urban groups was more than balanced by the heightened demand for other major crafts. Most of the history of what has often been loosely termed *the working class* in the early Industrial Revolution is in fact a history of artisans. Workers in the crafts were increasing far less rapidly than workers in the factories, but they long continued to dominate in numbers, wealth, social cohesion, and purpose.

Stability of Habits

Before 1870 artisans were fairly distinct from factory labor. They usually worked in different places; artisans still relied on traditional skills and techniques and worked on their own or in very small units. Even residentially, there was only limited contact between the two classes. There were relatively few factory workers in major artisan centers such as London and Paris and in large numbers of traditional towns. Furthermore, artisans had traditional quarters of residence, usually in the center of a city, which factory workers did not fully penetrate. Sections such as the Faubourg Saint-Antoine in Paris remained artisan preserves. However, particularly in factory cities, there were opportunities for contact. Artisans sometimes saw factory workers as important potential allies in such movements as unionization. To a certain extent they served as mentors to the new class, and workers often imitated artisan movements. But most artisans viewed workers with some suspicion as well. Although individual artisans took high-paying jobs in factories, most craftspeople abhorred the factory system and its products, and they distrusted the coarseness and the violence of the working class. Ultimately, they found some kindred interests with the skilled elements of factory labor, but rarely before 1870 did they identify with the working class as a whole.

Artisans remained a relatively stable class in personal habits and family structures. They had traditions in their work and in their city life to which they constantly referred. Even new artisans coming in from the countryside were assimilated to artisan values. Many had a craft background in the village that gave them a sense of status and dignity that few other workers had.

Many observers noted that even poor artisans were often better off than factory labor because they avoided showy spending on drink and on clothing. Thread twisters in Lille, for example, who earned about half the wage of factory spinners, frequently had better diets and cleaner housing and depended less on charity during crises. They were thriftier in good times, worked more steadily, drank less. Artisans generally, though they earned little more than workers, were far more inclined to save money. Similarly, their family structure was tighter. Artisans retained an interest in establishing their children in their own trade and educated them accordingly. Married women worked in the home, not in the factory. Most artisans carefully limited their family size by delaying marriage until their late twenties, in the interest of maintaining their material well-being and caring properly for the children they had. While some factory workers did the same, on the whole artisans were a more cautious group.

The material standards of artisans still varied greatly. Single women had to work long hours to earn enough to survive. Craftspeople facing mechanical competition received low wages for increasing hours of work. Many Lyons silk workers labored sixteen or eighteen hours a day for pay that was barely sufficient to sustain life, though artisan masters usually had some comforts. Among the leading crafts, pay levels usually rose slightly. Carpenters or butchers could afford more stylish clothing and furnishings and could often save. They seldom needed to put their children to work until they were in their teens.

There were still many hardships. Construction workers and some others suffered from long periods of seasonal unemployment. Personal disasters, such as illness or age, could reduce a family to dire poverty. Artisans suffered severely in economic crisis. Their wages fell, and they often experienced higher levels of unemployment than did factory workers. The need for artisan products, often in a semiluxury category, fell far more rapidly than did the need for factory staples such as clothing. And this crisis of falling wages and rising unemployment was, of course, usually accompanied by rising food prices. Only bare subsistence expenditures, appeals for charity, and sale or pawning of furniture and even vital tools could permit survival in these conditions. But the leading groups of artisans were not ordinarily impoverished; they had a small though insecure margin above subsistence. An elite group was even able to experiment with new consumer products such as pianos.

Forces of Change

Beyond the ups and downs of their immediate material conditions, artisans faced profound changes in the larger political and economic environment in which they lived. In times of prosperity as well as times of crisis some of the foundations of artisan economic and social values were being undermined, and far more radically than in the previous period.

Most basically, the principles of the rising new industry clashed with the principles of artisan economy. Artisans relied on stable skills; industry involved rapidly changing methods and the use of large numbers of unskilled workers. Skill and training were not eliminated in industry, but they were new and on the whole more easily learned; in few cases, for example, was prolonged apprenticeship required to enable a worker to perform a job adequately. The artisan's pace of work, involving frequent breaks and holidays, was threatened by the new machines.

Artisans traditionally tried to protect themselves against competitive pressure by restricting both techniques and the size of the labor force. In industry limitations were removed; workers were hired as they were needed, machines introduced at will. The artisan interest in restraining the degree of inequality within manufacturing was also ignored in the new factories. Factory owners often acquired great wealth and tried to expand this wealth without clear limit. The gap between them and their workers was great, and it was rare for a worker to rise to the ranks of the manufacturer. The novelty of the factory system was a real shock to the artisan stress on stability — to the artisanal definition of a moral economy.

Few urban artisans, of course, were forced outright into the factories. The threat of the factory system was more subtle. The rise of mechanized industry displaced artisans from a fundamental control of the urban economy. Their numbers rose, and their earnings grew slightly, but their relative position steadily declined. The working class expanded far more rapidly than did the ranks of the artisans, four times as rapidly in Germany by mid-century. The wealth of the new elements of the middle class eclipsed any increase in artisan pay; even some factory workers earned more than craft labor. Furthermore, factory industry was obviously dynamic and expansive. It had displaced many workers and might displace more. There was real concern among artisans, even those remote from branches of industry touched by machines, that the new principles of production might spread to their own trade.

The realization of the new challenge to artisan economic values caused many attacks on the factory system. Some artisans, directly threatened by mechanical processes, tried to destroy the factories themselves. Most areas went through a period of Luddism by urban artisans as well as some domestic workers. Nottingham glove makers destroyed a thousand new stocking frames in 1811–1812, and Yorkshire wool finishers attacked machines also. French wool finishers destroyed several machines after 1820. Craftspeople in Barcelona attacked new spinning machines between 1854 and 1856. Artisan newspapers, pamphlets, and petitions to the government often urged removal of machines. Pamphlets in Germany in the 1860s attacked the stock exchange, department stores, and the principle of division of labor. The Parisian newspaper *L'Atelier* warned constantly of the evils of factory industry. Hostile to much new technology, artisans could also oppose the profit-seeking emphasis of capitalism more generally, as it contradicted the values of small-scale quality production.

Artisanal conditions were changing greatly even as factories posed their challenge. Not only guilds but also all worker associations were outlawed in Britain and France by the end of the eighteenth century. The French Revolutionary government spread the abolition of guilds wherever its armies conquered, and in most cases the abolition was retained even after the Revolution. By 1815 many west German and northern Italian states, and the Low Countries, had eliminated the guilds. Spain abolished guilds by 1836.

Most of Germany, particularly Prussia, was slower to act. Conservative governments continued to enforce guild exclusions until mid-century. In the 1840s the Prussian government, without abolishing guilds, removed the official support from guild exclusiveness; workers could now enter crafts without guild permission. After the revolution of 1848 aristocrats tried to ally themselves with discontented artisans by restoring the legal position of guilds. Only in 1868 did the Prussian government again allow work in the crafts without guild permission. The German guilds did not die as a result; they continued privately to enforce some exclusions and to serve as centers for defense of professional interests. Their fundamental powers were nevertheless radically limited. But the tardiness of the attacks on the guilds allowed German artisans to remain attached to a traditional, even conservative, outlook that set them off significantly from artisans in the West.

In addition to the general trend toward abolishing the guilds, the relationship between journeymen and masters changed rapidly during the nineteenth century. Although the number of artisans grew steadily, the number of masters did not. Masters increasingly tried to protect their own social and economic position in a changing economy by limiting their ranks. Some became employers rather than masters, for they had enough workers to avoid most manual labor themselves and concentrated instead on arranging for materials and sales. In the construction industry, large crews were formed with the master serving as a contractor. Masters in this situation increased their capital for the purchase of supplies and equipment, and thus made it more difficult for a journeyman to rise. The social relations between artisan and master were changed. It became less common for journeymen to be housed and fed by the master. The gradual development of a purely and permanently wage-earning status for journeymen, though not entirely new, was a profound shock to artisan tradition. All of this also reflected the vast immigration to the cities, for urban journeymen faced massive competition from village-trained craftspeople now that guilds could no longer regulate craft size.

In other instances, masters and journeymen alike were forced into virtual employment by merchant capitalists. This was particularly common in the textile industry, where industrial capitalism was spreading rapidly, but it also occurred in some construction work and in some branches of metal work. Embroiderers, knife makers, and the like were increasingly assigned tasks by a supervisor employed by a large merchant. They might work in their homes or in a master's shop, but their conditions were set outside the artisan system. Again capitalism pressed for more impersonality and less equality at work, against cherished artisanal values.

Finally, many new employers, whether merchants or masters, showed some tendency to neglect traditional methods of apprenticeship. If they hired children, they expected them to work more than to learn. Journeymen themselves, involved increasingly in a wage system, were often reluctant to delay their work by training a child. Apprenticeship continued except in a few decaying trades such as lace making, for the old traditions were not entirely violated. In a limited way, however, aspects of industrial organization were being applied to the crafts without a real introduction of a factory system. There were also efforts to speed the pace of work.

The social as well as the economic position of the artisans was changing. Artisans lost the social contact of the guilds at the same time that their links with the masters were declining. Their place in the city was also slipping as factory workers became more numerous and as new elements of the middle class rose to prominence and took a growing role in city government. Neither destitute nor uprooted, artisans were nevertheless faced with major challenges.

The Reactionary Impulse

Artisans reacted to the challenge to tradition in a number of ways. There were some efforts to retain the old customs. The various attacks on machine industry, sometimes physical but more often verbal, were an important sign of traditionalism. A number of groups tried to maintain the guilds. British joiners and shoemakers retained some guild structure into the nineteenth century. This retention was primarily for social purposes, as the organizations raised few economic demands. Similarly, French carpenters joined traditional secret groups called *compagnonnages,* which were related to the guilds. The *compagnonnages* dealt with matters of apprenticeship and working conditions but again were primarily social organizations. They arranged for the traditional tours of France by young journeymen and provided an elaborate ritual for the entertainment of their members. The importance of these various guild remnants gradually declined and never involved more than a minority of the class as a whole. Guild traditions did, however, help prepare newer ideas of economic organizations, such as craft trade unions.

Only in Germany and Austria was there a persistent effort to preserve the guilds, for only in Germany did conservative classes have sufficient power to allow some hope of success. Hence the major demand of German master artisans in the revolution of 1848 was for full restoration of the guilds, which had after all only recently been threatened in states such as Prussia. The German artisans, spurred by two previous years of intense economic crisis, rioted in many cities, petitioned the revolutionary government, and even assembled a national congress of their own in June 1849, in an effort to win their demands. They wanted guilds to restrict the number of workers, wanted regulations and taxes to limit the output of factories, and wanted the state itself to guarantee work. In Prussia during the 1850s the restoration of the guilds simply encouraged the master artisans' attachments to a conservative social order. Having been rebuffed in their revolutionary demands by the middle-class assemblies, which sought economic freedom instead of guild restrictions, they turned against middle-class liberalism. The attacks by artisan pamphleteers on new industrial and commercial methods increased even in the 1860s; and as they acquired the vote, many German artisans attached themselves to conservative parties.

The German case represented an extreme of the general suspicion of modern trends. Even in Germany artisans west of the Rhine, where guilds were abolished during the Napoleonic period and where regimes were relatively liberal, did not concern themselves greatly with restoration of the guilds. Less formally, however, journeymen as well as masters almost everywhere tried to retain some guild benefits through other associations. German journeymen, now at odds with their masters' restrictiveness, did not ask for guilds in 1848 but they did want the right to associate to control their wages and conditions of work. In many towns even journeymen continued to be able to monopolize certain occupations. In Marseilles several trades were dominated by sons following their fathers into work; hence 69 percent of all masons had been born in Marseilles, as against 50 percent of the skilled labor force in general. So we need not exaggerate the disruption of artisanal traditions. The adaptation of most artisans consisted of a clever mixture of older habits, based around defense of a rare skill, and newer goals; craft unionism was ultimately one product of this mixture.

The Self-Help Impulse

At the opposite pole from the reactionary impulse, many artisans adapted older habits in an effort to seek individual improvement. Traditions of training could convert to a new interest in education; habits of saving might be diverted from purchase of a mastership to the establishment of a more modern small business. Here artisans could adapt to middle-class values and even enter the middle class.

Most commonly industrial artisans attempted to earn more money by working hard and improving themselves within their craft. Many developed a great interest in education, and artisan groups and publications commonly stressed this as a means of self-improvement. In Britain, mechanics' institutes were established to provide a variety of technical and commercial training. Courses in accounting, chemistry, practical mathematics, and the like, established in most French cities, were attended particularly by artisans, although often intended by their middle-class founders to benefit factory workers.

The vast majority of urban artisans were now literate, and some purchased and read books and newspapers fairly regularly. By the 1840s a number of artisan newspapers were appearing in Britain and France, often with great stress on political and social problems. Artisans sought entertainment above all from their reading, however, and cheap novels and periodicals were more popular. They stressed sentiment and sensation, and they purveyed tales of supposed aristocratic immorality. Some industrial artisans, however, were impressively self-educated, familiar with a wide array of reading.

Artisans also tried to improve themselves by saving. Savings banks spread fairly widely during the period, and artisans and servants were their principal patrons among the lower classes. Many artisans undoubtedly banked the funds that in an earlier period they would have devoted to buying a master's position. Elements of the artisan class were patterning themselves on the values of the rising middle classes. The interest in self-improvement, education, and saving was frequently urged by the middle class, in speeches and in pamphlets, as the path to happiness and success. These recommendations undoubtedly caught the attention of a class that had a sense of pride and that sought a respected place in a society increasingly dominated by the middle class.

Some artisans rose out of their class altogether. It was not unrealistic, once guild restrictions were lifted, to start a small business on one's own. In an artisanal city such as Vienna small firms proliferated in the first stage of industrialization, ironically reducing the average size of the firm (to only 1.3 workers per company). Many little shops failed; a few started their owners on the ladder toward middle-class status; still more swelled the ranks of the lower middle class, for a tailor or shoemaker was proud of the small family business. And artisans interested in mobility were found entering the noncommissioned army officer corps in France, the priesthood, and some of the lower professions. Far more artisans sought mobility than found it, without doubt, but this was a questing group and even hope for advancement might long sustain a journeyman. Finally many artisans left the shop for the factory. Early industrialization required masses of skilled workers, and the artisanry was a vital source of recruitment. Particularly in machine and metal factories, artisans with training as blacksmiths or locksmiths were in high demand. They could earn more money than their journeymen brethren, and although they were subjected to more rigorous supervision, their values of skill and pride in their work were not lost.

Many artisans thus had some range of choice in reacting to industrialization. Although pressed increasingly into the status of paid labor, journeymen were not yet fully proletarianized; even when they entered the factories their earnings and mutual interactions made them an aristocracy among labor.

Political Interest

Artisans also tried to raise their political and social status. They increasingly wanted the vote, particularly in western countries where the middle classes possessed or actively sought suffrage. In Germany, where political interest even in the middle class was relatively low, artisans were also less active. During the revolution of 1848 they made some demands on the government, including free state education, provision of credit for artisan shops, and support for the ill and maimed; but they showed little interest in political rights or in changing political forms. Even so, there was political consciousness: In the city of Halle in 1848, 81 percent of the artisan masters and 71 percent of the journeymen voted, compared to 46 percent of factory labor.

In France, where the Revolution had provided a brief experience of universal suffrage and political action, especially in Paris, and in Britain, where the middle class sought and gained the vote in 1832, political activity made even more sense to many artisans. French artisans who filled the streets in 1830 were acting specifically against the existing monarch and for a change in the political system. During the July Monarchy some artisans joined Republican groups and pressed for universal suffrage. British artisans were even more persistent before 1848 in seeking the vote. Before the Reform Bill of 1832 many joined with middle-class elements in associations and meetings to promote an extension of the suffrage. After 1832 artisans, particularly in London, took the lead in forming the Chartist movement to seek universal male suffrage and other political reforms. They held meetings, passed resolutions, sometimes threatened violence, and circulated gigantic petitions to further their cause. On three occasions, in years of economic crisis, the movement drew a great following, including factory workers as well as artisans. In 1839 a Chartist petition was signed by 1,280,000 people, and in 1842, some 3,317,702 people signed a new appeal. After a final abortive effort in 1848 the movement collapsed, and many artisan organizations turned away from politics.

The artisans sought political change for many reasons. They wanted the state to aid their self-improvement efforts by providing educational facilities. They hoped that their votes would induce the state to take economic action in their behalf. The Chartists, for example, had a vague belief that political reforms would result in the ending of poverty. Parisian artisans in 1848 felt that their control of the government would bring a new organization of work that would restore artisan forms of production and eliminate unemployment. They might see political action as a way to overturn the capitalist economy and work structure. Finally, artisans sought political participation as one means of obtaining respect from other elements of society. The German artisans in 1848, who insisted that they be addressed with the formal *Sie* instead of the familiar *du*, were expressing a general desire to be treated as equals by employers and other members of the upper classes. The search for political equality was an important effort along the same lines. In an age when established social positions were eroding, when economic inequality gained ground daily, artisans attempted to assert their place in new ways.

Mutual Aid

In addition to efforts at self-improvement and at political reform, artisans utilized a variety of methods to better their economic position and provide greater social cohesion. These efforts continued some of the artisans' economic traditions and moral economy values but in a new framework. They involved cooperation in the interest of collective economic security. They were organized along craft lines and were usually local.

The simplest and earliest form of artisan cooperation was the mutual aid group or friendly society. Most major cities had a variety of such groups for the leading crafts, which grew up quickly after guilds were abolished. The groups were far more extensive among the artisans than among factory workers. They provided aid in sickness and in death and often established technical courses, libraries, and recreational programs. Occasionally, aid groups conducted strikes as well.

Many crafts also formed unions to protect their economic interests, usually a few decades after aid groups began to form. Artisan union movements waxed and waned in most countries according to economic conditions. However, some individual locals persisted from the 1820s or 1830s in Britain and France. Groups such as printers' and carpenters' unions began in Paris in the 1830s and in London even earlier. Lyons silk workers had several large unions in the early 1830s, but government repression eventually reduced the movement. Printers and hatters formed short-lived associations in Italy in 1848, and in the 1860s more permanent unions grew out of aid groups.

In Britain artisan union efforts were unusually elaborate, aided by the easing of legal restrictions in 1824. In the early 1830s about half a million workers, led by members of the building trades, joined the Grand National Consolidated Trades Union under the leadership of Robert Owen. This group went well beyond the purposes of ordinary artisan unions and tried to reconstitute the economy on cooperative lines. After the failure of Chartism in 1848 and with the rising economic prosperity of the 1850s, the union movement among artisans and skilled workers increased substantially. Carpenters, iron founders, engineers, and the like dominated this movement, known as New Model Unionism; and they intentionally ignored the mass of factory workers. These unions attempted to be respectable and solid. They had large funds and professional officials. They urged temperance, saving, and hard work on their members and provided the benefits of a friendly society. They preferred to negotiate with their employers for improvement of wages and hours and conducted strikes only with reluctance. This was a quiet, exclusive movement operating on principles of collective benefits for members, very much in the artisan tradition but with no desire to challenge overall economic structure.

The New Model Union movement was the most extensive and elaborate union effort developed among artisans before 1870, and the only one that went beyond purely local associations for more than a brief time. But the methods of New Model Unionism were quite common. Parisian groups and the shorter-lived Lyons unions tried to established solid gains for their members in terms of wages and hours. They attempted to bargain collectively with their employers and a few cases did succeed in winning contracts that set the conditions for the whole occupation in the city. Whether unionized or not, many artisans attempted strike movements that had a similar novel ring in seeking new gains to compensate for altered working conditions. Although not yet typical of artisanal protest, many small strikes in France as early as the 1830s were designed to take advantage of prosperous years to win better wages and shorter hours. In Italy, similarly, the first modern strike movement developed with printers in the 1860s. And always, in this first industrial period, the artisanal strike rate was higher than that of other workers. Some artisans were thus learning to use organization and moderate protest to win gains within the new economic order and to regain the voice in job conditions that they had lost with the collapse of the guilds.

One other form of organization elicited considerable artisan interest, though again only a minority of the class was involved. By mid-century a cooperative movement of some importance had developed in western Europe. There were two hundred cooperative associations in Paris in 1851, principally among artisans. A number of similar groups existed in Britain, particularly in London, and involved tailors, hatters, and the like. These groups tried to establish a new system of production based on artisan principles. They stressed the need for a period of apprenticeship and limited entrance to their group. They hoped to eliminate competition and mechanization at the same time. Some of the groups collapsed, and even the successful ones failed to gain control of the economy as their founders had often hoped. Many groups did provide economic assistance and social contacts to their members, and a cooperative consumer movement, involving competition with private retail stores, had more enduring significance.

Protest

The first stage of industrialization everywhere saw massive artisanal protest. Many artisans, content either with maintaining sufficient traditions at work or with their individual adaptations, had no part in the protest. The Marseilles craftspeople who monopolized their jobs, for example, were slow to develop political protest, although artisans born elsewhere, precisely because they were excluded from the most prestigious jobs, began to react. Many artisans undoubtedly alternated attempts at adaptation with protest, depending on the state of the economy; for massive unrest occurred only after a slump. But there is no question that many artisans were concerned about the basic direction of society. The cooperative movement expressed such concern and frankly hoped to restore a more artisanal system of production as an alternative to capitalism. The Chartist movement vaguely sought a new organization of the economy. Movements such as the Grand National Consolidated Trades Union intended to take over the whole of industry and organize it on a cooperative basis; government itself would be put into the hands of the unions. These various movements enlisted only a minority of the artisans, for challenges to established order are always difficult to follow. Furthermore, laws against unions and political societies and arrests of key leaders, common in all early industrial settings, pitted the repressive police power of the state against artisanal protest potential. Protest groups represented, nevertheless, a significant impulse within the whole class. And there were many occasions when artisans defied the legal order by action as well as by doctrine.

Although most artisan strikes were relatively well organized and nonviolent, on occasion strike action took a more menacing tone. Huge strikes in the Lyons silk industry in 1831 and 1833 sought a minimum wage for the whole area, harking back to the craft tradition of mutual protection through joint action. Attacked by government troops and attracted by Republican propaganda, artisans actually took over the town for a period. Violent protests by Parisian artisans followed the ultimate repression in Lyons. In England, defeat of strikes in 1818 in Birmingham led many artisans toward political agitation. Luddite action, conducted by urban crafts workers such as cloth shearers, directly displaced by machines, had some strikelike aspects, for machine breaking had often been used to force employers to bargain over wages. But there was hatred of the machines as well, and English Luddites developed a vision of a utopian, egalitarian society run by artisanal units. Everywhere artisans sparked the bulk of the urban unrest that occurred during the first stage of industrialization. In western and central Europe their strikes and riots crested in the 1840s and flowed into the great revolutionary movement of 1848.

Artisans provided the street fighters in the three French revolutions of the nineteenth century, all of which were centered in Paris. Parisian artisans were distinguished from others in France and elsewhere by their number, their revolutionary tradition, and their exposure to the doctrinal and political ferment of the capital. In 1830, 1848, and after the siege of Paris in 1871, they rose in revolt. The 1830 revolution, though sparked by middle-class protest against the Restoration government, was manned by artisans. Members of the leading crafts composed the bulk of the street fighters, with carpenters and masons playing a particularly large role. During the 1848 revolt artisans rioted not only in February but also in the succeeding four months, and they manned the barricades during the bloody June days, along with a few skilled factory workers. Finally, in 1871, artisans and some small shopkeepers provided both the troops and the government personnel during the Commune.

Artisans played a major role in the rioting in Vienna and in Berlin during the 1848 revolutions there. Fighting in Berlin during March was concentrated in the artisans' quarters. Only a minority of artisans were ever revolutionary; of about 350,000 artisans in Paris in 1848, only 15,000 were on the barricades in June. Only a few other French cities stirred significantly during the same year. Nevertheless, the artisans provided a greater number of actual revolutionaries than did any other urban class.

Artisan revolutions occurred shortly after a major economic crisis, though usually after the worst point was past. In Paris before the Commune, 90 percent of the workers in some major crafts were unemployed. The 1848 revolution followed two years of intense hardship. The goals of artisan revolutions were quite broad, in the economy and usually in politics as well. In 1848 French artisans clearly pressed for the establishment of a democratic republic and in the Commune sought a new political regime for the city of Paris. In the economic sphere artisans sought protection from unemployment and government sponsorship for small artisan shops. In Paris in 1848 a significant number of artisans were acquainted with utopian socialist doctrines, particularly those of Louis Blanc and his book *The Organization of Work*. Blanc, like most other socialists of the day, offered doctrines with distinct appeal to artisan traditions. The stress of utopian socialism was on small, cooperative units of production working without elaborate equipment and distributing wealth equally among members of the unit. This was not the old guild system restored, but it urged some similar principles. Hence when Parisian artisans clamored for the organization of work in 1848, they were shouting for more than a system of relief from unemployment through public works. Public works were all they received, however, in the form of National Workshops; and even these were abolished in June, touching off the June Days. The leaders of the Commune, finally, were largely in the tradition of Proudhon, himself an artisan and a socialist. Here again the stress was on small, cooperative, egalitarian units of production and in this case also the abolition of the state in favor of self-government by these units.

Generally, the revolutionary movement tended to die after midcentury as artisans found new ways of dealing with their economic situation and realized they could not defeat the combined repressive power of the state and the capitalist middle class. In France, and later in Barcelona and parts of Italy, a utopian feeling lived on and was to reappear even after 1870. These were countries where industrialization had begun but proceeded slowly and where artisans were caught in the pressures of the Industrial Revolution for many decades without losing their sense of strength and tradition. A minority of them could continue to hope for radical change. Even Russia, though lacking in older urban craft tradition, saw new artisan groups like printers take a lead in voicing labor protest goals by the late nineteenth century. Before 1848 this utopian hope influenced artisans more generally in western Europe. It represented one aspect of the complex process of artisan adjustment to industrial society.

At the end of the first stage of industrialization artisans remained a distinct and growing class. They had fairly firm personal goals and had developed important collective institutions, including the first steps toward trade unionism, in their effort to adapt to change. A minority was periodically interested in more than this, in remaking the whole of society in the artisan image.

The early industrial decades formed a crucial period for artisanal life, as the foundations of the craft economy began to crumble. As the leading lower-class element in Europe's urban society, artisanal reactions were in turn crucial to shaping the early industrial period. Diversity and creativity were impressive. Artisans led implementing key middle-class values, like education, building on their own traditions of improvement. They led in articulating the impassioned defense of the traditional moral economy, against the capitalist ethic. They also led, slightly more haltingly, in developing new traditions of protest that would look toward political rights and toward material improvements, which might provide new advantages in work benefits and thereby compensate for some loss of control.

The Working Class

As a group, factory workers were distinct from artisans by their rapid rate of growth; their work on new, faster-paced machinery; their lack of collective tradition. Fewer were highly skilled; more entered the class from a peasant or agricultural laborer background. The units of employment were larger, averaging twenty workers and sometimes rising to the hundreds; inevitably this meant less personal contact with employers. Unlike journeymen, factory workers did not own their own tools; they were more completely propertyless. There were, as we have seen, former artisans in the factories but they generally skimmed off the top positions. In Mulhouse during the 1840s, for example, almost the only factory workers who had been born in the city were skilled machinists and cloth printers. Often this top group deliberately avoided social contacts with the mass of workers, many of whom served under their direction. So workers were deprived of a possible leadership element that could help them adjust to the newness of urban and factory life.

The industrial working class was at first rather small and very unevenly distributed in any country. In new factory cities such as Manchester, Mulhouse, or Essen, workers formed the majority of the population. But more traditional centers, such as Paris and London, long harbored very few factories. Other older cities did develop an industrial working class but only as one element of a diverse population. By 1902 approximately one-tenth of the inhabitants of Moscow and St. Petersburg worked in factories, and they tended to concentrate in a few sections of each city. By no means, then, did the working class dominate urban society in the early Industrial Revolution. Precisely because the new machines were so productive, they required relatively few workers; in the French wool industry of the 1840s there were 31,000 workers in the mechanized spinning factories, but weaving, with half a million workers, had been scarcely touched by new processes. Small wonder that by 1850 factory workers, numbering 400,000, constituted only a tenth of the French manufacturing labor force; even in Britain they had risen only to half the manufacturing force, with two million in the class.

Factory workers thus had special conditions setting them apart from all other workers. They were growing more rapidly than any other social group but their numerical importance must not be exaggerated.

The main source of factory workers was, of course, displaced rural labor, people who lacked land and could no longer continue as domestic manufacturers. Frequently it was only their misery that could have induced the new workers to abandon the countryside. Peasants often resisted factories even when the conditions of labor were exceptionally favorable. Manufacturers in Décazeville, a new industrial city in central France situated in an area of poor agriculture but extensive peasant smallholding, found it very difficult to recruit workers locally. The methods and discipline of the factory were simply unappealing even though the wages were much higher than in agriculture. In France more generally, the lack of severe population pressure on peasant tenure made it difficult to recruit a large labor force. There were, of course, individual cases of attraction to life in the factory and in the city. Some peasants were delighted at the opportunity of leaving the economic and social limitations of village existence. More commonly, however, the labor in the early factories was recruited by no positive attraction. Push, not pull, explained the arrival of new workers. Often there was little conscious choice at all. The hundreds of thousands of Irish people who crossed to English industrial cities, the Flemings who flocked to the mines of southern Belgium, and the Russian peasants who reluctantly left their villages in the 1890s were impelled by the increasing hardships of rural life. Often miserable and hoping only to return to the land, their origins were to exercise a profound influence over the early conditions of their class.

With little positive choice in entering the factories, faced with novelty on every hand, factory workers encountered anguishing problems of adaptation. The simple but basic question is: How did they make it through their lives? The first step toward the answer flows from their own origins. Their rural lives had already been disrupted; factory employment, for all its burdens, might provide welcome stability. Some had already begun a process of adaptation, by changing their sexual and consumption habits as domestic manufacturing workers. On the whole factory workers could continue these adaptation patterns. Without minimizing the shock of entering factory labor, it is vital to realize that few workers stepped directly from a purely traditional village into the city. Traditionalist areas, like Décazeville, simply did not provide much factory labor. Potential factory workers moved toward the city in stages. All this helps explain why, as in Germany, factory labor was hard to recruit even amid rapid population growth. It suggests that some of those workers who did take factory jobs saw some possibility of adaptation.

Material Conditions: Progress or Decline?

The second ingredient in an answer involves a subject long discussed by historians. Despite their many difficulties, most workers were better off in some respects than they or their parents had been in the countryside. The question of whether conditions deteriorated or were improved by early factory employment has been hotly debated, particularly in the case of the British industrial revolution. There is evidence on both sides. Many have tried to prove that early industry was evil; others have asserted its beneficence. Even during the Industrial Revolution itself the question was argued with much partisan feeling. The issue is not merely an academic one. In order to understand the workers themselves, it is vital to know whether they experienced a deterioration in conditions as they entered industry. That the workers were in misery from a modern point of view cannot be denied; that they were severely limited in their conditions is obvious; but whether they felt themselves to be miserable, judging by the standards they knew, is far from clear.

Several points must be considered as a preliminary to this major issue. In the first place, there are obvious national and chronological differences to be noted. The possibility of deterioration of conditions was greatest in Britain, for several reasons. The standard of living among the British peasantry was relatively high until the early eighteenth century at least; in rates of meat consumption and quality of housing particularly the peasants were better off than their counterparts on the Continent. Furthermore, British industrial growth and the corresponding urban crowding were very rapid, and this put pressure on the working class in the early decades that was less severe in France or Italy, where the process was slower. Also, British cities were far less regulated than those of the Continent; this affected housing and hygiene significantly.

Early British industrialization stressed the textile industry. This was a highly competitive industry, with small firms battling vigorously to stay alive and grow. It involved relatively little skill and employed large numbers of women and children. In contrast, later industrialization, as in Germany and Russia, involved more employment in large firms and in heavy industry. Competition was reduced because of the size of the firms, and the greater skill and strength required of workers encouraged better treatment. Finally, countries industrializing after 1850, when the supply of money was increasing rapidly, were less pressed by falling prices than industrializing areas had been in the earlier part of the century. Working conditions in Germany in the 1850s and in Russia in the 1890s were far from good. But there and even in France there can be little question of deterioration in material standards for workers entering factory industry.

Furthermore, in England and elsewhere, rural conditions had usually been declining before the Industrial Revolution began. This was, after all, the main impulse for peasants to accept factory jobs. Peasant standards of living were low anyway; preindustrial society was simply poor. And the people entering industry were often drawn from the lowest categories of the peasantry. These were the people who suffered most from expanding population and declining domestic industry. There was deterioration of material conditions in the early industrial period, but it occurred primarily in the countryside among the landless and the domestic producers and among the unskilled in the slums of cities like London. When they found factory employment, workers seldom could note a significant worsening of their situation: many factory workers actually gained some ground in standard of living.

The worst problem for factory workers, as for the poorer classes even in premodern times, was the instability of conditions. Sick workers were rarely paid and sometimes lost their jobs. With age workers' skill and strength declined, and so did their earnings. Old workers, lacking property to fall back on, suffered from falling wages and frequent unemployment. Machine breakdowns caused days and even weeks of unemployment. Most important, recurrent industrial slumps plunged many workers into profound misery. Wages fell, sometimes by as much as 50 percent; up to a quarter of the labor force lost their jobs. Some returned to the countryside to seek work or to roam in bands to find food. Some survived on charity; the charity rolls of manufacturing cities often embraced over half the working class, though only meager support was offered. Some sold or pawned their possessions. All reduced expenses by eating potatoes instead of bread and ignoring rent payments. Old age, finally, could bring disaster. Working-class life was thus punctuated by a number of personal and general crises, creating a sense of insecurity that haunted workers even in better times.

In prosperous years the worst feature of the average worker's material standard of living was housing. Rural cottages had often been flimsy and small, befouled by animals, but city housing was sometimes worse. Many workers had less than a room for their families in a filthy slum. More commonly factory workers could afford two rooms and sometimes even a garden if they lived on the outskirts of a city, where factories were most commonly located, or in a smaller factory town. Most factory workers thus were not the worst housed in the whole urban population. But their space was limited and related services, such as toilets and sewerage, were typically foul. Furnishings were also meager.

With poor housing and urban crowding, along with the pressures of factory work itself, many workers were in poor health. Rates of infant mortality were high, and many workers had a life expectancy at birth only half as high as that of their employers. Even as adults they suffered frequently from illness and often aged rapidly, becoming decrepit by age forty. But was their health worse than they would expect, according to their own previous experience? It is clear that urban health deteriorated in Britain between 1820 and 1840, improving thereafter, but this comment does not bear on factory workers specifically. In Lille, a fairly large industrial center in France, workers' life expectancy at birth rose from age twenty-eight to thirty-two during the early industrial decades. In this same area the rate of rejects from the army on grounds of health was higher in some of the poorer adjacent agricultural regions than in the factory centers. Health conditions were dreadful but it is not clear that workers could sense a deterioration.

For there were significant improvements in some aspects of life. Diets were limited, with food commanding three-quarters of the average budget; starches predominated, and much of the food purchased was of poor quality, for workers had little power to resist frauds or shoddy goods. Workers in metallurgy and mining earned enough to eat some meat regularly, which they needed to endure their strenuous jobs, but for other workers meat was a once or twice a week treat and half of all earnings went to buy starches. But meat consumption was higher than rural levels even so. Similarly, the working class increasingly ate wheat bread instead of black bread or potatoes alone. Here, admittedly, was an anomaly. White wheat bread was a symbol of better living and so was eagerly adopted, but it was less nutritional than other bread. Workers also consumed more coffee, sugar, and alcoholic drink. Clothing became more stylish and varied. There were workers in rags, coming to work barefoot, but far more had at least one change of clothing, including a pair of leather shoes. They liked to dress up on Sunday and no longer looked like the traditional urban poor. Machine-made cloth made clothes cheaper and more colorful. The same impulse toward fashion that distressed traditionalists in the middle class, who found the workers uppity, gave some pride and status to workers themselves. Workers were also able to afford new items such as forks and umbrellas.

Unquestionably factory wages were better than those of the countryside. Highly skilled male workers, many of them former artisans, were paid three to six times as much as ordinary laborers. For early mechanization did not eliminate the need for skill, though it reduced the percentage of skilled workers and changed the skills required. Hence the men who built and installed machines or puddled iron or ran the more complex spinning machines required years to learn their trade fully. But even lesser-skilled workers could command a money wage that was higher than what was available in the countryside or to the transient workers of the cities. There was little left over for purchases beyond food, housing, and clothing. A bit of tobacco or a small contribution to a mutual aid group were all that the ordinary worker could afford. However, wages tended to go up with time. They definitely rose in England after 1840. The main factory centers in France saw an increase in real wages in the 1830s and 1840s, and there was improvement in Germany in the 1840s and 1850s, in Russia in the 1890s.

So it is safe to conclude that material conditions, though bad, provided modest gains and some solace for many workers during the early industrial period as a whole. On the average, conditions were better than the new workers' traditions had led them to expect. Hence strikes for better wages were relatively rare. Factory workers did rise occasionally in slumps, often attacking bakers and other merchants in the traditional manner of the bread riot but sometimes asking for a restoration of previous wage levels. But material conditions were not, in normal times, the subject of articulate concern. Indeed many new workers were demonstrably uninterested in maximizing their wage gains. They enjoyed a few new amenities: better clothing, some changes in diet, and tobacco. But rural expectations were long preserved. This in fact allowed some workers a certain margin to adjust to other aspects of factory life. It was common, for example, for better-paid workers to stop work periodically to enjoy a period of leisure, instead of earning well beyond subsistence. Many French spinners and machine builders regularly worked only four or five days a week. Employers tried to put a stop to this by fines and other penalties, but they were not entirely successful, as workers preferred a bit of leisure over maximizing modest wages.

Workers were beginning to establish a culture of living for the present that would long endure. Savings had little meaning for them, and their use of savings banks was far lower than that of artisans. Immediate enjoyment was more to the point: buy a new suit or a cut of meat for Sunday dinner. The need to compensate for hard work, the uncertainty of an existence that was basically out of their control and dependent on the whims of employers, economic cycles, and disease, all help to explain a distinctive reaction. But it was work and family patterns, rather than consumer behavior, that best defined the new working class during the early industrial decades.

Work

Limited in material life, most workers faced even greater tensions in their job conditions. Here, industrialization showed its raw face. Factory life attacked the traditional work rhythm that the labor force brought in from shops and countryside with the new pace of the machinery and the dynamic work ethic of the entrepreneurs. Steady pressure was put on workers to discipline them to a new pace, and there was some change from one generation to the next. But workers were not just passive victims, and they preserved important elements of their own work tradition.

The physical environment of the factory was extremely harsh. Machinery was unscreened and it was not uncommon to catch fingers in it. Children had to crawl under textile machines to clean them while they were still in operation. Textile work involved heat, dust, and dampness; mining and chemical production involved exposure to gases. Few precautions were taken by manufacturers that would add to the expense or difficulty of production, and a host of accidents and occupational diseases resulted. There was some improvement with time. Bigger machines and rising profits encouraged manufacturers to build bigger, airier factories and reduce the level of dust. Some factory workers were accustomed to job hazards anyway. The craft tradition involved a variety of occupational diseases, and domestic spinning and weaving could be less salubrious than factory work. Workers were acutely conscious of job dangers, but they did not yet find new targets of blame.

Hours of work were long. In textile factories the average was about thirteen and a half hours, though with rest periods some workers spent fifteen hours at the plant and a few factories required that many hours of outright work. Metallurgical firms usually limited work to twelve hours so that two shifts could be set up for the whole day. Mining work varied but was usually under ten hours a day. There were few days off. Sundays were usually honored, although some employers required workers to show up briefly to clean their machines. A few traditional

The early factory setting and the new machine-driven nature of work. This drawing, from 1835, describes an English power-loom weaving plant, staffed by women workers under the supervision of a male foreman. *(The Bettmann Archive/BBC Hulton Picture Library.)*

saints' days were celebrated in Catholic countries, such as the festival of
Sainte-Barbe, the patron of miners. In Russia during the 1890s factories closed for more than forty such holidays. Generally, however,
work and walking to work consumed virtually all the waking hours of
the labor force, at least six days a week. The new sense of work time
was dramatized by the factory whistle, which piped workers to the job
each morning; fifteen minutes late and the factory gates were locked,
leaving tardy workers without pay and liable to a fine. Hours did decline a bit within twenty to thirty years after the beginning of industrialization. Manufacturers realized that long hours were not necessarily
productive, and child labor laws, regulating the workday for children,
prompted some to rethink their whole schedule. By the mid-nineteenth
century textile hours were down to twelve in Britain and France.

But even with such slight changes the long workday remained one of
the most vivid impressions of the early Industrial Revolution. How did
workers stand this? Countless workers undoubtedly hated the regimen
but felt powerless to fight it. But others did not find long hours unusual. They were accustomed to work from sunrise to sundown in the
fields, and as domestic workers they had sometimes labored up to eighteen hours a day. A slightly better diet could make the hours endurable,
and some of the machines lightened the purely physical burdens of
labor.

What was novel was not hours but pace. The machine operated at
considerable speed. Supervisors were set to supervise workers and shop
rules insisted that workers be diligent. Machines did not allow workers
to take a break when they wished; if one stopped, the whole machine
might have to shut down. Through fines, supervision, and the use of
inducements such as the piece rate, which would reward workers who
produced more, employers sought to enforce this new assiduity. Unquestionably workers were troubled by this, but they found some
means to counteract it. New workers wandered around the factory,
even at risk of fines. When their wages permitted they took days off.
And, at least while they were single and in their earning prime, they
often quit their jobs. Job changing was one of the most important de-
fenses workers could mount against the new work pressures. It gave a
chance to look for better conditions but above all it provided a precious
interval between jobs. Many new factories faced up to 100 percent turn-
over a year except during slumps; an important minority of workers
was stable, but many young men and women, not yet burdened with
families, switched jobs often.

So the vaunted new factory discipline was incomplete. Workers were
pressed but not yet forced to adopt a totally new work ethic. They took
individual measures to keep some of their traditional sense of control
and of relief from steady labor. Obviously the poorer workers could
not afford the luxury of quitting. New conditions, such as the sheer din

of machines, sorely troubled workers who were accustomed to sing and talk on their jobs. But for many there were means of keeping the job within some bounds of traditional expectations.

Other aspects of factory life might facilitate adaptation. The paternalistic employer who had a kind word for the workers he knew and who helped them out in sickness or sent a gift for the child's communion corresponded to some traditional standards of upper-class behavior. Small wonder that many former German peasants transferred their sense of deference from landlord to industrialist or that some French workers, given the vote in 1848, went to their employers for guidance.

Factory workers, in sum, had some important cushions against total novelty on the job, in vestiges of tradition and in their own abilities to modify arrangements—often infuriating employers in the process. A minority also found other ways to adapt, gaining new skills or accepting positions as supervisors, which gave them modest social mobility.

Yet there was a war on the shop floors of early factories, between what workers thought work should be like and what it was like. They labored in impersonal settings, with strangers. They were ordered not to mix leisure with their work, by rules that forbade chatting and singing. They were bossed and supervised, as industrialization steadily extended the number of people who worked under others' control. Small wonder that, when they could, they shifted jobs or even went back to the countryside. For some, work was losing meaning.

Servanthood

While thousands of women endured factory labor conditions along with men, though at lower skill and pay levels, many working-class women encountered a different setting. The largest employment category for urban women was servanthood, throughout the early industrial period. The number of servants rose massively in all the urban centers. Most servants were born in the countryside but no longer supportable there. They would typically have worked as servants for a peasant or farmer before marriage in preindustrial rural life, so it was logical to seek the same kind of job in the cities. Servanthood was thus the counterpart of factory work for redundant rural females, and because it kept women in a home environment it was in many ways less of a jolt.

Servant women faced long hours and sometimes abusive employers. Rarely did they have time off. With scrubbing, marketing, and cooking they had a hard job. Their rooms were cramped and ugly, if indeed they did not have to sleep in a hallway or kitchen, and their diets were meager. But there were compensations, and servanthood can be seen as an important means by which women made the transition to city life.

The "servant problem" — middle-class standards and clumsy cleaning. Problems with servants were a cartoon staple in the nineteenth century. (*The Bettmann Archive.*)

In the first place, though money wages were low they were higher, in combination with board and room, than what female factory workers could earn. So many servants saved money. Some sent it back to their family, in the traditional pattern. But others saved it toward a dowry, and a significant minority of servants were able to marry shopkeepers or established artisans, in what constituted upward mobility in society. Many learned household skills, new habits of cleanliness, and other middle-class values. Not a few were taught to read. Even those who married workers, which was the most common pattern (for only a minority of servants remained single and found servanthood a lifelong career), could bring some new values to the family. They might think about caring for their children in new ways, as the middle class was beginning to do, about educating their children and trying to help them move up in society, even about limiting their birthrate. Some of these impulses would have a clearer effect on the working class in the next stage of industrialization.

Servanthood also taught docility, for the servant was told to be respectful to the master and mistress. This could confirm traditional deference within the working class; it helps explain why many working-class married women accepted orders from their husbands without complaint. To be sure, servant women might compensate for harsh discipline by stealing from their employers or changing jobs, again a close analogue to factory behavior. As in the factories, a minority of servants could not stand the pressures of the new life. Some took to drink. More committed suicide than in the overall lower-class population. Some turned to prostitution, often after having been made pregnant by an employer but sometimes because prostitution provided a way to earn more money with less nagging supervision.

Servanthood, though domestic in setting and in one sense highly personalized, had several drawbacks in common with factory work. It placed servants under the supervision of a middle-class employer—the woman of the house—whose standards of work were different from those of the working class. Here, too, there was a battle over the nature of work, with homemakers insisting on unfamiliar habits of cooking, cleanliness, and child care, and with some servants rebelling privately—by shifting jobs or by ironic sabotage such as, in a few documented cases, urinating in the family soup.

Family Life

Given the disorienting aspects of factory labor and servanthood, life off the job was crucial to survival. Here too there were new pressures, in the conditions of the cities and the sheer fact that work was so dramatically separated from the family. For some workers, family stability suffered. Many, however, managed to construct new kinds of family patterns that made some sense. The working-class family innovated in a variety of ways to adapt to city life but also to preserve recognizable versions of traditional roles and functions. This complex combination helps explain why middle-class observers, adapting differently, so often criticized what they thought they knew about workers' private lives.

There were of course immense problems in the first generation of industry. Many workers came into factory towns alone, unmarried or leaving their families behind. Many in fact confidently planned to return to the countryside after earning a bit of extra money, and during the early years an important minority did go back at least to do harvest work. This retarded the development of new expectations. But single young people in the cities obviously faced many problems of adjust-ment even if they thought their lot temporary. Female factory workers, paid a low wage, were frequently forced to add prostitution to their working day in order to survive. Where men and women worked in a steamy room, often in partial undress, sexual temptation ran high. Men often abused factory women, taunting them sexually, sometimes coercing them outright.

But the most lurid stories of worker immorality were exaggerated, and as workers themselves often noted, sexual behavior had become at least as loose among the rural poor. It was true that many working women had one or two illegitimate children before marriage, with no great stigma attached. But these were often fathered by the same man; Wendel Holek, a German worker, described how he lived "on trial" with a woman for seven years, siring two children, before they married. Workers thus continued the sexual revolution; they did not begin it.

It was at least as significant that workers developed high marriage rates often at a rather early age, at least for women. Because of better money wages, marriage rates in the factory towns could be higher than those of the countryside, though some workers held back to avoid too many children or to contribute longer to parental households. In a strange city the family developed an emotional importance that it had not assumed in the preindustrial countryside. There were no property considerations to block a marriage that, at least at first, was based on love or sexual attraction. But the working-class family also maintained economic functions, as had been true in preindustrial traditions. Par-ticularly in the early factories the family was able to work as a unit. Children served as aides and apprentices to their father or mother. Use of child labor was high, particularly in textiles, for children's wages were low and they were held to be adept at operations like tying thread on machines. There was immense exploitation here, for long hours hurt children's health. And children were often beaten to keep them alert. But much of this system was regarded by workers, as well as employers, as perfectly natural. Children were supposed to work. What upset workers came a bit later, when more advanced machinery either cut off children's jobs or forced them into separate units of the factory, away from parental supervision. At this point, as in the 1820s in Britain, many workers decided that child labor was inappropriate and pressed for legislation limiting it. But long past this point the family and work were closely associated.

The same applied to some working-class married women. In textiles, a large percentage of the labor force was female, and when child labor was reduced by legislation and technical developments, female employ-ment went up. Unmarried and married women alike were thus able to contribute to the family economy. Their wages were lower than those of men, as was true in domestic service, but this did not matter greatly to most women because they were working not as individuals but as part of the family unit. Teenagers and young adults of both sexes, though theoretically free to leave home and earn their own wage, surprisingly often stayed back until marriage or even beyond, again contributing to the family economy. Even grandparents might have their role to play, taking care of young children while the intermediate generation worked. Grandmothers, especially, were more likely to live with a married child (usually a daughter) than had been customary in Western society, as workers reestablished an extended family to meet new needs.

The ongoing relationship of women to the family economy was complex, however. Outside of the textile industry the employment of married women was relatively low. Some young women were employed in the British mine pits, and women often could do some surface work at the mines, but this was not a female preserve. The same was true of metal and machine work. And male workers, outside of textiles, showed an early desire to pull their wives out of the factories and domestic service. Because women could not normally work alongside their husbands, the unity of the family economy would be disrupted by their work. It early became an important sign of failure for a family if the married woman worked outside the home; a sick man or one unusually low paid, an unskilled worker, a drunkard—these were the only men whose partners were sent out to work. More commonly married women continued to do work in the home, making lace or clothing or doing laundry. Many took in boarders. Women were expected, even if they did not earn money themselves, to keep their male partners fit. Some had to cut down on their own consumption in order to give their husbands enough to keep going. This made sense when the family was seen still as an economic entity. By the same token the male worker, along with the children, normally turned over most or all of his earnings to the wife, who was responsible for buying food, paying the rent, indeed serving as a consumer agent in the working-class version of division of family labor.

The working-class family quickly developed wider ties to other relatives, again re-creating many aspects of the extended family. Usually it was the wife's relatives who were most important, in contrast to the village situation where the man as inheritor of property set up the family network. The workers' extended family met for social gatherings and served, again, key economic purposes. One family member could help another get a job or lend money in times of trouble.

Aside from specific adaptations necessary to preserve a rather traditional set of family functions, the working-class family faced one key problem: how many children to have. Some long viewed children as a pure economic asset, when factory jobs for children were plentiful. But the factories changed, as we have seen; increasingly the family had to bear the expense of raising children until they were twelve. It took time to adjust to this situation. Some workers kept their family size low through late marriages or abortions; hence in Nottingham in 1851 the average working-class family was only a bit bigger, with 3.6 members, than the middle-class family. But a general working-class conversion to reduction of family size, by any means, was still in the future. Here was another responsibility for the working-class woman, and not always a pleasant one. Wendel Holek's wife, soon the mother of six, was not surprised by having to endure so many births; this, after all, was traditional. But she was surprised that none died, for death had traditionally reduced the burden of child care. Small wonder that she berated her husband when he came home from work.

Leisure and Values

At the family level and on the job, working-class adaptations remained difficult if only because fundamental conditions remained beyond the control of the class. The impulse to use traditional values to counter novelty, although surprisingly successful, produced strain. And to a substantial extent the working class was alone in its effort to hack out a response to factory and urban life, as customary community ties declined. Village festivals were gone, except for those workers who made it back to the countryside. Although an important minority of workers continued religious observance (the Welsh miners who were devoutly Methodist or the Alsatian textile workers who remained Catholic), the relevance of religion declined for the working class as a whole. Urban churches were too fancy, their rituals strange for people accustomed to peasant religion. Workers did not necessarily lose their faith—if they went back to their village they would often resume churchgoing—but they lost their habit of regular church attendance. Small wonder that the English religious census of 1851 revealed that only half the population attended church. And certainly the government was no help. With rare exceptions workers encountered agents of the state only as police officers, in cases of riot; or during slumps, when on the Continent many city governments revoked work licenses to send potentially disorderly unemployed workers out of the city; or, on a more limited basis, as a do-gooder trying to limit child labor or require education or insist on vaccinations. For a long time the state was either a hostile or an irrelevant force for the working class.

As in so many aspects of life, worker impulses and middle-class standards clashed in the leisure sphere, with a result that, while not producing complete middle-class triumph, restricted recreational outlets. Middle-class officials were suspicious of leisure as distraction from work and defined as valid only pastimes that generated self-improvement.

Workers saw leisure as a means to form social links and escape from ordinary realities. Yet new laws and police intervention limited not only festivals—seen as a waste of time and money, and politically menacing in the cities—but also animal contests, gambling, and unruly games. The result was to reduce the amount and variety of popular leisure to historically low levels.

Workers were not powerless. Some developed singing groups. Many enjoyed family strolls. At least for many young men, sexual expression took on a new importance.

Finally, in a discouraging environment with few recreational outlets and little money to spend, many workers turned to drink. The bars that spread quickly in working-class neighborhoods were mean and crowded, but they did provide some social life and escape from an ugly room. Many workers spent Sunday drinking, and Monday too when they could afford it; women sometimes joined in. Consumption of alcohol rose 40 percent among Russian workers between 1904 and 1913. In Lille during the 1830s some parents doped their children with laudanum so that they would be free to spend long hours in the bar. Here at least they might find temporary solace.

Overall, working-class leisure life showed some ability to respond to new constraints and needs, but decline of the traditional range of outlets far outweighed novel opportunities and creativity. At a time when work was being redefined by outside forces, recreation hardly compensated.

Discontent and Protest

Working-class life thus presented a host of ambiguities in this first stage of its development. The ability of this class to adapt traditions was impressive and some outlines of a durable working-class culture were forged quite quickly. But adaptation could not meet all the problems encountered, and many people were clearly disoriented. Ironically, both adaptation and disorientation inhibited protest. Workers proud of supporting their families, with their children grouped around them at the machine, might be loath to risk a strike. Workers who sought solace in liquor might storm off the job in anger, but go to the bar to discuss their problems, down a few drinks, and return to work in a day or two, somewhat the worse for wear but incapable of articulating their discontent.

There were genuinely angry workers. A British cotton spinner in 1818 wrote of his employers: "They are literally petty monarchs, absolute and despotic, in their own particular districts; and to support all this, their whole time is occupied in contriving how to get the greatest quantity of work turned out with the least expense."[7] Comparable expressions of class consciousness could be found in many factories. But

[7] E. P. Thompson, *The Making of the English Working Class* (New York, 1963), p. 177, quoting a Manchester factory operator.

the same cotton spinner admitted that most of his fellows were "docile and tractable," though he explained this by the fact that all their energies were consumed by their work. How many workers harbored articulate grievances about their condition cannot be determined. A variety of evidence indicates that most, if asked about their jobs, would have said they found no pleasure in them. British workers interviewed by parliamentary commissions during the 1830s reported many complaints. Many Germans polled around 1900, some still new to the factories and mines, said they had no enjoyment in work. But they did not necessarily expect pleasure, for traditional work had often been boring. And although they missed the opportunity to talk and sing freely, the ability to preserve the family might compensate in part. Further, even if aggrieved, it was hard to translate discontent into active protest.

  Of course there were formal barriers to unrest. Strikes and unions were illegal. The French Le Chapelier Law of 1791 and the British Combination Acts of 1799 and 1800 were typical of the measures that prohibited any association of workers. Strikes were treated as rebellions in most of Italy until 1859. Though England removed the harshest restrictions on unions in 1824, as Russia did briefly in 1906, most governments repressed worker agitation firmly in the early industrial period. Leaders of strikes were often arrested, and troops were used to break up any major demonstration. Employers also resisted expressions of discontent. They fired potential leaders and sometimes blacklisted them locally. They called in government troops, when agitation was merely threatened. And if a strike did occur, they typically tried to outlast it or to retract any gains they might be temporarily forced to grant.

  However, these barriers of repression did not inhibit artisan protest to the extent characteristic of early factory labor. It was true that workers had more sense of being among strangers, with fewer familiar faces to appeal to in times of anger. They were also less literate than artisans. Although reading ability spread rapidly in industrial centers—if only because employers had reason to encourage literacy, which would improve the ability of their workers to read directions and shop rules—many workers had no schooling and others who went to school were taught briefly and badly. So workers were less open than artisans to political propagandists; utopian socialists, for example, made little headway among them by 1848. Most important, workers lacked the organizational tradition that even inadequate guilds had provided. Hence workers were slow to organize mutual aid societies, although a few developed among the highly skilled soon after industrialization began. Beyond this, partial adaptation, traditional resignation and deference, and the sheer novelty of factory life differentiated workers from artisans in protest action. Far more workers expressed their discontents individually, through stealing materials from the plant or changing jobs, than could combine for action.

Worker agitation was infrequent and poorly organized during the early years of the Industrial Revolution, usually for at least the first four decades. There was little worker unrest in Belgium until the 1860s. The whole of French factory labor produced only eight strikes a year during the 1830s and 1840s, and these were usually small and brief. The most common action was more a riot than a strike, occurring during a slump that brought violent attacks on merchants or employers. Only a few groups broke through this pattern. Miners conducted several large strikes in France and Germany, fairly early on. They had more leisure and funds to plan an effort; their dangerous work easily stirred them to anger; and they had a nucleus of traditional mine workers who helped shape goals, for most mine areas had conducted small operations for decades before the Industrial Revolution. Many of the early strikes concerned work conditions and relations with employers. Silesian miners, for example, first stirred over changes in traditional work patterns and a reduction of customary benefits from their companies, such as free heating coal. Only later would large numbers of industrial workers turn to issues such as hours and wages, except in cases of massive deterioration. But strikes to preserve customs were hard to win, for employers were insistent on their right to command greater efficiency; so this discouraged strikes even further. Gradually, of course, more workers acquired the ability to protest. The revolutions of 1848 spread new consciousness to some; in Paris some workers in the new railroad yards even joined the artisans during the June Days. Factory strikes during the French Second Empire involved increasing numbers of metallurgical and textile workers. But the rate was still low, and few permanent organizations arose within factory labor to give leadership and coherence to worker discontent.

Britain offered a slightly different pattern. Again, there was little agitation for the first forty years. Factory workers showed no interest in machine breaking, for example, because this was their livelihood and they could build family work around the new equipment. But in the decades when urban material conditions deteriorated they did stir, often following the lead of artisans. Strikes by bricklayers and carpenters in Birmingham, for instance, were imitated by cotton workers in 1818. Britain was just pulling out of a slump, and workers struck against unemployment and reductions in pay. As in France, then, the first efforts were defensive, to protest deterioration. But here some workers had gained enough experience to go on to form unions, and important organizations developed among cotton spinners and miners, lasting into the 1830s. Workers also participated in the Chartist movement. Chartism gave them a way to protest economic slumps, and the movement in the industrial areas was more violent than where urban artisans were in firm command. But with the failure of Chartism and the advent of more prosperous times in the 1850s, worker agitation fell off once more. Only the highly skilled workers pulled away, in the sedate New Model Union movement, but this simply reduced the chances for general unrest. Major, persistent agitation among factory workers throughout western and central Europe was not to develop until the 1870s or 1880s.

The same pattern did not hold true for industrial workers in Italy, northern Spain, and Russia in their first industrial decades at the end of the nineteenth century. Large strike waves occurred, along with surreptitious unions, as early as the first or second decade of industrialization. Workers raised not only economic but political demands, asking for parliamentary reform and voting rights. A massive general strike was the backbone of the 1905 revolution in Russia, yet industrialization was only fifteen years old. Milanese workers conducted a major rising in 1898; Barcelona textile workers surged forward a decade later. This agitation had immense political implications, when joined to rural unrest and middle-class demands; in Russia it was to overturn the government and ruling class in 1917. Several factors explain the different working-class potential, including of course the fact that the political regimes in these countries were unusually backward and repressive:

1. Workers in all these areas were recruited from a peasantry that was extremely aggrieved. This obviously played a major role in Barcelona, where workers were recruited from the south and brought their peasant anarchism along with them; this was the only case in which large numbers of factory workers were anarchist. But peasant unrest formed a vital backdrop for workers in Italy and Russia too.

2. There were far more revolutionary doctrines and propagandists at work than was the case earlier in the West. Socialists, communists, anarchists—this was a rich menu to choose from. In Russia, at least, workers were probably more widely literate than their western counterparts seventy years before. Over 60 percent of the whole population could read by the 1900s, thanks not only to schools but also to training in military service. Comparable levels were reached in France only by 1870, at a much later stage of industrialization. Again this opened factory workers more easily to radical literature.

3. Factories and equipment in these early industrial revolutions were almost as sophisticated as those in the West at the same time. In Russia the average factory was larger than anywhere else in Europe by the 1900s, employing a thousand workers. Workers here lacked the ability to defend traditional work patterns that had been possible in smaller shops with slower machinery.

4. The artisanal tradition itself was less solidly developed than in western Europe. This meant that skilled workers like printers

had fewer guild habits to fall back on or to revive. They, and other discontented groups, such as middle-class intellectuals, turned more quickly to a larger working class for support in protest movements. In early industrial Britain, in contrast, we have seen that artisans and factory workers might combine occasionally but that the more persistent tendency was for artisans to emphasize their exclusivity, at most allowing a larger skilled labor aristocracy to join their efforts.

But if, in Russia particularly, unrest was a vital theme for the early industrial working class, the more general point still must be the limitations on working-class protest potential in its formative years. Protest required a sense of community and tradition, which workers often lacked. Hence, whether satisfied or not, whether benefiting by perceptible improvements in living standards or not, workers had to try to adapt to their new situation. This was true even in the areas where major protest surged. Workers could not successfully oppose the Industrial Revolution and, unlike the artisanry, few even tried. So the effort to find new sources of status and pleasure, as in clothing; or to reestablish traditional values in altered form, as in family life; or to wish for novel forms of protest set an enduring tone for the working-class culture.

Early Industrialization and Protest

The early industrial period stands out, in the history of social protest, for the frequency and vigor of agitation. This was not a rising of the whole society. The very poor, both in city and countryside, were largely left out. Factory workers participated only haltingly, with a few major exceptions. But large numbers of artisans and peasants were attempting to call a stop to change. They might hark back to an idealized village or guild or they might use anarchism or utopian socialism to paint a new society based on the same principles of egalitarianism and small-group organization. Neither the forms nor the basic goals of the protest were new in most cases. The usual form was a riot, the goals were traditional, pointing to old rights that had been challenged rather than new ones deserved. Hence the timing was usually associated with an economic crisis, when conditions deteriorated; when times were good it was hard to form goals, for the present had to be seen as worse than the past for this protest to be possible. Much of the protest involved elaborate rituals, hallowed symbols, and mythical leaders such as Ned Ludd or Captain Swing. Yet the depth of feeling involved should not be minimized. Though triggered by economic problems, the major protests involved fundamental hostility toward those held responsible for change.

Yet the protests failed to halt change. Often unpolitical, they rarely attacked the state directly. Peasants and artisans worked separately. Even when they rose in the same year, they did not join hands. Furthermore peasants, focusing particularly on the manor lords, were attacking an old enemy, not the source of commercial and industrial change. They were spurred by newer developments such as population pressure and the growing commercialization of agriculture, but they did not attack these directly. This was why they often won their leading demands, for the innovative forces, and particularly the middle class, could readily agree that manorialism was evil. But this simply opened the way for further change, as the aristocracy was weakened and the traditional legal structure of the rural world overturned. Artisans hit at the modern economy more directly, by attacking the principles of the capitalist order. Alone, they could not prevail. They were hampered not only by the separate action of the peasants but also by the positive hostility of the rising middle class, which seized control of the leading revolutions. The middle class might not win its revolutions either, preferring defeat rather than the artisan victory that would mean a return to the old order, but it could certainly block the craftspeople. Artisans were also hampered by the ability of many of their number either to defend tradition without revolution or to find individual ways to profit from the new economy.

Partly as a result of repeated failure, the last great wave of traditional protest ended during the early industrial period. Already in England the Chartist movement suggested an adaptation of protest to more political goals. Some Chartists might dream of a return to a craft economy, but others, asking for votes and education, were ready to try to improve the new economy. The revolutions of 1848 marked the end of preindustrial protest in France and Germany. The peasants in central Europe won the abolition of manorialism, as those in France had done earlier. The artisans were defeated. New elements were beginning to enter the protest scene, like the railroad workers who participated in the June Days. Here, too, protest was becoming more political; when artisans and agricultural workers rose in several parts of France in 1851, to oppose the abolition of the republic, they were trying to defend their new political rights, not to return to the past. All of this was tentative still, and many elements would still hanker for the past. But in terms of overt collective action, a major turning point was sketched.

The 1850–1870 decades, however, brought a strange return to calm. These were prosperous years for most elements in society. Famine had ended in western Europe, thanks to improved agriculture and transportation; this classic trigger of protest was gone. Some traditional protest groups were now vanishing—the middling peasant, the domestic manufacturing worker. Artisans were still vigorous but were turning to new forms of action and adaptation. Governments, frightened by the

1848 risings, became more adept at handling crowds; police forces were bolstered, their weaponry improved. And the middle class turned against protest. It was winning partial political gains, as parliaments and constitutions spread through central Europe. Even leading conservatives conceded that the state should further, not oppose, industrial growth. The Prussian government thus turned from a policy of discouraging industrial investment, in the 1840s, to supporting giant investment banks. The peasantry was quiet, with population pressure reduced and manorialism gone. When protest resumed, it would be on quite another basis.

The fate of early industrial protest in eastern and southern Europe was rather different. Sharecropping in southern Italy and Spain, the continued limitations on the peasantry in Russia until the Stolypin reforms prevented the calming of the countryside that occurred in western Europe. Rural agitation remained endemic in Spain into the 1930s, in Italy into the 1920s. In Russia the peasantry might have followed the western pattern after 1906; certainly rioting decreased. But the hardships of World War I, in a situation where adaptation had just begun, roused the peasants once more. The early contributions of the working class to protest also marked this area. And the middle class was weak. Lacking a large, independent business group, liberal professionals tried to master the revolutionary current, as their counterparts had done in the west in 1830 and 1848, but they could not. Finally, with the western experience behind them, revolutionaries like Lenin were far more adept than the smaller band of avowed revolutionaries in 1848 had been. So revolution triumphed in Russia in 1917. Agitation rocked Spain and Italy for decades.

In western and central Europe, many established institutions of society emerged from the early industrial period in apparently good shape. The leading churches had the firm support of the aristocracy, and with a prosperous agriculture some landlords were able to contribute large sums to religion. Middle-class elements, sincerely pious or eager for respectability, also gave money. This was a major period of church building and restoration of ancient edifices. Money went into missionary activity as well, and on the intellectual level there was a revived interest in theology. In England the nineteenth century has, with reason, been called a great age for religion, and the phrase could with some justice be applied elsewhere.

In fact, religion was declining as a social cement. The churches retained most of their hold on the peasantry, though in key areas peasants attacked the clergy along with the rest of the established order. But the peasantry was a shrinking majority of society. Middle-class interest in religion was ambiguous at best. The class ethic ran counter to traditional belief. Its optimism and belief in individual ability implicitly undermined the tenets of original sin and damnation. The middle class did not really believe in hell. Its faith in science overshadowed its interest in theology. With the popularization of the theory of evolution after 1859, even greater doubts spread about the validity of religion. The middle class, particularly in Catholic countries, also distrusted the church as an institution, allied as it was with the aristocracy and suppression of freedom of speech and expression. Middle-class leaders, as in the French revolution of 1830, readily countenanced a reduction in the political powers of the church. Religious freedom was declared in every major revolution and church property was often seized, following the example of the French Revolution of 1789. Even in England the political rights of the Anglican church were steadily diminished.

The states of western and central Europe were in better shape. With few exceptions they had weathered the amazing wave of revolutions that hit almost every country between 1820 and 1848. They had not been required to give over full power to the middle class. But they had introduced an important series of changes to retain what they could of stability and the old order. They had established parliaments and broadened the vote to include some of the middle class or, as in Britain in 1867, the working class or even, as in France and Germany by 1870, the whole adult male population. They had developed a host of new functions. The abolition of manorialism put the state in direct touch with every citizen for tax collection, military recruitment, and preservation of order—all rather traditional functions now expanded; but the state was also in touch with citizens for technical training, extension of credit, and, increasingly, primary education. At least in the cities the state inspected housing and factories. It licensed doctors. It kept census records and took over the functions of registering births, deaths, and marriages. This was a state capable of new initiatives even when, ironically, not fully controlled by a modern social class. Even when in conservative hands it now promoted change. It no longer relied on repression alone, even against the lower classes, as it abortively attempted, even in Britain, for a few years or decades after 1815.

If the state was expanding, other traditional institutions had loosened their hold. Guilds, by 1870, had either disappeared or were voluntary. When peasants could freely leave for the city, villages had lost their traditional control. Despite new state functions, despite even the powers of new institutions such as the paternalistic factory, individuals were freer than before. Some, in desperate misery or confused by the new order, saw freedom as confusion. Not only the very poor but the middling class had reason to question the process of modernity, and even with the decline of traditional protest society was not lacking new voices urging a halt to change. Other groups adapted more successfully to a situation in which individual choice was heightened. For choice meant not only middle-class decisions about what kind of professional education was best or what new machine was most reliable, it also meant homemakers' decisions about what to buy amid a growing array of consumer goods, workers' decisions about what job to take or what city to go to, and a woman's decision about whether servanthood, factory work, or perhaps prostitution would best serve her interests. The lower a person went on the social scale the more choice was hemmed in by restrictions, of course, but behavior patterns were far less closely guided than before.

To adjust to this situation, the family proved of key importance to most of the major social classes. It, too, was freer in important ways. Children or young adults, able to earn on their own, could leave home at an early age, and some did, defying their parents. Choice of mate was more open, even in the middle class. But despite some signs of disorganization, such as the still-rising illegitimacy rates among the rural and urban propertyless classes, most people chose the family. The nineteenth century was a marrying century. By 1850 in England 859 per 1,000 females reaching the age of fifteen would marry by the time they were fifty, and this figure long held steady. It was much higher than in premodern society. The family remained an economic necessity. Its producing role had changed, though not entirely disappeared; married women were less commonly producing agents than before. But, with the middle class guiding the way, it was increasingly becoming a consumer unit, with women here taking the leading role. It was not yet clear how these changes would balance out for women, but for the moment there was neither time nor widespread interest for questioning the importance of new functions, and it was significant that a higher percentage achieved the status of marriage than ever before.

What was happening, overall, was a change in balance among institutions. Traditional small-scale institutions that had fostered face-to-face community contacts largely declined, except for the family which gained new roles. Families were, however, increasingly separate from other aspects of community life, in part because of the domestic focus of women as chief family agents; the middle-class emphasis on distinctions between public and private spheres enhanced the split. Among the larger public institutions, in turn, it was the state that most clearly gained ground, even beginning to assume some functions, such as training the young, that had traditionally been left to the family, community, or church.

This rebalancing of institutional strengths further assured the need for a redefinition of protest, for the growth of the state necessitated more explicit attention to the political content of social movements, including demands for voting rights, while the decline of traditional institutions added to the need to shift away from traditional claims to assertions of new rights. The result of this new combination would become visible in western Europe after 1870, for the experience of various lower-class elements in learning new protest tactics and language was another vital product of this first contact between the forces of industrialization and those of social unrest.

Gender

The social divisions that described the various values and behaviors of the early industrial decades were not the only new rifts in European society or the only basis for protest. The key responses to early industrial conditions involved heightened distinctions between the genders. The differences between men and women, in both roles and perceptions, to some extent cut across class. Despite the huge gulf between the middle-class married woman and the working-class female servant, the two shared a number of characteristics, including confinement to domesticity and growing distance from the world of men. Though they could not unite in protest, women might unwittingly share grievances about their powerlessness and vulnerability to male abuse.

Growing gender distinctions in early industrial society stemmed in part from the new separation between work and home, in almost all the urban sectors, and in part from widespread desire to use gender identities to compensate for some of the new uncertainties of industrial life.

Gender relations had not changed systematically during the previous decades, despite population upheaval and spread of domestic manufacturing. In eighteenth-century France men began to shy away from domestic service, leaving the jobs increasingly to women, which suggested some novel male ideas about pride and independence. However, domestic manufacturing provided opportunities for wage earning, productive work for both men and women — and for shared insecurities, given the absence of property for the growing proletariat. In some aristocratic and middle-class circles, more democratic ideas and a new taste for romance invaded family life, reducing some of the patriarchal inequalities between marriage partners. Conditions were hardly revolutionary. The great French revolution of 1789 was noteworthy for its insistence on traditional gender relationships, despite some calls for new rights for women. Revolutionary law codes confirmed the dominance of men in families and carefully extended new political rights to them only.

It was the Industrial Revolution, however, that most clearly brought innovation to gender relations, making the middle decades of the nineteenth century a crucial turning point in western Europe in this regard. Industrialization challenged patriarchy, in that work now took men away from the daily conduct of the home for long stretches of time. Extensive interaction with children, particularly young children, was literally impossible for men. They might still claim to be the primary disciplinary authority and they still offered some moral guidance, as with the middle-class fathers who read uplifting stories to their children on Sundays. Men who brought their sons into their business offices for training, or who employed their sons as assistants on a factory machine, maintained important economic contacts. Nevertheless, primary authority over children increasingly passed to others—to schools to some extent, but even more obviously to mothers.

Most women, for their part, lost ground in terms of their roles in the economy. Middle-class women often assisted their husbands in the first generation of a new factory or store, and this collaboration continued among small shopkeepers. Generally, however, later generations of businessmen pulled their wives out of any formal work roles. As middle-class households drifted to the suburbs, women found themselves busy at more purely domestic tasks. And women were not encouraged to work prior to marriage. In this culture unmarried women faced a difficult economic prospect, for there were very few jobs regarded as respectable. The working-class pattern was different. Young women here did work, in factories and as servants. They too, however, were usually expected to abandon their jobs at marriage or soon thereafter. They continued to earn some money in tasks performed at home, but the central breadwinning role went to the man, aided by his employed children.

In an economy that depended increasingly on jobs outside the home, and on earning money, women were either excluded outright or reduced to a transient or supplementary role. It was no accident that mechanization spread most rapidly in branches of production, like spinning, that had been most heavily female-dominated. Early factory legislation both reflected and furthered this process, as women's hours of work were regulated while men's were left untouched. Men from various social classes easily agreed that women were the frailer sex and that their paid employment must be restricted in the interests of home life. Male workers, defining their respectability in terms of a primary earning role, welcomed further relief from women's potential competition. Relatedly, they usually (though not invariably) discouraged women workers from participation in their trade unions.

Faced with declining work opportunities, many working-class women also became more sexually vulnerable to men. Working-class men who sired illegitimate children with no intention of marriage, or who were impeded from marriage, but not from sex, by their need to move from town to town in search of work, were joined by middle-class men who visited prostitutes or exploited the household servant. The ongoing sexual revolution allowed some women to gain new participation in sexual pleasures, but it far more generally encouraged men to regard sexual prowess as a vital badge of masculinity. At a time when traditional demonstrations of masculinity, through mastery of customary work skills or acquisition of property, were becoming more difficult, the growing importance of sex helped fill a genuine need.

The middle class developed a larger gender ideology to explain and reinforce changes in male–female relationships. Many in the class assumed that their gender ideas were highly traditional, but in fact they were in many respects extremely novel. Middle-class beliefs stressed of course the difference in presumably appropriate roles for men and women. Men were destined to work, women to guard the hearth. Distinctions in education followed from these goals. Men needed training in practical subjects, women not only in household skills but also in graceful arts such as piano playing. Women were also encouraged to take active part in charitable activities, serving as representatives of the family conscience even as their businessmen-husbands blithely furthered the exploitation of their labor force.

Distinctions in male and female roles flowed into wider judgments about gender attributes. Men were by nature aggressive and rational. They had strong sexual drives, although they should discipline these drives in the interests of family harmony and birthrate control. Women were seen as more emotional, but they were also loving, nurturing, and morally pure. While most middle-class people did not go so far as some extremists in arguing that "proper" women had no sexual appetites at all—one authority did argue that sex held no joy for women, who should endure it only for the sake of procreation ("close your eyes and think of England")[8]—almost all claimed that women had low-level drives. This meant that highly sexed women were considered evil, and that "proper" women were considered the natural regulators of sexual relations in marriage, for a social class that needed careful attention to restraint as a means of birth control. Culturally, particularly in Protestant countries, women gained ground on men in terms of moral status, so long as they lived up to respectable standards.

Emphasis on gender distinction affected leisure activities, again across social-class lines. Working-class men treasured walks with their families, but they also went to bars that were usually exclusively male preserves. Middle-class men patronized all-male chambers of commerce and professional associations, and they joined men's clubs for further separate leisure. Casual contacts among youth were strictly supervised in the middle class as well, particularly on the Continent. An American woman doctor, studying in Paris in 1867, described the overall gender rift in France: "The French social system is constructed . . . entirely on the principle of keeping young men and women as far apart as flame and gunpowder."[9]

Gender differentiation clearly was a pervasive response to industrial conditions. It facilitated a division of labor in which women took charge

---

[8] William Acton, *The Functions and Disorders of the Reproductive Organs in Childhood, Youth, Adult Age and Advanced Life, Considered in Their Physiological, Social, and Moral Relations* (London, 1862), p. 18.

[9] Marion Harland, *Eve's Daughter, or Common Sense for Maid, Wife, and Mother* (New York, 1882), p. 11.

of child care and shopping tasks as a response to the new urban separation between work and home. It provided both genders with some sense
of special functions and identities in a rapidly changing environment.

Some women were, however, far from happy with the new arrangements. A minority, in the working class, insisted on working after marriage, and vehemently denied charges that their children and homes
suffered as a result. A few testified actively, though in vain, against the
reforms of women's work that reduced their ability to compete freely
with men. Women workers also occasionally conducted strikes on their
own, in an attempt to improve conditions of labor. Some middle-class
women attempted to define new spheres of activity as well. An impressive number of women novelists emerged in the first half of the
nineteenth century, particularly in Britain and France. During the revolutions of 1848 women took an active role and in some cases developed organizations to demand women's rights. A democratic women's
club formed in Berlin, though it raised few specific demands. In Paris an
array of women's political organizations formed and also a feminist newspaper, *Voice of Women*. French feminists demanded a vote for women.
Their numbers were not large, drawing mainly on women intellectuals
and schoolteachers; and they were easily crushed, by a ruling that wom-
en could not attend political meetings. Their efforts made it clear, however, that the growing disparities between men's and women's public
roles could generate yet another basis for protest in industrial society —
precisely because the most dominant protest models were now masculine.

The early industrial emphasis on gender brought some gains to
women even aside from protest. Freer on a day-to-day basis from male
control in family life, women did develop new functions in childrearing
and family budgeting; they increasingly served as the centers of larger
kin networks, against the patriarchal traditions that had seen wives move
to their husbands' extended family relationships. Middle-class ideology,
in giving women the claim to greater family morality and sexual virtue,
provided the basis for important new assertions of authority, at least
within the domestic context.

Women also gained ground rapidly in basic education. While they
rarely went beyond primary schooling, and often were taught separately from boys, girls did begin to close the literacy gap. This meant
in turn a growing women's audience for books and magazines and a
growing role in influencing general culture.

The gender response to early industrialization was by no means inevitable. The advent of industry in eastern Europe, late in the
nineteenth century, did not produce such extreme differentiation. In
this poorer society a larger number of married women continued to
work even in the cities. The Russian middle class did, however, replicate some earlier patterns from western Europe, in developing new
standards of domesticity while also extending educational opportunities

to women, at least up to a point. A Russian feminist movement also emerged from this mixture.

In general, and most obviously in western Europe during the early industrial decades, the growing real and imagined differences between men and women formed a vital part of social and personal life. They complicated class divisions, in allowing each gender to close ranks slightly over a few key issues. Whatever the resultant mixture of gains and losses for both men and women, the insistence on separate spheres had powerful effects on the ways most urban people lived. Transmitted through childrearing, schools, and general culture, the redefinition of gender would continue to affect European society in the decades to come.

Conclusion

The early industrial period generated a host of crosscurrents in European society. Details should not obscure some basic patterns, visible first in western Europe and later in eastern and southern Europe in broad outline. These decades saw the first steps in a major conversion of the European economy—from agriculture to industry, from human and animal power to the power of fossil fuels. It witnessed also a revolution in human residence, from countryside to city as normal habitat.

Inevitably, changes of this significance produced a variety of discontents and protests. They also produced a complex welter of social groupings, with the new divisions of gender added in as well. Basic class structure increasingly pitted property owners against wage earners. But each social grouping was complicated by ongoing rural–urban divisions as well as by profound internal rifts between people who on balance welcomed innovations—in business but also in farming or machine-tending—and people who sought to preserve or restore traditions. Warfare between the middle and working classes was joined by battles within each group over definitions of status and appropriate work. Complexity of this sort was the inevitable result of initial adjustments to radical new technological and commercial forces.

The early industrial decades also yielded a mixture of durable and transient trends. Redefinitions of family life varied greatly from one social group to the next, but the process of moving the family from its traditional service as a production unit to other functions was quite general—and this process would continue in the future. Work was reshaped, toward greater specialization and faster pace, under the aegis of a middle-class work ethic and the spur of new machines. Again, the nature of work varied greatly across economic sectors, occupations, and social classes, but common trends emerged that would continue and deepen as industrial patterns took fuller hold.

However, the differentiation of gender roles, which gained such momentum in early industrial society, did not prove permanent even though its effects linger even today. The restrictions of traditional leisure and efforts to shape recreation toward self-improvement were understandable results of middle-class values and the overwhelming concern with industrial production. These patterns would not endure, though, even in the middle class. New requirements inherent in the fuller development of industrialization would force a considerable reversal in leisure's role.

The unifying thread was rapid innovation, creating new social groups without eliminating older impulses, prompting some durable new trends but also some initial adjustments that would have to be rethought. The early Industrial Revolution, in fact, invited a rather different pattern of struggle and adaptation from what would follow — and these new patterns of social response began to emerge in western Europe after about 1870.

CHAPTER 5

Mature Industrial
Society

Within sixty to eighty years after the beginning of the Industrial Revolution in any country, most people had become accustomed to some of its effects, or at least resigned to them. It is useful to think of an industrial society as mature when about half its population lives in cities, a situation reached in England as early as 1850, in western Europe around 1900, in Russia around 1950. For this substantial urbanization means that most people remaining in the countryside have converted to market agriculture and are exposed to other urban influences. It means that most urban workers are no longer brand new to industry; increasing numbers have lived in cities and worked in factories for several generations. Even the middle class, though most optimistic about the possibilities of industrialization, has had a chance to adapt more fully. By the late nineteenth century the west European middle class was relaxing a bit, able to enjoy the fruits of earlier labor; from this class in fact would emanate a new ethic of leisure. At various levels of society people, now accustomed to their new work and setting, began to become more articulate about their goals. They no longer had to apply purely traditional standards to their life, but were able to formulate new demands. Protest levels mounted, but they operated within an industrial framework more than against it. Crime rates stopped increasing so rapidly in the late nineteenth century. Changes in the characteristics of crime continued, in that property crimes, particularly thefts, continued to gain over crimes of violence. Rates of assaults and suicides declined in several areas. It was after 1870 also that illegitimacy rates stabilized or even dropped slightly. In some areas, the dislocating effects of World War I reversed some of these trends; crime in England and Wales began to rise from 1920 onward. But it is legitimate to see personal dislocation as declining at least until the war and in some cases beyond.

Mature industrial society involves more, however, than the fact that some of the novelty had worn off the industrialization process. Important new developments were occurring that make the mature industrial period a new break in the course of industrial development. From about 1870 to 1940 in western and central Europe, basic structural changes were taking place in economy and society alike. This chronology is approximate; industrialization was far newer in Germany than in England by 1900, so that a second wave of change was less clearly distinguishable from the initial impact of industrialization. Many German workers were still coming into factories for the first time; they had to adjust to a second generation of technology and business organization simultaneously with their first reaction to city life. But for purposes of generalization, the idea of a new seventy-year span covering all those areas where industrialization had been well begun before 1870 has considerable validity.

Of course, in the midst of this period, an unprecedented world war occurred. World War I sharpened many of the trends visible already, bringing a near collapse of mature industrial society. The special effects of the war must be discussed, but only after the more fundamental trends of industrial maturation have been established.

Some of the features of industrial maturation spread to eastern and to a lesser extent southern Europe around 1900. Big business could be copied; so could socialism. But real industrial maturation took shape in Russia and Italy only toward the middle of the twentieth century. Again one can see important common elements to the maturation process, but at discrete chronological intervals.

A number of key topics define when a new break has occurred in the ongoing development of industrial society. Mature industrial society involved a new kind of social protest. It developed a new class structure, particularly with the rise of white-collar labor. More fundamentally a new basis for class structure was suggested, though just in embryo; property declined as a measurement of social stratification. Mature industrial society brought a new stage in the decline of religion and the rise of alternate loyalties and beliefs. It saw a new definition of work, though building on earlier industrial principles, and of work's relationship to leisure. It represented a distinct new demographic period. In mature industrial society the birthrate fell rapidly. Population kept growing for a time but at a much slower pace, and only because of a drop in the death rate plus the cumulative effect of earlier growth. Quickly, however, population headed toward a zero growth rate. France led the way here, as not only the urban classes but also the peasantry, eager to protect their land holdings from the divided inheritance that French law required, cut their birthrates early. By 1820 the major period of French population growth was over. But this pattern emerged by the mid-nineteenth century in Britain, by the 1870s in Germany, and by the 1920s in Russia and Italy. Thus, at a very early stage of industrial maturation, or even slightly ahead of its advent, population growth slowed dramatically. This reflected important changes in family including gender definitions, and it had significant effects on the economy and politics. By the 1930s under the impact of World War I and the Depression, population in Britain and Scandinavia had totally ceased to grow, and in France the native population was actually shrinking, with birthrates lower than death rates; France expanded only by admitting large numbers of immigrant workers.

All of these developments, particularly the new class structure and the new demography, form a vital part of the definition of mature industrial society; several must be explored further, in their relationship to specific social groups. But there are four more obvious criteria for measuring this period off from the first stage of industrialization. The nature of technology changed. So did the organization of the economy. So did the nature of key economic problems, as Europe clearly moved out of the traditional economy of scarcity. So, finally, did the relation of people to the government.

Technology

Although nothing so dramatic as the application of steam power to manufacturing marks off the maturation of industrial society, technology was changing sufficiently that the late nineteenth century has often been termed the scene of a second Industrial Revolution. The pace of technological change within existing factory industries speeded up, with a new generation of inventions. And machines now spread to literally every branch of the economy.

Between 1870 and 1890 the application of inventions such as sewing machines transformed many craft industries. By 1900 most shoes and many items of clothing were made in factories or in sweatshops. In the food-processing industries machines prepared, processed, and canned many products. Even the baking of bread was partially mechanized, although factory production was not installed. Printing developed automatic composing machines that greatly speeded production. Cranes and electric saws were introduced in construction work, which, along with the use of metal scaffolding for the larger buildings, altered many traditional skills. Cranes also changed the nature of dock work. Crucial to many of these developments was the utilization of electric and gasoline motors, which gained ground particularly after about

1890. Now even small shops and homes could use powered equipment. And regions distant from a coal supply could industrialize, although the heaviest concentrations of industry were still attached to mining centers. Areas with potential for hydroelectric power, such as the Alpine regions, experienced a real burst of industrial development after 1890.

Technological change was not confined to manufacturing. Agricultural producers increasingly applied mechanical equipment to their work. Cream separators in the dairy industry along with cultivators and harvesting machinery spread even to many peasant producers. In office work, typewriters and telephones reproduced some of the impact of the early machines in factory industry: work became more routinized, faster-paced, and noisier. A host of producers thus had to adapt to new equipment, really for the first time. Some were displaced; artisanal shoemakers and tailors increasingly had to concentrate only on luxury production and repair work. The total size of the artisan class, particularly outside the construction industry, began to stabilize or decline after 1870. Even where artisanal forms still predominated, as in baking, craftspeople might fear later displacement by some new invention, and almost everyone had to accept some changes in the methods of work. The same was true of many factory workers. In textiles machinery became increasingly sophisticated. Multiple looms were developed for weavers, allowing them to work first two or four looms and then, with the Northropp loom invented in the United States, as many as sixteen or thirty-two. The new machines did not spread immediately, for there was much resistance, but productivity did rise in the industry. This meant not only a new pace of work but also, given the limited market for textile goods, a stabilization or even slight shrinkage of textile employment.

Other factory industries were growing more rapidly, but here too technical change loomed large. Heavy industry was massively transformed. In 1856 the Bessemer process allowed the elimination of carbon from iron ore by chemical means. This increased the possible size of blast furnaces and also permitted the reintroduction of carbon to make steel on a widespread basis for the first time. The Gilchrist–Thomas process, developed in the 1870s, allowed the utilization of iron ore rich in phosphorous; this opened the iron ores of Lorraine to industrial exploitation and pushed the metallurgical industries of Germany and France to unprecedented levels. Such technical developments vastly increased the potential output of metallurgy and at the same time raised the capital needed by any metallurgical firm; the new devices were extremely costly. By the 1890s digging machines were gradually applied to mining. More important, the machine tools industry was transformed by the introduction of automatic lathes, riveting machines, and the like. These processes greatly reduced the skills necessary in the manufacture of machines and ships, while encouraging a more rapid pace of work. By about 1910 similar devices were changing automobile production from a small-shop, almost artisanal operation to a major factory industry.

New technology propelled the manufacture of electric equipment and the chemicals industry to new heights. By the 1920s these industries were replacing less dynamic branches such as textiles and even mining as the manufacturing leaders. Not only new methods but also new products such as rayon and radios challenged traditional industries severely. Mining found a vigorous competitor in petroleum products. The vitality of the industry declined even before 1914, and by the 1920s this was a sick branch. New technology thus brought displacement home to factory workers themselves. Where workers and manufacturers tried too hard to cling to traditional methods, as occurred in some branches of textiles, productivity did not increase rapidly enough to match the dynamism of other industries or competition from other regions. Whole areas of traditional industry, such as Lancashire, South Wales, and the mining districts of Belgium and northern France, seemed permanently blighted, as the emphasis switched to new regions such as Lorraine or southern England. By the 1920s unemployment stood at 16 percent in British mining and textiles. More generally, the new equipment first slowed down the growth of the working class and then brought it to a virtual halt by the 1920s, as demand could now be met by increased productivity per worker.

The key symbol of the new technology became the assembly line. Suggested before World War I, mainly by experts from the United States, assembly line methods spread increasingly in industries such as automobiles and machine tools. Semiskilled workers, using electric-powered equipment, repeated simple operations such as riveting bolts as a part of an engine or chassis moved by them on a conveyor belt. Not all factory skills were lost. In 1914 a full 60 percent of British machine tools workers were skilled, the rest evenly divided between semiskilled and unskilled. But the challenge was there. Factory workers, even more than artisans or office help, had to adjust to new methods and the fear of technological displacement. Overall, the semiskilled worker, trained to carry out repetitive tasks in a restricted work area, became increasingly prominent in the labor force.

Many people, some enthusiastic and some appalled, began to sense that European society was now driven by technological change without concern for human impact. A tendency spread to equate technology with progress, even during the 1930s Depression, and the attitude became a staple of popular advertising, part indeed of the definition of an up-to-date home.

Big Business

The assembly-line mentality involved more than technology. Whereas new technology set much of the framework for social developments in the early industrial decades, organizational changes were now more important.

The leading branches of industry grew more steadily concentrated after 1870, and the new industrial magnates thought in terms of rationalization in all aspects of their operation. Technological change helped spur big business, for the new machines, particularly in heavy industry, were extremely expensive and required a massive investment. But the big business outlook outstripped technological change. The chemical industry, for example, developed gigantic firms at least a decade before costly equipment was introduced. There was a new spirit in many branches of industry, a spirit that tried to use size to modify competitive pressure and even to reduce risks of failure during business crises.

A big firm with extensive capital at its disposal could afford a research staff; technical improvements could be produced more regularly, and the dependence on competition for occasional inventions could be reduced. A large professional sales force decreased the hazards of the market. Greater size allowed the integration of more operations to assure supplies and to eliminate dependence on any single product for profits. Finally, a sufficiently large firm could have direct control of much of its market. It could partially dictate terms to its buyers rather than rely on the forces of supply and demand, which were difficult to predict and control.

By the 1890s well over half the labor force in Germany, Britain, and Belgium was employed in firms with more than twenty workers. By 1910, 88 percent of Russian manufacturing labor worked in firms with more than fifty employees. Everywhere the number of large companies increased at a far faster rate than did the number of small enterprises. The trend of expansion touched virtually every industry, but the most significant development was the giant firm. In an extreme example of size, the German electrical industry was dominated by just two firms, the *Allgemeine Elektrizitäts Gesellschaft* and the Siemens concern, which controlled over 90 percent of German production and had important international links as well. Each firm could set the terms for many leading buyers on the strength of its great size; beyond this, the firms made agreements with each other on market allocation, which made price fixing even simpler. In the German chemical industry the I. G. Farben company possessed a tremendous influence over its own sales, because of its size alone. Few firms approached outright monopoly, even in Germany; and the concentration of German industry was greater than that of Britain or France. Nevertheless, the trend was general. The steady growth of firm size allowed the utilization of more massive and efficient equipment. It also allowed a greater possibility for profits, even aside from efficiency, by permitting greater control of research, supplies, sales, and position in the market.

The development of huge firms was significant in itself. The position of labor in such firms inevitably differed from the situation in small factories. New techniques of management had to be devised to administer the giants. Equally important, the large firm required new methods of finance. These methods altered the nature of industrial ownership and increasingly encouraged the formation of still larger economic units.

A few firms grew large and wealthy by judiciously plowing profits back into the business. Old metallurgical companies such as Le Creusot in France expanded and developed a variety of new operations without changing their fundamental structure of family ownership. Even there dependence on bank loans increased, and the prodigious expansion of industrial banking aided capital formation of all sorts. With the rise of railroads and heavy industry, the association of the financial power of banks with industry became absolutely essential. During the 1850s Napoleon III encouraged the *Crédit mobilier* as an investment bank to support the development of ports, railroads, and urban clearance. The bank ultimately failed, but in the next decade similar banking enterprises, such as *Crédit lyonnais*, were formed to channel funds into industry. In the German areas the association of banks and industry was even closer. The Vienna *Kredit Anstalt* was formed in 1856 specifically to lend to industry. The German Darmstadter Bank and *Diskontogesellschaft* arose in the same decade, along with a number of less solid banks that collapsed after contributing to a speculative mania. Other investment banks, such as the Deutsche and the Dresdener, arose in the prosperous period of the early 1870s, when the French war indemnity was filling German coffers. The Dresdener Bank developed close ties with the Krupp industrial complex and served as a major source of Krupp's funds. In Germany particularly, but to some extent everywhere, industrial investment banks greatly increased the amount of capital available and thereby promoted the development of larger firms.

The most important source of funds for large enterprises came, however, from the growing use of the corporate form. Banks might contribute to stock purchases, but funds could be drawn from an even broader base, from hundreds and sometimes thousands of investors, large and small. Corporations spread rapidly in every area toward the end of the century, and the rate of corporate formation increased as well. In France corporations required special authorization from the government until 1867, when a change in law encouraged a first burst of corporate growth; but the slow pace of French industrial advance restricted the number of corporations until the 1890s. By then the expansion of French heavy industry required massive financial support and so required extensive use of the corporate form. During the 1890s up to a thousand corporations were formed every year in France. Rates of corporate formation in Germany and elsewhere were rising in the same period, although Great Britain maintained a lead in the sheer number of corporations.

The use of corporate forms greatly increased the size possible for an individual enterprise, either new or old, by extending the amount of capital available. It also changed the nature of ownership, reducing personal control over a firm and substituting divided and substantially anonymous ownership and responsibility. Along with investment banking, the growth of corporate organization tied industry to essentially novel financial forms. This development was almost as important as the growth of the sheer size of firms.

Capping the growth of big business was a search for organizational forms that could bridge the gap even among giant firms. Lobbying associations were formed, such as the *Comité des forges* in France, to coordinate the relations between a major industry and the government. More important, cartels were developed to restrict or eliminate competition within an industry. The *Stahlwerkverband* in Germany, created in the 1890s as a successor to several smaller steel cartels, allocated set market quotas on some goods for each member of the association and fixed limits on all other types of production. In the 1890s a cartel was established among coal producers in the Rhineland–Westphalia region. Each company had votes in the cartel proportionate to its output, and a central commission was established to set production quotas and to determine prices. By 1900 there were three hundred cartels in Germany, and many more were created before World War I. A similar, if less intense, movement developed in Britain, Russia, and elsewhere.

Many governments favored cartels as a means of providing more rational direction to industry. Big investment banks encouraged them; many cartels and even trusts were formed by banks that owned shares in several concerns in an industry. Most important, however, the cartels developed because manufacturers increasingly realized that they could control market conditions through association as they never could in isolation. The movement began in Germany as a result of the depression of the 1870s, which provided a clear motive to seek more rational organization in industry. It was taken up almost exclusively in industries dominated by large firms; hence cartels were common in coal, steel, and chemicals but literally unknown in textiles. Large firms could make contacts easily because of the small number of units in the industry. Their owners recognized the value of size and coordination and were not committed to a system of family control and mutual rivalry. Increasingly, the principal branches of factory industry were dominated by a small number of giant firms with various mutual links. Coordination and control rather than competition provided the motive force for much of the economic activity within most industrialized countries.

Rationalization and concentration continued steadily during the 1920s and 1930s; World War I heightened the trend, if anything. Giant new combines arose, such as the *Vereinigte Stahlwerke,* which controlled almost half of the German steel industry. The role of industrial investment banks increased. Cartels proliferated, some on an international basis.

Big Business: Some General Social Effects

The rise of big business was obviously important for the working class. Growing firms needed new workers, often in tasks requiring considerable strength and skill. Reduction of competitive pressure gave many large firms greater margin for increasing wages and other benefits to their workers. With the great growth of heavy industry up to 1900, those same firms had to offer better conditions to attract the quality of labor they required. Big firms were normally inclined to extend the paternalistic approach to labor that had been suggested earlier. They liked to tie workers to the company by elaborate housing programs and pension schemes. They hoped thus to reduce protest, for big industrialists were particularly angered by any effort at interference from labor. They also hoped to reduce costs, for benefit programs were often cheaper than the equivalent improvements in living standards through higher wages, given the economies of scale in company housing; paternalism, which maintained a rather traditional view of what workers were and deserved, meshed with the rationalizing mentality.

At the same time the development of large units of employment reduced any opportunity for personal contact between workers and owners. It was easier for workers to see the owners as enemies than it had been in the days when the character and even the hard work of owners had been personally known. The huge profits of big corporations invited attack in the hope of obtaining a larger share for labor. Yet workers became increasingly accustomed to large organization. They learned to abide by certain rules; they learned to operate as part of a mass of fellow workers. Many of the causes of new unions and other groups among factory labor can be directly attributed to experiences in huge enterprises that encouraged both the ability and the motivation of workers to take action to improve their lot. But the power of the giant firms was such that successful action would be difficult if the firms chose to resist. The resultant conflict contributed to the rising tide of social tension before World War I.

Big business created new groups of employees during this period. Huge firms, directed by professional managers, required large bureaucracies and growing numbers of clerks. In commerce, large enterprises required clerks and salespeople. A new middle class was being formed that neither owned property nor worked as manual labor and whose members were salaried, but did not work with their hands. This new class was one of the most important social results of the development of large economic units dependent on masses of paperwork for their successful administration.

For the industrialists and bankers, the most obvious result of the new business structure was a great increase in profits. Larger enterprises and larger investments permitted an unprecedented concentration of profits. With the reduction of competitive pressure, the bulk of the vast new wealth industry was creating went to the owners of big business. Wages rose, to be sure, but not nearly so rapidly as production increased. During the period 1870–1900 the workers' share in the gross national product declined by 26 percent in Britain and by 55 percent in Germany. But the owners of industry had larger incomes than ever before. Their investments rose; giant firms became ever more gigantic. And their standard of living became more luxurious. The upper middle class attained the highest level of material prosperity it had ever known.

Other members of the middle class were disturbed by the trends toward concentration and impersonal ownership. They harked back to the pioneering days of industry, when a man could be personally associated with every phase of his enterprise, when his economic effort had a direct relation to his family. Ironically, small businesses steadily increased in number. Between 1882 and 1895 shops employing one to five people grew 24 percent in Germany, and companies with six to ten workers increased 66.6 percent. And this was the famous center of big business. After 1900 the rate of small business formation slowed; in England the number of firms actually began to decline in manufacturing by 1906. But still the small owner held on. In Germany there were still as many master artisans in 1926 (about 1.5 million) as in 1895, and many were organized in voluntary guilds. Small electric motors and the rise of new goods that could be serviced by small units—the bicycle repair shop, the automobile parts manufacturer—kept the form alive even in new fields. Some small owners hoped to expand and rise into the central or upper reaches of the middle class. But more maintained a more traditionalist mentality, as the existence of guilds in central Europe suggests. Some were directly threatened by big business, for the growth of small firms concealed many individual failures. Others realized that small firms were no longer proliferating rapidly enough to provide for more than one son; a large family would have to find something else for many of its children to do. The sense of insecurity was heightened beyond any actual displacement, for the relative decline in importance of small ownership followed from a growing cleavage in the values businessmen professed. Modest ambition and direct family control now clashed with a rationalizing mentality in a battle that was unequal from the first. It might have been kinder had small businesses been killed outright, but the industrialization process had never been kind to traditionalists. A confrontation was brewing that could prove to be just as important as the obvious conflict between business and labor.

The growth of formal organizations, though most striking in the area of big business, extended to many other aspects of European life from the late nineteenth century onward. Trade unions and expanding schools provided other settings for impersonal organization. So did the growing use of hospitals, converting, under the impact of improved sanitary procedures and crowded urban housing that complicated home care for the sick, to places where people might voluntarily go to seek treatment. No longer the last alternative for poor people about to die, hospitals nevertheless offered yet another case of extensive institutions that intruded on intimate aspects of ordinary life.

Economic Redefinitions

The economic emphasis of the first phase of industrialization was on production, for in a poor society increasing the goods available was essential for any further change. Now, as production continued to expand, the emphasis shifted to problems of distribution. Here was the third great structural shift that redirected European society after about 1870.

In every branch of manufacturing there were more goods to dispose of than ever before. World pig-iron production tripled between 1870 and 1900. French output of iron and steel expanded more than fourfold between 1890 and 1913. Coal output soared in the last three decades of the century, until affected by the growing use of oil. Britain doubled its already massive production, France tripled its production, and Germany raised its production fifteen times. New needs for acids, dyes, fertilizers, and explosives caused a rapid boom in chemical production. Germany's output of sulphuric acid increased three hundred times by the end of the century. Expansion of older areas of production and the addition of new branches created an unprecedented, though not uninterrupted, industrial boom during the latter part of the nineteenth century.

Many new products were designed for individual consumers. The chemical industry began to discover new kinds of cloth. Novel products such as bicycles, telephones, and automobiles began to flood the market. Here was an extremely significant development, for the early Industrial Revolution had concentrated primarily on goods already in use. The nature and amount of these goods had changed with their mechanical production, as in the growing use of cotton cloth. The growth of general wealth and of technical knowledge now allowed the development of totally new consumer items. Some, such as automobiles, were reserved for the wealthier classes. Others, such as telephones and electrical lighting, were seldom purchased by the lower classes but affected their way of life as public telephones and lighting systems developed. Finally, some items, such as bicycles, spread to many workers directly.

The dislocations of World War I interrupted the surge in production but only for a time. The French economy continued a substantial boom. Growth in Britain and Germany was slower, but even here new goods received wide currency. The ownership of radios, for example, spread well into the middle class. There were new fibers for clothing, new cosmetics; the list of consumer items grew increasingly long.

The expansion of industrial and also agricultural production spurred new developments in marketing and transportation. Railroads were extended. Western and central Europe, having completed the development of trunk lines, began to concentrate on local lines. The speed and capacity of railroad transport were brought to increasing numbers of small towns and even villages, expanding both market opportunities and social contacts for rural residents. In eastern and southern Europe trunk lines were now built; the virtual completion of the trans-Siberian railroad in the 1890s was the most notable example of the spread of railroad transport to the European hinterland and beyond. Oceanic shipping expanded greatly in the same period. Metal steam-driven ships dominated ocean transportation for the first time, raising the capacity and speed of shipping. The development of refrigeration allowed perishable items to be sent long distances. Oceanic cables and, late in the century, the radio combined with new shipping to allow increasing international trade. Exports and imports rose massively. European business sought, and often found, new markets in all parts of the world. Even within cities, transportation facilities increased greatly. Electric subways and trams speeded the movement of people. Larger trucking companies and the growing use of gasoline-powered trucks and cabs transformed urban transportation.

New marketing methods followed naturally from the increase of production and the expansion of transportation and communication facilities. Large wholesaling firms arose to supply major cities with consumer products, including foodstuffs. Department stores and even chain stores played a growing role in retailing. Expansion of business structure was a vital part of commerce as well as of industry. Advertising increased, particularly in the mass press, as a means of speeding the circulation of goods. Newspapers and other publications were filled with large, presumably eye-catching notices.

Expanding production obviously produced new wealth. New marketing techniques depended on this wealth, for increasingly industry required a mass market above the subsistence level. Despite growing inequalities, average wages rose significantly during the latter part of the nineteenth century. During much of the period wage increases were accompanied by a drop in prices. Between 1870 and 1914, for example, the wages in French industry rose 14 percent and prices dropped by the same amount; the result was a major expansion of purchasing power. The cost of housing continued to mount because cities remained crowded, but the declining prices of food and clothing more than compensated for this change.

In Britain real wages rose by a third between 1850 and 1875; between 1870 and 1900 they rose 45 percent. German real wages increased 30 percent in the last three decades of the century; French wages rose 33 percent, and Swedish workers benefited by a 75 percent gain. The expansion of purchasing power for workers was a general phenomenon even in Russia, where industrialization was just beginning; major differences in standards of living remained, of course, and the older industrial countries offered far higher standards than did newer arrivals such as Germany.

For the first time in human history real poverty, life on the margins of subsistence, was a minority phenomenon in the industrial regions. In Britain only a third or less of the population lived really near subsistence by 1900; a century before, two-thirds had done so. Wealth remained unevenly distributed; in fact, disparities between the middle and lower classes increased as the profits of industry soared. Nevertheless, the masses had gained.

The rise in real wages was translated into a number of improvements in living standards for the lower classes in the countryside and particularly in the cities. Diets became more varied. Consumption of starches tended to stabilize, and the quality of starch improved, especially through the growing use of wheat for bread. Milk and milk products came into greater use. In France the consumption of butter rose 50 percent between 1870 and 1884. Meat consumption increased notably. In Britain meat consumption per person rose 20 percent between 1880 and 1900, whereas the rate of bread consumption remained unchanged. Germans bought an average of 59 pounds of meat per person in 1873; by 1912 they were buying 105 pounds per person per year. The consumption of tobacco, tea, coffee, and sugar increased. British consumption of sugar rose 33 percent between 1880 and 1900, and Germans tripled their average consumption (from 12 pounds to 34 pounds per person) between 1870 and 1907. The use of drinks such as beer increased; German consumption of beer rose from 78 liters per person per year in 1872 to 123 liters in 1900. There were still cases of grossly inadequate nutrition, particularly among some agricultural workers and the large group of irregularly employed in the major cities. Class differences were reflected in the fact that, as late as 1930, the average British male worker was 2 to 4 inches shorter than his middle-class counterpart. For the majority of the lower classes, however, diets were above the levels of mere subsistence. This was an important precondition for the new vigor that elements of the lower classes showed in many aspects of behavior.

With rising wages and declining food prices, the masses could devote less of their budget to food and still purchase more and better food than ever before. By the 1890s in France only about 60 percent of the average budget was used for food instead of the previous 75 percent. The amount and stylishness of clothing reflected the greater resources that the masses could devote to their attire. Furthermore, prices of shoes and clothing fell rapidly. Cotton goods in France cost 50 percent less in 1896 than they had in 1873. By the late nineteenth century it was virtually impossible to determine a person's exact station by his or her clothing. The steady democratization of costume, though by no means complete, was an obvious symptom of the rising purchasing power of the masses.

Housing for the masses was still cramped and expensive after 1870, especially in the larger cities. An increasing portion of the budget had to be devoted to rents, but the teeming tenements of the early industrial period vanished from the most advanced industrial nations. In Prussia over 6 percent of the families still had only one room, but in Britain this was true for only 1.6 percent of all families; indeed 94 percent had three rooms or more. Clearly, housing construction had begun to catch up with the worst needs of the new cities even though rents rose.

Even with all the significant gains in food, clothing, and shelter the lower classes increasingly had money left over for other expenses. Purchases of newspapers and inexpensive novels became common among the masses. Many workers could now pay union dues and contribute a portion of their wage to insurance programs. Popular theaters and music halls arose in the cities to attract the masses; after 1900 moving pictures provided entertainment as well. Sports events, such as soccer football, became commercialized in this period because the urban masses could afford tickets. Railroads offered Sunday excursions for a clientele drawn from the lower classes, and hundreds of thousands of workers and clerks in western Europe bought bicycles, the most expensive consumer good not related to basic needs that had ever been available to the masses. At the same time small savings accounts increased rapidly, and new facilities such as postal savings systems were established to handle them.

The rising average wealth of the masses undoubtedly brightened the lives of most people. The increasing opportunities for diversion were a major new element for the masses in the cities. With more wealth, there was less chance of absolute economic disaster, even during a depression. Savings accounts and sometimes insurance programs provided some protection against illness and old age. There was still great economic insecurity but no longer so many risks of absolute destitution. Better housing and food promoted noticeable improvements in health. This was the period, after all, in which declining mortality rates provided the bulk of the continued expansion of population in western Europe. Increasing numbers of people began to think in terms of improving their health, buying new medicines, and consulting doctors when sick; traditional resignation toward illness declined.

Finally, the fairly steady increase in well-being encouraged a new interest in material enjoyments among the European masses. The masses, particularly in the cities, began to expect further improvements in the standard of living. They developed a concern for new technical devices that would make their lives more pleasant. They were gradually affected by the same attachment to material and technical progress that the middle class had developed earlier. The popular press, even the union movement, both encouraged and reflected this attachment. However, the rising standard of living, significant though it was, did not take the European masses into an era of abundance. A substantial minority remained desperately poor. Many others had only a small part of their budget free for expenditures beyond the necessities. The conflict between rising expectations and continued limitations on means was to affect both social and economic developments for many decades.

A certain margin, however modest and insecure, now characterized the economic life of most social groups, in contrast to the predominant scarcity of the early industrial decades. Improvements in living standards and the larger shift in economic emphasis from concern for production to a greater need to arrange for distribution generated a new climate for popular culture. The work-first attitudes of dominant elements in the early industrial period shifted now to tolerance, then active promotion of certain leisure interests. The result was an important range of innovations that created new opportunities and new stresses alike.

Weaknesses in the Economic Structure

The new economic trends brought with them certain recurrent difficulties, as opportunities for production were not matched by consistent and comparable opportunities for sale. Ongoing changes in technology and the organization of work, plus the growing list of major industrial nations, assured steady expansion of output. Despite innovations in sales and advertising, buying power did not consistently keep up. Social structure, and particularly the distribution of income, did not hold pace with the explosive power of the economy.

In the first place, the new demographic structure meant that population growth no longer provided the rapid and almost automatic extension of the internal market that had existed during the earlier period of the Industrial Revolution. Furthermore, important elements of the existing population were severely limited in their ability to buy. Despite rising wages workers could not increase their purchases as rapidly as production was rising. At the same time, the income of agricultural producers was relatively stagnant. Agricultural prices were falling as competition from fertile new regions increasingly pressed farmers. The price drop was partially compensated by major improvements in agricultural equipment and methods during the period, but the incomes of peasants and other landowners did not rise significantly. It was difficult, then, to extend the sales of industrial products among this group. Some new tools and machines were sold because farmers often went into debt to try to improve their production. But again, there was no increase in buying power comparable to the rise in industrial output.

In fact, the only major social group whose income was growing at a huge rate was the business community. Businesspeople increased both their consumer and investor purchases during the period. However, they did not spend their money as rapidly as production rose, for they were not pressed by primary needs and were therefore inclined to hold much of their income for a time before deciding to spend. The wealth of Europe as a whole was rising rapidly, but its distribution was such that the principal gains in purchasing power fell to groups that spent rather slowly. Europe had developed the capacity for massive production but had not yet made the change to a mass-consumption economy.

The disparity between production and market was by no means constant. Utilization of new export opportunities, the high rate of investment in new productive facilities, and the expansion of purchasing power allowed a rapid increase in sales. However, there were periods of slump even before 1900. Each of the last three decades in the century saw several years of depression in most areas. The crisis of the 1870s was particularly severe because it came after a period of great confidence induced by the building of basic railroad lines and other outlets for heavy industry.

The slumps of this period were new in some respects, reflecting the novelty of industrial development. They were triggered not by agricultural failures but by financial crises. The increasing investment of banks and private individuals in stocks could create an artificial speculative mood. The values of stocks soared not because of any corresponding increase in the possibilities of production and sales but because of the rising demand for the stocks themselves. Eventually the speculative bubble burst, sometimes through the failure of a major firm or even a bank. Investors then became more cautious and funds for further investment harder to obtain. Firms producing capital goods, which depended on investment for their sales, would be forced to reduce their production and employment. This would affect other industries in turn, as the purchasing power of workers and others declined, and the spiral of depression would take its course.

Although levels of unemployment rose during every crisis, suffering among workers was not as intense as it was in earlier depressions. More workers had some savings, and they were not plagued by a concomitant rise in agricultural prices. The inevitable fall in industrial prices made life easier as well. Nevertheless, living standards did decline during the major slumps. And many depressions, such as that of the 1870s, lasted for several years. If crises were not as intense as they had been before, they were more prolonged. Only gradually would the level of investment be built up again as capitalists tried to dispose of their funds; only gradually would sales recover, spurred by lower industrial prices.

The frequency and duration of economic crises contributed an important symptom of the weakness of the industrial market. It was far easier to invest in industry and produce industrial goods than it was to find corresponding sales opportunities. The growth both of investment and of production continued at a high rate during the period as a whole. Tremendous boom periods, such as much of the 1890s, compensated for periods of difficulty. Nevertheless, a certain structural imbalance in the economy was not removed.

Hence, even the industrialists showed some concern about the tightness of the market for industrial products. Well before 1900 it was clear that many felt international competition was increasing and economic activity was becoming more difficult. The feeling of growing pressure was deliberately exaggerated to obtain public support, but there was real and growing worry. Industrialists and their lobbying associations began to demand new political measures to protest existing markets and promote other sales. They sought tariff protection with greater insistence than ever before. In Germany groups such as the German Industrialists' Union joined hands with protectionist Junkers to press for tariffs on both agricultural and heavy industrial goods. Their greatest success came with the Bülow tariff of 1902, which put a 25 percent duty on many food and metal products. France passed a high tariff in the 1890s, and Russia, Italy, and most other countries increased or established high levels of protection. Only Great Britain resisted the new wave of economic protectionism until after World War I, despite the growing demands of British industrialists for high tariffs. There was a general desire to mark off national economies and protect the internal market, but in practice tariffs often worsened the situation by making exports more difficult. The pressure for tariffs, however irrational, was symptomatic of the growing anxieties for the future that prevailed among the captains of industry.

The owners of industry urged other panaceas for their marketing problems. Industrialist groups were among the principal promoters of imperial expansion. They argued that colonies would provide both protected sources of, raw materials and great markets for finished goods. These arguments were largely incorrect. Some raw materials were drawn from the new colonies, and certain firms profited hugely from empire. Most of the colonies cost more than they earned, however, and almost none provided adequate markets. Trade continued to be most active among industrial countries rather than between an industrial nation and a poor, semipastoral colony. Nevertheless, the intensity of the desire to find secure supplies and markets was another indication of the changing attitudes of industrialists.

Certain industrial groups were also active in promoting increased military expenditures by their governments. This was another, and very realistic, effort to obtain new markets for goods, particularly the products of heavy industry. In Germany owners of metallurgical firms joined with military leaders in the Navy League in a successful effort to stir up public support for the creation of a large navy that would both reflect Germany's national greatness and use an encouraging amount of iron and steel.

After 1900 the symptoms of economic imbalance became more pronounced. Industrial production faltered, as we have already seen in the case of mining. There were two recessions, in 1901–1902 and 1908–1909; though not particularly severe, they caused high unemployment levels. More novel was a nagging inflation that began with the turn of the century. New sources of gold, in South Africa, helped raise prices, but more than this was involved. High tariffs pushed food costs up. Big business, increasingly able to manipulate markets, could also help keep price changes ate up the gains. In Britain, real wages actually fell by about 4 percent before World War I. Profits continued to rise significantly because of the growing vigor of big business. But high profits about 4 percent before World War I. Profits continued to rise significantly because of the growing vigor of big business. But high profits would not help sales as much as mass purchasing power, and this was now challenged.

World War I brought the inflationary spiral to incredible heights. The new pressures were based on governments' printing of new money and extensive borrowing during the war. In essence this increased the demand for goods without any corresponding improvement in the ability to produce goods. Held down by government controls during the war itself, prices nevertheless doubled or tripled in some countries by 1918. Thereafter, except in Britain, which deflated prices by returning to the gold standard, inflation spread like wildfire.

In Austria the cost of living was 2,645 times higher in July 1922 than it had been in 1914. In Germany the inflation of the early 1920s made money virtually valueless as prices rose to astronomical heights. The process was stopped only in 1924 when the government set the mark at a more realistic, but far lower, level than ever before. In France inflation later in the decade was ended only in 1928 by pegging the franc at a quarter of its previous value. Inflationary pressures of this sort affected most groups. Some elements of the working class suffered, for their wages rose less rapidly than prices. Unions were massively damaged as their treasuries were depleted both by the inflation and by the subsequent government devaluation of money. Members of the middle and lower middle classes now suffered even more. A few, to be sure, seized on the inflation as a chance to borrow money cheaply for speculative investment, but the larger element that relied on savings saw their holdings virtually wiped out. This encouraged an interest in enjoyment rather than in saving. But the price rises during the war itself, the new taxes imposed by many governments, and the postwar inflation severely reduced opportunities to spend. The loss of savings was also a blow to the confidence, to the very sense of identity, of many in the middle class, which relied on property ownership to provide wealth and status. A new fearfulness arose in the class, which could be translated into active discontent. The class did not lose its esteem for property and its sense of separate status, but it recognized that these values were increasingly threatened by the workings of the economy itself.

Production continued to increase in most countries, though wartime disruption limited gains in some areas. Britain found it hard to recapture export markets that had been lost to the United States or Japan during the war. Germany suffered from the loss of key resource areas. Austria and Czechoslovakia, industrial states, were now cut off from areas like Hungary, their traditional agricultural hinterland. New European boundaries, drawn with no thought to economics, hampered sensible development. Along with inflation itself, this encouraged much unsound investment. Many new business combinations, particularly in Germany, were formed for their speculative possibilities, their potential drawing power for investments, rather than for any improvements they would make in production or distribution. New promoters such as Hugo Stinnes found it easy and profitable to buy firms of extraordinary diversity as vehicles for attracting speculative investments. The rapid price rise of the early 1920s made it easy to borrow with the expectation that the sum would be less valuable when the time for repayment came. Furthermore, massive American capital was available for speculative investment, particularly in Germany, Austria, and the new states of eastern Europe. These funds were not always directed to projects with real productive possibilities (some went into building fancy townhalls), but this simply heightened the speculative spiral. Shaky investments could be bolstered only by further investments, which would raise the value of a stock whether production possibilities were good or not. The result was an economic structure highly vulnerable to shock. When American capital was withdrawn after the 1929 financial crash and when the faith of European investors in their own holdings was correspondingly reduced, collapse of the speculative bubble was inevitable.

For long before this, it had become increasingly difficult to market goods. Wartime interruption of established trade added to the problem. By the mid-1920s areas that produced raw materials entered a severe depression; this was true of agricultural regions in Europe, such as the Balkans, but also of the colonial territories. Raw materials were being issued more rapidly than industrial production rose; so their prices fell, which in turn reduced the ability of these areas to buy industrial goods. These new developments were added to the older weaknesses of the mature industrial economy. Agricultural incomes remained low as competition reached new levels. Elements of the working class suffered from unemployment or poor wages, particularly in the older industries. The further reduction of population growth removed yet another possible market. Tariff barriers, which even England now adopted, continued to distort export opportunities.

With this disparity between industrial capacity and the possibilities of sales, production on the Continent as a whole increased only 1 percent a year after 1923, in contrast to a 3 percent annual rise before 1913. In a few countries, such as Germany, the speculative boom created a façade of prosperity, but it was highly vulnerable. With the collapse of export possibilities after 1928, and then with the financial crash in the United States and the withdrawal of American capital, Europe entered, inexorably, a period of unprecedented economic depression. The depression was the same type as those before World War I, but much worse than any of its predecessors.

The depression touched every aspect of economic life. It represented a financial crisis. Many banks closed, and credit was restricted; coming on the heels of inflation, faith in money and in financial institutions was severely shaken. Sales fell off sharply even with massive reductions in prices. As a result, production tumbled; German production had fallen 39 percent by 1932. Profits declined, wages fell, and unemployment increased tremendously. All major social classes suffered. Members of the middle class were hit by declining profits and by loss of stock investments. Their morale was shaken by the mere fact of depression; confidence and optimism about the economic system were reduced. Many managers and recent university graduates suffered from unemployment or were forced to take jobs beneath their station. The lower middle class, similarly, lost many jobs. Peasants were able to sell fewer agricultural goods because of the decline in urban income, so their earnings were reduced still further. But it was the working class that bore the brunt of unemployment and loss of income. In Britain 22 percent of the workers who had some social insurance were unemployed by 1932. Over six million people in Germany and 850,000 in France, not exclusively workers, were out of work. This massive unemployment made recovery from the depression difficult, because it proved hard to stimulate sufficient demand to set the economy in motion once more. And the fact or fear of unemployment greatly weakened public morale. The unemployed survived on some insurance payments and on charity, but they could do no more than survive. Consumption levels fell drastically. Prolonged joblessness reduced many to apathy and stirred others, including those with jobs who feared unemployment for themselves, to new anger.

European economies recovered only slowly and partially from the crisis. The depth of the depression was reached in 1932–1933, although France experienced its trough a bit later. Production after this low point rose; by 1938 the British economy was turning out more goods than ever before. Yet even then more than 1.5 million were still unemployed. France did not manage to recover its previous levels of production or employment before World War II. Germany under Hitler did restore full employment and greatly increased production, largely through state programs of investment, military purchasing, and labor service. Wages, however, did not rise to their earlier levels.

The Major Economic Forces

The culmination of the mature industrial period in massive global depression should not obscure the diversity of overall economic developments between 1870 and 1940. Improving living standards and the rise of mass leisure generated a host of positive changes. Other shifts required more complex adjustments. The new round of technological change challenged established habits, in a wider array of jobs than ever before. The growth of impersonal organization created new power alignments and established a complex tension between values of individualism and an increasingly bureaucratized environment at work. There was irony in the fact that growing prosperity, plus shifts in family values, allowed many German workers to provide separate bedrooms for their children by the 1880s—thus promoting fuller self-definition for the children involved—precisely as the typical workplace came under the sway of efficiency engineers, trained to organize the labor force as it would organize equipment. The new version of the industrial economy could function when greased by growing prosperity, though it yielded protest aplenty, but it made no sense at all when underlying imbalances brought a return of mass impoverishment.

Political Change

The Rise of Democracy

The final ingredient of the basic structure of European society between 1870–1940 involved the emergence of new relationships between state and citizen. In one sense, political changes were less fundamental than they had been in the late eighteenth and early nineteenth centuries: nothing altered the structure of society as had the legal abolition of manorialism and the guilds. The state, however, began to interact with society as never before on a regular basis. There was a steady expansion of government functions. This exposed people to another source of impersonal organization but also increased reliance on the state in key respects. At the same time, new political rights increased interest in the political process. Popular grievances were now routinely brought into the political arena, and the direction a group's politics took indicated a great deal about its basic values. In periods of economic collapse, when it became clear that government functions had not changed to match new expectations, politics threatened to become polarized between groups that wanted to use the state to turn back to an earlier society and those that wanted to press forward.

The revolution of 1848 had extended the vote to all males in France and, temporarily, to all males in Germany. French voters had little real choice, however, during most of the Second Empire. Only in the 1860s was there any real opportunity to vote against official candidates; with the establishment of the Third Republic during the 1870s the choice became more free. The new German Empire, created in 1871, granted universal suffrage for the lower house of the national parliament. Great Britain extended the vote to urban workers in 1867 and to most other males in 1884. Belgium established universal male suffrage in 1892. Italy extended the vote in 1882 and made it universal for males in 1912; Austria established universal male suffrage in 1907. Finland and Sweden even allowed women to vote in the 1900s. Britain and Germany did so after World War I. By this time all industrial countries had parliaments with at least one house elected by universal suffrage.

Furthermore, the powers of elected parliaments tended to increase, and parliamentary bodies were established in many nations where no regular instrument of popular representation had existed before. In 1911 the British House of Lords was stripped of the right to veto legislation, fully establishing the House of Commons as the basic authority in British government. The formation of the Third Republic during the 1870s established the supremacy of the French parliament over the executive branch. Elsewhere parliaments were less powerful. In Germany, for example, the functions of the elected Reichstag were severely limited, and Prussia, the leading German state, retained a class voting system for its own legislature until 1918. Even in Germany, however, the government paid careful heed to the political composition of parliament, and the masses received increasing attention. They did not rule, but they did not rule in other countries either. It remained generally true, except in Spain and eastern Europe, that the masses gained a regular political voice for the first time during this period; the spread of democratic parliamentary structures was the basis for that voice.

Other reforms promoted effective mass political power. Ballots were made secret in most countries, making it less easy to control votes. Parliamentary representatives began to receive pay, so poor men could serve. By the 1870s most parliaments contained a small number of representatives of working-class origin.

Conservative-liberal rivalries prompted both aristocrats and middle-class politicians to broaden the vote in the hope of finding support among the masses. Lower elements of the middle class as well as workers actively supported voting reforms as a means of obtaining political rights for themselves and others. Mass agitation preceded belated democratizing suffrage reforms in Italy, Belgium, and Austria around 1900.

There was often, nevertheless, a conspicuous lag between the extension of suffrage and the development of any clear new political trends. The masses were not accustomed to the vote, and political rights remained meaningless for many. Initial voter participation in German elections was low. Up to a third of all British adult males were excluded from the vote, even after 1884, because of residence requirements; they moved about too often, yet they showed few signs of resenting their deprivations. Those in the lower classes who did vote normally turned first to established political parties and leaders. In France the crisis of the Franco-Prussian War caused many peasants to support local landlords in the election of 1871; the result was a royalist parliament. In Germany democracy caused little change in the political spectrum for a decade. Only in eastern Europe, where the vote was extended amid early industrial conditions and intense rural population pressure, did new political patterns emerge quickly; during the 1920s a host of peasant parties arose to seek land reform to benefit the rural masses.

Even in western Europe, however, universal suffrage had its impact on established political parties. By the 1880s the professional politician had begun to emerge. Older groups, such as aristocrats or university professors—the "honorable people" of preindustrial society—began to drop out of parliamentary life. Only lawyers retained their place, for democratic politics meant active campaigning, talking to the people, raising campaign funds. So a new group began to enter political life, often as a means of mobility, for parliamentary service paid money, and there were opportunities for profitable contacts beyond this. Ideologically, too, the major political currents had to adapt. Conservative parties by the 1880s had begun to beat the drums of nationalism, even though this was historically a middle-class tradition. Because conservatives wanted no major changes in the social structure, they converted to a cause that might rouse the passions of the masses, and with considerable success. Increasingly, conservatism survived by appealing to, and promoting, nationalist loyalties.

Middle-class parties were also altered by the need to obtain mass backing. Liberal politicians obtained the support of many elements of the lower middle class, artisanry, and even the working class by offering support for the extension of free education to the masses and many important measures of industrial legislation and social welfare. The parties were still committed to the protection of middle-class economic and political interests, and on the whole liberal parties found it difficult to win or retain mass support.

The most distinctive result of the new political power and consciousness of the masses was the rise of the socialist parties, a new political force that represented the interests of growing segments of the working class. The socialist parties also appealed to some members of the lower middle class and to professional groups such as teachers. The rise of socialism did not follow immediately from the extension of the suffrage, for socialist leaders were not always ready to take advantage of the new opportunities, and the industrial workers were certainly not prepared for such a novel use of their new political rights. In Britain the Labour party developed real strength only after World War I, although it had eighty representatives in parliament after 1906; the Liberal party continued to win the support of most workers before the war. German socialist activity began in the 1860s but was slow to attract voters until the 1890s, when it regularly polled about 1.5 million votes. By 1913 the party received 4 million votes and had 110 deputies in the Reichstag; it was the largest single party in Germany and the strongest socialist party in the world. French socialists, split into several groups, had forty-nine representatives in parliament as early as 1883 and about a hundred by 1913; a socialist had even entered the cabinet in 1899. Socialist parties in Italy and Austria remained smaller because the laboring class was smaller and gained the right to vote only after 1900. Even on the basis of middle-class support, socialists gained importance in parliament, only to become the largest single party once universal suffrage was extended.

Mass Education

The spread of political democracy formed the most notable new link between the masses and government, but it was not the only one. Impressed by the power of Prussia's conscript armies, most Continental governments instituted systems of universal military conscription during this period. By the 1900s most healthy young men of all classes spent two, sometimes three years in military service. This service gave the lower classes experience in discipline and organization and provided important training in national loyalty. Many people, torn from village attachment, learned what the nation meant for the first time, as they were sent to serve in a different region or even to battle Africans or Asians as Europe's colonies expanded. The Russian army even taught its recruits to read and write. Everywhere military service provided new experiences for many individuals and tended to standardize certain habits regardless of class or region. Particularly for the peasantry, it loosened the force of localism and tradition. Just as military life and tactics changed greatly because of the development of massive conscript armies, so the military experience became an important part of the lives of the masses.

In most countries governments took over functions of record keeping and even marriage from the clergy, usually during a time of church–state conflict. The state registered births, deaths, and weddings for all its citizens.

Most important, the state in all western and central European countries developed free universal public education systems during the period and required school attendance by every child. Education had, of course, been increasing steadily among the masses even before 1870; government expenditures on schools had risen. But many schools remained in the hands of private groups, particularly the churches, and the quality of education before 1870 had been spotty. Many teachers were ill trained, and there were only loose regulations for entry into the teaching profession. Many children who attended school retained little from their experience, often not even the ability to read, and many children could not attend at all because of long hours of work in the city or their distance from schools in the country. Less attention was paid to the education of girls than to that of boys. Most schools charged small fees, which deterred many parents. Literacy rates rose in industrial countries, but a large minority still could not read.

By about 1870 this situation began to change rapidly. Governments developed a great concern for the education of their citizens, as part of the growing consciousness of the importance of the masses. If the masses were to vote and serve in armies, they would have to be educated. It was vital to attach the loyalties of citizens and soldiers to their governments through education. Middle-class politicians supported educational improvements actively, and the middle class had increasing political influence in this period. The interests of industry also created a greater need for mass education. Industry required growing numbers of people who could read instructions and do simple calculations. It also increasingly needed a population that could read advertisements. Like the state itself, industry required some participation by masses of people who had a basic education. Finally, groups within the urban lower classes, such as artisan unions, pressed for the extension of public education. This was an old demand given greater force by the new political power of the masses.

For a variety of reasons, then, the nations of western and central Europe developed systems of universal primary education during the 1870s and 1880s. Even in Russia primary schools spread rapidly, and in the West schools were available for all. They were quickly made both free, as in Britain in 1891, and compulsory, for girls as well as boys. By 1900 most of western Europe required school attendance until fourteen years of age, and states were providing technical and secondary schools for later years of education. There was even a small movement to broaden university education. New provincial universities were established in France. University extension-course movements and institutions such as Britain's Ruskin College were set up in the hope of drawing talented workers to the universities. These movements had little effect except to extend university training to more members of the middle class. More important was the opening of secondary schools and universities to women. The expansion of higher educational facilities continued after World War I, though again without breaking down basic class barriers.

But mass primary education did have a major impact. It was often of poor quality still. Early schoolmasters frequently thought that disciplining the wild beasts produced by the lower classes was their most important function; not a few school riots broke out among working-class children. Peasants long remained reluctant to send children to school at all, for strangers had no right to interfere in their families and no advantage was seen in book learning. Gradually, however, education became accepted and the quality of schooling improved somewhat. The most important result was the extension of literacy to virtually the whole population of industrial countries. In 1900 two-thirds of the people in Spain and Portugal, half of those in Italy and Hungary, and a third of those in Austria still could not read. In all those countries education and literacy were spreading, but the development was too recent to have eliminated extensive illiteracy. Often it required a generation of schooling for a family really to absorb education to the point of being literate, and this generation had not passed in these areas. In the mature industrial societies, however, nearly universal literacy was obtained. Britain rose from 66 percent literacy in 1870 to 95 percent in 1900,

France rose from 60 percent to 85 percent, and Belgium from 55 percent to 86 percent. The masses could read, and they did so increasingly. Newspapers preferred by the masses attained circulations sometimes in the millions. Inexpensive books and other publications were widely read also. Mass education, simply by creating the ability to read, was fundamental to the new interests and activities of all the lower classes.

Mass education required significant changes in the organization and curricula of education, which in turn guided the cultural development of the lower classes. In the first place, the educational systems were increasingly standardized under the control of the state. Central bureaus developed uniform course programs, textbooks, and teachers' qualifications for use in all public schools throughout the nation in countries such as France, where the government was highly centralized, or throughout a state in a federal nation such as Germany. The French ministers of education boasted that at any given moment the same lesson was being taught all over France. Local dialects and other parochial interests were specifically fought. One French minister stated that "for the linguistic unity of France, Breton should disappear." Not only Breton, but also Basque, Flemish, Provençal, and, after World War I, Alsatian were attacked by the French school system. Local customs as well as languages were combatted by an educational program consciously designed to provide uniformity. Peasants, obviously, were most affected by these trends, as their localism had been more intense, but all classes were involved. An expectation of uniformity and some cultural guidance from above were among the most important products of the new public education.

The systems of public education also encouraged secularization of the attitudes of the masses and the reduction of religious influences. In most countries the period was marked by major conflict between church and state over the degree of religious influence permissible in the schools. In Germany education was largely secularized during the *Kulturkampf* of the 1870s. Priests and pastors were removed from the schools, and a number of Catholic teaching orders were suppressed, although Bavaria continued to give public support to church schools. Teaching orders, especially the Jesuits, were suppressed in many other countries during the 1860s and 1870s. Belgian Catholics lost a long and bitter political struggle with middle-class liberals for control of education. In France laws establishing public primary education in the 1880s banned priests from teaching in the public schools and closed all Jesuit schools. The state in most countries sought full control of the education of the masses, though some religious education did survive. The state was supported by large elements of the middle class who traditionally combined an interest in education with a dislike of religious influence. The result was an educational experience for the masses that was largely secular in all countries and entirely, even militantly, secular in some.

In place of predominant localism and religion in education, the new systems promoted useful patriotic subjects. Courses in civics and national history were intended to provide the knowledge necessary to a good citizen and particularly to encourage national loyalty. Systems of public education were one of the most important forces in the development of mass nationalism during this period. Training in the national language and literature supplemented the nationalist orientation of the social sciences.

Otherwise, the new education systems pointed toward economic unity. Mathematics, particularly arithmetic, and some technical and scientific training (including discussions of better agricultural methods, in the countryside) completed the typical curriculum. Girls were carefully taught domestic subjects, such as cooking, and were urged to plan for their adult roles as mother and spouse in the family.

Education had a number of diverse implications. By spreading literacy and breaking down tradition it opened the lower classes, male and female alike, to new kinds of propaganda. But only a minority — perhaps 5 percent of the adult working class, according to several surveys — developed intensive new reading interests. Mass politicians, including socialists, long found that speeches were essential to capture their constituency, for the oral tradition remained strong. Reading ability might lead others to seek self-improvement, by obtaining an office job instead of factory work; educational achievement began to be a factor in social stratification among the lower classes. This was not incompatible with radical politics, for an aspiring worker might be an ardent socialist, and indeed leadership ranks of socialist parties and trade unions served as a means of mobility for many bright young workers. But against these dynamic implications of education was the fact that few members of the lower classes had either desire or ability to rise very high on the educational ladder, for schooling was a foreign experience. And the nationalistic tone of the educational systems helped turn many people away from any effort to rock the boat; here was a new form of deference.

Welfare Reforms

The advent of democracy and the rise of socialist parties prodded governments to a series of social reforms. By the 1890s the burning political issue was known as the "social question," which meant, fundamentally, what to do to keep the urban masses quiet. This replaced the dominant constitutional issues of the early industrial decades. Attention to the social question involved some traditional methods: police forces became ever more adept at riot control, and in most industrial countries major unrest called out the army. But governments expanded their role in other directions to deflate some grievances. The result was an important expansion of state functions, a major element in the growing bureaucratization of society.

With the growing political consciousness of the masses as a backdrop, there were many sources of support for limited reforms. Conservatives introduced many measures, such as the German insurance laws of the 1880s. A clerical, royalist majority in the French parliament passed in 1874 the first effective factory inspection law. Conservative parties hoped by these measures to win working-class support, and the idea of regulating middle-class business and extending paternal assistance to the poor still had some appeal for conservative aristocrats.

Far more support for welfare functions came from liberal middle-class politicians. There was opposition, of course. The liberal tradition was opposed to expanding the functions of government. Many businesspeople feared the expense of welfare programs; German industrialists, for example, opposed the initial social insurance laws of the 1880s. However, there was much middle-class support as well. Many came to see that welfare measures did not harm business interests; in Germany the business community supported some later welfare laws. Many saw welfare measures as a necessary response to the agitation of labor; the middle class was not inflexible in its attitude toward working-class desires. Finally, the humanitarian traditions of the middle class prompted some to see the justice of welfare measures, the need to eliminate some of the worst forms of material insecurity and abuse. Knowledge of the conditions of the poor was promoted by various public and private reports and by the propaganda of socialists and union leaders. There was some realization that reforms were needed not just to assuage labor but also to approach more closely middle-class ideals of general prosperity and opportunity.

Prior to 1870 or 1880 relatively little had been done by national governments to meet the social problems of industrial societies. There had been some protective legislation, covering particularly the field of child labor. National laws had permitted action, sometimes by localities, to protect certain minimal standards in health, housing, and education. Food and drug inspection began in the 1860s in much of western Europe. Municipal governments had led in developing new functions by providing parks, libraries, effective sewage disposal, and a wide variety of other facilities for their citizens. But the total amount of welfare activity was small and limited in concept. Most of it involved simply an extension of the middle-class idea of the state as police officer, removing abuses but not engaging in positive action to construct new conditions. Vigorous protection was extended only to categories of people, particularly children, who were clearly incapable of defending their interests.

After 1870 many older welfare concepts were extended, and new principles were developed, especially in the field of social insurance. Even relatively new industrial countries participated in the movements toward some welfare legislation, in imitation of the more extensive programs elsewhere. Germany was the first nation to develop a comprehensive welfare system. In 1883 a compulsory insurance program against illness was established for most industrial workers; up to thirteen weeks of sickness were covered. Both workers and employers contributed to the program, which was administered by local groups, including some old mutual aid societies. In 1884 accident disability insurance was passed, paid for entirely by the employer, novel recognition that the employer, not the worker, was responsible for accidents in the plant. Finally, in 1889, a program was passed to support the aged and invalid, with premiums paid half by employee, half by employer, with government subsidies if necessary. These three laws established the basic welfare program for Germany in the period. They were extended several times to cover more people, including agricultural workers. Between 1885 and 1900, some 50 million Germans received from the program benefits worth $750 million, $250 million more than the workers had contributed. Germany also passed various laws regulating hours of work and conditions of pay; even domestic workers were protected. The state promoted industrial courts to arbitrate disputes between employer and worker. With a massive program of social insurance and various other protective measures, the German state offered the most complete welfare program of any nation in Europe.

Britain, somewhat later than Germany, developed a series of measures almost as comprehensive. There was a great deal of regulation of sanitary conditions, of hours for women and children, even of the conditions of children in schools and in homes. In 1909 an eight-hour law was passed for miners, the first law directly regulating the hours of work for adult males. In 1912 a new type of protection was added, again for miners, with the establishment of a minimum wage. A 1905 law, passed by a conservative administration, admitted new state responsibility for unemployment by establishing state funds for the relief of deserving unemployed, and in 1908 a tax-supported pension plan was established. In 1911 the National Insurance Act was passed, the most extensive scheme developed in Britain before the war. It covered both sickness and unemployment and was compulsory for those categories of workers to whom it applied. A third of the funds for the program came from workers, a third from employers, and a third from the state.

Other European states developed welfare programs, often patterned on the German. Austria passed an accident-insurance plan in 1887 and a sickness-insurance scheme the next year. Denmark created similar programs between 1893 and 1903. Italy passed legislation providing insurance against accidents and old age in 1898, and Norway, Spain, and Holland established accident compensation in the 1890s. Most European states also passed laws limiting the hours of work; regulating the labor of children; setting minimum standards of ventilation, light, and sanitation in factories; and eliminating abuses in fines imposed on workers and in payments of wages in kind. In France insurance against illness and accident was passed, but coverage was voluntary rather than compulsory. A ten-hour day for factories employing both men and women and a six-day week were established by law. In 1910 a voluntary pension plan was set up by the state.

The welfare programs set up during the period all followed several general principles. They extended the concept of the state as police officer on guard against abuse by regulating many new aspects of factory and market activity. Some traditional limits on regulation remained, however, as in the general avoidance of direct regulation of the hours of adult males (with the exception of mineworkers). Another middle-class principle, self-help, guided the insurance programs of the period; participants in most of the programs paid most of the costs. This self-help feature was acceptable to many workers, who could thereby regard the programs as something other than charity, and it helped make the programs more compatible with middle-class ideals, for it seemed to encourage self-reliance and also did not threaten to cost much in tax money.

Many of the insurance programs went beyond the self-help feature by making them compulsory for the categories of workers covered and by adding state or employer contributions. Compulsion was necessary to spread the risks from an insurance standpoint, but it did reduce the liberty of workers to go their own way. Few programs depended on workers' contributions alone. The 1908 pension plan in Britain relied entirely on general tax funds. There was an embryonic concept of the state as a redistributor of income through taxes, and most states established graduated taxes, although mainly to support military expenditures. The Lloyd George budget in 1909 established special taxes on land, raised the taxes on upper incomes and lowered them for the poor, and provided some deductions for children. The British tax schemes, in combination with tax-supported welfare programs, effectively set aside 1 percent of the national income each year for redistribution. This was only a halting step, but it was the most novel extension of state responsibility during the period.

The early welfare laws did a great deal of good. In Germany and elsewhere insurance programs contributed significantly to the resources of many workers in times of misfortunes. Regulations of conditions eliminated many abuses in factory conditions and were responsible for many of the gains in leisure time and in health by the working classes. However, most of the plans were quite limited. Regulations often applied only to factories and left artisans, shopkeepers, and rural workers unprotected. Insurance schemes, even where compulsory, often covered a minority of workers. The National Insurance Act in Britain was intended to be experimental and applied to only 2.25 million men. None of the plans covered dependents, widows, and orphans. The poorest people, such as rural labor or single women working at home, were left almost untouched by these various schemes; only in Germany did measures go significantly beyond factory workers alone. Even those who did benefit received relatively little. Pensions and insurance payments in Britain were set deliberately low to discourage idling. It was assumed that these plans would merely supplement other savings; but other savings did not necessarily exist. The little redistribution of income that occurred was more than offset by the growing gap between profits and wages that developed everywhere after 1900.

The welfare programs, particularly in their insurance aspects, were important indications of the new political power of the masses and the flexibility of the upper classes in response. They showed that some new ideas about government functions were developing. They were not, however, major contributions to the well-being of the masses. They did not notably stem the discontent that arose among factory labor and even among some segments of the peasantry during the period. The measures taken obviously accorded with the expectations of the masses for direct government aid; but they did not yet go far enough to assure contentment.

The limitations on government action were agonizingly apparent after World War I. In the first flush of enthusiasm following the war, often under the auspices of socialist parties that had grown in strength, new welfare measures were adopted. The French government, for example, proposed a compulsory social insurance program, though this was passed only a decade later. Germany extended its social insurance programs to new groups of workers, and in 1928 passed an unemployment insurance scheme. The hours of adult male workers were limited in several countries. But there was no major breakthrough, and when depression came government policies throughout western and central Europe initially ignored the pressing needs of the working and even the middle classes. Government employees were fired, unemployment compensation funds kept to a minimum. New taxes burdened shopkeepers, who were already angry that they received less attention from the state than the workers did. The general reluctance to use the power of the state to take any new economic initiative contributed to the worsening of the depression for several years. It was only in 1934 that the British government agreed to commit tax revenues to the unemployment insurance program, even though funds had run out long before under the impact of depression, and even then the duration of assistance was severely limited. Only toward the middle of the 1930s were there suggestions, often halting, of a new kind of state to match the novel problems of mature industrial society.

The New Relationships of State and Society

The limitations on political change between 1870 and 1940, but also the new contacts with governments that had emerged, obviously encouraged the politicization of grievances, whether new or old. Not only the working class but also middle-class and peasant elements developed new ways to express discontent as their political rights outstripped their active political power. For the new voting rights, the new parties and campaign methods, did not effect rapid changes in government personnel or outlook. Professional politicians altered the composition of parliaments, drawing in even a minority of ambitious or dedicated workers. But the ministries these parliaments produced were still predominantly middle class and aristocratic. Even top socialist leaders were usually middle class. Still more important, the bureaucracies behind the parliaments, and often substantially beyond their control, were drawn heavily from a conservative amalgam of aristocrats and traditional professional people, open in turn to the pressure-group activities of landlords and big businesspeople.

Adjustments to a new political experience and to the growing outreach of the state formed nevertheless a final ingredient in the basic framework of European social life by the late nineteenth century. While governments in no sense determined popular behavior across the board — popular insistence on cutting birthrates actually went against official government interest in promoting population growth — they did enter mass consciousness in new ways. The spread of nationalism as a powerful, visceral loyalty was one sign of this, as was of course the growing use of political parties to express group interests.

With new economic and political trends, new technologies and organizational forms, Europeans continued to be caught up in a process of fundamental change. Some reactions, developed during initial industrialization, continued, but in other cases initial impulses had now to be rethought. Not surprisingly, while appeals toward literally preindustrial values dimmed (though they did not disappear), a desire to recapture some of the qualities of earlier industrial life — before big organization took command, for example — now surfaced strongly.

The Upper Class

Every major social group was caught in some tension between old and new in the decades after 1870. Was impersonal economic and political organization acceptable? Were political rights useful, and how should they be employed? How could the class adapt to new economic opportunities and problems? The new tensions explain, among other things, why no social class produced a unified political response. The middle

The country life, noble style. The aristocracy works to maintain its distinctive style of life. This picture is from turn-of-the-century Russia, where aristocratic power and resources, though challenged, remained unusually strong. Some similar continuities could be found even in western Europe. Aristocratic devotion to leisure may also have helped Europeans more generally accept the legitimacy of nonwork enjoyments, though usually at a less opulent level. *(The Bettmann Archive.)*

class spawned socialists, liberals, and ultimately fascists, all in some abundance, for example. All the social classes that had been defined by the first stages of industrialization were now forced into a redefinition, depending on their relationship to the new forms of production.

Nowhere was this more apparent than at the top of society, yet nowhere was the complexity of redefinition greater. Not a few of the weaknesses of the economic and political structure derived from the curious nature of the European elite.

The aristocracy could no longer serve as the upper class. This, plus the rise of big business, might suggest that a new, rationalizing class of leaders took over upper-class status in mature industrial society. In part this is correct. What had been, before, the richest segment of the middle class now split off because of its immense wealth and political influence. But it did not take over sole control. It did not monopolize the state bureaucracies, for it preferred to deal with government through pressure groups. Government bureaucrats came mainly from a mixture of professionals (mainly lawyers) and aristocrats, and their outlook and training left them ill prepared to deal with the newer social and economic problems. Big businesspeople accepted direct partnership with the aristocracy in education and many political activities. There was increasing intermarriage between the two groups, and in many countries the great industrialists adopted or were granted aristocratic titles. The magnates of the Ruhr regarded their firms as something of a family fief, despite the rise of the corporate form; hence they often named mine pits "The King" or "The Baron." And of course their paternalistic outlook toward the lower classes resembled that of the aristocracy. Big businesspeople, in sum, although adept at utilizing new technology and new organizational forms, did not form an entirely novel upper class. They retained admiration for the prestige of noble birth and for the sumptuous life-style of the landed magnates. Their great mansions and hunting parties, in which aristocrats increasingly intermingled, maintained other elements of an older tradition.

The aristocracy suffered important new setbacks during the mature industrial period that forced it to accept membership in the amalgamated upper class. The key to its dilemma was the unprecedented crisis in agriculture that opened up after 1875. Huge imports of grain, especially wheat, from areas outside Europe reduced grain prices steadily. Aristocrats, dependent on grain sales to the market, suffered along with the peasantry. Not only their earnings but also land values tumbled. At the same time political changes, including parliaments that gave power to middle-class politicians and then new suffrage systems that enfranchised the masses, threatened the class's political hold. But it was through politics that the class salvaged something from its agony, for the state could help preserve the land and give compensatory jobs and power beyond this.

The aristocracy confirmed its grasp on key bureaucratic jobs. Aristocrats could no longer buy offices. Civil service reforms in all the industrial countries opened the bureaucracy to competitive examination around 1870. This was one reason aristocrats increasingly intermingled with middle-class bureaucrats. But with their wealth, even if dented, and social connections it was still easy to get into the better schools and universities. Moreover, the schools that trained for government service retained a significant amateurish element that the aristocracy found congenial. England offered a classic case in point. Middle-class efforts to reform the great public schools were largely abandoned in the 1860s once these schools admitted the sons of wealthy businesspeople along with aristocrats. The schools added a bit more emphasis on science and modern languages, but continued to stress the classics, games, and a nonutilitarian approach. Knowledge of Latin, plus the social graces, were far more important in gaining access to the top civil service job than was specialized training in economics. Small wonder that here, as on the Continent, aristocrats were heavily overrepresented in the diplomatic corps and the military and that middle-class elements who served with them took on much of their culture.

Positions in the bureaucracy gave aristocrats pay and the means to influence government in their favor in other ways. Militarism and imperialism, so dominant in the policies of the European states during the mature industrial period, owed much to the aristocracy's desire for new bases of power and new ways to express older values. Imperialist pressure groups in France, beginning with the "geographical societies" of the 1870s, were led by aristocrats. Big businesspeople played their role, supporting imperialism because of presumed market benefits. But the imperialist movement owed at least as much to a new aristocratic reaction as to advanced capitalism, and many aristocrats won jobs in colonial administrations.

Aristocrats also entered the political arena, even when they did not run for office directly. They retained a dominant influence in conservative parties. They could still appeal for peasant support on the basis of traditional deference. Groups like the German Union of Agriculturalists advocated high tariffs on grain even though many peasants, converting to stock breeding, bought grain and suffered from any movement toward higher feed prices. Yet they won peasant support on the basis of the unity of agricultural interests and, increasingly, the invocation of nationalism. Traditionally hostile to nationalism, aristocratic interest groups, along with conservative parties, began converting to it in the 1880s because it let them retain political influence despite democracy. The nation's interest, spokespersons argued, demanded protection for agriculture, a strong military, and an expanding empire. Beneath all these resounding arguments were benefits to the aristocracy.

The Prussian Junkers managed to obtain state subsidies for rye; along with the high tariff protection this allowed them to continue fairly traditional agricultural methods, employing a low-paid agricultural labor force, and keep some hold over the large estates. In Russia a Nobles Land Bank was established in 1885; by 1900 aristocrats had borrowed 660 million rubles, much of which they used simply to maintain their standard of living.

Both political and economic efforts brought the aristocracy into growing unity with the upper middle class. Big businesspeople and bureaucrats bought land. Some aristocrats moved into corporate directorships. Economic interests became increasingly intertwined. In politics the two groups agreed to scratch each other's backs. Big businesspeople, through their political influence, agreed to agricultural tariffs and aristocrats accepted protection for industry; the 1902 Bülow tariff in Germany resulted from this kind of agreement among Junkers and industrialists. Both groups supported military spending. Both increasingly united in opposition to socialism and other lower-class demands.

Again in Germany, aristocratic politicians enjoyed tweaking the noses
of businesspeople by supporting the social insurance laws of the 1880s.
But when workers refused to be quietly grateful, when they pressed
into the socialist party, the aristocracy took fright. By the 1900s a solid
alliance of aristocrats and big businesspeople resisted any major labor
gains.

The size of the new upper class is hard to determine. Radical politicians talked of two hundred families in France controlling French industry and banking, and certainly there were great concentrations of
power in a few hands. In the 1930s, some 144 men served as directors
of at least ten French companies, and many of their families were intermarried. It was also true that many aristocrats went under in this
period, which further limited the size of the upper class. Some lost
their land; others huddled on small estates in poverty, damning the
modern world but unable to maintain the political flexibility that the
upper class now required. But in all probability the upper class was
larger than the traditional aristocracy had been. In 1900 in France 2
percent of all the people who died left 50 percent of the wealth that
was passed on. In Britain between the wars, 5 percent of the population
controlled over 75 percent of all earnings from private property. The
upper class had great political power, dominant wealth, and not incon-
siderable numbers. Partly because of their inclusion of the aristocracy
the class enjoyed wide social prestige. Popular newspapers were filled
with reports of the marriages and parties of the wealthy, stirring some
readers to envy but more, perhaps, to a bedazzled admiration. For this
new upper class benefited from much of the deference many groups
had long given to the aristocracy alone.

One final element enhanced the power of the upper class in the
mature industrial period. Its emergence coincided with a prolonged
crisis in the older professions, which drove many professional people
into tacit or direct alliance with upper-class political efforts. As university enrollments soared (they rose from 14,000 in 1870 to 61,000 in
1914, in Germany) the number of jobs for lawyers and doctors did not
keep pace. Many were only too eager to ally with aristocrats in the state
bureaucracy. Many sought parliamentary careers (not only lawyers but
unemployed doctors took this course), and although some served as
political radicals, even socialists, others worked easily with the interest
groups representing landed and big business interests. Many also filled
the ranks of nationalist and imperialist groups like the Pan-German
League, under upper-class leadership. Most important, the older professions did not insist on further reforms in preprofessional education.
They were content with the classical orientation of the leading secondary schools and universities, taking their cue from the respectable culture of the upper class that in turn derived so much from the aristocratic tradition of genteel amateurism. The result enhanced the difficulty government bureaucrats and politicians had in coping with new

economic problems. The French parliament, filled with lawyers, dealt successfully neither with inflation nor with depression during the 1920s and 1930s. Not the least of the reasons for this was the fact that law schools offered only an optional course in economics.

The new upper class, with its allies from the older professions, was no more malevolent than upper classes in other periods of history. But it was somewhat ill adapted to the needs of mature industrial society. It stressed property ownership—the big business fiefs—and a traditionalist education, with an overtone of a still more traditional esteem for gentle birth. Adept at political manipulation, it avoided outright revolution, and in this sense might be counted rather successful. But it could not manage the economy that it so largely controlled and it could not stem growing political challenge.

The upper class was damaged by World War I. The aristocracy had supplied many army officers, whose death rates were higher than those of ordinary troops; its ranks were seriously depleted. Professionals of good education also generally became officers and suffered greatly. The result was something of a demographic crisis in the leadership ranks, which reduced the quality of bureaucrats and politicians, drawn from a less competitive pool of newcomers, and damaged morale. Aristocrats were also frightened by the example of the Russian Revolution, where the class was expropriated and eliminated by law. The example of refugee nobles serving as doormen and taxi drivers in Paris or Berlin hardly inspired confidence.

Outside of Russia, aristocratic landlords in eastern Europe faced new challenges after 1918. New states and old set up democratic regimes. Middle-class politicians talked about liberal land reforms while militant peasant parties pressed hard in the same direction. Actual change was slight. Only in Romania were the large estates broken up, and even there aristocrats received substantial compensation that allowed them to invest in business. Elsewhere, even in relatively liberal Czechoslovakia, less than 10 percent of the land was redistributed. Furthermore, in all these areas, including Romania, aristocrats were able to forge much the same alliance with the upper middle class that had occurred in western and central Europe earlier. For both groups grew frightened by peasant and worker radicalism. In combination they were able to replace the democratic, parliamentary regimes with an authoritarian state everywhere except in Czechoslovakia. Much the same pattern developed in Spain. A republic was established in 1931, vaguely talking of land reform though doing little. This frightened aristocrats, and growing socialist and anarchist agitation terrified leading business and professional people. Here a bloody civil war resulted, but the upper classes retained their hold through the ultimate victory of the Franco regime.

The upper class was less beleaguered in the more advanced industrial areas of Europe but it had distinct problems. The continuing agricultural crisis hit the landed estates in the 1920s. Prussian Junkers had to find ways to persuade the new republican government to give them special subsidies, although their success was a testimony to the continued efficacy of upper-class action. Big businesspeople might pile up speculative profits during the 1920s, but investment patterns were disrupted. Big French investors lost heavily from the collapse of tsarist Russia and the Hapsburg monarchy, for they had poured funds into both areas. The Depression hit individual big businesspeople hard. There was no general collapse, but there was growing uncertainty. It was not surprising that the French upper class turned eagerly to a new book, published in 1935, entitled *The Art of Managing and Protecting One's Fortune*. For the upper class, in its capacity as economic and political leader, could not resolve the economic and political crisis of the interwar period. Its immediate reaction was defensive. Big businesspeople and landowners in Germany, Italy, and France began to support authoritarian political parties that might restore order in their troubled countries. Rarely fascist, for they recognized fascism as an attack on the existing social structure, they often subsidized fascist parties in return for a promise of noninterference in big business. True to their word, Mussolini and Hitler supported big business profits and made no move against the large estates.

So the upper class struggled through the 1930s. Its fortunes were fairly clearly tied to those of the new regimes in central and eastern Europe and, after 1940, to the reactionary Vichy government in France. Elsewhere its political role was less reactionary but it was no more successful in resolving the basic economic problems of the Depression. Politically potent, master of large business empires, the new elite turned stale, in part because of the insistence on defending aristocratic as well as big business interests.

The Peasantry

Important support for the new elite, during much of the mature industrial period, came from elements of the peasantry, who could combine some traditional deference to rural notables with a new desire to define interests separate from those of the city. Not a dramatic period in rural life, compared to the upheavals of the early industrial decades or the sharper transformation of the past half-century, the mature industrial era nonetheless did see important adjustments among various peasant groups. In areas where aristocrats remained particularly strong and active, peasants could come into substantial conflict with elites.

The separateness of the peasant classes continued despite expanding political and economic connections with the cities. West European peasants did accept a formal system of education during the late nineteenth century as a standard part of the life experience; growing agricultural competition and falling prices opened them to new interest in technological training. School systems gave them contact with authorities outside home and village, which was particularly novel for peasant women. Their local dialect yielded somewhat to more standardized language, which allowed them to understand urban politicians and other outsiders. But all of this took time, and there were other forces working against change among the peasantry. Emigration damaged them. Although the massive exodus to the cities had now slowed, the more enterprising young peasants were still prone to leave the village. In many areas the peasant population aged rapidly as a result, which reduced their ability to adapt to change. Peasants did alter their methods and their organizational structure to deal with the persistent agricultural crisis. In both respects they moved in ways parallel to ongoing industrial development, for their technology became more complex, their economy more impersonal. But there was a defensive element as well, when peasants asked for special favors from the state to reduce their need to change. Similarly, peasants learned the value of politicization, but again they usually gave it a special form; their most distinctive contributions to politics came through efforts to defend rural tradition, including the small family farm.

There could be no question of the challenge posed by the competition of cheap imported foods. Beginning in the 1870s, falling grain prices hit earnings directly and tumbling land values threatened the basis of peasant status. Many had to borrow heavily to survive.

All over western and central Europe peasants tried to counteract the agricultural crisis by improving the efficiency of their methods. Never before had peasants been so eager to try technical innovations. They purchased new tools, including seed drills and even threshing machines. After 1892 most wheat fields in France, large or small, were cultivated and harvested with machines. Danish dairy farmers began to use cream separators after 1870. Everywhere the utilization of fertilizers increased. The result of the quest for efficiency was a general and significant improvement in yields. French production of both wheat and wine increased after 1890 even though the amount of land devoted to each of those crops declined. An interest in technical advances began to penetrate the peasantry, promoted both by education and economic pressure, and the spread of new methods definitely helped the peasants to improve their economic position in the face of falling prices.

Peasants also began to change the crops they raised. They increasingly abandoned grain, in which competition was most intense, in favor of meat, dairy, and truck products. In Germany the raising of animals, particularly hogs, increased rapidly, especially in the small-holding areas. Danish peasants intensified the specialization in dairy farming that they had begun before the crisis. British farmers curtailed the amount of land devoted to arable farming, and their production of wheat actually declined. They concentrated instead on meat and dairy goods, as did farmers in Normandy. The peasants of Brittany and several other regions of France specialized in truck farming, though France as a whole retained a higher level of wheat production than any European country except Russia. Generally, the conversion to more marketable crops was an important result of the agricultural crisis. The growing demand of the urban masses for meats and dairy products assured an excellent market for the new specialties. Peasant attunement to the market, already well developed, was clearly increasing.

Most peasants converting to mechanized farming or to a specialty crop ran into important difficulties. Mechanized equipment was beyond the means of many individuals. Conversion to stock raising or dairy farming required far more capital than was necessary for grain production. The growing dependence on the market posed certain problems in itself. Peasants were economically weak in comparison with the producers of agricultural equipment and fertilizers; they could easily be victimized in their transactions. They were weak also in relation to the wholesalers who bought their crops. Some peasants entered into contracts with breweries, sugar refineries, and canneries in an effort to assure their sales; too often these contracts left the peasants in virtual servitude to the manufacturer. Peasants who borrowed money to buy new equipment or stock were often exploited by the lenders. For a variety of reasons peasants found it difficult to respond to the agricultural crisis and adopted new equipment and crops only hesitantly, despite the great need for change. In France, most notably, peasant agriculture remained extremely inefficient, with inadequate use of fertilizer and modern equipment. Much peasant adaptation simply continued older patterns: a gradual consolidation of plots into slightly larger holdings, which might or might not facilitate new methods, along with a reduction of common lands and of village decisions on how to farm. And even this change was slow; in 1892 about 71 percent of all French farms had five hectares of land or less; by 1929 the figure was still 54 percent. But change was essential, and it had to go beyond a mere acceleration of earlier commercialization. By a new organization of the peasantry that combined peasant resources, capital could be provided, supplies purchased, and even marketing arranged to the advantage of each producer. An extensive cooperative movement arose in direct response to the new economic needs of the peasantry.

Cooperation and Peasant Politics

The first cooperatives were established before 1850 as savings banks and lending agencies for the members. The Raiffeissen banks in Germany, begun in 1846 as a response to the agricultural crisis of that

year, and the Schulze-Delitzsch credit cooperatives did a great deal to
reduce interest rates on loans and to provide more ample funds for
German peasants. Savings and loan organizations were the most popular rural cooperatives, and their membership grew rapidly after 1870
in Germany and elsewhere. Purchasing cooperatives were also formed
to buy expensive supplies and even heavy machinery for shared use.
After 1870 Danish cooperatives helped purchase cream separators; the
first French cooperative was founded in 1881 to buy fertilizers. Other
groups in France were established to acquire vines from the United
States to replace the diseased French stock. Cooperatives extended
their purchasing functions even to such consumer goods as clothing. By
grouping the purchasing power of individual peasants, cooperatives
lowered prices, assured high quality, and allowed technical improvements impossible to the individual peasant. Finally, some cooperatives
developed storage and processing facilities for agricultural goods and
served as sales agents for their members. Again, the cooperative organization had far greater power in the market than did individual
peasants.

The cooperative movement spread widely; 750,000 French peasants
were in cooperatives of some sort by 1910, and over a quarter of the
German peasantry was enrolled. In Denmark, which adapted most successfully to the new agricultural situation, cooperatives played a major
role. Nevertheless, cooperatives demanded important sacrifices from
the peasants. They violated the individualism many peasants had developed during the earlier period of adjustment to market agriculture.
Cooperatives also demanded administrative skills that few peasants possessed. The movement, although it spread constantly, did not touch the
bulk of the peasantry during the period. In France, where peasant individualism was unusually intense, no more than a tenth of the agricultural population joined cooperatives before World War I, and many
who did only joined credit cooperatives, which were in business to finance individual, not collective, effort.

Peasant political consciousness inevitably rose in the period as education and voting rights were extended. In a few cases peasants used
their vote to express radical discontent. There were important pockets
of socialist voting in southwestern Germany. Around Bologna, where
large estates were formed in the 1860s on newly drained land, peasant
support for socialism developed before 1900. In certain French wine-
growing areas, active socialist voting took firm root. Landless laborers
in several industrial countries began, somewhat hesitantly, to strike and
unionize. Their position was made ever more desperate by the agricultural crisis, as wages fell and their employers became more demanding.
With the richer peasants fighting for more land, more people were
forced into this dependent position. One French laborer described how
his landlord employer called him "Thing," not bothering to remember

his name: "Obey and Work: I ask nothing else of you."[1] Small wonder
that major strikes broke out among agricultural laborers in France after
1900. The same impulse carried about 100,000 rural laborers into the
French Communist party when it formed in the 1920s. The rural proletariat began to touch base politically with its urban counterpart.

Generally, however, peasants in industrial countries were not attracted by extremes of this sort. They developed new political interests
but remained conservative. In France peasants traditionally had supported monarchist notables and Bonapartists; only in a few areas had
they ever developed an interest in republicanism. During the 1870s
republican campaigners, led by Léon Gambetta, tried to persuade peasants that a republic could maintain order and protect private property;
most French peasants therefore became firm republicans, but were still
hostile to major social initiatives. Elsewhere traditionalism was not modified even to this extent. Peasant voters in Austria rejected the political
control of the landlords by voting for the Christian Socialist party, but
they were still supporting a conservative party favorable to religion.
Many German peasants still voted as the landlords told them to. Gradually, however, peasants did become aware of the possibility of using their
votes, usually in a conservative way, to win economic assistance from
the government.

Governments offered various programs to farmers during the
period. They extended advanced technical training in agriculture. German universities offered night courses to peasants, in the villages, on
the principles of scientific agriculture, and the British government established similar training after 1900. The British government in 1900
also allowed county councils to buy land for rental in plots of moderate
size in an effort to encourage small farming. The German government
promoted consolidation of land and also purchased some estates to assist
small farmers. The French government lent money to the cooperatives,
and governments generally tried to develop the credit facilities in the
countryside.

Of greatest interest to the peasants was the possibility of establishing
tariff protection for agricultural goods. Most countries had abandoned
significant duties on food prior to 1870. Agricultural producers who
depended on exports, such as the Junkers, supported free trade, but
the peasants took little interest in the issue. As the crisis in agriculture
began, pressure for tariff protection rose. The peasants did not initiate
the pressure; issues of this sort were unfamiliar, and peasants were not
accustomed to political action of any kind. In Germany the Junkers
launched the agitation by forming their Union of Agriculturalists to
spread propaganda for tariff protection and to serve as a vigorous
lobby. In France not only large landowners but also some industrialists

---

[1] Victor Griffuelhes, *Voyage Révolutionnaire* (Paris, n.d.), p. 238.

pressed for new agricultural tariffs; the industrialists hoped to promote a general return to protective policies. These various interests began to appeal to the peasants for support in their campaigns. Conservative politicians sought peasant votes by pointing to the need to defend the nation's agriculture against foreign competition. Propagandists from the German Union of Agriculturalists talked of the unity of agricultural interests and the need to defend agriculture as a whole. As we have seen the group persuaded many peasants to urge tariffs that were sometimes against their own economic advantage.

More generally, peasants supported tariffs, once the idea was presented to them, as a means of reducing the need for change. With high duty on food imports, old methods and traditional products could still be profitable. In France, Germany, and elsewhere tariffs undeniably protected methods and crops that were economically wasteful. The French tariff of 1892 returned France to a position of almost complete agricultural self-sufficiency, despite the fact that French peasants could not produce grain as economically as farmers in the New World. The main victims of this system were urban buyers of food, however, not the peasants themselves, who saw their incomes and habits alike defended by the tariff system.

Peasant attachment to tariff advocates was intense. Along with continued political traditionalism, it helped maintain the conservative political orientation of most of the class. Peasants in France voted generally for moderate republicans because they offered tariffs, governmental sympathy for the church, and a firm defense of private property. German peasants usually voted either for the Catholic Center party, urged on by their priests, or in Protestant areas for conservative groupings controlled by the Junkers. Both of the parties receiving peasant support in Germany were staunch advocates of agricultural tariffs. The peasantry became accustomed to the idea that their inefficiency—they would argue their role in preserving the land and rural values—should be supported by the rest of the nation. In France peasant interest groups successfully advocated specially low taxes along with other favors. Beyond this, peasants, constantly told by conservatives that their way of life was more moral than that of the cities, were encouraged to believed that the old ways were of benefit to the entire nation.

The defensive adaptation helped keep peasant living standards low. There was some improvement, as more urban products became available. Clothing was usually factory-made now. Bus service allowed peasants to attend movies in the nearby town. But diets and particularly housing remained well below urban standards. This poverty drove some peasants away, for the city was a constant temptation. In France and Britain the absolute number of peasants began to decrease for the first time, and some land was taken out of cultivation. The spread of education and military service, which gave peasants dramatic experience of other regions of the country, encouraged this movement. But all this simply enhanced the self-satisfaction of the peasants who remained. Except for the stirrings among landless laborers, the attachment to traditional work and the land, the village festivals and games, and, usually, the continued interest in religion gave sufficient satisfaction.

The peasant way of life thus yielded only reluctantly to the pressures for change. Peasants proved surprisingly resilient in their defense of tradition, and in learning new ways to express older values they had an important impact on European politics and economic life. Their response, and the echo it found in other troubled segments of society, prevented any real solution for the basic difficulties of European agriculture.

World War I

World War I and its immediate aftermath heightened the pressures on the peasantry, causing their defensive political stance to alter into positive reaction. The war itself was a great shock. Peasants provided a disproportionate number of infantrymen, for factory workers were too valuable to spare in such numbers. Few peasant families, therefore, would be without a death to mourn, for the slaughter was appalling. Many peasants who did survive chose not to return to the countryside. Some of the land torn up by the war was not returned to use. Disruption of habits showed in the decline of religious practice in German villages, long bastions of traditional ways.

Ironically the war briefly interrupted the basic economic crisis of agriculture. A period of prosperity continued during the first years after the war before production was fully restored. Many peasants managed to pay off their debts and raise their personal consumption. French peasants borrowed to buy more land, Germans to buy new equipment. But by 1923 or 1924 pressure on agricultural prices returned, and the new debts became a great burden. The Depression made matters worse by reducing agricultural prices up to 50 percent. In France peasant buying power compared to 1913 was down 10 percent by 1930, 28 percent by 1933. Peasants continued to introduce some technical improvements in an effort to meet this pressure. Still, material levels remained low. In France the average peasant's house was at least a hundred years old. Government programs allowed some improvements, particularly by extending electricity to most villages. But only a minority of peasants had indoor plumbing facilities.

During the 1920s there were few signs of increased peasant discontent. Political patterns remained largely traditional and conservative. French peasants often elected conservative estate owners, the traditional notables, to newly created agricultural bureaus. Some new farmers' lobbying groups were formed in both Germany and France, but there was little significant change. With the advent of depression and the new political movements in the cities, peasant political patterns began to alter somewhat. Leaders of both the Left and Right began to solicit peasant support more actively. And peasants themselves had a greater desire to express their material discontent and, often, their distrust of the growing power of urban workers.

In France communism made some headway among peasants, while the left-wing trade union confederation (the *confédération générale du travail,* or C.G.T.) had 180,000 peasant members by 1936; in 1937 many farm workers struck for collective bargaining. More important were the gains of agricultural parties and groupings on the Right. A Peasant Front was formed in 1934 that stressed the need for a political system more attuned to the needs of agriculture. The Front was soon split, but important currents of activity in defense of specifically peasant movements remained.

There were also some cases of direct action. Demonstrations occurred in several areas, and in 1934 a peasant group marched to Paris. A milk strike occurred in the same period, the first time that peasant owners, as opposed to agricultural workers, had banded together for protest action. Cooperative movements continued to grow. Whereas before the war only a tenth of the French peasantry had belonged to cooperative groups, by the 1920s a full third of the class was enrolled. The cooperative movements continued to provide important assistance in matters of credit, purchasing, and processing; they also reflected the new willingness and ability of peasants to join together in matters of mutual concern. Finally, a new Catholic youth group developed, urging better technology and a new outlook, and thus helped train the new kind of peasant who came into prominence after World War II. The various efforts by peasants to better their lot had only limited success. Material conditions remained poor. Governments offered some new technical assistance, and in 1936 the Popular Front ministry established a Wheat Office to support wheat prices and improve peasant incomes. Various other subsidies were extended. For the most part, these measures relieved but did not remove the major economic difficulties. Increasing peasant activity was not yet sufficient to win substantial material improvements.

German peasants also developed some distinctive political expressions during this period, particularly after the Depression brought new and widespread hardship. As in France, the basic grievances concerned falling prices and lack of capital. There was also some general resentment over the declining status of the peasantry in society as a whole, the growing dominance of big business, and the rise of communist and socialist movements that threatened private property and seemed to give the workers undue influence. As a result of these various sources of discontent, many peasants proved vulnerable to Nazi propaganda. The first areas to offer majorities to the Nazis were regions such as

Thuringia, which lacked a substantial industrial population and were dominated by peasant small holding. Traditional, tightly organized villages were particularly liable to turn to the Nazis.

To many peasants the Nazis offered protection against change. They promised to support peasant tenure. They praised the peasantry as the true bearer of German tradition and promised to promote peasant traditions of dress and behavior in an effort to return to the essence of German culture. To be sure, peasants did not win what they wanted; the Nazi regime, once in office, continued to pay lip-service to a peasant ideal, but in the interests of efficiency it busily furthered consolidation of agricultural holdings and the displacement of the smaller peasants. Peasant confrontation with change remained an unfinished agenda, to be resumed during and after World War II.

Urban Society

Urban society became numerically predominant in western Europe during the mature industrial period, as the peasantry declined relatively and in some cases absolutely. Cities were divided between middle and working classes, even as the upper stratum of the middle class tended to pull into the new elite. Precise class definitions changed greatly, however, and the middle class, now growing most rapidly, took some unexpected new turns.

The Middle Classes

The mature industrial period produced important shifts in middle-class behavior and outlook, and even in the definition of the class itself, though many features continued from what had seemed successful adjustments in early industrial society. Middle-class people in the main developed new leisure activities, even a leisure ethos, in marked contrast to earlier narrowness. They modified gender beliefs, under the spur of important changes in women's lives. They adapted to democratic politics and, despite recurrent fear of worker radicalism, could often define some areas of limited collaboration. With all this, middle-class adjustment to change had some limits, and there were important divisions within the class. Above all, changes in organizational structures, which seemed to reduce opportunity for individual property ownership and initiative, troubled many middle-class people. When subjected to outright economic pressures, some of these people would direct their discontent against scapegoats, such as Jews, and support fascist movements.

The mature industrial middle-class poses, then, something of a co-nundrum. It modified its previous style of life in seemingly fruitful ways, and it also could support a new reaction. How can this duality be explained?

Variations in time are involved. The middle classes worked on their leisure ethic in good years, turned more to politics in bad. Variations in place play a role. Middle-class political reaction was strongest in Germany, next in France and Italy, while Britain and Scandinavia were not greatly affected; the leisure ethic emerged most clearly in England. But the most important single factor was the differentiation of the middle ranks of society into several distinct groups. The true middle class could be defined in terms of income; it was the second wealthiest group in the population, but earning, at its upper limit, less than 25 percent as much annually as the lower level of the upper class. It could be defined increasingly in terms of education, for this was a class that now went regularly into secondary school. Beneath this core middle class was the old shopkeeper group, now increasingly disgruntled, and a really new, white-collar group, propertyless but with values that over-lapped with the middle class. From the middle class and new lower middle class came the new life-style. From the traditional remnants of the shopkeepers came the main thrust toward new politics. This com-plexity is essential in understanding the period, for while products of disgruntlement captured the political arena during the 1930s, the up-dated middle-class culture was, in the long run, more significant.

There were of course points of overlap among the constituent groups in the middle class. The children of one might feed into another. The son of an embattled shopkeeper could easily become a clerk or a store manager. He might carry over some of his father's sense of grievance against the modern world, but he would also begin to develop other interests. The middle classes had some common prob-lems throughout the period. It became progressively harder to find servants. This caused much complaint but may not in fact have been totally resented, for servants had been a mixed blessing and new house-hold appliances helped replace them. Many middle-class families, in-creasingly close-knit, may have preferred to live without a stranger in the house. Urban rents rose dramatically, which burdened the middle-class budget and forced increasing numbers into the suburbs. There were new sources of income, too, and the middle class also defended living standards by dramatic additional reductions in birthrates. Educa-tional opportunities became more obviously important to middle-class definition than in the early industrial decades. Professional people still went further in their education than businesspeople, but both remained more highly educated than the lower classes. In France and Germany about 10 to 15 percent of the population went to the most prestigious

secondary schools, the *lycée* and the *Gymnasium*. Perhaps more important, new secondary schools were developed to offer a more pragmatic
training in science and modern languages; the German *Realgymnasium,*
in particular, drew many students from lower middle-class ranks,. Educational opportunities in England remained more haphazard until the
development of a state-supported secondary school system after 1902,
but here too the middle classes steadily improved their educational level.
A growing handful of middle-class women entered universities and
professional schools in fields such as medicine, though against bitter
male resistance. In all major cases most of the middle class received
primary education under the auspices of the secondary schools and so
was separate from the lower classes at all stages.

Middle-Class Disgruntlement

A variety of situations could produce middle-class anxiety. The middle-
sized industrialist, who believed in the family firm, was increasingly
squeezed by larger corporations. Some might decide that it was safest
to sell out and become a manager in one of the giant firms. But this
involved a crucial loss of property ownership, and with it much of the
traditional sense of status; hence in 1899 almost 20 percent of all
British industrial managers felt they had been downwardly mobile in
entering their new career, whereas another 40 percent had not, in their
opinion, improved their status over that of their fathers. The middle
class was often tempted into new investments, as the stock market expanded, yet these could easily fall through. Financial failures like that
of the 1870s ruined many. Fraudulent investment schemes robbed
others of their savings even in prosperous years. The Panama Canal
scandal in France affected almost half a million investors.

But it was from the older professions, not the business groups, that
the most persistently aggrieved segment of the middle class emerged
throughout the mature industrial period. Several factors were involved.
First, the professions did not keep pace with the new upper class in
income and status. Some slipped badly, like the French university professors who, miserably paid, spent much of their time discussing their
hatred of upstart businesspeople. Second, the older professions were
producing more people than there were jobs. Many groups continued
to measure society in terms of older occupational status rankings and
so urged their sons into law or university teaching. Professionals themselves wanted their sons to follow their footsteps, for entry into business would be degrading; hence 65 percent of German university professors were sons of university-educated fathers. Shopkeepers or even
successful businesspeople might opt for this older success ladder. The
son of a second- or third-generation industrialist who turned against
his father's money-grubbing was another common phenomenon. As

soon as they were free to enter the professions, Jews in central Europe flocked in; by 1890, only twenty-three years after their legal emancipation, Jews constituted 34 percent of all university students in Vienna. To the prestige of the older professions was added one new element in this period: Those professionals who entered state service, which was itself a traditional goal, now after retirement received pensions. French civil servants, for example, were covered by pensions after 1853. Interest in protecting one's old age became an increasingly distinguishing feature of this segment of the middle class, for this was a group that expected to retire with some security. Consciousness of the importance of old age was in itself an extremely promising development, but for the time it helped feed an excessive supply of people toward the civil service.

In law, teaching, and to an extent medicine, the professionalization process had broken down in key respects. Provision of elaborate training and state licenses were supposed to prevent oversupply. It still did in newer areas such as engineering; French and German engineers prospered during this very period on the basis of their training, which was increasingly suited to the managerial and research needs of modern industry. But, lacking the traditional cachet, they drew fewer recruits than there were jobs. Professional restraint still worked in England, if only because university expansion was limited, and the crisis of the professionals did not reach there, although only expansion of jobs in the Empire prevented unemployment. On the Continent, more people could acquire training than the old professions could accommodate. Secondary school teachers grew fearful of new competition; this was one source, in Germany, of opposition to women's entry into teaching careers. Primary school teachers were unable to professionalize at all because of oversupply. Entry into the ranks of university professors was difficult, for their numbers did not expand rapidly; the average German professor was fifty-four in 1907. Lawyers, with their largely classical training, did well on civil service examinations, but there were not enough posts. So many, as in Germany, served as mere file clerks. They also, of course, played a disproportionate role among parliamentary politicians, but this provided relatively few jobs overall. And lawyers lacked the specialized training that might make them useful in business management, which is where the newer opportunities lay.

The case of doctors is still more interesting. Here was a profession that seemed able to modernize successfully. It had its associations, licensing, and professional journals. It developed one specialization after another: surgeons, gynecologists, obstetricians, and by the end of the century specialists in pediatrics and geriatrics. But all of this rested on a very shaky base in terms of knowledge. Two kinds of medical knowledge advanced particularly in the nineteenth century. The germ theory, developed first by Pasteur in the 1860s, was vital for improvements in public health; it also helped cut deaths on the operating table or in the delivery room, always assuming that the doctors believed in the theory and remembered to wash their hands. The other main advance came in pathology; there was a real gain in knowledge of what diseased organs looked like, through discoveries in autopsies. But none of this helped treat sick people very much. There were some gains, of course. Gynecological surgeons were able, by the 1890s, to operate successfully on ovarian cysts and other problems that previously would have killed their victims. The growing use of obstetricians instead of midwives did reduce both infant death and maternal death in childbirth, though mainly toward the end of the nineteenth century. But the simple fact was that doctors were not responsible for most of the health gains that occurred during the nineteenth century, which resulted more from changes in diet and improvements in public sanitation—like the purification of water that spread in cities during the second half of the century and gradually eliminated typhoid. The further fact was that adult health did not really improve very much. Life expectancy at age twenty was little better in 1900 than it had been in 1800 and a host of adults, even in the middle classes, endured unpleasant chronic illnesses, even when nonfatal, like the 80 percent of all French women who suffered from leucorrhea in 1865. And the final fact was that doctors really did not have very much special knowledge to offer their patients before the 1930s, unless of course the patient died, when they became increasingly adept at identifying the causes. Professionalization had outstripped knowledge. Doctors themselves often doubted their own training. As late as the 1930s many French doctors returned to Neo-Hippocratism, attacking official medicine and claiming that the real causes of many diseases were still unknown and that the doctor should stress an appreciation of the individual temperament of each patient. Homeopathy continued to win converts among trained doctors. From the standpoint of potential patients, there was little to distinguish the professional doctor from the charlatan. Not only did peasants resist new medicine in favor of traditional cures, but urban residents often went to magnetisers, hypnotists, or herbalists as well, for these were in fact little different from the doctors who, around 1900, were still advocating cancer cures through living on a boat in the Rhone River and playing music during meals.

Most people went to doctors only in the late stage of an illness, if at all. Only the few doctors with a clientele among the upper classes, who had been more fully converted to medicine, made much money, along with some who offered consultations by correspondence. There were more trained doctors than could find even a marginal medical practice, almost 8 percent more in France. Still larger numbers found their income and prestige precarious. In 1901 it was estimated that only half the doctors in France considered themselves prosperous.

A large segment of lawyers, teachers, and doctors was thus alienated, their achievements well below their expectations. They could ally with some other professions or near professions that were also in trouble. Priests and pastors lamented the decline of religion in the modern world, which meant a decline in their own prestige. More directly, the rise of the state school system, with its symbol—the secular school teacher—reduced the local prestige of clerics. Journalists, though not professionals in that anyone could try a hand at the game, were badly paid and irregularly employed in the larger cities.

Finally, many professionals had contacts, if only through their student days and subsequent reading, with discontented intellectuals, many of whom came from professional families. Until the eighteenth century European intellectuals were mainly priests, or were under noble patronage. The advent of a more commercial society did not initially bother intellectuals, who could support themselves by writing or painting for a middle-class audience. This happy marriage dissolved around 1850, particularly for artists and avant-garde writers. Many intellectuals drew away from the middle class, deriding their taste and their suspicion of Bohemian unconventionality; poets and painters often expressed an inner vision, drawing only a small audience in the process. A gulf between innovative styles and public taste widened, into the twentieth century. Seeking alternatives to middle-class values, including politics, and trying to express discontent with their own marginal position and with the materialism of the society around them, some articulate intellectuals blasted modern values. Particularly on the Continent, they espoused ardent nationalism or authoritarian politics. Their works found a considerable audience among the literate and troubled ranks of the alienated professionals. Intellectuals varied greatly, to be sure; some were scientists and found themselves lionized by an appreciative public, which linked their work with broader progress, and some supported left-wing politics. It was revealing, however, that the predominant tone among students in medicine and law, in late nineteenth-century France and Germany, reflected the new intellectual politics of discontent.

Shopkeepers: The Borderline Middle Class

The horizons of many shopkeepers and master artisans were little changed in the mature industrial period. The owner of a German barbershop expected his worker to live in his home, and to work fifteen hours a day seven days a week, uncomplainingly. He would join with other owners in a voluntary guild to lament, still, the disrespect that was spreading among the lower classes. Parisian shopkeepers and artisans liked to think of themselves as the "little people" of society; one of their favorite newspapers was appropriately called *Le Petit Parisien*. As we have seen, the ranks of the small property owners expanded gradually but steadily during these decades. Their average incomes did not improve, but they were not bent on maximizing their earnings anyway. They continued to build their life around the shop, putting in long hours, with their spouses serving as cashiers and accountants.

What was changing was the world around these traditional operations. Although some workers might be content with the traditional bed and board, others wanted more independence. Small bakers and barbers even faced unionization among their employees, which infuriated them, although they often had to make concessions. Most notably, competition from department stores and other large commercial units reduced the significance of the small shop in the cities. Shops continued to handle most foods and many other goods. But the shopkeeping element, both retailers and master artisans, were driven out of the clothing industry except for the luxury trade. They could see they were losing ground relatively even when they were not displaced, and the threat of displacement was always there.

Shopkeepers readily exaggerated their dilemma, often claiming imminent displacement even as their number grew. Some, of course, continued a modest, private existence. Many British shopkeepers were on good terms with their working-class clientele, though they stood apart somewhat by their status and their somewhat unmasculine avoidance of manual labor. Even in Britain, however, the shops faced competition from consumer cooperatives, and some sense of threat and unfair treatment spread widely.

Signs of Discontent

Manifestations of anxiety among the shopkeepers and the disgruntled middle class were rather scattered before 1914. Some, in both groups, became socialists, for the early socialist parties drew much support from the middle ranks of society. Here was even a chance for some intellectuals to seek a new political role, although as theoreticians they were usually shunted aside somewhat when the parties gained a mass base. A small-town socialist meeting in France would often be attended by a doctor, a journalist, a teacher, two grocers — and one worker. Even aside from support for socialism, professional people and shopkeepers might help in workers' strikes, for they saw big business as their enemy too. Many a French strike received some guidance from a liberal newspaper editor and food and credit from local shopkeepers.

This movement toward the political Left should not be minimized, but the more typical expression of middle-class anxieties came in support for nationalist causes and anti-Semitism that had rightist implications. Nationalism was respectable. It associated people who felt lost in industrial society with a larger cause. News of imperialistic victories in

Africa and Asia gave excitement to otherwise drab lives. Extending the doctrines of racial nationalism, anti-Semitism provided an outlet for some of the specific grievances of shopkeepers and professional people. Jews could be blamed for much that was disturbing in the modern world. The prominence of Jews in finance and as owners of department stores made them a target for the growing hostility to big business. Many shopkeepers in Paris, for example, belonged to the Merchants' Antisemite Leagues, which worked to limit the commercial competition of Jews. Similarly, students in the professional schools often joined nationalist and anti-Semitic groups.

Intense nationalism generally and anti-Semitism in particular occasionally led elements of these groups into outright disorder. A number of riots occurred over imperialist crises, such as those in London in 1898 over Fashoda and Rome in 1911 over the issue of conquering Tripoli. These riots were stirred up by the excitement of the popular press and were often led by professional nationalist agitators; but they attracted a certain number of shopkeepers, master artisans like butchers, and their young assistants, who provided the bulk of the popular support for the agitation. The large riots over the Dreyfus case in Paris in 1898 drew participation directly from the lower middle class and students. The initial riots over Zola's letter claiming that Dreyfus was innocent were spurred by the desire to protect the honor of the national army against an officer assumed to be traitorous partly because he was a Jew. The popular press was uniformly hostile to Dreyfus, and some anti-Semitic papers, such as Drumont's *La France Juive,* called for riots. Students answered this call first, but they were not alone. Riots in January and again in October called forth many grocers, pastry-shop owners, waiters, and small investors in stocks and bonds. Along with medical and law students, these groups provided most of the participants in the riots and drew most of the arrests. This sort of nationalist and anti-Semitic agitation was not typical. Only a minority of the middle class participated, largely in capital cities, and only infrequently. Political parties organized on anti-Semitic lines, such as the group organized by a Lutheran pastor, Adolf Stöcker, in Germany during the 1890s, attracted only a small number of votes. (Stöcker's party drew about 400,000 at its peak.) Only in Vienna did a Christian socialist party draw mass support from the shopkeeping element; yet despite an anti-Semitic platform the party in power concentrated on improving urban transportation facilities and municipal insurance programs, suggesting that had governments given more attention to the material problems of the middle class they might have won its disgruntled elements from extremism altogether.

What was a slender current before World War I thus became a massive tide of discontent thereafter. During the 1920s the formation of small firms slowed notably under the pressure of large commercial and

industrial combines and the low rate of economic growth. The unemployment of professional people reached new heights. In 1926,
some 14,000 of 48,000 trained physicians in Germany were not able to
practice medicine and were engaged in clerical jobs instead. In Germany, where the problems of these elements of the middle class were
greatest, it was not uncommon by 1929 to see newspaper advertisements proclaiming personal misery: "Thirty years old, married, three
children. Nothing earned for three years. Future: Poor house,
madhouse, or the gas jet."[2] In many European countries rising rates of
suicide reflected the extremes of despair.

Most important was the damage caused by inflation and the subsequent Depression. In Germany inflation destroyed over 50 percent of
the capital of the middle class by 1925. The whole notion of the value
of savings and prosperity was undermined. Pensions were reduced and
many retired bureaucrats lived in near misery; some actually starved.
Even such an eminent professor as Ernst Troeltsch subsisted in retirement only on aid from friends. The government prohibited the raising
of rents during inflation, so many small property owners saw their incomes lag behind prices. Half a million people were forced into factory
work during the 1920s as a result of economic pressure. And all the
while the incomes of the wealthy capitalists were visibly increasing. A
hatred of big business and of labor, already evident before the war,
inevitably increased.

The Depression heightened this distress. Many shopkeepers suffered
as their clients' purchasing power declined. Increased taxes on small
business, as in Germany, added to the problem. Professional people
had difficulty finding work. In Germany 7,000 engineers lost their jobs,
and by 1930, some 300,000 German university graduates were competing for 130,000 positions. European governments fired literally hundreds of thousands of bureaucrats and clerks as tax revenues declined
during the crisis. Thousands of teachers were unemployed (40,000 in
Germany alone). Furthermore, unemployed members of the middle
class did not receive the social insurance benefits and union protection
accorded to the workers, and their resentment of the working class
increased as a result.

In general, important segments of the middle ranks met economic
disaster during the period, particularly during the Depression. Some
were entirely out of work; others had to accept jobs beneath their levels
of training and their social status. An even larger segment suffered
from the decline in economic growth during the period. A class that
had based its position on professional training or property ownership
now found both eroded by apparently uncontrollable trends in the
economy, even though recovery after the trough of the Depression

---

[2] Karl Dietrich Bracher, *Die Auflösung der Weimarer Republik* (Villingen, 1957), p. 169.

brought renewed profits to many shopkeepers and restored employment for numerous professional people.

Here was the background to a mighty explosion of protest. Still loath
to engage directly in violence, many discontented artisans, shopkeepers,
and professionals supported political parties whose mission was violence. What they sought from nazism and other rightist movements,
and what many of these movements seemed to promise, was a return
to an older economy, in which the family firm would have its due. The
promises to attack big banks and department stores were never really
kept, though for a time guilds were revived in Nazi Germany—as social
organizations. But from the standpoint of the supporters involved, not
only of nazism but of radical rightist movements like the *Croix de feu* in
France, the promises were long believed. Under pressure of unprecedented economic shock, the disgruntled middle class turned against
industrial trends and against the presumed incompetence of parliamentary government. Only countries like England, where the liberal impulse was strong and the guild tradition unusually weak, avoided a
strong current of right-wing middle-class protest. Ironically, these
rightist movements attacked not only modern economic forms but also
important elements of the new middle-class culture, such as changing
roles for women.

The disgruntled middle class was by no means the only support for
rising fascism, and its own goals were mixed. Middle-class fascists might
attack liberalism and Jews, department stores and cosmopolitan women.
They also saw fascism as a means of dislodging the upper class, creating
new jobs in the bureaucracy or universities for aspiring professionals.
And they treasured fascism's assertion of strong national purpose, even
adventure. They were not bent simply on restoring an imagined past.

The Middle Class and Its Values

Nationalism and protest were not the characteristic expressions of the
middle class during most of the mature industrial period. Certainly
before World War I, and to an important degree between the world
wars, the bulk of the middle class remained thoroughly committed to
industrial society and the progress it seemed to entail. This middle class
had few political grievances, for civil liberties seemed adequately protected while the parliamentary form prevailed. It had faith in modern
science; it believed in advancing prosperity. And although this mainstream middle class might not actively oppose anti-Semitism, it was not
sympathetic to it. The magazines most popular among the class, such
as the durable *Gartenlaube* in Germany, preached the ethic of liberal
humanitarianism and progress. Even socialism was not viewed as a total
threat, for it proved compatible with the parliamentary system, and

many middle-class politicians could easily cooperate with socialist representatives on specific projects of reform at the national level and even
more in municipal government, where both were interested in improving the physical facilities of the cities.

The optimism of the middle class was captured in 1900, when newspapers and other publications, looking back on the developments of the
past century, could only be impressed with the progress that had been
achieved. The economic situation had been transformed by the revolution in technology and the massive increase in output. New products
were available to almost everyone. Advances in health and increases in
population were evident. Political changes had brought new liberties
and opportunities for participation to the middle class and even to the
masses. Knowledge had advanced as education spread, and scientific
discoveries challenged the forces of ignorance and superstition. In
terms of the values held by most of the middle class, progress seemed
undeniable, and there was little doubt that further advance would
come.

Even the optimistic middle class viewed the lower classes with some
anxiety, as news of strikes and socialist agitation spread. Individual employers resented worker demands for a voice over conditions and
grumbled about ingratitude. Middle-class leaders, as they had to back
off from purely paternalistic policies, sought new ways to guide and
control workers. Youth groups were formed to moralize this segment
of the working class. New definitions of juvenile delinquency
criminalized vandalism and other disorder—another control directed
mainly at young workers. At the same time the middle class believed
the masses could and should advance, once they were better educated,
and they accepted, in the main, democratic voting rights for men. At
once anxious and superior, the middle class nevertheless did not view
workers solely through the lens of class warfare, at least not until after
World War I.

Who was in the middle class? Successful lawyers and doctors, middle-
level industrialists, mainstream and other independent businesspeople—all the groups that had been represented before in middle-
class ranks. Increasingly, however, the middle class was expanding on
the basis of specialized training and managerial skills rather than property ownership. Giant corporations required a complex layer of managers, beginning with the director of the individual plant or mine.
Their research needs created the technician, who could apply scientific
training to industrial products; hence the industrial chemist, alongside
the engineer. This kind of expansion meant upward mobility for many.
Forty-three percent of new British managers, for example, had improved their status. New educational opportunities allowed many to
rise through technical training. Not a few shopkeepers' and artisans'
sons took advantage of these opportunities to enter the middle class, for

small owners were alert to educational advantages in a period when their own economy seemed shaky. Here was an important junction between old and new groups. Mobility into the middle class slowed during the 1920s, given reduced economic growth. A large number of managers now came from established managerial families. In Britain the result was a decline of almost 50 percent in the number of managers who had risen from the lower classes, whereas in Germany there were many complaints that the few new positions available were given to outsiders, sometimes relatives of the owner, instead of being used as channels for promotion from within. The mainstream middle class was thus not immune to major difficulties. On the whole, however, the mature industrial period saw the chance for considerable expansion and redefinition.

The Lower Middle Class

One key to the power and complexity of the middle ranks was the emergence of an essentially new lower middle class that formed the most rapidly growing segment of society, based on the explosion of white-collar jobs.

There were several major sources of white-collar employment. The new wealth of upper and lower classes alike increased the demand for services not connected with manufacturing or with manual labor. Services such as teaching, the staffing of hotels and resorts, and banking expanded rapidly in the period and played a major role in the extension of lower-middle-class jobs.

The expansion of large organizations required an array of lower-level bureaucratic personnel. Huge corporations needed quantities of secretaries, clerks, and other white-collar workers. The spread of large factories increased the demand for foremen to supervise and direct the labor force. In earlier industry many of these tasks had been handled by employers and their families. Women had often done accounting and secretarial work for their husbands, and manufacturers had supervised workers directly in many small plants. With the expansion of firms, bureaucratic personnel became absolutely essential. Furthermore, this new bureaucracy was not confined to private enterprise alone. Governments also expanded their administrations during the period; they too participated in the movement to develop more massive organization, particularly in the economy. Expansion of government functions created thousands of new jobs. New taxing powers, including tariffs and even income tax, required massive paperwork and the clerks to handle it. Government education systems demanded teachers. New factory inspection laws called for inspectors and their clerks to execute them. Postal services expanded. By 1900 at least 5 percent of the labor force in France was employed by the government in white-collar jobs.

The expansion of bureaucracy, both public and private, was the most important single source of the growth of the lower middle class.

The surge of white-collar employment was extremely rapid. Britain had 7,000 female secretaries in 1881, 22,200 in 1891, and 90,000 in 1901. By 1871 the lower middle class constituted about 10 percent of the British population, up from roughly 7 percent in 1850. By 1900 the British lower middle class was a full 20 percent of the population. Comparable development took place in other industrialized countries. A significant clerical class began to rise with the spread of corporate bureaucracies even in countries such as Russia, where 3.5 percent of factory employment was in the white-collar category by 1900.

The lower middle class drew its new numbers from several social groups. To sons of beleaguered displaced businesspeople and artisans white-collar positions seemed relatively attractive alternatives, befitting their educational levels and sense of respectability. People from craft backgrounds were particularly numerous and welcomed the chance to avoid factory work; one survey showed that over half the sons of German printers had entered the lower middle class. The thousands of women who found white-collar employment came from a wide variety of social groups, including factory workers, for clerical positions were less demanding physically and more respectable socially than factory labor. On the whole, more white-collar women than men came from working-class backgrounds, which suggests the importance of these jobs for female mobility. This was one reason servanthood declined, as better education and the white-collar jobs opened new opportunity for working-class women. But certain white-collar positions were filled by male members of the working class; foremen, particularly, usually rose from the ranks. Sometimes they retained the attitudes and interests of the labor force, but more commonly they assumed a lower-middle-class orientation. Certain white-collar jobs also attracted middle-class women into the industrial labor force; nursing and school teaching were respectable enough to let a minority of women in this class break new ground. Very few lower-middle-class jobs were filled by people of rural origin. This was an urban class, as its culture was to indicate.

As with the middle class, the lower middle class declined somewhat as a source of mobility between the world wars. Large numbers of workers still sought to switch; half a million German workers moved into lower-middle-class ranks right after 1918. But this new supply tended to reduce wages; by 1929 at least a million white-collar workers earned no more than a skilled factory hand. Moreover, the Depression brought considerable unemployment. Again in Germany 600,000 of four million salaried employees were out of work by 1933, almost as high a proportion as in the working class. It was tempting to respond along with disgruntled shopkeepers or professional people, and some clerks and technicians undoubtedly swelled the ranks of supporters for nazism or other radical causes.

Economic Values and Social Status

Even before this there had been links between white-collar workers and the shopkeeping element. Some stemmed from the fact that many white-collar workers, particularly males, came from a shopkeeper background. This was a distinct group, in that its position was not based on property ownership. But it valued the idea of ownership and tended to distrust people, such as socialists, who advocated its destruction. In addition, it was slightly harder to unionize white-collar workers than to unionize their factory counterparts. Some of the unions that were formed were unusually conservative. The German Federation of Salaried Commercial Employees, formed in 1893, attracted a quarter of all private salaried personnel by 1914 and actively sought favorable legislation on hours and wages for white-collar work. It was not a working-class type of union, however, and it was hostile to the socialist labor movement. It shunned strikes, issued anti-Semitic propaganda, and sought above all to promote its members' sense of status. This sort of development has led some observers to lump white-collar workers with shopkeepers in a single large, potentially fascist, lower middle class. But this is not really accurate. White-collar workers often organized in radical unions. This was true of postal workers and primary school teachers in France; the former even conducted a major strike before 1914. British white-collar workers unionized rapidly around the turn of the century. Unionization spread still farther in Germany during the 1920s, and although the biggest groupings were non-socialist, a large socialist union found favor with many.

The lower middle class is best understood as a new group, separate from older propertied groups. It was certainly not working class, either in conditions or aspirations, though individuals and groups, as in France, might sympathize with the labor movement. White-collar work appealed to the age-old distinction between manual and nonmanual labor. Clerks were able to dress well on the job, indeed they were typically required to dress rather formally. This set them off from workers. They were paid by the month and had more job security; this set them apart economically even when their listed wage rates were no higher than those of workers. Some, undoubtedly, treated workers with scant respect. Foremen were often peremptory, pay clerks sometimes insulting. Many workers had ambivalent feelings about the lower middle class, hating their social pretensions but unable to deny that they were indeed a socially superior group.

Much of the distinctiveness of the lower middle class came from its origins. In the early Industrial Revolution and before, business clerks had considerable prestige. Many, indeed, were the sons of owners and would rise to a managerial position with age. This gave clerks a sense of participation in management that a manual worker could not have. As bureaucracies expanded the literal association of clerks with managers largely disappeared, but a sense of contact remained. At least this was the case for male employees; female secretaries were considered separate and unequal. But even the female worker might have dreams of marrying the boss, and a romantic, largely inaccurate, literature quickly developed around this theme. For males, separation from management in terms of dress and friendly greetings in the morning was far less sharp than for the working class. Big companies carefully preserved this linkage, setting up special benefit programs for office personnel in order to limit any sense of proletarianization. In Germany, even national insurance schemes were segregated, which suited the aspirations of the clerks admirably. By their own choice they were middle class, not workers.

That there was a great deal of bluff in all this is obvious. Working conditions in the offices, and still more for female department store clerks, were often similar to those in the early industrial factories. Long hours combined with harsh shop rules that dictated dress and behavior. One German office manager installed a steam jet in the employee's toilet, timed to go off every three minutes, to prevent idling. New technology became more and more routinized. Many clerks resented the intrusion of typewriters. Here was a precious opportunity for women, who, not having had secretarial positions before, had less reason for concern; women monopolized typing from the first. Complaints about the routinization of office work became still sharper in the 1920s. This was a potent cause of the unionization movements. Yet still the lower middle class found its work situation distinctive, and self-delusion was only part of this. Speed-up efforts and time clocks could never eliminate the possibility of socializing on these jobs. Clerical work retained a slower pace than manufacturing. Moreover, the fervent belief in middle-class status could be translated into reality. A substantial minority moved further upward in society. Thirty-five percent of the managers of British industry named between 1900 and 1920 came from the lower middle class, but only 25 percent from the far larger laboring classes.

By the 1920s, if not before, the lower middle class was beginning to define a new relationship of work to life. Legislation and unionization efforts pushed hours of work down. The continued sense of responsibility on the job, plus the relatively relaxed pace and social contacts, made the work seem pleasant; almost certainly far more clerks than workers would have defined their jobs as satisfying. But clerks were also bent on making work only one segment of their lives. One sign of this was in the growing interest in formal retirement plans, particularly of course among government employees such as postal workers and teachers. Far earlier than businesspeople or workers, the lower middle class pushed for formal retirement, with pension plans to make this possible. In France some groups won a retirement age of fifty-five, by the 1930s; in Britain and elsewhere sixty-five was more common. An old age free from work was just one aspect of the life-style this class sought. More than the middle class, which was still more likely to be wrapped up in the job, the lower middle class sought a pleasant life in and around home and family. Earnings did not yet extend to massive consumer purchases; only about half of this group owned a radio in the 1920s. But there were suggestions of a new consumer style.

The lower middle class was distinctly more concerned about good housing and furnishings than workers were. Different consumer standards reflected the desire of this group to follow a middle-class lead in defining respectable material life; lower middle-class people would devote more of their budget to rents even when their earnings were no higher than those of the workers. Their housing interest was thus distinctly middle class, and clerks imitated middle-class taste in furniture and home decoration when possible. To make sure they could afford good housing as well as to promote their children's mobility opportunities, the lower middle class reduced its birthrate notably below middle-class levels. By the 1920s many couples remained childless by choice. They also purchased large amounts of life insurance, to assure security. But this was not a conservative group, clinging defensively to a dated respectability. The lower middle class not only spent more heavily on recreation than the middle class but also spent more for it than workers. Members of the lower middle class led in the rising interest in motion pictures and radio, whereas the middle class was longer attached to older entertainment forms such as concerts. They also led in the growing expenditures on tobacco. They were, in sum, at the forefront of a new definition of middle-class, off-the-job culture by the 1920s.

The Leisure Ethic

Well before this, the mainstream middle class had begun to relax. The work ethic remained valid and many managers and professionals worked long hours with great intensity, from their student days onward. As industrial pioneers were replaced by managerial bureaucracies, however, the hours of work went down for the middle class overall. New leisure, plus at least a modest affluence, permitted the development of new habits. Distinctive lower middle-class interests added to the mix. At first the shifts were rather tentative, precisely because the hold of the work ethic was strong. English recreational magazines, which began to appear in the 1850s, urged sports and vacations because of their role in improving work performance. A man who exercised and got out into the pure country air would be able to do his job better. But gradually leisure was recommended for its own sake.

Middle-class recreational interests took many forms, with a strong element of faddism apparent in most. The class believed in change; the new leisure had scant traditional base. So one enthusiasm followed another. One channel was dancing. As early as 1860 there were sixty-eight dance halls in Paris. This was a new kind of dancing. Couples held each other closely and one style followed the other: the *maxixe,* the cakewalk, and then in the 1920s the Charleston. Sports formed another interest, with England leading the way. Horse racing drew new crowds. The first adult soccer football club was formed in 1858. Rugby grew more popular. Croquet had its day during the 1860s, tennis and roller skating came in during the next decade. By the 1880s bicycling was the reigning passion, and the automobile craze soon followed. In the 1920s boxing and car racing were added to the list of spectator sports. In yet another development seaside resorts drew new numbers of people. Some new leisure interests privileged men, most notably the rough sports. Women gained ground also, through family recreation and also sports such as tennis and bicycling.

These new leisure interests cut middle-class devotion to religion; though there were intensely pious segments, church attendance began to fall overall. Some pastors, eager to keep up with the times, suggested drive-in services for bicyclists, but there was really no remedy. Middle-class leisure was a big business, and followed some clear commercial patterns. Codification was one: old sports, like rugby and soccer, were given clear rules for the first time. Advertising was another. Specialized magazines grew up around every new interest, and notices in the general press were urging Europeans, by 1900, to smoke cigarettes, drink *apéritifs,* go to the beach, build muscles, or buy a newer-model bicycle.

The new leisure activities tended to loosen the public attitude of the middle class toward sex. The plays and, a bit later, the movies that the class helped patronize grew frank in their discussions of sexual matters; a popular play in Paris in the early 1900s stressed the desirability of premarital intercourse. The bicycle and the automobile helped change courtship patterns. An older chaperone might try to keep pace with a courting couple on bicycle, but it was a losing battle. Women's clothing changed, becoming looser and more revealing; the short skirts of the 1920s culminated a long trend here. For the new dances, for bicycling, the restrictive costumes of the early industrial middle class simply would not do. Indeed the whole notion of what a woman should look like evolved as part of the leisured life-style. The woman should be slender, a bit athletic though not heavily muscled. Imperfections in face or hair should be modified by cosmetics; older women should take care, using similar products, to look as young as possible. The battle against graying and weight gain had begun.

There were areas of the new leisure from which women were long excluded. Only in the 1920s, after World War I had further loosened traditional standards, was it good form for women to smoke and drink. Overall, however, the middle-class recreational patterns were notable

New ideas in the later nineteenth century: vacations, beach resorts, and more public romance. This picture is from the British resort Yarmouth, taken by Paul Martin in 1892. Costume did not initially keep pace with changing habits and expectations. *(Gernsheim Collection, Harry Ransom Humanities Research Center, The University of Texas at Austin.)*

for their inclusion of women. This same interest applied to sexuality. Women's sex drives received new attention and women themselves sought new pleasure. Middle-class women in England during the 1920s wrote in the thousands to a sexual expert, Marie Stopes, who advised methods of achieving orgasm. They made it clear that marriages did not depend on heightened sexual pleasure, but they also made it clear that they were intensely interested.

Middle-class leisure interests linked also to a more exuberant consumer ethic. Women, with some money to spend, flocked to the proliferating department stores, where they were served by deferential clerks. A minority pioneered a new disease—kleptomania—that found people,

The windows of consumerism. Store displays designed to encourage appetites for fashion became a vital part of urban life, particularly though not exclusively for the middle classes. This collection, aimed at proud parents, appeared on a fashionable Paris street in 1925. *("Magasin avenue des Gobelins," photo by Atget. Museum of Modern Art, NY.)*

mainly middle-class women, compulsively shoplifting items they did not need. Household finery gained new standards, as the middle class enjoyed purchasing mass-produced Turkish carpets and oriental lamps. Expression through consumption advanced steadily in its importance in middle-class life.

The Middle-Class Family

Like mainstream values, many features of the middle-class family had been launched in the previous period; they were now consolidated. Limitation of the birthrate became steadily more pronounced, aided by improvements in the quality of birth-control devices. By the 1930s the single-child family was a commonplace. There was still tension between the discipline regarded as desirable in dealing with children, particularly on the Continent, and a growing affection. Parents wanted to be honored and loved at the same time. But the general trend was toward ever-growing affection and attention, and the leading child-rearing manuals urged parents (fathers as well as mothers) to have fun with their offspring: "How simple it is to be happy . . . to be loved all one's life by a being one loves."[3]

In this context the middle class discovered a new problem by the 1890s: adolescence. Never before defined as a particularly remarkable period of life, adolescence was now seen as fraught with untold problems and tensions. This was a leading theme in the psychology of the day, but in actual family behavior as well. Improvements in education extended schooling into adolescence; this was new for the bulk of the middle class. It kept teen-aged children out of the work force; it also made them more knowledgeable than their parents. Here was a built-in generational tension as part of educational gains. Much of the new leisured culture gave special opportunities to teenagers: the dance crazes, and looser courtship patterns affected them particularly. It was easy for parents to disapprove, again a tension that has continued to be part of modern life. Finally, the age of puberty kept declining, yet the middle class did not clearly redefine its premarital sexual ethic. Premarital sex was in fact becoming more common, at least for boys. In France secondary school students regularly patronized brothels, which helped support tens of thousands of prostitutes in Paris by the end of the nineteenth century. Others took working-class or servant girls as mistresses during their years before marriage. But it was still widely believed that sexual intercourse too early in life, or too frequently indulged in, was harmful to health, and masturbation and homosexuality were held in horror, though undoubtedly widespread in boys' schools. Some adolescents, particularly girls, were kept in sexual ignorance as a result; one girl believed she had become pregnant after a man put his arm around her on a train. Generally, however, the sexual problems of adolescence, as seen by parents, seemed acute. At the same time the definition of adolescence as a difficult age actually helped parents cope

[3] Charles Lefebvre, *La Famille en France dans le Droit et dans les Moeurs* (Paris, 1920), p. 182.

with some fears that before had been hard to understand; hence fulminations against masturbation, which had gone so far as morning checks of sheets to make sure a youth had not offended, declined by 1900. By the 1930s the spread of Freudian psychology further eased concern about signs of adolescent sexuality, particularly among males.

The development of the concept of adolescence had a number of more general results. Schools and other institutions, even in dealing with lower-class youths, tried to stress conformity and discipline. Fear of adolescent wildness led to the new preoccupation with juvenile delinquency, the rates of which rose largely because definitions of improper behavior became more rigorous. A variety of movements were developed to channel adolescent energies. The youth group became an obligatory branch of institutions ranging from churches to socialist parties, while the Boy Scouts emerged as a distinct organization. Adolescents themselves began to see themselves as a group apart. Many hiking and athletic organizations arose after 1900, for in general the emphasis on adolescence related to a stress on action over thought.

Through most of the mature industrial period adolescence loomed large as a family problem for the middle class. In a sense it was the counterpart to the growing affection lavished on children in typically small families. With few brothers or sisters to deal with, the child was in rather constant contact with doting parents, whose love, by the time the teenage years were reached, could seem cloying. The problem of relating the family as a unit of affection to the need for individual independence was severe.

The middle class faced a related concern about old age, though this was far less clearly articulated. With some improvements in health, there was growing realization that survival into one's sixties or seventies was likely. Yet age was conventionally seen as a time of debility. There were some erroneous cultural impressions involved in the view of old age; for example, it was almost universally believed that sexual intercourse was likely to be fatal for anyone over fifty-five or so. In other words old age was assumed to be a period of more rapid and complete physical deterioration than was in fact necessarily the case. But this view encouraged important segments of the middle class to develop the notion of retirement; in addition, of course, bureaucratic managers were eager to get rid of older employees because they were believed to be inefficient. So the older parent, living on an often rather meager pension, became an increasingly common family problem. Contact between adults and their parents developed widely in the middle class, at least loosely reproducing an extended family network. With the telephone and the automobile the contact was facilitated. In the 1920s, older people began to develop new activities of their own, seeking recreational opportunities and companionship. The pattern of living with an adult child declined, a sign of greater prosperity and independence.

Between marriage partners a final set of ambiguous developments occurred. Marriage age declined slightly, which was the reflection of new courtship patterns. But in the middle class the husband was usually considerably older than the wife and, as already suggested, more likely to be sexually experienced. Furthermore, the business aspect of marriage remained important, particularly on the Continent. Dowries and formal marriage contracts were regular practice in France. As one observer noted, "For the great majority of the bourgeoisie, marriage is the greatest financial transaction of their lives."[4] This led to continuing tension in some families, as the male sought sexual enjoyment with a mistress rather than with his spouse. Some women were frightened by sexuality, which they endured only to have a child or two. Others might be frigid with their husbands, when marriage seemed merely a business arrangement, but sought affairs of their own; a few even worked secretly as part-time prostitutes, to supplement their household budgets. So there were problems in integrating the growing recognition of the importance of sex into middle-class marriage. But marriage manuals increasingly urged the importance of sexual compatibility in marriage, stressing the need for mutual orgasm. Better birth-control information and the growing emphasis on romance in courtship could facilitate ties of affection in many families.

Certainly divorce, which was legalized or, if already legal, made easier during this period in most countries, did not significantly dent the middle-class family. In France the divorce rate rose until 1920, then stabilized; during the 1920s and 1930s, about 5 percent of all marriages ended in divorce, but more commonly in the working class than in the middle class. It was also notable that formal marriage contracts declined in France, as the link between family and property loosened. The mixture of affection and financial arrangements, whatever the proportions of each, gave middle-class marriage a continuing vitality. The growing connection of the family with new recreational outlets provided an additional focus.

Middle-Class Women

The family remained the center of most women's lives. The married woman increased her importance as a consumer agent, for the decline of servants was matched by new purchases such as vacuum cleaners and washing machines. Housework was still a major challenge, for standards of cleanliness became even more demanding, bolstered now by the germ theory as well as the desire for a respectable home. Good

---

[4] Paul Bureau, *L'Indiscipline des Mouers* (Paris, 1927), p. 60.

appearance was another challenge, and homemakers paid growing attention to diet as well as to fashionable clothing and cosmetics. Health improved with less childbirth and more careful sterilization procedures by doctors and midwives; maternal mortality declined rapidly after 1890. There were ambiguities in this situation. With fewer children, who were in turn more often in school, the maternal role lessened somewhat. Movement to the suburbs left many homemakers alone during much of the day, although their visits or calls to relatives might compensate somewhat. A traditional crutch was removed as growing restrictions on drugs reduced the availability of opiates. New forms of recreation helped, as attendance at the movies and the rise of women's sports suggested, but some pastimes, such as dancing, were more accessible to women before marriage than to homemakers. Married women rarely worked in the middle class, so this was not an available outlet; even the impact of inflation and depression did not force many middle-class women to defy family respectability by taking a job.

More dramatic developments occurred for single women in the middle class, though it must be remembered that these were a minority as marriage continued to dominate the goals of most women. Better education and legal reforms opened professional careers to some middle-class women. Able to obtain a university education (by the 1900s about 12 percent of all university students were female in France), some pushed for admittance to law, medicine, and the civil service. Numbers here were still small, and far more women were channeled into only semi-professional jobs, such as primary school teaching. Where relatively large numbers were concerned with careers of this sort, a new feminist movement arose around 1900. Britain led the way here, for by this time there were almost 200,000 professional women. The feminists called for equal pay for equal work and insisted on gaining the vote. They obtained hundreds of thousands of signatures on their petitions and shortly before World War I conducted a number of massive demonstrations and acts of violence. The movement did not address itself to the concerns of the homemaker, nor was it particularly successful in attracting working-class support. This helps explain why, after the right to vote was granted to women in two stages, 1918 and 1928, feminism subsided rather quickly. On the Continent individual feminists were active during this same period, and socialist parties advocated a number of new rights for women.

French feminists attacked double-standard sexuality, urging greater restraint by men. Scandinavian feminists won voting rights before 1914. Women's protests, thought most dramatic in England, became an important new political ingredient. They signaled the tension between changes in women's lives, including educational levels, and continued limitations associated with largely family roles.

Women's new public recreation and their political demands roused the ire of the disgruntled segments of the middle class. Some professionals feared women as possible competitors. Many lamented the moral decay that, to them, the leisure ethic represented. When life was filled with games, and movies displaced concerts, civilization was sorely threatened. Themes of this sort were visible before 1914; a number of anti-Semitic movements, for example, included blasts at women's rights. With the shock of World War I, followed by the further elaboration of the leisure ethic during the 1920s, traditionalist outrage mounted. One of the appeals of the Nazi movement was to return women to the home and curb modern fashions. The peasant *Dirndl* was to replace the flapper's outfit, as the middle class continued to be divided on their basic orientation toward life. In this area, too, the middle class displayed its tensions between tradition and change.

The Working Classes

The working classes remained extremely diversified during the mature industrial period, though the balance among the major elements was shifting. The artisanal element remained strong. Large numbers of bakers and metalworkers still lived with their masters. Although sorely pressed by the spread of factories even the domestic manufacturing system hung on; almost 5 percent of all German manufacturing workers still labored at home in 1907. A number of French women, rural and urban, manufactured textile products at home. The growth of the working class was concentrated, however, in three major segments.

1. *The urban crafts: woodworking, many kinds of metalwork, printing, and so on.* These were increasingly centered in units of about fifty workers, well above traditional artisanal size. This meant that journeymen shared some of the problems factory workers had, in terms of more impersonal organization and the introduction of new technology. We will see, however, that the journeymen's situation remained distinctive. Except for construction, where the number of workers increased rapidly, this was the slowest-growing section of the working class, but it retained considerable importance.

2. *Factory work and mining.* Here growth was more rapid. But some sectors stagnated, such as textiles before World War I and both textiles and mining afterward. This meant that many workers, or their children, had to shift into the expanding industries—machine tools, electrical equipment, for example—or face unemployment. Reshuffling, rather than rapid growth, now characterized this central segment of the working classes. While an important minority of factory workers was highly skilled—like the artisans who built cars in small shops, at the outset of this industry—the growing majority fell into semiskilled ranks.

3. *The unskilled.* This category embraced some factory workers who simply moved goods, but it was particularly important in construction and transportation work. This group of workers faced some of the greatest changes of any working-class element during the period. Indeed they increasingly moved from the category of faceless, transient poor into the mainstream of working-class life. They had some new job opportunities. New equipment allowed untrained personnel to move into positions in metalworking or the manufacture of furniture. Wherever they worked they were now in contact with machines: loading cranes, trucks, taxicabs. And their units of employment grew more structured. The development of big shipping companies most obviously put the unskilled on the docks and on board ship in contact with big business for the first time. Many resented change. This was the only group that now produced any direct attacks on machinery, which was feared as a threat to jobs. In reaction to new business organization the unskilled became increasingly sensitive about their dignity; as some French sailors proclaimed, "We are not pariahs, and we have the same right as any man to aspire to improve our lot."[5] From the unskilled, then, came bursts of anger that were more profound than those of other sections of the working class. But the very ability to react showed that the unskilled were moving from their transient, impoverished life to a position similar to that of other workers. They still suffered problems unknown to other groups. On a normal day before World War I, 36 percent of all London dockers would be out of work; for factory workers the rate was nearer 2 percent, for artisans nearer 5 percent, except in depressions. But the rate of unemployment among the unskilled tended to decline, with the expansion of shipping and trucking and the other new jobs available. And the unskilled themselves were more settled, less likely to move about from one season to the next, and more likely to form families. As they worked with new machines, some moved into the semi-skilled category.

One final group of workers requires discussion. The job situation of women workers changed quite dramatically in the mature industrial period. During early industrialization women workers had essentially tried, or been forced, to concentrate on the same kinds of jobs they had always done. Large numbers still worked at home; the manufacture of clothing, for example, remained a predominantly home industry well into the late nineteenth century. Other women continued to manufacture textiles, even specializing in spinning just as they had before (for men quickly resumed their positions as weavers). They had to move into factories to do this, which was a big change, but as we have seen

---

[5] André Sayous, *Les Grèves de Marseilles en 1904* (Paris, 1904), p. 62.

they continued to function as part of a family economy. The largest group of women went into domestic service, again changing locations, by moving into the cities, but retaining a traditional role in many respects. This pattern of adaptation was now disrupted. The stagnation of the textile industry (which remained heavily feminized) meant that new numbers of women had to seek work elsewhere. Some home dressmakers held out but the industry was increasingly moved into shops. Above all, servanthood began to decline or at least stabilize. Millions of women still worked as servants; one of Adolf Hitler's more interesting and unsound moves during World War II was to allow middle-class families to retain a large number of women servants despite a desperate labor shortage in the factories. But nowhere did the female servant population keep pace with overall urban growth, in the mature industrial countries, and in France it began an absolute decline as early as the 1890s. With new household appliances middle-class families needed servants less. Wages tended to stagnate, making domestic service less attractive than factory work from a sheer economic standpoint. Furthermore, young girls, now accustomed to the city, began to prefer the independence other kinds of work could give them. Former servants in England reported they found "more life" in the factories, whereas comparable German women noted, "the foremen were not nearly so coarse as the gracious ladies."[6]

Whether prodded by economic change or attracted by new opportunities, women began to push into new branches of work, outside the domestic setting. Many moved into clerical jobs, as we have seen. But others took work in printing, machine building, and many other factory industries. Like the unskilled generally they benefited from the new machines that reduced the skill levels in such industries, forming an important part of the new semiskilled category. In some countries, such as Germany, even married working-class women took factory jobs in increasing numbers. World War I temporarily increased opportunities for women's work everywhere, though in the 1920s levels fell back again somewhat. All in all, however, many working-class women and some married women were gaining more diverse and independent work experiences than ever before.

The overall expansion of the working classes was now slowing up. They constituted 30 to 40 percent of the population of the mature industrial countries, but they were no longer the most rapidly growing segment. This meant that changes in the situation of one group might seem newly menacing to another, for not only craftspeople but also many skilled factory workers were accustomed to their jobs and their position in society. They wanted to pass their work on to their sons. The association of family and factory work had been consolidated over

[6] Adelheid Popp, *Die Jugend Geschichete Einer Arbeiterin* (Munich, 1930), p. 41.

the early generations and many workers took a proprietary interest in their jobs. All this reflected a natural maturing of the working classes. But it gave workers a somewhat defensive cast because change could only threaten the accommodations that had been made. So skilled workers resented the unskilled. Women's entry was particularly feared. A French printer noted: "They're too impulsive. One day they are enthusiastic for our work, the next day they've changed their minds. The only way perhaps to resolve the problem would perhaps be by absorption. Each male typographer would marry a female typographer. That would be a solution."[7] We have seen that, in the early industrial period, the working class survived its first exposure to the factories by adaptation of many key traditions. These traditions, including that of women's "proper" role, were now challenged.

A New Security

Obviously many of the worst problems of industrial life were ended or at least modified by the late nineteenth century, thanks to the adjustment that had already taken place plus greater prosperity. Many workers were still badly fed. Low wages plus traditional diets, which neglected fruits and vegetables in favor of meats and starches, caused much poor nutrition. But the food situation greatly improved. This, along with better housing and clothing, meant better average health; infants were less likely to die, adult workers more likely to live into their sixties. Average unemployment declined in years of normal prosperity, at least until after World I and the growing economic dislocation. New machines and methods frightened workers who were more conscious of their need for stable employment than ever before, but they displaced few workers directly. More common was an intergenerational change, in which the son or daughter of a weaver might have to decide to go into another line of work. This caused tension, but the fact remained that more workers had more regular work, year in and year out, than had been the case since the population boom of the eighteenth century. Child labor declined to almost nothing, if only because of legislation. Working-class children might resent the rigors of school, but overall they benefited from not having to start work until they were fourteen or so. And this helped release jobs for adults.

The picture of change should not be overdrawn. Less unemployment still meant that about a fifth of the skilled segment of the working class, not to mention the unskilled, were unemployed for part of each year, and rarely by their own choice. Illness or recessions made a mockery of any effort at complete stability, and the sense of unpredictability

---

[7] *La Typographie Française*, April, 1907, p. 14.

continued to be an important part of working-class culture. Child mortality declined but as late as 1900 the average working-class family would have to mourn at least one infant death. Workers themselves perceived their tantalizing position between a really new level of security and subjection to traditional hardships. Some mothers took the risk of loving their babies more fiercely than before, only to be plunged into sorrow when one died; others played it safer, finding death inevitable and a proper funeral adequate solace. Workers might talk in one breath about their aspirations for better jobs and more training, and then in another admit that life was out of their control and that they would end "where the wind blows me." In one case their hesitation to risk a change in outlook was positively damaging. Most workers refused to recognize that they were living longer, at least until they reached their fifties. They expected to die young and they associated old age, naturally enough, only with illness and suffering. They thus made little effort to push for pension plans or formal retirement programs, arguing that any pension that began at age sixty-five would come too late: "pensions for dead people," as the French trade unions proclaimed. Only with the Depression did the retirement rate of workers pick up, out of necessity. Until then older workers had to continue work or, if disabled, take advantage of the meager benefit programs available through state or company plans while hoping that their children would care for them. Important improvements in the workers' lot should not, then, be equated with genuine affluence.

Furthermore, workers' ongoing adaptation to industrial work removed some traditional remedies for dissatisfaction. It was harder to think about changing jobs or moving from one area to the next. New workers faithfully reproduced the traditional pattern. Many unskilled factory workers were now recruited from foreign laborers, another sign that traditional unskilled workers were finding new options. Italians who flocked to the mines and metallurgical factories of France and Germany and the Poles who poured into the Ruhr changed jobs frequently, often returned home for harvest work, and displayed a high rate of absenteeism. Women workers, as they entered new fields, were more likely to change jobs than men and of course still typically left the factories altogether when they married. For most factory workers, absenteeism and particularly job changing were less attractive than before. They had become attached to their jobs and they were conscious of their need to support their families. Most did not drift into factory work accidentally. Although their range of choice was limited, most skilled workers at least could give a reason for their work, citing the guidance or example of their parents or the interest they expected to take in their jobs. This kind of attachment could be immensely satisfying, for it meant that a worker saw a purpose in his factory labor and could hope to pass this same sense on to his sons. But it left workers vulnerable as well. Skilled workers increasingly refused to take other work even when unemployed, for this would be beneath their professional dignity. Sons could not always follow their fathers. Some undoubtedly enjoyed the chance to strike out on their own, particularly when they could earn a higher wage. But parents were upset, and laments about the decline of the trade and the heedlessness of the young reflected this common generation gap in the working class. Choice warred with a desire for stability. The conservatism of many workers was tragically revealed after World War I, when masses of miners and textile workers resisted retraining and relocation, preferring to hold out in hope that their own industry would revive. Even before this, the growing sense of attachment to work was challenged by the changing nature of work itself.

A New Kind of Work

Most workers entered the mature industrial period preserving something like a traditional pace of work. This was least true in England, where per-worker productivity was highest. It obviously applied more to journeymen than to factory workers, and to the unskilled most of all. Dockers, for example, alternated periods of intense labor, up to thirty-six hours at a stretch, with days in which they would not even bother to seek work, preferring to rest instead. But the notion of long periods of work, punctuated by rests, applied in most factories as well, as workers resisted official shop rules. British machine builders could take naps on the job as late as the 1870s. Many German metalworkers stayed twelve or fourteen hours at the factory in the 1890s, but had over three hours in rest periods and managed to limit their pace of work even aside from this; as a result they took work home after hours, turning out wire or simple tools in the evenings and on Sundays. Workers in many factories put on tremendous bursts of energy at the end of a week, hoping to boost their earnings right before payday, and were then so tired they had to sleep all day Sunday; to compensate for their lack of recreation, they would then take Monday off to get drunk, only to return blearily on Tuesday or Wednesday and begin the whole cycle over again. Obviously machines had speeded up the pace of work in the factories already, and the factory whistle was the symbol of the new sense of regularity that work was supposed to involve. But many workers still thought in terms of a relatively slow pace combined with long hours in the factory.

Only some big-city craftsmen, such as construction workers, had even pressed for a major reduction in the hours of work before the 1870s, partly because their pace was being forced but also partly because they wanted to spread the work and limit unemployment. Well into the late nineteenth century workers spent most of their waking hours on the job except for traditional holidays and rest periods, which they might supplement by taking some days off on their own.

Within this context some of the new developments of mature industrial society were not as bothersome as might be imagined. Technological changes might be welcomed. Artisans whose work was being taken over by the factories naturally howled; a Parisian shoemaker proclaimed: "If I want the revolution it's not to do any harm to people but to be able to destroy all these machines."[8] But many workers valued new equipment that reduced physical strain, particularly when they got some of the benefit of increased output in the form of higher wages. English cotton workers actually tried to prod their employers to provide more productive equipment. Even artisans could adapt when direct displacement was not involved. Printers worried about the new composing machines, but mainly in advance of their installation. Once they began work on them they found that they still had a sense of skill, if somewhat reduced, and enjoyed the extra money their higher productivity won. Machines worried most workers, although some were fascinated by them, but they did not make them feel dehumanized. The semiskilled workers who were upgraded by the possibility of machine work, including many women, could gain a new feeling of worth on the job. Skilled workers, whose numbers continued to increase, though more slowly, found their jobs a bit less interesting but were not completely antagonized. As a German machine shop worker noted, "One good thing about machines is that a person can at least think about other things."[9]

Big business forms had a similarly ambiguous impact. Artisans were concerned about their larger units of employment, though some welcomed their freedom from the master's personal supervision. The collective bargaining procedures that spread widely in construction and the crafts partially replaced person-to-person contacts. Printers, for example, could go to a shop representative, called the Chapel Father in England, if they had grievances, knowing that the representative could take it up directly with the employer. Factory workers were not so lucky. Big companies did develop grievance committees, but usually under strict employer control. Rarely did they let collective bargaining extend to on-the-job complaints, and as we will see, many big industrialists refused to have anything to do with unions at all. So as company size increased, workers might grow restive under the impersonality and remoteness of management. British miners talked of their friendly relations with supervisors in the past; but now the supervisor, pressed to keep production up, would simply refer them to the branch manager,

[8] Henry Steele, *The Working Classes in France, a Social Study* (London, 1904), p. 91.
[9] Marie Bernays, *Auslese und Anpassung der Arbeiterschaft in der Geschlossenen Grossindustrie* (Leipzig, 1910), p. 281.

who put on airs and said, "What the bloody hell do you want?" A German worker phrased his anger rather formally: "The consciousness of dependence on the employer embitters me. A gesture of the director is enough to make my blood boil."[10] So many workers did press for changes in factory organization that would give them greater voice over conditions. But most workers were less directly affected by the rise of big business. If their supervisor seemed fair they might find the job pleasant; personal clashes, more than disputes over remote management, were most common on the work site. Some directors were known to be fair, even friendly. The policies of paternalism continued by most big companies had their predictable effect of contenting some workers who valued the material benefits of housing programs or hospitalization plans and found it natural to defer to this management approach, while infuriating another group more conscious of personal freedom. Big business encouraged an atmosphere of class strife, particularly after 1900, but it was far from universal.

In combination with changes in organization and technology, a persistent pressure to intensify the pace of work affected a large segment of workers from the 1890s onward. Again, journeymen were largely immune. Their industries were not heavily involved in international competition and their strong craft unions prevented excessive innovation. Hence employers who tried to introduce piecework rather than daily pay, to encourage greater individual effort, were successfully rebuffed. In construction per-worker productivity actually declined as workers held their pace down. But in factories and in transportation the pace steadily increased. Machine workers, for example, were pressed to accept the piece rate, which by rewarding higher production with a higher wage stimulated faster work. Their unions objected, but to no avail; and a few workers found piecework more interesting precisely because of the motivation it provided. By the eve of World War I, particularly in the machine shops, time and motion studies were being conducted by outside engineers to determine how each worker could be compelled to greater efficiency. This was a foretaste of the assembly line system, in which workers in automobile factories and elsewhere repeated small operations on products as they moved past on the conveyor belt, the apotheosis of routinized, semiskilled labor. Spurred by the example of American productivity, the assembly line in Europe spread increasingly after World War I.

This kind of forced pace could drive workers to despair. "Why should we be asked to work under a system that indicates every movement of our elbow?" "We are driven like dumb cattle in our folly, until the flesh is off our bones, and the marrow out of them." "It seems to me that we are living to work, and not working to live." Other workers,

---

[10] Adolf Levenstein, ed., *Aus der Tiefe Arbeiter Briefe* (Berlin, 1908), p. 149.

however, continued to express pleasure in their jobs: "There is no work as interesting as that of a miner."[11] A 1928 poll in Germany showed that 65 percent of all skilled workers and 44 percent of all unskilled found more pleasure than distaste in their jobs. But work had changed. It was now intense, not leisurely; driven, not traditional. Even those workers who found pleasure in their work might complain of job tension, headaches, and sleeplessness. Nervousness was replacing physical hardship as the result of work, a key symptom of industrialization's further development.

One other change explains why workers could survive the new work system, even when they found aspects of it objectionable. The hours of work were now significantly reduced, as workers struggled to redefine their job life in light of the new pressures. New legislation pushed hours in textiles down to ten a day in most advanced industrial countries by World War I, and for miners the eight-hour day was established. Collective bargaining reduced hours to nine or ten for urban journeymen and had some impact in factory industry. Workers were implicitly agreeing that work might be intense, even abandoning traditional rest periods during the workday and reducing their absenteeism, in return for provision of time for life off the job. The idea of formal annual vacations gained ground from 1900 onward; French workers in the 1930s won a substantial yearly holiday.

Thus the traditional concept of work gave way, if only reluctantly. Workers still could find satisfactions in work but could no longer build their whole lives around it. They adopted, or were forced to adopt, a partially instrumental view toward work; that is, work was valued not only for its own sake but also for what it could provide toward life off the job. With the value of work now challenged, though by no means completely undermined, the quality of workers' existence depended heavily on what they could do with their new leisure time.

Life Off the Job

The working class could not, as a whole, seize as completely on a leisure ethic as the lower middle class did. Its resources were more meager; average earnings were lower and job instability greater. And work was hard. Many workers came home too worn out to use their leisure for much but sleep and light reading. Particularly for older workers leisure activities did not diversify greatly; the working-class recreational patterns were mainly for the young. There were important changes in behavior, but not enough, for many, to compensate fully for the alteration of work.

[11] Peter N. Stearns, *Lives of Labor: Work in Maturing Industrial Society* (London, 1975), pp. 286–310.

Big-city journeymen made the switch best. For their work was not really more intense, and their hours were shorter than before (though increased commuting time qualified this, as more and more moved to respectable suburbs). Quickly, around 1900, they reduced their family size, almost to middle-class levels. This protected their standard of living while also helping to assure that they could place their children properly now that the crafts were expanding more slowly. Artisans in London joined clerks in going to the new music halls, as well as finding social diversions in pubs. Their recreational life was increasingly dissociated from the job, and music hall humor helped make work and family bearable by poking gentle fun at class divisions, in-laws, and so on.

Workers more generally developed new interests in sports. Young miners played football and saved their money to attend a Saturday match. Belgian workers raced pigeons and bet on the results. Many workers took excursions on the railroads. Some enjoyed trips to the beach, though in England, it was only in the 1920s that workers normally were able to swim. Movie houses spread widely in working-class towns even before World War I. But there was long a certain tentativeness to this leisure ethic. Many workers turned increasingly to use of traditional outlets. Drinking went up in France and Germany; Paris, with 30,000 bars, had more than any other city in the world. This reflected job tensions but also the absence of a diversified recreational tradition to refer to.

German workers polled shortly before World War I listed gardening and walks in the countryside as their favorite pastimes. Sports interests were spreading among the young, but again traditionalism played a continued role. And this in turn qualified the workers' ability to take an instrumental view toward work. Many of their recreational interests were rather inexpensive, particularly after they married. This followed from their modest wages, but it also discouraged elaborate new wage demands. It was not automatic, therefore, for workers to respond to changes on the job with demands for more money. Workers still responded to a windfall wage gain by bringing home a new present for the kids or a bigger piece of meat for Sunday dinner, not by changing their basic pattern of life. The balance between change and tradition thus remained complex.

The same was true of family life. The working class began to reduce its birthrate by the 1890s. It still had larger families than the middle class, and some male workers believed that their masculinity required them to sire many children. Many women as a result had to resort to abortion; in Berlin around 1910, a survey showed that 24 percent of all working-class women had undergone at least one abortion. Women did not otherwise exercise control over the birthrate in this class, for the only control device commonly used was the condom and its employment obviously depended on the cooperation of men. Withdrawal or outright abstinence were even more common methods among married couples, reducing opportunities for sexual expressiveness. With regard to children, the working-class reduction of birthrate constituted a sensible but historically significant realization that children were no longer an economic asset; hence a family should have fewer of them and for different reasons. Mothers began to lavish more affection on their children. But the father's role changed less clearly; many fathers were authoritarian, even brutal, with their children.

And there were some signs of new tension between spouses, quite apart from possible arguments over birth control. Working-class women were in an anomalous situation. Their education was improving, their jobs before marriage becoming more diversified. But once married their roles remained rather traditional. They were still responsible for the main consumer expenditures of the family, and when living standards began to stagnate with the inflation after 1900 this could prove a demanding function. They still formed a kinship network with their relatives. A classic theme in music hall comedy was the working man returning home only to find his spouse surrounded by her mother and other relatives, from whom he would flee in horror to the nearest pub. But new roles were not available. There was only a slight increase in the percentage of married women working outside the home, for this was still frowned upon in working-class culture. When women took new jobs during World War I they created tensions in the family. A French railwayman wrote: "Women no longer want to obey.... We talk about marriage between men and women as people talk of peace between the Germans and the French."[12] For their part most of the new recreations men were developing were exclusively masculine: they played soccer or went to the races alone.

The working-class family was not in serious trouble. It was a distinctive statement, different from middle-class styles while sharing certain trends. Marriage rates remained high (higher than in the middle class) and the marriage age relatively young. The young working-class woman might enjoy her new independence in a factory or office job, but she busily saved her money to be able to furnish an apartment once married; her work was thus family-centered. She might attempt to get pregnant to win a husband, and for both sexes courtship was regarded as more fun than marriage. But working-class culture, now bent on defining its own version of respectability, saw to it that the man did marry. A small minority of unions ended in divorce; the rate jumped up after the disruption of World War I but then fell back again. Gardening and excursions allowed the family to serve as a recreational unit. What had not occurred, however, was the kind of qualitative improvement in family relationships that might compensate for new tensions on the job. Indeed strain at work caused many men to come home so nervous and exhausted that they could not treat spouses and

---

[12] Guy Chaumeil, *Histoire des Cheminots et de Leurs Syndicats* (Paris, 1948), p. 138.

children with the affection they intended. Traditional relationships were still valid; some new interests were developing, but the mixture was not entirely satisfactory.

Discontent

The situation of workers both on and off the job readily explains the most obvious feature of working-class life during the mature industrial period: the emergence of new protest forms and organizations. It also explains some of the constraints on this protest. Most workers were not thoroughly dissatisfied with their jobs or their lives off the job. Hence they were not attracted by movements that attacked the industrial system in the name of older values; here was one key difference with the unrest of the previous period. In France and to a lesser degree in Britain, the revolutionary syndicalist movement echoed earlier protest themes. Syndicalists believed that trade unions should work toward a general strike that would overturn the political and economic system alike; they admitted the classic revolution was now impossible because the ruling classes had the strength of a modern military apparatus behind them. But if all workers everywhere stopped work, capitalist society would collapse. Syndicalists looked to a future society in which there would be no government. The economy would be organized on the basis of small, egalitarian units that recalled idealized guilds. Syndicalism did have some attractions for the working class but its greatest gains were in Italy and Spain, where workers were confronting industrial society for the first time. In France the syndicalists won control of the major trade union federation, the *Confédération générale du travail* (C.G.T.); they proved particularly appealing to the revolutionary tradition of Parisian artisans. But most unionized French workers, including craftspeople, were not convinced syndicalists and syndicalism was on the wane by 1910. Distrusting modern organization, the syndicalist unions were weak, underfunded, and lacking in bureaucracy. They could not successfully confront employers. More basically, most workers in the mature industrial countries did not now think in terms of replacing the industrial system; they protested within it.

Mature industrial protest thus differed from its early industrial predecessor, in that it looked toward new demands rather than to the restoration of past forms. In addition, it produced direct action more in good times rather than in bad. Workers had learned that action during depressions just invited defeat, for employers had no reason to make concessions. So they waited, now able to form demands even in prosperity. The key weapons of mature industrial protest were politics and strikes. Neither necessarily involved violence, although both might bring clashes with police or recalcitrant workers. With strikes, at least, violence tended to decline as workers gained experience and organization. Even more than with goals, the methods and organization of working-class protest changed massively in this peak period of class conflict.

Strikes

The modern labor movement took shape in western and central Europe from the late 1880s onward. A rising rate of strikes was one key element, and strikes revealed much about the nature of the new tide of protest.

Organized strikes became easier to conduct in this period. Politicians, eager to win popularity among newly enfranchised workers, loosened the limitations on unions and strikes. France relaxed the restrictions in the 1880s and removed them finally in 1884. In 1874 Britain repealed the laws making strikers liable to arrest. Germany withdrew similar limitations in 1881 and Belgium did so in 1868. There were still important legal barriers; the British courts, for example, attacked the right to picket and the political activities of unions in the 1900s, and only after some difficulty were these rulings overturned through legislation. French and German law forbade any interference with the right of individuals to go to work, which made it difficult for labor leaders to compel obedience to a strike call. The result was frequent arrest of strikers and recurrent conflicts with police. Direct action was no longer illegal, as it had been in the days when the lower classes had to rely on riots to express their goals, but it remained difficult.

In a broader sense the new outburst of protest depended, ironically, on the greater resources, leisure, and education of the labor force. Workers could read propaganda. Perhaps more important, because reading interest was still not widespread, their understanding of standard French or German opened them to the speeches of radical leaders. Higher wages allowed strike funds; greater leisure gave time for planning. This is why protest became more frequent and regular than ever before in history, though these same improvements might limit its goals. However, strikes, more than union membership or protest voting, still involved real hardship. Loss of wages was rarely compensated for by strike funds, and there was a real risk of dismissal and possibly arrest. Employers, even governments, viewed strikes with great fear, and for many workers these strikes expressed profound grievances.

In 1892 French workers struck 261 times against 500 companies. Most individual strikes were small and local, usually affecting only one company, though a few larger efforts pushed up the number of companies attacked; even so, only 50,000 workers were involved. By 1906, the peak French strike year before the war, there were 1,309 strikes with 438,466 participants. The British strike rate was higher than the French; here a massive wave of agitation brought out over two million workers between 1909 and 1913 alone. Although this was unusual, a rising level of strikes developed in all the mature industrial countries. Most major kinds of strikes also appeared in the same period. The average strike was small (in Germany it involved only 119 workers), but industrywide strikes developed in mining, railroads, the merchant marine, and on the docks. National general strikes occurred in Belgium, Holland, and Sweden. Citywide strikes were still more common. Even some of the small strikes were carefully planned, as workers sought to attack one company at a time to break down employer resistance.

Yet most workers struck rarely and many strikes were still quite primitive. Only miners were likely to conduct repeated, massive strikes. The danger of their work and their cohesion in mining villages explain their unusual performance. Most other workers never struck at all before World War I. Journeymen were much more active than factory workers, but even they rose repeatedly only in the biggest cities. Many workers were satisfied with existing improvements in their lot. Others were intimidated by employers, still others too deferential to rise. Many strikes that did occur reflected this tentative consciousness. They often followed from a specific incident, such as an insult from a supervisor that personally angered a group of workers. This is why so many movements were small. It was only after World War I that strikes began consistently to take on more formal structure. They became less frequent but larger and better organized. In part this occurred because employer resistance stiffened; workers had to be more careful if they were to have any chance of success. But it also followed from the time required for workers to learn to curb spontaneous anger in favor of a more organized approach, for in the mature industrial period protest too had to be bureaucratized.

The most experienced workers conducted careful strikes even before World War I, and their demands reflected similar sophistication. Miners and urban journeymen, particularly printers and skilled construction workers, asked for shorter hours and higher pay. For most factory workers, including miners in their earliest strike activity, demands were more diffuse. There was often an initial impulse to use strikes to protest changes in working conditions. As late as 1897 British machine builders tried to attack the spread of the piece rate and other speed-up measures. On the whole, however, strikes over working conditions became rare if only because they were almost impossible to win; employers simply would not yield on those vital issues. Furthermore workers often disagreed over what conditions were appropriate. But this meant that those workers who found their jobs increasingly dismal could not turn to strikes in direct response. Their only outlet was the strike against a hated supervisor or a worker who set too fast a pace, and these strikes, though small and usually abortive, continued at a high rate. The most common strikes related to working conditions more indirectly. Some asked for union recognition, which was designed to give worker representatives some voice; for the journeymen this was a highly successful ploy, but for factory workers union recognition, if won, rarely touched day-to-day working conditions. Other strikes sought a reduction of hours, which was a vital part of the accommodation to the new pace of work. But more than anything else, strikers worked to defend their wages.

Many strikes asked for higher wages than ever before, to compensate for new methods of work. This was the instrumental approach: I'll accept possibly more disagreeable work if I'm paid more. Printers used this approach widely in reaction to the new composing machines. But other workers were not yet ready for this. They undoubtedly wanted higher wages, though their consumption goals were not always clear, but they had much more fundamental concerns. Most wage strikes were designed to protect an established, if rising, standard of living rather than to ask for more. They occurred when prosperity returned following a slump, seeking restoration of wages that had been cut. After 1900 they increasingly reacted to inflation; this was the key cause of the massive British strike wave right before World War I. Workers had to have higher money wages simply to make ends meet.

The immediate demands raised in strikes, along with most of the methods used, reflected a rather moderate labor force. Adaptation to work was sufficient, enjoyment off the job adequate for workers to refrain from rocking the boat too vigorously. Only if their adjustment was seriously threatened, as in the British inflation, would they threaten to turn strikes into massive disruption. This was a far cry from the violent, politically conscious strikes occurring during these same years in Russia and Italy; even the average strike rate was lower in the mature industrial countries, when measured against the total number of workers.

Trade Unions

The development of trade unions followed from many of the impulses that went into the strike movement. Indeed many unions were initially formed as organizations for combat and only gradually developed other functions. Trade unions were not new, of course. Many crafts had formed local unions by the mid-nineteenth century. In France and Germany they were long loosely organized. The German Hirsch-Duncker movement was of national scope, but it had attracted only 66,000 members by 1892. In the 1880s French craft unions linked locally around the labor exchanges (*Bourses du travail*), which briefly formed a national organization. Only in industrially advanced Britain, through the Trades Union Congress, had craft unions developed strong national representation before the end of the nineteenth century.

Some craft unions maintained a radical stance; the French *Bourses du travail* were a major source of syndicalism. But the typical craft union, even in France, worked for pragmatic gains for its members, adapting guild techniques to modern economic life. They usually shunned political activities as irrelevant to their function. The British movement, in the 1860s, even opposed the extension of suffrage to workers. Craft unions stressed large benefit funds to help members in sickness, old age, and unemployment, thus continuing the mutual aid tradition on a larger scale. Many provided travel support for journeymen to move from one area to the next seeking work. Most used strikes only sparingly, preferring calm collective bargaining with employers. Between 1851 and 1889 the British Amalgamated Society of Engineers paid out £3 million in benefit funds, while spending only £88,000 on strikes. Many were successful in getting local collective bargaining agreements that would guarantee a minimum wage for each type of work, a maximum level of hours, and extra pay for overtime and travel. They also tried to restrict the number of apprentices in their craft so to guarantee traditional training and limit the number of new craftspeople, though here their success was limited. Finally, craft unions worked for respectability and self-improvement; this was one reason they disliked resorting to strikes. They sponsored union libraries, and urged temperance and good habits on their members. Craft unions reflected the kind of adaptation to industrial society that artisans had been developing even in the first stage of industrialization. The form could be found at the origin of virtually every union movement. When typographers in Bosnia, for example, established the first trade union, in the 1900s, they carefully reproduced the purposes of craft organization, including the cautious approach to strikes.

Until the 1890s craft unions predominated, though in Britain there were important organizations among miners and cotton workers as well. The craft approach deliberately left most workers out, for it relied on exclusive skills for its bargaining power. In the 1890s, however, two related developments occurred. A new kind of industrial union arose, and the craft unions modified their own tactics.

In 1889 the successful London dockers' strike, conducted by thousands of unskilled workers, made it clear that even the poorest elements of the labor force could organize with success, and the union movement caught fire and spread quickly to most types of workers in industry and transport. A similar trend developed soon after this in France and Germany. Not all the new unions were durable; British maritime employers, for example, beat down the dockers' union in 1893, and it revived more durably only in 1911. Many workers themselves, hostile to organizational controls, moved in and out of unions during their first decades. But among miners, factory workers, railroad workers, and ultimately the maritime trades the union movement became a persistent part of working-class life.

Industrial unions were huge. National mining and railroad federations had hundreds of thousands of members. British unions collectively had more than a million members in the 1890s and more than three million a decade later. Germany had almost 1.5 million members by 1906. France lagged a bit with a smaller labor force and smaller firms, but French unions had half a million members in the 1890s and twice that many a decade later. Nowhere did unions embrace more than a minority of the labor force. Some workers objected to the movement because of its risk; others, who approved of unions but resented their dues, found they could benefit from union activity without joining. However, the unions became the largest active organizations ever developed in Europe, and they reflected the attitudes of a massive segment of the working class.

The industrial-union movement brought important changes to the organization of unions. Local unions embraced all types of workers in an industry, not just a single skill, and the locals were joined in a strong national federation within the industry. Sheer weight of membership was the key to union power. The industrial federations linked into a national union organization, which brought in many craft unions as well. The German and Austrian movements, influenced by the Marxist stress on organization and by the concentration of industry, were particularly centralized. Links among British unions, which centered on the Trades Union Congress, were looser but still significant, and individual industrial federations had considerable central power. In France the C.G.T. was founded in 1895 and embraced the *Bourses du travail* movement in 1902. It long failed to attract the majority of French unions, and its central powers were relatively weak until after World War I. Many industrial federations in France, however, had effective central organization with substantial funds and strong professional leadership. This was true of the northern miners' group, the railroad union, and the textile federation in the north. In Italy the *Confederazione generale del lavoro*, formed in the image of the C.G.T., was limited in power, but again some federations had great central strength. Massive membership and considerable direction from the center characterized the industrial-union movement, a sign of workers' class consciousness and response to the new organization of industry itself.

Industrial unions had none of the compunctions about strikes that the earlier craft unions had manifested. They existed above all to improve the wages and working conditions of their members. Hence they formulated general goals, stressing better pay, shorter hours, safer working conditions, and union recognition. Because big industrialists were loath to deal with them, strikes were an essential weapon for the industrial unions. However, the initial combative tone of the industrial unions waned with time. To win durable worker support the unions found that they had to develop benefit programs. They also organized social functions, such as dances and picnics; unions thus became an

important part of the lives of many members. Strikes remained significant but union leaders had to curb any radical enthusiasm; for strikes
cost money and, if they lost, they cost members as well. So the industrial unions increasingly preached moderation and careful planning.
Ultimately their promptings caused the growing sophistication of strike
tactics already discussed, but there was often a disparity between their
caution and the anger groups of workers could develop on the job.

During this same period, partly because of the example of the industrial unions, craft unions changed their approach. Individual artisans
were vital in providing leadership for the newer efforts: the London
dock strike, for example, was led in part by radical dissidents from the
Amalgamated Society of Engineers. So there was from the first a link
between the craft and industrial approach. Furthermore journeymen
now used their unions as a counterweight to the important changes in
their own job conditions. As their firms became larger and new
machines were introduced, they became quite ready to strike, when
necessary, to impose collective bargaining. They also grouped nation-
ally, a logical response to the heightened organization of their employers. By the 1900s the difference between craft and industrial unions
had diminished. The crafts still stressed exclusivism and protection of
skill. But both movements were well organized, usually linked through
a national confederation. And both were relatively moderate.

The cautiousness of unions was a common theme. Where unions
existed as part of a socialist party, they invariably played a moderating
role, advising against risky tactics or revolutionary efforts. Workers expected their unions to provide benefits here and now. Rarely were they
attracted to unions that advocated political action alone. Hence in Germany initial socialist unions, under firm party control, drew only
350,000 members (in the mid-1890s). Unions had to develop their own
goals and methods, and as the German movement escaped political
control, a separation formalized by the Mannheim agreement of 1906,
they quickly increased their membership. But more often than not the
tail could wag the dog. But the 1900s German union leaders played a
key role in reducing the revolutionary zeal of the socialist party. Because, with rare exceptions, they won support only through immediate
gains within the system, union leaders became naturally cautious. They
also had their own position to consider. Most were of working-class
origin and could be proud of their rise to power in a mighty bureaucracy. On occasion, at least, their desire to avoid jeopardizing their position antagonized their membership. Workers could find union
bureaucrats too remote, too concerned with protecting the organization's treasury, and strikes against union orders became common before World War I. However, although some workers urged a more
radical union approach, on the syndicalist model, their dissidence did
not prevail.

Socialism

As political rights spread, workers increasingly learned to use their votes to express discontent. Here was an obvious vehicle for workers who found their jobs appalling, for whom unions and ultimately strikes became too tame, or who found political support essential even to win trade-union goals.

New political doctrines spread to the working class from outside leadership. Socialist parties were almost uniformly founded and long led by members of the middle class, usually people with a professional background who used socialism in part to express their own discontent as well as genuine ideological fervor. Jules Guesde and Jean Jaurès in France, Karl Liebknecht in Germany, Filippo Turati in Italy were all lawyers or journalists with advanced education. So was the initial French syndicalist leader Fernand Pelloutier; even anarchism was founded by a Russian military officer. The Labour party in Britain had genuine working-class leadership, but its ideology, which was adopted only gradually, came from the eminently middle-class Fabian society. Middle-class leaders had the understanding of doctrine and organization that could impel a political movement.

Early socialism, in fact, won few workers. Socialism has a rich history before the 1880s, but its membership was limited to a small minority of the working class. Often, in fact, middle-class idealogues were too abstract to catch on at all; hence efforts to establish a Marxist group in Britain failed almost totally, save in London itself. Early socialism helped build up a leadership group, devoted to pure, usually Marxist, socialist doctrine and to preaching the revolution.

By the 1880s socialist parties grew rapidly, mainly on the basis of working-class support. The British Labour party was formed in the 1890s to represent the working class specifically, although it cooperated with the Liberals to fight for welfare legislation and other government assistance to labor. On the Continent socialist parties were larger than in Britain. France had more than a hundred socialist deputies by 1913; the German party was receiving almost 1.5 million votes by the mid-1890s and four million by 1913. The Austrian socialist party rose to a similar position of strength and socialist movements in Scandinavia, the Low Countries, and even Italy drew the support of increasing numbers.

Most of the Continental socialist movements were Marxist, though some native traditions, such as the French, did persist. In Germany and Austria the socialists were characterized by tight organization and strict control from the top, after the pattern Marx himself had established in earlier stages of the movement. Elsewhere, in France, for example, there was a constant tendency to splintering within the movement, although a Marxist orientation was accepted by most socialists at least in theory.

Under Marxism the Continental socialist parties rose to great prominence; they were supported by most of the working class and urged the
abolition of capitalism by means of revolution and the establishment of
a new working-class society. Without doubt, many workers believed the
existing economic and political system unacceptable. Many found the
idea of a radically new society based on worker rule and on equality of
wealth extremely attractive. Most workers had not developed their criticisms and hopes very explicitly, but they certainly found Marxist leaders compelling. However, hopes for revolution and for a future utopia
were not dominant in the minds of most working-class supporters of
Marxism, though they continued to influence many leaders. For the
socialist movement changed significantly as it developed mass support.
A German worker expressed his thoughts this way:

> "You know, I never read a social democratic book and rarely a news-
> paper. I used not to occupy myself with politics at all. But since I got
> married and have five eaters at home I have to do it. But I think my own
> thoughts. I do not go in for red ties, big round hats and other similar
> things. All that does not amount to much. We really do not want to
> become like the rich and refined people. There will always have to be
> rich and poor. We would not think of altering that. But we want a better
> and more just organization at the factory and in the state. I openly ex-
> press what I think about that, even though it might not be pleasant. But
> I do nothing illegal."[13]

There were many kinds of working-class socialists, ranging from devoted ideologues to people who looked to socialism simply for specific
reforms. Every large socialist party had to blend fervent revolutionaries
and wary pragmatists. On the whole workers wanted direct benefits
from the movement. They did not expect to change the whole society,
even preserving some idea, as the German worker suggested, that a
social hierarchy was natural enough. They did hope that socialism
would bring them a new voice over job conditions and that, through
socialism, the state could turn from enemy to supporter of working-
class needs.

Partly in response to majority sentiment, most socialist parties began
to work for reforms more than for outright revolution by the 1890s; it
was no accident that they began picking up mass support at the same
time. In the 1880s a Possibilist party split from the Marxist movement
in France, specifically renouncing revolution and proclaiming the possibility of reforms through parliamentary means. In Germany a bit later
Eduard Bernstein stated that Marxist predictions of increasing poverty

---

[13] Paul Göhre, *Drei Monate Fabrikarbeiter* (Leipzig, 1913), pp. 348–349.

under capitalism were not true and that the revolutionary approach in general was inaccurate and needless. He urged cooperation with middle-class parties for reform.

The socialist movements in general renounced these new doctrines, known formally as *revisionism*. Both the German and the French movements asserted the continued validity of Marxist teachings. In practice, however, socialist behavior became increasingly revisionist. German socialists worked primarily for new welfare measures and for political reforms, especially in the Prussian voting system, that would increase democracy. They talked of revolutionary Marxism, but they did nothing. In France, similarly, socialists such as Jaurès struggled to defend the republican form of government against attack. French socialists talked of the principles of the new society, but their efforts were increasingly bent toward welfare legislation, laws protecting unions and strikes, and other measures that would aid labor. A similar reformist approach developed in most Continental countries, and in Britain the party was not revolutionary even in theory.

By 1914 the socialist movement, trade unions, and strike activity all presented much the same tone of vigorous moderation. Articulate workers had a firm sense of their rights, though there were still many who found every aspect of the labor movement irrelevant or dangerous. The articulate workers, their numbers growing, wanted their own political representatives, and through them they sought new dignity as well as improved welfare protection. It was socialist pressure above all that encouraged the elaboration of national welfare programs after 1900. Equally important, in many factory centers socialists gained power in urban government and were able to put through improvements for working-class schools and neighborhoods. Workers did not feel fully a part of the existing political and economic system; they did not find their rewards appropriate. But they worked within this very system to improve their situation.

Socialist parties also provided the more active members with a vigorous social life, particularly when combined with a kindred union movement. Socialist halls offered loans, dances, libraries, picnics, even advice to the lovelorn. Though most workers preferred popularized mass entertainment to the strictest socialist fare, the movement contributed to a vigorous working-class subculture in the mature industrial decades.

A minority of socialists found this pragmatic approach inadequate. Workers more generally, although only rarely rebelling against party or union directives, might yearn for a protest that would express their resentment at their continued dependence on employers, their lack of voice over conditions basic to their lives. They might thus welcome revolutionary rhetoric even when they had no intention of launching a revolution. Or they might simply hope that someday, somehow, conditions more appropriate for revolution might come about.

World War and Depression

The turmoil of the world war and the exciting example of the Russian Revolution briefly opened up a new period of agitation when the fighting ended. Some workers, ironically, were drawn to the labor movement because it had gained new respectability during the war. Union and socialist leaders served in coalition governments after war broke out, proving their own moderation and making them seem less fearsome to more timid segments of the working class. But the tension of wartime existence and deteriorating material conditions at the war's end, which in Germany amounted to near starvation, brought still more workers into the labor movement in a quest for radical changes in their existence. The French C.G.T. quadrupled its membership by 1920, rising past the two million mark. In Britain the Labour party rose for the first time to a position of major importance, displacing the Liberals as one of the two principal parties in the country. Everywhere unions grew and socialist parties received more support, while strike levels reached an all-time high.

Many workers sought new kinds of control over their lot. German workers, imitating the Russian revolutionaries, formed councils, or soviets, in many factories, hoping to take over management directly. Workers in Italy in 1920 conducted sit-down strikes, refusing to work but trying to seize control of their factories. British workers talked of entrusting power in the plant to elected shop stewards, and miners and other groups pressed for nationalization of their industries in hopes of gaining more open and responsible management. At least temporarily, the war brought to the surface the radical impulse harbored by important elements of the working class. This was heightened by the disgust of some socialist and union leaders at the moderation of the main body of labor, particularly after the events in Russia convinced them that revolution was feasible.

Generally, however, the most specific revolutionary efforts did not win wide support. When syndicalist leaders in France, in their last independent gesture, called for a general strike in 1920, hoping to topple the social order, they drew only some railroad workers who were mainly interested in attacking a single company over disciplinary problems. Radical German strikes were put down by the new government, under the direction of the moderate socialists. Everywhere the recession of 1920–1921 dampened workers' ardor. Some were frightened by the outburst that had developed; others were disillusioned that revolution had not come. From this radical period one durable development did emerge: In France, Germany, and some other countries the labor movement split into socialist and communist wings. This confirmed socialist parties and the main union movements in their moderate, non-revolutionary approach; but now there was a specifically revolutionary movement to their left.

   Throughout most of the 1920s, however, the working class reverted
to earlier protest patterns. The communist organizations drew only
modest support. In Germany they continued to strive directly for revolution until 1923, but their final abortive risings were rather contrived
affairs attracting only a handful of party faithful. The advent of communist parties did affect national politics, but more because of their
tactics than because of their popularity. Most workers stuck with the
moderate socialist approach. Union membership dropped down near
prewar levels. Strike activity returned to prewar patterns also, except
for the improvement in organization and strategy. Goals focused once
again on wage demands, inspired by the intense inflationary pressure.
The one major exception occurred in Britain, where miners and others
afflicted by significant unemployment and insistent on government
support launched the largest strike movement in British history. The
1926 general strike involved 2.5 million workers. But it failed; in fact
strike movements generally encountered more resistance from employers and the public during the 1920s. This, plus generally satisfactory
economic conditions in most countries, reduced direct action. Political
support for socialist or communist movements remained more solid, in
part because employers were so intransigent, so the decade did produce a tendency toward further politicization for working-class demands. Even the British general strike was really aimed at government
action in the mining industry, not the employers directly. To be sure,
socialist and labor parties could not win undisputed national political
power during the 1920s, but their importance increased and they often
served in coalition governments. Their control of city governments
gave them even greater power, for here they could extend direct benefits to their constituents.
   The tendency of workers to turn to political action became abundantly clear during the Depression, but the mood changed decisively.
Only in England, where so many workers were already unemployed
and disillusioned and where the Labour party had proved inept, did
the Depression fail to produce a new surge of protest. Elsewhere the
Depression, with its searing effect on both incomes and morale, capped
the development of mature industrial protest. Workers stepped forward, though impelled by catastrophe, to demand new rights.
   The Depression challenged much of the adaptation workers had developed during the mature industrial period. Their standard of living
was obviously jolted as wages fell. Workers who had learned to enjoy
aspects of their jobs and value a certain professional dignity now faced
unprecedented crisis. In 1932 a Silesian mine was closed by the state
after three hundred workers were asphyxiated by gas, but the surviving
workers petitioned that it be reopened: they preferred the danger of
death to the demoralization of unemployment. In some cases women,
with their lower wages, found it easier to keep work than men; this
challenged yet another value in working-class culture.

Union membership rose as one expression of the new and vigorous sense of grievance. By 1937 French unions had grown from 785,000 to over five million members. In 1936 an important series of strikes was conducted for improvements in wages and hours. Factories were occupied, often for several weeks, and the workers won their point. The action had been spurred by the election of a Popular Front government controlled by the socialists, for workers wanted to make sure that the government would take the corrective action they wished.

The principal focus of working-class protest against the Depression had to be political. Union action, particularly strikes, was of little avail in this depression, as in any other; what was needed was a new kind of government action. The result was a major increase in support for socialist and, in some areas, communist parties. Elements of the middle class and peasantry, themselves suffering intense economic hardship, also gave some support to these parties, but the major impetus came from the workers. Even in Britain support for the Labour party steadily grew in the later 1930s and the party's victory in 1945 was a continuation of this movement. Scandinavian socialist parties received clear majorities and took control of the governments. Votes for the French socialists increased, but even more notable was the steady rise in communist political power; in the 1936 election, the number of communists in the Chamber of Deputies rose from ten to seventy-three, and they had become a major political force for the first time. Spanish socialist parties in the industrial areas of the north steadily increased in strength, and a small communist movement was founded. In Germany the communist party provided a particularly vigorous expression of working-class grievance. German workers had long supported the socialists; to express their new discontent, some of them naturally turned to a more radical movement. By late 1932 communists had almost 17 percent of the total vote.

The new political efforts of the working class had varying results. In Germany the Nazi victory decapitated the labor movement. In Scandinavia the socialist parties were able to introduce a variety of social-insurance schemes and increased governmental control of the economy. Political backing was given to cooperatives and to unions; collective bargaining became general in Scandinavian industry. Public housing was developed and greater assistance given to large families, to the aged, and to the sick. Under this administration the effects of the Depression on the working class were soon eliminated; production rose and relatively full employment was restored. The working class was more protected and more prosperous than ever before, and the attachment to socialist parties was solidified.

The French labor movement won only limited results. Only in 1936, after the Depression had already made major inroads, did the socialists gain control of the government, and that control was extremely shaky.

The socialists depended on the cooperation of the middle-class Radical party, and this was soon withdrawn in opposition to the various economic measures that the socialists took. The perpetual division between socialists and communists further weakened the government. Communists supported the government at first but refused to participate in it; and gradually their support lessened. The Popular Front government was doomed to failure, and many of its measures were subsequently rescinded. It did attempt, however, to counter the effects of depression and to provide an economic structure more favorable to the working class. There was some effort to guide the economy, particularly by government operation of the Bank of France. Most important, the government tried to meet the demands of the workers, expressed in the strikes of 1936, for significant improvements in working conditions. It sponsored a series of compulsory collective bargaining arrangements, the Matignon agreements, between employers and unions. The possibility of providing the workers a greater voice in industry, with government assistance, was a notable feature of the settlement. The agreements set higher wages, established a minimum wage and a forty-hour week, and guaranteed two weeks paid vacation a year. These gains were not well administered, and some, such as the limitation on hours of work, were soon abandoned. The discontent and material hardship of the workers were not eliminated and they were reflected in the steady increase in communist popularity. Nevertheless, the Popular Front had introduced some new principles into French industrial life. It represented the sort of approach workers clearly sought and supported.

The impact of the Depression on workers and on their political habits proved enduring. The new voting patterns were maintained well after the peak of the Depression and even after World War II, except in countries such as Germany, where the leftist political movements were disbanded by government action. Workers and their leaders continued to seek programs, centering around greater government action, that would guarantee full employment.

Working-class life developed on many fronts during the mature industrial period. The growing cohesion of the class followed from increasingly similar working conditions. New leisure interests expressed a thirst for enjoyment and release from the tension of ordinary life. The protest surge was the most distinctive reaction, as large numbers of workers cast about for new ways to gain some control over the economic and political framework of their existence. Workers wanted a better material life and they wanted a serious modification of the power structure of industrial society. Never had class consciousness loomed so large, and never had unrest so consistently marked European society, decade after decade. Through their new protest muscle, as through their labor and their cultural style, workers inevitably touched the whole society, even though they could not capture it.

Mature Industrial Society and Eastern Europe

During most of the period in which mature industrial society took hold in western and central Europe, the east and south were experiencing their own version of an early Industrial Revolution. The most obvious result was a pattern of agitation even more deep-seated than that of mature industrial society, an exacerbated version of the early industrial upheavals that had occurred a century before in the West. Here, outright revolution loomed, even though protest incidents were less frequent than in the West. A small middle class, composed primarily of professional people, espoused liberal and nationalist goals, sparking insurrections from the Bosnian and Bulgarian risings of 1875 through the Russian revolution of 1905. In 1904, as Russia suffered from its war losses to Japan, groups of teachers, lawyers, and doctors formed unions to work for liberal political reform, ultimately creating the Kadet party to push for effective parliamentary government.

But the middle class was too weak to control agitation in these areas; hence, in Russia, the short-lived liberal phase of the 1917 revolution. More serious was peasant grievance, which continued into the post–World War I years in the form of peasant parties in eastern Europe, persistent anarchist agitation in southern Spain (including attempts to seize estates when civil war broke out in 1936), and rising rural crime in many areas plus endemic banditry in the Balkans. The massive political and economic power of the landlords, except in Russia, combined with low agricultural prices and economic pressure to maintain tension. In Hungary 0.7 percent of the population owned 48.3 percent of the land; in Poland, 0.6 percent owned 43 percent. Overall, 70 percent of the peasants in eastern Europe possessed less than 12.5 acres of land, enough for a bare subsistence at best. In Romania, the one non-communist country where land reform did occur after 1918 (only 7 percent of the land remained in large holdings), 50 percent of the peasantry held less than 7.5 acres. Without capital or education, Romanian peasants were unable to produce for the market and returned to a near-subsistence economy. Here and elsewhere up to a third of all children still died before reaching two years of age, reflecting the impoverished housing and diet available.

Added to rural unrest was the unusual agitation of early factory workers. Russian workers conducted thousands of strikes between 1895 and 1914. Various socialist doctrines spread there and among workers in Poland, southern Italy, and many parts of Spain.

Eastern Europe, particularly Russia, thus displayed the basic tensions of early industrial society—expressed earlier in the nineteenth century in the West. The expression was, however, even more vigorous because of unusually unfavorable rural conditions and the advanced organizational forms of the new factory sector. The possibility of importing protest ideologies from the West added further to the brew. Not surprisingly, then, it was Russia that experienced outright revolution, first in 1905 and then more sweepingly, under the spur of hardship during World War I, in 1917—despite the fact that protest movements were, on the surface, better organized in Western countries.

All of this again serves as a reminder of the major differences in stages of development between the two principal zones of Europe. But something of a mature industrial society was to develop in these areas, and although its nature can be pursued in the assessment of Europe after World War II, an outline can usefully be suggested now. In eastern Europe, initially in Russia, mature industrialization arose under the guidance of communist regimes. This altered some of its basic aspects. Most obviously the upper-class amalgam of big businesspeople and aristocrats so important in the West was absent, for the new regimes gave primary power to dedicated communists drawn from diverse social origins but including a substantial segment from working-class and peasant backgrounds. By reforming higher educational facilities, using scholarship funds to open them to talented students from various classes, and spreading primary and secondary schools widely, the communist regimes for a considerable time kept the ruling class open to accessions from below.

The Russian revolution and the civil war that followed set Russia's early industrialization back for several years, but by the 1920s, and particularly under Stalin's planned economy after 1928, industrial development resumed. Other parts of eastern Europe, though experiencing difficult political adjustments between 1918 and the end of World War II, also expanded their industrial sector. This was most obviously the case in Czechoslovakia and Poland, where some industrial development had taken root before the dislocations of World War I and its aftermath. Growing cities and factory concentrations signaled the ongoing process, as key parts of eastern Europe moved beyond an experimental early industrial phase.

For as Russia neared industrial maturity by the 1930s and certainly after World War II, it replicated some social characteristics developed earlier in the West. The same was true of other communist countries after World War II, where rapid efforts at industrialization or, as in Czechoslovakia and East Germany, consolidation of earlier industrial progress created a new society. A managerial and professional class developed. Like its counterpart in western Europe earlier it restricted its birthrate to protect its own standard of living and to maximize opportunities for the children born. This class made strenuous efforts to place its children well in school in order to launch them on appropriate professional careers.

The entry of women into key professions was more significant than in mature industrial society in the West, but there were some comparable problems of status. Although fields, such as medicine, were dominated by women in Soviet Russia, they were less prestigious and lower-paying than their western, male-filled counterparts.

The professional–managerial class in eastern Europe, although requiring many of the same planning skills and manifesting many of the same personal traits as its western counterpart, could not develop along exactly similar lines. It was not distracted by the anxieties of an anarchistic shopkeeping element. State controls over most retailing, although painfully imposed by the communist regimes (in Russia, Lenin had to allow some reversion to private ownership during the 1920s, but this was reversed under Stalin), eliminated what had always been a small urban middle class. At the same time opportunities for development of a leisure ethic were limited. The managerial class could enjoy small country homes and regular vacations, but a work ethic, sedulously fostered by communist states bent on rapid industrialization, continued officially to hold sway. Costumes and cultural activities remained, by western standards, rather traditional and somber.

For the working class the communist regimes provided a more carefully guided entry into mature industrial structures than had been true in the West, in certain respects at least. Communist parties and unions gave individual worker representatives a voice in management decisions; they also prevented the development of spontaneous protest outlets, for independent organizations were forbidden. Workers were constantly told of their importance to society; they could not feel as isolated as some of their western counterparts. They were required, however, to adapt to rapidly changing technology and consistent pressure to speed up their pace of work. Prizes given to unusually productive workers in Russia during the 1930s, modified piece rate systems and differential pay for differential skills, careful supervision by foremen, all reproduced the trappings of advanced factory production. Provision of recreational facilities, usually at communist party headquarters, and annual vacations compensated workers somewhat. So did pension plans and other social security benefits that were more comprehensive than their western analogues during the mature industrial period. However, limitations on the production of consumer goods, including very restricted housing facilities, prevented some of the individual work compensations workers in the West came to know. This was long a function of the greater traditional poverty of these regions, as well as the more collectivist impulses of the communist system. Along with the absence of protest outlets it did raise questions about the ability of these societies to transcend the earlier phases of industrial maturation. By the mid-twentieth century, persistent signs of worker alienation and a stagnation of per-worker productivity harked back to the problems faced in western Europe around 1914.

For the peasantry, the communist version of transition to a mature industrial society was decidedly different than that of the West, and on the whole less successful. Some traditional problems were removed; notably, advancing industry reduced population pressure on the land. The spread of education brought peasants closer to urban attitudes in other respects. The new regimes made concerted efforts to disseminate more advanced agricultural technology. But traditional peasant adaptation possibilities were cut off by the collectivization of land ownership. There was every sign that peasants wanted their own control of the land and might best have adapted at their own slow pace, once this was achieved, as western peasants had earlier. This had already been suggested, in Russia, by the favorable reception given the Stolypin reforms. Under the impact of the 1917 revolution Russian peasants seized more land from the large estates, and some of the poorer peasants attacked the richer ones. But the Russian peasants kept their individual holdings only briefly. By 1918 the Soviet government attempted to press for greater collectivization of agriculture and particularly for new state controls over output and distribution. The peasants resisted, largely by restricting their production to their own needs. In 1921 the government, as part of Lenin's New Economic Policy, relaxed its pressures, and the peasants enjoyed a new period of private individual holdings. Earlier trends toward the concentration of land in the hands of a minority of wealthy kulaks continued, and agricultural production rose once again. At the end of the decade, however, renewed repression, including the extermination of the kulaks, attacked the peasant agricultural system, and collectivization was fully imposed. Again, some poorer peasants joined the attack on the kulaks but only in the interest of acquiring land themselves; the policy of collectivization thwarted them just as it did the more substantial farmers. Overt resistance to the new system was limited, but in the early 1930s many peasants destroyed their livestock and smashed equipment before entering the unwelcome collectives. Although the government imposed its will by military force, the peasants' traditional desire for individual holdings remained unquenched.

Similar tensions developed with the imposition of communist regimes in the smaller eastern European countries after World War II. Everywhere the conflict between official policy and peasant interest was reflected in low rates of agricultural productivity that kept a far higher percentage of the population on the land, in order to assure food for the cities, than was true of contemporary western European society.

But even this fact recalls the applicability of some aspects of a mature industrial model to both the principal zones of Europe. In both cases, despite the radically different forms involved, there was a disparity between peasant values and those of the urban world. Peasant agriculture in France remained unnecessarily inefficient. Nowhere, save where a peasant mentality had never really developed (as in the United States) or where the peasantry had essentially been eliminated (as in England) did mature industrial society successfully deal with the problem of agriculture. None of this is to argue that eastern Europe toward mid-century can be interpreted in the same terms as the mature industrial society we have more fully outlined for western and central Europe. Some key problems were avoided, notably through the more thorough, if sometimes brutal, elimination of traditionalist urban and upper-class elements. Some important advantages were also missed, and this issue must be addressed more fully in dealing with contemporary European society. Most notably the outline of a new leisure ethic was far different. Urban groups in eastern Europe did develop something of the same separation between work and leisure that came to prevail elsewhere; this included some similar interests, as in mass sports. But the impulse was more collectively controlled and far more somber than western Europe had developed by the 1920s. A youth culture was frowned upon, in favor of youth groups organized for disciplined exercises and marches. Women, although given important new job and educational opportunities, did not play the same role in a consumer society; not for them, to the same degree, the bright dresses, cosmetics, and faddish dances of England or Germany. To many communists the absence of Western-style garishness and sexual exploitation was another sign of the superiority of their version of industrial society.

Mature Industrial Society: An Interim Assessment

A number of evaluations of European society during the mature industrial period have emphasized discontinuities in rates of change as a key interpretive tool. The argument has been applied to western Europe generally, but particularly to societies such as Germany where industrialization gained ground so rapidly without full adjustment in the social realm. Some suggestions of a similar discontinuity may aid in the interpretation of the crisis in eastern Europe later in the twentieth century, when lags in some social and political sectors began to complicate continued development in other areas.

For parts of western Europe in the decades around 1900, the argument runs as follows: Fairly steady and fundamental change continued in technology and organization, challenging the adjustment of many groups and institutions. Many groups simply failed to keep up. A new upper class was formed but not entirely on the basis of industrial expertise; the aristocracy was not decisively renounced. Peasants, though adapting creatively, remained peasants in most cases, and stayed unduly isolated from the main trends of mature industrial life. The disgruntled segments of the middle class constantly threatened attack in the name of real or imagined traditions. Men failed to rethink the kind of dominance they had forged during the early industrial period. Combining patriarchal claims with the economic power they held as primary breadwinners, men did not resist all advance by women, but they refused to yield on the central issue of work. Despite important educational and political gains, as well as actual entry into the labor force in new numbers during World War I, women remained largely confined to the domestic sphere. Again, a classic opportunity for breakthrough was delayed.

Failure to adjust society to the ongoing changes in its framework explains the recurrent temptation to seize on scapegoats as targets for widespread hostility to "modern" conditions. For elements in the upper class, peasantry, and middle classes, Jews could thus symbolize big business, modern aristocratic trends, looser leisure forms, as well as trade unions and socialism. Traditionalism in Britain, though not assuming severe political forms, began to retard further industrial gains, as the British leadership and middle class clung to images of rural life or individual entrepreneurial business styles. Germany, in contrast, proceeded full steam with up-to-date technologies and organizational forms, but many social groups refused fully to adjust. The contest, under the special stress of defeat in World War I and ensuing economic dislocation, entered the political arena, with the rise of nazism the ultimate product. Nazism, ironically, drew support from groups that wanted to recall the past but proceeded to advance Germany's technological and organizational changes, particularly by giving big business fairly free rein.

The idea of discontinuities in change, with society lagging behind technology and organization, focuses inevitably on the huge dislocations of the two decades between the world wars, when much of Europe was near collapse—a process discussed at the end of this chapter.

Discontinuities in change must not be pressed too far as an interpretive tool. The concept may imply that there is some ideal standard of modernity by which all alternative versions are judged as failures. European society, though more successful in many ways since 1945 than during the first half of the twentieth century, still has problems, shortcomings, and deep-seated conflicts.

Evaluating the mature industrial period as a special case of inadequate adaptation risks ignoring, finally, the many important changes that did take place in the social realm. This was the period when European society came to terms with a new demographic structure, accepting a low birthrate accompanied by a low child death rate— along with the United States, the first society in the world to make this shift. New embraces of consumerism showed a capacity to adapt behavior on another front, as people learned new forms of expression through acquisition. The rise of organized labor, though it could generate paralyzing class conflict, revealed the creative power of many segments of the working class in defining new rights and new methods of action. It was the mature industrial period also that saw the emergence of modern mass leisure, revising the trends of the early industrial period and devising leisure forms quite different from those offered by preindustrial example. Here, too, despite important limitations, there was significant creativity from below.

Mass Culture and the Leisure Ethic

For one of the most durable innovations of the mature industrial phase in western and central Europe, along with the suggestions of a new, nonpropertied class structure, was the new definition of life off the job and what to do with it. Contemporary observers, most of them disgruntled intellectuals, saw the rise of a new mass culture. The term *mass culture* is acceptable if we make several obvious qualifications. Although "the masses" had vast new opportunities, from politics through spending money, they were not homogeneous. Quite apart from the rather recalcitrant peasantry, urban groups differed widely in their definition of leisure time or politics. The most obvious new culture was in fact a mutation of middle-class values, in which the new lower middle class and the upper segments of the working class played a key role. Mass culture reflected a reshuffling of class lines but not their obliteration. Traditional leaders, bemoaning their loss of political influence or the decline of the classics, undoubtedly had the impression of a barbaric, undifferentiated mass, but they exaggerated its unity and ignored the extent to which their own sons and daughters, newly interested in pleasure, shared some of the new cultural values.

The new mass culture manifested class divisions quite apart from the fact that many workers could not afford the range of activities available. A certain tension still existed between middle-class leisure ideals, which involved some self-improvement, and working-class desires to see leisure as an escape, an alternative to reality. Many workers introduced a kind of spontaneity into recreations, an earthiness, that the middle-class might value without being able to replicate. Middle-class and upper-class patrons often went to working-class shows to enjoy the bursts of humor and sensuality available there. Another division was revealed in sports. Worker games were rough, even brutal, against the more genteel amateur habits of middle-class players. Workers saw their games as a chance to express anger and passion, as an opportunity possibly to make money as professional players. When working-class soccer teams played university groups, they literally drew blood—and had a good bit of fun shocking well-bred spectators in the process.

Mass leisure was not entirely class-bound, however, in part because it provided occasions when different groups could learn from each other.

Worker theater toned down a bit, as it drew middle-class patrons, and middle-class criticisms of workers' rowdiness abated in return. New technical forms blurred class distinctions. As films replaced live song and theater increasingly after 1900, they created a more homogeneous audience and also, in the darkness of the movie houses, a more impersonal one. Without eliminating separate, often hostile social classes, with distinct value systems, the new mass culture of the cities produced some overarching themes.

Decline of Traditional Values

Overall, the rising urban culture involved two elements: a decline in traditional systems of belief and their possible replacement by new ones, and a change in personal values. Organized religion tried to adjust to mature industrial society but on the whole it was unsuccessful. Many people still went to church, but in the cities this was now part of individual choice, not an systematic community of belief; and in fact church attendance declined steadily among middle and working classes alike.

Many Protestant organizations tried to react by establishing settlement-house facilities to aid the urban poor. They sponsored scouting groups and various efforts in social work to offer recreational facilities and material assistance to the lower classes. In Britain a new Protestant movement, the Salvation Army, was founded in 1880 to provide material as well as spiritual solace to the poor and downtrodden.

Catholic programs were also developed to promote material well-being and thereby attract working-class groups to the church. Many Catholic unions were founded in Germany, France, and elsewhere. Far more moderate than other union movements, they stressed mutual aid and bargaining without strikes. They won only modest membership but they revealed the new level of Catholic interest in the needs and demands of workers. More generally, Pope Leo XIII tried to modify the Catholic church's earlier opposition to modern political and social movements. He admitted the acceptability of democratic and even republican regimes, urging French Catholics, for example, to rally to the support of the French republic. Further, while attacking socialism and insisting on the importance of private property, he urged greater attention to social justice. In the encyclical *Rerum novarum*, issued in 1891, he approved of the union movement and of government welfare programs and recommended that employers better the conditions of their workers.

On the whole, however, the churches had begun effective adjustment to the new position of the lower classes too late. An important minority of workers were attached more firmly to the church by the new programs, but far more were left untouched. Important rural and aristocratic elements in the churches resisted many of the programs of reform, so efforts to woo the masses were small and were often contradicted by conservative action by Christian leaders. Many French Catholics, for example, ignored the pope's appeal to support the republic and seized on the Dreyfus affair as an excuse to attack republican principles. Catholic army officers, aristocrats, some members of the upper middle class, and certainly many members of the hierarchy continued to view religion as a force for social conservatism. It was significant, nevertheless, that efforts by both Protestant and Catholic churches to woo the masses were based on recognition of the need to combine religion with social reform. The working of religion in the world, beyond mere charity, became an increasingly important part of church activity.

The hold of religion on the urban lower classes was weakened by developments in church-state relations and in intellectual life. The middle-class political attack on church privileges continued, and middle-class parties had greater power than ever before because of the rise of parliamentary structures. And they were aided by the new socialist parties, which where almost uniformly hostile to Christianity. Together the parties launched a major attack on the churches, especially the Catholic church, in most countries. The German *Kulturkampf* of the 1870s suppressed many religious orders, secularized much of the educational system, and established civil instead of religious marriage. In Italy and France the government and the liberal parties were in a virtual state of war against the Catholic church; many religious orders were suppressed, and the church's role in education was curtailed. After the Dreyfus affair the attack was renewed in France, for the church seemed attached to the enemies of the republic. Religious orders and schools were weakened further, and in 1905 the church was separated from the state; state funds and protection were entirely withdrawn.

The political clashes weakened the churches in several ways. The churches lost institutional power and many traditional functions. Their educational role was reduced; traditional charity was diminished by the advance of secular welfare efforts. The Christian marriage ethic and influence over the family were hampered by new laws permitting divorce and civil marriage. Furthermore, the political disputes distracted many Christian leaders from the pressing problems of dealing with the newly awakened lower classes. The continued concern with defending institutional privilege often furthered the impression that the churches were conservative, out of date.

This impression was heightened, finally, by the spread of new scientific doctrines, such as the theory of evolution, and by the popularization of attacks on the historical veracity of the Bible. These new doctrines were published widely in the press and were often taught in the school systems; they confirmed many members of the middle and working classes in their view of religion as superstitious and irrelevant.

Despite the decline of religious interest, the churches showed considerable vitality during the period. The new scientific doctrines were answered by a revival and revision of Christian theology. The churches gradually accepted new political regimes; Catholics adjusted to the new German state after the 1870s and even to the separation of church and state in France. There was a huge burst of missionary activity from Catholics and Protestants alike. Many churches were gaining in wealth; the Irish and Spanish churches, particularly, were richer than ever before. The decline of religion was thus ambiguous; the churches were still receiving support and seemed to be gaining in vigor despite growing indifference among major groups.

The power of the churches came largely from nonindustrial classes, many of whom turned to religion with renewed interest in reaction to hostile industrial trends. Many peasants remained loyal to the faith and were often guided politically by local priests. The churches were vital to aristocratic conservatism and, in most countries, to shopkeepers and other elements of the middling class. Missionaries, for example, were recruited from small-town elements that found it easier to preach the faith to heathens than to adjust to what was, to them, the strange new society around them. Largely nonindustrial regions, like southern Germany, or whole countries, such as Ireland, were the bastions of religious fervor. Religion was increasingly a refuge for people who were being reduced in status by the classes most directly associated with the leading economic forms. Where antimodern political movements developed, they usually had Christian overtones and appealed to many Christians. The conversion of many French priests to anti-Semitic movements and the association of many German Protestants with anti-Semitism were extreme forms of Christian protest.

Of course sincere religious belief was found among individuals in every part of society, and the association of religion with traditionalist elements was incomplete. But the churches were declining and, although this was not entirely new, their decline raised important questions of alternatives for the leading urban groups.

New Beliefs

Some people sought an alternate, encompassing loyalty, as religion lost ground. It has often been pointed out that socialism provided religious-like values for certain of its adherents: It had a Bible (Marxism), martyrs, a heaven to come in the future, and often important rituals. A German miner, describing the role of socialism in his life, proclaimed religious fervor: "What is my meaning in this great world plan where brutal physical and psychological forces feast themselves in orgies? Nothing! Only Social Democratic activities could give me goals. . . . so that I may attempt my plans. I therefore adhere to socialism with every fiber of courage and idealism."[14] In eastern Europe, the later rise of communist loyalties could replace religion. Everywhere some individuals

[4] Levenstein, *Aus der Tiefe*, p. 104.

made the transfer quite directly, abandoning traditional churches as irrelevant but switching their entire devotion to socialism or communism.

Nationalism might serve something of the same purpose. It was more likely to be combined with religion, as conservative leaders came to support both loyalties by the end of the nineteenth century. But workers might unite nationalism with socialism, like the German who declared himself "a good socialist and a good soldier of the Fatherland, both at the same time."[15] Some intellectuals certainly attributed religiouslike importance to their devotion to the nation; this was particularly true in multiethnic areas where one's nationality could so easily seem oppressed by others, as in the Hapsburg monarchy where Slavs resisted the dominance of Germans and Magyars.

Critics of mass culture noted the rise of new loyalties with disfavor. Both socialism and nationalism were manipulable by calculating leaders. Both could rouse masses to blind, sometimes violent enthusiasms. Roaring mobs, shouting obedience to a rabble-rousing speaker skilled in playing on their emotions, vowing death to an enemy class or race, constituted recurrent features of mature industrial society.

Most people, even nationalists and socialists, replaced or supplemented religion with a more informal set of values. Most socialist workers really wanted a new society but they did not see socialism as all-encompassing; hence, among other things, they were mildly nationalistic too, as their loyal performance during the first years of World War I was to indicate. Most middle-class people, although believing in nationalism, also believed in science and material progress and a host of other values. For the majority of all urban groups the culture that really replaced religion was hedonistic, a commitment to a range of individual choices about what pleasures to seek when work was done.

Nothing more clearly mirrored and shaped the new popular culture than the mass press that developed at the end of the nineteenth century. Working-class literacy of course attracted a variety of socialist newspapers that provided political information and guidance to their members and maintained a high level of excitement about current problems. Though significant, these were not the papers that gained a really mass following, their circulation being limited to a small number of the faithful.

The truly mass press had a twofold basis. First, it was able to lower prices drastically. This was due partly to major improvements in printing, but particularly to the development of huge advertising revenues. Second, the new press catered to people whose reading habits were not sophisticated and who sought entertainment in what they read. In both respects the press reflected the new search for pleasure. Older journals of course continued, appealing to the upper classes with their serious

---

[15] Göhre, *Drei Monate*, p. 349.

accounts of political and cultural events, but their readership was limited. By 1900, however, *Le Petit Journal* in Paris sold two million copies
a day. The Berlin *Lokal-Anzeiger* had a million readers, as did both the
Daily Mail and the *Daily Express* in London. The size of these giants
allowed steady reductions in cost and development of various new features to keep the readers entertained; both tended to increase the
readership even further, cutting across strict class lines.

The entertainment function of the mass press was expressed in many
ways. Stories of crimes and of personal melodrama proved increasingly
popular. This contrasted with the older middle-class press, which had
devoted space to short stories with a moral message and to comments
on theater, music, and the like. Special features were developed to appeal to the interests of various groups. Women's sections discussed social
news and other matters of concern to female readers. Accounts of
sporting events were greatly expanded. And in all the features of the
paper, writing was simplified, headlines made more sensational.

The political content of the new papers differed from the older middle-class press and from the working-class press. Little attention was
given to internal politics. The great interest in editorializing, which
typified older middle-class papers, declined as the enlarged reading
public showed little concern for elaborate discussions of issues. However, the papers did have a political tone, almost uniformly conservative. The publishers and the advertisers were businesspeople; they had
a definite interest in turning the masses away from social discontent.
And they discovered quite quickly that appeals to national loyalty, particularly in accounts of imperial ventures, appealed to readers. Stories
of national empire could be filled with excitement and the lure of the
strange, and they promoted a comforting sense of importance among
readers who saw their nations dominating inferior peoples.

After World War I the entertainment functions of the mass press
became still more prominent. Newspapers found that only their frivolous
articles attracted readers. They provided intensive coverage of particularly interesting crimes, the activities of the socially fashionable (including
the affairs and divorces of film stars and aristocrats, whose amusement
value almost gave the class a new function), and other phenomena that
were diverting in their peculiarity, such as nudist movements or the
tales of the Loch Ness monster. Sports sections were expanded, covering
the new range of athletics and also expanded betting possibilities, for
gambling on horse racing and football games won growing popularity.

In addition to the mass press, music halls and, after 1900, films provided new entertainment outlets. The radio, available in bars if not in
all private homes, offered yet another set of standardized entertainment
fare. All in all a formidable array of diversions was available. Bars retained popularity, though the level of public drinking now declined in
places like France, as earlier in Britain. Dancing, sports, shows, gambling,

light reading, and excursions all contributed to the pleasure-seeking culture of the 1920s.

It is easy to criticize this new culture. It was highly commercialized, for the leisure industry was big business. It was sensationalist in many respects. Mass culture did not spring from tightly-knit communities, though it could create crowd loyalties. The main organs of mass entertainment were standardized. This was a passive culture in most of its manifestations, involving watching other people perform or hearing about disasters that occurred someplace else. Professional players and entertainers gained status and, sometimes, considerable fortunes. But this was not really the deterioration of some glorious tradition of popular entertainment, for leisure was itself a new development. Older popular festivals were periodic occurrences, not regular chances for enjoyment, and they themselves were highly stylized and custombound, restricting individual initiative on the part of participants. Many of the weaknesses of the new leisure culture derived from the inevitable fumbling that occurred as people adjusted to the use of unaccustomed funds and free time. Although standardization and control by rapacious businesspeople trying to play on poor taste in order to make money were legitimate targets of criticism, from the viewpoint of the masses the culture provided unprecedented scope for choice. Not everyone read newspapers; some preferred the radio. Although some thronged to soccer games, others preferred bicycling.

Interpretation of mass leisure continues to be difficult, even aside from the biases of the turn-of-the-century educated elite, who derided base taste. This critical elite included not a few socialist leaders, who found mass leisure an opiate that distracted from serious protest. The standardized forms and rules did not prevent individuals and groups from finding special meanings. A French peasant village, for example, gaining access to movies for the first time (on an irregular basis; there was no theater), watched an epic about a Roman, Marius, over and over again, not because it was popular in the cities, where audiences had long since turned to other things, but because its heroic values seemed relevant to the way these particular people set their own ideals. Homogenization and autonomy were at war. The new leisure stressed innovations, fads, and crazes that could appeal to the taste for progressive novelty and sell new goods. But some of the most popular sports, like soccer and football, had old traditional roots, and many people continued to treasure other customary pastimes—like the bowling games brought from the countryside to city parks by rural migrants into the working class. Tradition and innovation were at war. Much new leisure emphasized fixed forms, like the rules and referees that defined modern sporting events. But many people, watching an earthy comedy or even seeking pleasure in sex, found opportunities for release. Regimentation and spontaneity were at war. The new leisure was, in sum, ambiguous in its meanings and social effects. Whether it provided people the meaning they needed, especially as work became more routine, whether it offered community ties as against the possibilities for urban loneliness, whether it offered distinct class, ethnic, and gender groups a way to maintain or to lose their group identities—these are important questions open to debate. What is clear is that a novel urban culture was taking shape, though still in gestation during the mature industrial decades, that captured growing attention from otherwise varied groups.

World War I and the Collapse of Industrial Society

Although it suggested a popular culture that has received much fuller development in recent decades, the period of industrial maturation had a number of inherent weaknesses. We have already sketched the serious structural imbalances of the economy that led to recurrent crises well before World War I; we have dealt with the incomplete adaptation of the upper class and of tensions within as well as between the middle and lower classes. Where this would have led without the catastrophe of World War I is anybody's guess. Advanced industrial countries that were not involved in the war, such as Sweden, made the transition toward a new set of policies relatively smoothly, without great tension. Sweden moved quickly toward a welfare state in response to the economic problems of the 1930s. Possibly, then, the malaise of the 1920s and 1930s was not inevitable. However, the World War itself arose in part from social tensions. This was obviously the case in Russia and the Hapsburg monarchy, where the initiative for war first rested. Social tensions in both countries had reached such heights that diplomats were vowed to use diplomacy to distract from the dislocations of early industrialization; if this meant war, so be it. But even in Germany and Britain, upper-class leaders, frightened by the belligerence of the working classes, had become partial victims of their own nationalism. They too had used diplomacy as a political panacea, first through imperialist ventures and more recently through internal military buildups. Many German officers, dissatisfied with their position in modern society, wanted war. British diplomats who used the threat of war to stop strikes, claiming that agitation would damage the nation, were milder but perhaps almost as unsure of their position in a changing economy and a changing culture. At the very least they were guilty of leaving the diplomatic initiative to unstable states such as Russia. Ironically, important elements of the middle and lower classes also welcomed war at first. Youth responded to the idea of adventure and action; soldiers left eagerly for the front, convinced that this would be a fun war of short duration. Most socialists loyally entered wartime governments, abandoning all pretense of protest.

Aspects of mature industrial society thus promoted war, though it is hard to argue that it was an inevitable product of this stage of industrialization. In any event the results of the war transformed the necessity for change, to deal with the weaknesses of industrial maturation, into catastrophe, and another bloody purging was needed before Europe could right itself.

The war proved to be one of the most frustrating, certainly one of the most brutal encounters in European history. It killed millions and sapped the morale of millions more. On the western front battle lines established within the first few months shifted only slightly during the next four years. Day-long battles could result in the loss of tens of thousands of lives. New war machines were introduced that were unprecedented in their destructive power. Submarine warfare attacked even civilian shipping. The use of gas, tanks, and flame throwers provided awesome proof of the power of technology to injure and destroy. Airplane warfare, including some bombing of major cities, brought the horrors of war directly to some civilians. Destruction seemed endless and without clear purpose.

The total death rate was staggering. Germany lost 2 million people; France lost 1.7 million, a full 5 percent of its total population. Italy and Britain lost a million each, and Russia was to lose a full 17 million in war and the revolutions and famines that followed. In all, 16 million people died or were lost during the war and 20 million more were wounded. Most families had to mourn the death of at least one close relative. Much of a whole generation was wiped out, which would long reduce the vitality of European leaders by limiting the competition of the able young for established positions in society. Above all the very fact of such wanton slaughter made a mockery of the optimistic tone of Europe's popular culture just a few years before.

The people most affected by the shock of the war were, of course, those who fought in it. The armies on both sides embraced millions of soldiers; in war as in other activities, the age of the masses had clearly arrived. These millions were directly faced with the daily pressures of shelling and with the frequent anguish of bloody but inconclusive battles. Soldiers felt that their efforts deserved some sort of special recognition from society, that their hardships should result in a changed world and a better life. During the war itself many troops believed that civilians, particularly politicians and war profiteers, were not responding properly to the situation at the front. Important mutinies by troops, from 1917 until well after the war's end, indicated the discontent of those fighting.

After the war, troops returning to civilian society continued to feel abused and somewhat separate. They faced inevitable problems of adjustment to civilian life after the bloody stress of war. Many were wounded, others psychologically marred. Veterans also faced economic difficulties, for the national economies adapted only slowly to the influx of returning workers and peasants. The problems of veterans were heightened in some countries, notably in Germany, by the reduction even of professional military ranks, so that officers as well as troops were thrown out of their accustomed positions. Again, it proved easy to focus the frustrations of peacetime on civilian society, on the politicians, on the capitalists.

Some of these frustrations very early assumed a political form; veterans formed organizations designed to remake society. Many supporters of communist groups in the postwar years were veterans, and the massive strikes and attempted revolutions were sparked by returning troops. At the other extreme the founders and followers of rightist movements were veterans who could not find a suitable place in civilian life. More general veterans' organizations, such as the German *Stahlhelm* or the French *Croix de feu*, became active proponents of radical and nationalist conservatism.

The shock of the war affected civilian populations as well as soldiers. Civilians in frontline areas, such as Serbia, Belgium, and Poland, were subject to the same pressures of bombardment and attack as soldiers themselves. Civilians everywhere were actively involved in the war effort. The economies of Europe had to convert almost totally to wartime production. Rationing of foods and some other products was introduced. Most countries suffered from a lack of consumer goods, particularly food. In Germany and eastern Europe the conscription of peasants into the armies and the difficulty of importing food led to real hardship for most civilians by 1916. Diets were reduced to subsistence levels, with primary dependence on potatoes and other starches. In Russia outright famine reappeared in some areas. These reductions in standards, coming after a period of rising material expectations, produced a psychological as well as a material shock to the millions affected.

Involvement in the war economy was not confined to consumption patterns. More and more people were drawn and even forced into war industries. Many countries, including Britain and Germany, set up compulsory labor procedures to channel workers into the most vital branches of production. This brought new experiences to many people, including large numbers of women who found jobs of unprecedented importance open to them. It also brought a sense of involvement in the war itself and in its frustrations.

Moreover, governments were not content with requiring economic participation of civilian populations; they insisted on moral participation as well. War in industrial Europe brought not only the creation of armies of unprecedented size but also the subjection of civilians to centrally directed propaganda designed to instill uniform and active loyalty to the war effort. Earlier changes in state functions and organizational capacity now transformed the meaning of war, just as industrial technology transformed its methods. Censorship of all forms of publication and arrests

Women in the labor force during World War I. These workers, doing heavy industrial jobs traditionally reserved for men, were cleaning fittings for the Glasgow (Scotland) Gas Department in 1918. Work of this sort generated great debate about previous gender differentiations on the job, and about how much change should be institutionalized for the future. *(Imperial War Museum.)*

of dissidents became commonplace. Governments also planted news in various media, without particular regard for truth. The German government tried to instill firm belief in German victory and war aims and in the evils of the opposing powers, with such success that many Germans were unaware that the tide had turned against them in 1918. British and French propaganda painted the Germans as barbaric Huns whose defeat was essential to Western civilization. All governments tried to promote a constant sense of excitement and tension that would lead to more vigorous support of their cause. The propaganda efforts were not totally successful. Particularly among the working classes, partially hostile to the established order before the war, movements of protest developed as material conditions deteriorated. On the whole, however, extraordinary loyalty was maintained. After the conflict was over, the emotional and economic involvement with the war brought to civilian elements some of the frustrations that afflicted veterans.

Partly because of the tension and expectations promoted during the war, the aftermath disillusioned most people everywhere. Some had put faith in Wilsonian principles of a democratic society free from war. They were quickly disillusioned because Wilson's efforts were partially thwarted. Far more people, spurred by government propaganda, had expected massive national gains. The French hoped not only for the return of Alsace-Lorraine but also for permanent protection from Germany; they were disappointed. Italians dreamed of great acquisitions in the Balkans and the Near East; they were frustrated. Germans had expected huge gains in both east and west; instead they lost much of their own land in both areas. Newly created states in eastern Europe, though excited by their existence, were almost uniformly discontented about territory that they did not receive.

For various reasons, then, there was a widespread feeling that the war and all the strain it involved had led to failure. Radical socialists gained mass support by pointing to capitalists as the scapegoats. German nationalists began to preach that revenge was necessary, that Germany had lost only because of the disloyalty of politicians or labor leaders or Jews. Italian groups, including the new fascist party, made rapid gains by citing the failures of the parliamentary government to win significant new territory. Even in a less agitated nation like Britain many leaders urged that the war had been a mistake and that Britain should pull out of its Continental involvements; again, these views correspond to sentiments held by a wide public.

To the horror of the war itself was added a widespread disillusionment about the peace. It became more difficult to maintain the confidence and optimism that had dominated much of the prewar mood. The bloodshed and the apparent futility of the war efforts helped to change the tone of European thinking. Some groups, particularly in the defeated countries, preached the need for revolutionary change to right the wrongs of the war. Far more people, in most social classes, were vaguely embittered and disillusioned as a result of the shattering conflict, and their uncertainty about traditional goals and principles dominated much of the behavior of the interwar period.

Economic Effects

With the war's end, pessimistic intellectuals found a new audience for their predictions of doom, for it was plausible to believe that civilization had come to an end. Books like Oswald Spengler's *Decline of the West*, if not widely read, were at least widely known. On the surface, however, after a few important years of disruption, popular culture regained a certain equilibrium. Workers protested violently for two or three years after the war, revealing new aspirations plus their discontentment with wartime privations, but after employers and governments repressed their efforts, workers returned to more moderate protest patterns. Elements of the middle and working classes took advantage of the new pleasures open to them as mass culture resumed its progress. The 1920s was not simply a restoration of prewar Europe, however, though many people wanted nothing better. There were new, enduring tensions. The rise of communist parties reflected the politicization of important lower-

Vacations for the masses. French interest in seaside vacations grew steadily in the 1920s, and again in the later 1930s in the wake of government-mandated holidays. Many urban workers saw the sea for the first time. Crowding increased accordingly—a common part of mass leisure. The scene above is a popular beach developed on the French Riviera. (*The Bettmann Archive.*)

class grievances, just as the advent of rightist groups played on the frustrations of former military men or the disgruntled middle class. Even the popular culture of the decade, with its heightened faddism and pleasure seeking, can be judged a superficial, really frenzied effort to conceal the inevitable collapse of European society.

Probably Europe could have recovered from the shock of war itself. The extreme Right and extreme Left in Germany, for example, remained minority phenomena and even receded after 1924, and Germany was the country hardest hit by defeat. But to the shock of war was added economic catastrophe, for the war exacerbated virtually all the structural weaknesses of the economy. Serious economic problems were inevitable anyway; the war seemed to make them virtually insoluble.

Population growth had been slowing; the war brought it to a virtual standstill in western Europe. This reduced the market for goods. Actual devastation in the war was considerable, for approximately one-thirtieth of Europe's assets were destroyed. Physical damage was greatest in France, Belgium, Serbia, and eastern Europe. The worst damage could be made good, for reparation payments plus government aid allowed actual upgrading of equipment in France and Belgium. There were, however, other points of weakness. Wartime demand for food stimulated production elsewhere, in the United States for instance, and even in combatant nations such as Britain, which reversed its earlier tendency to abandon farming. By the mid-1920s, however, traditional producers had for the most part returned to their earlier levels of production. There was a greater surplus of agricultural goods than ever before, and farming income suffered accordingly; here was another market damaged.

The war also drastically altered the economic position of Europe in the world. The diversion of production and shipping to war needs made it impossible for European industry to supply its export markets. Non-European powers, led by the United States and Japan, entered these markets and retained part of their hold on them after the war. To these material difficulties was added a blow to morale as traditional views of European superiority were weakened.

Europe's credit position was also drastically altered. The need for foreign supplies, especially from the United States, compelled many countries to abandon their investments abroad in order to pay for needed materials. Foreign investments were also lost, particularly by France, when the Russian revolutionaries renounced their foreign debts. For both Britain and France the loss of these investments was accompanied by new borrowing. Germany also borrowed significantly during and after the war; its debts also were increasingly owed outside Europe, especially to the United States. Thus Europe was transformed from a creditor continent to a continent considerably in debt.

Finally, the peace settlement was economically disruptive. A few nations profited economically from the settlement, notably France, which gained the remainder of the iron ore resources of Lorraine. Even for the victors, however, the new boundaries were drawn on the basis of nationalist impulse rather than economic reality. The new states in eastern Europe were for the most part economically weak. They were too small, and they quickly increased their economic isolation by the nationalistic policy of high tariffs. Russia lost Polish industry and the oil resources of Bessarabia. Germany lost part of its coal resources in Upper Silesia and was deprived of the coal fields of the Saar for fifteen years; and it lost three-quarters of its iron reserves as well as merchant shipping, railroad rolling stock, and cash in the reparation exactions imposed upon the country. The various deprivations of markets and resources, heightened by the protective tariffs adopted by all European states immediately after the war, decreased the economic possibilities for mature and emerging industrial nations alike.

All of this meant that economic crisis was not only inevitable, short of new government policies that no state aside from communist Russia was able to take, but that it would be far more extensive than its prewar counterparts. As we have seen, large sections of Europe—from the outdated industrial regions of Britain to the agricultural nations of the Balkans—were in severe depression by the mid-1920s. Unemployment was rising in Germany early in 1928, and of course inflation had earlier taken its toll. The Great Depression, stemming directly from the collapse of American finance, massively heightened Europe's economic problems, but it did not create them.

Social Chaos

From depression, in turn, came an almost complete polarization of European society. Lines had been hardening during the 1920s. The middle classes and upper class, their morale damaged by the war, were frightened by the Russian Revolution and rise of communist movements in most European countries. Here seemed proof that the workers could take over. Accounts of Russian communist atrocities appeared quite frequently, and conservative parties played on the communist threat; in France, rightist groups during the early 1920s had great success with a poster showing, without comment, a red hand holding a dagger dripping with blood. In the context of growing class war, businesspeople became more resistant to workers' strikes, so despite the improved organization of many unions the rate of strike victories and compromises declined. In Britain the general strike of 1926 provided a clear illustration of hostility to the demands of labor, for it was marked by willingness of members of the middle class, including students at Oxford and Cambridge, to replace workers in loading jobs, in the running of trains, and in other functions. There was a clear desire to keep the economy operating sufficiently to defeat the strike; and the middle class won its victory. In the following year legislation was passed forbidding sympathetic strikes and weakening the general bargaining power of labor. Class interest was now predominant.

The active defensiveness of the middle class was clearest, of course, in the political field. From the early postwar period middle-class voting patterns displayed greater conservatism than had been typical of the prewar period. Traditional middle-class political vehicles such as the British Liberal party declined rapidly, as the class switched its votes to the Conservatives. The French Radical party retained substantial middle-class support only because of its resistance to any real social reforms. Furthermore, under stress major segments of the middle ranks of society turned to other political movements. In Italy after 1919 certain middle-class elements joined with other groups in support of the fascist party. To the middle class fascism offered an acceptable defense against working-class revolution, in the name of national unity; the Italian middle class was interested in nationalist causes anyway and had been disappointed by the lack of gains from the peace settlement. Fascism also proclaimed a need to protect small business against large stores and industries. It promised an end to antagonistic labor unions and parties and a solution to economic difficulties. Italy was wracked by the postwar depression, the rise of a militant socialist party, and a wave of strikes. These developments induced some members of the middle class to support fascism directly and others to acquiesce in the fascist takeover. Crucial to the fascist government was an arrangement with big businesspeople whereby the control and profits of industry remained in the hands of the upper middle class, despite the earlier anticapitalist talk of the party.

In Germany the Nazi party was formed in the years following the war. It attracted little initial support. Only in 1924, at the peak of resentment over the inflation, did a coalition of which the Nazis were a part poll nearly two million votes. With the onset of depression, however, Nazi power rose rapidly, and the party achieved far more massive direct support than the Italian fascists ever knew. The party polled 37.3 percent of the vote in 1932, largely at the expense of traditional middle-class parties. It attracted many members of the disgruntled middle class by its promises of full employment and welfare aid and its attacks on communism and big business alike. Even more than Italian fascism, the movement appealed to the middle-class desire to protect the small firm against modern capitalism as well as against the power of organized labor. It was particularly popular, therefore, in the smaller towns. At the same time, as in Italy, the party depended for its final seizure of power on an agreement with business leaders in which protection for business was promised in exchange for financial support. The upper middle class was not committed to nazism, but it saw in the movement a chance to defeat the rising threat of communism; many upper middle-class voters opted for the Nazi party in 1932. Thus, for various reasons, by 1933 substantial elements of the German middle classes had turned to nazism.

Elsewhere in Europe middle-class support for fascist movements was more limited; conservatism remained more powerful. And a minority of the class turned left to protest; by 1936 some of the most ardent supporters of the French socialist party were clerks and teachers. On balance, however, the rightist impulse predominated in middle-class France. As the economic crisis deepened and as socialist and communist parties grew in strength, semi-fascist groups like the *Croix de feu* and, after 1936, the *Parti populaire français*, obtained the backing of hundreds of thousands of members of the middle classes. These groups appealed to the new desire for economic protection against both depression and the leftist threat to private property, and cited the need for attention to the nation instead of to the divisive elements of class warfare.

The new reactionary parties, drawing from small property owners (including peasants in the more traditional villages) above all, also could attract support from some professional people, students and other youth eager for action, even some workers who were disappointed with the political Left. In Germany nazism drew more votes from women, who perhaps saw in it a protection for their traditional roles, than from men; it also attracted more new voters than experienced voters. Religious affiliations could play a role. The Nazis fared better in Protestant regions than in Catholic ones, since well-organized Catholic parties and trade unions kept many traditional supporters in the fold, at least until 1933 when Hitler's government set out to destroy all independent political parties. The new parties were thus socially complex. All in all they did primarily appeal to a desire to go back to a simpler but more structured society, free from advanced capitalism, organized labor, and the new fads and fashions. Spurred by their own suffering during the Depression, the propertied elements could turn against even the remnants of a liberal political tradition, denying the virtues of liberty and the parliamentary system, denying even the rationality of individuals in favor of leaders who stressed the need for physical activity, violence, and war.

For its part the Left, drawing mainly from the working classes but with some rural and middle-class support, added to what became a political vicious circle. Even relatively small leftist groups, by using new political tactics, stimulated the fascist or semi-fascist response, and vice versa. The agitation of Maximalist Socialists in Italy right after the war helped create the basis for fascism, though unintentionally, by rallying the forces of order around Mussolini's claim to be able to restore social harmony. Communist demonstrations and strong-arm tactics in France in the 1920s stimulated the growth of the first paramilitary organizations on the right. In Germany and France the increase in communist voting strength resulting from the Depression fostered fascist gains, which in turn brought new vigor to the Left; the French Popular Front was a direct response to rightist agitation in 1934–1935.

Class warfare involved violence. Communists and even socialist groups occasionally broke up political meetings. In Spain the perpetuation of the anarchist tradition among many workers and peasants led to even greater violence, including murders, during the republican period. On the whole, the methods of the Left were not so violent as those of the Right. Worker parties and unions relied on their increasing strength of organization and growth in numbers to pursue their purposes. Major strikes, such as the British general strike or the French sit-ins in 1936, involved almost no violence at all. Workers and their leaders were also afraid of the repressive power of the troops and the police, whose officials were usually conservative in inclination and notoriously more ready to repress workers than to attack rightist demonstrations. Working-class protest, therefore, was limited primarily to the polls, to strikes, and to many gigantic but calm street demonstrations.

The Right was more unruly, particularly in Spain, Italy, Germany, and France, where significant fascist movements arose. Fascist rioting, beatings, and murders were common during the period of greatest social tensions. Fascists themselves praised violence as a true expression of the human spirit, and they tried to attract attention to themselves by its use. They hoped to create sufficient chaos to provide an opportunity for the seizure of power and recruited large, uniformed forces to stimulate such chaos. Brownshirts in Germany, Blackshirts in Italy, and several different colors in France did create considerable disorder. The fascist shock troops were drawn from young unemployed professional people, unemployed workers, clerks, and the like. In Spain massive participation of the military in the conservative cause brought about a bloody civil war, the extreme expression of the class conflict that had developed. In Germany and Italy considerable fascist rioting and demonstrations preceded the actual takeover. France saw large demonstrations and some rioting early in 1934, which culminated on February 6, when thousands of Parisians rioted against the parliamentary regime, attacked police officers and deputies, and stormed government buildings. Labor groups responded with counterdemonstrations, and France came close to civil war. This was the worst outburst in France during the decade, but demonstrations and beatings continued even later.

It was in the political arena proper that the principal manifestations of class conflict took place. Only a minority was involved in violence on either side. Fascist leaders themselves recognized, except in Spain, that they could not take power by force alone. In many countries leading elements on both Left and Right refused to accept the existing regime and took all possible measures to bring about its downfall. In Germany massive communist and fascist parties in the early 1930s helped paralyze the government. Similar chaos existed in Italy in the early 1920s, while French politics were stalemated as well during much of the 1930s. Everywhere a dynamic political center was missing. The middle class and its allies largely withdrew allegiance from parties that were interested in bridging the social gap between them and the workers. Workers, for their part, supported either socialist parties, which were reluctant to become too involved with the existing regime, or communist parties, which rejected the regime altogether. Even in England, where political extremes were less marked, there was a tendency toward polarization of parties on a class basis. In the major Continental countries the polarization threatened to become total. The only link between Left and Right was a common hostility to the existing situation.

In most countries extreme social chaos lasted for only a few years. The Scandinavian nations, which, like Britain, were not afflicted by the most radical political hostilities and in which, furthermore, the Depression was not severe, resolved many of the tensions by their welfare policies. These policies were sufficiently effective to alleviate workers' grievances and to prevent their recourse to more vigorous action. At the same time, the measures were mild enough not to provoke the hostility of the middle class. Conservative elements were distressed by most of the new programs, but their resistance was expressed only though the normal channels of parliamentary action.

In other European countries, however, social tensions were relieved most clearly by the total victory of the extreme Right. This was the pattern in Italy, Germany, Austria, Spain, and to an extent the authoritarian states of eastern Europe. The new fascist or semi-fascist regimes obviously protected the interests of large landowners and the leaders of industry. Despite the anticapitalist elements of fascist doctrine, little was done to control industry or profits; landed estates were left untouched. Only in Germany were certain limitations placed on private industry, in the interest of increasing the economic power of the state; but even there private ownership and substantial profits were not affected. For the lower classes, even those that had opposed fascism, the new regimes offered numerous benefits, though they never won wholehearted working-class support. Full employment was restored in Germany, and public works in Italy improved the economic position of many workers, although the Depression did cause some unemployment. The governments of both countries offered subsidies to large families in the interest of promoting demographic growth, and in Germany an increase in population growth rate resulted. Organizations such as the "Strength Through Joy" movement in Germany tried to fulfill the workers' desire for leisure and recreation by promoting hikes and outings. New state unions sought to give workers a sense of participation in decisions about labor conditions, though the interests of management remained dominant. Beyond this, the fascist state organized an elaborate propaganda and police apparatus that actively promoted public satisfaction with and loyalty to the regime. Educational systems were altered to stress fascist principles. A state of national tension was maintained through the many news media under government control, which induced ever greater attachment to fascist leaders. Further, organizations with a potential for protest were quickly and completely eliminated. This affected the working class particularly, for workers represented the class most hostile to fascism before the takeover. Communist and socialist parties were outlawed, and many labor leaders were arrested. In Spain the execution and exile of thousands of leftists removed the possibility of worker protest in a similar, if bloodier, manner. Unions were disbanded and replaced by the state organizations.

Thus the new regimes stifled protest by a combination of benefits and repression. Almost no active resistance to the fascists developed. Class warfare had been ended by an alliance of the upper classes and dynamic middle-class leaders. The resulting regimes proved impossible to dislodge except by war.

In Britain and especially in France hardly any solution to social conflict was discovered during the interwar period. The British government, under Conservative party control, did take steps to alleviate social and economic distress. Increased government economic activity was developed to retrain workers, to channel investments, and to promote exports. The extension of earlier social insurance programs, notably unemployment insurance, did allow some redistribution of income. Before World War I workers had paid more in dues and taxes than they had received in government aid. By 1935 the working class paid in only about 80 percent of the money it received in benefits. British suffering from the Depression, though intense, was alleviated by an economic boomlet during the later 1930s. Renewed attention to new industries, such as the production of automobiles, refrigerators, and even a modest number of television sets, brought new prosperity to southern England; there was also a housing boom, as suburban development resumed. But in other areas there was much unemployment still. England's moderate political traditions, plus the partial recovery, kept class tensions within bounds, but rising support for the Labour party on the local level, before World War II, showed that class antagonisms might yet affect the state.

In France the government was far more completely paralyzed by a network of political and social divisions. The promising measures of the Popular Front did not relieve working-class grievances, for economic conditions continued to deteriorate. Communist strength mounted steadily. At the same time, larger elements of the middle class were attracted to radical conservative movements; by 1938 the *Croix de feu* claimed two million members, and several other groups had formed on the extreme Right. Economic difficulty and the perpetual conflict between Right and Left made it impossible to undertake any significant action or reform after the failure of the Popular Front.

Furthermore, internal social conflicts affected diplomatic policies. Social divisions in Britain and France paralyzed both countries internationally during the 1930s. The rise of Nazi Germany was recognized as an international threat, but the western nations lacked the will to act. The political Right, although not for the most part favorable to the Nazi regime, feared communist Russia as the primary enemy. The political Left was willing to take action against fascism but was not strong enough to impose its will. Divisions over foreign policy first became clear during the Spanish Civil War, when the French Popular Front was forced to remain idle while its Spanish counterpart was gradually crushed. Powerful conservative movements opposed action in coordination with Russia and against the advocates of private property and religion, and they could not be overcome. From that point onward, the governments of France and Britain worked for peace at almost any price, for they lacked the internal strength to do otherwise. The results of their efforts, the Munich agreements of 1938, were hailed by large elements of the citizenry.

When renewed war came, it caught Europeans in a far different mood from that of 1914. There was no confidence, no belief that the war would be easy or pleasant. At best, there was a grim determination to see it through; at worst, the alienation of important groups from the established order hampered the war effort itself. In contrast to 1914, important segments of the labor movement resisted participation in the war because a Nazi-Soviet pact (1939) neutralized communist hostility to Germany. The social conflicts of the period were carried over into the war itself in France, where the Vichy regime drew much support from traditionalist elements despite its acceptance of France's defeat. Yet, curiously, the developments during and after the war alleviated many of the social and economic problems of the preceding period. The mood of hopelessness so clearly apparent in western Europe before the war receded, and a new period of social development began.

CHAPTER 6

The Consumer Society

After a brief though important period of dislocation following World War II, Europe began to reverse many of the most disheartening trends of the interwar years. This achievement differed from what had occurred after World War I. Then Europeans had encountered disastrous inflation in the early 1920s before plunging a decade later into economic depression. Fascist regimes took power in Germany and Italy. Class tensions, reflected in politics, seemed to paralyze the western countries. After World War II, however, Europeans embarked on a path of unprecedented economic growth. Class tensions diminished to an important degree and some of the most bitter opposition to change was eliminated. Nationalism declined and with it the likelihood of European war. New movements of cooperation, most notably the Common Market (or European Community, as it was later called), reflected a desire to innovate, overcoming a legacy of economic and military rivalry. Prosperity and cooperation bred a new sense of confidence. When confronted with nationalist movements after World War II in Asia and Africa, Europe largely divested itself of colonies. Whole civilizations, including the Greek and the Roman, had foundered on the corruption of internal society through a desire to cling to colonies when their age had passed. Postwar Europe was perhaps fortunate in being too weak to make the effort, although decolonization was resisted even so, particularly in France. From a larger perspective, however, decolonization reflected a willingness to concentrate on building a strong domestic society that had been wanting during the interwar years. And although some members of the upper class grumbled at the undeniable loss of world stature the former colonial powers suffered, few people cared much about empire by this point. Europeans focused their collective attentions on the choices involved in rebuilding their own societies.

What emerged in the postwar era, especially in western Europe, was an advanced industrial society that many observers came to call a *consumer society*. More people than ever before turned to the marketplace

Café Life in Contemporary Madrid. Since the nineteenth century cafés have provided social and bodily nourishment. Regular patrons typically gave cafés a class character. In a society where the homes remained intensively private (and crowded), cafés served as a public space for meeting friends and taking part in the small town life of a big-city neighborhood. (*UPI/Bettmann Archive.*)

to satisfy their needs and desires. Leisure became more a matter of mass consumption than before, as more and more workers, and not just middle-class Europeans, took advantage of restaurants, holiday resorts, spectator sports, and the movies. Radio, television, and the advertising that saturated their air waves gradually became commonplace in everyday life. Consumption became a more important avenue of personal expression—how people presented themselves became more and more a matter of what they bought. Even such intimate aspects of life as childbirth and child rearing became entangled in a growing market of goods and services. Spiritual matters, once the province of the church, became services for purchase as well—from doctors, teachers, social workers, and psychologists. And the economic well-being of the society depended increasingly on the mass consumption of goods and services as well as the continuous invention of new products.

Consumerism, in short, became both a mentality and a state of the economy. To be sure, Europe's emergence as a consumer society did not happen suddenly; it had been developing all along with commercial and industrial growth. Nor did mass consumption pervade the various regions and social strata of European society with equal speed and intensity. But the relative prosperity of the postwar era accelerated trends already underway, which brought most Europeans into a more comprehensive dependence on the marketplace than ever before. In some respects, such as in institutionalizing the extended annual vacation, postwar Europeans came to lead the world in elaborating new forms of consumption.

Before Europeans could concentrate their energies on the renewal of their societies after 1945, they first had to come to terms with the immediate human costs of World War II, which took a devastating toll, especially in Germany and eastern Europe. If combat in the swiftly changing battlefields of this war did not produce as many casualties in western Europe as did the murderous trench warfare of World War I, civilian death rates were far higher. Hitler's policy of mass murder took eleven to twelve million victims. The Soviet Union lost twenty million people, and Poland lost at least 13 percent of its population. Millions of people who survived bombing and shelling died from overwork, malnutrition, or epidemic disease. Material destruction was substantial as well. Nearly all the larger towns of Germany and England suffered heavy bombardment, though the military effectiveness of strategic bombing fell short of air force claims. Only a tenth of Germany's productive capacity was destroyed; bombers proved more adept at hitting houses than industrial targets. Still, the widespread destruction of bridges, harbors, and rail lines, and the leveling of urban districts across much of the Continent created chaos. For three or four years after 1945 Germany was reduced to a near-subsistence economy. Its people endured severe shortages of food and fuel. Inflation reduced the value of money to almost nothing. Nonmonetary units of exchange, such as cigarettes, replaced normal currency. Even in France and England, where wartime casualties were more modest than in 1914–1918, postwar hardships proved immense. In central and eastern Europe postwar burdens were greater still, as millions of refugees wandered the Continent in flight from disbanded concentration camps or Soviet occupied territory. Millions of Germans fled or were excluded from the eastern part of Prussia, now given over to Poland, and millions fled the communist regime of East Germany. All these refugees had lost property, many were ill and weak, and they all faced difficulties integrating into the countries where they sought to make new lives.

The war and its aftermath left their mark on European society. Wartime mobilization expanded the role of government in the economy and in the regulation of social life. Much of this change proved lasting. Gender roles shifted as well, if often just temporarily, as many women entered the work force and presided alone over families with absent fathers. Divorces increased, the inevitable result of years of separation and hardship, though the rate descended again after 1950. Crime rates rose in many areas, and this proved to be a more durable trend. Many penniless young women in Germany had to resort to prostitution, and juvenile crime and crimes of violence began a gradual increase everywhere. Workers responded to postwar hardships with renewed capabilities for collective action. Strike waves mounted throughout western Europe, except in Germany where workers were too demoralized to join the trend. In France and Italy workers in growing numbers lent support to communist parties, which were to remain major players in French and Italian politics for decades to come. In countries that had been ruled by fascist or collaborating regimes during the war, the postwar period brought new leaders to the fore, not just in politics but in business and the professions as well. Many of these newcomers first made their mark in resistance movements, which sprouted across the Continent from France to Poland against Nazi domination. Soviet success in creating satellite regimes in eastern Europe brought a new bureaucratic elite into power, bent on recasting the economies of these countries along socialist lines within a Soviet empire. Even the emergence of a new elite in both eastern and western Europe, however, did little to dispel the widespread feeling during the first few years after the war that the European future was bleak.

Yet prosperity did return, especially to western Europe, and the Continent did not sink into the morass of self-pity that some observers expected right after the war. By 1948 the peak of postwar unrest had passed. By 1952 the worst threat of a new war was over, for Russia and the United States began to balance each other out and pursued their rivalry in other regions of the world. Under this fragile umbrella of the cold war stand-off, the countries of western Europe could stake out their own development. Ironically, in some ways western Europe became freer to adapt to economic growth and social change than did its American ally. Between the wars it was America that led the way toward a new culture of mass consumption: American dances, American films, American music, American methods of advertising, management, and mass production. By the 1960s the tide had partially turned, and the United States was busily importing European miniskirts, the Beatles from Liverpool, and what Americans were wont to call pornography from Scandinavia. By the 1980s the Atlantic Ocean had become a two-way exchange route in nearly every respect, as European companies became multinationals on American soil and European investors became major customers on Wall Street. Western Europe, which had been far from successful in meeting the challenges of mature industrialization during the early decades of the century, came to embrace the opportunities of a consumer society at least as confidently as did America and Japan.

The factors that shaped Europe's advanced industrial society, in addition to the forces involved in postwar recovery, included many of the same elements that had promoted change during the mature industrial period. Once again, Europeans combined new technologies with new organizational forms, ranging from more extensive rural cooperatives to larger international business conglomerates. Government policies played an active role, along with advances in material conditions. If these patterns were familiar, however, the specific forms that they took were new. The functions of the state, moving beyond education to more elaborate welfare policies, took greater priority than before. Prosperity now meant not simply a margin above poverty but real affluence for many social groups. Earlier trends, like the expansion of mass leisure, continued but took new directions. The resultant society had problems and protests that were novel in comparison with those of the mature industrial period.

As in the United States, the emergence of an advanced industrial society in western Europe did not eliminate older conflicts in class, ethnic, and gender relations. Nor did the achievement of postwar prosperity spare Europe from encountering new kinds of tensions over the costs of maintaining high levels of mass consumption. Moreover, by the late 1970s prosperity itself became an uncertainty as Europeans learned they had to find new ways to adapt to fundamental changes in the global economy. West Europeans, in short, went a long way after 1945 toward overcoming some of the social conflicts that had set the stage for the two world wars, but they by no means found their way to the kind of harmonious equilibrium some social commentators were predicting in the early 1960s. New tensions surfaced, particularly from the late 1960s onward, as the momentum of building a new version of industrial society slowed, though without reversing direction.

Eastern Europe in the meantime took another path. Under Soviet domination, communist regimes tried with some success to accelerate the industrialization of a region that had long lagged behind much of western Europe. But none of these regimes made the leap to high levels of mass consumption, nor did they accommodate widespread aspirations for democracy and national autonomy in the region. By the late 1980s these failures, combined with popular pressures and a protracted economic crisis in the Soviet Union itself, paved the way for a dramatic collapse of communist rule in one Eastern bloc country after another. By the late 1980s Europeans on both sides of what had been called the Iron Curtain looked forward to a new era of social and economic integration across the Continent.

Toward a New Social Structure

In western Europe the remarkable process of renewal after 1945 involved more a continuation of earlier trends in social restructuring than a major break with the past. For one thing, the new consumer society did not usher in a new stage of demography. There was a change from the doldrums of the 1920s and 1930s, and this had brief significance. East European countries, particularly Poland, continued to have a higher birthrate than western Europe, though their growth steadily slowed after the typical recovery from wartime losses. West Germany's population increased more rapidly than it had during the interwar decades. The same reversal was even more dramatic in Britain and France. Britain's population grew from 45 million to 47 million during the war itself, and by 1960 had passed 52 million; the rate of expansion was a steady 0.5 percent a year. Scandinavian population rose in similar fashion, and the Netherlands, another highly organized country, jumped to first place in demographic vitality in western Europe. The greatest surprise was France, Europe's traditional laggard. Between 1945 and 1954 French population grew by three million, the fastest growth rate the country had enjoyed since the early nineteenth century.

This population spurt reflected a new confidence in Europe's economic prospects. It was the direct result of new welfare systems that provided state payments to support larger families. The population boom encouraged economic revival by providing new markets for goods, though it caused obvious problems of housing and the provision of new school facilities. But although all of this formed an important backdrop for Europe's social history through the mid-1960s, it did not reflect a permanent change in demographic structure. By the early

1960s birthrates began dropping sharply, returning most European countries toward demographic stability, though overall growth continued as the result of previous expansion. It was clear that the advanced industrial societies tended toward zero population growth, though they were capable of moderate increase on occasion. The east European countries had obviously entered the same stage. Most striking of all, by 1990 even Greece, Spain, Portugal, and Italy had become sufficiently integrated into the social patterns of industrialized Europe to have some of the lowest fertility rates on the Continent.

Just as demographic change involved no fundamental shift from trends already in motion, so too was technological change more a story of evolutionary, not revolutionary, development. To be sure, the postwar era brought important new technologies in every field of engineering and medical science. The harnessing of the atom for electrical power and military destruction had an important impact on European economics and politics. By the 1980s the phenomenal growth of computer technology and improvements in mass communications gave analysts the justifiable right to proclaim a new "information era," in which the economic prospects of a nation depended on its capacity to incorporate the new computer technology. From the 1970s on engineers found ways to use robots and computers in manufacturing, at the social cost of destroying working-class jobs. Computers brought similar changes to the service sector. But none of these innovations produced the same degree of social transformation that had come with the Industrial Revolution. Though postwar technology did have important social effects, it did not trigger the kind of wholesale recasting of the class structure that had taken place in western Europe a century before.

Some important changes in social structure, however, did occur after 1945 through the acceleration of earlier trends. Transformations in the composition of the elite, improvements in social mobility, shifts in the occupational structure, and the expansion of mass consumption all contributed to a more dynamic and open society, though one where important forms of inequality persisted. The aristocracy, which had continued to make its weight felt in many countries in the interwar period despite the decline of agriculture and legal privilege, was virtually removed as a coherent political force. Communist regimes in eastern Europe confiscated estates and eliminated noble titles. The social power of the German Junkers, based as it was on estates in eastern Germany and positions in the military and civil service, was finally destroyed. New educational opportunities in both eastern and western Europe gave people with middle-class and sometimes working-class origins access to high government posts. Stiff property taxes imposed by postwar welfare states hit hard at landed holdings. Some aristocrats hung on ingeniously, opening their homes to gawking but paying tourists or even converting ancestral grounds into open-air zoos. Titles remained in western Europe and had a certain prestige in the popular press. Until the collapse of right-wing authoritarian regimes in Spain and Portugal in the 1970s, aristocrats there had real power. But elsewhere the class, if identifiable at all, had become little more than a museum piece.

The displacement of the great industrialists and financiers was less decisive. Some, like the car manufacturer Louis Renault who had collaborated with wartime fascists, were stripped of power. Nationalizations right after the war took their toll. Other business families died out or lost interest in business control. The giant Krupp concern, for example, revived after the war, but direction fell out of tight family control. A new breed of managers emerged in both the public and private sector who increasingly came from middle-class backgrounds and were trained as economists, lawyers, or engineers. These technocrats, as they came to be called, were more interested in long-range planning, new markets, stable labor relations, and new institutional arrangements (such as nationalized enterprise and the Common Market) and less in some of the traditional trappings of social prestige.

Alongside this new business elite something like a new political class also emerged by the 1970s. University-educated technocrats of middle-class and well-to-do backgrounds became increasingly important in both left-wing and right-wing parties. While the politician typical of the late nineteenth and early twentieth centuries — with local roots in the small-town trade union, schoolhouse, family business, or medical practice — had by no means disappeared from national politics, many of the same effects of bureaucratization and educational credentialing that were changing the managerial ranks of big business were transforming political parties as well. Many aspiring European technocrats built administrative careers by migrating between business enterprise and government service while keeping well connected to the leading left-wing or right-wing party of the country.

Changes at the top of society should not be exaggerated. An elite, albeit quite differently structured from the one that had ruled Europe at the beginning of the century, still enjoyed enormous influence in society. And an upper class, in terms of wealth, could still be identified in western Europe. By 1975 the top 5 percent of the population in Britain owned nearly 50 percent of the wealth, a decline from 79 percent in the early 1930s but a sizable share nonetheless. Still, the upper class changed after the war with new blood and new attitudes. It contained no major element that, like the aristocracy as late as the 1930s, felt threatened by modern society. After witnessing the great upheavals of the Depression and World War II, the postwar upper class became more realistic about the need to conciliate the lower classes, accommodate the democratic spirit, and make concessions to the welfare state. Upper-class recalcitrance, which had contributed a great deal to social polarization and political instability in the interwar period, diminished after 1945.

Below the top echelons of society something of a leadership revolution occurred in western Europe during the postwar period. As a result of fascist attacks on tradition before World War II, the war itself, the rise of resistance movements, and wider social changes after the war, new leaders asserted themselves at nearly all levels of society. In many villages a younger generation pushed aside old peasant notables and embraced the cause of agricultural change. In business and government young people took advantage of a dramatic expansion of the educational system to win access to middle-level jobs. Even the Catholic church, long a bastion of conservatism in Europe, found renewal by the 1950s with an infusion of new energy and new outlooks from a younger generation inspired by the wartime resistance.

The combination of educational opportunity and economic change created greater mobility from below. Whereas in the nineteenth century mobility rates in Europe had lagged modestly behind norms in the United States, by the postwar period European rates had become virtually the same despite popular impressions to the contrary. European mobility in the twentieth century had become a bit more closely tied to education than was the case in the United States. Almost everywhere in Europe illiteracy nearly vanished, and more and more students continued on to secondary education. The number of high school students almost quadrupled in Belgium between 1945 and 1970, while tripling in Czechoslovakia and doubling in Greece. Throughout Europe governments used schools to build something of a "meritocracy" where training and talent, rather than wealth and birth, would provide access to jobs. In addition, gradual changes in occupational structure, building on earlier trends, created new opportunities as the size of the agricultural work force diminished and the service sector expanded. The greatest changes took place in eastern and southern Europe, which had lagged behind in industrialization. By 1980 only 20 percent of Bulgarians worked on farms, down from 80 percent three decades before. In Spain that figure dropped to 20 percent in 1979, down from 52 percent in 1940. Shifts in the industrial work force were enormous as well. In less industrialized countries, such as Yugoslavia, the proportion of workers in manufacturing shot up from 16 percent in 1951 to 52 percent in 1980, while in industrialized western Europe the change was reversed. In Britain the proportion declined from 49 percent in 1951 to 38 percent in 1980. The service sector expanded everywhere, though much more so in western Europe where jobs in trade, communications, insurance, health, education, public administration, and other services accounted for 55 percent of employment. These major shifts in occupational structure created new possibilities for the children of poor agricultural families to find urban jobs in manufacturing or services. Many children of skilled and semiskilled workers sought their futures in white-collar work. From 1950 on overall income inequalities declined throughout Europe, largely as a result of welfare provisions and economic growth.

Still, the class structure continued to limit opportunities for social mobility. By the 1980s the son of a blue-collar worker still had only half the chance of ascending into the middle strata of society as those who had been born at that level. Ascent into the upper strata was obviously harder: one-seventh the probability of that for a son whose father was already there. While the educational system had opened doors shut tight to most people before 1950, it still fell short of the egalitarian ideal. Although the number of university students had risen sharply to 24 percent of the 20–24 age group in western Europe in 1978, up from less than 4 percent in 1950, children from the lower strata continued to be underrepresented in higher education. In France the proportion of university students from working-class families actually fell from 13 percent in 1974 to 9 percent in 1979. The survival of elite qualifications for high-level positions, such as the second state examination for lawyers in West Germany or graduation from the *grandes écoles* in France, further limited mobility. In most countries secondary education remained sharply divided into vocational and academic tracks. Mobility had improved since 1950, but important barriers remained.

The persistence of inequality did not prevent most west Europeans from taking part in the consumer society. A substantial growth of real wages in western Europe, which ranged from a threefold increase in Britain to a sixfold increase in France between 1950 and 1980, gave working-class families the means to buy cars, refrigerators, televisions, cinema tickets, and in some cases even homes. Some reduction in the work-week and greater observance of the weekend gave workers more time for leisure. The vitality of the consumer society depended on extending the consuming practices of the interwar middle class, if not necessarily its tastes and consumer choices, into the postwar working class. Brand-name goods, chain stores, consumer credit, savings accounts, spectator sports, mail-order purchasing, advertising, and the ubiquitous presence of radio and television broadcasting eventually found their way even into isolated rural settings. Mass consumption by no means eliminated established distinctions between classes. In some respects consumer choices and leisure activities provided new ways to express longstanding differences. Nor did mass consumption necessarily diminish people's sense of nationality or ethnic identity. But by the mid-1970s, three decades of unprecedented economic growth, the rise of the welfare state, and the proliferation of consumer goods had raised the living standards of most west Europeans even if these changes did not eliminate inequality.

The postwar decades, in sum, brought important changes in European social structure without producing the kind of fundamental transformations that had occurred during industrialization. Modest shifts in demographic patterns, combined with significant, if not revolutionary, innovations in technology helped fuel economic growth. The decline of the old landed aristocracy and the rise of new business and technocratic elites fostered a greater openness to change at the peak of the social hierarchy. Greater educational opportunity and shifts in the occupational structure, especially the decline of agricultural employment and the expansion of the service sector, improved the prospects for social mobility, even though barriers to upward movement remained and inequalities endured. These changes in social structure made it possible for more and more people to participate in the expanding domain of mass consumption.

The Expanding Role of the State

Long-term shifts in class structure, which enhanced the size of the industrial working class and the salaried middle class, combined with the shock of the war itself and political developments in the 1940s, help explain the emergence of new state functions. Europe's political spectrum swung to the left. Fascism was discredited by its excesses and defeat; only in impoverished southern Italy were neo-fascist parties able to gain significant support. Several of the traditional but more moderate right-wing parties on the Continent had been tarnished by right-wing extremism as well, leaving the way open for new, more progressive leaders to come to the fore after the war. West European countries, though quite varied politically, generally developed a more flexible conservatism, often in the form of Christian Democratic parties, that was willing to see the state play a larger social and economic role.

At the same time socialist and communist parties emerged from the war with new vitality. In France and Italy in particular the resistance gave left-wing parties unprecedented opportunities to refashion the government's role in their societies, while in Britain the Labour party had a similar chance to champion social and economic reform. Broadly speaking, a powerful resurgence of left-wing parties made workers just after the war more insistent than ever on state action to prevent the hardships they had endured during the Depression. Even the middle class approved of a larger role for the state, partly to reduce class tensions and partly to provide benefits for the middle class. As a result, the early postwar years became a decisive occasion for expanding state functions both in social welfare and in managing the economy. This expansion proved durable, for the most part, despite important challenges to welfare policy and state-centered economic management after the mid-1970s. And it was paralleled in eastern Europe by an even greater transformation of state–society relations under the aegis of communist regimes.

Although most of the forms of state intervention that expanded after World War II had ample precedents in the nineteenth and early twentieth centuries, the state had rarely played as central a role in social change as became the case throughout Europe in the postwar period. State initiative had proved important in enabling Germany to industrialize quickly after 1850, and this was even more the case in Russia after 1890. Several European governments expanded their functions, if only temporarily, during World War I in their efforts to coordinate production, regulate labor relations, and ration consumption. But for the most part the role of the state remained relatively circumscribed in Europe before the 1930s in comparison to what developed thereafter. The crucial sources of social change during industrialization and even through the mature industrial era came mainly from society at large rather than from the more narrow confines of the state. By contrast, the central role of the state in stimulating change after 1945 helped distinguish the postwar era from previous periods.

The Welfare State

Before World War II a wide range of social insurance schemes had emerged in virtually every European country to help workers offset the burdens of sickness, accident, and old age. Bismarck's Germany had paved the way in state-supported social insurance in the 1880s, largely in the hope of diminishing the appeal of a rising socialist movement, and most countries in western Europe had made some innovations in social legislation by World War I. But even by 1940 such programs still fell far short of providing the majority of citizens with comprehensive protection against misfortune or the prospects of an adequate living standard in retirement. State provisions varied markedly from country to country, and nowhere had social insurance been established as a citizen's right. By 1948, however, a revolution in social provisioning had taken place, as one European country after another established comprehensive social insurance programs that lay at the heart of the modern welfare state.

The process was clearest and most immediate in Britain, untouched by direct invasion and where social tensions had been relatively moderate before 1940. The war immediately reduced party frictions in Britain, and all major political elements were represented in the wartime cabinet. The Labour party won new respectability. At the same time, the war provided greater opportunities for social contact among members of different classes. There was a sense of unity against the enemy. Military service and war work offered common experiences, and rationing allocated scarce consumer goods on the basis of per capita need, not per capita income, so that the gap in living standards between rich and poor narrowed. The wealthy accepted these measures in the interest of national defense. Many people realized that new policies were needed to cure the unhealthy social situation of the interwar period and to reward the working classes for their wartime loyalty.

It was in this context that the wartime government began planning ways to maintain the high levels of employment and rising wages that the wartime economy was providing, as well as to establish better ways to guarantee the general welfare. The Beveridge plan of 1942, drawn essentially in the spirit of middle-class humanitarianism, called for expanding and revamping the coverage for health, poverty, unemployment, accident, and pensions. It also charted a new form of family allowances. Underlying the whole plan lay the bold new principles of universal participation, comprehensive coverage, and equality of contributions and benefits. The Beveridge plan placed the state at the center of a system of social insurance, even though employers and individuals would continue to play an important role in financing contributions to the system.

The Labour party's electoral triumph in 1945 enabled the wartime vision of the welfare state to become a reality. Having come to power with overwhelming working-class support and the endorsement of a full third of the middle-class voters, the Labour party expanded the system of social insurance along the lines Beveridge had recommended. A national system of health care was instituted, giving virtually free medical attention to all citizens, with the bulk of the funds coming from tax sources. The government embarked on an ambitious program of public housing, partly to compensate for wartime damage, partly to improve living conditions and respond to population growth. By the 1950s over a quarter of the British population was housed in structures built and run by the state. Educational needs attracted attention as well. The government began a large-scale postwar program of building schools, expanding universities, and funding scholarships for higher education. The school-leaving age was raised to fifteen years, then to sixteen. Most importantly, popular support for these measures endured. When Labour lost power in 1951, the Conservative party did nothing to dismantle these reforms in social welfare, national health, housing, and education that served as the pillars of the British welfare state.

On the Continent, under the heel of Nazi occupation, wartime conditions were obviously far different from the British situation, but attitudes and programs eventually took shape that were not very different from those across the English Channel. In fact Continental wartime governments themselves introduced some measures that were to endure as part of the postwar welfare state. The Nazi government promoted full employment and family allowances in Germany. The Vichy regime of occupied France extended a system of family allocations that was instituted in the late 1930s and that was to become a major element of the French postwar welfare program. However, it was in the resistance movements that much of the impulse to establish postwar welfare measures arose. Even though the resistance drew on support from a wide social spectrum, the political coalitions that stood behind the movement generally intended to foster ambitious social reforms at the end of the war. They hoped to modify the capitalist system (some hoped to topple it) in the interest of social justice. They wanted to use government to establish greater economic equality and security, and create a new Europe freed from the national and social conflicts of the past. If postwar realities quickly disappointed many of the idealists of the resistance, their plans nonetheless provided an essential stimulus to the reforms that governments eventually made.

The most complete new welfare program emerged in France, which had long lagged behind most of western Europe in social legislation. A coalition government of communists, socialists, and left-leaning Catholics established the country's first real social security program. Hospital costs were insured, and coverage was provided for old age and unemployment. Workers, both in industry and agriculture, were compelled to participate in the programs. They paid a part of the cost, but employers paid 30 to 40 percent of the cost and the state contributed as well. An ambitious family-assistance program supplemented these basic measures. Aid to families increased with the size of the family, regardless of income, so that by the 1950s a working-class family with low earnings and five children, admittedly an unusual brood by this point, could improve its income by as much as 40 percent through family allowances. The French state also participated in educational reform and public housing. By the 1950s France had more than made up decades of conservative foot-dragging in social policy. The various social security programs alone had come to account for 16 percent of the French national income.

Nearly three decades of strong economic growth after the war enabled all countries in western Europe to expand and elaborate their welfare systems. In every country the welfare state had emerged from the 1940s as a product of compromise. Its emphasis varied from one nation to the next. But by the mid-1970s a good deal of convergence had taken place among national systems. In 1975 in every country except Greece, Portugal, and Spain, over 70 percent of the economically active population was covered by accident, health, old-age, and unemployment insurance. In the 1980s southern Europe was catching up as well.

Some diversity still remained. Britain continued to have the most comprehensive medical program, France the most extensive program of family aid. The cost-sharing pattern for social insurance varied as well. Although the average apportionment of costs in western Europe in 1974 was 30 percent to the insured person, 37 percent to the employer, and 29 percent to the state, in France and Italy employers covered over half the costs, partly because they financed the entire cost of family aid. These differences, however, paled in significance when compared to the basic similarity of the programs across western Europe and their success in the first postwar decades.

Throughout western Europe, too, the growth of the welfare state was associated with the expansion of the government's role in labor relations. Scandinavian countries had already experimented before World War II with trilateral bargaining, where government officials participated along with unions and employers. After the war, governments in France, Italy, Belgium, and elsewhere became directly involved in national negotiations between labor and management. In Austria the government even went so far as to invite the leading organizations of business and labor to play a formal and continuous role in discussions about economic policy. Everywhere in western Europe government became more important in legislating matters of employee safety, work hours, vacation policies, and other working conditions. Everywhere, too, the prospects of employment became increasingly tied to a government's fiscal and monetary policy. Government played a new role within the enterprise as well. In 1945 the French government established mandatory "enterprise committees" designed to give worker representatives a voice in at least some aspects of company policy. In 1951 Germany launched supervisory boards with a strong voice for workers in heavy industry, which proved to be a precedent for later experiments in worker representation, or "co-determination," in German enterprise. These efforts to give workers more say in the workplace met with only modest success. Employers were careful to keep serious issues off the table, and in many instances the trade unions regarded these experiments as threats to their own power. But on the whole the new wave of labor reforms and government involvement in industrial relations gave workers greater protection from workplace hardships and greater power in the industrial economy than they had had before.

Through the mid-1970s welfare programs enjoyed remarkable popular support throughout western Europe, largely because they provided aid for citizens at many income levels. Working-class families and the poor had initially stood the most to gain. The welfare state finally delivered basic levels of financial protection that socialists had long advocated. But the middle class benefited as well, certainly from family aid and state medical insurance, and even disproportionately so from expanded educational systems and university scholarships. By providing new jobs for professionals and new educational opportunities the welfare state helped the middle class directly. Although some aspects of the welfare state redistributed income by financing benefits through graduated income taxes, the welfare state did not make a major change in the structure of the class system. The redistributive effects of the welfare state even diminished over time as governments turned increasingly to indirect taxes to finance the system. The "value-added" tax system, which levied taxes on each stage of the production process, became particularly prominent after the 1950s, and as a kind of super-sales tax ultimately paid by consumers it did little to promote redistribution. The welfare state proved consistent with a substantial range of economic inequality. And since unemployment insurance, health care, public housing, and a state-financed educational system served to maintain and train the labor force, private employers stood to benefit from the welfare state as well, even if they shared the costs.

In eastern Europe governments also made important strides in social provisioning, but with purposes and results that differed from what was achieved in western Europe. Communist governments in the east did not aim to establish the welfare state in the sense of establishing a separate set of semiautonomous programs designed to provide a level of general welfare to which each citizen, as an individual, had a right. Instead, social insurance was regarded as an element of the state's central budget and as an instrument for the larger project of building an industrialized socialist society. In most countries the state and its enterprises covered the entire cost of social insurance. Individuals did not make independent contributions, except in East Germany and Hungary. Self-employed people and peasants were initially left out of the system on the grounds that they were not as essential as were workers and state employees to the goals of building a socialist state. Polish peasants only gained access to the national health system in 1972 and to the state pension plan in 1978. Social insurance certainly improved the economic security of most people in eastern Europe in comparison to what it had been before 1945. A variety of state-sponsored vacation schemes supplemented the insurance programs. But benefit levels fell a good deal short of what people in western Europe came to expect. Pensions were not indexed to the rise in cost of living. And pension levels generally remained sufficiently low to compel many people to work well past the official age of retirement. These limitations in social provisioning in eastern Europe derived in part from the different orientation that governing regimes took to welfare policy, and in part from weaknesses in the economies of the Eastern bloc. Per capita gross domestic production in these countries, which fell far short of what had ᵐe the norm in the wealthier nations of western Europe, placed ₌t constraints on social insurance.

The Crisis of the Welfare State

If the welfare state of western Europe proved to be superior to its counterpart in eastern Europe, the former was not immune to crisis. After the mid-1970s a number of adverse pressures began to converge. The first was demographic. Advanced industrial societies were producing the oldest population known in history. This accomplishment followed in large part from the birthrate pattern that had developed by the 1930s. With fewer babies being born and life expectancy rising, the average age of the population climbed. The postwar population spurt modified this trend but did not supersede it. An aging population meant new expenses for medical care, and more retirees increased the number of people drawing from, rather than contributing to, social security.

Another problem was the matter of costs. For thirty years governments sought to increase the benefit levels and the range of programs that citizens could enjoy in the system. Left-wing parties fought to use the welfare provision and education to address persistent problems of poverty and inequality. Middle-class voters supported measures that expanded the general level of benefits, and politicians of various political stripes were eager to comply. In the meantime medical costs climbed, as new pharmaceuticals and new technologies drove up the price of health care. The average expenditures for social welfare in western Europe rose from 9.4 percent of national product in 1950 to 22.4 percent in 1977.

Economic problems compounded these difficulties. When the great growth boom of the 1950s and 1960s gave way to tougher economic times in the mid-1970s, governments found it harder to raise the tax revenue to meet climbing costs. High unemployment overburdened the system as well, with greater demands for relief benefits. By the 1980s in one country after another conservative parties with largely middle-class support championed the cause of cutting back government spending on social welfare. No country was spared these pressures. When the conservative Christian Democrats came to power in West Germany after over a decade of Social Democratic rule, they cut back welfare payments to the unemployed and retirees by about 6 percent. Conservatives even made headway in Scandinavia, a bastion of Social Democracy since the 1940s, on the promise of reducing welfare expenses and holding down taxes. The socialist government of François Mitterrand in France, after flirting with an expansion of the welfare state in the early 1980s, bowed to economic pressures in 1983 and joined the ranks of those governments searching for ways to trim social expenditures.

The most dramatic challenge to the welfare state emerged in Britain, where Margaret Thatcher and the Conservative party used major electoral victories in 1979, 1983, and 1987 to steer the most right-wing course the British had seen in their country in the twentieth century. Thatcher advocated not merely tinkering with the welfare state but substantially reducing it in the interests of lower taxes and greater private initiative. During the 1980s government investment in education and public housing declined. By the end of the decade the Thatcher government toyed with an attack on the National Health Service. Even in Thatcher's Britain, however, the basic foundations of the welfare system — social security and insurance against illness, injury, infirmity, unemployment, and abject poverty — proved too popular to dismantle. The new relationships between state and people embodied in the welfare state created expectations that defied major alterations. Throughout Europe, including Britain, government budgets for social welfare diminished little in the course of the 1980s. As the European economy gradually began to recover some of its vitality late in the decade, political pressures to cut expenditures ebbed, even if no one was prepared, especially in the face of the future aging of the population structure, to declare an end to what still seemed to be the permanent crisis of the modern welfare state. The expansion of state functions that had taken place in the 1940s had transformed the contacts between citizen and state in too profound a manner to enable the more doctrinaire critics of social welfare provision to reverse the postwar achievement.

Nationalization and Economic Planning

Right after the war political leaders throughout Europe also expanded the functions of the state in the economy. Here was another facet of the state's new role in shaping society and another deliberate attempt to alter social conditions that had prevailed in the mature industrial period. Most postwar governments nationalized some sectors of transportation, energy, and industry. In Britain and France early postwar nationalizations brought about 20 percent of the capital of industrial enterprise under state control. In France, moreover, direct state ownership extended into the insurance industry and over many of the country's largest banks. The early postwar enthusiasm for nationalization in Europe had many sources. Businesspeople in the private sector momentarily lost power and prestige for cooperating with fascist or collaborationist regimes during the war. The liberation of continental Europe brought left-wing groups into power that had long nurtured hopes that nationalized enterprises would both promote industrial growth and serve as models of progressive labor management.

Many nationalized industries in fact proved effective in the decades that followed. State-run rail systems were costly but efficient and helped reduce pressure for the kind of massive highway development that made Americans more dependent on automobiles in the postwar era. Whereas some nationalized companies limped along in declining industries, and none was spared labor conflict as some reformers had hoped, a number of major nationalized firms flourished profitably. In France nationalization retained enough credibility as an economic instrument and enough symbolic appeal as a left-wing innovation to lead François Mitterrand's government in 1981 to make a host of new nationalizations in banking and industry.

By the same token, conservative parties harbored plenty of critics of public enterprise. In Britain, the Conservative party denationalized steel in the 1950s. More importantly, in the 1980s the Thatcher government launched an all-out assault on much of what the public sector thought sacrosanct since the early 1950s. "Privatization" came into vogue as the government sold to private investors a large number of state enterprises, including British Gas, British Petroleum, Britoil, as well as airports, water companies, electrical utilities, and the state-owned telecommunications system. When French conservatives won control of Parliament and the prime ministership for a two-year period in 1986, they too pursued a similar, though much more limited, policy of privatization. By the late 1980s, however, the tide of privatization ebbed as the declining popularity of conservatives and the turbulence of European stock markets made it a risky strategy. For western Europe as a whole, the overall balance of public and private enterprise that had been struck in the early postwar period remained largely intact, except in Britain, and direct state control over finance and industry remained much greater than in the United States.

Alongside nationalization, new economic planning agencies also expanded state economic controls in the postwar era. After 1944 the British government used its power to tax, spend, and regulate the money supply to maintain a high level of employment through the 1950s and 1960s. The Italian government used the giant state-owned holding companies that Mussolini had created in the 1930s to promote ten-year plans for railroads, the iron and steel industry, and the construction of schools, universities, and worker housing. The Italian government also channeled investment toward the economically backward south, though with limited success. France went furthest to experiment with state economic planning. A *Commissariat du plan,* or national planning office, was established in 1946 to help steer capital toward economic branches believed to be important for long-term economic growth. The French called it "indicative" planning, in contrast to the coercive planning of the socialist bloc, and private entrepreneurs remained free to run their firms as they pleased. But the French state had impressive powers to channel investment through nationalized industries and banks, as well as through building permits, loan guarantees, and the considerable authority that the finance minister came to exercise over investment credit in the private sector. The rapid development of French industry during the three decades following World War II lent credibility to this system of state-guided planning. And although rougher economic waters after 1973 led conservatives and socialists alike to give some ground to the free (and increasingly international) market for investment capital, the French government remained the foremost practitioner of central planning in the capitalist West. As in Italy, moreover, the government made efforts to steer economic activity toward underdeveloped areas in southern and western regions.

This style of economic interventionism that emerged with such force after 1945 did not take hold everywhere in western Europe. West Germany in particular steered clear of nationalization after the war and created what Germans came to call the "social market economy," which combined the social supports of the welfare state and a voice for the trade unions on company boards with a free-enterprise economy in which the state had little directly to do with industrial management. A small group of powerful private banks, rather than the finance ministry, assumed the major role in coordinating investment in a rapidly expanding industrial economy. Although long periods of conservative Christian Democratic government lay behind this aversion to nationalization and planning, a major period of left-leaning Social Democratic rule in West Germany in the 1970s and early 1980s did little to alter this basic pattern.

State economic intervention in eastern Europe after 1945 was of another magnitude entirely. Communist regimes went to great, and coercive, lengths to impose the Soviet model of centralized state planning everywhere in the Eastern bloc. By the late 1940s the vast majority of the industrial work force throughout eastern Europe found itself working in state-owned enterprise. By the early 1950s all of these regimes had gone a long way toward collectivizing agriculture. Only in Poland were peasants and small farmers successful in resisting these policies to the extent of maintaining private holding as the principal form of agricultural property in the country. Everywhere in eastern Europe communist party leaders established a hierarchy of planning committees that linked enterprises and local planning bodies to regional and highly centralized state planning committees, which allocated resources, set prices and wages, and determined production goals. Important variations in this model did emerge, most notably in Yugoslavia where an experiment in decentralized planning and worker-management brought mixed results, and in Hungary where the government's "new economic program" in 1968 gave greater autonomy to individual enterprises. During the Krushchev era of the late 1950s and early 1960s, some experimentation with decentralization and enterprise autonomy was even tried in the Soviet Union. By and large, however, state-centered socialist planning remained the defining characteristic of soviet bloc economies until the precipitous collapse of eastern Europe's communist regimes in the late 1980s.

State initiatives, in sum, played an unprecedented role in setting a framework for material conditions and social relationships throughout Europe after 1945, in patterns that proved durable. State–society interactions differed considerably, however, between the eastern and western regions.

Economic Development

After World War II the European economy expanded rapidly during almost three decades of unprecedented growth and prosperity, and then slid into a more turbulent period of high inflation, industrial contraction, and slower growth in the 1970s and 1980s. These two phases in postwar economic life reflected in part a dynamic of intra-European economic development and in part the patterns of growth and crisis in the larger global economy.

Postwar Growth

Neither the first phase of extraordinary growth nor the second of "stagflation" and modest recovery were easy to foresee. It would have been difficult, as late as 1950, to predict a major economic advance. Wartime dislocation kept production levels down; disruption of transportation facilities was particularly damaging. With production low and governments attempting to increase industrial investment, massive inflation developed, for demand inevitably exceeded the supply of goods. Germany stabilized its currency only in 1948; Italy did so in 1952, but only by pegging the lira at one-fiftieth of its previous value. French inflation ultimately reduced the franc to one-twenty-fifth of its postwar level. Britain, too, suffered a substantial devaluation. All of this discontented workers, when wages lagged behind prices and wiped out savings; many entrepreneurs also questioned the future of the economy. Inflation plus the need for foreign, particularly American, food and industrial equipment left the European countries in perpetual deficit in their balance of payments; observers predicted that the "dollar gap" would reduce Europe to permanent economic dependence on the United States.

But in 1947 the United States launched the Marshall Plan program to provide funds for redevelopment, hoping not only to aid Europe but also to stem the growth of communist movements of protest. This was the first step toward rapid recovery. But it was also apparent that much of the wartime damage and confusion could be quickly repaired. Once its transportation network was rebuilt and its currency stabilized, for example, Germany was ready to move ahead in what Germans rather ostentatiously proclaimed an "economic miracle." Postwar economic advance was not simply the result of American aid or the resumption of earlier growth. Something new was afoot, a more vigorous desire for economic change. Government planning and assistance aided the movement but so did new expectations of business managers and workers alike. A freer trading environment with lowered tariff barriers also played a role in stimulating growth, especially after Germany, France, Italy, and the Low Countries created the Common Market in 1957. Germany's miracle was soon matched and even eclipsed by the rapid development of French and Italian industry. Only Britain, of the major non-communist countries, expanded at a modest pace.

Beginning in Germany in 1948 and in France and Italy in the early 1950s, an economic advance of vast proportions began that continued through the 1960s. It was not completely uninterrupted and there were years of reduced growth. But in contrast to previous industrial history there were no real recessions. Even recessions in the United States merely resulted in a slower pace of growth, not in a cessation. State guidance helped channel resources to points of actual need and prevented speculative overdevelopment. The provision of minimal standards for all classes and the maintenance of full employment opened a new mass market for many goods. Thus economic growth was unprecedentedly steady as wartime damage was repaired and production soared to new heights.

Growth was also rapid in most countries, exceeding the rates of the interwar years and also the decades before World War I. It also surpassed the rates of the more troubled American economy from the mid-1950s onward. The German economy expanded at an annual rate of 6 percent during much of the 1950s. During the early part of the decade significant unemployment persisted, tolerated by the trade unions in the interest of using resources for new investment. But by the end of the 1950s German industry was crying out for more workers and growth continued at a high rate during most of the 1960s. In 1973 expansion had returned to a 6 percent level.

France attained an 8 percent annual growth by the end of the 1950s. Expansion continued at a somewhat slower pace during the 1960s, rising again in the early 1970s to over 7 percent a year. By 1959 the Italian economy expanded at the rate of 11 percent a year, propelling Italy into the ranks of advanced industrial nations, though serious labor troubles reduced expansion again by the 1970s. Growth rates in Scandinavia and particularly in Britain were somewhat lower. The British economy grew at a rate of about 4 percent a year in the 1950s. British workers and entrepreneurs both seemed more resistant to technological change than their counterparts on the Continent; as a result, the British standard of living declined in relation to France and Germany.

But even in Britain there was significant advance, in contrast to the stagnation of the interwar years.

Certain traditional industries continued to decline throughout western Europe. Textiles and particularly mining suffered. Some mines were completely closed, unable to compete with petroleum fuels. On the whole, however, this decline was more than balanced by the advance of petrochemicals, electronics, and heavy consumer goods such as automobiles and appliances. There was a marked increase as well in the service sector of the economy, as the need for teachers, sales personnel, and the like expanded. Indeed the growth of the service sector rapidly outstripped that of the classic working class. In France in 1968 half of all salaried workers were in the service sector; by 1973 this proportion had risen to 53 percent. An affluent society needed new services. Bureaucratization demanded educated, nonmanual personnel. Improved technology in manufacturing allowed production advances without a rapid increase in the size of the working class. All of this of course involved substantial social mobility. It was estimated that 30 percent of the French working class had moved into white-collar jobs in the twenty years after World War II.

These shifts in turn altered the regional balance of national economies. Italian industry continued to be centered in the north, despite the location of a few important firms elsewhere. In France and Britain, however, the coal regions, the traditional centers of manufacturing, declined. Many of the newer industries preferred to locate in regions free from the grime of the mining areas. Service industries, such as insurance, and many company bureaucracies tended to settle in the capital cities or other financial centers. Paris, London, and Frankfurt, and the regions around them, expanded rapidly. Southern England, long eclipsed by the industrial north, was now reversing the process. A few traditional factory areas in Britain and the coal districts of Belgium were afflicted with noticeable levels of unemployment. But generally the expansion of the economy more than sufficed to compensate for lagging areas and industries. All this meant greater geographical as well as social mobility.

Agriculture participated strongly in economic growth. Increasing numbers of peasants abandoned the countryside for the city, where industrial growth assured them of jobs. The result was less rural poverty and more efficient farm units. Governments encouraged more productive methods on the farms, providing better training and information on new techniques. They promoted the consolidation of small plots into larger, more efficient holdings and they actively backed the cooperative movement. Improved equipment, including tractors and other agricultural machines, spread widely, resulting in a sharp increase in crop yields. West Germany, cut off from the agricultural east, raised agricultural productivity rapidly; by 1952 West German wheat yield per acre was 1.2 tons, compared to 0.4 in the United States. French agricultural gains were in many ways still more dramatic, and output rose rapidly. European farmers were not as efficient on a per-worker basis as those of North America, where farming was far more mechanized. Their increased output added to the problem of excessive agricultural production in the industrial nations of the world and this output could be maintained only by tariff protection and subsidies. Nevertheless agriculture was not the invalid it had been during the previous half century. It was less of a drain on the economy as a whole and provided better-quality food to Europe's cities.

The economic expansion and rising prosperity of Europe's traditional industrial heartland in Germany, France, Britain, northern Italy, and the Low Countries also helped stimulate the long delayed economic development of Mediterranean Europe. By the 1960s Spain, Portugal, and Greece all benefited from loans and investments from western Europe and the United States. Southern Europeans found an expanding market for exports in the rapidly growing economies to their north. And labor shortages in France, Switzerland, West Germany, and elsewhere attracted a steady flow of immigrant workers from Europe's southern tier, workers who often sent earnings to families back home. Tourism blossomed as a growth industry in sunny summertime climes of Greece, southern Italy, and the Iberian Peninsula. Although southern Europe still lagged behind economically in the 1970s, postwar growth integrated the region more tightly into the Europeanwide economy, a trend that eventually brought Greece, Spain, and Portugal into the Common Market.

Throughout western Europe, growth in most major sectors of the economy brought prosperity, particularly to the middle classes in the form of rising salaries and profitable investments. Continuing a well-established trend, the size of businesses grew steadily and the managerial ranks expanded accordingly. Companies also became international, as the establishment of the Common Market encouraged firms to establish factories and sales operations beyond national borders. Small wonder then that earnings rose, often more rapidly than wages.

Even so the working classes did win a share of the general prosperity, despite government efforts to fight inflationary trends in the economy through wage restraints. Rising working-class incomes brought working-class families more firmly into the habits of mass consumption that fueled the postwar economy. Unemployment, moreover, was virtually eliminated after the economic boom began, though there was a lag in Germany, where more than two million workers were unemployed as late as February 1954. After the mid-1950s, unemployment rates of no more than 2 percent were maintained in France and Germany, which meant that most of the unemployed were simply in transition from one job to the next. By the 1960s both countries came to rely extensively on immigration from North Africa, Turkey, and southern Europe to fill the soaring demand for workers created by economic growth.

Growing numbers of women found employment as well, which boosted family income. In Britain the number of working-class women with jobs rose two times over the level of the 1930s. By 1973 women constituted 39 percent of the employment population in France. And this was not a traditional kind of advance. Employment of teenaged girls fell steadily because more and more were prolonging their schooling. It was adult women, many of them married, who were entering the labor force; in France the employment of women aged twenty-five to fifty-four, 52 percent in 1972, had risen past 53 percent in 1973, a rate of growth far higher than that of the labor force as a whole. Women played an important role in the factories but they were particularly concentrated in the ranks of the service sector. Never, in fact, since the population explosion of the eighteenth century had such a high percentage of the adult population been regularly employed over such an extended period of time as was the case in the 1960s and early 1970s.

Full employment and the steadily rising demand for workers naturally produced a rise in wages. Demands by individuals and unions for new raises met only moderate resistance. By the early 1960s wage rates were rising fast, which brought the urban lower classes of western Europe unprecedented affluence. Whereas per capita disposable income rose 117 percent in the United States between 1960 and 1973, it increased 258 percent in France, 312 percent in Germany, and 323 percent in Denmark. New spending money rapidly translated into huge increases in the purchase of consumer goods. By 1969 two of every ten people in Britain, Sweden, West Germany, and France owned an automobile. Ownership of television sets became virtually universal. In France and elsewhere consumers indulged in a mania for household appliances. Shopping malls and supermarkets spread at the expense of traditional specialty shops. Recreational opportunities increased as work hours diminished, and most workers were legally guaranteed two or three weeks paid vacation.

Despite the remarkable economic advances, there were weaknesses in Europe's new economic structure. The British economy, although expanding, did not take part fully in the boom. Having suffered less from bombardment during the war, its industries benefited less from postwar investment. And having urbanized so extensively in earlier decades, Britain did not experience the same automatic improvements in productivity that urbanization and agricultural modernization brought to much of the Continent. Slower growth rates and a dependence on massive imports of food and other goods created a chronic balance-of-payments problem for Britain that dominated national policy by

the 1960s. In order to produce more for export and adjust the payments' balance, the government periodically imposed restrictions not
only on imports and travel abroad but also on consumer spending at
home. These policies reduced domestic demand, prompted recessions,
and forced the government to reflate the economy and reproduce the
balance-of-payment problem. "Stop–go" policies of this sort drew widespread criticism and failed to redress the underlying structural deficiencies of the British economy.

The scale of American investment in postwar Europe worried Europeans in Britain and on the Continent alike. American aid had been an
important boon to postwar recovery in the early 1950s, but by the
1960s the growing presence of American multinational corporations
aroused concern. Although western Europe had surpassed the United
States in overall rates of postwar economic growth, Europeans had not
come close to matching the Americans in technological innovation or in
the creation of the large industrial enterprises that were coming to
dominate the capitalist economy. In 1969 a French politician and journalist, Jean Jacques Servan-Schreiber, published *The American Challenge,*
which quickly won attention for sounding the alarm. The argument
was hard to assess because the Europeans clearly had strengths—
stronger social supports for employees, balanced government budgets,
a better track record for exports, and some flexibility in industrial
structure, which would later prove to be an asset in the 1980s. American investment in Europe, moreover, had helped spur the postwar advance. It was not clear, then, who was lagging behind.

Inflation emerged as the most important problem in the burgeoning
postwar economy by the late 1960s and early 1970s, even in stable,
inflation-averse Germany. Some observers blamed the flood of unwanted dollars from American investors and speculators, but other important factors were also involved. Food prices climbed in part because
tariffs and subsidy programs limited agricultural competition. Large
firms with considerable market power sometimes pushed up prices.
Consumer demand shot up as well, despite continuing income inequality and important pockets of outright poverty. By the early 1970s prices
were rising up to 10 percent a year in several countries, and government efforts to control the trend had little effect.

Economic growth, however, made it relatively feasible to absorb the
burden of inflation. Well into the mid-1970s most of western Europe
continued to enjoy the fruits of the postwar boom. There seemed little
reason to doubt that the advanced industrial West had found its way
beyond the destructive boom-bust cycles of an earlier era. Although
Britain continued to suffer from its protracted decline as a world
economic power, most economists and government planners on the
Continent remained cautiously confident that the basic principles of

countercyclical demand management—the careful expansion and contraction of government spending and the money supply—could keep the postwar economy on an even keel.

Even eastern Europe participated in the boom of the 1950s and 1960s, when every country in the Eastern bloc enjoyed an unprecedented period of economic growth. Much of this vitality derived from an expansion of the service sector, a concentration of investment in heavy industry, and a shift in the employment structure away from agriculture. Some regions that had long lagged behind finally began to catch up. In Bulgaria per capita production increased fivefold between 1950 and 1970. Industrial output in Romania increased 120 percent from 1963 to 1970. Although achievements such as these did not produce the same levels of prosperity that prevailed in most of western Europe, they did raise living standards in much of the Socialist bloc. By the 1980s in Hungary there was one private car for every three households, not spectacular by Western standards but a thirtyfold increase since 1960. The Soviet economy grew about 5 percent annually during the 1960s, and by the late 1970s Soviet industry produced seven times more than it had thirty years before.

Despite success, however, Eastern bloc economies had their distinctive maladies. Consumer goods remained scarce, even after periodic and sometimes large-scale popular protests forced government planners to shift investment capital into consumer industries. Trade within the Eastern bloc remained anemic, as each government, following the lead of the Soviets, strove for national economic self-sufficiency. When trade improved, it was often with western Europe rather than with eastern neighbors. Above all, agriculture remained inefficient. Most governments in the east channeled investment capital into industry at the expense of agricultural modernization. Collectivized farming and centralized pricing failed to stimulate greater efficiency. Even in the case of the Soviet Union, where the government poured a great deal of money into agriculture in the 1960s and 1970s, farm productivity languished. In Poland, where private landholding predominated, farms remained too small and investment capital too scarce for a breakthrough in per capita output. To be sure, the agrarian record in the Eastern bloc was not entirely bleak. The Bulgarian government's investment in farm equipment, rural schools, and electrification helped transform a backward agricultural economy. Farm yields there doubled and the agrarian work force diminished by half in the course of the 1950s and 1960s. By the 1980s a mixture of collectivized and private farming in Hungary had created a healthy export trade for the country and gave Hungarians the best foodstuffs in eastern Europe. But overall, agriculture remained a serious drag on Eastern bloc economies during the growth decades of the 1950s and 1960s.

A New Age of Troubled Economies

In the mid-1970s west Europeans discovered that their capitalist economies were no longer as immune to serious structural ills as they had
seemed to be during the first postwar decades. Soaring inflation, poor
growth rates, and rising levels of unemployment brought western
Europe, along with the United States and much of the rest of the
world, into a new era of stagflation. Conventional economic policies no
longer seemed to work. Efforts to spur investment to end the stagnation pushed prices up, while anti-inflationary measures only worsened
unemployment. In 1974–1975 total output declined in almost all the
west European economies for the first time since the 1930s. Another
recession between 1979 and 1982 proved particularly damaging.

Part of the problem stemmed from rising prices in the global markets for primary materials, especially oil. In 1973 the nations on which
Europe was dependent for oil, headed by the Organization of Petrol-
eum-Exporting Countries (OPEC), cut production and raised prices,
initially in response to a Middle Eastern war with Israel. Oil prices
remained high through the 1970s and rose again in another energy
crisis in 1979, triggered by a revolution in Iran. High energy prices in
turn fed the inflationary pressures of the European economies and led
to setbacks in manufacturing and overall employment.

The crisis, which remained severe in much of western Europe into
the mid-1980s, had deep-seated causes in addition to oil prices. European industries faced new competition from East Asia and other areas.
The iron and steel industry, for nearly a century a cornerstone of the
British, French, and German manufacturing sectors, cut back dramatically as cheap, high-quality steel entered world markets from Japan,
Korea, and Brazil. The European automobile industry suffered similarly. And Europeans in the new growth industry of consumer electronics
found it difficult to keep up with American and Japanese manufacturers. But competition was not the only problem. The overall demand for
European products no longer grew at the rates manufacturers had
come to enjoy in the 1960s. Within Europe population growth declined
and with it the demand for consumer durables. World demand for
European exports declined with the slowdown of the global economy.
By the 1970s, moreover, the European economy no longer had the
advantage of relatively low wage levels, which had boosted Europe's
competitive position in the 1950s and 1960s. Nor could many west
European countries go much further in shifting employment from agriculture to industry, a shift that had done a great deal to increase
productivity in the earlier decades. By the 1980s it was clear that there
was no simple path to the easy growth that had characterized the postwar decades.

The stormy economic climate of the 1970s and 1980s led to a
number of important changes in the economic life of western Europe,

some of which had been already underway. The service sector continued to expand as the most dynamic part of the economy. The introduction of computer technology into banking, insurance, corporate administration, and the communications industry transformed white-collar work, not always for the better, and improved productivity in these sectors. Similarly, manufacturers looked to computerized processing and electronic robots as a way to cut costs and respond to the pressures of foreign competition. By the late 1980s large steel plants that once had employed ten thousand to twenty thousand workers now could produce as much steel with two thousand people. Manufacturers also altered the organizational structure of their firms. More and more European companies became multinational by building plants and acquiring firms not only in Europe but overseas as well. At the same time small specialty firms found new ways to thrive in the competitive global markets of the 1980s by finding small but profitable niches in a rapidly changing market for high-quality goods, be they metal alloys or high-style furs.

The crisis had important geographical effects. Many older industrial regions, such as the British Midlands, northeastern France, and the Ruhr district of West Germany, declined. These erstwhile centers of industrial growth became persistent pockets of unemployment. Many areas on the southern and western periphery of western Europe, such as southern Italy, Portugal, and the French southwest, faltered once again after regional development projects in the 1960s and 1970s had given new hope to backward areas. Other regions flourished as growth centers of a restructured economy — places like London and southern England, Paris and its burgeoning southern suburbs, and a number of cities in southern West Germany and northern Italy. Cities well endowed with professionals, skilled technicians, and affluent consumers attracted new investment, both foreign and domestic, while old, half-used ports like Marseille and Liverpool struggled with the problems of the desperately poor. When the west European economy began to show renewed vitality in the mid-1980s — inflation rates dropped, growth rates climbed — it became clear that the economic landscape had changed.

By the late 1980s a spirit of cautious optimism about the west European economy returned. To be sure, plenty of uncertainty remained in a world of volatile financial markets, fierce competition from Japanese and American firms, and continued dependence on Middle East oil. But the rich nations of western Europe had emerged from the crisis well supplied with essential ingredients for further economic development — an educated work force, a wealth of investment capital, a dynamic network of public and private enterprises, and political stability. The resilience of the west European economy, and its reservoir of resources, stood in sharp contrast to the weaknesses of the east European economies, which failed to recover from the prolonged crisis of the late 1970s and 1980s.

By the end of the 1980s something else surfaced in western Europe to galvanize the economic potentialities of the region—"1992." The governments of all twelve members of the European Community agreed to eliminate most of the remaining barriers to the free flow of capital, goods, and employees between member countries by the end of 1992. The creation of a common currency for western Europe, which would have seemed utopian a decade earlier, became a realistic objective. Since the 1950s trade within Europe had been a major stimulus to economic growth. The very prospect of a single market of over 320 million people inspired new investment and a powerful wave of international business mergers and acquisitions, as governments and enterprises positioned themselves for the intensified competition of an economically unified Europe. Just what a true common market would mean for particular regions and economic sectors, to say nothing of immigration patterns, welfare policies, and employment practices, remained unclear. But the symbolic power of "1992" both reflected and enhanced the tendency for Europeans to see their economic fate in continental rather than in national terms.

Social Change

The forces reshaping European society, especially economic growth, shifts in the occupational structure, the new functions of the state, and the expansion of mass consumption, were no mere abstractions. They touched every major social group, altered social relations, and pushed people to see themselves in new ways. For some groups the changes of the postwar era even transformed forms of social identity that had been forged during the Industrial Revolution or before. The peasantry in particular encountered powerful pressures of social change, though portions of the working class and middle class did as well. Social experiences varied, of course, between western and eastern Europe. So too did the pace of change, as postwar recovery gave way to rapid economic growth, followed in turn by economic difficulties and new kinds of social conflict.

The basic structure of social classes did not change radically. Peasants, the middle class, and workers all continued to embrace earlier values and outlooks. Each of these groups, however, had to adjust to major change, and some novel subgroups, such as a rapidly expanding unskilled immigrant labor force, acquired new importance in the social structure. Relative numbers changed as well. The rural population shrank, and so did the working class as a percentage of the total labor force. The middle class gained ground numerically, though this change came largely through an expansion of the employee group whose conditions resembled that of blue-collar labor.

A Vanishing Peasantry

The peasantry, as a distinct social class with its own culture, came close to extinction in the decades following World War II. This was partly a matter of dwindling numbers. In western Europe the size of the farming population continued to shrink steadily as migration to cities continued. In eastern Europe, and even in Spain and Portugal, postwar industrialization reduced peasant numbers as well, although not to the same extent as in West Germany, France, and the Low Countries. Just as important as demographic change, however, was a shift in values in rural areas. Except in the most remote areas of Southern Europe and the Iberian Peninsula, people in the agrarian sector came to share similar values with their urban counterparts about economic and social life. By the 1980s radio and television became as commonplace in the countryside as in the city, which brought rural peoples into closer contact with the urban world and its mass entertainments and consumer tastes. In economic terms a great many peasants gradually became more and more like commercial farmers, who had more in common with the small businessperson than with the near-subsistence producer of a century before. In 1970 it was possible for a leading French sociologist to speak with authority of the "vanishing peasantry."[1]

This process of change, well underway before World War II in some areas, took place gradually in the postwar era and unevenly among regions. In the early 1950s the commercial farming economy of England, Denmark, and Holland still contrasted sharply with the survival of very large pockets of a strong peasant culture in the villages of France, southern Europe, and even West Germany. Peasants still had larger families and lower divorce rates. Even as late as 1970 a French survey showed that only peasants continued to define a successful family in terms of the number of children it had. Peasants in many areas remained attached to age-old but inefficient economic habits, such as the scattering of small plots of land around a village. And peasant traditionalism was maintained by the continued departure of many younger, ambitious peasants to cities; as before, the rural population was older than the national average.

By the late 1970s much of this peasant world had disappeared. In eastern Europe the communist attack on large estates and the collectivization of agriculture produced enormous cultural change in rural life. The spread of new social services, closer contact with cities, and the interaction of rural people with the burgeoning bureaucracy of a centrally planned economy undermined rural life as a separate cultural experience. Of course, longstanding values and loyalties did not disappear entirely. The Catholic church, for example, remained a quiet

---

[1] Henri Mendras, *The Vanishing Peasant* (Cambridge, Mass., 1970).

force in rural Poland despite state harassment. But in general in eastern Europe, antireligious policies took their toll on traditional rural custom.

In western Europe conditions changed almost as rapidly. The welfare state provided new material benefits for peasants, such as social security, family subsidies, and insured medical care. Literacy spread in remote areas where rural education had lagged behind. Although peasant incomes did not reach urban levels, they did improve, giving families the means to buy new products and household conveniences and to invest more strategically in production. With government encouragement, peasants showed a growing interest in economic change. Observers noted a virtual revolution in the attitudes of younger French peasants, who took a keen interest in new methods and new machines. Tractors became a more important status symbol than land itself. Some peasants preferred to use capital to acquire equipment rather than land, which they might then rent—an unprecedented recasting of their values toward a strict cost-benefit calculation of their business. The cooperative movement continued to spread, aided by government subsidies. This, too, brought new organizational experience, as did elections for the leadership of cooperatives and local state agencies, which in turn altered the nature of village politics. Political contests became a subject of lively, even bitter debates, as traditional village leaders were pushed aside by a younger, more forward-looking generation.

The shift from a peasant to a commercial farming culture did not diminish the capacity or inclination of agricultural groups to engage in popular protest. Farm leaders did not become quiet lobbyists in Europe's agricultural ministries. The Italian and French communist parties found important sources of voting support among peasants, small farmers, and agricultural laborers. From the 1950s on farmers of both right-wing and left-wing persuasion in western Europe frequently engaged in dramatic, disruptive demonstrations to call for price subsidies and protective tariffs, even within the liberalized trading environment of the Common Market. Tractor-driving farmers often blocked the traffic of city dwellers leaving on vacation, barricaded highways to protest imports, or marched on government buildings in administrative capitals and in Brussels, the seat of the Common Market. Sometimes farm protests turned violent, as in 1990 when French farmers burned, poisoned, and contaminated British sheep being trucked into France and a French truck driver was beaten in England in retaliation. Although small in size, the agricultural voting bloc put strong pressure on government policies throughout most of western Europe. Agricultural policy remained the chief source of conflict among member nations of the Common Market, and farm subsidies persisted through a complex transfer of Common Market funds to many farmers, a practice that kept farm prices less competitive than they would have been otherwise.

Farmers did not, to be sure, simply merge into an urban-defined social structure. They were less likely to travel extensively and remained more likely to be religious. Despite government programs for land consolidation, some peasants clung to small plots. And although their festivals were hollow echoes of older tradition—filled with urban band music and bus loads of city tourists—rural people retained at least a vague sense of attachment to village rituals and old habits. But by the 1980s the peasantry as such had nearly vanished in all but the more remote areas of western Europe.

The Middle Class

Postwar economic development and the rise of the welfare state gave most people in the west European middle class greater security and more opportunity than even before. Indeed, during the 1950s and 1960s it seemed to many observers that the middle class was exerting so much political and cultural influence that Europe itself was becoming a homogenized, middle-class society. Working-class affluence seemed to blur the lines at the bottom end of the middle class, and the rise of upper middle-class executives and professionals into positions of economic, cultural, and political leadership clouded distinctions at the upper end. But by the 1970s and 1980s this rosy image of middle-class power and security gave way to a more realistic view of what had been happening all along: Various middle-class groups fared differently in postwar Europe, and alongside prosperity new problems and pressures arose that complicated the rather simple portrait of the postwar decades as an age of middle-class triumph.

For example, small shopkeepers and tradespeople continued to suffer from the slow but steady economic decline that came with the advance of grocery chains, department stores, and mass production. This group by no means disappeared but it lost ground more rapidly than before despite collective efforts to the contrary. In France in particular small shopkeepers supported a highly visible protest movement in the 1950s, and had enough influence to curb supermarkets by law in some center cities. But the long-term decline of the old lower middle class continued, forcing many of the sons and daughters of small independent proprietors into the scramble for places in other middle-class occupations.

The new middle class of clerks, managers, sales personnel, and bureaucrats expanded markedly in the postwar era and offered avenues for advancement in a service-oriented economy. But organizational realities in the bureaucratic world of the corporation, hospital, school system, and government agency brought frustrations along with opportunities. Some jobs became routinized, work hierarchies became rigidified, and employees' special abilities were sometimes ignored. Personal contacts more than talent might push one's colleague up the organizational ladder, while the sheer weight of procedure could disgust someone who in the classic middle-class manner wanted to get to the top. Supervisors kept tabs on employees, and new office machinery made certain skills — for example, rapid arithmetic ability — outmoded. In many cases white-collar salaries did not keep pace with the growth of factory pay, so the lines between middle- and working-class living standards increasingly blurred.

Under these circumstances it was not hard for many middle-class people to develop a new sympathy for the labor and socialist parties. The bulk of the class did not vote left wing, but many middle-class people did; and most found socialist parties, even communist parties, a legitimate part of the party system. Just as important, many middle-class employees turned to white-collar trade unions as a means to improve their leverage at the workplace. By the 1960s unions representing teachers, nurses, bank employees, and government workers had become some of the most vigorous and expressive organizations in the labor movement. Even doctors, as virtual employees of the welfare state in many countries, found in the organizational tactics of the labor movement new ways to express a voice. White-collar employees and middle-class professionals played a prominent role in the massive general strike in France in May 1968. Although middle-class unions did not become quite the bastion for left-wing resurgence that some observers were predicting in the 1970s, they remained resilient during the tough economic period of the late 1970s and 1980s.

Even though middle-class employees challenged their superiors on a much larger scale than had been the case before World War II, they did not reject the work ethic that had long figured so centrally in industrialized Europe. Middle-level managers gave themselves extensively to their jobs. Professional people did the same. Benefiting from improved training in medical and law schools, even members of the older professions found satisfaction in their work. University professors for the most part abandoned their nostalgia for the good old days of classical education and accepted an emerging intellectual world of competitive, specialized work in scientific or social scientific research and teaching. All professionals found new job opportunities with the expansion of state functions. One sign of work satisfaction on the part of professionals and higher-level managers was a relatively late retirement age.

The lower middle-class culture of work was somewhat different, as it had been in the earlier decades of the century. With fewer opportunities to rise to the top of an organization or a career, and fewer avenues for expressing themselves creatively on the job, many people in this group paid a great deal of attention to life off the job. Retirement age was relatively low. But there was job satisfaction for this group, too. Most polls suggested that 70 to 80 percent of clerks enjoyed their work. Some people did in fact move up the ladder. The expansion of state educational systems, particularly at the secondary school and university levels, gave many sons and daughters a real chance to gain higher status through training. Many developed social contacts with friends on the jobs. And of course job satisfaction was enhanced by the steady advance of middle-class earnings.

Furthermore, the middle class retained decisive advantages over the working class in terms of income, status, and life chances. Those in the middle class who depended on a sense of superiority could take satisfaction in their social position. Despite new working-class prosperity the average pay level of the middle class was distinctly higher. More important, middle-class pay came in the form of salary, not wage. Middle-class employees were paid a monthly or yearly rate and had more job security, more freedom from temporary layoffs, than workers whose earnings were based on hourly rates or daily performance. Most European systems based entry into the most prestigious secondary schools— those that would enhance later advancement into universities for the ablest students—on an examination taken around the age of eleven. Success in this early testing depended heavily on home environment, the encouragement parents could give their children to do well in school. And here the middle class, again taking advantage of its traditional ethic, continued to thrive.

The middle class in postwar Europe also used its prosperity and sense of job security to expand on a culture of leisure acitivity that had already taken hold in the early decades of the century. Far more clearly than before, the middle class learned to have fun. Ample leisure time and regular annual vacations of at least three weeks—and in some countries five or six weeks by the 1980s—enabled middle-class families to create a new life-style. Clerks as well as bankers became Continental travelers. Every summer millions of middle-class Germans, Britons, Scandinavians, and French poured into Mediterranean Europe to bask in the sun. The bronzed body became an important status symbol now that more people worked indoors, in contrast to the nineteenth century when fashionable women strove to preserve the whiteness of their skin. New attention to leisure activities altered middle-class spending patterns. More money went to vacations, camping equipment, and ski holidays. Affluent families bought up the country houses that a declining agricultural population no longer could maintain. And by the 1980s west Europeans, like their American counterparts, took a keener interest in physical fitness, healthy diets, and athletic activity—a trend that fed on the popularization of medical advice and the middle-class ethic of leisure.

New attitudes toward retirement emerged as well. Europeans were urged to think of their later years as a "third age," in which they expected to be healthy and engage in a host of activities they had been too busy to enjoy during their adult, working years. The middle class was particularly able to take some advantage of this advice, even though some segments retired relatively late. More than was the case with the working class, middle-class people professed to find retirement enjoyable. The extension of the life span and the economic security of middle-class retirement also kept older people involved in mass consumption. Advertisers appealed to—and indeed helped foster—the image of the spry grandparents amply equipped to purchase the full array of food, liquor, real estate, and holiday tours that the middle-aged and young were expected to enjoy.

If the middle class took a leading role in the elaboration of a consumer society in western Europe after 1945, the same could not be said in the Eastern bloc. Indeed, the very notion of a middle class found little currency in socialist societies where elite status was tied more to educational achievement, bureaucratic standing, and party loyalty than to private property. However, socialist societies in eastern Europe all had an intelligentsia of managers, legal and economic experts, teachers, doctors, and scholars, who often (though certainly not always) had family roots, educational opportunities, and leadership positions that Westerners would associate with the middle class. Industrial growth and state expansion enhanced the size and prominence of this social group, enabling its members to experiment in a limited way with a new recreational culture not altogether different from what was emerging in the West. While the east European managerial and intellectual elite lacked the wealth and property of the west European middle class, it did have a similar kind of cultural capital—educational credentials, intellectual training, and cosmopolitan sophistication—that gave the group advantages over the working class. Despite these similarities, however, the Eastern bloc managerial and intellectual elite was too small and too limited in economic power and political autonomy to play the cultural role of a Western, consumption-oriented middle class.

The Working Class

Postwar growth brought unprecedented prosperity to workers in western Europe, and the new era of political and social stability in the West that followed World War II did a great deal to integrate the working class into advanced industrial society. But class distinctions did not disappear and class conflicts persisted. Some workers, moreover, benefited much more than others from the booming economy of the 1950s and 1960s. And when rapid growth gave way to crisis and a restructuring of the European economy in the 1970s and 1980s, it became obvious everywhere in western Europe that social inequalities and class tensions remained enduring features of even the most advanced industrial societies.

There is no gainsaying the fact, however, that workers shared in the fruits of postwar affluence. The social security provisions of the welfare state gave working-class families greater protection from hardship than ever before. More important, high employment rates in the 1950s and 1960s, combined with rising real wages, increased the standard of living for most workers and reduced the number of them who were desperately poor. With more to spend working-class families took part in the postwar consumer revolution, bringing home the appliances, televisions, and low-priced but increasingly stylish standardized clothing that made the young in particular keen observers of fashion. It even became possible for workers to partake of that crucial symbol of middle-class consumption, the automobile — an important development in a Europe that had lagged behind the United States in this respect. In addition, the spread of low-priced government housing and improvements in public schooling often meant better living conditions and better prospects for children in what had been working-class slums in the interwar years.

Working-class leisure changed as well. With legally guaranteed vacations and better pay, workers took advantage of the postwar boom in holiday travel. Some even joined the traffic jams on highways toward the sea. New recreational patterns emerged that resembled the middle-class tendency to make leisure a more private and family-centered domain. Neighborhood bars, cafés, and pubs declined in number and patronage, in part because the traditional, isolated working-class neighborhood was declining as well. Television, too, played a role as many workers went home after work to enjoy what quickly became the favorite evening pastime. Gardening, tennis, and the family vacation took workers away from older habits of group activity. Class-centered leisure by no means disappeared. Chances were that a working-class tennis enthusiast used a trade union-run court in the outskirts of Paris, rather than the "bourgeois" court in the Luxembourg gardens. Still, working-class consumption and leisure had its integrating effects. A Danish union-owned brewery that had long relied on working-class loyalty to sell its product closed its doors in the 1960s because workers no longer found solidarity reason enough to shun better-tasting beer from capitalist firms, and they had the money to indulge their palates.

Some observers claimed that, because of affluence, mass consumption, and the welfare state, along with less authoritarian structures on the job, workers were coming to resemble the middle class in a process known as *embourgeoisement*. They pointed not only to overlaps in consumer and leisure behavior from class to class, but also to more shared family values. Indeed, there were signs of a reduction in class conflict during the 1950s and 1960s, in comparison to the earlier decades of the century. Strike rates remained high, especially in France and Italy, but strikers usually aimed at winning concrete concessions in collective bargaining rather than major changes in economic organization. Although working-class support for socialist and in some cases communist parties surged after the war and remained high thereafter, most of these parties focused on reform and not revolution. Furthermore, many former working-class militants devoted more of their time to new leisure interests, or to overtime work to pay for a new car or better apartment, effectively reducing their political commitments. Trade-union membership, rising into the 1950s, stabilized and then began to drop relative to the size of the labor force in the 1970s.

Yet despite some mobility for a minority of workers who rose to white-collar status or sent their children into the university system, and despite some lessening in class hostilities, the working class did not merge with the middle class. Housing, health care, and education may have improved, but working-class families still suffered from social and economic disadvantage. Public housing was often drab, isolated, and poorly constructed. The path to higher education was still a good deal straighter for middle-class students, who usually had better schooling, more time to devote to their studies, and greater encouragement at home. While many workers expressed hopes for their children's upward mobility, they did not really expect their children to advance and so did not push them to succeed in school. Most workers' children remained in the lower educational tracks and entered trade school or apprenticeships in their mid-teens. Furthermore, income inequalities persisted. In 1972 the average manager in France earned a salary that was four and a half times greater than the average unskilled worker's.

Although the bitterest class hostilities did decline, workers were quite aware that they were different from most people in the middle class. They differed in their consumer tastes and in their political values. They often relied more heavily on family, including extended kin, for their social contacts, rather than on outsiders. Most important, workers maintained a sense of class identity and did so with pride. In contrast to the United States, where 85 percent of the population claimed to be in the middle class, most urban Britons or French said they were working class and (somewhat) proud of it.

Workers, more than other urban groups, also maintained an ambivalent outlook toward their jobs. Skilled workers usually took considerable pride in their skills and derived satisfaction from the work they accomplished. But they also typically believed that they were bossed around by incompetent managers; they resented the structure of authority at the workplace. Semiskilled workers complained less about bosses but also showed less indication that they expected or found much pleasure in their work. Most workers admitted to some satisfaction in work or its material reward, though in surveys a minority of up to 31 percent did not. Most workers also said that had they to do it over again, they would choose another line of work. On the whole, workers found the workplace less open to them as a domain through which to advance and fulfill themselves than did the middle class.

The New "Underclass"

An important segment of the postwar working class—the "underclass"—still had to deal with poverty and social isolation. Many workers remained unskilled and earned just enough to get by. And after 1950 this group became increasingly associated with a new wave of immigration from southern Europe, Africa, Asia, and the Caribbean—a host of peoples attracted to the low-level jobs being created in the surging economies of central and western Europe. Large numbers of Turks, Yugoslavs, and Italians were brought in to work in West Germany. In France hundreds of thousands of North Africans became street sweepers, transport workers, or construction workers, or they took up assembly line positions in the factories of Renault. Close to two million Pakistanis and West Indians poured into Britain. Large numbers of Spanish and Portuguese women migrated north to become domestic workers in middle- and upper-class households. And a majority of these immigrants, euphemistically labeled *guest workers* in West Germany, were often residentially segregated, poorly paid, and victims of prejudice, racial violence, and discrimination. They formed something of a separate labor force, confined for the most part to menial jobs and hardly benefiting from the prosperity of the society around them.

By the 1980s immigrant workers and their families had become a significant minority in the working classes of the richest West European countries. Although many immigrants had initially planned to work in Europe temporarily, and indeed some did return to their homelands, most stayed, established families, or had family members they had left behind come join them. With the end of the economic boom in the mid-1970s, the flow of immigrant workers slowed considerably, and in the deep recession of the early 1980s many immigrants lost jobs and were compelled to return to their native country. Still, the great majority stayed and their families grew. For a second generation of immigrant children, Europe, however hostile, was home. By the late 1980s illegal immigration was on the rise, and by 1990 over twelve million immigrants were living in the twelve nations of the Common Market, most of them in Britain, France, and West Germany. Islam became the second religion of France. Of course, the European working class had always had its share of intra-European immigrants. The Irish had peopled the mills of the British Midlands, Poles had dug coal in the Ruhr, and Italians had staffed the giant ironworks of eastern France. But postwar immigration added a new dimension entirely. Working-class Europe became multiracial and multicultural to an unprecedented degree.

Immigration also served to reinforce a general trend toward political moderation in the west European working class. New immigrants in the 1950s and 1960s took the most poorly paid jobs and at least initially had little access to the usual channels of protest—strikes, trade-union membership, and support from left-wing parties. Discriminated against by native workers and employers, often deprived of basic citizenship rights, and divided by language and custom, unskilled immigrants kept the lower, most desperate segment of the working class quiet. Only by the 1970s did trade unions begin to take immigrant workers seriously as part of their future and, as strikes at the Renault autoworks most dramatically revealed, did immigrant workers show a significant capacity to demand incomes and opportunities comparable to those of native workers. If by the 1980s trade unions had gone a long way to recognize the virtues of multiethnic solidarity in the labor movement, racial and cultural divisions could still hamper collective action.

Changing Patterns of Protest

A number of factors, alongside immigration, tended to make working-class protest appear more moderate in the postwar era. Ironically, the very success of the labor movement and the left after the war put a damper on the revolutionary tradition. In Scandinavia workers could count on the powerful influence of the labor and socialist parties to secure through parliament the gains they had previously fought for in strike movements and on the streets. The highly unionized work force of West Germany found similar advantages in using trade-union influence at the company and industry level to win concessions that employers would never have granted in the earlier, more turbulent decades of the century. Even in strike-prone Italy and France, strong communist parties and communist-dominated unions served more to ritualize and regularize informal methods of bargaining among workers, employers, and the government than to radicalize their working-class constituents.

But postwar affluence and the integration of left-wing parties and trade unions into the institutional mainstream of western Europe in the 1950s and 1960s did not cut off workers entirely from their traditions of protest. When inflation began to dig into working-class incomes in the late 1960s, strike rates rose in several countries. And when students set off a wave of defiance in Paris in May 1968, French workers seized control of factories and offices throughout the country and eventually produced the largest general strike in the history of France. They ultimately returned to work with wage hikes and new rights for their unions, but not before many strikers had called into question basic principles of managerial authority. After May 1968 "autogestion" or worker "self-management" became a clarion call for workplace organizing, not just in France but throughout much of western Europe.

In the early 1970s observers described a resurgence of working-class protest virtually everywhere on the Continent. Britain, too, felt the change, as British workers produced several important waves of strike activity, sometimes against union leadership as well as management. In Spain and Portugal industrial strikes in the mid-1970s took on even greater political significance, as workers quite self-consciously contributed to the successful effort to transform longstanding authoritarian regimes into the newest democracies in western Europe.

Once the economic climate changed for the worse in the mid-1970s the focus of working-class protest shifted toward protecting jobs and sheltering incomes from the ravages of high inflation. Workers in nationalized industries in several countries struck against government-imposed wage restraints. Italian unions mobilized ten million workers in 1982 for a one-day protest for higher wages. In perhaps the bitterest strike of the 1980s British miners spent over a year fighting government efforts to reduce the industry. French steelworkers spent much of the late 1970s and early 1980s trying to push the government to salvage jobs in their languishing industry—a struggle that culminated in the plundering of public buildings in the eastern town of Longwy in 1984 when the mills there were finally shut down. Even German metalworkers, rarely inclined to strike, conducted an unprecedentedly bitter strike in the mid-1980s for more of a say over working conditions and for better pay.

There were other forms of protest as well. Working-class youth frequently displayed a restiveness that could not be captured by conventional strikes or demonstrations. Young workers were responsible for a growing wave of spectator violence at British soccer matches, for example, during the 1970s and beyond. Anti-immigrant violence, though by no means perpetrated exclusively by working-class youth, also gave expression to frustration at a life haunted by unemployment and dwindling opportunity.

None of these forms of protest, however, whether organized strikes or back-street brawling, offered workers a way out of the defensive position in which political and economic changes since the mid-1970s had thrust them. The contraction of major industries such as coal mining, shipbuilding, and steel, and the automation of much of the manufacturing that did survive the recession of the early 1980s, wreaked havoc on many traditional working-class communities. High rates of unemployment weakened the unions, as did nearly a decade of conservative rule in major countries such as Britain and West Germany. Union membership declined generally throughout western Europe. The once-powerful communist parties of France and Italy saw their electoral support dwindle steadily in the 1980s. Though trade unions often managed to win government support for worker retraining programs and early retirement pensions, and in a few cases government bailouts did succeed in reviving troubled companies, working-class families faced enormous pressures to adapt to changing labor markets on their own. The postwar era of prosperity and crisis, while in many ways standing out as a high-water mark for working-class progress in Europe, perpetuated longstanding patterns of diversity in the class. By the end of the 1980s the living conditions and life chances of workers varied enormously depending on country, region, skill level, occupation, gender, and native or immigrant status.

Eastern Europe

Workers in eastern Europe also experienced the postwar era as a mixture of good fortune and adversity, though they did so under quite different conditions and without the same level of affluence as in the West. Working conditions and living standards certainly improved for most workers in the Eastern bloc after 1950. Rapid industrialization and steady economic growth produced high levels of urban employment, and in this respect eastern Europe resembled the West during its period of rapid industrial consolidation in the late nineteenth century. New social security protections and the constant official insistence on the importance of workers in a socialist society had their benefits as well, and here experience in the East differed from earlier Western patterns. In terms of prestige, if not always in income, skilled blue-collar workers generally ranked higher than low-level white-collar employees, contrary to the usual west European pattern. New educational opportunities gave working-class children possibilities their parents could not have dreamed of for themselves. In 1961 in Poland, 42 percent of blue-collar workers enjoyed a higher social position than their parents had. Eastern Europe was probably more egalitarian than the West from a blue-collar point of view.

However, workers in eastern Europe bore the burdens of one-party states and restricted economies focused strongly on heavy industry. Consumer goods were often scarce and store lines long. Because the state prohibited independent unions and the right to strike, workers had no independent outlets for protest. High rates of drinking, absenteeism, theft on the job, and deliberate efforts to slow down the work pace suggested that workers had plenty of grievances and serious problems with motivation. There was little indication that factory labor itself was either more or less pleasant under communism than under capitalism. What was clear was that off-the-job compensations lagged behind, on the whole, in eastern Europe. To be sure, workers sometimes found ways to give expression to their aspirations. When construction workers in Berlin went on strike in 1953 they triggered a wave of strikes and riots throughout the country. Polish and Hungarian workers played an

Prague, 1968. When the communist head of government, Alexander Dubcek, gave the people of Czechoslovakia a chance to experiment with decentralized decisionmaking, workers' councils, and free debate, the Soviet Union moved a half-million soldiers and thousands of tanks into the country. Czechoslovakians resorted to passive resistance on a massive scale to no avail. Communist regimes remained in power in eastern Europe another two decades. (*Josef Koudelka/ Magnum Photos, Inc.*)

important role in a chain of protests that eventually led to the failed Hungarian revolution of 1956. Czech workers, taking advantage of a liberal atmosphere during the Prague Spring of 1968, eagerly participated in new factory councils, only to have their hopes crushed by Soviet tanks. A Polish uprising in 1970 against price hikes and food shortages began with worker protests in the Lenin shipyards of Gdansk and riots in the country's Baltic ports. Labor protest over prices erupted again in Poland in 1976, over food shortages in Romania in 1977, and over job security in Hungary in 1980. Strikes and riots even broke out in the Ukrainian region of the Soviet Union in 1972, a scantily reported episode that brought strikers and rioters severe sentences. Workers would also play a crucial role in the political upheaval that transformed eastern Europe in the late 1980s.

The pressures workers placed on their regimes in the Eastern bloc during the 1970s, combined with some expressions of discontent in the intelligentsia and managerial class, fed expectations similar to those that had ultimately helped produce the consumer society in western Europe. East Europeans could not help but compare their lot with the higher living standards of the West. Television and radio broadcasts in the border areas of the West, if nothing else, made the differences patently clear. Young people in the East became enamored with Western fashions, from blue jeans to rock music, insofar as they could learn about them. Styles of dress, dance, and music that were popular among Western youth had a devoted Eastern audience, despite officials' denunciations of bourgeois decadence. And whereas workers and their families were by no means the only group pushing governments in the East to respond to consumer dissatisfaction, it is not surprising that they played a central role. When western Europe went through its comparable period of rapid industrial development in the nineteenth and early twentieth centuries, urban workers also had figured prominently in the politics of popular protest.

Gender Relations and the Family

Along with change in the major social classes of Europe, family life and gender relations altered greatly in the course of the postwar decades. Older patterns by no means disappeared. Women still found themselves trapped in longstanding forms of subordination to men. The family, while under stress from a number of directions, remained the fundamental institutional bridge between individuals and the larger society. Yet, by the 1980s, women had done a great deal to challenge, and in some respects diminish, traditional gender inequalities, and family life had changed in important ways.

New Roles for Women

The most pervasive force for change in gender relations was the entry of women into the work force. World War II brought women into factory jobs and clerical positions, just as the previous world war had done. After a few years of decline in female employment after 1945, the upward trends continued. From the early 1950s on, the number of working women rose steadily in western and eastern Europe, just as it did in the United States. What was especially striking about this movement into the work force was the rise in the employment of married women. By 1980 about 42 percent of married women had paid employment in West Germany, up from 25 percent in 1950. In 1979 the proportion rose to 60 percent in Britain and to 64 percent in Sweden. The highest levels of female employment were found in eastern Europe, where a socialist commitment to employment opportunity and a chronic shortage of labor in the industrial and service sectors pushed female employment up to 90 percent.

Several factors contributed to the rise in women's employment in western Europe. Earlier educational gains by women, combined with the postwar expansion of educational opportunity, qualified more women for work. Moreover, the growing number of service jobs created a need for additional workers—and women, long associated with clerical jobs and traditionally paid less than men, were deemed ideal candidates. Part-time employment also expanded for women, in part because women who were juggling family responsibilities found the option suitable, and in part because employers found it a cheap way to take advantage of an underunionized segment of the work force. Improvements in public child care and the curtailment of childbearing in an age of declining family size also gave married women more freedom to enter the labor force. Many women took jobs as a means of adding to personal or family income; others sought employment as a means of personal fulfillment in a society that associated worth with work and earnings.

This fundamental trend in women's employment was not, to be sure, a full stride to job equality. Women's pay continued to lag behind men's. In Britain pay inequities actually widened for awhile in the 1970s when women in manufacturing earned only 57 percent of what men earned, down from 62 percent in the 1960s. As late as 1982 women's gross hourly wages in industry in West Germany were still only 73 percent of men's. Throughout western Europe most women who worked were concentrated in clerical jobs, rather than spread through the occupational spectrum on a par with men, despite a growing minority of middle-class women who were entering the professional and management ranks. In eastern Europe women were encouraged more than in the West to take manual jobs, so it was easier in the East for women to enter apprenticeships in the trades and to find their way into professional and managerial careers. In the Soviet Union women came to dominate the medical field by the mid-1970s, by which point three-fourths of the country's doctors were women. Still, these achievements in eastern Europe should not be exaggerated. Medical work commanded less prestige in the Soviet Union than in the West, and the general pattern in the East was to relegate the most poorly paid jobs and the vast majority of clerical work to women. Still, in both regions in Europe, the postwar era brought a profound shift away from the longstanding tendency in industrialization to keep married women isolated in the family and outside the labor force.

Other new rights for women accompanied the shift in employment patterns. Women finally secured the right to vote in France in 1945. By 1970 Switzerland was the only European democracy to refuse women the franchise at the national level. By the 1980s it was no longer uncommon for women to compete for positions in political parties and to run for political office, though European parliaments and high government posts remained overwhelming male domains. In 1983 only about 10 percent of the members of the German Bundestag were women. Women also took increasing advantage of higher education. By the 1980s the proportion of university students who were women had risen to 40 percent in West Germany and 46 percent in France, up sharply from an overall west European average of 22 percent in 1950. Engineering, science, and management training, however, remained heavily male. Only 10 percent of the students in the elite French engineering school, the Ecole Polytechnique, were women. Women did win some legal gains in the 1970s. Divorce laws were liberalized so that divorce by mutual consent became easier and women had a better chance than before to win equitable property settlements. Abortion was legalized, even in Catholic Italy and France, which had lagged behind Britain and Scandinavia in this respect. Reproductive rights made an enormous difference in France, where as late as the 1960s perhaps as many as twenty thousand women were dying each year from clandestine abortions.

In addition, women achieved a greater degree of sexual freedom after the 1950s. The development of new birth-control methods, such as the contraceptive pill introduced in 1960, plus greater knowledge and acceptance of birth control, decreased unwanted pregnancies. Sex and procreation became increasingly separate considerations. Even in the 1950s advertising had become more sexually explicit, pornography more widespread, and male promiscuity more openly accepted in European culture. By the late 1960s and 1970s female promiscuity became more accepted as well, as young women more frequently called into question the traditional double standard. For a time, rates of illegitimate births rose as a result of greater sexual freedom. But as young people gained more access to contraception, unintended pregnancies declined, in contrast to patterns in the United States. Europeans generally accepted the new sexual freedom, which marked an especially important change for unmarried women. Although women continued to differ from men in sexual outlook and behavior—over twice as many women as men, for example, hoped to link sex, marriage, and romantic love, according to polls in the 1960s—more women than before tended to define sex in terms of pleasure. Taboos against sex before marriage largely fell by the wayside as young people in their twenties very frequently chose to live in free union outside of marriage. Polls in West Germany in the 1980s suggested that about 40 percent of couples between the ages of eighteen and thirty-five lived in this way. Homosexuality among both women and men, though still stigmatized, became more readily tolerated in western Europe in the 1970s and 1980s.

The various changes in the status of women had an obvious impact on the family. With women working and contributing to the family income, they often acquired more power to make family decisions. Legal rights empowered women as well. Greater equality between man and woman in the family could create tension, but it could also enhance the sense of companionship in husband–wife relations. The man who claimed to be boss became viewed as an anachronism. In reality genuine equality rarely reigned in the more egalitarian family, even in the 1980s. Working women still usually bore more of the responsibility for childrearing, household chores, and family management, despite greater efforts by men to share the tasks. But even as early as the 1960s some observers argued that the contemporary European family had evolved into a new type, different both from the preindustrial and the industrial model: In this "symmetrical family" both spouses worked outside the home and contributed income, and both shared power and consumer satisfaction as earnings were pooled for joint decisions about what to buy and what to do for vacation.

Innovations in the Family

Family life in the postwar era evolved in new directions in response to a variety of crosscurrents. The emergence of the consumer society diminished family functions. As children spent more time in school and, from the 1950s on, ever-greater amounts of time in front of the television, the role of parents as agents of their children's socialization in some ways declined. Moreover, the family became small, a continuation of earlier trends. Once the postwar baby boom ended in the early 1960s, a rapid decline in the birthrate ensued. By the 1970s some countries, led by West Germany, had such a low birthrate that, were the trend to continue, by the twenty-first century they would not be able to avoid absolute population decline except through impressive rates of immigration. The tendency for greater numbers of married women to work and pursue careers, combined with the desire to use income to satisfy higher standards of consumption, reinforced the long-term trend to reduce family size, particularly in the middle class where birthrates were lowest. Young children, moreover, were sent in increasing numbers, often at an early age, to day-care centers, one of the amenities of the European welfare state deemed particularly essential as new fears surfaced about population decline. Child-care facilities and preschool education were sometimes of quite high quality—the French system, for example, paid teachers and care providers handsomely by American standards in the 1980s—but here again this innovation marked a shift of functions away from the family.

Some observers even worried that European society, and family life, were becoming indifferent to children. In Germany a new word, *Kinderfeindlichheit*, was coined to describe hostility to children and parental responsibilities. It was suggestive that the leading resort club founded in postwar Europe, Club Med, focused on single people and couples, not on families with children, although facilities for the latter were eventually developed; in contrast, the American resort chain, the Disney complex, was oriented toward the family holiday from the start. It was certainly true that children were built less solidly into the European definition of family success than had previously been the case, and less solidly than was true in the United States.

Yet, at the same time, the postwar European family tended to become more nurturant and less authoritarian. In this respect the middle class led the way. Middle-class families relaxed their discipline of children. Fathers became less severe and remote and were more inclined to play with children and take an active role in their care. This trend was already evident by the 1950s and 1960s; it had accelerated by the 1980s when men with working spouses became more responsive to the notion that both parents should share heavily in childrearing. The French remarked on *le nouveau père*, or the new father. In several countries, most notably Sweden, fathers acquired legal rights to paternity leaves, as working mothers had for maternity leaves, to care for newborns. The middle class eased its rigorous toilet training of young children. Teenagers were allowed as never before to socialize with people of their own age and enjoy a specific youth culture in terms of fashion, music, dance, and other forms of mass entertainment. Whereas greater autonomy for teenagers sometimes created new tensions within the family over matters of politics, sex, and drug abuse, many observers argued that parent–adolescent relations improved on the whole in the postwar era. The European middle-class family remained more disciplined than its American counterpart, partly because more crowded housing required stricter regulation and more parent–child contact. But the authoritarian middle-class family, never entirely a reality, became a rarity.

The working-class family evolved along the same lines, though more slowly. As in the middle class, the family became more important after World War II as a recreational unit in the working class and as a haven for personal growth. Although some workers still complained that they came home from the job too exhausted to behave decently to their families, more viewed the family as their main focus in life: "That's my life, wife and children."[2] This was not an entirely new sentiment, but it was one that workers had increasing time and money to develop. By the 1960s workers were spending more time at home — taking up hobbies, making home improvements, watching television — and less time in the bar or café. Mothers and fathers alike tried to express greater affection for their children. Working-class children were still subjected to greater discipline than their counterparts in the middle class, if only because their parents had less free time and patience to coddle them. Toilet training, for example, occurred at a younger age. Cramped housing, more limited facilities, and the fact that the working-class family was still larger on average than in the middle class accounted in large part for this difference. But the working-class family became child-centered to a greater degree than before. And this trend, while beneficial to children, had its ambiguities as well. Many teenaged sons, while acknowledging how different their affectionate fathers were from their fathers' fathers, felt a new kind of burden: It might be harder to free oneself from a loving parent than from a taskmaster.

Family relations outside the nuclear unit also remained intense in the postwar era, although the trend toward separate residences for the elderly, launched in the 1920s, continued. In contrast to the United States, where greater physical mobility across the great distances of the continent tended to weaken ties between siblings, cousins, and grandparents, in Europe the bonds were easier to preserve. Working mothers in both the middle and working classes depended heavily on grandparents to care for children. The automobile and greater leisure time allowed families to see even distant grandparents and other relatives with some frequency. Social insurance and other supports from the welfare state, while by no means eliminating all the economic burdens of old age, did ease some of the tensions that had long prevailed in the relations between the adult generations.

Family stability and rising expectations for the quality of emotional life within the family also opened new cracks. The European divorce rate soared after World War II, then declined and stabilized, though at a higher rate than before the war. Divorce rates remained well under American levels, particularly in the 1950s, suggesting greater familial stability and even conservatism. But with women in greater numbers entering the work force and making a living, and with new legal freedoms for women, divorce became a more attractive option than it had

2 Ferdynand Zweig, *The Worker in an Affluent Society* (New York, 1963), p. 194.

been before for men and women alike. In 1961 about 9 percent of all British marriages ended in divorce; by the late 1970s a third of all British marriages would end that way. Countries with a Catholic background had patterns of greater marital stability, but even there the rate inched upward. Large demographic trends played a role here as well. With urban growth and the decline of the peasantry, the strict community enforcement of traditional marital norms gave way to greater individualism. As had occurred in the United States earlier, so too in Europe a rising divorce rate had its own momentum: As divorce became more common, the stigma associated with it declined.

Aside from divorce, though, the family remained a focus of contradictory expectations. Polls taken of German women in the 1960s indicated that a solid majority believed that mothers with children under twelve should stay home, even though a solid majority of such mothers were working. By the 1980s the working mother had become both more common and more accepted, but the stresses of negotiating the competing demands of work and family had scarcely diminished. Men, too, though rarely full partners in handling family pressures, increasingly felt similar strains. Continuing gaps between ideals and practice suggested that the family, like the gender roles that were being played out in it, remained in a state of dynamic transition toward directions that were far from clear.

The New Feminism

A new surge of feminist protest in the postwar era gave expression to the aspirations and frustrations that women felt as they challenged established norms. Although employment opportunities expanded for women, pay inequities endured as did barriers to promotion and positions of power. Divorce too often led to impoverishment for women struggling to combine work and child care without sufficient institutional support. In the 1960s even left-wing organizations devoted to improving conditions for workers and the poor frequently seemed impervious to the burdens women were systematically forced to bear. And even apart from specific material injustices, many women sought supporting values and organizations to help them define new identities less tied to the domestic roles and accommodating images of previous decades.

The new feminism had important roots in World War II, when wartime economic mobilization, military service, and the creation of resistance movements enabled many women to play a more active role in the work force and in local political life than they had played before. Peace and postwar reconstruction brought a resurgence of pressure to conform to the domestic ideal—to children, family, and the home— which many women were willing to do. But beneath the surface of domestic conformity some women, or their daughters a decade or two later, became receptive to feminist ideas challenging the legal, institutional, and cultural practices that reinforced the subordination of women. The new feminism began to take shape in 1949 when the French intellectual Simone de Beauvoir published *The Second Sex*. Echoed in the 1950s and 1960s by other works, especially in the United States, a new wave of women's rights agitation arose after three decades of relative calm. Just as the feminism of the late nineteenth and early twentieth centuries had done before, the new movement sought specific legal gains for women, especially in education, the workplace, and reproductive rights. The new feminism differed from its predecessor, however, in more frankly confronting the image of female domesticity that had gained such force in industrializing societies in the nineteenth century. Feminists in the early twentieth century, for example, had often argued that women deserved the vote because they were more moral, peaceful, and nurturant than men. In contrast, the new feminism insisted on equality as a right in itself, and called into question the very legitimacy of traditionally conceived masculine and feminine norms that served to reinforce gender inequality.

By the 1980s it was obvious that the new feminism had an important impact on European society. To be sure, feminist leaders and thinkers did not win support from many women, even in the middle class where the movement had its most responsive audience. Nor did feminism by itself produce some of the most sweeping social changes that were altering gender relations, such as the growth of female employment. But feminism certainly reinforced these trends, and it was crucial in influencing the way women and men came to understand the new role women were coming to play in public life. Feminism also had a political impact, as European governments felt increasing pressure to address issues of economic equity, abortion, child care, and gender discrimination that previously had been absent from the political agenda. Feminism had an impact too in shaping the way men and women reconsidered their own roles in the family. In a real sense, later twentieth-century feminism seemed to respond to the same desire for individuality and work identity in women that men had aspired to earlier as part of the new mentality suitable for a commercialized economy. But postwar feminism was more than just an effort to give women equal life chances as men, for it also raised new questions about the relationship between men and women, public and private, work and family, that few Europeans had faced squarely before. Finally, the new feminism placed some women more solidly in the ranks of social protest than had been the case since the Industrial Revolution began. Earlier feminism had partially compensated for male dominance in work-based protest, but it had been overshadowed by the great class struggles of the late nineteenth and early twentieth centuries. By the 1970s, with working-class protest somewhat muted in comparison to the past, the feminist voice sounded loudly.

New Forms of Protest

Alongside feminism, a variety of other movements emerged in western Europe to challenge established values, especially from the late 1960s on. To be sure, popular protest took place in the 1950s and early 1960s, but it was relatively moderate in scope and conventional in its objectives. Trade unions periodically mounted large (and usually short) strikes to win concessions from business and governments. Left-wing parties, especially the communist parties of Italy and France, led demonstrations against the American military presence in Europe, notably in the early 1950s, but they did not press too far against the existing system. A small but visible movement against nuclear weapons captured attention as well. However, none of these forms of protest did much to disturb a western Europe remarkable for its political stability and for its rapid economic recovery from the ravages of World War II.

By the late 1960s new forms of protest began to challenge mainstream political and cultural values that had flourished in the early postwar era. They also challenged the protest currents that had dominated mature industrial society, and in so doing implicitly demonstrated how dramatically social conditions had changed since 1945. Student movements called into question the structure of authority and the very materialism of advanced industrial societies. Feminism, as we have seen, rejected conventional assumptions about gender. By the late 1970s an environmentalist movement gathered considerable strength in several countries, as did a surprising new wave of regional and ethnic activism, which disputed the authority of central governments and in some cases even longstanding assumptions about the immutability of existing nation-states. Racial and ethnic conflict also gave rise to riots, racial attacks, antiracist demonstrations, and divisive debate over citizenship rights and immigration, especially in the 1980s. None of these developments led to the kind of general political crisis that toppled regimes in the interwar years. But collectively they fed and reflected serious, ongoing tensions in societies that optimists in the early 1960s had erroneously predicted had settled into a long social peace.

Student Protest and a New Radicalism

The first major stride into a new form of protest politics came with the youth rebellions of the late 1960s. The spread of youth protest—primarily among secondary school and university students—was almost

a global phenomenon. Young people in the Americas, Africa, and eastern and western Europe questioned the authority of adults, from parents
and teachers to national elites. In an era of rapid change, young people
may have come to believe that elders had less to teach them. International issues played a role as well, as students in many countries rallied
to the idea of opposing imperialism, and especially the American war
against communist rebels and their allies in Vietnam. In western
Europe issues closer to home were important too. Despite the economic
boom of the 1950s and 1960s, western Europe still had plenty of poverty
and economic inequality to jar the social conscience of middle-class students. Educational conditions, moreover, created discontent. Students
in the late 1960s faced crowded schools and classrooms, as the baby-
boom generation surged into outmoded facilities. The authoritarian
character of the European university, which provided little contact with
the faculty, angered students as well. Many young people feared for
their own futures, especially in crowded fields where job prospects
seemed insufficient for large flocks of graduates.

Serious student protest burst forth in a number of European centers.
In West Germany student demonstrations disrupted universities frequently from 1967 to 1971. Italian students protested with similar determination, even clashing from time to time with right-wing organizations.
British universities, where faculty–student contact was more extensive,
encountered less trouble, but students at the London School of Economics mounted an important series of protests. By far the most spectacular rebellion took place in Paris in May 1968. What began as a
skirmish between radical students and campus administrators at a suburban campus of the University of Paris escalated into classroom sit-ins
and overreactions by the police. By mid-May thousands of students had
barricaded the university quarter on the Left Bank of Paris to hold off
a police attack. Inspired by events in Paris, students elsewhere in
France seized their campuses, and more important still, young workers,
especially in technically advanced sectors such as aviation and automak-
ing, began a huge wave of factory occupations reminiscent of the giant
French strike movement of June 1936. Before the month was out ten
million employees in nearly every branch of the economy had joined in
the biggest strike in the history of France.

Student goals varied in May 1968, as they did generally in the European student movements of the period. As in any major protest movement the participants aspired to practical objectives as well as more
sweeping ideological goals. Students and many faculty members sympathetic with their cause called for thoroughgoing reforms in the university system. Students also voiced their criticisms of capitalism, big
business, imperialism, and the state bureaucracy—the usual targets of
discontent for a protest movement inspired in part by traditional left-
wing ideology. But many students went even further in their rejection

Paris, 1968. Students took to the streets in a monthlong rebellion in France that climaxed in the largest general strike in the history of the country. The upheaval was part of a worldwide pattern of youth revolt, but it also had sources in the rigidity and centralization of French institutions. *(Bruno Barbey/Magnum Photos, Inc.)*

of conventional norms; they reacted against the lures, deceptions, and shallowness of mass consumption. They attacked the materialism of the consumer society and the individualistic ethic of the middle class. And they rejected the dominant rationalism and pragmatism of Western culture. In their stead, students appealed to spontaneity and action with slogans such as "Imagination has seized power" and "Be realistic: Demand the impossible."[3] These aspirations were heartfelt—a reflection of deep-seated tensions between restraint and release in modern Euro-

[3] Alain Touraine, *The May Movement: Revolt and Reform* (New York, 1971).

pean popular culture. And this vision dovetailed to some extent with calls for "autogestion" or worker self-management, which galvanized much of the strike movement in May. Just as students struck out against a faceless, impersonal educational bureaucracy producing trained graduates like so many widgets, so too were many blue- and white-collar employees eager to voice their concerns about job routinization, blocked advancement, and a sense of powerlessness at the workplace.

The government of Charles de Gaulle, initially caught by surprise by the magnitude of the rebellion, found ways to dissipate the movement. The alliance between students and workers was fragile from the beginning. Many union leaders and most communist party politicians had no sympathy for the anticonsumerist radicalism (and the middle-class backgrounds) of university rebels who indeed viewed traditional left-wing organizations as part of the problem with contemporary society. Workers and students in fact had little common experience to build on. De Gaulle's government offered workers a handsome pay hike and other practical concessions. Elections in June, moreover, gave de Gaulle the chance to rally a solid majority, as frightened voters, including many communists, sought to preserve their postwar gains against the disruption of a month of economic paralysis and against the vague and uncongenial aspirations of student radicalism. Having failed to establish meaningful ties to workers, and having failed to develop a sophisticated political organization that would have violated the very spontaneity and antibureaucratic principles of their own movement, students had nothing to match de Gaulle's political machine. By the end of June the revolt was over.

Student protest, in France as elsewhere, nonetheless had a number of durable effects. Consumer society was exposed as a vulnerable social construct, a product of values and assumptions open to question rather than a natural, inevitable development. University life underwent a quiet revolution in the 1970s. Governments took student grievances seriously and began to give students and young faculty members greater voice over university affairs. In France in particular, the upheaval of May 1968 inspired people in many walks of life to make the institutions in their lives more participatory and less rigidly bureaucratic. The official trade unions and political parties of the Left, though often criticized by student radicals, generally benefited from the movement as young people turned to these organizations in the 1970s as channels for protest. A few student radicals went on to establish small fringe parties or even terrorist groups. In 1971 young Italian radicals created the Red Brigade, which carried out bombings and kidnappings through the 1970s. The Red Army Faction, or Baader-Meinhof Gang, gained similar notoriety in West Germany. Instead of arousing popular discontent and accelerating the breakdown of the existing order as these groups hoped, terrorism alienated people initially sympathetic to their aims. Overall, student protest did not fundamentally alter European society, but it did play an important role in reinvigorating certain left-wing parties, in widening the boundaries of political debate and cultural criticism, and in creating a greater sense of uncertainty about the future than had been the case during the early postwar "renaissance."

Student radicalism also had an impact on the popular culture of young people in the late 1970s. Rock music in the late 1960s had already given lively expression to a youthful desire to ridicule adult, middle-class, mainstream respectability. From Britain the Beatles brought an authentic working-class touch in their scoffing at authority and hierarchy, and in their preference for impulsiveness over traditional British reserve. They also expressed a good-natured desire to enjoy the pleasures of life, and in this respect they reflected, more than rejected,

London youth in the 1970s. Punk styles flourished in Britain in the 1970s and spread abroad. As a repudiation of conventional dress and hairstyle, punk was more a generational than a class phenomenon, but it often had strong appeal for working- and lower middle-class youths who harbored deep resentments toward mainstream society. (*Alon Reininger, Woodfin Camp and Associates.*)

the consumption ethic of the postwar era. Celebrations of sexuality also linked such music with larger social trends. By the early 1970s political radicalism often found its way into the song lyrics, cinema, and literature being absorbed into the popular culture and the academic culture of university students. Even apart from politics, rock music sometimes turned to themes of despair in ways that suggested the alienation of some youth from the wider culture. By the late 1970s middle-class conventionality had come under attack from a wide variety of cultural directions—in the searing critique of bourgeois society in the New German Cinema, in the popularity of radical thinkers such as Michel Foucault and Roland Barthe in France, and in the shocking colors and cuts of the "punk" movement in Britain. During the 1980s much of this radical irreverence lost its appeal with young people, in part because economic difficulties encouraged middle- and working-class youth to focus instead on how to launch their lives in troubled waters. Even so, the cultural radicalism of the 1970s, like the student movements often associated with it, left an enduring mark on European society.

Environmentalism, the Peace Movement, and the "Greens"

The new radicalism of the late 1960s also contributed to a growing awareness of the environmental damage industrial growth was leaving in its wake. The environmentalist movement in western Europe, as in the United States, drew strength from a number of sources. Some student radicals channeled their disdain for consumerism and corporate capitalism into new campaigns against water and air pollution, airport expansion, and nuclear power. New knowledge about the harmful effects of pesticides, pollutants, and toxic waste, and greater understanding of the fragility of the earth's ecological balance, gradually made the public more aware of environmental hazards. A few major ecological disasters had an effect as well. Between 1967 and 1980 the northwestern coast of France suffered from six large oil spills and tanker accidents, the worst of which, the wreck of the *Amoco Cadiz* in 1978, washed nearly a quarter of a million gallons of crude oil onto Breton shores. The following year the nuclear accident at Three-Mile Island in Pennsylvania, though a long way away, had a chilling effect on Europeans and gave further impetus to a growing protest movement against nuclear power. The nightmare of nuclear contamination became a European reality in 1986, when a Soviet power plant at Chernobyl exploded, sending a cloud of radioactive dust adrift over northern and central Europe. Acid rain also became an urgent concern. In 1984 the West German government issued a report that admitted sulphur dioxide and nitrogen oxide, largely from coal-burning power plants and automobile emissions, had damaged 50 percent of the country's forests. By the end of the 1980s environmentalism had entered the mainstream of European political life. Every political party felt the need to address popular concerns about the medical and ecological consequences of industrial production and mass consumption.

The environmentalist movement had an important impact on government action. By the 1980s every country in western Europe had taken some steps to improve air and water quality, and the growth of nuclear power was sharply curtailed. After the oil shock of 1974 several European governments had stepped up their efforts to build nuclear plants in hopes of diminishing dependence on foreign oil. But by the late 1970s popular protest against the building of new nuclear facilities forced the West German government virtually to halt new construction. In 1978 a referendum in Austria put a stop to nuclear power altogether. A similar referendum in 1980 led the Swedish government to cut back its nuclear program as well. France, in contrast, stuck with nuclear power in the 1980s. The French communist party had always supported the nuclear program, and even the more environmentally oriented socialist party, when it came to power in 1981, was reluctant to stop the program since nuclear power had long been associated with the country's military independence and its postwar accomplishments in high technology.

Concern for nuclear safety also spilled over into another wave of protest that gained considerable momentum during the first half of the 1980s — the European peace movement. In 1979 NATO foreign and defense ministers adopted a policy of modernizing the nuclear arsenal of the Western Alliance by stationing 572 American medium-range nuclear missiles in western Europe from 1983 onward. American and western European leaders made this decision partly in keeping with the evolution of NATO policy, which was to see Europe as the stage for a possible "limited" nuclear war, and partly in response to the Soviet deployment of similar weapons in the late 1970s. The decision to deploy American Pershing IIs and cruise missiles in Europe came at a time of renewed cold war tensions. The Soviet invasion of Afghanistan, troubles in Poland, superpower rivalry in Central America, and a major American military buildup under President Ronald Reagan destroyed whatever goodwill had remained in East–West relations from an era of détente in the 1970s. This shift in the international climate renewed European fears of a nuclear war on European soil, and it was in this context that people in several countries joined by the hundreds of thousands in marches and demonstrations between 1980 and 1986 to protest the deployment of American missiles.

The peace movement drew supporters from a variety of social groups and it flourished more in some countries than others. It was relatively weak in Italy and virtually lifeless in France, which as a non-

NATO power did not face the prospect of American missile deploy-ment. In Britain, however, the Campaign for Nuclear Disarmament (CND) had a wide following, including support from the clergy and church groups and a sizeable wing of the Labour party. When the United States began deploying cruise missiles at Greenham Common, outside of London, the CND besieged the site for months in continuous protest. In the Netherlands polls in 1985 showed that a majority of the Dutch people opposed the deployment of American missiles in their country. The campaign there and in neighboring Belgium, which in both countries cut across class and age strata and garnered significant support from religious groups, was strong enough to force governments to postpone deployment until the mid-1980s.

Nowhere was the movement more significant than in West Germany, and for understandable reasons. The Germans believed that in the event of war their country would become the nuclear battlefield, an ironic fate for a nation prohibited since the end of World War II from having nuclear weapons. The peace movement in West Germany at-tracted support from much the same array of social groups as in the Low Countries, but it also became a vehicle for small, vocal minorities to express sentiments peculiar to West Germany's past—resentment over America's continuing postwar military presence in the country, a revulsion against militarism, and hopes for a neutralist stance in East–West relations. The campaign in West Germany did not succeed in preventing the conservative government of Helmut Kohl from eventually approving the missile deployment. But it did have a profound effect on public opinion. Polls conducted in 1983–1984 suggested that whereas 75 percent of the West German people wanted the country to remain in NATO, 86 percent opposed the deployment of cruise and Pershing II missiles in Germany.

The movement in West Germany and elsewhere did not succeed in forcing NATO officials to reverse their policy. But it did play an im-portant role in encouraging Soviet and American officials to reach an agreement in late 1987 to dismantle the medium-range missiles that had catalyzed the peace movement a decade earlier. Soviet and Ameri-can officials found themselves competing with each other for popularity in western Europe by advocating ways to reverse the military confron-tation on the Continent.

Environmentalism, the antinuclear movement, and the peace move-ment fed on and drew sustenance from a new kind of political organi-zation that emerged in Europe during the late 1970s—the Green parties. Ecology activists, frustrated by the failure of political parties to respond to environmental issues, organized their own parties in a number of countries. Green parties, though first and foremost environmentalist in origin, quickly became more than single-issue organizations. They at-tracted support from (mostly middle-class) radicals who were interested in feminist issues, defense and foreign policy matters, and the relationship of the West to the Third World, and who were disillusioned with mainstream left-wing parties.

The notion of establishing an "antiparty party" was particularly strong in West Germany, where the Green movement thrived best in the Europe of the 1980s, in part because of the poignancy of environmental and peace issues in Germany and in part because many of the ex-student radicals of the early 1970s had been uninspired by ten years of Social Democratic rule. German Greens, in fact, entered parliamentary politics with some misgivings in the beginning, and instead put considerable stock in extra-parliamentary activity such as local citizen initiatives, rallies, sit-ins, and the creation of ecologically sound, nonprofit farms, workshops, and communal enterprises. The Green party also made an extraordinary effort to remain decentralized and grassroots-oriented. The Greens kept paid party posts to a minimum and tried to maintain the principle of a rotating leadership. Women exercised a good deal of influence in the movement. Electoral lists were drawn up on the basis of the "zipper principle," by which male and female candidates alternated down the list. As a decentralized party ambivalent about its role in parliamentary politics, the Green party had its share of internal conflicts, especially between so-called realists, willing to make compromises to establish the party as a significant force in parliamentary politics, and so-called fundamentalists, reluctant to jeopardize party principles. Still, by the mid-1980s the Green party had demonstrated its staying power, and in 1987 garnered over 8 percent of the electorate in national elections. Perhaps most important, the Green party in West Germany and other west European countries had won enough of a following to force the mainstream parties, even conservative ones, to become sensitive to environmental issues.

By the early 1990s the prospects for the Green movement remained unclear. To a degree the movement was a generational phenomenon; its core of support came from young people in their late twenties and thirties who had come of age in the era of student activism in the late 1960s and early 1970s. Younger cohorts showed signs of being more conservative, less hungry for political alternatives. In addition, the more the Greens succeeded in pushing mainstream parties into advocating environmental reform the harder it became to distinguish themselves from German Social Democrats or French Socialists or British Labour. At the same time, however, the mainstream parties could hardly claim to have come to terms with environmental problems, many of which had only grown in magnitude in the course of the decade. What was more, Green parties continued to capitalize on voter rebellions against traditional parties, as seemed to be the case in 1989 when Green parties picked up several new seats in the elections for the European Parliament. If the Green movement was too weak to produce a fundamental shift in European politics in the 1980s, it nonetheless provided the means for a significant minority of Europeans to advocate positions on environmental quality, energy policy, mass transportation, and other matters that clearly had broader appeal. And the Green movement also exposed the extent to which conventional political parties had failed to recapture the loyalty of a segment of the middle class that had abandoned them after the 1960s.

Ethnic Nationalism and Regionalism

Another form of protest that surged in western Europe with surprising force came from ethnic minorities. From the mid-1960s into the 1980s Welsh and Scottish nationalists in Britain, Bretons, Alsatians, Corsicans and Occitan nationalists in France, South Tyrolians in Italy, and Basques and Catalans in Spain fought for greater autonomy in the nation-state, and in some cases aspired to make new nations of their regions. Almost every country in western Europe encountered some form of ethnic protest, usually in areas where language minorities occupied well-defined geographical territory. Although not all of the fifty or so ethnic minority regions in western Europe became sites of regionalist or nationalist movements, enough of them did to mark the 1970s as a highwater mark for ethnic activism in postwar western Europe.

Few observers would have predicted what one scholar of ethnic nationalism later described as the "unexpected rebellion."[4] Central governments, after all, had worked hard for at least a century—and in Spain, France, and Britain for several centuries—at stamping out regional differences. Since the late nineteenth century most states in Europe had used public schooling to promote linguistic and cultural uniformity in countries that in reality were a patchwork of diverse peoples. Yet, despite the continuing process of state centralization in the course of the twentieth century, a sense of ethnic or regional distinctiveness did not wither away. World War I, which in its earliest days did so much to foster a sense of national unity, in the end served to stimulate ethnic nationalism. The heavy toll of the war sharpened tensions between some regional groups and the central state, and when many ethnic regions in eastern Europe were given the chance to create new nations in the peacemaking process after the war, some ethnic groups in the West thought they too should aspire to separate nationhood. A number of ethnic nationalist groups, such as the *Plaid Cymru* in Wales and the *Parti Autonomiste Breton* in Brittany, had their origins in the 1920s.

---

4 William Beer, *The Unexpected Rebellion: Ethnic Activism in Contemporary France* (New York, 1980).

World War II and the challenges of postwar reconstruction put a damper on ethnic movements in the 1940s and 1950s, but soon thereafter a number of conditions converged that proved to be a stimulus for ethnic activism. By the mid-1960s ethnic groups in some areas of western Europe had become acutely aware of regional economic disparities that had widened rather than narrowed during the postwar boom. The decline of coal and steel in Britain brought chronic unemployment to southern Wales. Similar distress in the heavy industry of southern Belgium made the French-speaking minority, the Walloons, more willing to press claims on the Flemish majority. In France the continuing economic underdevelopment of the west and southwest fed a sense of grievance in Brittany and in the towns and villages of Languedoc, where Occitan activists tried to create a following. The Scottish highlands continued to suffer from a longstanding pattern of economic stagnation that seemed to grate all the more when parts of southern England were blooming in postwar prosperity. When North Sea oil was discovered in the early 1970s, the Scottish Nationalist party won substantial support by claiming it was Scotland's oil. Not every case of ethnic nationalism arose in economically disadvantaged regions; the Basques and the Catalans lived in the most industrialized and dynamic areas of Spain. But most of these movements, and to some extent even the Basques and Catalans, argued that the central state was depriving their regions of their economic due.

Cultural and political developments in the 1960s and 1970s also played a role in stimulating these movements. Ethnic nationalists became all the more invested in preserving their linguistic traditions when radio, television, supermarkets, multinational corporations, and mass marketing seemed to conspire in blotting out provincial distinctiveness. At the same time, decolonization and the proliferation of nationalist movements in the Third World served as sources of inspiration to some ethnic radicals inclined to see their regions as internal colonies. As more and more middle-class Breton, Welsh, and Basque young people became university educated in the postwar era, a kind of ethnic intelligentsia grew in size that played an important role in promoting the language and cultural heritage of their regions. Many of these people also built new political organizations, or reinvigorated old ones, which advocated either a regionalist strategy of greater political autonomy within the nation or a nationalist strategy of separation altogether. Some of these ethnic activists also drew inspiration from the new student radicalism of the late 1960s, which, after all, had also questioned the authority of the central state and extolled the virtues of decentralization and citizen action. Although regionalist organizations varied a great deal in political ideology, in general they leaned to the Left in the 1970s and found left-wing parties sympathetic to their aspirations. Environmentalists and regionalists also had occasion to join forces, as was the case in the mid-

1970s when sheep farmers, Occitan regionalists, and ecologists spent years fighting off the efforts of the French army to create a tank-firing range on the Larzac plateau in southern France. In 1980 a similar alliance of Breton nationalists, local villagers, and ecologists from several countries battled police on and off for six weeks in the village of Plogoff to protest the building of a nuclear plant. Ethnic regionalism and nationalism, in short, while having deep roots in the past, flourished in the context of other forms of protest that had emerged in the 1960s.

Ethnic movements, though sharing similar circumstances, differed

After an IRA bomb explosion in Belfast, Northern Ireland, 1972. Centuries-old conflict between Catholics and Protestants in Northern Ireland erupted in the early 1970s and made the region a continuous battleground thereafter. The troubles there had deep roots but they also were part of a western European-wide resurgence of protest in the 1970s by ethnic and regional minorities who sought greater power in or autonomy from the central state. *(Abbas/Magnum Photos, Inc.)*

from one another in important ways. Welsh nationalists were less concerned with establishing political autonomy from London than with reviving the Welsh language and a sense of regional identity. Scottish
nationalists had no linguistic issues at stake but aimed at economic,
administrative, and potentially even full political independence from
England. The Catalan movement in Spain, in its moderate, even patient,
approach to regionalism, contrasted sharply with the more militant
Basque movement, especially the clandestine organization *Euskadi Ta
Azkatasum* (ETA or Basqueland and Liberty), which after 1967 resorted
to kidnappings, bombings, sabotage, and the assassination of dozens of
government officials in the name of the nationalist cause. In France
Corsican activists also used violence, though not nearly to the same
degree as the ETA. Breton nationalists set off a bomb at the Palace of
Versailles. None of the movements, however, came close to producing
the kind of violent and unrelenting conflict that emerged in Northern
Ireland, where longstanding antagonism between a Protestant majority
and a Catholic minority degenerated into something bordering on permanent civil war. In the late 1960s a nonviolent civil rights movement
by Catholics gave way to violence, the revival of the radical Irish Republican Army, the rise of Protestant paramilitary organizations, and,
by the early 1970s, a British military occupation of the region. Nearly
twenty years later little progress had been made. Terrorism continued
through the 1980s, as did recalcitrance on both sides.

Northern Ireland aside, most ethnic movements in western Europe
could claim some positive achievements by the early 1980s. In 1979 the
Spanish government introduced a sweeping decentralization plan that
granted considerable legal and administrative autonomy to the country's
regions. To placate Welsh nationalists, the British government sanc-
tioned the creation of Welsh-language schools, and by 1984 the region
could boast of 344 of them at the primary level and 36 at the secondary level. A Welsh-language television station was created as well. For
the first time since statistics on such matters had been kept, the number
of Welsh children who could speak Welsh actually began to rise in
the 1980s. Meanwhile in France the socialist government of François
Mitterrand expanded the teaching of minority languages, enforced the
use of these languages in official dealings, and sponsored television and
radio programs on ethnic themes as well as ethnic festivals and projects
in ethnomusicology. A government plan to decentralize decision making,
though not on the scale of the Spanish model, did give ethnic regions
a bit more autonomy. While most of these efforts still fell short of what
many regionalists had envisioned as political autonomy, there was no
denying that the movements of the 1970s had had an effect.

By the mid-1980s the tide of ethnic nationalism activism had ebbed.
Government concessions to a modest degree of regional autonomy and
government support for cultural and linguistic programs dissipated

much of the militance in these movements. Hard-core nationalists remained unsatisfied but they represented only a minority view. Plaid Cymru, the Welsh nationalist party, saw its electoral support in Wales dwindle to 8 percent in 1983, and the Scottish National party garnered only about 12 percent of the Scottish parliamentary vote in the same year after having had 30 percent in 1974. Regionalist sentiment by no means disappeared in Wales and Scotland, but it lost much of its sting; more and more voters chose the British Labour party, which had become more responsive to regional issues, as the guardian of regional interests. Similarly, with the exception of the Corsican movement, regionalism in France peaked in the 1970s. Even Basque nationalism declined in Spain, where the new autonomy statute cut public support for the separatist cause. The ETA continued its terrorist tactics through the 1980s, but it lost much of the sympathetic hearing it had once enjoyed among Basques.

If militant movements declined, however, popular support for partial regional autonomy, ethnic cultural revival, and linguistic survival remained strong. Just as the Greens lost some of their steam in the 1980s as mainstream parties took up the cause of environmentalism, so too the ethnic movements of the 1970s paid a price for seeing conventional parties incorporate regional aspirations into their programs. Of course, no one could say what the long-term prospects really were for sustaining cultural and linguistic distinctiveness in the many regions in the face of the undeniably powerful pressures of national and even international cultural integration in Europe. Nor was it clear in the 1980s what tighter economic and political integration of western Europe through the agency of the European Community (EC) would mean for the regionalist cause. The rising power of supranational institutions in the EC could isolate Bretons, Welsh, and Catalans forced to swim in a much enlarged (European) sea. But many ethnic and regional activists welcomed the newfound momentum behind European integration that emerged in the late 1980s. A strong Europe, they argued, could further weaken the grip of central governments, and it might lead to a new kind of European federalism in which regions would play a larger role than before. There were signs, too, that many EC bureaucrats and planners in Brussels and Strasbourg were eager to establish stronger ties with regional authorities and regional elites. Not surprisingly, in the late 1980s many regional activists set their sights on securing representation in the increasingly important European Parliament.

Ethnic nationalism in the broadest sense, then, by no means faded from view. Even after the major movements declined in the 1980s most observers were left with a continuing appreciation for the durability of ethnic and regional identities, once thought to be mere historical vestiges doomed to rapid decline. Today the nation-state indeed remains the most powerful political structure in Europe, as in the world at large, and nations still command the loyalty of the vast majority of their citizens.

But loyalties have remained complex in Europe. Not only did ethnic and regional identities revive unexpectedly in the postwar era; the notion of a Europeanwide identity also gained currency, especially among young people in smaller countries and in West Germany, where nationalism fell into disrepute after Hitler. Whether people defined themselves first by region, nation, or as Europeans varied enormously depending on peoples' region, their social class, and their own individual predilections. By the end of the 1980s one thing was clear: ethnicity, a distinctive language tradition, and regional loyalty remained important to many west Europeans, and this reality could continue to have unpredictable cultural and political consequences.

The new forms of protest that surfaced from the 1960s through the 1980s—feminism, student radicalism, environmentalism, and ethnic nationalism—did not produce a fundamental break in the political order or social organization of postwar Europe. Nor did they congeal, despite the efforts of Green parties to draw together the themes of several movements, into a single, comprehensive effort at change in the economic order. Because of their novelty and diversity it was not easy to characterize the new protest currents in simple terms. Even their prospects for durability remained unclear. Taken as a whole, however, they did share a few common features. The new protest movements drew heavily from the diverse and expanding middle class, in contrast to the worker-dominated protest movements of the mature industrial era. These new movements, moreover, while not at all reactionary in the conservative sense, did seek to modify long-term trends in industrial society—consumerism, environmental despoliation, political centralization. Feminism attacked not only longstanding gender arrangements but also the newer gendered divisions of labor and family strategies that had emerged with industrial capitalism. In fighting for new values and policies to govern the relationship between women and men, nature and society, state and region, these movements all sought to redefine fundamental features of the advanced industrial order. So too did one other new form of protest—activism by, and against, immigrants of non-European origin—which became increasingly important after the 1960s and brought to the fore basic issues of cultural pluralism.

Immigrant Rights, Racism, and the New Ethnic Minorities

The immigration of peoples from Africa, Asia, and the Caribbean into western Europe led to new ethnic conflicts potentially more explosive than those that had pitted Europe's old, indigenous ethnic groups against the central state. Although the flow of newcomers slowed after

Postwar immigration. Economic expansion in western Europe fueled the migration of workers from Africa and the Middle East. In the 1960s most immigrants were men looking for work. By the 1970s women and children had become an important part of this demographic movement. These North Africans, arriving in Marseille in 1974, are having their papers checked by French immigration inspectors. *(UPI/Bettmann Archive.)*

the early 1970s due to economic hard times and government restrictions on immigration, it continued nonetheless. More important, a second generation of immigrant children, many of them born in western Europe, were coming of age with desires for the rights and opportunities of European citizens. Too often, however, they faced the prospects of poverty, underemployment, discrimination, police harassment, and inadequate housing and schooling. By the 1980s the newcomers and their offspring—a host of different peoples and cultures, but especially North Africans in France, Turks in West Germany, and West Indians and Pakistanis in Britain—were no longer immigrants on temporary stay; they had become the new ethnic minorities of Europe, and they had become more capable of defining and defending their collective aspirations. By the same token, xenophobic, anti-immigrant movements on the far Right had emerged as well, and in some countries gained significant electoral support. In the 1980s ethnic, racial, and religious conflict surfaced in western Europe as a major source of tension.

Citizenship rights and public policy toward the new ethnic minorities became central issues in political debate.

Anti-immigrant movements on the Right derived some of their strength from the effects of economic turmoil in the 1970s and 1980s. As unemployment rates rose, leaders of the National Front in Britain, which flourished in the 1970s, and of Jean-Marie Le Pen's National Front in France, which took off in the 1980s, argued that immigrants were hoarding jobs that the native unemployed really deserved. A variety of far right-wing parties in West Germany made the same point: "Two million foreign workers equals two million German unemployed, so send them all home!"[5] Immigrants were also portrayed as a drain on the overburdened welfare state. Most immigrants in fact worked as janitors, street sweepers, nurses aides, and maids doing menial, poorly paid jobs that native Swiss, French, and German citizens had long since forsaken. But in an age of painful economic restructuring and chronic unemployment, the simplistic image of immigrants stealing jobs had a certain force.

Anti-immigrant parties also drew on a reservoir of racial fears and cultural prejudices that had a long history in Europe. Since the nineteenth century European political and intellectual leaders had justified colonial expansion and foreign aggression by promoting notions of racial, religious, or national superiority—the "white man's burden" in Britain, the "civilizing mission" in France, the propagation of anti-Slavic and anti-Turkic ideas in Germany. Prejudices against Muslims and Jews had sturdy roots as far back as the Middle Ages. Although the Holocaust, decolonization, and greater intercultural exchange in the postwar era had done a great deal to sensitize people to the dangers and fallacies of such prejudice, it still held some appeal. In the 1980s it was still not uncommon in West Germany to see "Germans only" or "Europeans only" in newspaper ads for jobs and apartments. Faced with the realization that non-Europeans had come to stay, and that a great many of them had their origins in Muslim rather than Christian countries, many Europeans viewed immigrants as a threat to their ethnic, religious, and cultural traditions. Anti-immigrant parties also exploited people's fears about AIDS, drugs, and crime—problems that tended to be associated with the poverty and high rates of youth unemployment that immigrant families often had to endure. While the majority of Europeans rejected the explicitly racist claims of the anti-immigrant movements, fear, prejudice, and economic insecurity created fertile enough ground for groups like the National Front to grow.

Like the Green movement, the anti-immigrant movement had an impact on mainstream parties. This effect was especially clear in France

---

[5] Quoted in John Ardagh, *Germany and the Germans: An Anatomy of Society Today* (New York, 1987), p. 246.

where Le Pen's National Front, which called for repatriating immigrants, obtained enough support (11 percent of the vote in the European Parliament elections of 1984) to inspire mainstream conservatives to adopt a more anti-immigrant stance. When the conservative Jacques Chirac became prime minister in 1986, he tried to stiffen requirements for obtaining citizenship. Protests by human rights organizations, church groups, and immigrant associations that viewed the legislation as racist eventually forced Chirac to withdraw his bill. Still, anti-immigrant opinion in France remained sufficiently strong to encourage even the socialist government in 1990 to back away from its plan to enable non-citizen immigrants to vote in municipal elections.

At the same time, however, discrimination and the rise of the anti-immigrant parties inspired a variety of protests on behalf of immigrant rights. Although as newcomers immigrants initially found it difficult to mount collective action, by the 1970s it became more common for immigrants to join together in work stoppages and rent strikes to protest working conditions and dilapidated housing. They created distinctive immigrant associations as well. In the mid-1970s young blacks in Britain were in the vanguard in developing organizations and using public demonstrations to combat racial prejudice and anti-immigrant assaults. By the mid-1980s immigrant activists in France and West Germany made similar efforts. The leading antiracist organization in France, *S.O.S.-Racisme,* used marches, educational programs, and the support of celebrities to make immigrant issues a popular cause, especially among the young. For a brief time buttons bearing the slogan *Touche pas à mon pote* ("Hands off my buddy") became a fashionable badge of solidarity for the antiracist campaign in France.

Alongside immigrant organizations a number of conventional institutions added their weight to the effort. Trade unions, which had been slow in the early 1970s to respond to immigrant concerns, tended by the 1980s to support immigrants, who after all had become a more significant presence in their memberships. Churches, too, became more involved. Religious organizations played an important role in defeating a government effort in West Germany to reduce from sixteen to six the maximum age at which children who remained abroad could reunite with their immigrant parents. Teachers and social workers also became active in promoting bilingual education and reforms in immigrant housing and social services. And left-wing parties, though usually joining the chorus of calls for restrictions on further immigration, nonetheless tended to defend rights of existing immigrants and to cultivate immigrant voters.

Immigrant protest in some instances took the form of violence. To be sure, immigrants themselves were often the victims of violent assault. A government report in Britain estimated that in 1980–1981 there were at least seven thousand racially inspired attacks during a wave of anti-immigrant violence reminiscent of an epidemic of "Paki-bashing" in the 1960s. In 1990 the French witnessed a shocking sequence of fatal attacks against young North Africans. Moreover, relations between immigrants and the police often bordered on violence, since it was common practice for police to stop and search immigrants in public places. Hostility and suspicion poisoned the daily encounter between immigrant youths and the local police. Between 1980 and 1985 incidents involving the police triggered a series of violent riots in Bristol, Birmingham, and the Brixton section of London. Four days of rioting broke out in a predominantly North African neighborhood of suburban Lyons in France in 1990, when a young man died in a motorcycle crash with a police car. Investigations into these and similar civil disturbances revealed that while police harassment enraged immigrants, so too did the underlying sources of economic disadvantage—unemployment, poor housing, and school failure.

By the early 1990s the prospects for improving the condition of western Europe's new ethnic minorities were far from clear. Though the European economy rebounded noticeably after the mid-1980s, poverty persisted, unemployment rates came down only gradually, and the problems of urban blight touching the lives of so many immigrants remained severe. Many Europeans in the white majority, moreover, found it difficult to embrace the kind of cultural pluralism that a full acceptance of the non-European minority would entail. To complicate matters further, many Turks, North Africans, Pakistanis, West Indians, and other non-European ethnics remained ambivalent about just how far they wished to go in assimilating into the European cultural mainstream. Few Turks or North Africans aspired to become culturally German or French in the fullest sense. Islamic fundamentalists, who ironically had been stronger in West Germany than in Turkey where the government repressed them, rejected any concessions to Western culture that impinged on their strict religious practice and a separate Islamic identity. Many nonreligious North African and Turkish youth, like West Indians in Britain, found themselves at odds with both the white mainstream and the religious traditions of their parents' homeland. They struggled to create a new collective identity in which they aspired to formal integration and economic advancement within European society while defining themselves as culturally distinct from the white majority. Ambivalence on the part of both immigrants and the white majority, then, encumbered the quest for mutual understanding across the ethnic divide.

However difficult the search for new forms of ethnic pluralism is bound to be in western Europe, the relationship between white Europeans and the new ethnic minorities will remain in the forefront of European political life for some time to come. The Europe of 1992, featuring the lowering of economic barriers within the European Community, will also bring about the freer flow of peoples, both immigrants and white Europeans, across national borders in search of jobs, better pay, and new educational opportunities. Foreigners entering one European Community country will be able to travel freely to the others. Although the European Community may try to regulate the flow of peoples into Europe from the poorer, more populated nations of Asia and Africa, there is little doubt that a more open European economy will continue to serve as a magnet for immigration. Demographic trends within Europe point in the same direction. As birthrates fall and life expectancy rises, an aging European population will continue to need its newcomers from abroad to sustain economic growth. Like it or not, Europeans will persist in playing host to one of the largest population movements of modern times, a demographic shift transforming in its wake the very nature of social relations and popular values in western Europe.

Revolution in Eastern Europe

New forms of protest in western Europe in the 1970s and 1980s neither toppled governments nor gave rise to new political regimes. In this respect western Europe remained politically stable, remarkably so in contrast to much of the rest of the world. Only in Spain, Portugal, and Greece, where democratic movements succeeded in replacing dictatorships in the 1970s, were the basic structures of government transformed. Eastern Europe, however, was another story. After forty years the communist monopoly on power in the Soviet satellite states, from Poland in the north to Bulgaria in the south, collapsed with astonishing speed in 1989 through a revolutionary process that no one had predicted.

The democratic revolution in eastern Europe, like the upheavals of 1848, drew people into an international wave of protest in ways that reflected the particular circumstances of each country. In Poland, where the process of change began, a deepening economic crisis and eleven years of bitter conflict between the government and an independent trade union movement, Solidarity, finally forced the regime to agree to free elections in June 1989. Solidarity, as the main opposition political party, won enough votes to dominate a new coalition government. Drawing lessons from the Polish example, communist reformers in Hungary, likewise prodded by economic troubles and opposition pressures, cut the barbed wire barriers at the Austrian border and gingerly steered the country toward multiparty democracy. In October 1989 the party abolished itself to become a Western-style socialist party. Elections the following spring brought a new coalition of democratic parties into power. Meanwhile, East Germans, especially the young and educated, took advantage of the open Hungarian–Austrian border to emigrate by the tens of thousands to West Germany. By October 1989 this gaping hole in the Berlin Wall, combined with gigantic, peaceful demonstrations in the larger East German cities, brought that regime to the brink of collapse. When the government opened its borders on November 9, the citizens of East and West Berlin made the wall that had divided them since 1961 the site of an immense celebration. Soon thereafter the communist party lost its grip on power. One day after the Berlin Wall opened, the communist party of Bulgaria pushed out Todor Zhivkov, the party strongman who had ruled the country for thirty-five years. Czechoslovakia came next, when students and dissident intellectuals led a series of massive demonstrations that in less than a month brought the government down. Only in Romania, the last regime to fall, did the peaceful revolution take a violent turn. Several days of fighting between the government's security forces and the army, which had refused orders to fire on peaceful demonstrators and then sided with the popular rebellion, finally brought down the regime. By year's end every country in eastern Europe, Albania aside, had embarked on a new and difficult course toward multiparty democracy, a market economy, and the rule of law.

The extraordinary events of 1989 owed a good deal to a fundamental change in Soviet policy. Mikhail Gorbachev, the Soviet leader since 1985, had embarked on a program of economic liberalization and democratic reform to rejuvenate a Soviet Union mired in serious problems—a deteriorating economy, low morale, ethnic conflict, demands for self-determination in a number of regions. Gorbachev had also sought better relations with the West. Arms agreements brought badly needed cuts in the military budget. A new era of cooperation brought the prospect of trade and investment. When faced with change in eastern Europe, Gorbachev chose not to intervene and even encouraged communist reformers to negotiate a transition to democracy. Suddenly, communist regimes that had banked on the support of a half-million Soviet soldiers in East bloc barracks faced the prospect of using only their own armies to counter the hundreds of thousands of peaceful demonstrators who gathered nightly in the public squares of their own cities. Gorbachev's decision to cut loose of the Soviet empire in eastern Europe lent courage to protesters; no less important, it helped break the will of the party bosses to repress the movement.

But if Gorbachev's astute accommodations to change made 1989 possible, the origins of the revolution lay in the social fabric of the Eastern bloc countries themselves, including the Soviet Union. Economic problems plagued eastern Europe from the mid-1970s on and only worsened in the course of the 1980s. After World War II, state-run systems had been able to channel resources into heavy industry effectively enough to expand these economies and improve living standards. Essentially, state direction had enabled the Eastern bloc countries to complete the basic stage of industrialization but then stymied them in their efforts to move to a further stage. After the mid-1970s central planning proved less effective for adapting to the new technologies and rapidly evolving consumer demands of the sort emerging in the West. Relatedly, it was difficult for closed, repressive regimes to introduce the new computer and information technology that by the 1980s was doing so much to stimulate economic growth in the capitalist West. Problems with worker motivation, which had plagued Eastern bloc economies all along, remained severe. In the West, the routine jobs and intense discipline of modern work had been cushioned, at least to an extent, by access to consumer pleasures. In eastern Europe, though welfare systems provided security, consumer goods remained scarce by Western standards. Flagging rates of worker productivity, plus growing levels of alcoholism, suggested that motivational problems had worsened. In the 1980s growth rates in eastern Europe slowed to about 1 percent a year, less than a third what they had been in the 1960s and 1970s. In Hungary, by no means the sickest of the east European economies, inflation forced the real value of pensions to drop by at least 40 percent in the 1980s. Trapped in a long depression, faced with a mounting foreign debt, Eastern bloc governments searched in vain for ways out of economic malaise. Even the Hungarian effort to promote a second, more privatized economy alongside the state-planned one failed to spark a recovery. Throughout the region people faced the prospect not simply of a widening economic gap between East and West but of outright decline in comparison to their own past.

The revolution of 1989, however, was far more than a reaction to economic failure. It was above all a revolt against political oppression and an expression of the popular desire for national self-determination. For this purpose the survival of a tradition of political dissent proved essential in generating the events of the late 1980s. Here the Polish people set an example. In 1980 a group of industrial workers, intellectuals, and Catholic laypeople and priests created the Solidarity trade union, the most successful effort in eastern Europe to organize an autonomous political institution outside the orbit of the communist party. When the government imposed martial law in 1981, Solidarity was driven underground. But the effort to create a mass movement continued, largely under the protective shelter of the Catholic church. By 1988 over sixty independent groups, parties, and movements had sprung from this underground effort to build an alternative set of symbols and loyalties in opposition to the communist regime. When the government felt compelled to legalize Solidarity once again, a highly organized alliance of workers, peasants, students, and intellectuals emerged to give political muscle to the opposition movement.

Elsewhere in eastern Europe a culture of political opposition surfaced as well, though nowhere with the strength of Solidarity. In Hungary hundreds of independent circles and groups had emerged by the late 1980s, including at least twenty oppositional political organizations, which gave many people an identity and sense of direction outside the purview of the state. In Hungary, too, plans to build a dam on the Danube triggered an environmental protest movement that brought together scientists, ecologists, and an assortment of mostly middle-class citizens who argued vigorously against the government. In Czechoslovakia many of the dissident intellectuals who in 1977 had signed an opposition manifesto, Charter 77, continued to foster small independent groups in one of the most repressive of the Eastern bloc states. The Catholic church also staged a revival in Czechoslovakia. More than 600,000 people signed a petition in 1987 for religious freedom. In East Germany the Lutheran church played a similar role of providing quiet support to a small underground opposition of ecologists, peace activists, and dissident intellectuals. Networks of this sort provided the basis for the new organizations—New Forum in East Germany, Democratic Forum in Hungary, Civic Forum in Czechoslovakia—that suddenly crystallized during the revolution of 1989 to steer negotiations to democracy.

Even beyond the shadowy world of underground political opposition important features in the popular culture of eastern Europe, both old and new, also weakened the grip of communist regimes in the 1980s. Religious institutions not only sheltered the opposition: they also implicitly challenged the ideological influence of the state. Many priests and pastors made their church buildings available for independent performances, exhibitions, and debates. Exposure to the West had a corrosive effect on the regimes as well. Scientists, doctors, scholars, and other professionals made more frequent trips West for conferences and intellectual exchanges. Travel restrictions were eased in some countries. Most important, radio and television brought nightly access to Western entertainment, Western products, and a consumer ethos that dramatized the deficiencies of the Soviet bloc. Western music attracted a keen audience in eastern Europe in part because it came to symbolize free expression. In Czechoslovakia in the early 1980s the Jazz section of the Musicians Union became a center of dissident culture, until the government dissolved it. Rock music enthusiasts in Prague painted "You have your Lenin, give us our Lennon" in tribute to slain Beatle John Lennon. And as the events of 1989 were to show, many people harbored memories of a popular culture closer to home—a sense of historical tradition as conveyed through songs and anthems, folk heroes, and slogans that the authorities had suppressed since the 1940s. These symbols came back to life in 1989 when a sea of people took to singing and chanting in the public squares of Warsaw, Leipzig, and Prague.

Although the revolutionary upheaval of 1989 had solid roots in the social, cultural, and political life of these countries, there was nothing inevitable about what happened. It still took the unexpected convergence of popular pressures, economic crisis, and a willingness at the top to yield to the democratic movement to produce the largely peaceful transition to new regimes. Nor was it clear what would emerge from the transformation. Czechoslovakia alone had a history of successful democracy in the interwar period. It would take time for new governmental structures, new parties, and new habits of popular participation and civic tolerance to take hold even in that country, to say nothing of a Romania or Bulgaria that had barely known a democratic past. Multiparty democracy, moreover, promised to give fuller expression to social conflicts than had been possible under one-party rule. The Polish electoral campaign of 1990, for example, brought to the surface antagonisms between workers and intellectuals and between city dwellers and farmers that had been buried within the subsoil of the Solidarity movement.

More difficult still, the transition to a market economy held the prospect of painful dislocations and unprecedented adjustments. Even in relatively well-off East Germany, which in the fall of 1990 became part of a reunified Germany, the shift to a market system and the collapse of state-run enterprises produced a startling rise in unemployment. In Poland, where the new post-communist government chose price hikes and austerity as the most direct path to capitalism, people faced a further decline in their living standard, at least for a time. Economic deterioration in Bulgaria brought food and fuel rationing and scheduled power blackouts. In Hungary angry truck drivers and taxi drivers blockaded the streets of Budapest to protest a 65 percent rise in the price of gasoline—a rough change for everyone in a country where inflation already reached 30 percent. Economic insecurity throughout the region made the consolidation of democracy that much tougher.

No less troubling, the collapse of communist regimes brought a resurgence of ethnic rivalries that forty years of authoritarian rule had held in check but scarcely erased. Every country in eastern Europe had ethnic minorities fearful to one degree or another of discrimination, prejudice, and in some cases even physical assault. Age-old rivalries between Islamic Turks and Christian Bulgarians took the form of violent clashes in Bulgaria within months of the fall of the old regime. The Hungarian minority in western Romania feared similar recriminations. Observers in several countries noted a rise in anti-Semitism. Religious minorities, too, though grateful for an end to persecution under communism, now faced new worries about discrimination by religious majorities. Protestants and Orthodox Christians in a largely Roman Catholic Poland protested a new government decree allowing priests to teach religious classes in all schools. Catholic Slovaks sought new laws on abortion and religion in schools that ran counter to the views of less religious Czechs. Catholic Croats and Slovenes came into increasing conflict with Orthodox Serbs in Yugoslavia. There were even signs that the disappearance of the Iron Curtain could intensify ethnic conflict in western Europe, as immigrants from the East competed for jobs with non-European workers. Already in 1990 East Germans were beginning to displace Turkish-Germans from their jobs. A Europe of open borders, between East and West as well as within the European Community, certainly reduced the prospects of international conflict and European war. But it also increased the likelihood of ethnic, religious, and racial conflict within the borders of many nations.

If ethnic conflict, the transition to a market economy, and the creation of a new democratic political culture posed big challenges to the peoples of Poland, Czechoslovakia, and the other former satellite states of the Soviet Union, those problems were greater still in the Soviet Union itself. Remarkably, the Soviet leadership successfully accommodated pressures to democratize the political structure in the late 1980s so that by 1990 paper parliaments had become real ones and free and open elections were taking place. But the consolidation of democracy

Awaiting election results in Red Square, Moscow, 1990. Mikhail Gorbachev's reforms in the late 1980s played a pivotal role in enabling people in eastern Europe to create new democratic regimes. Change came much more slowly in the Soviet Union, but even there a measured shift toward parliamentary government and popular elections marked a sharp break with the past. (*Wojtek Laski/SIPA Press.*)

and the transition to a market economy, though formally embraced by the Soviet leadership in 1990, posed an enormous challenge in a gigantic socialist economy on the verge of collapse. Communism in the Soviet Union, in contrast to the satellite states, had not had a forty-year run through an externally imposed regime; it had taken root through revolution, civil war, and over seventy years of social and institutional development. Party officials were much less willing to give up power than in eastern Europe, and much more able to circumvent reforms. Long-entrenched habits of central planning, bureaucratic inefficiency, and dependence on the state were difficult to shake. Ordinary citizens in the Soviet Union viewed capitalism and market freedom with greater suspicion than did their counterparts in eastern Europe. And indeed, the very notion of entrepreneurship ran against the grain of an ethos, with deep roots in the nineteenth-century Russian peasantry and not just communist ideology, that disapproved of efforts to surpass one's peers. Moreover, the sheer scale of the undertaking—of privatizing a vast empire of state-owned assets, of breaking up huge state monopolies, and of liberalizing a well-established pricing system—made the notion of transforming the Soviet economy much more daunting than elsewhere.

Economic stagnation plus new political openness produced outright social conflict within the Soviet Union. Workers feared the prospect of unemployment if inefficient state operations were cut back. Despite government opposition, major labor strikes, often spearheaded by coal miners, sought better wages and conditions; a determined miners' movement in 1991 defied a Gorbachev strike ban. Resentment of privileged communist party officials fueled other protests. The new assertiveness of labor, reminiscent of industrial conflicts at earlier points of western European history, revealed how the East, like the West, remained a class-divided society. It also raised challenges that were difficult for the existing regime to satisfy.

On top of it all, the very notion of the Soviet Union as a unified state faced serious challenge as one republic after another declared its intentions of becoming an autonomous entity. In late 1989 the Lithuanians began the trend, which the other Baltic states of Latvia and Estonia soon followed. By the end of 1990 fourteen of the country's fifteen republics, including the vast Russian Republic, had taken similar steps to assert the primacy of local rule over that of the central government. Once again, in the wake of the collapse of the communist party's monopoly on power, and in the face of near chaos in the economy, people reasserted their ethnic and territorial loyalties, much as they had in eastern Europe but with graver implications. Soviet Republics even faced minority revolts within their borders, as, for example, in Soviet Moldavia, where the Gagauz people asserted their claim to autonomous status. By the early 1990s, in short, the Soviet Union not only confronted unprecedented economic difficulties; its centralizing institutions threatened to split apart as well.

Despite the uncertainties that hung over eastern Europe and the Soviet Union, one thing was clear: The sharp ideological and military divide that had split Europe since 1945 had disappeared. Nearly everyone in Europe hailed the end of the cold war as a new and hopeful beginning for both halves of the Continent. As if to reinforce this sense of being part of Europe again, and not of a separate Soviet bloc, the peoples of Poland, Czechoslovakia, and Hungary now spoke of themselves as east central Europeans in rejection of the very notion of an eastern Europe. They, like their neighbors in Bulgaria, Romania, and Yugoslavia, pinned their hopes on eventually becoming part of the European Community, which had served western Europe as an engine of economic growth. It remained to be seen how quickly the troubled economies of the East could be integrated into the relatively prosperous EC, and even how soon the EC would accept the task. But it was a measure of how much Europe had changed, both East and West, that so soon after reasserting their claims to national self-determination the peoples of eastern Europe embraced the notion of a new era of European unification.

Conclusion

The theme of European identity that greeted the final decade of the twentieth century owed its strength to more than the end of the cold war or even the economic integration of western Europe. No less important, postwar economic growth had done a great deal to bring the more impoverished regions of Mediterranean Europe, and isolated areas within many of the prosperous nations, into the consumer society. Although continued differences in political experience and standards of living reflected the longstanding social divide between eastern and western Europe, the changes induced after 1945 by more active governments (communist and non-communist), by the general decline of the aristocracy and the peasantry, and by shared features of industrialization and urbanization made social differences between the East and West less acute than at any time in centuries. To be sure, great disparities of wealth and opportunity remained in Europe—not only between the East and West, and the North and South, but within every nation. The uneven effects of economic recovery in the late 1980s in fact widened the gap in many countries between the rich and the poor, and between the East and West. But the promise of further economic and monetary union in the 1990s within the European Community, and hopes for the much more difficult integration of the eastern countries into some kind of enlarged economic community sometime in the future, gave Europeans from the Atlantic to the Urals a renewed sense of their common destiny. This affirmation of Europe as a single economic and potentially political entity also reflected a new understanding in the intensely competitive global economy of the late twentieth century: No country could go it alone and hope to prosper. The international economy, along with the powerful market pressures of mass consumption within Europe, had made "Europe" not just a noble idea but a practical necessity.

This is not to say that Europeans had transcended important forms of social conflict or shed their identities as national citizens or as members of groups defined by class, ethnicity, religion, gender, or age. Far from it. Although changes in the social structure since 1945 had all but eliminated the aristocracy and greatly diminished the peasantry, the basic class divisions that had emerged from industrialization remained. A great many Europeans, including now an immigrant underclass, remained relatively impoverished, poorly educated, unemployed, or burdened by the continuing proletarianization of industrial and service-sector work. Class conflicts, though less intense than they had been, still played an important role in the political culture and social experience of Europeans. So too did the search for gender equality, as men and women struggled with the enduring legacy of a patriarchal past. Ethnic, religious, and racial tensions also showed little sign of abating. On the contrary, the end of communist rule in eastern Europe brought a renewal of ethnic and religious rivalry, while in western Europe ethnicity, religion, and language remained important sources of identity for minorities who continued to agitate in their own behalf. Immigrants and their offspring—Europe's new ethnic minorities—posed an even more acute challenge to a continent that had yet to remedy the ills of poverty, discrimination, and prejudice that these newcomers often faced. Environmental problems also continued to provoke conflict as Europeans, like their counterparts elsewhere in the world, disagreed over what was entailed in protecting human health and the natural world from the effects of industrialization. Europe, in short, though largely liberated from the imminent threat of a third world war on its own soil, nonetheless had yet to overcome the long-term sources of conflict within industrial society and the newer forms of conflict that had emerged since the 1960s.

Nor had a narrow consensus emerged over the nature and role of the state. To be sure, when the leaders of the United States, Canada, and nearly all the nations of Europe, including the Soviet Union, gathered in Paris at the Conference of Security and Cooperation in Europe in 1990 to pledge their commitment to democracy, human rights, and economic liberty, they closed a long chapter of ideological division that had polarized the Continent for several generations. But significant differences of opinion remained within each country over what kind of balance to draw between public and private authority in social life. Disagreements remained too over how much to trust the market, or to regulate it, whether to improve or reduce welfare provisioning, and how much to relinquish the authority of the national government to supranational bodies in the European Community or subnational bodies at the local and regional level. These questions were not just technical issues for politicians and bureaucrats; they impinged on the interests of ordinary citizens, businesspeople, trade unionists, and farmers, who continued to fight for their interests in the increasingly complex maze of Europe's governmental institutions. Not surprisingly, then, competition between political parties remained as intense in the 1980s as it had been in the early postwar decades, even though the ideological divisions had narrowed.

But if Europe remained a conflictual society, Europeans nonetheless settled into patterns of social and cultural life that underlined the stability of the consumer society as it had evolved since 1945. The place of sexuality, for example, had changed significantly in the course of the century, and in ways that were largely accepted by most Europeans. Sex was now associated more explicitly with pleasure, leisure, and self-expression, and it was openly exploited in advertising and popular entertainment. Europeans, moreover, appeared less conflicted about this change than were their counterparts in America, where the impact of conservative religious traditions still held considerable sway. The place of religion, too, had changed in Europe after World War II, and here too in ways that most Europeans tacitly approved. Earlier in the century confessional issues had been a major source of social conflict in Europe. They largely ceased to be thereafter, at least in the West. This fundamental change derived in part from the cumulative effects of secularization and mass education, in part from the breakdown in the 1930s and 1940s of the close association of the Catholic church with political conservatism. After World War II churches lost political influence virtually everywhere in western Europe. Even in Catholic Italy the church failed to prevail in plebiscites on divorce and abortion in 1974 and 1981. Religious leaders bemoaned the rising use of cremation, instead of traditional funerals, as a sign not only of secularism but also of modern superficiality. It was not that religion declined inexorably. Many Europeans, including young people, remained devout, and many more participated in the religious rituals of baptism, marriage, and burial—though simple, secular ceremonies were the rising trend. In eastern Europe, where churches revived through their association with political opposition, it remained to be seen whether the Western pattern of declining confessional politics would eventually prevail. But a general understanding emerged in Europe that religion and the church, if important in many people's private lives, no longer played a major role in public life or in shaping the general culture.

Above all, the growth of mass consumption proved essential in reinforcing Europe's social and cultural integration in the postwar era. Especially in the more open and prosperous West (though to some extent in the East as well), Europeans continued to support a rich array of consumer interests—from ritualized vacation getaways and fashion-driven shopping habits to the pastime pleasures of video games, television, and the movies. The automobile became nearly as important a tool and symbol in daily life as in the United States, despite the higher cost of fuel. The consumption of mass-produced goods and services formed part of virtually every aspect of life from work to leisure, from street to home. Consumer interests to some extent served Europeans as compensation for dissatisfactions at work or in other aspects of their lives. They also served to stimulate people to demand better wages and a more equitable system of rewards, and in this respect consumerism could fuel as well as dampen social conflict. And superficially at least, a shared culture of mass consumption, along with the rise of a large service sector, inspired more informality in casual personal relationships, as older, rigid social hierarchies receded and newer hierarchies encouraged a more accommodating interpersonal style.

As in the United States, mass consumption in Europe inspired numerous critics who spoke of the darker side of the consumer society—the stress on conformity, the manipulative appeals of advertisers, the shallowness of what people watch on television, and the effects of television on learning and family relationships. Since the late 1940s Europeans often voiced these concerns through laments about the "Americanization" of Europe—the fear that American fast food, movies, music, and television programs would drive out what was decent and indigenous in European culture. As recently as the 1980s Europeans debated proposals to limit imports of American broadcast programming (the second largest U.S. export, after aircraft). But ironically, as Europe continued to participate in the elaboration of a consumer culture, and as it created more of its own brand of mass consumer products, the fear of "Americanization" appeared to decline. Although some Green activists called for a radical scaling back of consumer activity, most Europeans showed no sign of altering their behavior. And the tendency of east Europeans in the upheaval of 1989 to equate freedom with consumption suggests that consumerism will likely grow, not diminish, as a fundamental feature of European society.

If the growth of consumerism integrated Europeans into a European and increasingly global marketplace and into elements of a shared popular culture, it by no means eliminated protest nor forced people into a homogeneous cultural mold. Moreover, the expanding marketplace also made it possible for small producers, and not just big ones, to prosper in the postwar era, and in this respect the consumer society could sometimes support local customs and ethnic traditions. Nor should it be assumed that particular classes, ethnic groups, or regions conformed to some uniform set of consumer behaviors. Still, new habits of mass consumption, the economic integration of the Continent, and the rise of new forms of protest did change the meaning and in some cases the importance of the older social distinctions. As in earlier stages of industrial development, people called on old identities to face the challenges and opportunities of social change, and in the process they came to have new understandings of themselves and their neighbors. In this respect Europeans in the postwar era remained a people in transition to an uncertain future, and the Continent, while stable, remained far from immune to new and unexpected forms of upheaval.

CHAPTER 7

Conclusion: Patterns and Complexities

The process of creating an industrial society went through several stages in Europe, from the eighteenth century onward. After 1750, population pressure, the impact of new beliefs, and the expansion of a commercial economy prodded west Europeans into new behaviors ranging from their sexual practices to their work habits. In the early nineteenth century technological changes paved the way for a profound restructuring of economic and social life, though other forces continued to play a role as well. A new series of technological innovations also helped usher in a more mature industrial period after 1870—during which time eastern Europe began to industrialize—but on the whole it was the expansion of organizations and the spread of secular ideas that most affected the way Europeans changed their lives in the late nineteenth century. The spiral of war and depression soured mature industrial society in the first half of the twentieth century. In response, European governments took a more active role in shaping social and economic relationships. This pattern, along with the economic and cultural changes associated with the advent of an affluent consumer society, set the tone for Europe's entry into an advanced industrial stage.

It is possible to see a few consistent patterns of change through these various stages. From 1750 onward, though with important oscillation, the economy became more productive, increasing Europe's total wealth. Technological innovation played an important role throughout the process, though it was by no means the only or even at times the most important stimulus for change. In a general way, too, each phase of European industrialization reduced the importance of local and personalized organizations in favor of larger and more formally structured ones—factories, big business, big unions, commercialized sources of leisure fare, the expanding state. Even family functions diminished as part of this trend. A few changes in popular beliefs also moved in roughly common directions from one period to the next—namely, the trend toward secularization and science at the expense of religion and superstition.

The idea of common directions of change must not, however, be pushed too far. Each major period had its own dynamic. New wealth created in the early industrial period had the primary effect of enlarging the middle classes and widening the gap between the affluent and the poor. By contrast, in subsequent periods, expanding wealth created a more generalized, though still class-divided, consumer society. Although European beliefs steadily became more secular, this trend could produce fervent adherence to ideologies like socialism and nationalism in one period, a more hedonistic materialism in another. Furthermore, a host of trends shifted direction from one period to the next. The early industrial period, though it introduced a few promising innovations in leisure activity, was noteworthy for its attack on traditional leisure forms and its restriction of opportunities for play. Only in the mature industrial period did Europeans reverse the trend by creating a new kind of leisure culture.

The complexity and shifting character of social divisions constitute a second barrier to easy generalization about the directions of change in European social history. At key points, particularly but not exclusively in the early stages of industrialization, Europeans divided between those who, on balance, sought to preserve or restore traditional social relations and those who tended to welcome innovation. Class divisions became especially sharp in the late nineteenth and early twentieth centuries and continued to leave their mark after World War II. Working-class and middle-class people shared in certain kinds of change—in adjusting to the power of more formal organization, in reducing the importance of religious belief—but they did so in different ways and at a different pace. An accurate but very general point—that sexual interest and activity increased as part of Europe's development as an industrial society—must immediately be qualified by the distinctive timing of rural and urban, worker and middle-class participation in the phenomenon and by the varying forms of sexuality that persisted into the late twentieth century. Gender roles, themselves subject to change over time, and differences in age group experience, complicated class relations by forming other social divisions. What new work patterns or emotional expectations meant to the men and women of the nineteenth century varied greatly from place to place and up and down the social hierarchy. Furthermore, and particularly in the twentieth century, important racial divisions formed yet another barrier to easy generalizations about European society.

Finally, the differences among Europe's regions bedevil any effort to venture categorical statements conveying what European society was all

about, or even what it is about today. Europe's regions differed a great
deal from one another at the onset of industrialization, and these differences affected the timing and shape of subsequent change. The gaps
between eastern Europe, initially locked in harsh serfdom and slow to
industrialize, and the more urban, commercial western region were already particularly marked in the eighteenth century. The divergence of
East and West continued in the form of early and late industrializations,
non-communist and communist regimes, and the differing intensities
of discontent that surfaced in the 1980s. This was not, however, the
only regional distinction that counted. It was possible in the 1980s to
see in the difference between English and French divorce rates or
feminist fervor the contemporary echo of older distinctions in family
forms and the continuing legacy of Protestant and Catholic pasts.

The process of industrialization certainly encouraged a host of conver-
gences among Europe's various regions. The creation of urban society,
the decline of the birthrate, and the erosion of the traditional peasantry
cut across regions. The Europe of the late twentieth century, seeking
to build larger institutions under the umbrella of the European community and its possible extension toward new regimes in the former
Soviet bloc, relied to some extent on common patterns and impulses
that had reduced local particularisms from the late nineteenth century
onward. Yet not only traditional loyalties, manifested in ethnic conflicts, but also new diversities complicated the process of convergence.
Germany, through most of the industrial period a relatively vigorous
society demographically, had by the 1970s become Europe's leader in a
birthrate reduction that threatened outright population decline. This
trend made Germany newly different from Holland or even France.
The Italian surge into rapid industrial growth created unprecedented
differences between that nation and Britain, which struggled in the
decades after World War II with slow economic growth. Britain's early
and extensive urbanization, to take another example, marked this nation
off from France or Denmark, where the agricultural sector remained
more vital through the twentieth century.

European society had long been a complex entity, and its complexities,
though changed by industrialization, hardly disappeared. Simple ana-
lytical formulas, then, do not capture the process of change. Yet, the
evolution of Europe's recent social history was not random. Europeans
transformed their institutions, values, habits, language, and social relations in ways that are open to coherent historical analysis. But to grasp
the transformation requires the hard work of mastering not only the
nuances of change across several discrete periods but also the subtleties
of social divisions and regional distinctions.

The twists and turns of Europe's social history also warn against
facile predictions for the future. Continued expansion of prosperity
seems likely at least for western Europe, but even this forecast cannot

be asserted with certainty, and what may be done with prosperity is even harder to gauge. Further aging of Europe's population seems likely, given low birthrates and increasing longevity, but the consequences of this trend remain unknown. Nor is it clear how Europeans will handle the obvious tension between sharing common institutions and continuing to rely on ethnic and national loyalties to provide identity in a new era of change.

Europe in the 1990s had come to share a number of features and prospects with other advanced industrial societies, notably the United States and Japan. At the same time, Europeans had also carved out their own version of what an advanced industrial society could be like. Their educational and political systems were designed to maintain a different balance between identifying and training an elite and encouraging democratic participation than was the case in the United States. Their commitment to leisure, as embodied particularly in the lengthy annual vacation, exceeded that of both the Japanese and the Americans. Less prudish than Americans in their willingness to tolerate teenage sexuality, for example, Europeans were nonetheless more restrained than the Japanese. Europeans also demonstrated a capacity to endure adversity and adjust to change. A society that only forty years before had been judged lucky if it could follow the United States into a new era of affluence and mass consumption had, by the 1980s, revealed its impressive creativity and no small measure of unpredictability in shaping a consumer society and helping to restructure the global economy. This capacity for innovation, combined with the renewal of Europe's importance in the world and the complexity of its own internal tensions, were all products of Europe's social past.

Appendix. Class Structure, a Chart of Major Changes

Premodern Society	Early Industrial Society	Mature Industrial Society	Consumer Society
Aristocracy magnates gentry	Aristocracy magnates gentry	Upper Class aristocracy big business	Managerial upper class
Peasantry farmers middling owners near-landless laborers Rural Merchants and Professionals Rural Artisans	Peasantry farmers middling (being squeezed) laborers: agricultural and domestic/manufacturing	Peasant-Farmers Agricultural Laborers	Farmers
Bourgeoisie Artisans Servants	Middle Class Shopkeeping Class Master Artisans	Middle Class (business and professions) Shopkeeping Class Lower Middle Class	Middle Class: Middle Managers, Technicians Lower Middle Class
	Journeymen Working Class (including female servants)		
Urban Poor	Urban Poor	Working Classes journeymen factory workers semiskilled and unskilled	Working Classes skilled semiskilled unskilled, including immigrant labor

Bibliography

The following bibliography is intended to fulfill a dual purpose. It provides a basis for further reading in the major topics of modern European social history, where such reading is available. In this category preference has been given to studies of broad geographical or chronological scope and to work in English. At the same time, there is some indication of the most important monographic material, with preference here to recent work. Monographic studies can offer insight into subjects and methods far beyond the limits of the topic itself; they provide important guidelines for further efforts. Certainly much exciting work has recently been done in a variety of aspects of modern European society, and there is both opportunity and profit in additional exploration.

At the same time, many of the major subjects of modern European social history remain open to further inquiry. In a few cases, an excellent study can be cited for one area and time period but no general work has been done. In other instances, central problems have scarcely been treated at all. Only a few topics, such as labor organization, can offer a really full bibliography. Leading categories, such as the peasantry, have received only scattered treatment; even the middle class, so often cited, has rarely been studied. The social history of popular beliefs is just beginning to receive attention. The bibliography offered here is not of course an exhaustive list; it inevitably reflects gaps in our present knowledge. The openness of modern social history and the prospect of vital works yet to come enhance the basic excitement of the field.

I. Journals

Much of the most exciting work in social history appears as journal articles rather than books. The following journals are particularly important for the field: *Journal of Social History; Comparative Studies in Society and History; Interna-*

tional Review of Social History; Past and Present; and *Journal of Interdisciplinary History.*

Among the foreign language journals see *Annales, Ecomomies, Sociétés, Civilisations; Mouvement social; Revue d'histoire économique et sociale; Vierteljahrschrift für Sozial und Wirtschaftsgeschichte;* and *Zeitschrift für Geschichtswissenschaft.*

II. General Works

Several works provide a framework for interpreting modern social history. Barrington Moore, *The Social Origins of Dictatorship and Democracy* (Boston, 1966), is an important comparative study. A number of works by Michel Foucault are useful; see *Discipline and Punish: The Birth of the Prison* (New York, 1977), and *Madness and Civilization* (New York, 1965), for key examples. Charles Tilly, *Big Structures, Large Processes and Huge Comparisons* (New York, 1984), offers one view of major themes in modern social history; see also *Contentious French: Four Centuries of Popular Struggle* (Cambridge, Mass., 1989). Another modern social history is John Gillis, *The Development of European Society, 1770–1870* (Bethesda, Md., 1983).

A number of national social histories provide excellent orientations. See Harold Perkin, *Origins of Modern English Society, 1780–1880* (London, 1969), and his second volume, *The Rise of Professional Society in England Since 1880* (New York, 1989). Also on Britain see F. M. L. Thompson, ed., *The Cambridge Social History of Britain 1750–1950* (Cambridge, Eng., 1990). On France see Theodore Zeldin, *France 1848–1945: Vol. 1: Ambition, Love and Politics* (Oxford, 1973), and *France 1848–1945: Vol. 2: Intellect, Taste and Anxiety* (Oxford, 1977); on the Mediterranean see J. G. Peristiany, *Honour and Silence: The Values of Mediterranean Society* (Chicago, 1963); and on the Balkans see Traian Stoianovich, *A Study in Balkan Civilization* (New York, 1967).

Several topical studies survey a substantial period and introduce a wide swath of European social history. On various core subjects see Harvey Graff, *The Legacies of Literacy, Contentions and Contradictions in Western Culture and Society* (Bloomington, 1987); John Beattie, *Crime and the Courts in England, 1600–1800* (Princeton, 1986); V. A. C. Gatrell, Bruce Lehman, and Geoffrey Parker, eds., *Crime and Law: The Social History of Crime in Western Europe Since 1500* (London, 1980); Lawrence and Jeanne C. Fawteir Stone, *An Open Elite: England, 1540–1830* (Oxford,1984); and Paul Hohenberg and Lynn Hollen Lees, *The Making of Urban Europe, 1000–1950* (Cambridge, Mass., 1985). A lively introduction to leisure theory and history is Johann Huizinga, *Homo ludens: A Study of the Play Element in Culture* (New York, 1988).

Survey work is particularly rich on family and women's history. On women see Bonnie Anderson and Judith P. Zinser, *A History of Their Own: Women in Europe from Pre-history to the Present* (New York, 1988); Bonnie Smith, *Changing Lives: Women's History Since 1750* (Lexington, Mass., 1988); and Sheila Rowbotham, *Hidden from History: Rediscovery of Women in History from the 17th Century to the Present* (New York, 1975). On family see John Gillis, *For Better, for Worse: British Marriages, 1600 to the Present* (New York, 1985); Edward Shorter, *The Making of the Modern Family* (New York, 1975); James Casey, *The History of the Family* (New York, 1990); Jack Goody, *The Development of the Family and Marriage in Europe* (Cambridge, Eng., 1983); Lloyd de Mause, *History of Childhood* (New York,

1974); Ivy Pinchbeck, *Women Workers in the Industrial Revolution* (London, 1930); and Margaret Hewitt, *Wives and Mothers in Victorian Industry* (London, 1958).

An important series, covering various aspects and periods in social history is George Duby and Phillippe Ariès, eds., *A History of Private Life*, 4 vols. (Cambridge, Mass., 1987).

III. Preindustrial Economy and Demography

A fine sketch of demographic history is E. A. Wrigley, *Population and History* (New York, 1969). See also Michael Flinn, *The European Demographic System, 1500–1820* (Baltimore, 1981), for an excellent overview. For more detailed treatment see E. A. Wrigley and R. S. Scoffield, *The Population History of England, 1541–1871: A Reconstruction* (Cambridge, Mass., 1981); and Peter Laslett, *Household and Family in Past Time* (Cambridge, Eng., 1972). See also O. J. Willigan and Katherine Lynch, *Sources and Methods of Historical Demography* (New York, 1982); and Carlo Cipolla, *Economic History of World Population* (Baltimore, 1962).

On issues of age structure see David Troyansky, *Old Age in the Old Regime: Image and Experience in Eighteenth-Century France* (Ithaca, N.Y., 1989); and Peter N. Stearns, ed., *Old Age in Preindustrial Society* (New York, 1982). A fascinating monograph on nutrition and population is John Komlos, *Nutrition and Economic Development in the Eighteenth-Century Hapsburg Monarchy: An Anthropometric History* (Princeton, 1989).

For economic patterns, a classic study is Fernand Braudel, *The Mediterranean and the Mediterranean World in the Age of Philip II* (2 vols., New York, 1972) and *Capitalism and Material Life* (New York, 1974). On the protoindustrialization framework see Peter Kriedte, Hans Medick, and J. Schlumbohm, *Industrialization Before Industrialization* (Cambridge, Eng., 1981). See also Maths Isacson and Lars Magnusson, *Protoindustrialization in Scandinavia: Craft and Skills in the Industrial Revolution* (New York, 1987). On the Russian economy see Arcadius Kahan, *The Plow, the Hammer and the Knout: An Economic History of Eighteenth-Century Russia* (Chicago, 1985). On western technological patterns see David Landes, *Revolution in Time: Clocks and the Making of the Modern World* (Cambridge, Mass., 1983). On Europe's world economic position see Immanuel Wallerstein, *The Capitalist World Economy* (Cambridge, Eng., 1979).

IV. Preindustrial Social Structure

General studies include Peter Laslett, *The World We Have Lost* (London, 1965), which has a pronounced British and even more pronounced nostalgic slant; and Pierre Goubert, *Louis XIV and Twenty Million Frenchmen* (New York, 1969).

On the aristocracy and bourgeoisie see Eliner Barber, *The Bourgeoisie in Eighteenth-Century France* (Princeton, 1955); G. R. Mingay, *English Landed Society in Eighteenth Century* (Toronto, 1963); Robert E. Jones, *The Emancipation of the Russian Nobility, 1762–1785* (Princeton, 1973); Hans Rosenberg, *Bureaucracy, Aristocracy, and Autocracy; the Prussian Experience, 1660–1815* (Cambridge, Mass., 1958); and Mack Walker, *The German Home Towns: Community, State and General Estate* (Ithaca, N.Y., 1971). See also T. J. A. LeGoff, *Vannes and Its Regions: A Study of Town and Country in Eighteenth-Century France* (Oxford, 1981); and Hoh-cheung and Lorna Mui, *Shops and Shopkeeping in Eighteenth-Century England* (Montreal, 1989).

On the urban lower classes and the poor see Olwen Hufton, *The Poor of Eighteenth-Century France* (Oxford, 1974); Colin Jones, *Charity and Bienfaisance: The Treatment of the Poor in the Montpellier Region, 1740–1815* (Cambridge, Eng., 1982); Cissie Fairchilds, *Domestic Enemies: Servants and Their Masters in Old Regime France* (Baltimore, 1984), and *Poverty and Charity in Aix-en-Provence, 1640–1789* (Baltimore, 1976); Mary Lindemann, *Patriots and Paupers: Hamburg, 1712–1830* (New York, 1990); J. Jeanne Hecht, *Continental and Colonial Servants in the Eighteenth Century* (Northampton, Mass., 1954); Michel Sonenscher, *Work and Wages: Natural Law, Politics and the Eighteenth-Century French Trades* (New York, 1989); Catharina Lis, *Poverty and Capitalism in Preindustrial Europe* (Atlantic Highlands N.J., 1979), and *Social Change and the Laboring Poor: Antwerp, 1770–1860* (New Haven, 1986); and Katryn Norberg, *Rich and Poor in Grenoble, 1600–1814* (Berkeley, 1985).

Literature on the peasantry is particularly extensive. For France, classic studies include Emmanuel Le Roy Ladurie, *The Peasants of Languedoc* (Urbana, 1974); and Marc Bloch, *French Rural History* (Urbana, 1974). Alan MacFarlane, *The Origins of English Individualism* (New York, 1979) and *The Culture of Capitalism* (London, 1987), argue for a distinctive English rural society; see also Joan Thirsk, ed., *The Agrarian History of England, 1500–1640* (Cambridge, Eng., 1967); and Keith Wrightson and David Levine, *Poverty and Piety in an English Village* (New York, 1979). Charles Tilly, *The Vendeé* (New York, 1967), shows the impact of economic change on peasants and divisive results during the French Revolution. See also on France, Patrice Higgonet, *Pont-de-Montvert; Social Structure and Politics in a French Village, 1700–1914* (Cambridge, Mass., 1971); and Thomas Sheppard, *Lourmarin in the Eighteenth Century; A Study of a French Village* (Baltimore, 1971).

For distinctive aspects of Russian society see Richard Hellie, *Slavery in Russia, 1450–1725* (Chicago, 1982), and *Enserfment and Military Change in Muscovy* (Chicago, 1971). Social interpretations of the French Revolution include Georges Lefebvre, *The Coming of the French Revolution* (Cambridge, Eng., 1964); and Lynn Hunt, *Politics, Culture and Class in the French Revolution* (Berkeley, 1984).

V. Preindustrial Family and Gender

The preindustrial family and its changes are beginning to receive considerable attention. A pioneering work, with an important general thesis about the development of the modern family, is Phillippe Ariès, *Centuries of Childhood: A Social History of Family Life* (New York, 1962). A good summary is Michael Anderson, *Approaches to the West European Family, 1500–1914* (London, 1980). On family structure see Peter Laslett and R. Wall, *Household and Family in Past Time* (New York, 1972). See also David Hunt, *Parents and Children in History: The Psychology of Family Life in Early Modern France* (New York, 1970); Randolph Trumbach, *The Rise of the Egalitarian Family* (New York, 1978); Jean Louis Flandrin, *Families in Former Times: Kinship, Household and Sexuality* (Cambridge, Eng., 1979); and Lawrence Stone, *The Family, Sex and Marriage in England, 1500–1800* (New York, 1987). Linda Pollock, *Forgotten Children: Parent–Child Relations from 1500 to 1800* (Cambridge, Mass., 1984), is a revisionist work claiming that parental outlook was little different in 1600 from what it is today; see also Steven Ozment, *When Fathers Ruled: Family Life in Reformation Europe* (Cambridge, Mass., 1983).

Another lively argument against the common grain is Alan MacFarlane, *Marriage and Love in England, 1300–1840* (New York, 1986). A useful if more sober survey is Michael Mitterauer and Reinhard Sider, *The European Family: Patriarchy to Partnership from the Middle Ages to the Present* (Chicago, 1982). Specialized studies include James S. Traer, *Marriage and the Family in Eighteenth-Century France* (Ithaca, N.Y., 1980); and Roderick Phillips, *Family Breakdown in Late Eighteenth-Century France: Divorces in Rouen, 1792–1803* (New York, 1980). On marriage patterns see Jacques Dupaquier, E. Heelin, P. Lasslet, M. Livi-Bacci, and S. Sogner, eds., *Marriage and Remarriage in Populations of the Past* (New York, 1981).

For women's work patterns see Martha C. Howell, *Women, Prosecution and Patriarchy in Late Medieval Cities* (Chicago, 1986); and Mary Wiesner, *Working Women in Renaissance Germany* (New Brunswick, 1986).

VI. Preindustrial Mentalities

An excellent overview is provided by Sheldon Watts, *Social History of Western Europe, 1450–1720* (New York, 1984). Central issues in mentalities history are covered in Robin Briggs, *Communities of Belief: Cultural and Social Tensions in Early Modern France* (New York, 1989).

For an understanding of premodern attitudes, including popular religion and magical beliefs, see Christopher Hill, *The World Turned Upside Down: Radical Ideas During the English Revolution* (New York, 1972); Alan MacFarlane, *The Family Life of Ralph Josselin* (New York,1970), and *Witchcraft in Tudor and Stuart England* (New York, 1978); and Natalie Davis, *Society and Culture in Early Modern France* (Stanford, 1975). An interesting effort to correct new ideas with early industrial technology is A. E. Musson and Eric Robinson, *Science and Technology in the Industrial Revolution* (Toronto, 1969)

Key studies in preindustrial mentalities include Peter Burke, *Popular Culture in Early Modern Europe* (New York, 1978); Edmund Leites, *The Puritan Conscience and Modern Sexuality* (New Haven, 1986); David Sabean, *Power in the Blood: Popular Culture and Village Discourse in Early Modern Germany* (New York, 1984); and Robert Darnton, *The Great Cat Massacre* (New York, 1985).

Other crucial studies are Robert Muchembled, *Popular Culture and Elite Culture in France, 1480–1750*, trans. Lydia Cochrane (Baton Rouge, 1985); Keith Thomas, *Religion and Decline of Magic* (New York, 1971), and *Man and the Natural World: A history of Modern Sensibility* (New York, 1983). On emotional culture see Carol Z. Stearns and Peter N. Stearns, eds., *Emotion and Social Change: Toward a New Psychohistory* (New York, 1989); and Jean Delumeau, *Sin and Fear: The Emergence of Western Guilt Culture, 13th–18th Centuries* (New York, 1990).

Other features of preindustrial mentalities are covered under various topical rubrics. A vital study on leisure trends is Robert Malcolmsen, *Popular Recreations in English Society, 1700–1850* (New York, 1973). Other important mentalities issues are addressed in studies of punishment, death, and disease: see Pieter C. Spierenburg, *The Spectacle of Suffering: Executions and the Evolution of Repression: From a Preindustrial Metropolis to the European Experience* (Cambridge,

England, 1984); Phillippe Ariès, *Hour of Our Death*, trans. Helen Weaver (New York, 1981); John McManners, *Death and the Enlightenment: Changing Attitudes to Death Among Christians and Unbelievers in 18th-Century France* (New York, 1981); Roy Porter, *Patients and Practitioners: Lay Perceptions of Medicine in Preindustrial Society* (Cambridge, Eng., 1985); Michael MacDonald, *Mystical Bedlam: Madness, Anxiety and Healing in Seventeenth-Century England* (Cambridge, England, 1983); and George Rosen, *Madness in Society* (New York, 1968).

Recent attention has focused also on the rise of consumerism: see Neil McKendrick, John Brewer, and J. H. Plumb, eds., *The Birth of a Consumer Society: The Commercialization of Eighteenth-Century England* (Bloomington, 1982); Lorna Weatherill, *Consumer Behavior and Material Culture in Britain, 1600–1760* (London 1987); and Colin Campbell, *The Romantic Ethic and the Spirit of Modern Consumerism* (New York, 1987)–this last with a theoretical structure ranging from preindustrial to contemporary.

VII. Economy and Demography During the Industrial Revolution

Concerning the Industrial Revolution, basic studies include David Landes, *The Unbound Prometheus: Technological Change and Industrial Development in Western Europe from 1850 to the Present* (Cambridge, Eng., 1969); Kingston Derry and T. I. Williams, *A Short History of Technology* (Oxford, 1961); Phyllis Deane, *The First Industrial Revolution* (Cambridge, Eng., 1965); and Rondo Cameron, *France and the Economic Development of Europe, 1800–1914* (Princeton, 1961). For eastern and southern Europe, see Alexander Gerschenkron, *Economic Backwardness in Historical Perspective* (Cambridge, Mass., 1962). A recent general survey is Peter N. Stearns, *Interpreting the Industrial Revolution* (Washington, D.C., 1991).

Somewhat more specialized economic studies include William O. Henderson, *The State and Industrial Revolution in Prussia* (Liverpool, 1958); Charles Kindleberger, *Economic Growth of France and Britain, 1851–1951* (Cambridge, Mass., 1962); and Richard Tilly, *Financial Institutions and Industrialization in the Rhineland* (Madison, 1966).

Issues of demographic change have received considerable recent attention. Thomas McKeown, *The Modern Rise of Population* (New York, 1976) deals with Europe's eighteenth-century boom. The key topic, on fertility decline, is surveyed in Ansley Coale and Susan Cotts Watkins, eds., *The Decline of Fertility in Europe: The Revised Proceedings of a Conference on the Princeton European Fertility Project* (Princeton, 1986). See also Michael Teitelbaum, *The British Fertility Decline: Demographic Transition in the Crucible of the Industrial Revolution* (Princeton, 1970); John E. Knodel, *The Decline of Fertility in Germany, 1871–1939* (Princeton, 1974), and *Demographic Behavior in the Past: A Study of Fourteen German Village Populations in the Eighteenth and Nineteenth Centuries* (New York, 1988). See also Ansley Coale, Barbara Anderson, and Erna Harm, *Human Fertility in Russia Since the Nineteenth Century* (Princeton, 1979). Less strictly demographic, but relevant on general outlook, is Angus McLaren, *Birth Control in Nineteenth-Century England* (New York, 1978). See also Michael Drake, ed., *Population in Industrialization* (New York, 1969), with essays on several key issues; Michael

Haines, *Fertility and Occupation: Population Patterns in Industrialization* (New York, 1979); and Etienne Van de Walle, *The Female Population of France in the Nineteenth Century* (Princeton, 1974).

Somewhat more general discussions on demographic outlook and policy include Angus McLaren, *Sexuality and Social Order: The Debate over Fertility of Women and Workers in France, 1770–1920* (New York, 1983), and *Reproductive Rituals: The Perception of Fertility in England from the Sixteenth Century to the Nineteenth Century* (New York, 1984); and J. A. Banks, *Victorian Values: Secularism and the Size of Families* (Boston, 1981).

Three specialized studies relevant to demography are Anthony Wohl, *Endangered Lives: Public Health in Victorian Britain* (Cambridge, Mass., 1983); Leslie Page Moch, *Paths to the City: Regional Migration in Nineteenth-Century France* (Beverly Hills, 1983); and Robert Woods and John Woodward, eds., *Urban Disease and Mortality in Nineteenth-Century England* (New York, 1984).

Several nineteenth-century social histories cover both economic and demographic developments: F. M. L. Thompson, *The Rise of Respectable Society: A Social History of Victorian Britain* (Cambridge, Mass., 1988); Edmund Royle, *Modern Britain: A Social History, 1750–1985* (New York, 1987); and Richard Evans, *Society and Politics in Wilhelmine Germany* (New York, 1978). An important if idiosyncratic interpretation of industrial society is William Reddy, *Money and Liberty in Modern Europe: A Critique of Historical Understanding* (New York, 1987).

VIII. The Aristocracy and the Middle Classes in the Nineteenth Century

The aristocracy has not drawn a great deal of recent research. Several earlier studies, however, remain very serviceable. See Alexander Gerschenkron, *Bread and Democracy in Germany* (Berkeley, 1943); Ernst Bramstedt, *Aristocracy and the Middle Class in Germany* (Chicago, 1964); John Gillis, *The Prussian Bureaucracy in Crisis, 1840–1860* (Stanford, 1971); Réne Rémond, *The Right Wing in France from 1815 to de Gaulle* (Philadelphia, 1966); F. M. L. Thompson, *English Landed Society in the Nineteenth Century* (London, 1963); and Richard Kelsall, *Higher Civil Servants in Britain from 1870 to the Present Day* (London, 1955). On eastern Europe see Jerome Blum, *Lord and Peasant in Russia from the Ninth to the Nineteenth Century* (Princeton, 1961). Frederick Jaher, ed., *The Rich, the Wellborn and the Powerful* (Urbana, 1975), contains essays on the upper classes of several countries.

For more recent work see Roberta Thompson Manning, *The Crisis of the Old Order in Russia: Gentry and Government* (Princeton, 1982); David Cannadine, *Lords and Landlords: The Aristocracy and the Towns, 1774–1967* (Leicester, 1980); Dennis R. Mills, *Lord and Peasant in Nineteenth-Century Britain* (London, 1980); David Spring, ed., *European Landed Elites in the Nineteenth Century* (Baltimore, 1977); John. A. Armstrong, *The European Administrative Elite* (Princeton, 1973); and Robert Moeller, ed., *Peasants and Lords in Modern Germany* (Boston, 1986).

Several studies of higher education deal both with the aristocracy and the middle class of the nineteenth century: see Fritz Ringer, Brian Simon, and Derek Müller, *The Rise of the Modern Educational System: Structural Change and Social Reproduction, 1870–1920* (New York, 1987); Konrad H. Jarausch, ed., *The*

Transformation of Higher Learning, 1860–1930: Expansion, Diversification, Social Opening and Professionalization in England, Germany, Russia and the United States (Chicago, 1983), and *Students, Society and Politics in Imperial Germany: The Rise of Academic Illiberalism* (Princeton, 1982); and Patrick J. Harrigan, *Mobility, Elites and Education in French Society of the Second Empire* (Waterloo, Ontario, 1980). On intellectuals see Fritz Stern, *Politics of Cultural Despair: A Study in the Rise of the German Ideology* (Berkeley, 1961); Richard Pipes, ed., *The Russian Intelligentsia* (New York, 1961); and Cesar Graña, *Bohemian Versus Bourgeois; French Society and the French Man of Letters in the Nineteenth Century* (New York, 1964).

Despite the frequency of generalizations about the middle class, there have been surprisingly few thorough studies of this group. Charles Morazé, *The Triumph of the Middle Classes* (New York, 1968), interprets modern history in the light of middle-class ascendancy. See also W. J. Reader, *Professional Men* (London, 1966); and R. S. Neale, *Class and Ideology in the 19th Century* (London, 1972). Social mobility studies bear heavily on the middle class; see Hartmut Kaeble, *Historical Research on Social Mobility* (New York, 1981). An excellent overview on middle-class development is E. J. Hobsbawm, *The Age of Capital, 1848–1875* (New York, 1975). Adeline Daumard, *Les Bourgeois et la bourgeoisie en France depuis 1815* (Paris, 1987), is a vital monograph, with unparalleled detail. See also Rolf Engelsing, *Zur Sozialgeschichte Deutscher Mittel — und Unterschichten* (Gottingen, 1973). The key issue of contacts between middle-class values and those of the lower classes is taken up in Reinhard Bendix, *Work and Authority in Industry: Ideologies of Management in the Course of Industrial Labor* (New York, 1956); Sidney Pollard, *The Genesis of Modern Management* (Cambridge, Mass., 1965); and Peter N. Stearns, *Paths to Authority* (Urbana, 1978).

Aspects of middle-class politics are covered in A. P. Donajgrodski, ed., *Social Control in Nineteenth-Century Britain* (Totowa, N.J., 1977); see also Katherine Lynch, *Family, Class and Ideology in Early Industrial France: Social Policy and the Working-Class Family, 1825–1848* (Madison, 1988); and John Gerrard, *The Middle-Class in Politics* (Farnborough, Eng., 1978).

Several recent studies focus on the middle class in the urban power structure: see Derek Fraser, *Power and Authority in the Victorian City* (New York, 1979); Gary Wray McDonogh, *Good Families of Barcelona: A Social History of Power in the Industrial Era* (Princeton, 1986); and John Gerrard, *Leadership and Power in Victorian Industrial Towns, 1830–1880* (Dover, N.H., 1983).

National studies include Leonore Davidoff and Catherine Hall, *Family Fortunes: Men and Women of the English Middle Class, 1780–1850* (Chicago, 1987); Alan Spitzer, *The French Generation of 1820* (Princeton, 1986); François Crouzet, *The First Industrialists: The Problem of Origins* (Cambridge, England, 1985); W. D. Rubenstein, *Men of Property: The Very Wealthy in Britain Since the Industrial Revolution* (New Brunswick, 1981); and Martin J. Wiener, *English Culture and the Decline of the Industrial Spirit, 1850–1980* (Cambridge, England, 1981), for an upper-class turn away from entrepreneurial drive. See also Alfred Rieber, *Merchants and Entrepreneurs in Imperial Russia* (Chapel Hill, 1982).

Important professional groups are treated in Matthew Ramsey, *Professional and Popular Medicine in France, 1770–1830: The Social World of Medical Practice* (Cambridge, England, 1988); and Anthony La Vopa, *Prussian Schoolteachers: Profession and Office, 1763–1848* (Chapel Hill, 1980).

Literature on the lower middle classes, long deficient, is improving rapidly.

See David Lockwood, *The Blackcoated Worker: A Study in Class Consciousness,* 2nd ed. (New York, 1989); Jürgen Kocka, *Unternehmer und der Deutschen Industrialiserung* (Göttingen, 1975); Robert Gellately, *Politics of Economic Despair: Shopkeepers and German Politics, 1890–1914* (Ann Arbor, 1989); Peter G. J. Pulzer, *The Rise of Political Anti-semitism in Germany and Austria* (New York, 1964); Michael Winstanley, *The Shopkeepers' World: 1830–1914* (Dover, N.H., 1983); Geoffrey Crossick and Heinz-Gerhard Haupt, *Shopkeepers and Master Artisans in Nineteenth-Century Europe* (New York, 1984); Shulamit Volkov, *The Rise of Popular Anti-modernism in Germany: The Urban Master Artisans, 1873–1896* (Westport, Conn., 1978), and Philip G. Nord, *Paris Shopkeepers and the Politics of Resentment* (Princeton, 1986). These studies divide, partly on national grounds, between a focus on political efforts and other aspects of lower middle-class life.

IX. Agriculture and the Peasantry in the Nineteenth Century

Peasant history for the period can be followed in a number of excellent recent studies: Richard J. Evans and W. R. Lee, eds., *The German Peasantry: Conflict and Community in Rural Society from the Eighteenth to the Twentieth Centuries* (London, 1986); Gregor Dallas, *The Imperfect Peasant Economy: The Loire Country, 1800–1914* (New York, 1982); Pamela Horn, *The Rural World, 1780–1850: Social Change in the English Countryside* (New York, 1981); Judith Devlin, *The Superstitious Mind: French Peasants and the Supernatural in the Nineteenth Century* (New Haven, 1987); Eugen Weber, *Peasants into Frenchmen: The Modernization of Rural France, 1870–1914* (Stanford, 1976); Roger Price, *The Modernization of Rural France: Communications Networks and Agricultural Market Structures in Nineteenth-Century France* (New York, 1983); Martine Segalen, *Love and Power in the Peasant Family: Rural France in the Nineteenth Century* (Chicago, 1983); James R. Lehning, *The Peasants of Marlhes: Economic Development and Family Organization in Nineteenth-Century France* (Chapel Hill, 1980); and Raphael Samuel, ed., *Village Life and Labour* (London, 1975).

On southern and eastern Europe see James C. Davis, *Rise from Want: A Peasant Family in the Machine Age* (Philadelphia, 1986);David Kertzer, *Family in Central Italy, 1880–1910: Sharecropping, Wage Labor and Co-residence* (New Brunswick, 1984); Rudolph Bell, *Fate and Honor, Family and Village: Demographic and Cultural Change in Rural Italy Since 1800* (Chicago. 1979); Sydel Silverman, *Three Bells of Civilization: The Life of an Italian Hill Village* (New York, 1975); Roland Sarti, *Long Live the Strong: A History of Rural Society in the Apennine Mountains* (Amherst, 1985); Peter Kolchin, *Unfree Labor: American Slavery and Russian Serfdom* (Cambridge, Mass., 1987)—an exciting comparative study; Steven Hoch, *Serfdom and Social Control in Russia: Pretrovskee, a Village in Tambore* (Chicago, 1986); Teodor Shanin, *The Awkward Class: Political Sociology of Peasantry in a Developing Society: Russia, 1910–1925* (Oxford, 1972); Elise Kimerling Wirtshafter, *From Serf to Russian Soldier* (Princeton, 1990); and Daniel Field, *The End of Serfdom: Nobility and Bureaucracy in Russia, 1855–1861* (Cambridge, Mass., 1976).

Somewhat older works are also helpful. See on Spain, Gerald Brenan, *The Spanish Labyrinth: An Account of the Social and Political Background of the Civil War*

(Cambridge, Eng., 1950); and Edward Malefakis, *Agrarian Reform and Peasant Revolution in Spain: Origins of the Civil War* (New Haven, 1970). On rural protest, Eric Hobsbawm, *Primitive Rebels: Studies in Archaic Forms of Social Movement in the Nineteenth and Twentieth Centuries* (New York, 1957), provides exciting case studies and a persuasive theoretical structure. Also see Theodore Hamerow, *Birth of a New Europe: State and Society in the Nineteenth Century* (Chapel Hill, 1983); Rudolph Braun, *Soziale und Kultureller Wandel in einem Landlichen Industriegebiet* (Earlenbach-Zurich, Stuttgart, 1965); Wayne S. Vucinich, *The Peasant in Nineteenth-Century Russia* (Stanford, 1968); Cecil Woodham Smith, *The Great Hunger: Ireland, 1845–1849* (New York, 1972); and E. J. Hobsbawm and George Rudé, *Captain Swing* (New York, 1968).

A number of anthropological studies on Balkan villages provide insight into peasant tradition and history: E, Friedl, *Vasilika: A Village in Modern Greece* (New York, 1962); J. T. Sanders, *Balkan Village* (Lexington, 1949), and *Rainbow in the Rocks: The People of Rural Greece* (Cambridge, Mass., 1926); Irene Winter, *A Slovenian Village* (Providence, 1977); and Vera St. Erlich, *Family in Transition: A Study of 300 Yugoslav Villages* (Princeton, 1966).

X. The Working Classes in the Nineteenth Century

Research on the European working classes prior to 1870 has focused heavily, in recent years, on artisanal groups, though the factory experience still receives attention; studies on the later nineteenth century are better balanced, in terms of the types of workers covered.

An excellent introduction, with comparative implications, is Ira Katznelson and Ariside Zolberg, eds., *Working Class Formation: Nineteenth-Century Patterns in Western Europe and the United States* (Princeton, 1986); see also, for the mature industrial period,, Peter N. Stearns, *Lives of Labor: Work in a Maturing Industrial Society* (New York, 1975). John Merriman, ed., *Consciousness and Class Experience in Nineteenth-Century Europe* (Oxford, 1985), is another good essay collection, dealing mainly with France and artisans. See also Patrick Joyce, ed., *The Historical Meanings of Work* (New York, 1987).

On Britain see the classic study by E. P. Thompson, *The Making of the English Working Class* (New York, 1964), dealing mainly with traditional worker categories encountering new economic structures. See also E. J. Hobsbawm, *Laboring Men: Studies in the History of Labor* (New York, 1964); Neil J. Smelser, *Social Change in the Industrial Revolution: An Application of Theory to the Lancashire Cotton Industries, 1770–1840* (London, 1971); Gareth Stedman Jones, *Outcast London: A Study in the Relationship Between Classes in Victorian Society* (Oxford, 1971), and *Languages of Class: Studies in Working Class History, 1832–1982* (Cambridge, England, 1983); Lynn Hollen Lees, *Exiles of Erin: Irish Migrants in Victorian London* (Ithaca, N.Y., 1979); Francis Hearn, *Domination, Legislation and Resistance: The Incorporation of the Nineteenth-Century English Working Class* (Westport, Conn., 1978); Paul Johnson, *Saving and Spending: The Working Class Economy in Britain, 1870–1939* (New York, 1985); Malcolm Thomis, *The Town Laborer and the Industrial Revolution* (New York, 1974); Richard Price, *An Imperial War and the British Working Class* (Toronto, 1972); José Harris, *Unemployment and Politics: A*

Study in English Social Policy, 1886–1914 (Oxford, 1972); and James Treble, *Urban Poverty in Britain, 1830–1914* (New York, 1979). Two excellent studies are Patrick Joyce, *Work, Society and Politics: The Culture of the Factory in Later Victorian England* (New Brunswick, 1980); and John Foster, *Class Struggle and the Industrial Revolution* (London, 1974).

French working-class history is also well served. See Robert J. Bezucha, *The Lyon Uprising: Social and Political Conflict in the Early July Monarchy* (Cambridge, Mass., 1974); Ronald Aminzade, *Class, Politics and Early Industrial Capitalism: A Study of Mid-Nineteenth-Century Toulouse* (Albany, 1981); John Merriman, *The Red City: Limoges and the French Nineteenth Century* (Oxford, 1985); Lenard Berlanstein, *The Working People of Paris, 1871–1914* (Baltimore, 1984); Alan Forrest, *The French Revolution and the Poor* (New York, 1981); William Sewell, Jr., *Structure and Mobility: The Men and Women of Marseille, 1820–1870* (Cambridge, England, 1985). Two important studies of working-class culture are William, Sewell, Jr., *Work and Revolution in France: The Language of Labor from the Old Regime to 1848* (Cambridge, England, 1980); and William Reddy, *The Rise of Market Culture: The Textile Trade and French Society, 1750–1900* (Cambridge, N.Y. 1984). See also Michael Hanagan, *The Logic of Solidarity: Artisans and Industrial Workers in Three French Towns, 1871–1914* (Urbana, 1980); and Donald Reid, *The Miners of Decazeville: A Genealogy of Deindustrialization* (Cambridge, Mass., 1985).

For Germany see David Crew, *Town in the Ruhr: A Social History of Bochum, 1890–1914* (New York, 1979); James Roberts, *Drink, Temperance and the Working Class in Nineteenth-Century Germany* (Boston, 1984); and Richard Evans, ed., *German Working Class, 1888–1933: The Politics of Everyday Life* (Totowa, N.J., 1982).

On Russian workers see Reginald Zelnik, *Labor and Society in Tsarist Russia: The Factory Workers of St. Petersburg, 1855–1870* (Stanford, 1971); and Robert E. Johnson, *Peasant and Proletariat: The Working Class of Moscow in the Late Nineteenth Century* (New Brunswick, 1979).

XI. Nineteenth-Century Social Protest

Concern with social protest formed one of the initial avenues into nineteenth-century social history, and it remains a lively area. Coverage of major protest movements obviously overlaps with attention to other topics, particularly concerning working-class life.

Several studies of nineteenth-century revolutions provide insight into broader social history, dealing with the full spectrum of society. An overview is provided in Eric Hobsbawm, *The Age of Revolution, 1789–1948* (Cleveland, 1962). On 1848, a survey, with extensive bibliography, is Peter N. Stearns, *1848: The Revolutionary Tide in Europe* (New York, 1974). Useful special studies include Domenica Demarco, *Una Rivoluzionne soziale, la republica romana del 1848* (Naples, 1944); K. Griewach, *Deutsche Studenten und Universitäten in der Revolution von 1848* (Weimar, 1949); Georges Duveau, *1848: The Making of a Revolution*, trans., A. Carter (New York, 1967); Roger Price, *The French Second Republic* (Ithaca, N.Y., 1972); and Karl Obermann, *Die deutschen Arbeiter in der ersten bürgerlichen Revolution* (Berlin, 1950). On the Paris Commune see Edward Mason, *The Paris Commune* (New York, 1930). The nature of lower-class unrest before the mid-nineteenth century has been analyzed by George Rudé, *The Crowd in History, 1730–1848* (New York, 1964). Important specialized studies of early industrial protest include J. P. Aguet, *Les Grèves sous la monarchie de juillet* (Geneva, 1954); Wolfgang Kollman, *Wuppertaler Farbergesellen-Innung und Farber gesllen-Streiks, 1848–1857* (Wiesbaden, 1962); and Malcolm Thomis, *The Luddites: Machine-breaking in Regency England* (Newton Abbot, Eng., 1970). See also John Bohstedt, *Riots and Community Politics in England and Wales, 1790–1810* (Cambridge, Mass., 1983); J. D. P. Dunbabin, *Rural Discontent in Nineteenth-Century Britain* (New York, 1974); Bernard Moss, *The Origins of the French Labor Movement, 1830–1914: The Socialism of Skilled Workers* (Berkeley, 1976); Edward Berenson, *Populist Religion and Left-wing Politics in France, 1830–1852* (Princeton, 1984); Mark Traugott, *Armies of the Poor: Determinants of Working-Class Participation in the Parisian Insurrection of June 1848* (Princeton, 1985); Ted Margadant, *French Peasants in Revolt: The Insurrection of 1851* (Princeton, 1980); and John Merriman, *The Agony of the Republic: The Repression of the Left in Revolutionary France, 1848–51* (New Haven, 1978). Three books provide models for mature industrial protest: K. G. J. C. Knowles, *Strikes: A Study in Industrial Conflict* (Oxford, 1952); Charles Tilly and Edward Shorter, *Strikes in France, 1830–48* (Cambridge, Eng., 1974); and James Cronin, *Industrial Conflict in Modern Britain* (Totowa, N.J., 1979).

See also Eduarde Comîn Colomer, *Historia del Anarquismo Español* (Barcelona, 1956); and Hugh A. Clegg et al., *A History of British Trade Unions Since 1889* (New York, 1964).

On the social basis of socialism see Guenther Roth, *The Social Democrats in Imperial Germany: A Study in Working-Class Isolation and National Integration* (Totowa, N.J., 1963); Vernon Lidtke, *The Alternative Culture: Socialist Labor in Imperial Germany* (New York, 1985); and Tony Judt, *Socialism in Provence, 1871–1914: A Study in the Origins of the Modern French Left* (Cambridge, Eng., 1979).

For a comparative overview see Dick Geary, *European Labor Protest, 1848–1939* (London, 1981); Charles Tilly, Louis Tilly, and Richard Tilly, *The Rebellious Century, 1830–1930* (Cambridge, Mass., 1975); and Barrington Moore, Jr., *Injustice: The Social Bases of Obedience and Revolt* (White Plains, N.Y., 1978) — an excellent theoretical work.

Particularly important recent work focuses on protest in some of the late-developing areas. See Samuel Clark and James Donnelly, Jr., *Irish Peasants: Violence and Political Unrest, 1780–1914* (Madison, 1983). On Russia see John Bushnell, *Mutiny Amid Repression: Russian Soldiers in the Revolution of 1905–1906* (Bloomington, 1983); Victoria Bonnell, *Roots of Rebellion: Workers' Politics and Organization in St. Petersburg and Moscow, 1900–1914* (Berkeley, 1983); and Gerald Surh, *1905 in St. Petersburg: Labor, Society and Revolution* (Stanford, 1989). See also Philip Gabriel Eidelberg, *The Great Rumanian Peasant Revolt of 1907* (Leiden, 1974).

Closely related to protest is the study of crime and other deviance, which also has a rich historical literature. Key studies in the history of crime are: J. J. Tobias, *Crime and Industrial Society in the 19th Century* (New York, 1976); Howard Zehr, *Crime and the Development of Modern Society* (Totowa, N.J., 1978); Abdul Lodhi and Charles Tilly, "Urbanization, Crime and Collective Violence in 19th-Century France," *American Journal of Sociology* 49 (1973), 296–318; and V. A.

C. Gatrell, Bruce Lehman, and Geoffrey Parker, *Crime and the Law: The Social History of Crime in Western Europe Since 1500* (London, 1980). Louis Chevalier, *Dangerous Classes and Laboring Classes* (New York, 1972), deals with perceptions, rather than firm statistics; also interesting is Mary S. Hartman, *Victorian Murderesses* (New York, 1975). See also Benjamin Martin, *Crime and Criminal Justice Under the Third Republic* (Baton Rouge, 1990). For some of the changes in twentieth-century criminal patterns that so complicate a modernization model for this topic, see F. H. McClintock and N. Howard Avison, *Crime in England and Wales* (New York, 1969). See also Gordon Wright, *Between the Guillotine and Liberty: Two Centuries of the Crime Problem in France* (New York, 1983); and Patricia O'Brien, *The Promise of Punishment: Prisons in 19th-Century Britain* (Princeton, 1982).

Various studies address the issue of insanity and important shifts in society's approach in the nineteenth century: Andrew Scull, *Museums of Madness: The Social Organization of Insanity in 19th-Century England* (New York, 1979); and Klaus Doerner, *Madmen and the Bourgeoisie* (Oxford, 1981). A single study, but an excellent one, deals historically with suicide: Olive Anderson, *Suicide in Victorian and Edwardian England* (New York, 1987); see also Herbert Hendin, *Suicide and Scandinavia* (New York, 1964).

XII. Women and Gender in the Nineteenth Century

The history of women is receiving growing attention and amid increasing sophistication. J. A. Banks has written *Prosperity and Parenthood: A Study of Family Planning Among the Victorian Middle Classes* (New York, 1954), and with Oliver Banks, *Feminism and Family Planning* (Liverpool, 1964). Patricia Branca, *Silent Sisterhood: Middle-Class Women in the Victorian Home* (Pittsburgh, 1975), is an important study of women and domestic change; see also Jeanne Peterson, *Family, Love and Work in the Lives of Victorian Gentlewomen* (Bloomington, 1989); and Leonore Davidoff, *The Best Circles: Women and Society in Victorian England* (Totowa, N.J., 1973).

Good general introductions to the history of women are: Martha Vicinus, ed., *Suffer and Be Still: Women in the Victorian Age* (Bloomington, 1972), and *A Widening Sphere: Changing Roles of Victorian Women* (Bloomington, 1977). Other valuable collections include Lois Banner and Mary Hartman, *Clio's Consciousness Raised* (New York, 1974); and Renate Bridenthal and Claudia Koonz, eds., *Becoming Visible: Women in European History* (New York, 1987). Bonnie G. Smith, *Ladies of the Leisure Class: The Bourgeoises of Northern France in the 19th Century* (Princeton, 1981), is a vital monograph. See also John C. Fout, ed., *German Women in the Nineteenth Century: A Social History* (New York, 1984); and Edward Shorter, *A History of Women's Bodies* (New York, 1952).

Some key trends among working-class women are discussed in Margaret Hewitt, *Wives and Mothers in Victorian Industry* (New York, 1958). William L. O'Neill, *Woman Movement: Feminism in the United States and England* (Chicago, 1969), is a good brief overview of this important movement at the turn of the century... An important survey is Joan Scott and Louise Tilly, *Women, Work and*

Family (New York, 1978). See also Patricia Branca, *Women in Europe Since 1750* (New York, 1978).

A number of studies deal with women's socialization patterns: See James C. Albisetti, *Schooling German Girls and Women: Secondary and Higher Education in the Nineteenth Century* (Princeton, 1989); Laura Strumingher, *What Were Little Girls and Little Boys Made Of? Primary Education in Rural France, 1830–1880* (Albany, 1983); and Linda Clark, *Schooling the Daughters of Marianne: Textbooks and Socialization of Girls in Modern French Primary Schools* (Albany, 1984)

Several monographs focus on women's work: See Rose Glickman, *Russian Factory Women: Workplace and Society, 1880–1914* (Berkeley, 1984); Theresa McBride, *The Domestic Revolutions: The Modernization of Household Services in England and France, 1820–1920* (New York, 1976); Pamela Horn, *The Rise and Fall of the Victorian Servant* (New York, 1975); Ann Oakley, *Women's Work: The Housewives, Past and Present* (New York, 1975); Mary Lynn Stewart, *Women, Work and the French State: Labor Protection and Social Patriarchy, 1879–1919* (Montreal, 1989); Jane Lewis, ed., *Labour and Love: Women's Experiences of Home and Family, 1840–1940* (New York, 1986); Angela John, ed., *Unequal Opportunities: Women's Employment in England, 1800–1918* (New York, 1986); Lee Holcombe, *Victorian Ladies at Work: Middle-Class Working Women in England and Wales, 1850–1914* (Hamdon, Conn., 1973); Barbara Franzoi, *At the Very Least She Pays the Rent: Women and German Industrialization* (Westport, Conn., 1985); and Gay L. Gullickson, *Spinners and Weavers of Auffay: Rural Industry and Sexual Division of Labor in a French Village* (Cambridge, Eng., 1986).

Other interesting studies of women include Gail Malmgreen, *Religion in the Lives of English Women, 1760–1930* (Bloomington, 1986); James F. McMillan, *Housewife or Harlot: The Place of Women in French Society, 1870–1940* (New York, 1981); Carol Dyhouse, *Girls Growing up in Late Victorian and Edwardian England* (London, 1981); and Deborah Gorham, *The Victorian Girl and the Feminine Ideal* (Bloomington, 1982).

Six books take up the issues of nineteenth-century prostitution: Frances Finnegan, *Poverty and Prostitution: A Study of Victorian Prostitutes in New York* (New York, 1979); Judith Walkowitz, *Prostitution and Victorian Society: Women, Class and the State* (Cambridge, England, 1980); Jill Harsin, *Policing Prostitution in Nineteenth-Century Paris* (Princeton, 1985); Alain Corbin, *Women for Hire: Prostitution and Sexuality in France After 1850* (Cambridge, Mass., 1990); Mary Gibson, *Prostitution and the State in Italy, 1860–1915* (New Brunswick, 1986); and Paul McHugh, *Prostitution and Victorian Social Reform* (New York, 1980).

Several recent books deal with women in Russia: See Barbara Alpert Engel, *Mothers and Daughter: Women of the Intelligentsia in Nineteenth-Century Russia* (Cambridge, England, 1983); Dorothy Atkinson, Alexander Dallin, and Gail Warshofsky Lapidus, eds., *Women in Russia* (Stanford, 1977); and Richard Sites, *The Women's Liberation Movement in Russia* (Princeton, 1978).

For a somewhat more theoretical approach to gender history, see Joan Scott, *Gender and the Politics of History* (New York, 1988); see also Dorinda Outram, *The Body in the French Revolution: Sex, Class and Political Culture* (New Haven, 1989).

Two books deal with men and masculinity in the nineteenth century: J. A. Mangan and James Walvin, eds., *Manliness and Morality: Middle-Class Masculinity in Britain and America, 1800–1940* (New York, 1987); and Peter N. Stearns, *Be a Man! Males in Modern Society*, rev. ed., (New York, 1990)

XIII. The Family During the Industrial Revolution

One relatively early study on the nineteenth-century family remains a fine introduction: Michael Anderson, *Family Structure in Nineteenth-Century Lancashire* (Cambridge, Eng., 1971). Two other good introductions are Richard Evans and W. R. Leeds, *The German Family: Essays on the History of the Family in Nineteenth-Century Germany* (London, 1981); and Steven Mintz, *A Prisoner of Expectations: The Family in Victorian Culture* (New York, 1983). See also David Ransel, ed., *The Family in Imperial Russia: New Lines of Historical Research* (Urbana, 1978).

Three excellent books deal with youth: John R. Gillis, *Youth and History: Tradition and Change in European Age Relations, 1700–Present* (New York, 1974); Stephan Humphries, *Hooligans or Rebels? An Oral History of Working-Class Childhood and Youth, 1889–1939* (Oxford, 1981); and Thea Thompson, *Edwardian Childhoods* (Boston, 1981). For a slightly later period see J. Robert Wegs, *Growing up Working Class: Continuity and Change Among Viennese Youth, 1890–1938* (University Park, Pa., 1989).

On old age see Peter N. Stearns, *Old Age in European Society: The Case of France* (New York, 1976); see also Simone de Beauvoir, *The Coming of Age* (New York, 1972), an impressionistic and gloomy study; Ethel Shanas et al., *Old People in Three Industrial Societies* (New York, 1968); and Jill Quadagno, *Aging in Early Industrial Society: Work, Family and Social Policy in Nineteenth-Century England* (New York, 1982), an excellent history of old age and policy. See also Steven Ruggles, *Prolonged Connection: The Rise of the Extended Family in Nineteenth-Century England and America* (Madison, 1987).

On familial emotion, including sexuality, see Peter Gay, *The Bourgeois Experience, Victoria to Freud* (New York, 1984), and *The Tender Passion*, (vol. 2 of *The Bourgeois Experience*, New York, 1986); and Catherine Gallagher and Thomas Laqueur, eds., *Making of the Modern Body: Sexuality and Society in the Nineteenth Century* (Berkeley, 1987).

David Ransel, *Mothers of Misery: Child Abandonment in Russia* (Princeton, 1988), deals with an important aspect of the family experience. See also Judith Lewis, *In the Family Way: Childbearing in the British Aristocracy, 1760–1860* (New Brunswick, 1986); Rachel Fuchs, *Abandoned Children: Foundlings and Child Welfare in Nineteenth-Century France* (Albany, 1984); and Gary Sussman, *Selling Mothers' Milk: The Wet-nursing Business in France, 1715–1914* (Urbana, 1982).

XIV. Popular Culture and Beliefs in the Nineteenth Century

Three classic studies of cultural trends are Raymond Williams, *Culture and Society, 1780–1950* (New York, 1958), and *The Long Revolution* (New York, 1961); and Rudolf Schenda, *Volk ohne Buch: Studien zur Sozialgeschichte der popularen Lesestoffe, 1770–1910* (Frankfurt, 1970).

Carlo M. Cipolla, *Literacy and Development in the West* (Baltimore, 1969), Geoffrey H. Bantock, *Culture, Industrialization and Education* (New York, 1960), provide a general background for the modern history of education. Two important recent studies apply to the topic of education's social impact on nineteenth-century Russia: Jeffrey Brooks, *When Russia Learned to Read: Literacy and Popular Culture* (Princeton, 1987); and Ben Eklof, *Russian Peasant Schools: Officialdom, Village Culture and Popular Pedagogy*, 1864–1914 (Berkeley, 1986). See also Fritz Ringer, *Education in Society in Modern Europe* (Bloomington, 1979). For France, Michilina Vaughan and Margaret S. Archer, *Social Conflict and Educational Change in England and France, 1798–1848* (New York, 1971), is good on the early period. E. H. Reisner, *Nationalism and Education Since 1789* (New York, 1923), deals with another important theme, the inculcation of nationalist values through the schools. On rural education see Roger Thabault, *Education and Change in a Village Community* (New York, 1971); and Robert Gildea, *Education in Provincial France, 1800–1914: A Study of Three Departments* (Oxford, 1983). See also Jo Burr Margadant, *Women Educators in the Third Republic* (Princeton 1990). English education has been extensively studied: See B. Simon, *Studies in the History of Education, 1780–1920* (London, 1960); Howard C. Barnard, *A Short History of English Education* (New York, 1955); and David Vincent, *Literacy and Popular Culture: England, 1750–1914* (Cambridge, Eng., 1989). R. D. Atlick, *The English Common Reader: A Social History of the Mass Reading Public, 1800–1900* (Chicago, 1957), deals with the uses of growing literacy. See also Harvey Graff, ed., *Literacy and Social Development in the West* (Cambridge, Eng., 1982).

On the leisure phenomenon generally see Peter Bailey, *Leisure and Class in Victorian England: Rational Recreation and the Contest for Control* (Toronto, 1978). For a brief general interpretation see Michael Marrus, *The Rise of Leisure* (St. Louis, 1976), and *The Emerging of Leisure* (New York, 1974). Peter C. McIntosh, *Sport in Society* (New York, 1963), and *Physical Education in England Since 1800* (London, 1969), are useful. See also J. A. Mangan, *Athleticism in the Victorian and Edwardian Public School* (Cambridge, Eng., 1981); William J. Baker, *Sports in the Western World* (Totowa, N.J., 1982); Kenneth Sheard and Eric Dunning, *Barbarians, Gentlemen and Players: A Sociological Study of the Development of Rugby Football* (New York, 1979); James Walvin, *Football—The People's Game* (London, 1975), and *Leisure and Society, 1830–1950* (London, 1978); and Richard Mandell, *The First Modern Olympics* (Berkeley, 1976). Hugh Cunningham, *Leisure in the Industrial Revolution* (New York, 1980), has a rich bibliography. On France see Richard Holt, *Sport and Society in Modern France* (Hamden, Conn., 1981). On a related leisure issue see Brian Harrison, *Drink and Sobriety in an Early Victorian Country Town: Banbury, 1830–1860* (London, 1969), and *Drink and the Victorians: The Temperance Question in England, 1815–1872* (Pittsburgh, 1972).

On consumerism see Michael Miller, *The Bon Marché: Bourgeois Culture and the Department Store, 1869–1920* (Princeton, 1981); and Rosiland Williams, *Dream Worlds: Mass Consumption in Late Nineteenth-Century France* (Berkeley, 1982).

On changes in emotional standards see Norbert Elias, *The History of Manners*, trans. Edmund Jephcott (New York, 1982)—a classic study; and Alain Corbin, *The Foul and the Flagrant: Odor and the French Social Imagination* (Cambridge, Mass., 1986).

On religion see Kenneth S. Inglis, *Churches and the Working Class in Victorian England* (London, 1963); Serge Bonnet, *Sociologie Politique et Religieuse de la Lorraine* (Paris, 1972); Ralph Gibson, *A Social History of French Catholicism, 1789–1914* (New York, 1989); S. J. Connolly, *Priests and People in Pre-Famine Ireland, 1780–1845* (New York, 1982); Thomas Kselman, *Miracles and Prophecies in*

Nineteenth-Century France (New Brunswick, 1983); Ralph Holbrooke, *Death, Ritual and Bereavement* (New York, 1989); and Ellen Badone, *Religious Orthodoxy and Popular Faith in European Society* (Princeton, 1990).

On other entertainment and popular values see John Walton, *The English Seaside Resort: A Social History, 1750–1914* (New York, 1983); Robert Eben Sackett, *Popular Entertainment, Class and Politics in Munich, 1900–1923* (Cambridge, Mass., 1982); Robert Storch, ed., *Popular Culture and Custom in Nineteenth-Century England* (London, 1982); Terry Parssinen, *Secret Passion, Secret Remedies: Narcotic Drugs in British Society, 1820–1930* (Philadelphia, 1983); Virginia Berridge and Griffith Edwards, *Opium and the People: Opiate Use in Nineteenth-Century England* (London, 1981); Ginette Dunn, *The Fellowship of Song: Popular Singing Traditions in East Suffolk* (London, 1980); William Weber, *Music and the Middle Class: The Social Structure of Concert Life in London, Paris and Vienna* (New York, 1975); Charles Rearick, *Pleasures of the Belle Epoque: Entertainment and Festivity in Turn-of-the-Century France* (New Haven, 1985); Morris Berman, *Social Change and Scientific Organization: The Royal Institution, 1799–1844* (Ithaca, N.Y., 1978); John Lowerson and John Myerscough, *Time to Spare in Victorian England* (Sussex, Eng., 1977); and Roger Cooter, *The Cultural Meaning of Popular Science: Phrenology and the Organization of Consent in Nineteenth-Century Britain* (Cambridge, England, 1984).

XV. Economics and Social Change in the Twentieth Century

Several general overviews of the economic and social history of twentieth-century Europe serve as useful reference books while offering insightful arguments about long-term trends as well. See, especially, Gerold Ambrosius and William H. Hubbard, *A Social and Economic History of Twentieth-Century Europe* (Cambridge, Mass., 1989); Frank B. Tipton and Robert Aldrich, *An Economic and Social History of Europe, 1890–1939* (Baltimore, 1987), and *An Economic and Social History of Europe from 1939 to the Present* (Baltimore, 1987). See also Derek Aldcroft, *The European Economy, 1914–1980* (London, 1982); and Hartmut Kaelbe, *A Social History of Western Europe, 1880–1980* (Savage, Md., 1990).

For an introduction to demographic change in the twentieth century see E. A. Wrigley, *Population and History* (New York, 1969); D. V. Glass and Roger Revelle, eds., *Population and Social Change* (New York, 1972); and T. H. Hollingsworth, *Historical Demography* (Ithaca, N.Y., 1969). More detailed material on population changes in interwar Europe can be found in Dudley Kirk, *Europe's Population in the Interwar Years* (Princeton, 1946); and Wilbert E. Moore, *Economic Demography of Eastern and Southern Europe* (Princeton, 1945). For a thoughtful exploration of the connections among demography, culture, and politics see Richard A. Soloway, *Demography and Degeneration: Eugenics and the Declining Birthrate in Twentieth-Century Britain* (Chapel Hill, 1990).

On specific periods see the several books published in the University of California series, *History of the World Economy in the Twentieth Century*, including Gerd Hardach, *The First World War, 1914–1919* (Berkeley, 1977); Derek Aldcroft, *From Versailles to Wall Street, 1919–1929* (Berkeley, 1977); Charles P. Kindleberger, *The World in Depression, 1929–1939*, rev. ed. (Berkeley, 1986); Alan S. Milward, *War, Economy and Society, 1939–1945* (Berkeley, 1977); Alan

S. Milward, *The Reconstruction of Western Europe, 1945–51* (Berkeley, 1984); and Herman Van der Wee, *Prosperity and Upheaval: The World Economy, 1945–1980* (Berkeley, 1985). The essays on economics, social change, and cultural trends in Stephen Graubard, ed., *A New Europe?* (Boston, 1963), are still a rich source of material on the 1950s and early 1960s. For the 1970s, and a more pessimistic perspective on the Europe of that decade, see two issues of *Daedalus* also edited by Graubard: "Looking for Europe" (Winter 1979), and "The European Predicament" (Spring 1979).

For economic policy and the role of interest groups and government in the economy, the essential starting point is Charles S. Maier, *Recasting Bourgeois Europe: The Stabilization of Germany, France and Italy After World War I* (Princeton, 1976). Andrew Shonfield, *Modern Capitalism: The Changing Balance of Public and Private Power* (Oxford, 1969), remains unsurpassed as a survey of economic policy and institutions in the early post–World War II era. For a sophisticated comparative examination of the relationship between politics and economics in the 1960s and 1970s see Peter J. Katzenstein, ed., *Between Power and Plenty: Foreign Economic Policies of Advanced Industrial States* (Madison, 1978). On specific countries see Karl Hardach, *The Political Economy of Germany in the Twentieth Century* (Berkeley, 1980); Stephen Cohen, *Modern Capitalist Planning: The French Model* (Berkeley, 1977); Richard F. Kuisel, *Capitalism and the State in Modern France: Renovation and Economic Management in the Twentieth Century* (New York, 1981); and Peter Hall, *Governing the Economy: The Politics of State Intervention in Britain and France* (New York, 1986). On the Common Market see John Paxton, *The Developing Common Market: The Structure of the EEC in Theory and in Practice*, 3rd ed. (Boulder, 1976); and Helen Wallace, William Wallace, and Carole Webb, *Policy-Making in the European Community*, 2nd ed. (New York, 1983).

The welfare state has inspired a growing literature, much of it comparative, especially since economic pressures have made social policies more subject to controversy since the mid-1970s. For a comprehensive introduction to the subject, with a focus on France and Britain, see Douglas E. Ashford, *The Emergence of the Welfare States* (Oxford, 1986). Important comparative explorations include Abram de Swaan, *In the Care of the State: Health Care, Education and Welfare in Europe and America in the Modern Era* (New York, 1988); Peter Flora and Arnold J. Heidenheimer, eds., *The Development of Welfare States in Europe and America* (New Brunswick, 1981); Peter Flora, ed., *Growth to Limits: The Western European Welfare States Since World War II*, 5 vols. (New York, 1986–1988); Hugh Heclo, *Modern Social Politics in Britain and Sweden* (New Haven, 1974); Wolfgang J. Mommsen, ed., *The Emergence of the Welfare State in Britain and Germany* (London, 1981); and Eric S. Einhorn and John Logue, *Welfare States in Hard Times* (New York, 1989). For the politics of British policymaking after World War II see Kenneth O. Morgan, *Labour in Power, 1945–51* (New York, 1985). Wilfred Fleisher, *Sweden: The Welfare State* (New York, 1956), remains important for understanding the Swedish experiment. Much work still needs to be done on how various social groups have related to social policy in the postwar era; however, on women see Elizabeth Wilson, *Women and the Welfare State* (London, 1977); on education see Fritz K. Ringer, *Education and Society in Modern Europe* (Bloomington, 1979); and R. Premfors, *The Politics of Higher Education in a Comparative Perspective: France, Sweden, United Kingdom* (Stockholm, 1980).

Relatively little historical work has been done on the structure and culture of business enterprise in Europe. For an essential introduction to the subject see

Alfred D. Chandler, Jr., and Herbert Daems, eds., *Managerial Hierarchies: Comparative Perspectives on the Rise of the Modern Industrial Enterprise* (Cambridge, Mass., 1980). For an exemplary study of a major company see Patrick Fridenson, *Histoire des usines Renault* (Paris, 1972). On business in the 1950s and 1960s see Raymond Vernon, ed., *Big Business and the State: Changing Relations in Western Europe* (Cambridge, Mass., 1974). Michael J. Piore and Charles F. Sabel, *The Second Industrial Divide: Possibilities for Prosperity* (New York, 1984), offers an innovative analysis of long-term trends in business organization and manufacturing techniques. A fresh examination of business enterprise in Germany, Britain, and the United States can be found in Alfred D. Chandler, Jr., *Scale and Scope: The Dynamics of Industrial Capitalism* (Cambridge, Mass., 1990).

For useful accounts of social change in major west European countries see Stanley Hoffmann et al., *In Search of France* (Cambridge, Mass., 1963); John Ardagh, *France Today* (London, 1988); Judith Ryder and Harold Silver, *Modern English Society, History, and Structure, 1850–1970* (London, 1970); Arthur Marwick, *British Society Since 1945* (New York, 1982); Ralf Dahrendorf, *Society and Democracy in Germany* (Garden City, N.Y., 1968); and John Ardagh, *Germany and the Germans: An Anatomy of Society Today* (New York, 1987).

On Eastern Europe see Joni Lovenduski and Jean Woodall, *Politics and Society in Eastern Europe* (Bloomington, 1987); Michael C. Kaser and E. A. Radice, eds., *The Economic History of Eastern Europe, 1919–1975*, 3 vols. (Oxford, 1986–1987); Daniel Chirot, ed., *The Origins of Backwardness in Eastern Europe: Economics and Politics from the Middle Ages Until the Twentieth Century* (Berkeley, 1989). See also Francois Fejtö, *A History of the People's Democracies: Eastern Europe Since Stalin* (New York, 1971); Jürgen Tampke, *The People's Republics of Eastern Europe* (New York, 1983).

On recent social and economic change in the Soviet Union and the crisis of the late 1980s, see Geoffrey Hosking, *The Awakening of the Soviet Union* (Cambridge, Mass., 1990); Basile Kerblay, *Gorbachev's Russia* (New York, 1989); Moshe Lewin, *The Gorbachev Phenomenon: An Historical Interpretation* (Berkeley, 1988); and for background see Stephen Cohen, Alexander Rabinowitch, and Robert Sharlet, eds., *The Soviet Union Since Stalin* (Bloomington, 1980).

XVI. Social Classes in the Twentieth Century

For a general introduction to the history of social theories about class and their applicability to twentieth-century Europe, see Anthony Giddens, *The Class Structure of the Advanced Societies* (New York, 1973). For a concise introduction to Marxist points of view and the main criticisms they have provoked, see Tom Bottomore, *Classes in Modern Society* (New York, 1966). Ralf Dahrendorf, *Class and Class Conflict in Industrial Society* (Stanford, 1959), remains an important critique of the Marxist view.

The literature on peasants and rural peoples has tended to focus on France. See, especially, Lawrence Wylie, *Village in the Vaucluse*, 3rd ed. (Cambridge, Mass., 1974); Henri Mendras, *The Vanishing Peasant* (Cambridge, Mass., 1970); Gordon Wright, *Rural Revolution in France* (Stanford, 1964); and Suzanne Berger, *Peasants Against Politics: Rural Organization in Brittany, 1911–1967* (Cambridge, Mass., 1972). For other countries see Robert G. Moeller, *German Peasants and Agrarian Politics, 1914–1924: The Rhineland and Westphalia* (Chapel Hill, 1986); Julian Pitt-Rivers, *People of the Sierra* (Chicago, 1971); Douglas R. Holmes, *Cultural Disenchantments: Worker-Peasantries in Northeast Italy* (Princeton, 1989); Leopold H. Haimson, ed., *The Politics of Rural Russia, 1905–1914* (Bloomington, 1979); David Mitrany, *The Land and the Peasant in Rumania* (London, 1950); Andrzei Korbonski, *Politics and Social Agriculture in Poland* (New York, 1965); C. M. Hann, *A Village Without Solidarity: Polish Peasants in Years of Crisis* (New Haven, 1985); and Jozo Tomasevic, *Peasants, Politics and Economic Change in Yugoslavia* (Stanford, 1955).

On workers and their relationship to middle-class culture see Ferdynand Zweig, *The Worker in an Affluent Society* (New York, 1962); and John H. Goldthorpe et al., *The Affluent Worker in the Class Structure* (Cambridge, Eng., 1969), which argues for the continuity of the working class rather than its assimilation into the middle class. For an important set of explorations into the sources of working-class radicalism after 1950, see Richard Hamilton, *Affluence and the French Worker in the Fourth Republic* (Princeton, 1967); and Duncan Gallie, *Social Inequality and Class Radicalism in France and Britain* (Cambridge, Eng., 1983). On working-class protest in the 1960s and 1970s see Colin Crouch and Alessandro Pizzorno, eds., *The Resurgence of Class Conflict in Western Europe Since 1968*, 2 vols. (London, 1978). On the reaction of workers to changes in technology and business organization, see Dorothy Wedderburn and Rosemary Crompton, *Workers' Attitudes and Technology* (Cambridge, England, 1972); Roger Penn, *Skilled Workers in the Class Structure* (New York, 1984); and Charles F. Sabel, *Work and Politics: The Division of Labor in Industry* (New York, 1982).

On authority relations in the workplace and the culture of work, Michael Crozier, *The Bureaucratic Phenomenon* (Chicago, 1964), is a classic. See also Robert Linhart, *The Assembly Line* (Amherst, Mass., 1981); Ronald Dore, *British Factory—Japanese Factory* (London, 1973); Marc Maurice et al., *The Social Foundations of Industrial Power: A Comparison of France and Germany* (Cambridge, Mass., 1986); and Michael Seidman, *Workers Against Work: Labor in Paris and Barcelona During the Popular Fronts* (Berkeley, 1991). On technical and white-collar workers see Serge Mallet, *The New Working Class* (Nottingham, 1975); Michael Crozier, *The World of the Office Worker* (Chicago, 1971); and Duncan Gallie, *In Search of the New Working Class: Automation and Social Integration Within the Capitalist Enterprise* (Cambridge, England, 1978). On workers in Eastern Europe see Jan Triska and Charles Gati, eds., *Blue-Collar Workers in Eastern Europe* (London, 1981); Howard M. Wachtel, *Workers' Management and Workers' Wages in Yugoslavia* (Ithaca, N.Y., 1973); and Leonard Shapiro and Joseph Godson, eds., *The Soviet Worker* (London, 1982). For readings on the labor movement, see section XIX, Social Movements and Popular Protest in the Twentieth Century.

The middle class and the elite have received much less attention than have workers. Useful studies include Heinrich Winkler, *Mittelstand, Demokratie und Nationalsozialismus* (Cologne, 1972); Herman Lebovics, *Social Conservatism and the Middle Classes in Germany, 1914–1933* (Princeton, 1969), R. V. Clements, *Managers: A Study of Their Careers in Industry* (London, 1958); Luc Boltanski, *The Making of a Class: Cadres in French Society* (Cambridge, England, 1987); Dean Savage, *Founders, Heirs, and Managers: French Industrial Leadership in Transition*

(Beverly Hills, 1979); Steven M. Zdatny, *The Politics of Survival: Artisans in Twentieth-Century France* (New York, 1990); Linda Weiss, *Creating Capitalism: The State and Small Business Since 1945* (Oxford, 1988); and J. Howorth and P. Cerny, eds., *Elites in France: Origins, Reproduction and Power* (London, 1981).

On social divisions in Eastern Europe see Milovan Djilas, *The New Class: An Analysis of the Communist System* (London, 1966); Walter D. Conner, *Socialism, Politics, and Equality: Hierarchy and Change in Eastern Europe and the USSR* (New York, 1979); Pierre Kende and Zdenek Strmiska, *Equality and Inequality in Eastern Europe* (New York, 1984); and Mervyn Matthews, *Poverty in the Soviet Union: The Life-Styles of the Underprivileged in Recent Years* (New York, 1986).

XVII. Women, Gender, and the Family in the Twentieth Century

Much work remains to be done on women's experience during the two world wars. Margaret Randolph Higonnet, Jane Jenson, Sonya Michel, and Margaret Collins Weitz, eds., *Behind the Lines: Gender and the Two World Wars* (New Haven, 1987), provides an excellent introduction to the issues and an important set of essays on women and gender relations in Europe and the United States. On women and work see Gail Braydon, *Women Workers in the First World War: The British Experience* (London, 1981); and Penny Summerfield, *Women Workers in the Second World War* (London, 1984). By contrast, women in interwar and Nazi Germany have attracted a good deal of scholarly attention; see Renate Pore, *A Conflict of Interest: Women in German Social Democracy* (Westport, Conn., 1981); Claudia Koonz, *Mothers in the Fatherland: Women, the Family, and Politics in Nazi Germany* (New York, 1987); Jill Stephenson, *The Nazi Organization of Women* (New York, 1981), and *Women in Nazi Society* (New York, 1975); Renate Bridenthal, Atina Grossman, and Marion Kaplan, eds., *When Biology Became Destiny: Women in Weimar and Nazi Germany* (New York, 1984); and Leila Rupp, *Mobilizing Women for War: German and American Propoganda, 1939–1945* (Princeton, 1978). For the role women played in resisting the Nazi regime, see Vera Laska, *Women in the Resistance and in the Holocaust* (Westport, Conn., 1983); and Margaret L. Rossiter, *Women in the Resistance* (New York, 1986).

For women's experience in specific countries over the longer sweep of the twentieth century, see Donald Meyer, *Sex and Power: The Rise of Women in America, Russia, Sweden, and Italy* (Scranton, Pa., 1987); Jane Lewis, *Women in England, 1870–1950: Sexual Divisions and Social Change* (Bloomington, 1984); Elizabeth Wilson, *Only Half Way to Paradise: Women in Postwar Britain, 1945–68* (London, 1980); Bonnie G. Smith, *Confessions of a Concierge: Madame Lucie's History of Twentieth-Century France* (New Haven, 1985); Ann Cornelison, *Women of the Shadows* (New York, 1977); and Utz Frevort, *Women in German History: From Bourgeois Emancipation to Sexual Liberty* (New York, 1989). Although much less work has been done on women in eastern Europe, Soviet women have received significant scholarly attention: see, especially, Gail Wartshofsky Lapidus, *Women in Soviet Society: Equality, Development and Social Change* (Berkeley, 1978); and Barbara Holland, ed., *Soviet Sisterhood* (Bloomington, 1985).

On feminist movements see Jill Lovenduski, *Women and European Politics: Contemporary Feminism and Social Policy* (Amherst, Mass., 1986); Claire Duchen,

Feminism in France: From May '68 to Mitterrand (London, 1986); and Jennifer Dale and Peggy Foster, *Feminists and State Welfare* (London, 1982).

For studies of the family in the early decades of the twentieth century, see Diana Gittins, *Fair Sex: Family Size and Structure in Britain, 1900–1939* (New York, 1982); and D. V. Glass, *Population Policies and Movements in Europe* (Oxford, 1940). There a number of important sociological studies of the family in postwar Britain: see, especially, Peter Willmott and Michael Young, *Family and Kinship in East London* (London, 1957), and *The Symmetrical Family* (New York, 1973). R. E. Pahl, *Patterns of Urban Life* (London, 1970), offers useful insights into family life in the 1960s. See also several general studies of the family, including Colin Rosser and Christopher Harris, *The Family and Social Change* (New York, 1965); Jacques Donzolet, *The Policing of Families* (New York, 1979); R. Chester, ed., *Divorce in Europe* (Leiden, 1977); and Alice Rossi, Jerome Kagan, and Tamara Haraven, eds., *The Family* (New York, 1978).

XVIII. The Social Impact of War, Revolution, and Fascism

For an introduction to the social history of the Russian Revolution see Marc Ferro, *October 1917: A Social History of the Russian Revolution* (Boston, 1980). On the revolutionary experience of specific social groups see Graeme J. Gill, *Peasants and Government in the Russian Revolution* (New York, 1979); Robert B. McKean, *St. Petersburg Between the Revolutions: Workers and Revolutionaries, June 1907–February 1917* (New Haven, 1990); and S. A. Smith, *Red Petrograd: Revolution in the Factories, 1917–18* (Cambridge, England, 1983). See also Roger Pethybridge, *The Social Prelude to Stalinism* (New York, 1974). On social upheavals elsewhere that came in the wake of the Russian Revolution, see Risto Alapuro, *State and Revolution in Finland* (Berkeley, 1989); and F. L. Carsten, *Revolution in Central Europe, 1918–19* (Berkeley, 1972).

On the social experience of World War I see Eric J. Leed, *No Man's Land: Combat and Identity in World War I* (New York, 1979); Jürgen Kocka, *Facing Total War: German Society, 1914–1918* (Cambridge, Mass., 1984); Jean-Jacques Becker, *The Great War and the French People* (Dover, N.H., 1985); J. M. Winter, *The Great War and the British People* (London, 1986); and Arthur Marwick, *The Deluge: British Society and the First World War* (London, 1965).

A number of studies have probed the social bases of nazism in the 1920s and early 1930s. See, especially, William Sheridan Allen, *The Nazi Seizure of Power: The Experience of a Single German Town, 1922–1945*, rev. ed. (New York, 1984), a fine local study; Theodore Abel, *Why Hitler Came into Power* (Cambridge, Mass., 1986), which analyzes the autobiographical essays of Nazi party members; and two careful electoral studies, Richard Hamilton, *Who Voted for Hitler?* (Princeton, 1982), and Thomas Childers, *The Nazi Voter: The Social Foundation of Fascism in Germany, 1919–1933* (Chapel Hill, 1983). See also Hans Speier, *German White-Collar Workers and the Rise of Hitler* (New Haven, 1986); Rudy Koshar, *Social Life, Local Politics and Nazism: Marburg, 1880–1935* (Chapel Hill, 1986); and Geoffrey J. Giles, *Students and National Socialism in Germany* (Princeton, 1985). On the social impact of the regime after Hitler came to power, see David Schoenbaum, *Hitler's Social Revolution: Class and Status in Nazi Germany*

(New York, 1966); Ian Kershaw, *Popular Opinion and Political Dissent in the Third Reich: Bavaria, 1933–1945* (Oxford, 1983); Christa Kamenetshy, *Children's Literature in Hitler's Germany: The Cultural Policy of National Socialism* (Athens, Ohio, 1984); and Detlev Peukert, *Inside Nazi Germany: Conformity, Opposition and Racism in Everyday Life* (New Haven, 1987).

On fascism in Italy see Victoria de Grazia, *The Culture of Consent* (New York, 1981); Luisa Passerini, *Fascism in Popular Memory: The Cultural Experience of the Turin Working Class* (Cambridge, England, 1987); Alice A. Kelikian, *Town and Country Under Fascism: The Transformation of Brescia, 1915–1926* (Oxford, 1986); Anthony L. Cardoza, *Agrarian Elites and Italian Fascism: The Province of Bologna, 1901–26* (Princeton, 1982); Frank M. Snowden, *The Fascist Revolution in Tuscany, 1919–1922* (Cambridge, England, 1989); and Frank Tannenbaum, *The Fascist Experience: Italian Society and Culture, 1922–1945* (New York, 1972).

For the social history of the Spanish Civil War see Gerald Brenan, *The Spanish Labyrinth: An Account of the Social and Political Background of the Civil War* (Cambridge, Eng.,1950); Ronald Fraser, *The Blood of Spain* (London, 1981); E. Malefakis, *Agrarian Reform and Peasant Revolution in Spain: Origins of the Civil War* (New Haven, 1970); Colin M. Winston, *Workers and the Right in Spain, 1900–1936* (Princeton, 1985); and Adrian Shubert, *The Road to Revolution in Spain: The Coal Miners of Asturias, 1860–1934* (Urbana, 1987).

World War II has yet to receive the kind of attention that social historians have devoted to World War I. For an introduction to the subject see Arthur Marwick, ed., *Total War and Social Change* (New York, 1988). Important studies include Angus Calder, *The People's War: Britain, 1939–1945* (New York, 1969); John F. Sweets, *Choices in Vichy France: The French Under Nazi Occupation* (New York, 1986); Alexander Werth, *Russia at War, 1941–1945* (London, 1964); and Susan J. Linz, ed., *The Impact of World War II on the Soviet Union* (Totowa, N.J., 1985).

XIX. Social Movements and Popular Protest in the Twentieth Century

On the labor movement and the Left several comparative studies offer useful introductions to the subject. See, especially, E. M. Kassalow, *Trade Unions and Industrial Relations: An International Comparison* (New York, 1969); Adolf Sturmthal, *Left of Center: European Labor Since World War II* (Urbana, 1983); and Hans Slomp, *Labor Relations in Europe: A History of Issues and Developments* (New York, 1990). France has received a good deal of scholarly attention: see Kathryn E. Amdur, *Syndicalist Legacy: Trade Unions and Politics in Two French Cities in the Era of World War I* (Urbana, 1986); Gary S. Cross, *A Quest for Time: The Reduction of Work in Britain and France, 1840–1940* (Berkeley, 1989); Tyler Stovall, *The Rise of the Paris Red Belt* (Berkeley, 1990); Herrick Chapman, *State Capitalism and Working-Class Radicalism in the French Aircraft Industry* (Berkeley, 1991); Annie Kriegel, *The French Communists: Profile of a People* (Chicago, 1972); and George Ross, *Workers and Communists in France: From Popular Front to Eurocommunism* (Berkeley, 1982). For systematic comparisons of the communist movements in France and Italy, see Donald L. M. Blackmer and Sidney Tarrow, eds., *Communism in Italy and France* (Princeton, 1975). On Britain see James

Cronin, *Labor and Society in Britain, 1918–1979* (London, 1984). Two excellent comparative studies of European labor since 1945 are Peter Gourevitch et al., *Unions and Economic Crisis: Britain, West Germany and Sweden* (London, 1985); and Peter Lange, George Ross, and Maurizio Vannicelli, *Unions, Change and Crisis: French and Italian Union Strategy and the Political Economy, 1945–1980* (London, 1982).

Accounts of youth rebellion and the uprisings of 1968 include Alain Touraine, *The May Movement: Revolt and Reform* (New York, 1971); and Raymond Aron, *The Elusive Revolution: Anatomy of a Student Revolt* (New York, 1969).

On postwar democratic movements in southern Europe see Raymond Carr and Juan Pablo Fusi, *Spain: Dictatorship to Democracy* (London, 1981); Joe Foweraker, *Making Democracy in Spain: Grass-Roots Struggle in the South, 1955–1975* (Cambridge, Eng., 1989); Jose Maria Maravall, *The Transition to Democracy in Spain* (London, 1982); and Nicos Poulantzas, *The Crisis of the Dictatorships: Portugal, Spain, Greece* (London, 1976).

Studies of the Green movement, environmentalism, and postwar campaigns for disarmament tend to focus on West Germany. See Rob Burns and Wilfried van der Will, *Protest and Democracy in West Germany: Extra-Parliamentary Opposition and the Democratic Agenda* (New York, 1988); E. Papadakis, *The Green Movement in West Germany* (London, 1984); and Fritjof Capra and Charlene Spretnak, *Green Politics* (New York, 1984).

On popular protest in eastern Europe see Timothy Garton Ash, *The Polish Revolution: Solidarity* (New York, 1983); C. Harman, *Class Struggles in Eastern Europe, 1945–83* (London, 1983); Roger Woods, ed., *Opposition in the GDR Under Honecker* (New York, 1986); and H. Gordon Skilling, *Czechoslovakia: Interrupted Revolution* (Princeton, 1976). Useful introductions to the revolutionary changes in eastern Europe at the end of the 1980s include Timothy Garton Ash, *The Uses of Adversity: Essays on the Fate of Central Europe* (New York, 1990), and *The Magic Lantern: The Revolution of '89 Witnessed in Warsaw, Budapest, Berlin and Prague* (New York, 1990); and Elie Abel, *The Shattered Bloc: Behind the Upheaval in Eastern Europe* (Boston, 1990).

XX. Immigration, Race Relations, and Ethnicity in the Twentieth Century

For an introduction to immigration and race relations in western Europe, see Stephen Castles and Godula Kosack, *Immigrant Workers and Class Structure in Western Europe* (London, 1973); and Stephen Castles et al., *Here for Good: Western Europe's New Ethnic Minorities* (London, 1984). Important specialized studies include Gary S. Cross, *Immigrant Workers in Industrial France: The Making of a New Laboring Class* (Philadelphia, 1983); Gary Freeman, *Immigrant Labor and Racial Conflict in Industrial Societies: The French and British Experience, 1945–1975* (Princeton, 1979); Michael J. Piore, *Birds of Passage: Migrant Labor and Industrial Societies* (New York, 1979); Robert Miles, *Racism and Migrant Labour* (London, 1982); Hans Christian Buechler and Judith-Maria Buechler, eds., *Migrants in Europe: The Role of Family, Labor, and Politics* (New York, 1987); and Ira Katznelson, *Black Men, White Cities: Race, Politics, and Migration in the U.S. and*

Britain, 1948–68 (New York, 1973). Jane Kramer, *Unsettling Europe* (New York, 1981), provides vivid portraits of immigrant families and other socially marginalized people in several European countries. For an insightful survey of how government policy and social scientific opinion about race have evolved in twentieth-century Britain, see Paul B. Rich, *Race and Empire in British Politics*, 2nd ed. (Cambridge, Eng., 1990).

On ethnic relations in eastern Europe and the Soviet Union see George Klein and Milan J. Reban, *The Politics of Ethnicity in Eastern Europe* (New York, 1981); and Bohdan Nahayo and Victor Swoboda, *Soviet Disunion: A History of the Nationalities Problem in the USSR* (New York, 1990).

For a general introduction to ethnic nationalism in western Europe, see William Beer, *The Unexpected Rebellion: Ethnic Activism in Contemporary France* (New York, 1980). Michael Hechter, *Internal Colonialism* (Berkeley, 1975), has stimulated important debate. See also R. D. Grillo, *Dominant Languages: Language and Hierarchy in Britain and France* (Cambridge, England, 1989); Tom Nairn, *The Break-up of Britain* (London, 1977); Katherine O'Sullivan See, *First World Nationalisms: Class and Ethnic Politics in Northern Ireland and Quebec* (Chicago, 1986); Anthony Smith, *The Ethnic Revival* (Cambridge, England, 1979); and E. Tiryakian and Ronald Rogowski, eds., *New Nationalisms of the Developed West* (Boston, 1985).

XXI. Popular Culture in the Twentieth Century

The study of popular culture and of the relationship between high and low culture in twentieth-century Europe remains relatively undeveloped in comparison to work on earlier periods. On the cultural impact of World War I see Paul Fussell, *The Great War and Modern Memory* (New York, 1975); and Modris Eksteins, *Rites of Spring: The Great War and the Birth of the Modern Age* (Boston, 1989). On the Soviet Union see Lynn Mally, *Culture of the Future: The Proletkult Movement in Revolutionary Russia* (Berkeley, 1990); and Timothy W. Ryback, *Rock Around the Bloc: A History of Rock Music in Eastern Europe and the Soviet Union* (New York, 1990). Robert Graves and Alan Hodges, *The Long Weekend: A British Social History, 1918–1939* (New York, 1941) remains a classic on popular culture in interwar Britain; see also D. L. LeMahieu, *A Culture for Democracy: Mass Communication and the Cultivated Mind Between the Wars* (New York, 1988). Important interpretative perspectives can be found in Raymond Williams, *The Long Revolution* (New York, 1961); and Richard Hoggart, *The Uses of Literacy* (London, 1957).

Film has obviously had an immense impact. A useful starting point for this subject is Paul Monaco, *Cinema and Society: France and Germany During the Twenties* (New York, 1976). For insightful overviews of popular culture since the 1960s see John Ardagh, *France Today* (London, 1988), and *Germany and the Germans: An Anatomy of Society Today* (New York, 1987); and Jane Kramer, *The Europeans* (New York, 1988).

Index

Abortion, 85, 194, 288, 381, 410
Adolescence, 84, 193, 275–76
  See also Children; Youth
Advertising, 221, 314–15, 333, 335, 366
Aged. *See* Elderly
Agricultural classes, in Industrial Revolution, 78–128, 242–56
  See also Peasants
Agricultural specialization, 107, 249
Agriculture, 16–25, 105–109, 213, 225
  enclosure movement and, 78–79
  market, 75, 79, 106–108, 110
  after World War II, 341, 353–54, 357, 362, 415
Albania, 402
Alsatian regionalism, 391
Amalgated Society of Engineers, 294, 296
"Americanization", 411
Amoco Cadiz, 387
Anarchism, 121–22, 180, 327
Andalusia. *See* Spain
Anti-Semitism, 20, 256, 262–63, 265, 269, 279, 405
Apprenticeship, 35–36, 172
Architecture, 160
Aristocracy, 25–33, 109–15, 226, 232–33, 238
  in early industrial society, 78–79, 87, 109–15, 142
  as no longer upper class, 232–33, 242–48
  after World War II, 337–41, 409
"Aristocracy of Labor," 175, 181, 185
Aristocratic titles, 115
Aristocratic women, 38–39, 63
Artillery, 32, 94
Artisans, 19, 35–36, 53–58, 78–79, 119, 167–80, 212, 213, 279, 285, 292, 294
Artists, 158
Arts, patronizing of, 109, 140, 158, 159–60
Assembly line, 214
Assembly of Notables of 1787, 31
Atelier, L', 170

Austria, 345, 388
"Autogestion", 370, 385
Automobiles, 214, 219, 221, 288, 348, 353, 367, 368, 379, 410

Baader–Meinhof Gang, 385
Baby farms, 85
Balance of payments, 323
Balkans, 22, 42, 69, 123, 147, 229, 294
Baltic region, 24, 109
Banking, 92, 216, 225, 348–49, 359
Barcelona, 130, 170, 180
Barthe, Roland, 387
Basque nationalists, 391, 392, 393–94
Beatles, 335, 386, 404
Beauvoir, Simone de, 381
Belgium, 99, 130, 147, 182, 214, 231, 235, 291, 339, 345, 353, 389, 392
Berlin, 129, 140, 141, 179, 372, 402
Bernstein, Eduard, 298
Bessemer process, 213
Beveridge Plan, 343
Bicycles, 219, 221, 223, 272
Biedermeier style, 155
Birmingham, 9, 129, 197, 400
Birth control, 38–39, 127, 163–64, 211, 271, 288–89, 309, 376–77
Bismarck, Otto von, 342
Blanc, Louis, 179
Bodies, 1, 74, 223
Bohemianism, 158
Bologna, 251
Boulton, Matthew, 71
Bourgeoisie, 14, 49–53, 77–80, 138
Bourse du travail, 293, 294, 295
Boy Scouts, 276
Bread riots, 38, 57, 120
Breton nationalists, 391, 392, 394
Bristol, 400
British Medical Society, 144
Brotherton, Joseph, 141
Budapest, 405

Bulgaria, 339, 357, 401–402, 405, 408

Bülow tariff (1902), 226, 245–46

Bureaucracy, 49–50, 80, 112, 135, 142, 202, 230, 238, 243–45, 264, 267, 290, 353, 361, 383, 385, 407

Burschenschaften, 148

Business, 140, 149, 215–20, 226, 410, 413
  small, 138–39, 219, 259–64, 363
  after World War II, 338, 354, 410
  See also Manufacturing

Businessmen, 25–27, 33, 50–51, 143
  See also Bourgeoisie; Business; Entrepreneurs; Industrialists

Buying power, 101–102, 227–28

Campaign for Nuclear Disarmament (CND), 389

Capitalism, 51, 88, 171, 383–85, 405, 407

Carbonari, 145, 148

Cartels, 217–18

Catalans, 391, 394

Center party, 253, 326

Change, 413–16
  forces against, in preindustrial society, 63–66
  forces for, from 1750 to 1820, 87–88

Charity, 27, 51, 81, 142, 240

Charter 77 (Czechoslovakia), 404

Chartism, 175, 197, 200

Chemical industry, 214, 215, 220

Chernobyl, 387

Child abandonment, 39

Child rearing, 39, 70, 163–64, 275–76, 377, 378–79

Children, 36, 51, 94, 162–64, 186, 192, 238, 271, 275–76, 378–79
  education of, 142–45, 173–74, 234–36, 271
  in sexual revolution, 74–75
  working-class, 186, 192, 379
  See also Adolescence; Family

Chirac, Jacques, 399

Christian Democratic parties, 341, 344, 347, 350

Churches, 31, 87, 155–57, 201
  after World War II, 339, 361–62, 399, 403–404, 410
  See also Clergy; Protestantism; Religion

Cities, 46–49, 53–59, 128–35, 166–167
  government in, 49, 132–34, 238
  as market for agricultural goods, 106–108

Class(es), 3, 6, 8, 10–11, 211, 220
  chart of major changes in, 417
  conflict between, 150–54, 189, 195, 201, 218, 286, 324–28, 335, 366–67, 405, 407, 409
  decline of traditional, after World War II, 336–41, 366–68, 409, 410–12
  lower, of cities, 58–59, 120–35, 166–67
  See also Lower middle class; Middle class;
"Underclass"; Upper class; Working class

Cleanliness, 162–63

Clergy, 50, 80, 139, 141, 234, 389

Clerical work, 211, 219, 267–70, 375

Clocks, 67

Clothing, 64, 82, 185, 223, 272, 278, 374, 386, 387

Club Med, 378

"Co-determination," 345

Collectivization, 306, 357, 361

Combination Acts of 1799 and 1800, 196

Commercialization, 15, 185, 223, 272, 278

Commissariat du plan, 349

Common lands, 23, 105–106

Common Market. *See* European Community

Communism and communist parties, 255, 302–303, 304–307, 313–14, 324, 334, 336, 341, 342, 344, 350, 351, 361, 362, 364, 370, 373, 385, 401–408, 409, 415

Compagnonnages, 172

Competition, 64, 216–20, 405, 407

Conception cycle, 83–84

Condoms, 164

Confédération générale du travail (CGT), 253, 290, 295, 300

Conservative groups, 94, 242–48, 339, 341, 350
  See also Fascism; Nazism

Conservative party (Britain), 343, 347, 349

Consumer(s), 64, 82, 145–49, 222–25, 270–71, 273–74, 365–66
  new products for, 222–24, 271, 367, 403
  society of, after World War II, 331, 333, 335, 340, 366, 367, 374, 410–11, 413, 416

Consumerism, 2, 64, 82, 270–71, 273–74, 306, 384, 403, 404, 410–12

Consumption and production, 101–102, 220–22

Cook, Thomas, 159

Cooperatives
  artisan, 177
  peasant, 126, 250–52, 255, 335, 362

Corn Law of 1815, 146

Corporations, 216–17, 267

Corsicans, 391

Courtship, 37, 43, 71, 272, 275

Craftsmen. *See* Artisans

Credit, 108, 216

Crédit mobilier, 216

Crime, 48, 51, 117, 120, 131, 135, 210, 315, 334, 398

Croix de feu, 265, 319, 326, 330

Crystal Palace Exhibition, 142

Culture
  aristocracy and, 31–33, 109–15
  popular preindustrial, 59–60

Czechoslovakia, 339, 373–74, 402, 404–406, 408

Dandyism, 27
De Gaulle, Charles, 385
Death and death rates, 60, 74–75, 104, 131,
    184, 211, 220, 224, 309, 410
  in preindustrial society, 36, 39, 58
  in World War I, 317–20
  in World War II, 333
Decazeville, 181
Decembrist revolt, 114
Decolonization, 331
Democracy, rise of, 231–32
Demography, 1, 72–77, 211–12, 309,
    336–37, 347, 401
  See also Population
Denmark, 249, 251, 361, 367, 415
Department stores, 102–103, 221, 264, 273
Depression(s)
  in mature industrial society, 225, 229
  of 1929–39, 229–30, 241, 248, 254–56,
    301–303, 329, 338, 341
Dickens, Charles, 155
Discontent. See Protests; Revolution(s);
    Riots
Disease, 36, 39, 58
Divorce, 277, 289, 334, 361, 374, 379–80,
    410, 415
Dockers, 280, 284, 294
Doctors, 50, 135, 144, 224, 259–60, 264,
    376, 404
"Dollar gap", 351
Domestic manufacturing, 48, 69, 80, 117,
    126, 171, 279
Domesticity, 162–63, 204–208, 237, 278,
    381
Dowry, 37, 57, 141, 160–61, 277
Dreyfus case, 263, 312
Drinking, 45, 118, 135, 185, 195, 288, 315,
    372
Dubcek, Alexander, 373
Duels, 27, 112

East Germany, 334, 346, 401–402, 405–406,
    408
Eastern Europe, 9–12, 34, 47, 117–18, 145,
    211, 232, 247, 415
  mature industrial society and, 304–308
  revolutions of 1989 in, 401–408, 409,
    411
  after World War II, 333, 334, 336, 342,
    346, 350–51, 357, 361, 366, 415
Ecole Polytechnique, 376
Economics
  of industrial society, 102–103, 109–11,
    149–52, 220–230
  middle-class, 149–52
  in 1700s, 17–18, 32, 36–38
  of World War I, 317–24
  after World War II, 351–60
  See also Agriculture; Business; Commer-
    cialization; Depression(s); Manufac-
    turing; Poverty; Taxes

Educated classes, 135, 142–45
Education
  mass, 153, 173–74, 339–40, 343, 344,
    346, 367, 368, 391, 399, 410, 416
  middle-class, 135, 244–45, 257, 364–65,
    368, 376
Elderly, 36–38, 184, 223, 225, 239, 276
  among peasants, 36–37, 38, 115–16
  after World War II, 365–66
Electricity, 212–13, 221, 337
Emancipation of serfs (Russia), 22, 23,
    105–109, 118
  See also Serfdom
Embourgeoisement, 367–68
Emigration, 73–74, 117
Emotional stress, 5, 162, 275–76
Employees. See White-collar workers
Enclosure movement, 28–29, 82, 92
Enlightenment, 5, 70
"Enterprise committees", 345
Entrepreneurs, 92
  lack of, 99–100, 407
Environmentalist movements, 387–91, 396,
    404, 409
Estates, large, 22–25
Estonia, 407
ETA (*Euskadi Ta Azkatasum*), 394, 395
Ethnicity, 335, 340, 369–70, 391–96,
    405–406, 407, 409, 411–12, 415, 416
  See also Immigrants and immigration
European community, 331, 338, 352, 354,
    359, 362, 395–96, 400–401, 406,
    408, 415

Factories, 90, 170, 183, 188, 413
  artisans in, 167, 174
Family, 15, 64, 160–65, 191–96, 203,
    273–77, 288–89, 413–14
  of artisans, 57, 204–208
  of bourgeoisie, 49–53
  middle-class, 160–65, 204–208, 273–77,
    378
  peasant, 38–39, 127
  working-class, 191–96, 204–208, 288–89,
    379
  after World War II, 343, 374–82
Family economy, 38, 203
Famine, 19–20, 76–77, 118, 319
Farm equipment, 107
Farming. See Agriculture
Farts, 62
Fascism, 248, 325–26, 334, 339, 341, 348
  See also Nazism
Federation of Salaried Commercial
    Employees (Germany), 269
Feminists, 207–208, 231, 278–79, 380–82,
    396, 415
Festivals, 21, 41, 45–46, 62, 116, 194, 363
Feudalism, 31
  See also Manorialism
Feuds, 46

Financial crises, in mature industrial soci-
    ety, 225, 229
Food, 20, 76–77, 184–85, 222, 282, 319,
    333
France, 20, 76, 99, 122, 129, 147, 211, 213,
    216–17, 228, 231–32, 235, 240, 246,
    255, 290, 295, 298–99, 312–13,
    323–24
  ethnic and regional conflict in, 391–94
  immigrants and racism in, 369, 397–400
  nationalizations in, 348–50
  student protest in, 383–85
  welfare program in, 342, 344–45, 347
  after World War II, 334, 336, 340, 351,
    353–54, 355, 358, 359, 361, 362,
    363, 367–68, 370, 376, 387, 388, 415
  See also French Revolution
Frankfurt, 353
Frederick the Great, 32
French Revolution (1789), 22, 32, 80, 85,
    87–88, 93, 122, 133, 171, 204

Gagauz people, 407
Gambetta, Léon, 252
Gambling, 114, 195
Gartenlaube, Die, 155, 265
Gdansk, 374
General strike, 290, 292, 300–301, 324
Gentry, 29
German Bundestag, 376
Germany, 8, 11, 74, 99, 129, 155, 173, 211,
    213, 228, 232, 235, 246, 255, 264,
    296, 297–98, 302, 312–13, 319–21,
    325–27, 331, 333, 342, 344, 415
  artisans of, 94, 173, 219
  big business in, by 1890s, 215–17, 226–27,
    229, 245–46
  land tenure in, 122–23
  riots in, 122–23
  welfare program in, 238–39, 342
  See also East Germany; Nazism; Prussia;
    West Germany
Gilchrist-Thomas process, 213
Golota, 28
Grand National Consolidated Trades
    Union, 176, 178
Grandes écoles, 340
Great Britain, 14, 18, 73, 129, 183, 197,
    226, 229, 231–32, 291–92, 294, 301,
    309, 317, 329, 415
  aristocracy in, 28
  ethnic and regional conflict in, 391–96
  immigrants and racism in, 369, 397–400
  Industrial Revolution in, 87–93, 98–99,
    183, 197
  nationalizations in, 348–50
  welfare program in, 239, 342–43, 347–48
  after World War II, 333, 334, 336, 338,
    339, 351–52, 353–54, 355, 358, 359,
    362, 370
Greece, 337, 339, 344, 401

Green parties, 389–91, 395–96, 398, 411
Greenham Common, 389
Grève, 59
Guilds, 54–56, 86, 87, 93, 112, 170–71,
    173, 202, 219
Gymnasium, 258

Haussmann, Baron, 133
Health, 58, 184, 222, 224, 259–60, 266
  middle-class, 163
  urban, 131, 134, 163, 184
Health insurance, 343–46, 348, 362
Hirsch-Dunker unions, 293
Hitler, Adolf, 230, 248, 326, 333, 396
Hobereaux, 28
Holek, Wendel, 192, 194
Holland. See Netherlands, the
Honor, 27, 112
Hospitals, 60, 220, 344
House of Lords, 32, 113, 231
Housing, 20, 57, 64, 132, 184, 223, 254
  in early industrial society, 132, 133,
    184–85
  after 1870, 223, 254
  after World War II, 344, 346, 348, 367,
    368, 399, 400
Hungary, 17, 68, 109, 113, 228, 304, 346,
    350, 357, 372, 374, 401, 404, 405,
    408

Illegitimacy, 83, 86, 131, 210
Immigrants and immigration, 130–212,
    283, 360, 369–70, 371, 378,
    396–401, 409
Imperialism, 227, 245, 312
Incomes. See Profits; Wages
Individualism
  new sense of, 68, 141
  self-help impulse of, 141, 173–75
Industrial Revolution
  causes of, 91–92
  early, 88–96, 97–209
  spread of, 91–96, 98–100
Industrial society
  early, 97–209
  mature, 210–330
  after World War II, 331–412
Industrialists, 92, 215–18
  See also Business; Businessmen
Industrialization, 2, 88–91, 97–209, 372,
    403, 413, 415
  in Europe (table 1–1), 10–11
  as term, 1–2
  late, 99–100, 415
Industry. See Business; Economics; Manu-
    facturing
Infanticide, 39–85
Inflation, 227–28, 244, 264, 333, 351, 356,
    358, 371, 403
Insanity, 46
Instrumentalism, 287, 293

Insurance programs, 223–24, 238
  See also Health insurance; Welfare state
Intellectuals, 144, 148, 158, 261, 381, 387,
  403–404, 405
Inventions, 89–90
  See also Technology
Investment, speculative, 49–53, 225
Iran, 358
Ireland, 43, 73, 77, 118, 130
  See also Northern Ireland
Irish Republican Army (IRA), 393, 394
Islam, 369, 398, 400, 405
Israel, 358
Italy, 11, 25, 99, 113, 198, 231, 321, 325,
  415
  riots in, 117, 121
  after World War II, 331, 334, 341, 345,
    351–52, 353–54, 367–68, 370, 376,
    383, 385, 388

Jacqueries, 44
Japan, 12, 124, 228, 304, 335, 358, 359,
  416
Jaurès, Jean, 297, 299
Jews, 20, 42, 112, 158, 256, 258–59, 263,
  398
Journeymen, 55, 56, 57, 79, 86
June Days, 149, 175–76, 176, 197
Junkers, 24, 32, 34, 109, 110, 112, 226,
  245, 252, 337

Kay, James, 151
Kinderfeindlichkeit, 378
Kleptomania, 273
Koechlin, Jean, 77
Kohl, Helmut, 389
Korea, 358
Krupp, 216, 338
Krushchev, Nikita, 350
Kulturkampf, 236, 312

Labor Unions. *See* Unions
Labor(ers)
  agricultural, 15, 81–83
  landless, by 1800s, 117
  unskilled, 58–59, 280–81
  See also Working class
Labour party, 233, 297–300, 302, 341, 342,
  390, 395
Land
  in early industrial society, 105–106
  lack of, in 1800s, 117
  use of, in preindustrial society,
    18–19
Land tenure, in preindustrial agriculture,
  21–24
Landless labor, 81–83, 106, 110, 117,
  251–56
Landlords
  aristocrats as, 24–25, 110
  peasants and, 41, 120–21

Larzac plateau, 393
Latvia, 407
Lazzaretti, 116
Le Chapelier law, 196
Le Pen, Jean-Marie, 398, 399
Legal privilege, 26, 87–88, 109–10
Leipzig, 404
Leisure, 2, 140, 310–11, 365, 367, 413,
  414
Leisure ethic
  in early industrial society, 140, 185,
    187–88, 194–95, 204
  in mature industrial society, 224, 271–73,
    287–89, 310–17
  in twentieth century, 310–17, 365, 367,
    410, 416
Lenin, Vladimir, 26, 404
Leo XIII, 311
Liberalism, 138, 146, 149, 232–33, 236–38,
  324–26
Life expectancy, 4, 36, 225
Literacy, 2, 43, 54, 65, 235, 339, 362
Lithuania, 407
Liverpool, 335, 359
London, 47–48, 183, 353, 359, 389, 400
Longwy, 371
Love, 71, 162–65, 275–77, 376–77
Lower middle class, 219, 233, 258, 267–69,
  339–40, 363–66
  See also Middle class
Luddism, 122, 137, 178, 199
Lycées, 135, 258
Lyons, 47, 48, 179, 400

Machines
  in early industrial society, 89–90, 163,
    183, 186
  effects of, 99–103, 183, 186
  farm, 109, 213, 249–50
  improved and new, in Industrial Revolu-
    tion, 89–90, 163
  in mature industrial society, 212–14,
    249–50
  workers and, 169–70, 282, 285
  See also Factories; Manufacturing
Madame Bovary, 157
Magic, 43, 65, 116
Magnates, 29–30
Maize (corn), 76
Managers, 266–67
Manorialism, 22, 34, 87–88, 110, 122–24,
  200, 202
Manufacturing
  in mature industrial society, 224–26,
    261–64
  in preindustrial cities, 46–47
  role of, in industrialization, 89–91
  after World War II, 353, 357, 358–59,
    402–403, 407
Marketing, new techniques of, in early
  industrial society, 101–102

Markets
  agricultural, 75, 79, 106–108
  in early industrial society, 102–103
  See also Competition
Marriage
  in changing society of 1800s, 87, 141
  in early industrial society, 102–103
  in mature industrial society, 277, 289
  in the middle class, 141, 160–63, 277
  among peasants, 36–38
  in the working class, 168, 192, 289
  after World War II, 377–380, 410
Married Women's Property Act (1870), 165
Marseille, 359
Marshall Plan, 351–52, 356
Marx, Karl, 143
Marxism, 297–300
Masculinity, 204–208, 282
Mass culture, 310–11, 314–15
  See also Consumer(s); Consumerism
Masturbation, 161
Mechanic institutes, 173
Medical Act (1848), 144
Medical eclecticism, 43, 60
Medical profession. *See* Doctors
Mentalities, 15, 64–65
Merchant, preindustrial, 25–27, 50–51
Merchants' Antisemite Leagues (France),
    263
Metallurgy, 90, 98–99, 185, 213
Middle class, 135–50, 256–79, 414
  big business and, 215–18, 226
  in early industrial society, 94, 135–50
    culture of, 154–59, 201–202
    economics of, 149–51
    families and women of, 160–65
    lower class and, 146, 150–54
    in politics, 138, 145–49
    in professions, 142–45
  in mature industrial society, 219–20, 225,
    228, 229, 256–79
  after World War II, 341, 345, 360, 363–66
  See also Lower middle class
Migration, in early industrial society, 128–30
Military, 31, 112, 227, 234, 247, 318–19,
    333–34, 388–89
Mining, 89, 98–99, 151, 193, 197, 213, 214,
    239, 284, 353, 371, 407
Ministers. *See* Clergy
Mittelstand, 53
Mitterrand, François, 347, 349, 394
Mobility, 25–27, 136, 141–42, 173, 181,
    185, 233, 237, 266–67, 268, 271,
    337–41, 364–65, 372
Modernization, 2, 143–44
Money lenders, 20
Moral economy, 44, 57, 94, 175–80
Mortality rates. *See* Death and death rates
Motherhood, 39, 163–64, 275–76, 374–82
Motte-Bossut, 137
Movies, 288, 311, 316, 333, 335, 387, 411

Music, 33, 140, 159, 223, 374, 386–87, 404
Music halls, 223, 288, 310–11
Mussolini, Benito, 349
Mutual aid groups of artisans, 176–77, 196

Napoleon, 25, 32, 94
Napoleon III, 216
National Front (Britain), 398
National Front (France), 398, 399
National Health Service, 348
National Insurance Act in Britain, 239, 241
Nationalism, 123, 147, 227, 233, 234, 237,
    245–48, 263, 314, 317, 331, 340,
    403, 405–408, 414
Nationalizations, 338, 348–50
NATO, 388–89
Navy League, 227
Nazism, 255, 265, 279, 329–30, 344
Netherlands, the, 18, 66, 336, 361, 389, 415
New Economic Policy, 306–307
New German Cinema, 387
New Model Unions, 177
Newspapers, for masses, 221, 223, 236,
    314–15
Nobles Land Bank (Russia), 245
Noblesse oblige, 27, 238
Northern Ireland, 393–94
Northropp loom, 213
Norway, 115
Nouveau père, le, 378
Nutrition, 20, 76–77, 184, 222

Obruk, 33
Occitan regionalism, 391, 392–93
Old Believers, 116, 155, 158
OPEC (Organization of Petroleum-Export-
    ing Countries), 358
Orgasm, 273
Owen, Robert, 176

Pacific rim, 12
Pan-German League, 246
Paris, 47, 48, 129, 133, 139, 167, 175, 207,
    275, 353, 359, 367, 370, 383–85, 409
Parlements, 31
Parliaments, 32, 113, 147, 202, 231, 406
Parti Autonomiste Breton, 391
Pasteur, Louis, 77, 259
Paternalism, 153–54, 218
Patriarchalism, 28, 40, 63
Patronage, 109, 140, 155–60
Peace movement, 388–89
Peasant Front (France), 255
Peasants, 16, 103–108, 114–28, 248–56,
    361–63
  attitudes of, toward justice, 44, 57
  in early industrial society, 79, 81,
    106–108, 127, 200
  in 1800s, 106–108, 114–28
    aristocrats and, 120–21
    land tenure and, 106–22, 211, 307

Peasants, *(continued)*
  rebellion by, 119–22, 200
  and industrialization, 106–26, 307
  in mature industrial society, 225, 229,
    232, 235, 248–56, 307
  in preindustrial society, 35–46
  tariffs and, 252–56
  after World War II, 346, 350, 360–63,
    409
Penot, Achille, 143
Periodization, 8–9, 210–26
Pharmacists, 144
Philippe, Louis, 147
Phylloxera, 107
Piece work, 286
Plaid Cymru, 391, 395
Planning, economic, 338, 349–50, 352, 403
Plogoff, 393
Poaching, 120
Poland, 17, 28, 113, 129, 130, 303, 304
  after World War II, 333, 334, 336, 346,
    350, 357, 362, 372, 388, 401,
    403–406, 408
Police, 132, 135, 205, 237, 400
Political reforms, 145–49, 231
Politicians, 232–33, 338
Politics, 44–46, 175, 178
  aristocracy in, 30–33
  city, 132–33
  middle class in, 138, 145–49
  in modern industrial societies, 231–32,
    238
  peasants and, 44–46, 126, 251–56
  after World War I, 231, 324–27
  after World War II, 341–51, 382–408
  See also Communism and communist
    parties; Fascism; Liberalism; Nazism;
    Parliaments; Political reforms; Pro-
    tests; Revolution(s); Socialism and
    socialist parties; State; Voting
Poor law, 151–52
Population
  city, in 1700s, 46–47
  in early industrial society, 72–77
    in cities, 128–30
  growth of, after 1750, 33, 413
  in mature industrial society, 211, 323
  after World War II, 336–37, 347,
    377–78, 401, 415, 416
Portugal, 337, 338, 344, 361, 371, 401
Possibilist party, 298
Postindustrial society, 9
Potato, 72, 76, 184
Poverty
  in cities, 58–59, 222
  decline of, 222
  in 1800s, 81–83
  in preindustrial society, 58–59
  after World War II, 348, 369–70, 398,
    400, 409
Prague, 373–74, 404

Preindustrial society
  and change, 14–15, 63–66
  in Europe, 14–66
Press. *See* Newspapers, for masses
Prices, lowered, 102, 222
Primogeniture, 28
Printers, 167, 176, 180, 212, 282, 289
Prison, 66, 146
Production
  increasing, in industrial revolutions, 94
  in mature industrial society, 220–22
    problems in sales and, 224–26
  not maximized, in predindustrial agricul-
    tural society, 18–19
  See also Manufacturing
Professionalization, 143–44
  of artists and entertainers, 159–60
Professionals, 49–50, 80, 142–45, 233,
    258–60
  disgruntled, 233, 258–60
  in mature industrial society, 233, 246,
    258–60, 264, 306
  preindustrial, 49–50
  upper class and, 50, 112, 142–45
Profits, 218, 225, 227
Proletariat, growth of, 15, 81–83, 180–82
Property. *See* Land
Prostitution, 162, 191, 204, 275, 277, 334
Protestantism, 21, 65, 68, 92, 155, 158, 311,
    415
Protests
  by artisans, 57, 176–80
  in early industrial society, 82, 119–21,
    195–203
  in eastern Europe, 44, 123, 124, 126,
    145, 147, 372–74, 401–408
  middle-class, 87–88, 148, 254–56
  new forms of, after 1960, 382–401
  peasant, 27, 42, 44, 86, 119–21, 227–29,
    362–63
  in preindustrial society, 27, 44, 57
  as result of industrialization, 94–96,
    291–300
  student, 144, 382–87, 396
  working-class, 176–80, 191, 195–203,
    291–300, 370–72
  See also Revolution(s); Riots
Protoindustrialization, 68–83, 89
Proudhon, Pierre Joseph, 179
Prussia, 25, 26, 32, 34, 80, 94, 106, 147,
    232
Puberty, 1, 83–85
Pugachev revolt, 44
Punk movement, 386, 387
Purchasing power, 102, 264
Putting-out. *See* Domestic manufacturing

Racism, 140, 269, 279, 312, 396–401, 414
Radio, 271, 333, 361, 374, 404
Raiffeissen banks, 250

Railroads, 99, 102–103, 221, 348–49
Reagan, Ronald, 388
Realgymnasium, 258
Rebecca riots, 122
Recessions, 103–104, 183–84, 225, 358–60
Red Brigade, 385
Reform Bill of 1832, 145, 146
Reform Judaism, 158
Reform movements
  artisans and, 175
  in 1800s, 153
Regionalism, 9–12, 34, 47, 305, 391–96
Religion, 15, 211, 236, 311–12, 403–406,
    409, 410, 414, 415
  in education, 155, 236, 312
  by 1800s, 86, 116, 155, 194, 201–202,
    211, 236, 311–12
  middle class and, 155–57, 201
  peasants and, 45, 116
  working class and, 60, 194
  See also Churches; Clergy; Protestantism
Renault, Louis, 338
Resistance, 339, 341, 380
Retirement plans, 268, 283, 365–66, 371
Revisionism, 298–99
Revolution(s)
  doctrines on, 146–48, 297–300
  of 1848 in Europe, 122–23, 145, 149,
    172–73, 175, 178–79, 207
  by end of eighteenth century, 87–88
  forces for, 87–88, 172–73, 178–80
  middle class in, 87–88, 148
  of 1905 in Russia, 42, 124, 126, 145, 147,
    198
  of 1989 in eastern Europe, 401–408
  peasants in, 42, 122–23
  See also French Revolution; Russian Revo-
    lution
Rightist movements, 265, 269, 279, 398–99
  See also Fascism; Nazism
Riots
  by artisans, 82, 146, 178–80
  racial, 400
  rural, 44, 86, 119–20, 180, 248–56,
    329–30
  See also Protests; Revolution(s)
Rituals, peasant, 40–41
Romania, 110, 123, 247, 304, 357, 374,
    402, 405–406, 408
Rural, as terms, 17
Rural classes, 25–43
Ruskin College, 235
Russia, 11, 16, 40, 65, 114, 117, 180, 198,
    201, 207, 318–19
  aristocracy in, 24, 31, 33, 114, 247
  early industrial society in, 99–100, 180,
    198
  land tenure in, 22–25, 118, 247
  mature industrial society in, 304–10
  riots in, 123–24, 126, 180
  after World War II, 333, 334, 336, 342,

    350, 357, 373, 376, 402, 406–408, 409
Russian Revolution, 201, 305–307, 324

S.O.S.-Racisme, 399
Sales of goods, 135, 138–39
Salvation Army, 311
Savings, 168, 174, 186, 223–24, 228, 241
Say, J. B., 146
Scandinavia, 278, 302, 317, 328, 335, 336,
    345, 352, 355
Schulze-Delitzsch cooperatives, 251
Science, 2, 70, 140, 157, 237, 252, 312, 337,
    414
Scotland, 391–96
Scottish National Party, 392, 395
"Second Industrial Revolution," 212
Self-help principle, 142, 152–53, 173–75,
    240
Semi-skilled workers, 214, 279, 368
Serfdom, 24, 415
  See also Emancipation of serfs; Feudalism
Servan-Schreiber, Jean Jacques, 356
Servants, 58, 81, 131, 154, 189–91, 204,
    281
Service aristocracy, 26
Sewage, 134
Sexuality, 1, 62, 153, 161–62, 204–208,
    272–73, 288–89, 414, 416
  in mature industrial society, 272–73,
    288–89
  middle-class, 153, 161–65, 204–208,
    272–73, 275, 277
  revolution in, by 1800s, 75, 83–85,
    192–93, 205
  working-class, 153, 192–93, 204–208,
    288–89
  after World War II, 376–77, 410
Shaftsbury, Earl of, 112
Sharecropping, 110
Shipping, 91, 103, 221
Shopkeepers, 135, 136, 138–39, 141, 257,
    261–64, 363
Smiles, Samuel, 142
Social history, nature of, 5–6
"Social market economy," 350
Social Security, 238–39, 242–48. *See also*
    Welfare state, after World War II
Socialism and socialist parties, 121, 178,
    196, 233, 237, 241, 246, 251, 265–66,
    278, 296–301, 313–14, 341, 344,
    347, 350, 364, 366, 368, 370, 385,
    390, 399, 414
Society
  consumer, 331–412
  early industrial, 97–209
  European, 1–12
  forces for change in, 67–96
  mature industrial, 210–330
  preindustrial, 20–66
  after World War I, 317–20
  after World War II, 331–412

Solidarity (Poland), 401, 403–404
South Tyrolians, 391
Soviet Union. *See* Russia
Spain, 11, 15, 25, 99, 110, 113, 232, 247, 302, 327, 337, 339, 344, 361, 371, 391–94, 401
  riots in, 121–23
Spanish Civil War, 329–30
Specialization, crop, 19, 107
Spengler, Oswald, 322
Spinning, 89, 181
Sports, 223, 272, 278, 288, 310, 315, 365, 367
"Stagflation," 351, 358–60
Stahlwerkverband, 217
Stalin, Joseph, 305
Standard of living, 64, 102, 168, 182–86, 222
  in eastern Europe, 372
  higher, for lower classes, 185–86, 222–24
    in mature industrial society, 222, 282–84
  after World War I, 227–28, 322–23
  after World War II, 340, 352, 354, 363–64, 367
Starvation and hunger, 19–20, 76–77, 319, 333–34
  See also Famine
State
  function of, in early industrial society, 132–33, 202
  function of, after World War II, 335, 341–51, 409–10
  role of, in industrialization, 71–72, 98–100, 231
  See also State and society; Welfare state, after World War II
State and society, 2, 65, 71, 100, 127, 132–33, 146–47, 202, 231–42, 341–51, 413
Status, 7, 25–27, 159
  of aristocracy, 29–31, 109–15
  lack of, of propertyless class, 81–83
  middle-class, 135–50, 159
Steam engines, 70, 89
Stinnes, Hugo, 228
Stöcker, Adolf, 263
Stolypin, Piotr, 126, 307
Stopes, Marie, 273
Stratification. *See* Class(es)
"Strength through Joy," 328
Strikes, 82, 176–78, 185, 196–98, 291–93, 294, 324, 334, 367–68, 370–72, 382–85, 407
  See also General strike
Student protest. *See* Protests
Suburbs, 134, 164, 275, 288
Suffrage, 111, 113, 145–49, 175, 231–32, 278
Swaddling, 39, 71
Sweden, 355, 378, 388
Switzerland, 354, 376, 398
Syndicalists, 290, 297, 300

Tariffs, 114, 146, 147, 149, 226, 352
Taxes, 88, 121, 240, 337, 346, 348
Teachers, 145, 233, 235, 259, 264
Technocrats, 338, 341
Technology, 64, 89–90, 99–103, 107, 163, 270, 335, 337, 353, 356, 359, 403, 413
Television, 333, 355, 361, 367, 374, 379, 404, 411
Ten Hour Law of 1847, 112
Tenure. *See* Land tenure
Textile industry, 89, 98, 167, 186, 192, 213, 280–81, 353
Thatcher, Margaret, 347–48, 349
Theater, 155, 157, 223, 310–11
Thierry-Mieg, Jean Ulric, 136
Three-Mile Island, 387
Threshing machines, 107, 249
Time, 67
Tocqueville, Alexis de, 31
Trade unions. *See* Unions
Trades Union Congress, 293, 295
Traditionalism, of artisans, 79, 168–69
Trans-Siberian railroad, 221
Transportation, 102–103, 221
Treaty of Vienna, 32
Typewriters, 270

"Underclass," 369–70, 409
Unemployment
  of artisans, 169
  in mature industrial societies, 214, 226, 239, 282
    during depression, 226, 230, 264
  by 1900s, 214
  after World War II, 347, 358, 398, 400, 407, 409
Union of Agriculturalists (Germany), 245, 252
Unions
  artisans in, 176–78, 293, 297
  craft, by late 1800s, 293, 297
  in 1800s, 176–77
  growth of, 176–78, 218, 413
  industrial, 218, 295–98
  middle-class, 269, 364
  in twentieth century, 218, 228, 293–98, 345, 368, 370–72, 382, 385, 399, 401, 403, 407, 410
United States, 12, 213, 228, 323
  after World War II, 334–35, 339, 351, 354, 355, 358, 387–89, 409, 416
Universities, 135, 235, 246, 258–59, 264, 340, 343, 368
Unskilled workers. *See* Labor(ers)
Upper class, 226, 242–48, 317
  See also Aristocracy
Urban poor, 58–59, 166–67, 280
  See also "Underclass"
Urban society, 47–60, 128–33, 256
Urbanization, 9, 128–30, 355, 415
Utopianism, 178, 180

Vacations, 271, 287, 345, 355, 365, 367, 377, 416
Values
  of aristocrats, 27, 112
  of bourgeoisie, 77–80
  of middle class, 154–59
  religion to encourage, 155–57
  sexual, by 1800s, 83–85
Veterans, 319
Vichy France, 328–30, 344
Vienna, 133, 136, 179, 263
Villages, 24, 40–42
Villermé, René, 151
Violence, 46, 96, 112, 120, 371, 399–400, 402
Viollet-le-Duc, 160
Voice of Women, 207
Voting, 111, 113, 145–49, 175, 231–32, 278, 377, 381
  See also Suffrage

Wages, 169, 185, 222, 282–84, 293, 340, 355, 365, 367, 368, 410
Wales, 391–96
Walloons, 392
Warsaw, 404
Watt, James, 70
Wealth, rising in mature industrial society, 215–22, 282–84
Weaving, 89, 181, 213
Weddings, 40, 410
Welfare reforms, 237–42, 299, 302–303; 317
Welfare state, after World War II, 336, 340, 341–48, 362, 367, 378, 379, 410
West Germany, 336, 340, 347, 350, 356, 358, 359, 361, 370, 377, 383, 385, 402, 405
  economic growth in, 351–54
  Green party and environmentalism in, 387–91
  immigrants and racism in, 369, 397–400
Wet nursing, 162
White-collar workers, 211, 213, 219, 267–69, 340, 353, 359, 363–64, 372
Widows, 63
Wilson, Woodrow, 321
Winegrowing, 9, 19, 85, 107, 251
Witchcraft, 15, 68
Women, 28–29, 160–65, 189–91, 204–208, 234–35, 277–79, 280, 414
  and industrialization, 81, 84, 189–91, 203, 204–208, 306

  middle-class, 137, 139, 140, 160–65, 204–208, 267–68, 270, 272–73, 277–79, 306
  and preindustrial society, 28–29, 38, 44, 54, 56, 63, 66
  as readers, 155, 234–35, 315
  as servants, 81, 189–91
  white-collar, 213, 267–68, 270
  working-class, 168, 189–91, 192–93, 204–208, 280–81, 289, 306
  after World War II, 334, 374–82
  See also Children; Family; Feminists; Marriage
Women's Club (Berlin), 207
Work, 7, 53–54, 94–96, 186–89, 286–87, 306
  conditions of, of working class, 186–89, 279–300
  new kind of, in mature industrial society, 285–87
  pace of, 53–54, 185, 188, 213, 270, 286–87
Work ethic, 7, 53–54, 94–96, 154–59, 189, 196, 364, 368–69, 403
Working class, 180–99, 279–300, 366–374
  conditions of, 182–89
  in conflict after World War I, 300–304, 324–28
  discontent and protest of, 196–98, 204–208, 370–74
  disorientation, 197–98
  family life of, 191–94, 287–90, 379
  in Industrial Revolution, 172–99, 306
  in mature industrial society, 230, 279–300, 306
  middle-class relations with, 150–54, 189
  urban poor and unskilled, 58–59
  work of, 186–89, 196, 306, 368–69
  after World War II, 340, 341, 345, 360, 363–64, 366–74
World War I, 201, 210, 211, 218, 227–29, 241, 254–56, 300–303, 317–30, 331, 333
World War II, 330, 331, 333–34, 338, 339, 342

Youth, 131, 382–87
Yugoslavia, 339, 350, 405–406, 408

Zadruga, 39
Zemstvos, 114
Zhivkov, Todor, 402
Zola, Emile, 263